Conversation Pieces

Mario Praz

CONVERSATION PIECES

A Survey of the Informal Group Portrait in Europe and America

The Pennsylvania State University Press
University Park & London

Published by The Pennsylvania State University Press

Library of Congress Catalogue Card Number 76-127380

Standard Book Number 271-00132-1

Printed in Italy

Layout by Carmine Siniscalco

On the cover: GEORGE STUBBS, *Colonel Pocklington and his Sisters* · Washington, D.C., National Gallery of Art.

CONTENTS

Acknowledgements

The purchase in 1930 at a Florentine auction of a family portrait erroneously attributed to Gauffier, but actually by Desmarais — an example of the peculiar technique sometimes used at the end of the eighteenth century of working in oil on paper glued on canvas — first stimulated my interest in the kind of compositions which I later saw described in Sacheverell Sitwell's *Conversation Pieces* (a copy of which I ordered from a Batsford catalogue of remainders shortly before the Second World War). I had occasion to purchase a few more paintings of the same type on the antique market, and during that time further volumes on the subject by R. Edwards, H. Kronberger-Frentzen, A. Staring, and L. Hautecœur gave me the idea of a general, systematic study based on the history and structure of the genre rather than, like Sitwell's book, on a survey of the individual artists and the families of the sitters. In this study I intended to approach more closely Edwards' work than that of the other authors of volumes dealing with this class of paintings. My search for examples of a type of composition which has only partially been studied has been greatly aided by the knowledge and friendship of art historians such as Federico Zeri, Ellis K. Waterhouse, Desmond Fitz-Gerald, Jørgen Hartmann, Serge Grandjean, Andrea Busiri Vici, and Elka Schrijver, as well as by the information kindly supplied by scholars and owners of private collections such as Giovanni Incisa della Rocchetta, the late G. B. Spalletti Trivelli, and Alessandro Contini Bonacossi, and by antique dealers such as Carlo and Marcello Sestieri, E. Rousuck, and the Wildenstein and Charpentier galleries. On the basis of information and help from these sources, I undertook a rather difficult search for permissions from owners of paintings relevant to my subject. A stay in Washington in 1967 enabled me to trace a number of English conversation pieces which had entered the collection of Mr. and Mrs. Paul Mellon, through whose courtesy I had access to invaluable illustrative material. I am also indebted to the staff of the Witt Library of the Courtauld Institute for their considerable help, and to the photographic archives of the Rijksmuseum in Amsterdam and the Nationalmuseum in Stockholm, to the Käte Gläser Archives at the Berlin Staatsgalerie, to the British Council, and particularly to Mr. A. Staring, who placed photographs of rare Dutch conversation pieces at my disposal.

My inquiries ought to have been extended also to Russia, but the difficulties I encountered when collecting photographs of paintings of interiors for my *History of Furnishing* have discouraged me from undertaking a similar search there for illustrative material pertaining to the present work. But to all of the above, and to the many owners of private collections who have generously consented to the reproduction of paintings in their possession — their names are recorded in the captions to the illustrations — I express my deep appreciation. Thanks to their permission, many conversation pieces are reproduced here for the first time.

The introduction to the present volume, which concerns the art of the bourgeoisie, is intended to present the subject matter discussed in the various chapters from a social and historical point of view. A suggestion from my Italian publisher, Ugo Bozzi — who has also supplied me with invaluable information concerning the illustrations — stimulated this approach. I would also like to thank my English and American publishers, Methuen & Co. and The Pennsylvania State University Press, for the help they have provided in improving the quality of the illustrations.

M. P.

Rome, January 1971

Just as, according to the Bible, the sons of Noah scattered throughout the earth and became the progenitors of the various human races, so, in the opinion of J.L. Borges, at the origin of every literature lies the great watershed of the *Iliad* and the *Odyssey*. The *Iliad* is virile, epic, and heroic; but the *Odyssey* is steeped in such a different, more tender, and more human climate that Samuel Butler — the bizarre and far-from-orthodox philologist who was also a bitter satirical novelist — ventured to maintain that it was written by a woman. This carries to an extreme Bentley's earlier suggestion that the *Iliad* was written for men and the *Odyssey* for women, as well as Shelley's remark that the *Iliad* is strong and the *Odyssey* sweet, and Gladstone's theory that family life supplies the woof upon which the thread of the poem of Ulysses is wrought.

Speculation upon the author's sex is pure fantasy, but not so the remark about the two climates — the heroic and the familiar — which respectively characterize the two poems. If there is such a thing as an aristocratic art, the *Iliad* is at the root of its pedigree; and what more authentic progenitor of bourgeois art than the *Odyssey* can be imagined? Aristocratic art tends to the schematisation of sentiments, to black and white contrasts, and to a certain abstraction which aims at the essential and neglects nuances and details. In this it has much in common with popular art. The *Iliad*, the *Chanson de Roland*, and the Sicilian *teatro dei pupi* are from the same stock: Roland is the counterpart of Ganelon, and the Clorindas and Erminias are complements of the Armidas and Alcinas. The hero is contrasted with the coward, the angelic woman with the *femme fatale*.

The effigies of the Pharaohs are standardized, and all that counts is the designation of their rank. Representations of the English kings of the Middle Ages are not intended to be true portraits; one king may easily stand for another, and the real significance lies in the dress and insignia. Clothes were of paramount importance as heraldic signs of social rank. Similarly, in the prints of Épinal or in Staffordshire ware the same figure may represent Napoleon or Wellington, Queen Victoria or the Empress Eugénie. The crucial point is the rank — of general, king, or queen. One has only to change the plume, the helmet, and the colour of the skin, and, presto! Roland becomes Sacripant. The realistic portrait was born around the fifteenth century; but why so late, we may ask? The answer may seem over-simplified: because at about that time bourgeois art began to assert itself. In mediaeval effigies, as we have said, faces were less eloquent than attire; indeed, Chaucer's Canterbury pilgrims are mainly described in terms of clothing. In Chaucer clothes are already expressive of the individual; their description summarily but perceptively enables us to judge his character from external signs. The details of dress, the physical peculiarities, and the habits of the Prioress, the Wife of Bath, and the Pardoner are observed with a miniaturist's eye. A century later, the great Flemish masters van Eyck and Memling brought to perfection this art of notable truth to life. There is a similarity of intention and presentation between Chaucer's portraits of the pilgrims and Jan van Eyck's portrait of his wife or of the Arnolfini couple, and, later, Memling's portrait of Barbara Moreel: a decidedly new point of view has made its way into art.

There is no such love of detail either in Dante or Giotto, in whom the terrestrial element is combined with the supernatural in a balance never before reached, because only in them do allegorical abstractions become incarnate in living creatures. They both, however, started from abstraction — Dante the aristocrat and Giotto the man of the people — and soared above the point of view of their respective social classes only because they possessed that rare virtue, genius, which cuts across every class and transcends it.

Chaucer was a great poet within his limits, but no genius. He began by imitating the French poets of the courtly tradition of Guillaume de Lorris, then turned to the more congenial Jean de Meung. In fact, we find in the *Roman de la Rose* another watershed parallel to that between the *Iliad* and the *Odyssey*.

The author of the first part of the *Roman*, written at the beginning of the thirteenth century, moved in aristocratic circles. For Guillaume de Lorris, romance had to be a code of courtly love, an *ars amandi* in Ovid's manner. He treated this subject destined for gentlemen and ladies of high rank with the method and in the spirit of the learned men who organized the doctrine and cult of love as a kind of amorous theology: there was an actual " church of love " which had its faithful and its heretics, its saints and its sinners. The taste for abstraction and didactic formulae found its proper medium in allegory; Guillaume, following already established conventions, built a great allegorical machine round the figure of the Rose, symbol of the beloved. The Rose is the ideal type, abstract and quintessential, of the beloved; her feelings radiate outwards into many external allegorical projections, just as later in the heroic period of the Renaissance the aspirations of gentlemen and warriors became crystallised into the symbolic figures of the heraldic devices.

Allegories and devices, those exquisite aristocratic crystals, are like the precious elements of a ritual, like tarots, or chessmen. Guillaume also created an enchanting background to this *jeu de cartes* or masked ball of human sentiments: the setting of the May morning, with the garden, the song of the birds, the sweet scents, the fountain, and the walled castle. To this artificial paradise, a pagan reflection of the paradise of Christian theology, the poet imagined himself to have been introduced in a dream.

Forty years later Jean de Meung added a further eighteen thousand lines to this graceful unfinished poem of little more than four thousand lines, and in the meanwhile a new point of view in art had dawned. It was neither aristocratic nor popular, because neither of those two classes ever thought of repudiating allegory. (Allegory was rejected neither by Dante the aristocrat nor — more than three centuries later — by John Bunyan, the visionary tinker, in that other pilgrimage, *The Pilgrim's Progress*.) Compared to the dreamy, aristocratic delicacy of Guillaume de Lorris, we have Jean de Meung's practical, positive, materialistic — in a word, bourgeois — spirit. Jean was a bourgeois and a pedant, but also an original thinker; in him the mediaeval world was dissected and broken up into its constituent parts. He was a realist who proclaimed the necessity of adhering to nature and who waged war against whatever strayed from it. This is not as yet the contrast between Don Quixote and Sancho, but something equally sharp: the affirmation of a concrete world, brooking no nonsense, caring for particulars, and curious as to details. Allegories were set in smiling or scowling masks, but Faux-Semblant and la Vieille are more than masks; the latter, together with the portrait of the woman given to making pilgrimages in Deschamps' *Miroir de Mariage*, was to serve as a model for Chaucer's woman in the flesh, the Wife of Bath.

Chaucer began, then, by following in the footsteps of the successors of Guillaume de Lorris, the artificial and vapid authors of the *Founteinne Amoureuse*, the *Livre Morpheus*, the *Espinette Amoureuse*, and *Méliador*, Machaut and Froissart. But even in the *Book of the Duchess*, which is indebted to the conventions of courtly poetry, the choice of models works in a certain direction. The poet imitated the May-morning vision, but not the allegories; the usual troop of personified feelings was left out, and he concentrated on the human figures. The same thing happens in the *Parliament of Fowls* and in the *Legend of Good Women*. In fact, the French models Chaucer found most sympathetic were Jean de Meung, his disciple Eustache Deschamps, and the *fabliaux*, and he succeeded in perfecting and surpassing them. Later he learned much from Boccaccio and Dante, but when he wanted to imitate an episode in the *Divine Comedy* directly (that of Count Ugolino), he disclosed not so much his weakness but his different point of view. What in Dante is a cosmic tragedy, with the famous invective against Pisa and the well-known apocalyptic vision of divine revenge, becomes in Chaucer a domestic tragedy: the tragedy of a family starving to death. Instead of the terrible pauses and silences and implications of Dante, we find the wailing of human beings in distress. Pity, a warm feeling of human sympathy, is one of Chaucer's characteristics; it is the central theme of the story of Griselda as well as of that of Troilus, and of the story of Ugolino's children as well as of that of the boy killed by the Jews. With Chaucer dawns the sensibility which centuries later was to culminate in Dickens, and this feeling can be called bourgeois. When Chaucer thought somehow to follow Dante's bold scheme of the *Divine Comedy*, he kept in mind the episodes of the Italian poem but not its structure. People in every station of life and of every kind of character from the lowest to the highest appear and talk to Dante, bent on his pilgrimage through the realms of the dead; all the modes and shades of the human soul find expression in the Italian drama. But a pilgrimage to the other world was not among the possibilities of England's bourgeois poet, who wrote:

> A thousand sythes have I herd men telle
> That there is joye in hevene and peyne in helle,
> And I acorde wel that it be so;
> But natheles, this wot I wel also,
> That ther is non that dwelleth in this contre,
> That eyther hath in helle or hevene ybe.
> (Prologue to the *Legend of Good Women*);

and also, speaking of the death of one of the characters in the *Canterbury Tales:*

> His spirit chaunged hous and wente ther,
> As I cam nevere, I kan nat tellen wher.
> Therfor I stynte, I nam no divinistre;
> Of soules fynde I nat in this registre,
> Ne me ne list thilke opinions to telle
> Of hem, though that they writen wher they dwelle.

Chaucer clings to the dear, everyday world, and brings down to the homely plane of common sense the situations which he finds in his models. Though trained in the school of French allegory, he opted for the concrete and rendered in rational terms the visions of philosophers and divines. There was no pilgrimage to the kingdoms of the other world for the man who was " no divinistre ", but instead an earthly pilgrimage to the shrine of the national saint. On this pilgrimage no demons or angels were to be met, but rather all varieties of human folk; Chaucer cared only for humans. The *Divine Comedy* begins with a meeting with allegorical heraldic animals; then follows an encounter with a symbolic person, Virgil, in a forest which is itself a symbol. The *Canterbury Tales* begins with the usual description of spring and then continues:

> Bifil that in that seson on a day,
> In Southwerk at the Tabard as I lay
> Redy to wenden on my pilgrymage
> To Caunterbury with ful devout corage,
> At nyght was come into that hostelrye
> Wel nyne and twenty in a compaignye,
> Of sondry folk, by aventure yfalle
> In felaweshipe, and pilgrimes were they alle,
> That toward Caunterbury wolden ryde.
> The chambres and the stables weren wyde,
> And wel we weren esed atte beste....

Then follows a description and inventory of the pilgrims, presented with the notarial accuracy we have already mentioned. The way is paved not so much for a pilgrimage to the shrine of Saint Thomas à Becket as for Balzac's *comédie humaine*.

From the *fabliaux* and the *Novellino* to the *Decameron* and the *Canterbury Tales*, to picaresque novels and stories of Elizabethan roguery and so on to Defoe's and Fielding's novels: this is the bourgeois mainstream. Boccaccio, the son of merchants; Chaucer, another son of merchants; Defoe, a merchant himself; Balzac, the son of an attorney's secretary and Dickens of a civil servant.... Of course we do not claim here that only the children of the bourgeoisie are capable of writing a certain type of fiction or of producing a certain type of painting. Talent and genius, an idealist philosopher would say, know no class or caste; but who would be such a besotted idealist as to deny that a definite social climate favours one rather than another tendency? Montemayor, Sir Philip Sidney, and Honoré d'Urfé, who enriched and gave sophistication to the Italian pastoral novel inaugurated by Sannazzaro (whose father was a nobleman) were gentlemen; also from noble families were Gomberville, La Calprenède, and Mademoiselle de Scudéry, who grafted the heroic tradition of the *Amadis de Gaule* upon the pastoral one. Their novels, in which the heroic-pastoral convention covertly suggests real events which could hardly be described directly in the court circles of the time, continue the courtly genre of the first part of the *Roman de la Rose*. Instead of an allegorical fiction, we have here an heroic-pastoral one; and instead of the conflicting passions embodied in symbolic figures — the Petrarchan love casuistry — Platonism is boiled down to a manual of civil conversation, the mannerist prolixity of psychological analysis in its infancy:

Celadon mesme eut opinion que j'aymois Lycidas, et moy je creus qu'il aymoit Phillis, et Phillis pensa que Lycidas m'aymoit, et Lycidas eut opinion que Phillis aymoit Celadon.

Thus d'Urfé. And here is Sidney:

... exceedingly sorry for Pamela, but exceedingly exceeding the exceedingness in fears for Philoclea....

Such verbal contortions and long speeches of *serpentinata* eloquence delighted the Hôtel de Rambouillet no less than the Countess of Pembroke, to whom Sidney's *Arcadia* was dedicated. The characters are puppets, automatons whose evolutions might amuse us up to a point but certainly do not delight us as they did the courtiers of yore; in fact, they are too sophisticated to retain a winning grace of infantile naïveté and not ripe enough to appeal to the more complex taste of today. In a later revision Sidney recast his novel on Heliodorus' pattern, rendering the phraseology more tortuous and behaving like the carver in the moral fable who, by cutting ornaments in his bow, caused it to break when it was bent.

D'Urfé's descriptions anticipate Boucher's abstract pastoral artificialities:

Regardez cette bergère assise contre ce buisson, comme elle est belle, et proprement vestue: ses cheveux relevez par devant, s'en vont folastrant en liberté sur ses espaules, et semble que le vent, à l'envy de la nature, par son souffle les aille recrespant en onde, mais c'est que jaloux des petits amours qui s'y trouvent cachez, et qui vont y tendant leurs lacs, il les en veut chasser. Et de fait voyez-en quelques uns emportez par force, d'autres qui se tiennent aux noeuds qu'ils y ont faits, et d'autres qui essayent d'y retourner, mais ils ne peuvent, tant leur aisle encore faiblette est contrariée de l'importunité de Zephir.

If, as Malraux has said, " la soumission au réel " is " une valeur bourgeoise ",[1] what are we to think of van Marle's assertion that " there is abundant evidence to show that no patrician house lacked the kind of decoration which confronted the eyes of its inhabitants with familiar subjects: their favourite occupations, the pleasures of their life, the persons of their family, and the romances and tales in which they delighted? "[2] Are we to consider these scenes as true to everyday life, like illuminations representing the occupations of the various months in the books of hours which anticipated van Eyck's art? Or were they not merely typical and generalised reductions of everyday life, such as we see in Bracciano Castle or in the Casa dei Borromei in Milan? In illuminated manuscripts we find scenes in which the lord is represented either sitting at table or at the ceremony of the presentation of a book; but as a rule these documents do not appear before the fifteenth century, when Jan van Eyck, Robert Campin, and Rogier van der Weyden inaugurated in their holy pictures the minute and faithful rendering of interiors which — with the first conversation piece, the *Arnolfini Couple* — marks the beginning of bourgeois inspiration in art. The Flemish illuminations of the *Roman de la Rose* and of the *Decameron* of Philippe le Bon by Guillaume de Metz, and those of the *Histoire du bon roi Alexandre* by Philippe de Maserolles — which reached their supreme blossoming in the *Grimani Breviary*, in the *Golf Book*, and in the *Heures de Hennesay* by Simon Bening[3] — anticipated genre painting

1. *Les voix du silence* (Paris, 1953), p. 296. Engl. ed. *The Voices of Silence*, transl. S. Gilbert (London: Secker and Warburg, 1954). 2. R. VAN MARLE, *L'iconographie de l'art profane au Moyen-Age et à la Renaissance*, I, *La vie quotidienne* (The Hague, 1931), Preface. 3. F.-C. LEGRAND, *Les peintres flamands de genre au XVIIe siècle* (Brussels: Éditions Meddens, 1963), p. 8.

and the so-called *tableaux de société* and *tableaux de moeurs*.
Thus in the bourgeois North arose the faithful portraiture of interiors and the conversation piece. Meanwhile, both in the north and south of Europe the figure of the donor had been extricated from holy pictures.

If there is an easily readable history, requiring almost no comment, it is that of the portrait in the Christian era.[4] The portrait began as an appendix to religious subjects, as the profile of a donor or devotee at first of almost Lilliputian proportions.[5] But the relation of the donor to the holy figure underwent a change at a certain moment: in Masaccio's fresco of the *Trinity*, painted ca. 1425, Lorenzo Lenzi and his wife have the same proportions as God the Father, the Virgin, and Saint John.[6] Around 1435 Jan van Eyck painted the Chancellor Rolin kneeling in front of the Virgin and Child, and the portrait of the devotee becomes almost the chief figure. In Italy, the portrait developed in the bystanders at sacred scenes in frescoes, such as those of Perugino, Botticelli, and Cosimo Rosselli in the Sistine Chapel; these may be read, as Pope-Hennessy says, on two different levels: as applied theology, or as a *Who's Who* for 1482.[7] It finally asserted itself as an independent work, first in Florence and then in Northern Italy under the influence of Antonello da Messina. And why is portraiture so rare in the Middle Ages and yet such a conspicuous feature of the Renaissance? The title of the first chapter of Pope-Hennessy's book, " The Cult of Personality ", might have been borrowed from Burckhardt's currently much maligned *Civilization of the Renaissance in Italy*.[8] It was in the name of this cult that the revolution of the Renaissance developed and also that the Romantic revolution was to develop a little less than four centuries later. And it was in the name of the negation of this cult that the present-day revolution of mass civilization began.
Although much has been written in modern times denying a real distinction between the Middle Ages and the Renaissance,[9] today a number of scholars think that Burckhardt's interpretation of the Renaissance is substantially well grounded. The face of the Renaissance was set according to a pagan-humanistic pattern which had as its goal a moral perfection, oblivious of the cardinal virtues of piety and humility as well as of the cardinal Christian doctrine regarding man's sinful nature and his fall from grace. Leonardo's formula " Man a model of the universe " (*L'uomo modello del mondo*) was not the belief of a single individual but was extensively shared: the sense of social hierarchy and of magnificence considered as a virtue, the thirst for honour, and the acceptance of apotheosis as a poetic convention inspired the behaviour of anyone who desired to distinguish himself. The representation of man was therefore concentrated on the individual, on a single person shown against a background such as a curtain or column which would not distract attention from him, but would rather suggest the magnificence to which he aspired. The painter suited the richness of the costume to the figure: Italian portraits do not give details of location, but of the dress of the sitter. In *Antony and Cleopatra*, Cleopatra's wish to present herself to Mark Antony at their final meeting in all the regal splendour of queenly pomp was not prompted by an exaggerated vanity, as the eminent Shakespearian critic Granville-Barker believed, but by virtue of the magnificence which the epoch, imbued with Aristotelian precepts, expected of a Renaissance sovereign.

4. See JOHN POPE-HENNESSY, *The Portrait in the Renaissance*, Bollingen Series, 12 (New York: Bollingen Foundation, 1966), passim. 5. See a few out of a number of such diminutive portraits of devotees in ITALO FALDI, *Pittori viterbesi di cinque secoli*, (Rome: Ugo Bozzi editore, 1970), figures 74, 84, 173. 6. *The Portrait in the*

Dress, as Thorstein Veblen maintained,[10] has its basis in sumptuousness achieved through the employment of costly materials and expensive means of production to create a garb which implies a leisurely way of life, designed to suggest that the wearer is removed from menial necessities. Sixteenth-century Italy was the wealthiest country in Europe; descriptions of the profusion of precious materials, of the labour — almost like a goldsmith's — dedicated to the adornment of clothes, of the richness of the noblewomen's trousseaux, and of the display in festivals and parades are apt to cloy the reader of chronicles of the time, no matter how infinitely varied and ingenious are the details. We note a taste for variegated, slashed, and embroidered fabrics in sixteenth-century clothes,[11] for a profusion of ribbons and " favours " typical of the Baroque — which with their various colours made dresses the rivals of the peacock's tail — for laces patterned like leaves and flowers, for pearls and gold and silver strips woven through embroideries, for codpieces boldly raised to stress virility, and for the display of women's breasts. All this pomp had a paramount role in sixteenth- and seventeenth-century life, such was the importance given to lavish display (costumes were even paraded by noblemen at their executions). Yet this was nothing other than the corollary of the heroic stature fixed by the code of Renaissance ethics as the ideal for man. Unfortunately, in Italy the counterpart of so much external display was a bankrupt political situation; hence a passage from *Troilus and Cressida* (V, viii) can be aptly quoted in this connection. Hector has pursued a richly armoured Greek, and when he has killed him, he says: "Most putrified core, so fair without, / Thy goodly armour thus hath cost thy life".

Iconoclasts who maintain that every aspect of the Renaissance was already present in the Middle Ages may well say that at the time of Frederick II portrait busts inspired by classical antiquity were made. This little renascence, however, must be reduced to its proper size; it was at most a limited anticipation of a phenomenon that took on gigantic proportions in the Renaissance. The whole history of the Renaissance portrait can hardly be reduced to a vogue for ancient medals and busts and to an infatuation with a chapter of Pliny's *Natural History* (35.2) dealing with the importance of portraiture to the Romans. There was an exchange of influences with Flemish portrait-painting: Florentine merchants knew the Flemish painters; Memling learned from Perugino and Perugino from Dirk Bouts; van der Weyden's *Entombment of Christ* was modelled on Fra Angelico's; and the famous Portinari altarpiece by van der Goes left a deep impression in Florence.
The main trend, however, was classical inspiration: from the Romans men learned how to perpetuate their effigies in an exemplary fashion. Pliny speaks of life masks as well as of death masks, and Rossellino applied the technique to his busts. In the case of women, the reduction to classical models was hindered by costume and hairstyles; and here the vein of free invention and the zest for catching fleeting facial expressions which was to be developed in the psychological portraits of Leonardo and Raphael intervened. It was in a female bust that Verrocchio boldly included the hands. The frequency of the profile in portraits of women was certainly due to the fact that it is more flattering (cf. Filippo Lippi, Pollaiuolo, Baldovinetti, and Botticelli), but the vogue for it was chiefly determined by Roman imperial coins. Artists studied these just as humanists applied themselves to the

Renaissance, p. 258. 7. Ibid., p. 17. 8. JACOB BURCKHARDT, *Die Cultur der Renaissance in Italien* (Basel, 1860). Engl. ed. *The Civilization of the Renaissance in Italy*, transl. S.G.C. Middlemore, rev. & ed. I. Gordon (New York: Mentor Books, 1960). 9. See my essay " Rinascimento e rinascenze ", in *I Volti del Tempo* (Naples: E.S.I., 1964). 10. *The Theory of the Leisure Class* (New York: Macmillan & Co., 1899). 11. See RO-

study of classical texts. From the Romans they also derived devices and mottoes, taking their inspiration particularly from the *Semper festina lente*, the anchor and dolphin of Titus' medal.
A special category of portraits, those of *condottieri*, offers the most obvious instance of classical inspiration as well as of the Renaissance cult of personality. Gioacchino Lanza Tomasi's *Ritratto del condottiero*[12] might also serve to illustrate the above-mentioned chapter in Burckhardt's book. Burckhardt, however, did not explain what Tomasi argues with subtlety, if at some length — i.e., why the *condottiero*, who in his purest form was a champion of brute force and unscrupulous behaviour, could become " the centre of a civic cult". He was the expression of a manner of waging war which Burckhardt had compared to a work of art (" War as a Work of Art "), and like many other aspects of the Renaissance, he had his roots in the bourgeois and mercantile society whose commercial activity had made Italy the most prosperous country of Europe. In mediaeval Italy the prosperity of trade created a powerful middle class, which at the time of the Renaissance (since, contrary to the opinion of certain modern critics, we believe that at a certain moment lay ideals prevailed over religious ones in the social structure) had reached the stage of enjoying its accumulated wealth and had absorbed new heroic ideals, thus becoming a new aristocracy and founding the various seigniories.
The danger of being taken prisoner and having to pay a heavy ransom prevented the Florentine merchant from bearing arms himself: hence the emergence of mercenaries who contracted to defend the State and ably undertook to damage the enemy economically, with the greatest possible saving of their own effectives. This function of war as a commercial enterprise yielded large profits, which were employed to favour the arts (cf. Sigismondo Malatesta at Rimini and Federigo da Montefeltro at Urbino), because the arts were not only a display of pomp but also a powerful means of advertising.
Certain passages of Poggio Bracciolini's *Historia convivialis* help us to understand how the humanists — whom some imagine as bent on purifying Christian dogma by injecting doses of Neoplatonism — could lend themselves to celebrating figures whom Tomasi compares to modern football champions in order to make their popularity comprehensible, though they were actually no better than gangsters. A quotation from Tomasi reads as follows:

> Only the populace and the rabble are bound by your laws; the ties of the law exist only for them. Grave, prudent, and decorous men need no laws. They themselves have formulated their own law of existence, conditioned as they are to cultivate virtue and good customs by their very nature and education.... As for strong men, they reject and break the laws suited for the weak, the mercenaries, the cowards, the wretched, the lazy, and those who have no means.... Indeed, all noteworthy and memorable enterprises are born from violence and injustice: in short, from the violation of laws.

Tomasi recalls Machiavelli, but one is also reminded of Nietzsche and of d'Annunzio's hero, Corrado Brando.
From the encounter of this military profession and the peculiar idea of *virtù* which proceeds from it, on one hand, with the humanists' dream of classical restoration on the other, was born the iconography of the *condottiero*. The latter no longer wished to be commemorated *gisant*, like a humble Christian resigned to God's will and lying atop his tomb. By this time even Christ began to be represented as triumphant rather than as nailed on the cross or laid in the sepulchre. Mediaeval *gisants* were portrayed as souls anxious for their

SITA LEVI-PISETZKY, *Storia del costume in Italia*, III, *Il Cinquecento, il Seicento* (Milan: Istituto Editoriale Italiano, 1966). The tradition of dressing well is still alive in Italy, particularly in the lower middle class. 12. Turin: Edizioni RAI, 1967.

own salvation; but the Christian attitude has already vanished in Cangrande's sarcophagus, in which the presentation of the dead warrior to God is omitted. The *memento mori* was abandoned, and its place was taken by the glorification of the worldly hero in the full vigour of action; art took up the task of exorcising death. The *condottieri* asked that their prerogatives should be respected in the realism of equestrian statues and in triumphal representations; the recumbent warrior (Guidarello Guidarelli) disappeared from art. What we noticed apropos of the Chancellor Rolin before the Virgin also happens here: in Altichiero's fresco of the presentation of the three Cavalli warriors to the Virgin (in the Cavalli Chapel in Sant'Anastasia at Verona), the armoured donor dominates the rest of the *sacra conversazione*. Federigo da Montefeltro, too, stands out from the rest of the composition in Piero della Francesca's altarpiece in the Brera: the supremacy of the holy figures is lost. Medals, busts, and equestrian statues were inspired by Roman models; the cult of Livy's mythical heroes replaced that of the seven mediaeval worthies. Then, at the beginning of the sixteenth century when the *condottiero* was humbled and displaced as a result of the introduction of firearms and mass armies, the courtier and the sacred prince in armour appeared in his place. Dosso Dossi's Alfonso d'Este (after 1528) is the symbol of an epos which was no longer real, a hero transfigured by the painted panegyric, who was not afraid of the smell of powder and whose shining weapons have been reduced to the mere insignia of nobility, like the collar of the Order of St. Michael he wears around his neck; Titian's Francesco Maria della Rovere is a *condottiero* only in his attire. A new idealization in the name of beauty replaced the grim-faced portraits of warriors which had required two generations of artistic development to reach their climax in Colleoni's bust.
In Italy, therefore, under the stimulus of the heroic ideals of the Renaissance and with the rise of the upper-middle-class to the rank of aristocracy, the representative portrait of the single person developed.

The mercantile prosperity which flourished in Holland in the seventeenth century had a different issue. Here, too, thriving trade brought about the blossoming of art; but if we compare the Dutch artistic production with that of the rest of Europe, we find ourselves in quite a different world.
The concept of Baroque, as Johan Huizinga has remarked in his well-known outline of seventeenth-century Dutch civilization, is hardly applicable to Holland during that period:

> There is indeed a figure, Vondel, who harmonizes with it almost perfectly. But most of the other manifestations and personalities of the period diverge from the pattern in a surprising manner. A landscape by Ruisdael or van Goyen, a genre piece by Jan Steen, a painting representing a Militia Company by Frans Hals or van der Helst, and also what really matters in Rembrandt, are all things breathing a completely different air and having a quite different temper. The Low Countries of that period in their most typical aspects have very little in common with the France, Italy, or Germany of the time. Neither precision of style nor magniloquent gesture nor majesty of carriage is characteristic of the Low Countries.[13]

Besides this difference, which seems almost as if it were due to a curtain separating Holland from the rest of Europe, the surprising thing is the echo of Dutch art throughout the

13. "Nederland's beschaving in de zeventiende eeuw", in *Verzamelde Werken*, ed. L. Brummel, W. R. Juynboll, J. G. Locher, II (Haarlem, 1948).

world. If we consider the extension of the territory from which this type of civilization radiated, we discover — as Huizinga has remarked — that " the civilization of the Low Countries in Rembrandt's time, in both its receptive and its creative aspects, was concentrated within a territory of a hundred square miles or little more ". This seems a miracle comparable only to that of a small city-state of the ancient world, Athens. And as Athens triumphed over Xerxes, so Holland triumphed over Philip II.
The political and religious conditions were peculiar. But first considering the geographical situation, we find that shortly after 1300 the provinces of Holland and Zealand were already maritime powers; supported a century later by the political strength of the Burgundian dukes who had extended their dominion over the Low Countries between 1384 and 1428, they could compete with the German Hansa in control of the seas. The geographical situation included a fortunate internal system of waterways, major rivers, and minor water-courses, allowing easy communication in a period in which the only motive power to compete with sails or oars was the horse. Huizinga also remarks: " The horseman or knight might go hunting on the moor, but he had little or no authority in matters of commerce; for this reason, the nobility already carried less weight with us than elsewhere ". In addition, the shape of the land hindered the development of large estates; the old landed nobility, whose income was comparatively modest, as a rule had preserved simple and patriarchal habits. Since the most important provinces were the maritime and mercantile ones, namely Holland and Zealand, the aristocratic class — which was still numerous in agricultural regions — carried little weight in the government of the republic. The clergy likewise had no great importance, in complete contrast to the situation in the southern Low Countries (Liège, Brabant, Flanders, and Hainault). For this reason the Reformation did not meet any serious obstacle in taking root in Holland, although one should not overestimate the influence of Calvinism on the development of the capitalistic system. The only dominant class, both for economic strength and intellectual ripeness, was that of the merchants: and it was from this class that the magistrates, to whom the government of the republic was entrusted, came.

The heyday of trade actually occurred during the critical period of the long war of independence against Spain, to which the Low Countries had been subjected under Charles V. The rebellion, which had started with William the Silent, succeeded in 1579 in giving unity only to the northern provinces; although *de facto* recognition had already been achieved with the twelve years' truce with Spain in 1609, *de jure* recognition had to wait until the Treaty of Münster in 1648. Under Maurice of Orange (1567-1625) — the son of William the Silent, stadtholder of the provinces of Holland, Zealand, Utrecht, Gelderland, and Overijssel, and captain-general of the Union — the United Provinces became the greatest naval power in the world, with large colonies in the East and West Indies which were a source of much wealth.[14] The ideas prevailing in Holland regarding the economy and organization were not more advanced than those of the other states; on the contrary, the system in force was still the pre-mercantilist one of the late Middle Ages. However, the free regime of the mediaeval communes still survived (the same which had permitted the commercial blossoming of the Italian republics in the Middle Ages), unim-

14. JAKOB ROSENBERG, SEYMOUR SLIVE, E. H. TER KUILE, *Dutch Art and Architecture, 1600-1800*, Pelican History of Art (Harmondsworth: Penguin Books Ltd., 1966), p. 5.

peded by the fiscal demands that hampered trade in countries of centralized administration — although in these very countries the first mercantilist experiments in the modern sense had developed soon after the end of the Middle Ages. The Dukes of Burgundy had wisely abstained from interfering, even to their own advantage, in an economic system which worked very well by itself. It was, in fact, the Hapsburg government's plans for centralization (advanced though they were in some respects, for example in the unification of penal law) which, by threatening to stifle free initiative, provoked the revolt. It was a conservative revolt, for the preservation of those mediaeval franchises which, in their turn, by favouring trade and the accumulation of wealth, produced the Amsterdam monetary market and consequently paved the way to advanced economic ideas. Amsterdam became the banking centre of Europe in a period when sovereigns were willing to pay high rates of interest for money needed for their wars. It also became the first centre of the antique market and of the great European auctions.

How a little country like Holland could have beaten a great power like Spain may perhaps be more easily understood today than in any other historical period by taking the war in Vietnam as an analogy. Even then the other states were beset by great difficulties so that they were unable to pursue an energetic foreign policy: the German Empire was paralyzed by the Thirty Years' War; France, having just emerged from the wars of religion, was engaged in defending herself against the Hapsburg power; England was busily concentrating her energies on the struggle for her own form of government. The Dutch were few but determined, and the Spaniards far from their bases and fighting against a hostile population.

Unlike other European countries, the centre of Holland's social and intellectual life was not the princely court at The Hague, which was actually very subdued in tone. Prince Frederick Henry (1584-1647) — younger brother of Maurice and his successor as stadtholder, captain, and admiral-general of the United Provinces — gave a few commissions to Rembrandt, but neither he nor other members of the House of Orange patronized Frans Hals, Vermeer, Ruisdael, Jan Steen, or any of the minor painters. The culture which flourished in other Dutch towns had no relation to court life. It was an essentially bourgeois culture and did not lend itself to the glorification of a race of sovereigns; thus, when the widow of Frederick Henry intended to decorate her country-house near The Hague, Huis ten Bos, with paintings celebrating the life of her deceased husband, she turned not to Dutch but to Flemish artists, and Jacob Jordaens had the lion's share in the undertaking.[15] Painters, as well as the military heroes of the nation like the great admirals (Tromp, De Ruyter, Piet Hein), came from the middle class and on the social plane were less esteemed than poets. Apart from Rembrandt, who had his moment of celebrity but later succumbed to financial catastrophe and died in poverty, none of the Dutch painters became a gentleman as did Rubens, van Dyck, and Velázquez. Only a few of them travelled to Italy, and their clients consisted not only of rich bourgeois but also of people belonging to a lower social rank. The Englishman Peter Mundy, who visited Amsterdam in 1640, has left this record:

As For the art off Painting and the affection off the people to Pictures, I thincke none other goe beeyond them, there having bin in this Country Many excellent Men in thatt Facullty, some att

15. Ibid., pp. 5-6.

presentt, as Rimbrantt, etts, All in generall striving to adorne their houses, especially the outer or street roome, with costly peeces, Butchers and bakers not much inferiour in their shoppes, which are Fairely sett Forth, yea many tymes blacksmithes, Coblers, etts., will have some picture or other by their Forge and in their stalle. Such is the generall Notion, enclination and delight that these Countrie Native(s) have to Paintings.[16]

In the following year John Evelyn visited the annual fair of Rotterdam and was amazed by the great numbers of pictures he saw, " especially Landscips, and Drolleries, as they call those clownish representations ". According to Evelyn, " The reason of this store of pictures and their cheapenesse proceede from their want of Land, to employ their Stock; so as 'tis an ordinary thing to find, a common Farmor lay out two, or 3000 pounds in this Commodity, their houses are full of them, and they vend them at their Kermas'es to very greate gaines ".[17]

The dwindling of sacred art as a consequence of Protestantism was a favourable circumstance for the development of the art of portraiture, of the interior scene, and of genre painting. What had been an accessory (the figure of the donor in a *sacra conversazione*) or background (landscape and small figures in it) became foreground by the very fact of the disappearance of the religious element. This tendency was already evident in Brueghel's sacred paintings; in his *Preaching of Saint John the Baptist* or his *Ascent to Calvary* he was not so much interested in the divine figures as in the picturesque variety of the crowd which clusters round them and almost prevents us from seeing them. The same is true of the *Ecce Homo* by Lucas van Leyden (1513), as well as of that by Frans Francken II, which has altogether the appearance of a genre painting.[18] Houses were decorated instead of churches, houses whose rooms became more and more embellished, though they remained small in size; hence the predominance of paintings of small proportions. More deliberately than anywhere else, art in Holland aimed at satisfying, delighting, and edifying an austere and prosperous social class. A contrast to people's higher spiritual life — which took place in the dry, abstract atmosphere of unadorned white churches— was provided by the vanity of seeing themselves represented in their own environment (even, as we shall see, in rooms more lavishly decorated than their own), in the bosom of their family or among their favourite chattels and pets. With the absence of an heroic ideal in the sense of Machiavelli's *virtù*, Dutch portrait painters did not attempt to invest their models with ideal qualities (unlike Flemish painters such as Gonzales Coques, who tried to give a Vandyckian air of distinction to his sitters). The subjects of the paintings remain what they were in real life; their traits did not have to conform to a set standard, either devout or warlike. They remain what they were, essentially bourgeois. Whereas Italy produced the aristocratic portrait depicting a person conscious of his rank, in Holland we find the bourgeois portrait, intended for communication, and the conversation piece, in which figures seem almost to invite the onlooker to share their domestic joys. Until the end of the eighteenth century, the conversation piece flourished in Holland exclusively in well-to-do bourgeois milieux, among professional men, merchants, and industrialists who, together with farmers and seamen, formed the backbone of the nation.[19] As we have

16. Ibid., p. 9; quotation from *The Travels of Peter Mundy in Europe and Asia, 1608-1667*, IV, *Travels in Europe, 1639-1647*, ed. Richard Carnac Temple (London: Hakluyt Society, 1925), p. 70. 17. Ibid.; quotation from *The Diary of John Evelyn*, ed. E. S. de Beer (Oxford, 1935), p. 39. 18. See LEGRAND, op. cit., pp. 10 ff: "Les 'Tableaux de moeurs' et la métamorphose du sujet religieux ". 19. See A. STARING, *De Hollanders Thuis*

noted above, this middle class provided the families of the oligarchy which ruled the United Provinces. The sitters in the paintings in question were never persons of the landed gentry.

Thus in Holland the conversation piece became a flourishing branch of painting which spread to other European countries, aided by the same social phenomenon which furthered the cult for interior decoration among the upper classes, as Lewis Mumford has explained.[20] The advent of absolutism in Europe during the seventeenth century diminished the importance of the bourgeoisie in public affairs (an importance which cannot be overestimated during the Middle Ages and the Renaissance). This was the main reason why the bourgeois, particularly those of them — and there were many — who belonged to persecuted religious communities, tried to find a compensating interest within the domestic sphere, the ritual of " conspicuous consumption " which involves the care of furniture.

The fixtures of the mediaeval household were equipment: chairs to sit on, beds to sleep in, icons to pray before: so much and no more. Furniture is really a re-invention of the baroque period, for by furniture one means useless or super-refined equipment: delicate vases to dust, inlays and precious woods to polish, metal work to keep shiny, curtains to be shaken and cleaned, bric-à-brac and curios to be washed. Display outstripped use; and the care of furniture commanded time that once went into the weaving of tapestries, the embroidery of garments, the making of useful household preserves, perfumes, and simples. These new burdens were inflicted upon housewives and domestics at the very moment that the form of the house itself had changed, multiplying the number of private chambers to be supplied with wood, coal, water, and raising the height of dwellings from two flights of stairs to five, one below ground. Up to the seventeenth century, at least in the North, building and heating had hardly advanced far enough to permit the arrangement of a series of private rooms in the dwelling. But now a separation of functions took place within the house as well as within the city as a whole.... The dining room was separated from the bedroom; and though in the seventeenth century a lady's bedroom still served as a reception room for her guests, whether or not the bed stood in an alcove, in the eighteenth century a special room for meeting and conversation, the drawing room, the salon, came into existence.[21]

It seems as if the pleasure of inventorying and of mustering a universality of things is behind both the accumulation of furnishings (which reached its climax in the Victorian era) and the cumulative representation of a whole family in a painting, as well as the minute — and often superfluous and cumbersome — descriptions of milieux in novels. One glimpses behind all this the figure of Marin van Reymerswael's merchant, counting money on his money-changer's desk.

As Max J. Friedländer has remarked, " the Dutch view of the world, taken by and large, is objective, modest and patient.... They knew what they were depicting and guarded against depicting anything they did not know ".[22] The Dutch were distant cousins of Chaucer, who felt able to deal with a pilgrimage to Canterbury, but not, like Dante, with a journey to the other world. Taking up the opposition outlined by Thackeray in his essay " Small-Beer Chronicle " (July 1861) between those who try to swell beyond their natural size (*vin ordinaire* giving itself the airs of port) and those who are content to show their genuine qualities, no matter how modest (namely, of the small-beer sort), we might venture to say that the Dutch were content to chronicle small beer, although no doubt they were mightily pleased with their neat furnishings and domestic affections. They practised

(The Hague: Martinus Nijhoff, 1956), p. 58. 20. *The Culture of Cities* (New York: Harcourt Brace & Co., 1938). 21. Ibid., p. 115. 22. *Landscape, Portrait, Still Life* (Oxford: Bruno Cassirer, 1949), p. 105.

what an English writer of our century, Denton Welch, had set himself as an aim: " I wish that people should mention the tiny things of their lives that give them pleasure or fear or wonder. I would like to hear the details of their houses, their meals and their possessions. I would like to hear the bits of family or intimate history they know ".[23]

The inspiration of the Dutch conversation pieces is earthly, or even *terre à terre*, but still it is enlivened with a neatness and tidiness which makes us aware of the resemblance of this kind of painting to the country which produced it. " Sky and clouds, then as today, were mild elements which unbend the spirit. The modest towns, girt by their green ramparts, rose in the midst of more green, and wherever there was no moor, there was water either in large rivers or small rivulets — water, the most ancient element in creation, over which first the spirit of God hovered; water, the simplest of terrestrial things. No wonder that in this region men also were simple in their thoughts and manners, their attire, and their houses ".[24]

With this character of the Dutch landscape summed up by Huizinga we may compare the following passage by William Morris on the landscape of England, the other country in which the conversation piece reached its highest development: " Not much space for swelling into hugeness;... no great wastes overwhelming in their dreariness, no great solitudes of forests, no terrible untrodden mountain walls; all is measured, mingled, varied, gliding easily one thing into another, little rivers, little plains,... little hills, little mountains ... neither prison, nor palace, but a decent home ".[25]

Lucien Goldmann might have produced detailed documentary evidence drawn from the mercantile history of Holland in order to throw light on the origins of the small-format painting called the conversation piece; here we have given only a short account of its origins, and we might conclude by stating that favourable conditions for the development of that type of genre painting existed in the North of Europe, but not in Italy.

23. *The Denton Welch Journals*, ed. Jocelyn Brooke (London: Hamish Hamilton, 1952), p. 141. 24. Op. cit., pp. 62-63. 25. "The Lesser Arts", in *The Collected Works of William Morris* (London: Longmans & Co., 1910-15), XXII, p. 17.

CONVERSATION PIECES

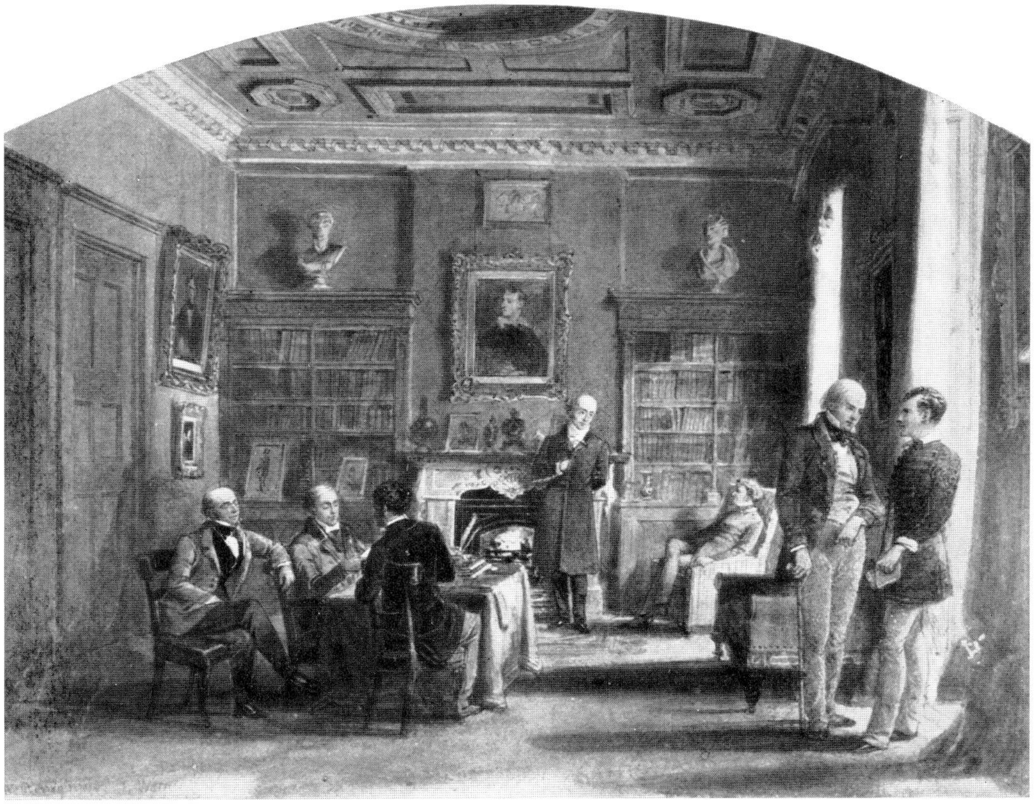

1 ANONYMOUS (19th century), *The Drawing Room of the Publisher John Murray at 50 Albemarle Street, London*, showing (left to right) Isaac D'Israeli, John Murray, Sir John Barrow, George Canning, William Gifford, Sir Walter Scott, Lord Byron. London, collection of John Murray, 50 Albemarle St.

PREFACE – FAMILY PORTRAITS

In the forties of the nineteenth century, at least three thousand five hundred portraits were painted in Berlin alone; of these only five hundred were known to Käte Gläser,[1] the keen scholar who has studied the Berlin portrait painters of that period. Where have all the family groups recorded in the exhibition catalogues of the time been concealed, and how have they disappeared? What has become of the works of four hundred portrait painters of whom nothing remains but their names? I asked Käte Gläser herself the reasons for this curious phenomenon when, many years ago, she happened to be in Rome while attempting to trace some of the missing portraits in various corners of Italy. Whereas Paris was the elementary school of art for the German painters of the Biedermeier period, Italy was its university; they often went there in order to study the great masters, eking out their livelihood by painting landscapes and portraits. Frau Gläser had thought that some of their delightful paintings would surely remain with Italian families, perhaps in Rome or Naples. I was unable to encourage her, because I had never heard of anything of the sort; but how was it, I asked her, that in the North — where there is such a cult for family records and where life is so much concentrated in the home — so many paintings painted only a century ago had vanished? The only reply she could give me was to quote a Berlin proverb, according to which a certain number of moves has the same effect as a fire: so many families were dispersed, and portraits dear to the generation which knew their originals meant nothing to later descendants. In addition, the growth of Impressionism in the second half of the nineteenth century brought about a revolution of taste, and the meticulous precision of the Biedermeier painters — who reproduced every detail of a room — came to be considered banal. The costumes of the sitters looked old-fashioned, and the minute realism which delighted in rendering headdresses, braids, and lace as if in a mirror was judged flat and dull. Even the fine, calm colours, each confined within its own field, appeared sour and cold to people whose vision was conditioned by the flickering and throbbing of Impressionist paintings, which aim at rendering the vibration of light.

1 KÄTE GLÄSER, *Das Bildnis im Berliner Biedermeier* (Berlin: Rembrandt Verlag), 1932.

I reminded Frau Gläser of a page from *Vanity Fair*, apropos of the portrait of the Osborne family:

There was a picture of the family over the mantelpiece, removed thither from the front room after Mrs. Osborne's death — George was on a pony, the elder sister holding him up a bunch of flowers; the younger led by her mother's hand; all with red cheeks and large red mouths, simpering on each other in the approved family-portrait manner. The mother lay underground now, long since forgotten — the sisters and brother had a hundred different interests of their own, and, familiar still, were utterly estranged from each other. Some few score of years afterwards, when all the parties represented are grown old, what bitter satire there is in those flaunting childish family portraits, with their farce of sentiment and smiling lies, and innocence so self-conscious and self-satisfied.[2]

Perhaps the same reason which had persuaded the Osbornes to remove the family portrait from its exalted position (and one may surmise that the next generation would have consigned it to the garret, and from there to the bric-à-brac dealer is but a step) would have urged many Berlin families to remove from sight the minor masterpieces of a Wach, a Magnus, a Hopfgarten, a Begas, a Schoppe, a Herdt, a Hummel, and so on; a whole legion of such painters exists, and although there is no genius in its ranks, on the other hand there is no lack of genuine and exquisite talents.

It is just for this reason that Thackeray's irony about family portraits appears unfair and superficial, as happens all too often with him. Unfairer still is Ivy Compton-Burnett's cruel irony (in *Daughters and Sons*, 1937): " 'I see why a portrait of a family group is called a conversation piece', said Roland coming to escort Miss Marcon — 'They do not generally have such good names for things'. 'Nor such dreadful ones. I daren't look at these pictures because of what I might read into them. It is really too morbid to paint family groups, with a father and a mother and children and no attempt to leave out anything' ". As for Thackeray, he should have been more indulgent in this case, considering how sensitive he was to the appeal of the old familiar faces and how well he knew the art of perpetuating the memory of everyday experiences (see his " Ballad of Bouillabaisse "), for wasn't it he who honoured the humble, humdrum virtues — in contrast with the Passions and Virtues in capital letters — and preached the wisdom of not pretending to be above oneself, and praised the goodness of genuine *vin ordinaire*? If there is a school of painters apropos of which one cannot speak of pretence and hyperbolic affectation, it is the school of portrait painters of the Biedermeier period and of its Victorian equivalent. Thackeray, who has been called the Apostle of Mediocrity, ought instead to have sung their praises. This was the period of diaries, of effusive dedications, of long affectionate letters, of albums of travel-sketches, of dried flowers kept within the leaves of books, and of curious and cumbersome souvenirs. Friendships were fostered with an almost daily exchange of letters; families were really united, clustering together as in these paintings — the father and mother in the centre, the eldest daughter at the piano and another singing a *Lied*, the children busy with their toys. It was the solidity and continuity of the family nucleus — a tiny *civitas* within the bigger one — which causes us through these pictures to imagine the period from 1820 to 1850 as extraordinarily calm and motionless. Instead it fermented with the germs of social and political revolutions: the foundations of the great modern industries were laid at that time; the first sparks of socialism were kindled in the factories; steam-power changed the sense of distance altogether and expanded the horizon to such an extent — a prodigy not unlike the incantation of Gogol's story — that suddenly the world's farthest corners were made visible, as if the air had become incredibly pellucid. All this was taking place, but the middle class in its heyday was proud of the new manner of life it had established in the world. Its members had themselves portrayed in everyday scenes, surrounded by beloved chattels, and with familiar views from the windows — even views of the factories which were the source of their prosperity; in the painting by David J. Bles of *The Family of Karel Enthoven* (1855) a picture hanging from the far wall shows a view of the rolling-mill from which the family had made a fortune (fig. 3). In the same way the aristocracy had once included some symbol of the family name, like the painting representing a fountain which Hogarth put into his portrait of *The Fountaine Family* (fig. 2).

In the eighteenth century aristocratic sitters would be shown with a park as background, in the shadow of a voluminous curtain swollen with a baroque wind; in the Empire period parvenus had themselves portrayed sitting on a curule chair in a columned hall, frequently with a classical bust as a protective deity nearby. Now the bourgeois family sat for the painter in the breakfast

2 THACKERAY, *Vanity Fair*, ch.xxiv.

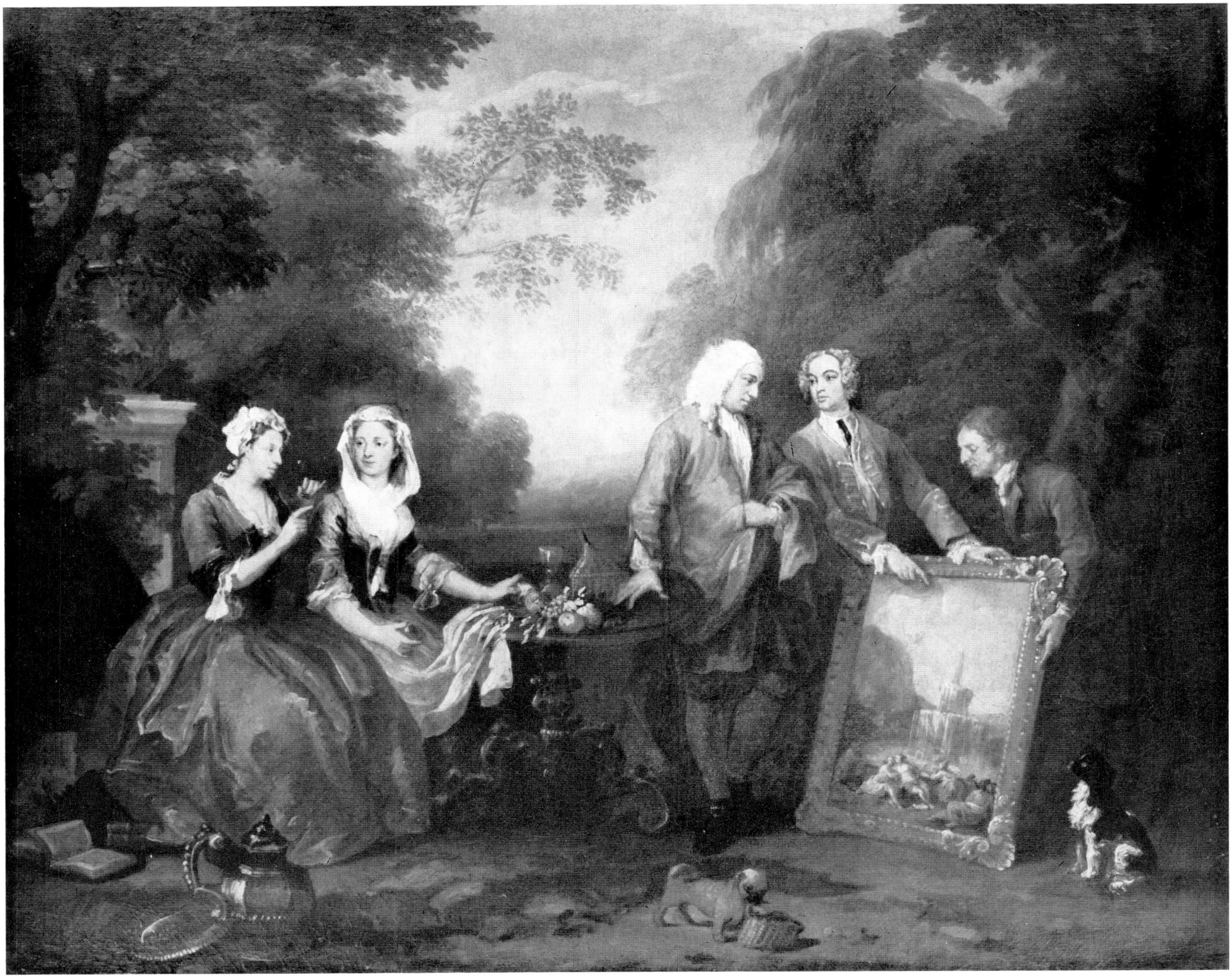

2

2 WILLIAM HOGARTH (1697-1764), *The Fountaine Family*. Philadelphia Museum of Art (John H. McFadden Collection).

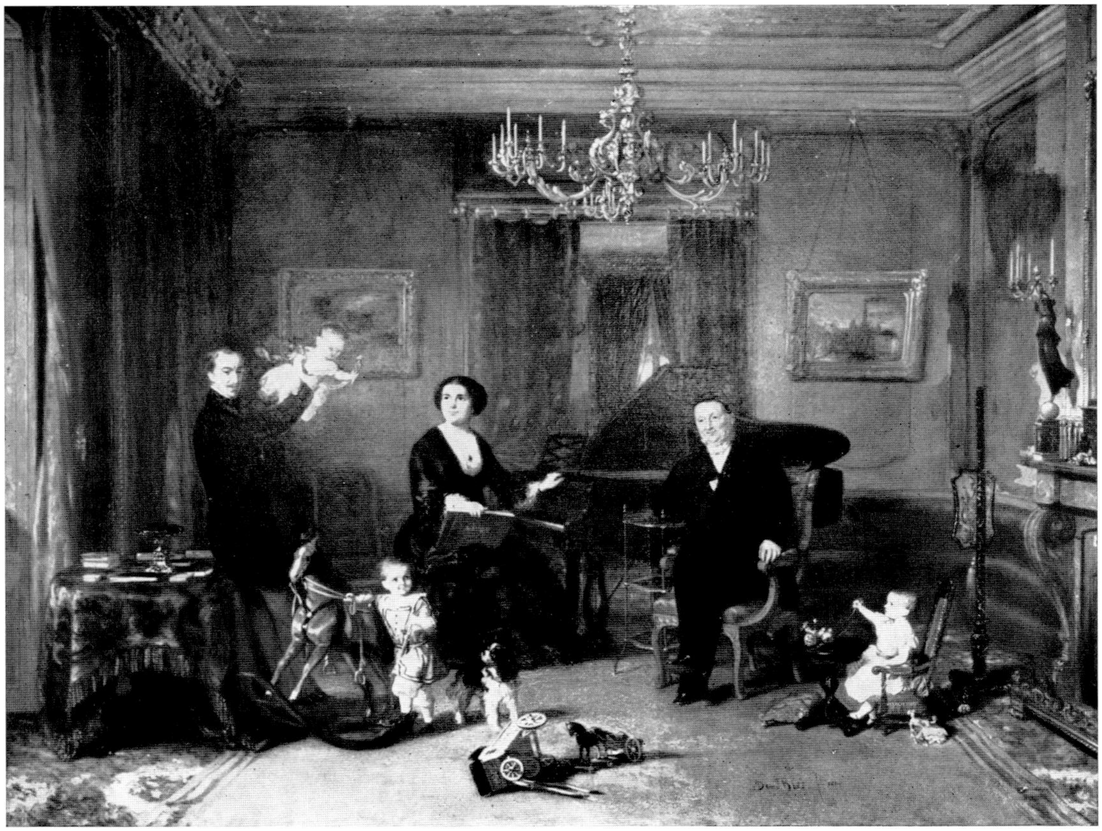

3

3 DAVID J. BLES (1821-1899), *The Family of Karel Enthoven*, 1855. Coral Gables (Florida), collection of Mr. and Mrs. Frank Enthoven Kerdyk.

room or in the small garden, with a view from the window of the steeple of the parish church, or of the street with the shop which was the centre of their activity, or of the modest urban orchard. The children of Parson Berduschek by Piotrowski greet their father and mother who, Bibles in hand and dressed in Sunday clothes (he with immaculate bands on the front of his gown, she wearing a freshly-ironed lace cap) are on their way to the parish church where the Parson will preach to the congregation — visible through the window — approaching the church gate; the air quivers with festive chimes (fig. 5). The family of Mathieu the gardener by Louise Henry sit round a table among the exotic plants they rear, behind which rise the spires of Potsdam. A melon and a few peaches lie upon the table, which is covered with a printed calico tablecloth; one of the daughters is busy filling a flower basket and the other slices off a salad stump. An equal serenity seems to emanate both from the human faces and from the large magnolia and rhododendron blossoms (fig. 4). There is no heroic pretence in these Biedermeier paintings. Even if the scene is a military parade, as in Krüger's famous one, the warlike display is turned into a peaceful spectacle: the painter delights more in painting the groups of well-to-do bourgeois who line the parade ground than the brilliant uniforms of the troops. Even royal personages remove their crowns and hold garlands in their hands, as in the portrayal of the Princess of the Low Countries by Wilhelm Wach.

Frequently the girls or women portrayed by these painters carry flower baskets or attractive nosegays (*Blumenbukett*), or wear or hold a garland. Little Wanda von Graefe by Julius Schoppe holds in her right hand a bunch of roses, lilies of the valley, and forget-me-nots and places her other hand on a flower basket, by the bank of a smooth canal in a park; young Eliza and Theodor Wegener sit under the shadow of an ancient tree, and Eliza has a basket of roses and pansies in the lap of her bright dress; the dancer Amalia Taglioni by Herdt, daisy-wreathed, hovers over a rose bush; the daughter of the painter Kretzchmar has a

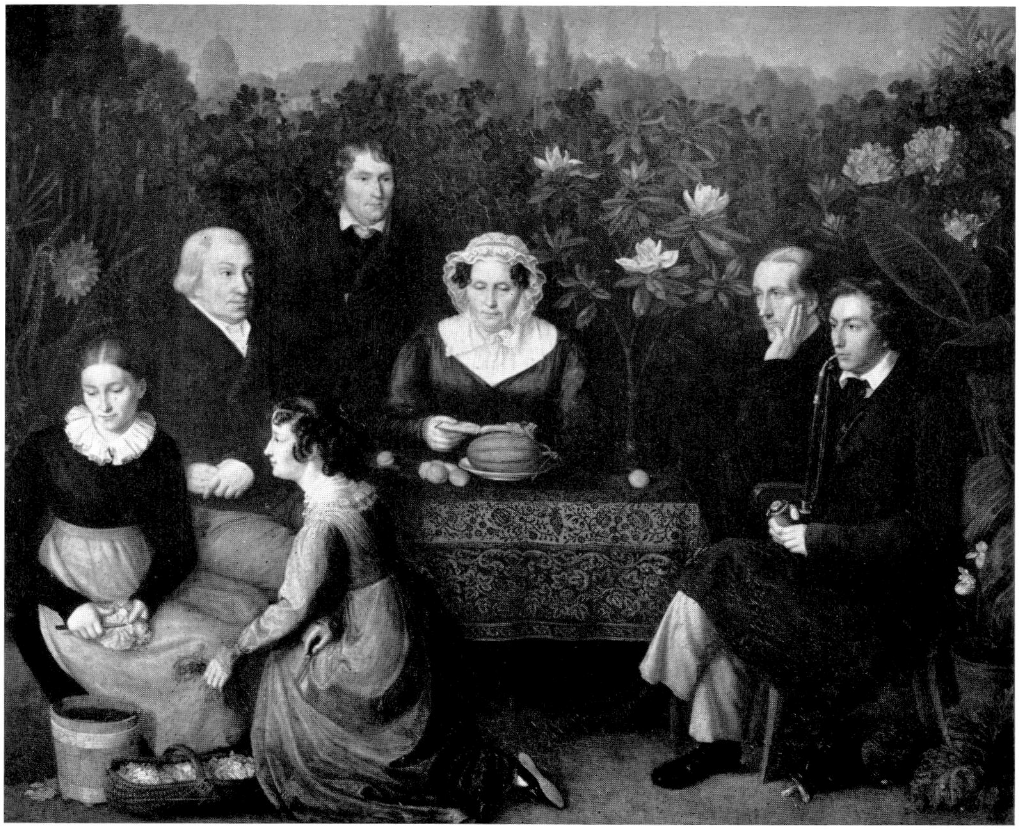

4 LOUISE HENRY (1798-1839), *The Family of the Berlin Gardener Mathieu*, c. 1820. Formerly in a private collection, Berlin; photo Nationalgalerie, Berlin: Käte Gläser Archives.

tame bird perching on one of her hands and lays the other near flowers contained in a crystal vase which, like a convex mirror, reflects the room; the little daughter of Magnus the banker places a flower basket on her mother's lap, and the sister-in-law of the painter Fielgraf crowns the artist's fiancée, who wears her wedding dress, with a wreath; Princess Charlotte of Prussia by Hensel wears a rose wreath, as does Princess Liegnitz by Hopfgarten. A subtle harmony of violet, mauve, and pink usually predominates in all these paintings. One could almost say that the age saw in the microcosm of a nosegay the symbol of its predilection for objects neat, pretty, agreeable to the senses, and arranged in a comely symmetry, almost as if the chief aspiration of these matter-of-fact and sentimental middle-class people was to see the society of men harmonized like a well-contrived bunch of flowers. If Pater felt that the spirit of the Renaissance was summed up in the portrait of la Gioconda, why should we not in our turn feel that the spirit of the Biedermeier style is summed up in the portrait of Princess Liegnitz who, in an attitude similar to that of Leonardo's mysterious lady, rises beside the calm waters of a park? That good-natured presence beside the waters is expressive of what, in the course of a hundred years, men had come to desire. It is a beauty wrought out from within upon the flesh, contrived by the prosperous mercantile commerce of the Age of Enlightenment, by Rousseau's love of nature and his optimism, and by the sentimentalism of the romantic " beautiful souls ". Here is the head upon which " the ends of the world " have become reconciled in a bland compromise: but her eyelids are not weary; she is fresh and adorned like the roses which crown her head, and all the past to her is but as the sound of the violin and harpsichord which accompanies the words of a simple and tender romance. Truly there are moments in which one feels more pleasure in contemplating this tidy doll, precious like a flower seen against a background of still waters, than in regarding the celebrated Monna Lisa, with her ambiguous smile teeming with magnificent and sinister allusions, standing before a background of waters seething in meanders and whirlpools among fantastic rocks.

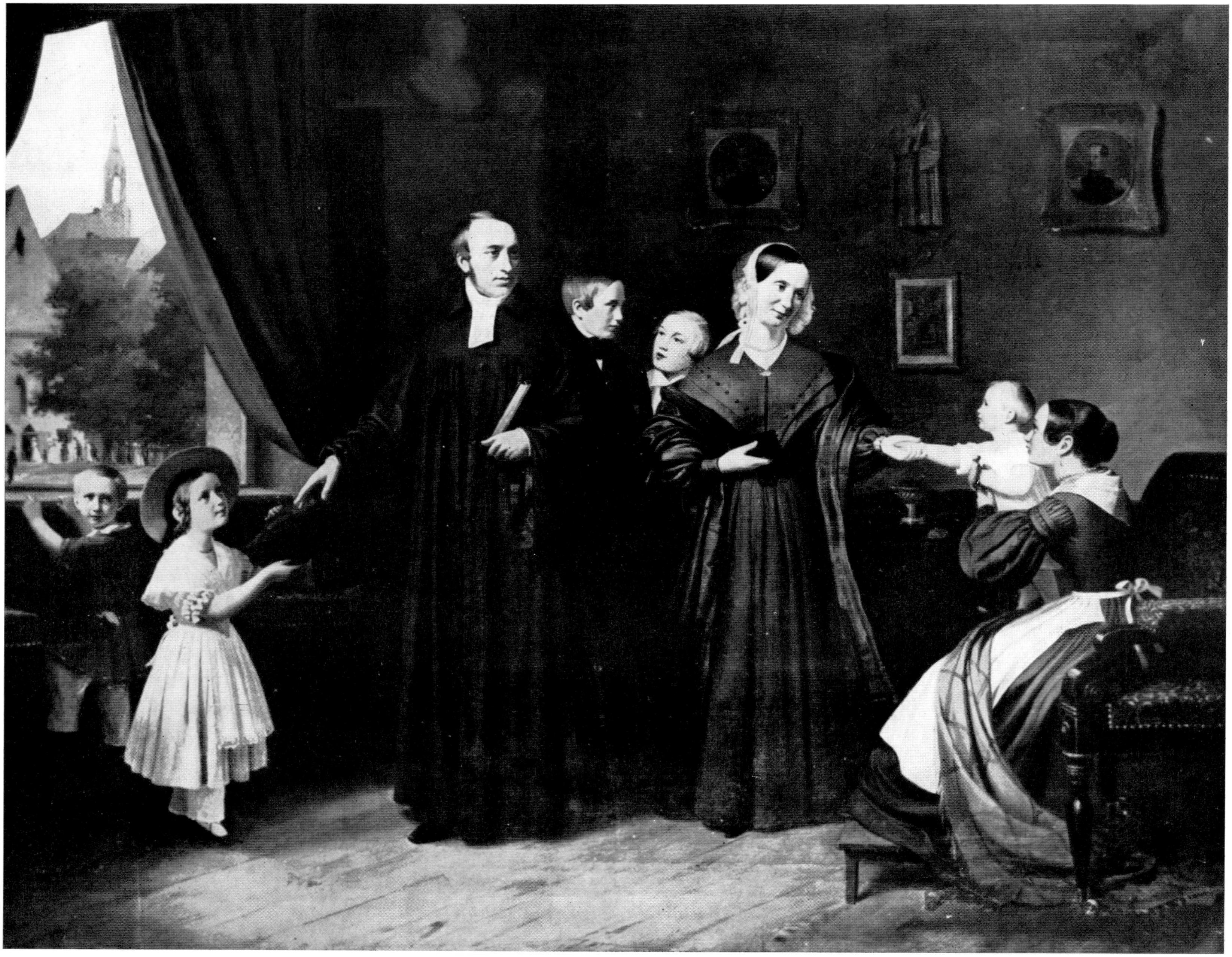

5

5 MAXIMILIAN ANTON PIOTROWSKI (1813-1875), *The Family of the Minister J.F. Berduschek*, 1842. Formerly in East Berlin, Märkisches Museum; destroyed during the war.

CHAPTER I – DEFINITION OF THE CONVERSATION PIECE

The term " conversation piece " is used in England for paintings, usually not of large dimensions, which represent two or more identifiable people in attitudes implying that they are conversing or communicating with each other informally, against a background reproduced in detail. We shall return shortly to this definition in order to make it even more precise; but first of all let us put the reader on guard against an error into which even a normally cultivated person might fall by imagining that the English term is an adaptation of the Italian *sacra conversazione*, by which one designates a group of saints gathered round the Virgin and Child enthroned, not necessarily signifying by their attitudes that they are conversing either among themselves or with the central figures. This was indeed the belief of an otherwise well-informed author of a volume on three centuries of Dutch conversation pieces: " A ' conversation ', in its original meaning, was adopted from the Italian word *conversazione*, denoting a group of figures, either holy or profane, engaged in quiet communication which might not necessarily be a conversation ".[1]

Although the Italian *sacre conversazioni* are much earlier than the " profane conversations " known as conversation pieces, no Italian dictionary registers the use of the term for a group of persons represented by a painting or a sculpture. Ralph Edwards states that " the secular use of *Conversazione* in the sense of a social gathering of people, or a club, is found in the title of Della Casa's *Trattato* (*Galateo*, *Rime et Prose*, Venice, 1558) ".[2] The long title of the *Galateo* actually reads: *Trattato nel qual, sotto la persona d'un vecchio idiota, ammaestrante un suo giovanetto, si ragiona de' modi che si debbano o tenere o schifare nella comune conversazione, cognominato Galateo, ovvero de' costumi.* It was translated into English in 1576 by Robert Paterson: *Galateo... or rather, A Treatise of the manners and behaviours it behoveth a man to use and eschewe, in his familiar conversation.* The word occurs also in the title of Stefano Guazzo's work, *Della civil conversazione*, which was widely circulated in England in a translation (*The Civile Conversation*) by George Pettie (the first three books, published in 1581) and Bartholomew Young (the fourth book, published in 1586). Florio

1 A. STARING, *De Hollanders Thuis* (The Hague: Nijhoff, 1956). 2 *Early Conversation Pictures from the Middle Ages to about 1730: A Study in Origins* (London: Country Life Ltd., 1954).

in his *Second Fruites* (1591) mentions Guazzo's book next to Castiglione's *Cortegiano* as " the two books most commonly read by those who desire to know a little Italian ". Whereas in the Italian dictionaries there is no trace of the use of *conversazione* to designate a picture of the type described, the English usage was established from the beginning of the eighteenth century. Vertue in his Notebooks reports that a Dutch artist who had come over to England, Egbert van Heemskerk, used to call his genre pictures in the manner of Brouwer " conversations ", and Buckridge writes in his *Essay towards an English School* (about 1706) that Marcellus Laroon the Elder was " fam'd for Pictures in Little, commonly called Conversation Pieces ". Cornelis de Bie in his verse eulogy[3] of the painter Christoffel van der Lamen (1606/7–1651/2), who painted gentlemen and ladies gathered together for the purpose of dancing, conversing, or playing society games, defined the artist as a *conversatie schilder*, that is, a painter of conversation pieces.[4] Thus the term was used in Holland earlier than in England to describe genre paintings portraying groups of persons, actually not very different from the Italian *bambocciate* — except for the depreciative tone the latter word derived from the nickname given to the Dutchman Pieter van Laer (" il Bamboccio ", active in Rome from 1625 to 1638). Vertue speaks of " conversations " by Teniers, Brouwer, and Brueghel, and the quotations in the *Oxford English Dictionary* are all of the same import, always alluding to Dutch genre paintings.

On the other hand, Jacob Burckhardt in his essay *Das Altarbild* (written in 1893-94) states that the term *sacra conversazione* is a fairly recent one, and that previously paintings of this kind were called *Madonna con santi;* hence Edwards concludes that the term *sacra conversazione*, instead of being at the origin of a " conversation piece ", " seems to have been adopted, probably *ad analogiam*, in comparatively recent times ".

Next to " conversation " the English vocabulary defines the Italian term *conversazione* in the sense of " assembly for conversation or social recreation ", a sense which was current in mediaeval Latin of the tenth century and in Italy from the thirteenth century on. Foreign travellers in Italy during the eighteenth century speak of this custom; thus Thomas Gray in a letter of 1740 to his mother: " The diversions of a Florentine Lent are... in the evening, what is called a *conversazione*, a sort of assembly at the principal people's houses, full of I cannot tell what " (OED); and Alexander Drummond in his *Travels through different cities of Germany, Italy, etc.* of 1754: " These *conversazioni* [at Florence] resemble our card-assemblies: — some played at cards, some passed the time in conversation, others walked from place to place ". The sense of a familiar gathering proper to the Italian word must have influenced the term " conversation piece " already current for a genre painting representing a gathering of people, so that in the course of time the sense of " conversation piece " was restricted to a painting portraying a family group.

Returning to the definition of the " conversation piece " — a word which has no Italian equivalent, strange as this may seem after what we have been saying — we may attempt to list its characteristics (in the same academic spirit that prompted Paolo Giovio to dictate the rules for a perfect " device "[5]) as:

First, two or more identifiable people, or at least persons appearing as themselves and not as types or fictitious characters; this rules out genre paintings such as the interior scenes by Metsu, Terborch, etc., and — in the eighteenth and nineteenth centuries — those by artists like Chardin, Boilly, or Marguerite Gérard illustrating situations or episodes whose participants are generic types.

Second, a background which describes the habitat of the family or group. We shall see that the taste for the representation of surroundings proceeds apace with that for the portrayal of the family group.

Third, action: a gesture signifying conversation or communication of some kind from at least a few of the components of the group.

Fourth, privacy (i.e., not a public or official function).

3 *Het Gulden Cabinet* (Lierre, 1661), p. 159. 4 See F.-C. LEGRAND, *Les peintres flamands de genre au XVIIe siècle* (Brussels: Éditions Meddens, 1963), p. 84.
5 See M. PRAZ, *Studies in Seventeenth-Century Imagery*, Studies of the Warburg Institute, 3 (London: The Warburg Institute, 1939), pp. 54-55 (new edition: Rome, Edizioni di Storia e Letteratura, 1964, p. 63).

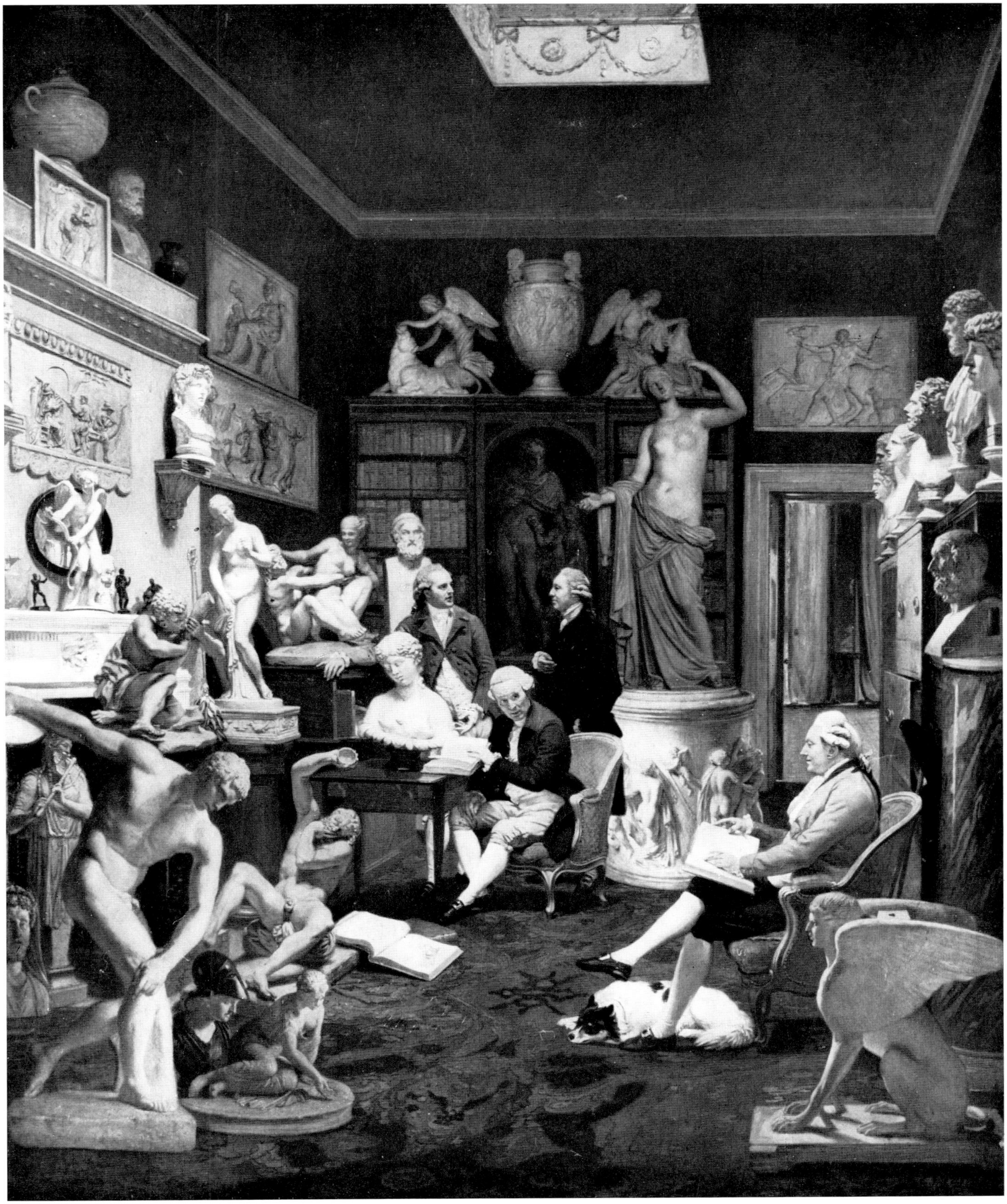

6

6 JOHANN ZOFFANY (1734/5-1810), *Charles Towneley and his Friends in his Library*, 1790. Burnley (Lancashire), Towneley Hall Art Gallery and Museum.

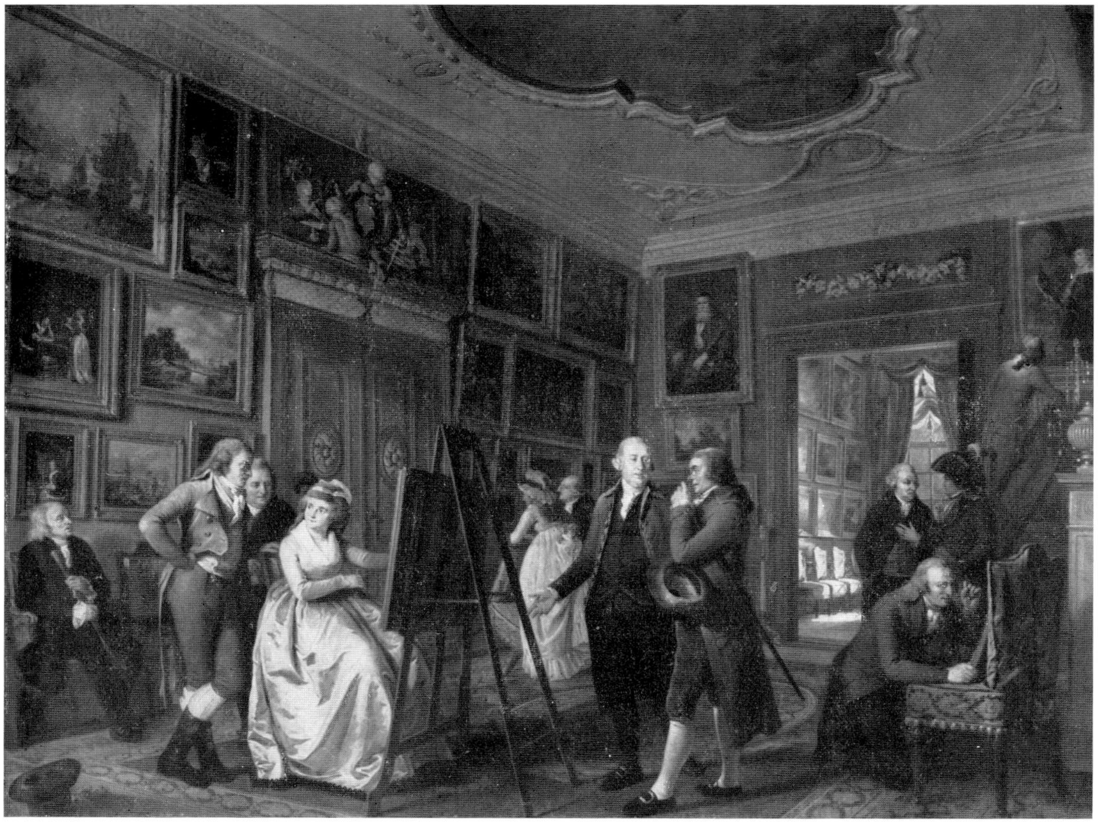

7 ADRIAAN DE LELIE (1755-1820), *Jan Gildemeester Jansz. in his Gallery*, 1794-5. Amsterdam, Rijksmuseum.

This eliminates portraits of sovereigns represented in their official roles (but not, of course, if they are represented informally, in the bosoms of their families), as well as scenes of balls, weddings, and assemblies of companies of militiamen (cf. works by Hals and Rembrandt, for example),[6] and imaginary (though probable) meetings of representative people. An example of the latter is the study of the publisher John Murray with Byron, Scott, Thomas Moore, and others (fig. 1). There are two versions of this painting, one of 1815 in monochrome (destroyed in the war), and a later one containing the same persons except one, J.W. Croker, in the same postures but grown older. Byron wears a frogged coat in the latter, which seems to point to a date very close to his departure to join the Greek insurgents in 1823. The reason for Croker's (1780-1857) exclusion may have been, rather than his notorious slashing of Keats' *Endymion* (1818), his unattractive personality (Macaulay detested him "more than cold boiled veal"). Since Byron never returned to England after 1816, the fictitious character of this conversation piece is evident.

The idea of bringing a conversation piece up to date would inevitably result, with the passing of years, in a painting like Paul Delvaux's *Squelettes dans un bureau* (fig. 380; 1944, Mr. and Mrs. Jerome L. Stern Collection, New York). We may mention in this category of imaginary conversation pieces also the painting in which another Murray, General Sir John Murray — a much-travelled connoisseur and modest collector — commissioned P.C. Wonder to include famous paintings[7] and the most famous art collectors of the time in groups in a single hall. The Flemish painters Francken and Gonzales Coques had depicted such interiors of galleries: see for instance Coques' *Interior of a Gallery of Paintings* (at Windsor Castle), executed in collaboration with van Ehrenberg, who provided the architecture, and a score of other painters who executed miniature reproductions of the paintings hanging on the walls. The Italian Panini had represented in some pictures the whole of Baroque Rome. Following

6 For groups of guild members see the standard work by A. RIEGL, "Das holländische Gruppenporträt", in *Jahrbuch der kunsthistorischen Sammlungen in Wien*, XIII (later impression Vienna, 1931, with notes by L. Münz, two vols.). 7 See S. SPETH-HOUTERHOFF, *Les peintres flamands de cabinets d'amateurs au XVIIe siècle* (Brussels, 1957).

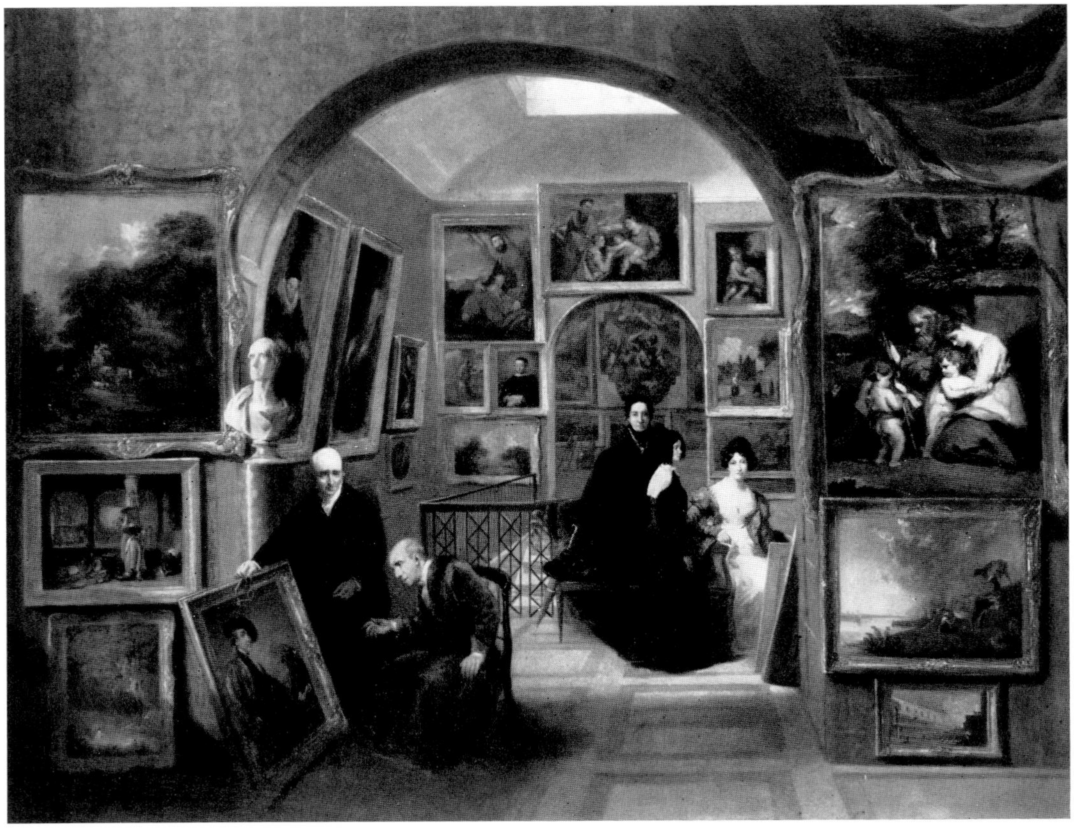

8 JOHN SCARLETT DAVIS (1804-1845/6), *The British Institution Gallery*, 1829. Washington, D.C., collection of Mr. and Mrs. Paul Mellon.

8

their example Zoffany had assembled in the Tribuna of the Uffizi the most celebrated paintings of the gallery[8] and in a single hall all the works of art in the Towneley collection (fig. 6). A. de Lelie in 1794-95 represented *Jan Gildemeester Jansz. in his Gallery* (fig. 7)[9] and Wybrand Hendricks in 1799 a gathering of Haarlem connoisseurs; J. Scarlett Davis painted *The British Institution Gallery* with Benjamin West and James Northcote gazing at Reynolds' self-portrait and with J.S. Harford and his wife Louise (the latter after two paintings by Lawrence; fig. 8).

Another instance of this type is the famous musical conversation painted in 1840 by Josef Danhauser which shows Liszt at the piano surrounded by Rossini, Paganini, Berlioz, Dumas, and George Sand; a bust of Schubert is against the window, and a portrait of Byron hangs from the wall. The paintings by Ignace Henri Fantin-Latour (*Hommage à Delacroix* and *L'Atelier de Batignolles*) depicting groups of celebrities of the time are comparable, and Courbet's self-portrait in his studio shows a crowd of representative men. All these paintings are closer to the imaginary assembly of geniuses in Raphael's *Parnassus* than to a conversation piece proper, whereas every self-portrait of a painter in his studio accompanied by his relatives belongs to the genre, as we shall see further on.

One should not apply these rules too strictly; otherwise, particularly in the early period and in Italy, one would exclude many significant paintings which waver between a juxtaposition of individual portraits and a conversation piece, or groups among whose members exists a harmony or communication of some sort.
What may appear odd is that, as there have always been families, the portrait of a family group with the characteristics we have listed only began to appear and spread after a certain epoch. We must now attempt to understand the reason for this.

8 See O. MILLAR, *Zoffany and his Tribuna* (London: Routledge & Kegan Paul for the Paul Mellon Foundation for British Art, 1967). 9 On this painting and on the identification of the pictures represented in it, see the article by C.J. DE BRUYN KOPS, " De Amsterdamse Verzamelaar Jan Gildemeester Jansz. ", in *Bulletin van het Rijksmuseum*, 1965, no. 3, pp. 79 ff.

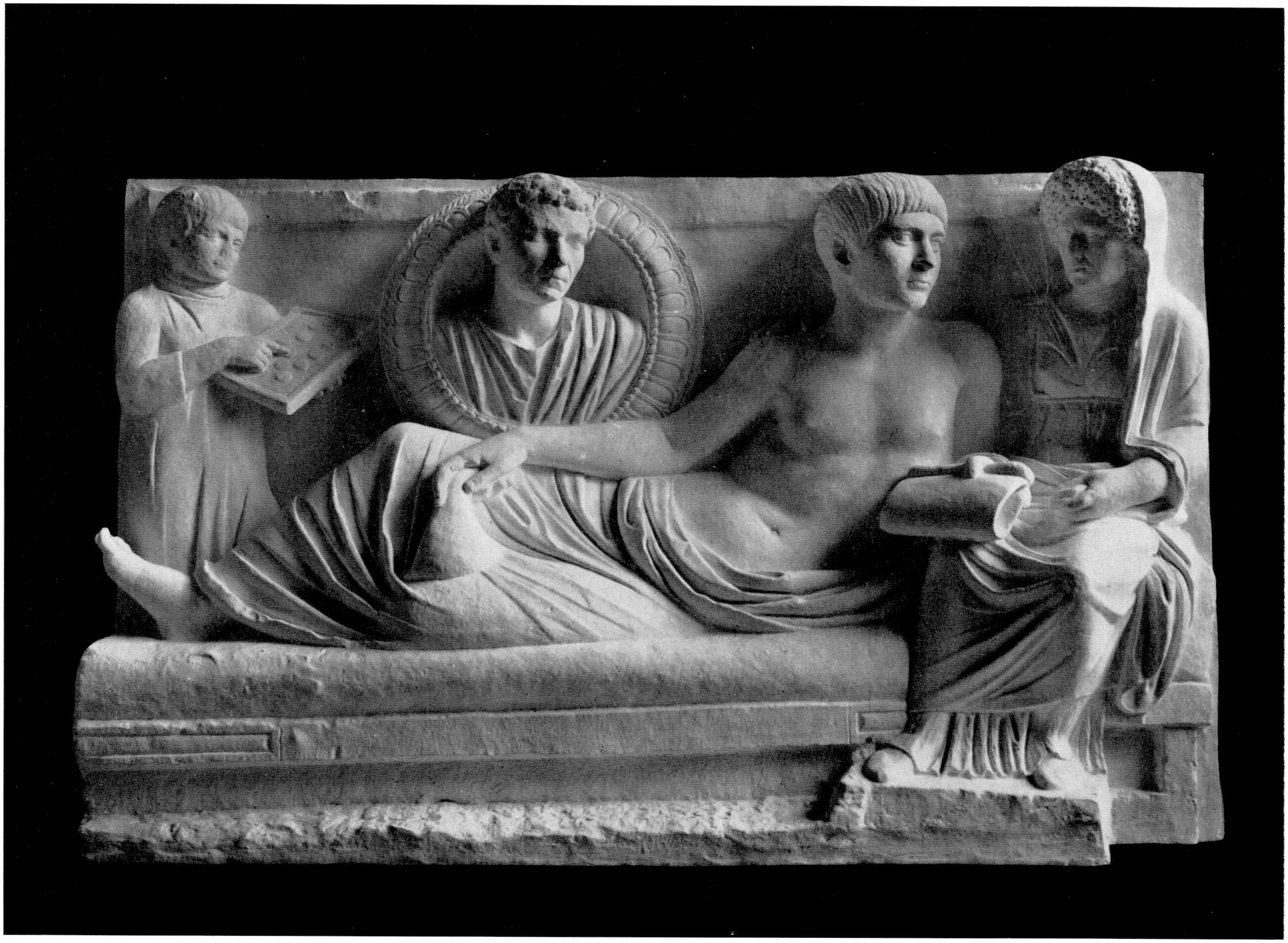

9

9 *Scene of the Drawing-up of a Will*, Rome, Capitoline Museums.

CHAPTER II – THE FAMILY PORTRAIT IN ANTIQUITY

We would not consider effigies of the dead (usually couples) from ancient Egypt and Etruria as family groups in the aforesaid sense. Rahotep and his wife Nofret, rigidly sitting — once in their tomb, but now in the Cairo Museum — do not communicate with each other. In the bas-relief of Khufu-Khaf and his wife, the wife takes her husband by the arm; with a similar gesture Mycerinus' queen touches her king's arm. In the Saqqara funeral chapel Mereruka and his two sons hold each other's hands. There is no lack of genre scenes: Egyptians hunting, inspecting cattle, harvesting, or picking fruit from the trees; but do we ever find a man and a woman depicted at ease in their home together with their children? Only the coloured ivory relief on the lid of a chest resembles a conversation piece: there Tutankhamen and his queen, radiant with youth, appear against a background of stylized plants in a garden, near a garlanded couch. The young woman clasps a bunch of flowers with her left hand and the king lifts his left arm as if for a caress. We might put in the young queen's mouth the words of an ancient Egyptian love song: "My arms are laden with persea, my hair with ointments. I am like a princess of the Lord of the Two Lands when I am within your arms".[1] But it is a far cry from this portrait of a married couple to the Arnolfini pair by van Eyck.

The Greeks used to portray human beings at their customary occupations after they had died and could no longer attend to them. A maid holds a box, possibly containing jewels, in front of Hegeso in the well-known Hegeso stele; Hegeso's hands clasp something, incapable though they are now of clasping anything (fig. 11). In a stele from the Ilissos (fig. 183) a young, athletic huntsman is ready with his stick, while the dog at his feet scents the ground and the sleepy slave boy rests his head on his arms, which are folded on his knees. But the youth's vacant eyes are not looking for game; they look beyond, as if he cared now for no other animals than those which give their names to the constellations, and his old father looks at him with knitted brows and silent sorrow. In another stele, a slave girl ties the sandals of Ameinokleia (fig. 184), who places her right hand on her head while she lifts her cloak with the other. An older slave woman presents to her the casket for the last touches of her toilet,

1 Translated from *Liriche amorose degli antichi Egiziani*, selected and translated by Boris de Rachewiltz (Milan: All'Insegna del Pesce d'oro, 1955), p. 21.

as she used to do daily but now does for the journey from which there is no return. Elsewhere, as in the stele of Korallion, wives shake their husbands' right hands in a last farewell, while other figures of relatives appear between them and from below a dog turns his head towards his mistress. In another relief, a deceased daughter takes leave of her parents, gazing into her mother's eyes (fig. 10). A high relief in the Capitoline Museum represents a man lying on a couch and next to him a matron with a scroll in her hand; at the man's feet is a smaller figure counting coins on a small slab, and from a round frame on the wall projects the effigy of another man (fig. 9). This is supposed to represent the drawing-up of a will: a family group, a conversation piece *in extremis*, and the prototype of a kind of monumental sculpture which continued for centuries — down to the funereal kitsch of the Staglieno cemetery.

The monuments of the Staglieno cemetery near Genoa are a telling corollary of genre painting, and since genre painting is a typical expression of the bourgeois spirit, these monuments are the quintessence of the bourgeois temper in the nineteenth century; they are almost a distillation of the maudlin sentimentalism of Edmondo de Amicis' *Cuore*. This was a time when every painting was required to tell a story, and thus at Staglieno every tomb tells a story. These dwelling-places of the dead, paradoxically enough, are a series of *tableaux vivants*; the figures are treated with an emphatic verisimilitude as if in a wax museum, with emphasis on the minutest details of attire: the buttons, medallions, trinkets, lace, combs, folds of material and shoe leather. A little girl, lifted in the arms of a young woman whose face twitches with sorrow, moves to embrace the bust of an elderly person, while a man in a bowler hat stands aside trying to restrain his anguish; two blind boys kneel before the effigy of their benefactor; relatives gather round a deathbed in various attitudes of despair and resignation, as if in a painting by that father of nineteenth-century genre painting, Greuze; a widow in elaborate weeds stands at the foot of a declaiming orator wearing a toga; other dead people wear shrouds draped toga-wise over their morning or evening clothes; a soul and an angel perform a twisting, convoluted dance; and also present is the poor cake-seller, a woman who throughout her life saved money in order to be represented in marble in the act of selling cakes for eternity. All this is very pathetic. Nietzsche felt it and dedicated two lachrymose little lines to the Staglieno cemetery: " Dich lieb'ich, Gräbergrotte! dich, Marmor-Lügnerei! "

The dusty and desolate cemetery of Staglieno may be termed a monumental mockery in Shakespeare's words; but what relationship exists between the maudlin bourgeois sentiment which inspired these monuments and the feeling that inspired the Greek stelae? Is it the relationship between a resigned but concise epigram and a morbidly sentimental story? If the Greeks felt the pain of parting from their loved ones, they must have tasted the joys of family life; why then did they not represent through visual images the kind of feeling which we find already expressed by Homer? " Having said this, proud Hector stretched his arms towards his son, but the child instantly withdrew and turned his face against the breast of the well-girdled nurse, terrified at the aspect of his father, dreading the shine of the armour and the horsetail crest he saw waving terribly from the top of the helmet. The loving father then laughed, and the august mother as well, and proud Hector at once took off the helmet from his head and put it shining on the ground, and then said... ".[2]

Is this not already a conversation piece? But when Greek art represented this and other episodes of the Homeric poems, it was as scenes of a story or legend, and not as everyday experiences. It was because Hector and Andromache appeared in them; if their subjects had been ordinary citizens of Athens or Corinth, the scenes would not have been represented.

The Roman paintings which survive show us specimens of every type, from heroic paintings whose characters are gods and mythical heroes down to genre painting, landscape — albeit only in outline and without perspective — and still life. However, one seeks in vain for scenes of family life or of groups of relatives gathered together informally. The *Aldobrandini Wedding*, with the bride led to the nuptial bed, is merely the image of a ritual. A baker is portrayed with his wife on the wall of a tablinum at Pompeii,[3] but these are merely two juxtaposed portraits whose subjects look in different directions. The portraits of a mother and her two sons in the golden glass disc in Brescia are also juxtaposed, almost as if three of the portraits covering mummies' faces at Fayum had been assembled. It would never have crossed Trimalchio's mind to have had himself portrayed with his spouse against the background of his pretentious surroundings as, on the contrary, it did in the case of wealthy Dutch merchants in the seventeenth century. Nevertheless, the Romans certainly enjoyed the pleasures of domestic life, as students of their

2 *Iliad*, VI, 461-473. 3 At the National Archaeological Museum in Naples.

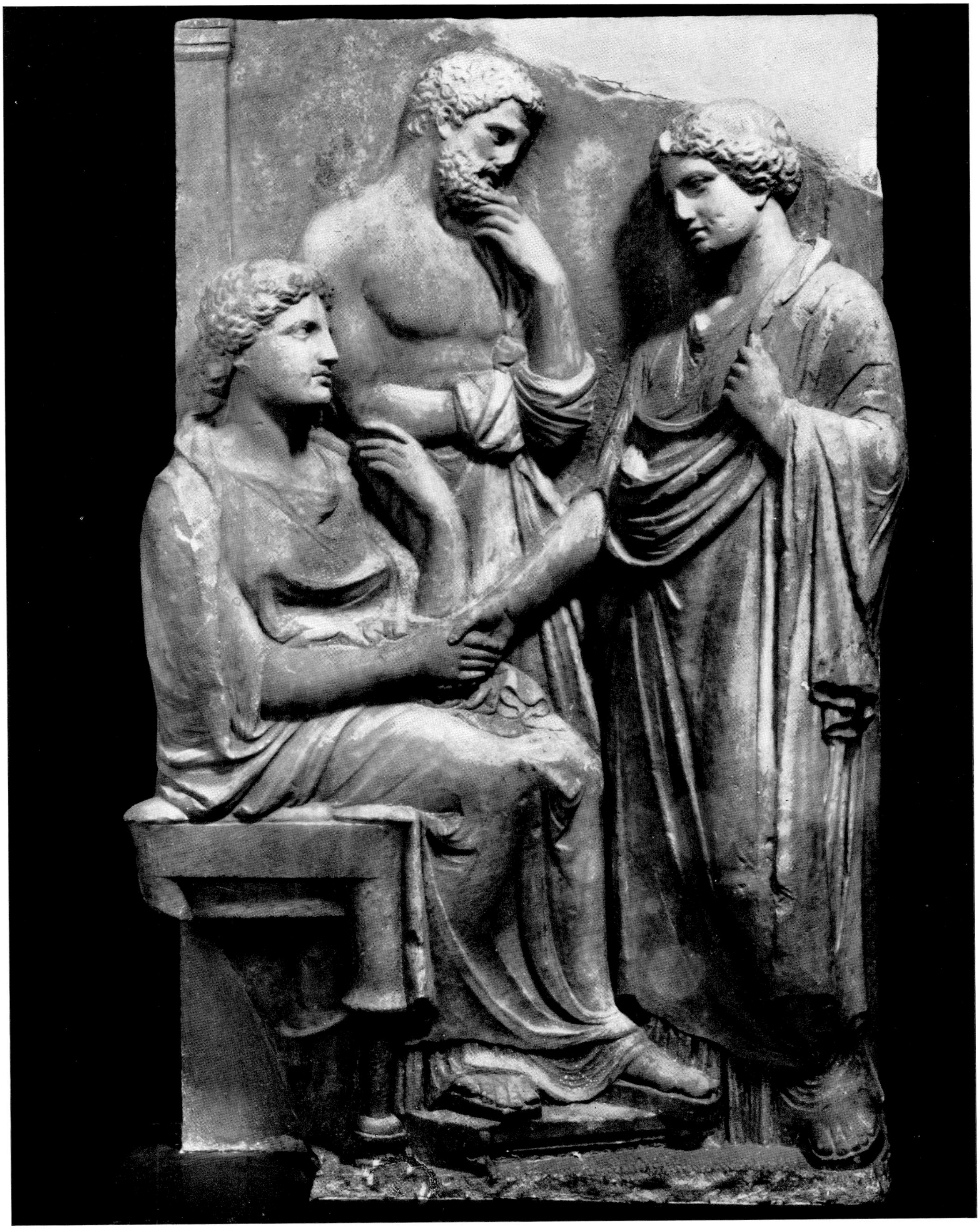

10

10 *Scene of a Departure from an Attic Stele*, Athens, Kerameikos Museum.

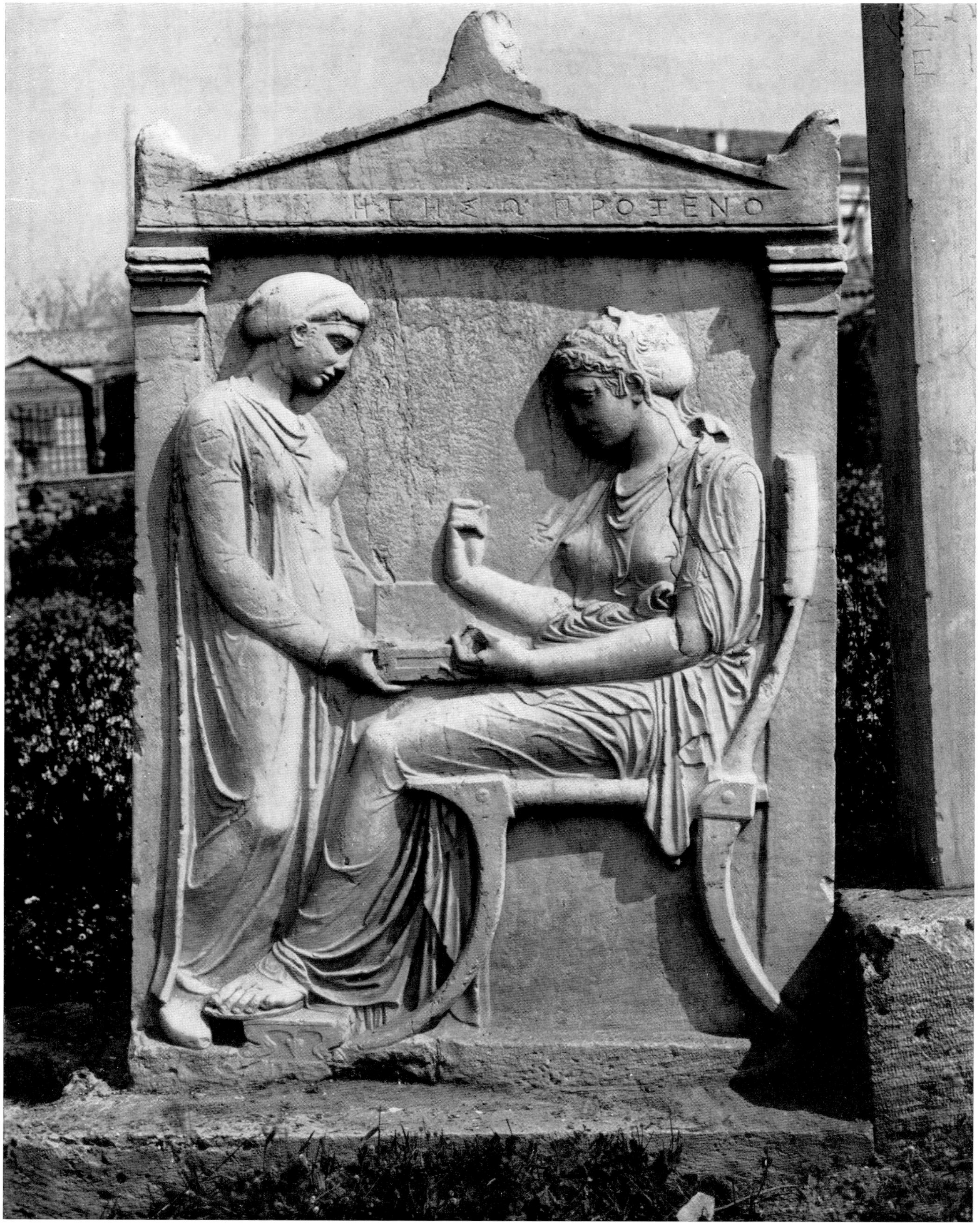

11

11 *Hegeso Stele*, Athens, Kerameikos Museum.

civilization never fail to point out. Birt writes, for example: " A second courtyard, this one open, was the rectangular one of the peristylium, consisting of a small garden surrounded by graceful colonnades, upon which the neighbouring rooms abutted as in the atrium. Here the family was enabled to taste the pleasures of a tranquil life, far from the noise of the street. The bedrooms and the dining rooms were close by. There was, in addition, the exedra, a corner designed for conversation, provided with massive seats and situated in a central place ".[4]

Conversations were thus involved in these family gatherings, but no one thought of recording them in an image. No painter has given us a visual counterpart of Pliny's description of Fundanius' dead little girl (*Epistolae*, V, 16): "With what grace she would hang from her father's neck! With what fond shyness she used to embrace us, too, the friends of her father! And how she loved her nurse and tutors! She was eager to learn, and even in the midst of childish games, which frequently are boisterous, she kept a moderate and quiet behaviour ". How many portraits of children with their charm and playfulness there are in the nineteenth century! But can we find any from the ancient world?

Jérôme Carcopino tells us that in Rome the paternal authority whose severe discipline had prevailed in the republican home slackened during the imperial period, and relations between father and children were inspired by an affectionate gentleness " not unlike the smiling friendliness that is customary with us nowadays ". The family was thenceforward based on the *coniunctio sanguinis*, " because, according to Cicero's happy anticipation in *De Officiis* (I, 17, 54), this natural community was the most suited to bind human beings by reciprocal benevolence and charity (*et benevolentia devincit homines et caritate*)".[5] The position of women made great strides forward, and there were partisans of feminism even in those distant times — like Musonius Rufus who, under the Flavii, claimed for women the rights to which they were entitled by their moral and intellectual equality with men. There is no surviving image which conveys to our eyes this well-balanced and delightful family life except, as with the Egyptians, Greeks, and Etruscans, the images of the dead. In the funeral pair once known as " Cato and Portia " the woman places her left hand on her husband's shoulder and her right hand on his; the signs of the domestic virtues of devotion and modesty are impressed on their faces. On the other hand, we read many descriptions of corruption and depravity in the Latin authors; Petronius, for one, fixed his attention on the seamy side of Roman life.

Having thus come to the conclusion that no painting in the classical West offers us an image of normal family life, can we find any in the Near East? In 1952 Jules Leroy discovered in the neighbourhood of Edessa, in Jebel Ahdar, an astonishing mosaic covering the whole floor of a room hewn out of rock, measuring 2.50 metres by 2.55. Against a greyish-white ground, a conventionally decorated frame stands out, within which seven members of a noble (perhaps princely) family are represented. All are seen full-length, frontally, and standing: an exceptional thing, because generally only busts are found in funeral mosaics. The portraits are of Moqîmû with his wife G'û and their children: they hold their hands close to their breasts, except for the last figure to the left (one of the daughters), who lays her arm against her brother's — a gesture frequently found in funeral sculpture. One of the group — Salmat, the daughter of Ma'nû and granddaughter of Moqîmû — is only partially shown. Two of the women wear fourfold tiaras topped with veils, but young Salmat has three combs placed crosswise. Three of the men wear turbans and one a Phrygian cap; the colours of the costumes are vivid and delicate. But this multiple portrait, dating from the second century of our era, is also a funeral image.[6] A Persian miniature by Mu'in represents a prince in the harem: female musicians play on their instruments and maidservants carry food, while more women peer from a door and a window. Have we here a family entertainment of some sort, or is this a genre painting? Both, perhaps more the former than the latter; in any case, the work stands for the type of conversation piece that might have been conceived in a society where the harem was the equivalent of life in the family. The same may be said of an Indian miniature by Aka Riza Mouzaffer, wich shows us a prince watching his women bathing. If we think back to the requirements which we have said are necessary to define a conversation piece, we shall see that they are more or less all fulfilled by this miniature: the prince is an identifiable person, the surroundings are represented, and the action which takes place — the customary visit of the prince to his women — is quite informal. This miniature was made in about 1608, and the Persian miniature described above also belongs to the seventeenth century. By this time the kind of picture of which we are speaking had already taken firm root in Europe.

4 THEODOR BIRT, *Zur Kulturgeschichte Roms, Gesammelte Skizzen* (Leipzig: Quelle und Meyer, 1909); from the Italian translation by Giovanni Decia, *La civiltà romana* (Florence: Tipografia Ariani, 1912), p. 47. 5 *La vie quotidienne à Rome à l'époque de l'Empire* (Paris: Hachette, 1939), pp. 98-99, 106-7. 6 See the magazine *Syria*, XXXIV, 1957, pp. 306 ff., and a colour reproduction in the *Illustrated London News*, 21 February 1953, fig. 4. I owe this information to Dr. J.B. Ward Perkins of the British School in Rome.

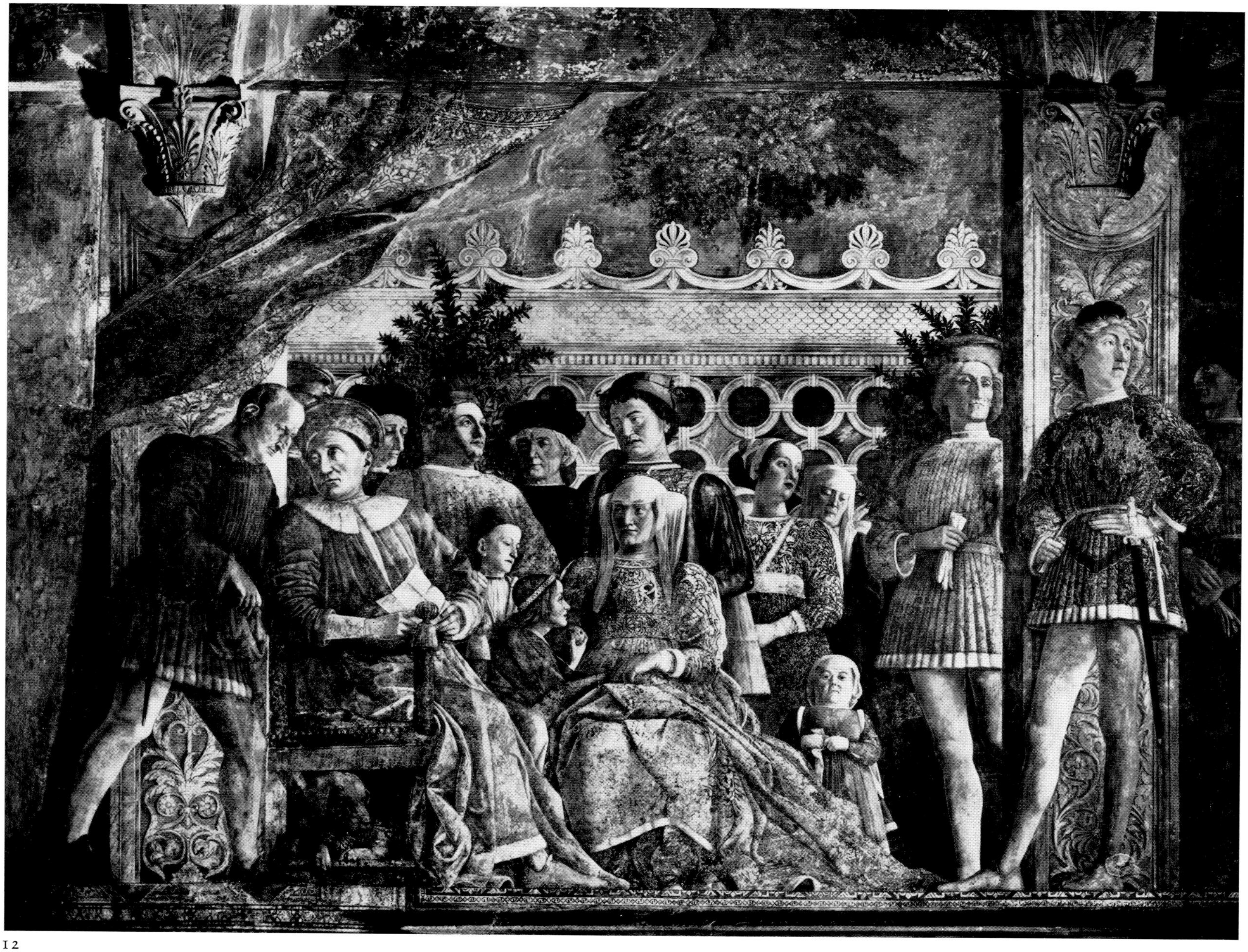

12

12 ANDREA MANTEGNA (1431-1506), *Ludovico III Gonzaga among his Relatives*, 1471-4. Mantua, Ducal Palace (Camera degli Sposi).

CHAPTER III – THE GROUP

During the fifteenth century, the donor — either alone or with his family — is portrayed in a corner of an altarpiece, kneeling in adoration. No doubt a conversation between these worshippers and the divinity is taking place, but no one would confuse this kind of image with the family groups of which we are speaking, represented at ease in their surroundings. The family of the Florentine merchant Tommaso Portinari in Hugo van der Goes' famous triptych, destined for the church of Sant'Egidio in Florence, is one of the best known examples of the representation of a devout family. The theme recurs in several Flemish and German paintings and on tombs of the Elizabethan period in England, in which whole families are seen kneeling in a line in order of size. In the triptych, the Portinari women are on one side and the men on the other, divided by sex as if in church.[1]
Van der Goes' triptych was painted in Bruges in about 1476, not long after Mantegna, in the Camera degli Sposi at Mantua (fig. 12), had portrayed Ludovico III Gonzaga among his relatives, in surroundings that are hardly significant but with a freedom of movement as in a real conversation. Barbara of Brandenburg gazes at her husband, who turns his rather tired face (with dim eyes denoting bad vision) towards his secretary, Marsilio Andreani, whose sharp profile is bent in the act of receiving instructions from his master. There are two delicate children: pale Ludovico with his thin neck, who was destined for an ecclesiastical career, and the precociously ripe Paola, with the sad face of a hunchback. She holds an apple in her hand, more as a symbol than as a desirable food, and her looks are perhaps even more pathetic than those of the female dwarf who appears behind the voluminous gown of the Marchioness. In the background are two young people: Barbara, in the full bloom of youth, and a vigorous young man (perhaps the fourth-born, Rodolfo) standing behind his mother.
Another scene in the Camera degli Sposi has a more official character. It represents the meeting of the Marquis, accompanied by some of his sons and courtiers, with his son, Cardinal Francesco, and probably commemorates the solemn visit the latter paid to his native town in 1472. But here too, as in the Schifanoia frescoes which record episodes of the court life of Borso

1 It was a standing rule which we see applied, for example, in Friedrich Herlin's *St. George* altarpiece of 1463 (Nördlingen, Stadtmuseum); in the diptychs by Bartholomäus Bruyn and his pupils in which one piece portrayed the mother and her daughters and the other the father and sons; in the *Madonna* of the burgomaster Jacob Meyer by Hans Holbein (Darmstadt, Schlossmuseum); in the *Retablo del Mariscal* (1555) by Pedro de Campaña in the Seville Cathedral, painted for the chapel of Don Diego de Caballero; in the Moreel altar in the Bruges museum; in the *Virgin* of Jacob Floreins by Memling at the Louvre; and so on. For Germany

d'Este (1469-70), it is by no means easy to determine how much of the informal character of the family group is to be found. The encounter of the Marquis with his son the Cardinal must have been attended by a certain solemnity, yet the Cardinal holds the future ecclesiastic, the delicate Ludovico, familiarly by the hand. Ludovico surrenders his other hand to the boy Sigismondo, dressed in white; another child who has an equally bulging forehead is behind him: Francesco, the first born of Federigo and the future fourth Marquis of Mantua, who was to marry the celebrated Isabella d'Este. Rather than a formal meeting, this looks like a casual encounter of people strolling: the grownups are talking while the children pull at their clothes, impatient to move on. We certainly cannot speak of family groups in the case of the Schifanoia scenes relating to the hunting activities of Borso d'Este, although they depict the customary occupations of the lord in the various months — occupations which actually amounted to a single one. In March the Duke is surrounded by a band of horsemen and falconers with goshawks and young falcons on their wrists; some hounds chase a hare, and at the horses' feet ducks fly from a pond flapping their wings. In April, beneath images of awakening nature (sparrows and finches in the trees and rabbits in the hedges), what is Borso d'Este doing? He is on horseback with his retinue, while a falconer looks at a hawk which has seized a heron and another falconer strokes a hawk which he holds on his gloved hand. And in June? Borso on horseback, preceded and followed by falconers and dogs, obviously going to the country to hunt. In July, in the hall of a palace, Borso receives a steward who, kneeling, hands him a paper; but one can see that the Duke is about to go hunting again, because mounted men with falcons and goshawks are waiting at the right and left. In August the lord talks to a falconer, and of what does he talk if not of hunting? In September he rides to one of his country houses with the usual retinue of hunting companions. In October he has just time to speak to an ambassador on the threshold of a sumptuous hall, near which gentlemen on horseback wait for him to make up a hunting party. Whether the Ram or the Bull was in the sky, or the Goat, the Virgin, or the Balance, Duke Borso always went hunting. Only in the episode in which the Duke, surrounded by courtiers, gives a coin to the court jester can we see some affinity with conversation pieces. But then one is also reminded of a lost painting by Masaccio, the large fresco of the *Sagra del Carmine* in the cloister of S. Maria del Carmine in Florence (destroyed at the end of the sixteenth century) which recorded the consecration of the church on April 19th, 1422, with various groups of persons appearing in the procession. And one recalls a painting by Domenico Giuntatondi mentioned by Vasari (who misnames him Giuntalochi) in his life of Niccolò Soggi, who was Giuntatondi's master. According to Vasari, " When he went to Rome he was so favoured by fortune that, having made the acquaintance of Don Martino, the ambassador of the King of Portugal, he went to live with him and made for him a painting on canvas with perhaps twenty portraits from life; these were all his relatives and friends, with himself in the middle conversing. The work so delighted Don Martino that he considered Domenico the first painter in all the world ".[2]

Meanwhile, outside Italy, Jan van Eyck (c. 1390-1441) had painted the portrait of Giovanni Arnolfini and Giovanna Cenami (1434; fig. 13), and before February 7th, 1527, Hans Holbein had made a sketch of Sir Thomas More in the midst of his family (fig. 14) from which he also made a painting, now unfortunately lost (there is a poor copy of it in an English private collection). In these works the family group portrait reached its complete definition. It seems so simple to represent a family in its surroundings; yet even Mantegna adopted a generically decorative background in the Camera degli Sposi (which must have inspired Holbein). In general, in the case of individual portraits, the surroundings failed to interest the Italians. Thus in a painting attributed to Paolo Veronese the family is represented against a wall with a door, the curtain of which is lifted by the maidservant (fig. 187). As I have already said, the family portrait follows a parallel course to the representation of surroundings; both are products of the bourgeois civilisation of the North.

One might say that in Italy the family portrait developed little by little, by a slow process of aggregation and juxtaposition of single portraits; we have a typical example in the portraits of the three Gaddi by a Florentine artist of the end of the fourteenth century (fig. 186), and an illustration of a slightly more articulate stage in the double portrait of a master and disciple (fig. 185) which can be ascribed to Filippino Lippi. Indeed, the Italians must have conceived of the group portrait in this way, for we read of Domenichino that he painted the portraits of his relatives " all in a single painting ";[3] it is natural that this should have happened, because the Italian idea was not to represent several people *in their surroundings*, but only several people together.

see HANNA KRONBERGER-FRENTZEN, *Das deutsche Familienbildnis* (Leipzig: Johannes Asmus Verlag, 1940), pp. 12-13 and figs. 1, 2, 3, 10, 11, 12; (cf. on pl. 17 the curious painting by Christian Richter, *The Family of Duke John of Saxony-Weimar* (1613; Gotha, Herzherzöglisches Museum). 2 VASARI, *Le Opere*, ed. G. Milanesi (Florence: Sansoni, 1906), VI, *Le Vite*, p. 27. 3 EVELINA BOREA, *Domenichino* (Milan: Edizioni per il Club del Libro, 1965), p. 67 and n. 72 (PASSERI, 1934 edition, p. 44; BAGLIONE, 1642 ed., p. 383).

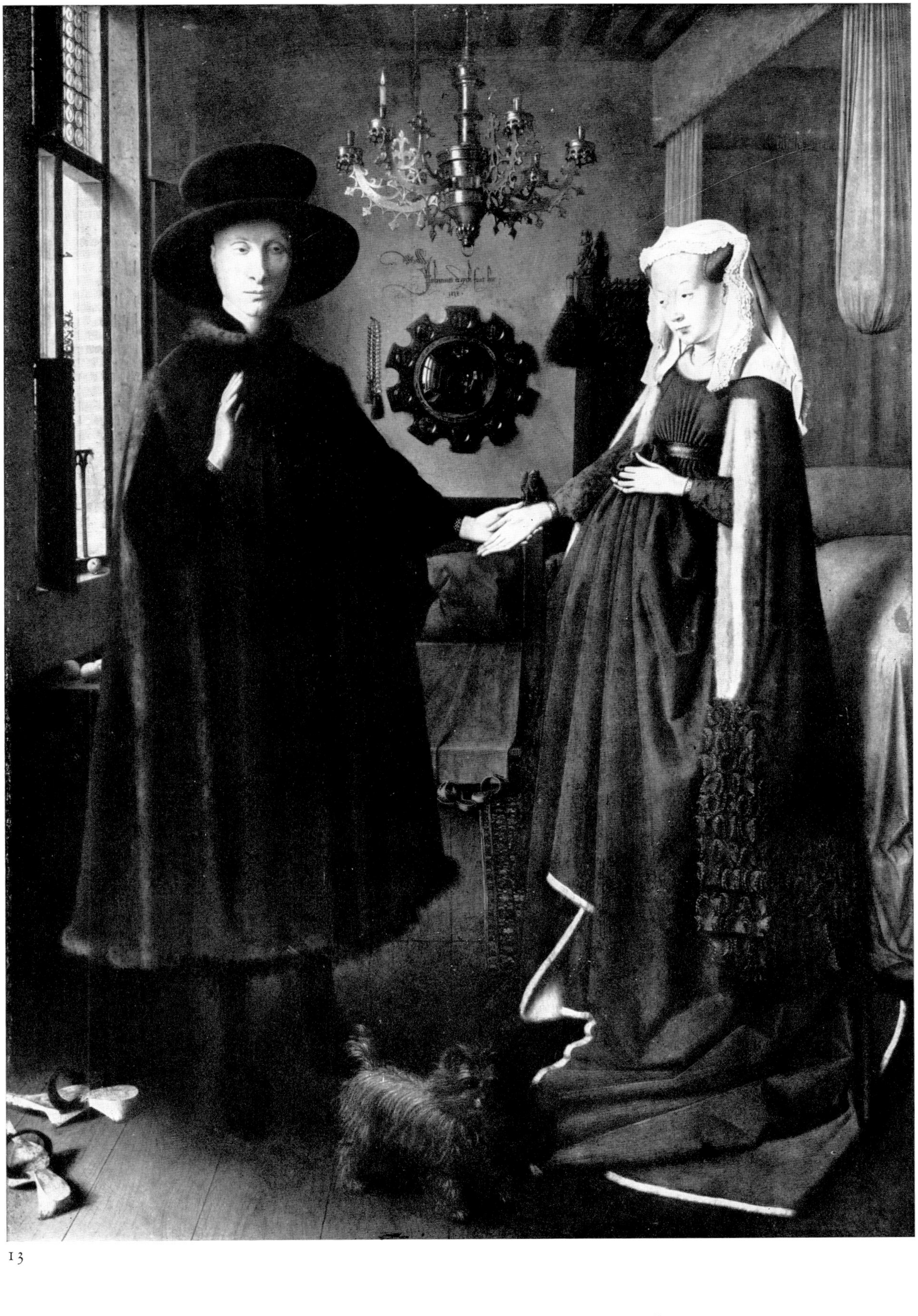

13

13 JAN VAN EYCK (c. 1390-1441), *The Marriage of Giovanni Arnolfini and Giovanna Cenami*, 1434. London, National Gallery.

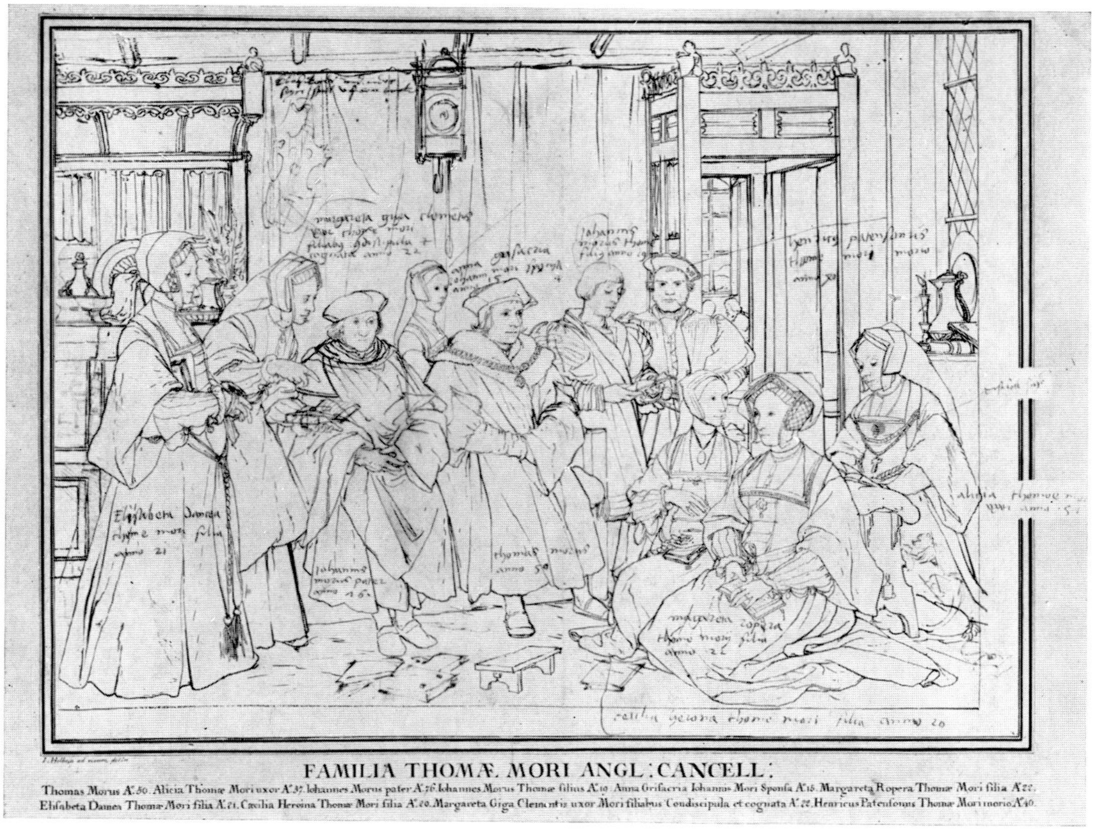

14

14 HANS HOLBEIN (1497-1543), *Sir Thomas More in the midst of his Family*, c. 1527. Basel, Oeffentliche Kunstsammlung (Kupferstich Kabinett).

The proportions of these persons were those of the waist-length individual portrait; they occupied the whole space of the painting, and were not seen full-length as in an episode of real life. Ignoring van Eyck and being unacquainted with Holbein's sketch of the family of Sir Thomas More, and forgetting on the other hand Mantegna's example in the Camera degli Sposi, they started from the point at which the multiple portrait had been left by the Romans. And if they approached the conversation piece in the portrait of Paul III and his nephews, or in that of a cardinal who consults a document with a counsellor (fig. 188), it was not through a new conception of the group portrait, but through a continuation on a more familiar plane of the representation of official scenes: such as that of Platina kneeling before Sixtus IV by Melozzo da Forlì, or of Federigo da Montefeltro with an open book and a courtier by Fra Carnovale. A case like that of Ghirlandaio's portrait of a pimply-nosed grandfather and his fond grandchild (Louvre) is exceptional and betrays a northern influence in the ruthless realism of the execution, which in no way tries to soften the old man's deformity. There is much less originality in another portrait by Ghirlandaio, also of an elderly person and a child, *Francesco Sacchetti with his Son Teodoro* of about 1480 (New York, Metropolitan Museum).
The surroundings are ignored; one finds at most a background like that of a *sacra conversazione* with its conventional festoon at the top and a section of landscape, as in *The Family of Uberto Sacrati* by Antonio Leonelli da Crevalcore. Uberto is shown in profile as in a medal (as we have said, the heroic ideal in portraiture is evidenced during the Renaissance by the innumerable medals of famous people). His hand is on his wife's shoulder, and she in turn places her hand on her son's back, almost as if to confirm the blood tie which the vacant faces give no sign of showing (fig. 15). The eloquence of the painting is limited solely to the position of the hands. The same may be said of the fine portrait of a *Father with his Daughter Reading* (fig. 16) from the Lombard school of the second half of the sixteenth century, which marks a step forward in the reproduction of a real scene portrayed from life; the girl lowers her eyes to the book and actually reads instead of just holding it and gazing at the onlooker,

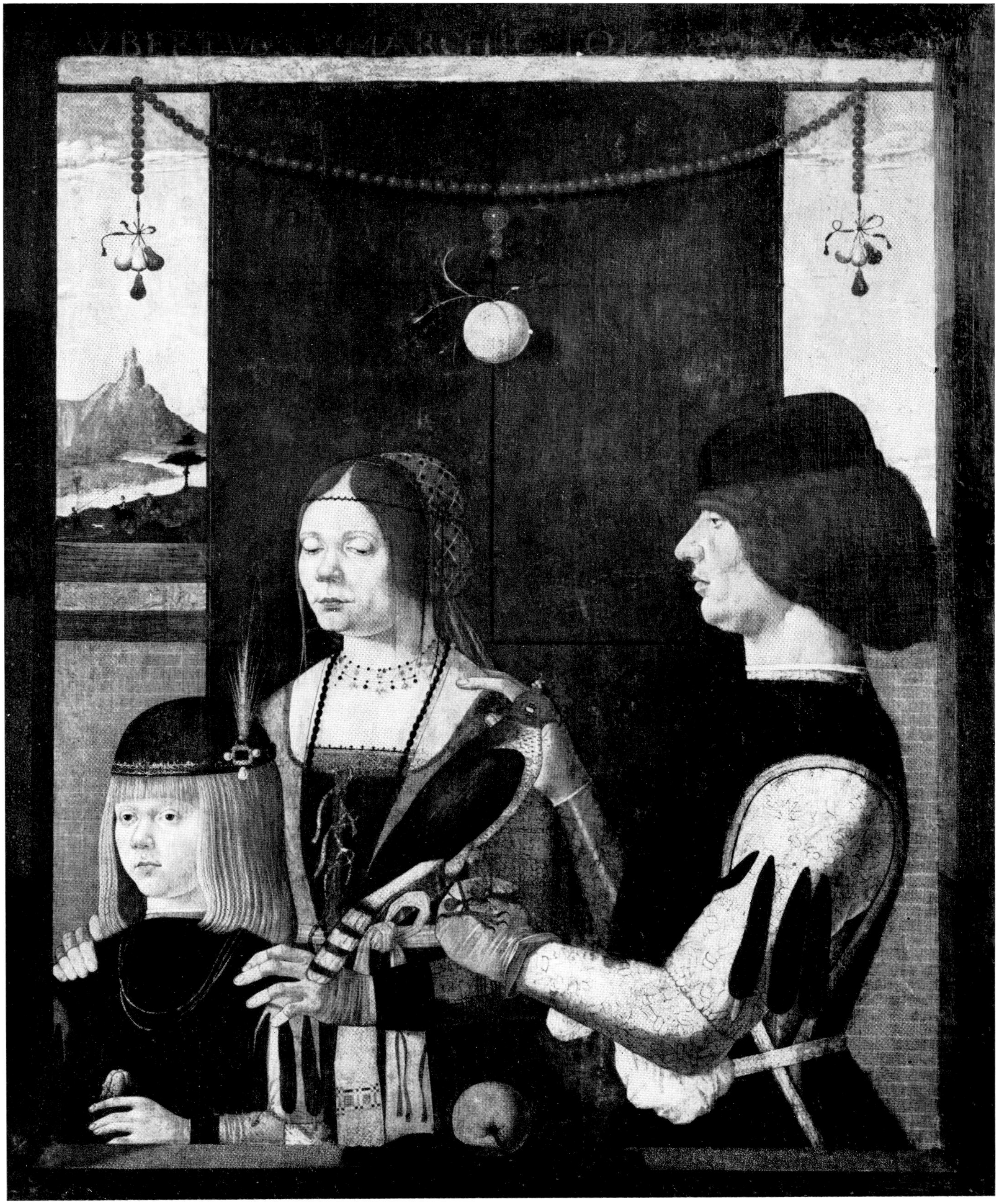

15

15 attr. to ANTONIO LEONELLI DA CREVALCORE (active in 1490, d. before 1525), *The Family of Uberto Sacrati*. Munich, Alte Pinakothek.

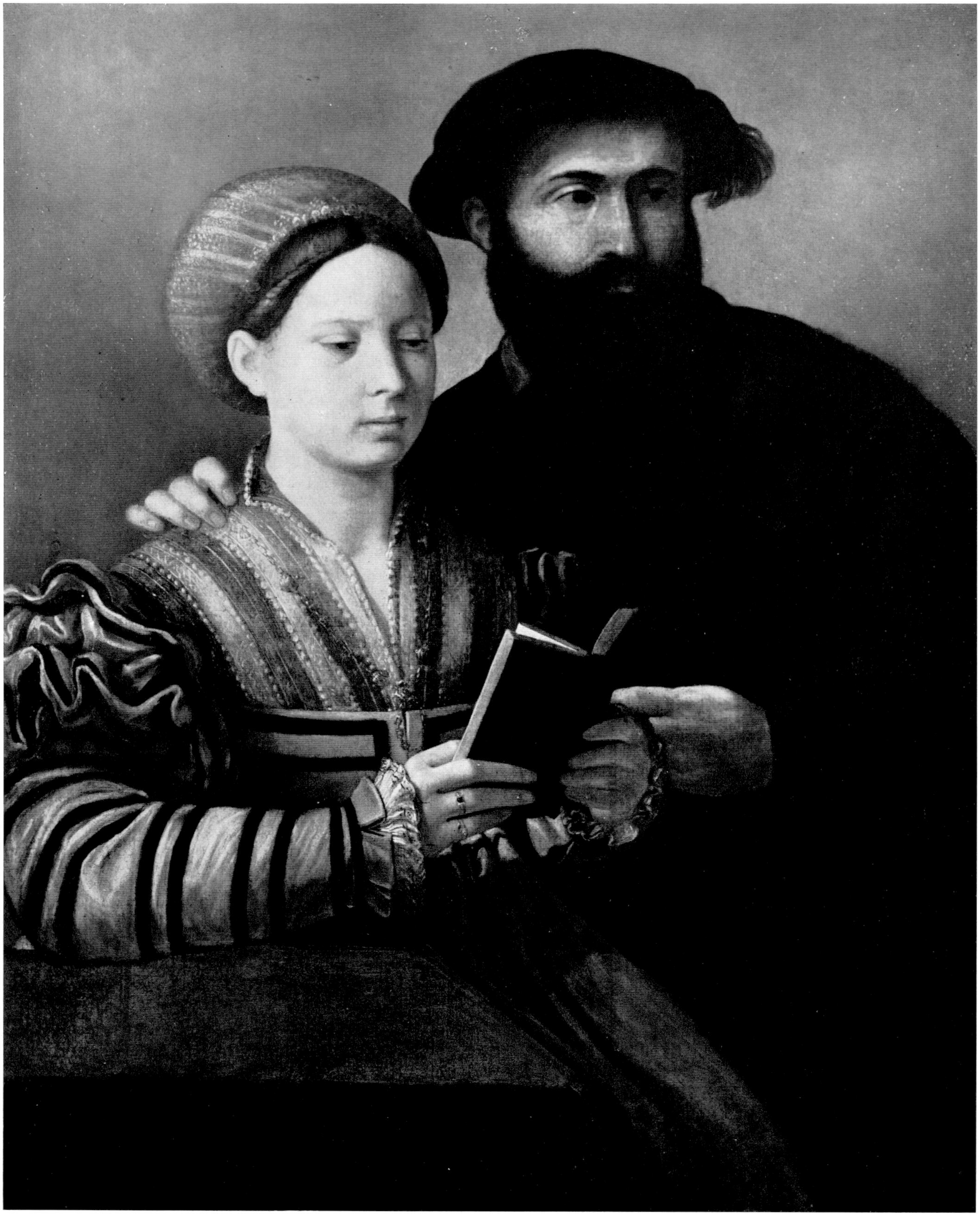 16

16 LOMBARD SCHOOL (16th century), *Father with his Daughter Reading*. Present location unknown.

as in the ancient Roman portrait of the baker's wife or in the more famous one (also at the Naples Archaeological Museum) of a girl holding tablets in her hand and raising a stylus to her lips. In another painting of the Lombard school, Sofonisba Anguissola's *Three Relatives* (fig. 192), the old man places his left hand on the shoulder of the boy, who keeps his right hand on the old man's, while the girl holds a nosegay against her breast. In Giambattista Moroni's *Portrait of a Widower with his Children* (Dublin, National Gallery of Ireland) the father's hands are on the shoulders of the little ones; the youngest conventionally holds an apple, and there is a hint at the surroundings in the form of a bookshelf. Salviati's *A Man and Two Women* (fig. 20), a young and an old one, also belongs to the sixteenth century. The young one places her fingers on the hand of the bearded man who holds a book and looks at her; the head of the matron is inserted between the two like an isolated portrait, not communicating with the others. Here also the gesture of the young woman is conventional: she is raising her left hand to the chain round her neck. The play of the hands is more meaningful in the *Portrait of a Cardinal and a Gowned Gentleman* (fig. 188) attributed to Girolamo da Carpi, who borrows the theme of Raphael's *Portrait of Leo X with Cardinal Giulio de' Medici and Lodovico de' Rossi* (Florence, Pitti); the pose of the Cardinal also imitates Raphael's portrait of Cardinal Bibbiena. The Cardinal holds a pen in his right hand and points his left forefinger at a paper, while the bearded gentleman touches the seal of a document, perhaps a treaty, with his left hand. At one time these figures were fantastically thought to stand for Caesar Borgia and Machiavelli! In Sebastiano del Piombo's group, *Cardinal Bandinello Sauli, his Secretary, and Two Geographers* (fig. 190), the collective portrait labours to free itself from the single portrait; whereas the two figures on the left repeat the formula of the secretary who receives instructions from his lord, the raised hand of the man on the right, with its pointing forefinger, resembles an irrelevant intrusion between the two men, who maintain an absolute lack of expression. In Pontormo's *Double Portrait* (fig. 17), one of the two persons severely dressed in black holds in his hand a paper written in Latin and points to the first line of it with his right forefinger. In the very fine portrait of *A Gentleman and Lady Playing Backgammon* by a Cremonese painter of the sixteenth century (fig. 18), the lady's hand is placed on the gaming-board, while the man makes a gesture as if calculating a sum. According to Vasari in his life of Garofalo, Sofonisba Anguissola also made a gaming-board the centre of a multiple portrait (fig. 19): "A painting very diligently made, three of her sisters playing chess[4] and with them an old serving-maid; such is the diligence and readiness of the execution that they actually look alive and only lack speech". (The portrait is now in the National Museum in Poznan.) The same type of half-size collective portrait is also found in a few Northern works, such as a South German painting of about 1570-80 (Munich, Bayerische Staatsgemäldesammlungen) showing a seated father who takes cherries from a dish presented by his child, on whose shoulders the mother places her hands with the same gesture as that found in the painting by Antonio da Crevalcore.

During the seventeenth century the half-length double portrait developed towards a greater freedom of attitudes and gestures. This is already evident in the *Portrait of Fra Luca Paciolo with a Bystander* (signed *Iac. Bar.*) by an unknown painter of the school of Alvise Vivarini; the friar, who is drawing a Euclidean demonstration on the blackboard, contemplates a neat crystal polyhedron as if in a magical rite (fig. 21). The same thing is true of the portrait of *Thomas Killigrew and William Murray* (Windsor Castle), dated 1638, in which the dramatist reads to a gentleman of the court, or in the double portrait of *J.B. de Champaigne and Nicolas de Platte-Montagne* in a painter's studio (Rotterdam, Boymans-van Beuningen Museum). Here the so-called bust of Seneca is on a shelf, and a viola da gamba is laid against the knees of one of the two intimate friends; with an expansive gesture of his right hand he indicates the other, whose hands are placed on a tablet holding a sheet of paper. In this painting the surroundings are included, insofar as space permits; but in the double portrait of the collector *John Tradescant Grasping the Hand of his Friend Zythepsa* by Emmanuel (?) de Critz (d. 1665; fig. 22), the still-life — a heap of shells from Tradescant's cabinet of rarities, triumphantly exhibited on the nearby table (he had collected shells during his travels in Northern Russia in 1618) — becomes the chief object of the picture, occupying half the space; this type of asymmetrical composition was to find expression chiefly in Dutch and English paintings representing couples sitting at the side of a landscape.

The half-length portrait with a faint hint of action (another instance is the portrait of *Arthur, First Baron Capel, and his Family*,

4 Actually only two of them are playing chess; the youngest looks at the one who is checkmated and smilingly acknowledges her defeat.

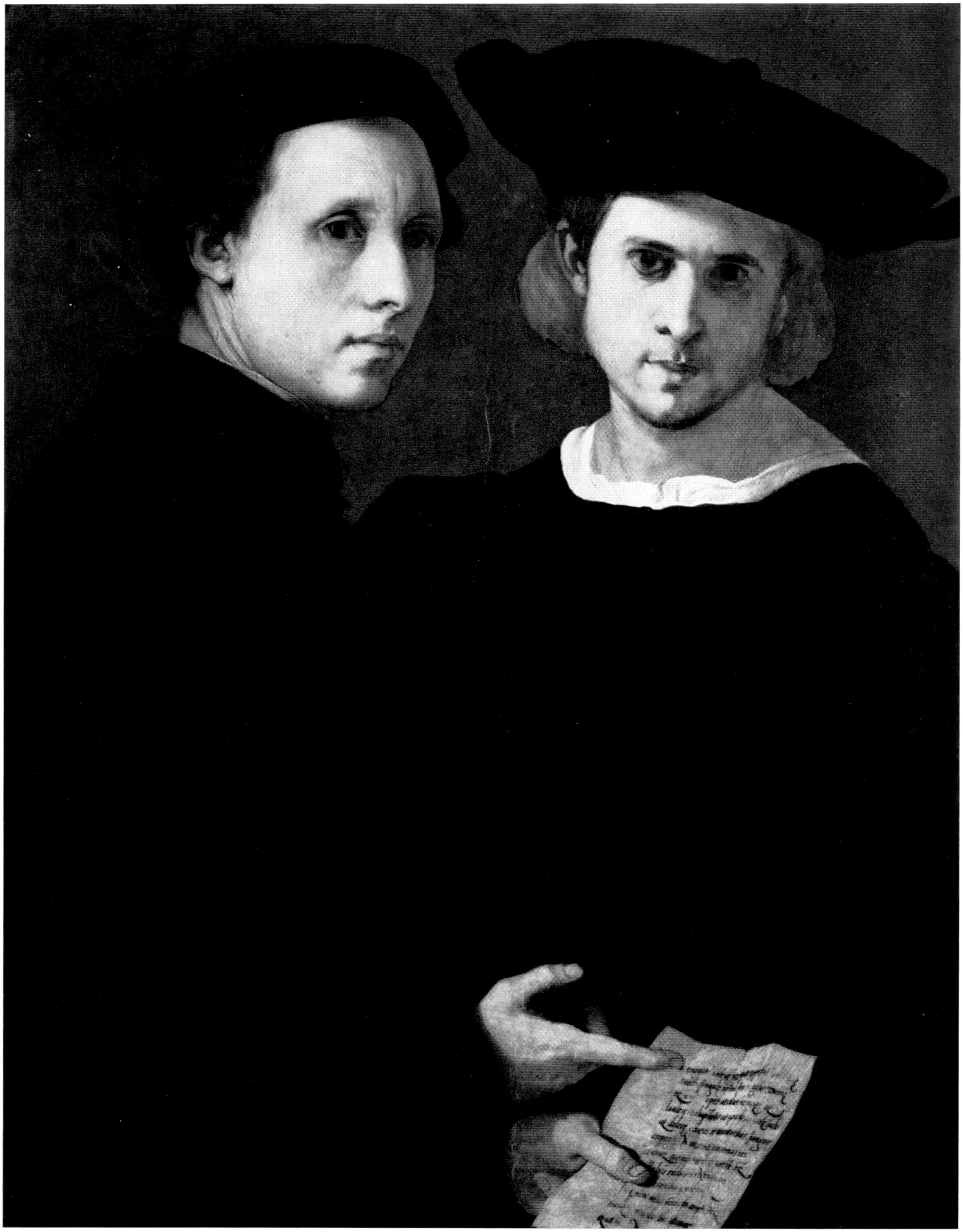

17

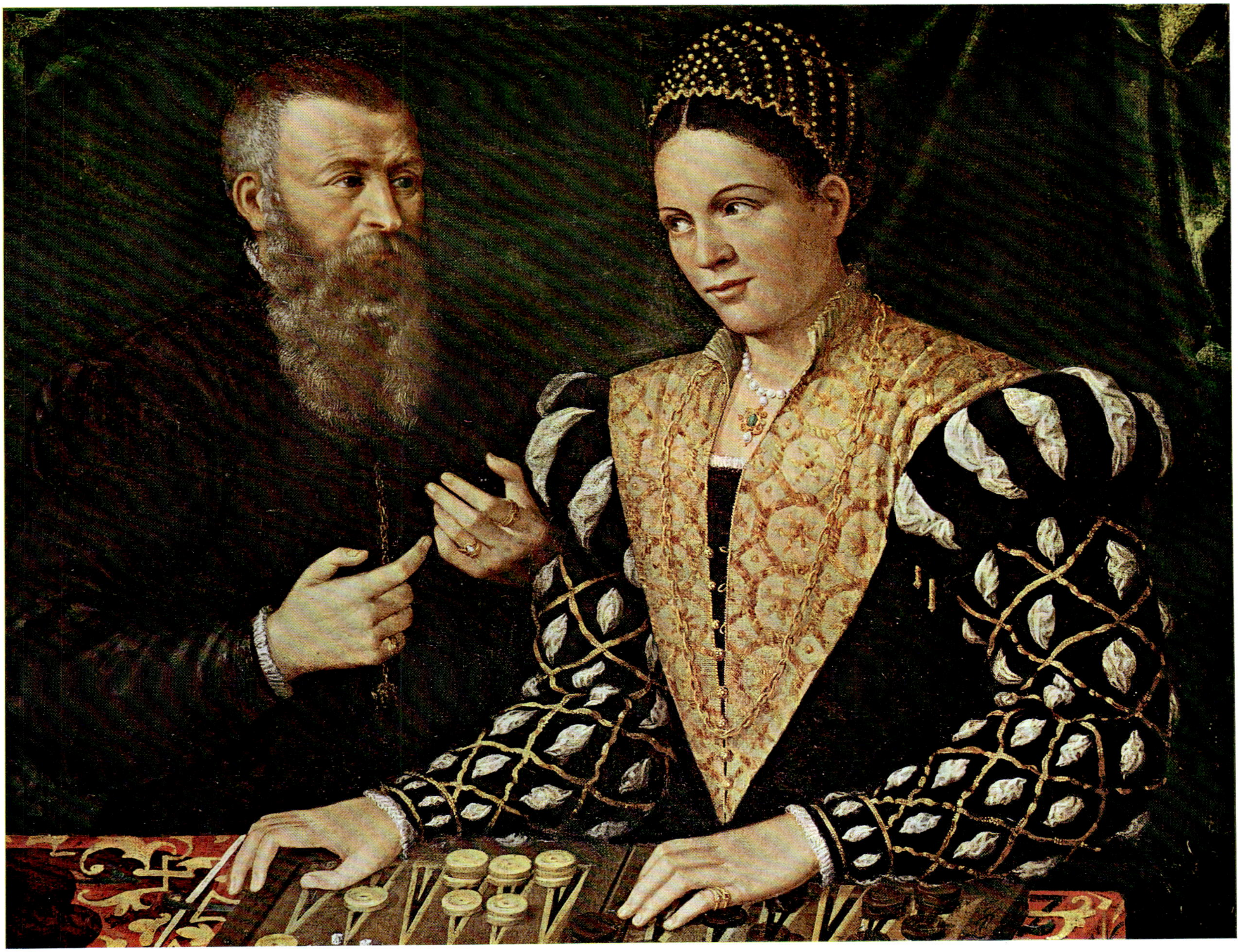

18

17 PONTORMO (1454-1556), *Double Portrait*. Venice, Cini Collection. 18 CREMONESE SCHOOL (16th century), *A Gentleman and Lady Playing Backgammon*. Venice, Cini Collection.

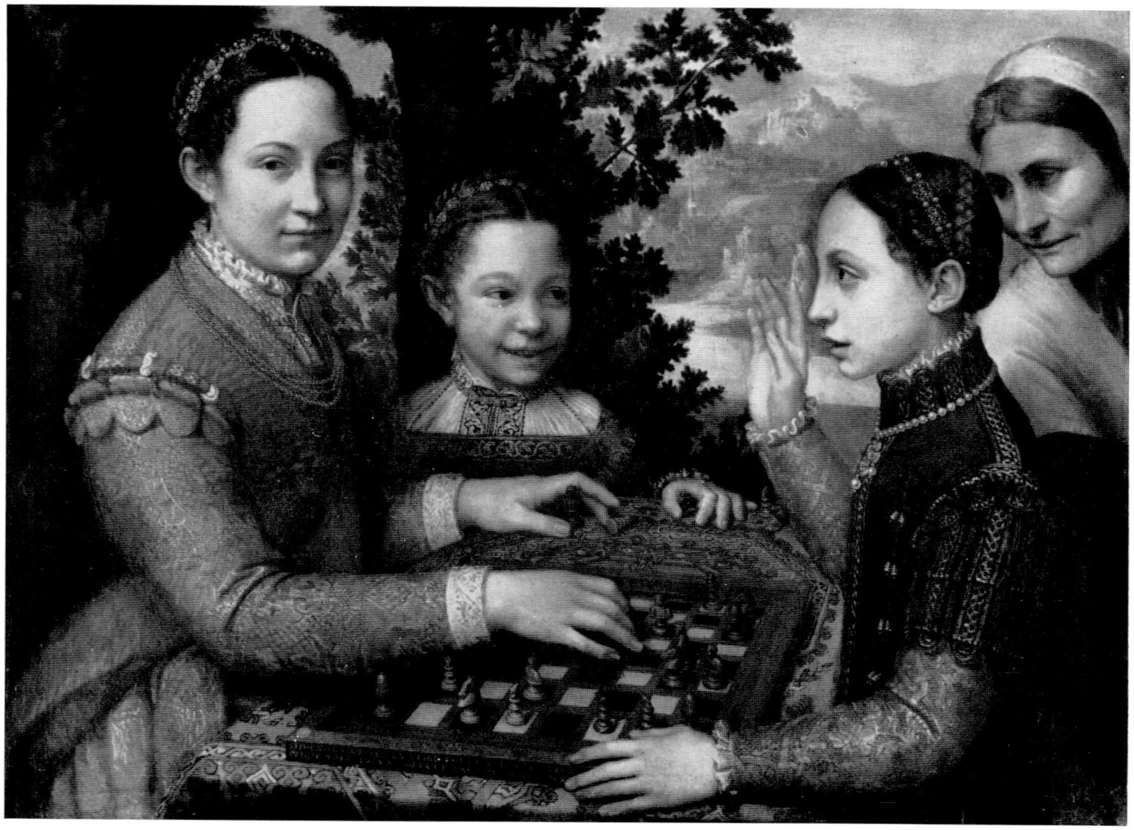

19 SOFONISBA ANGUISSOLA (c. 1528-c. 1624), *Three of the Artist's Sisters.* Poznan, National Museum. 19

by Cornelius Jonson [1593-1661; fig. 191]) bears the same relation to the conversation piece proper as puppets manipulated by a showman's hands do to puppets moved by wires: the figures look as if they were standing in front of windows rather than moving in space. But in a *Family Group* by Lorenzo Lotto (fig. 194) one already has the impression not of a collection of juxtaposed portraits, but of a group of persons caught during a moment of their daily life.[5] Across the table covered with an oriental carpet, the children — freeing themselves from their symmetrically leaning parents — playfully hold out their hands to collect cherries from those of their parents. The structure is still that of sacred scenes (cf. *The Mystic Marriage of Saint Catherine* at the Munich Alte Pinakothek, in which the Infant Jesus seizes an object that the kneeling saint has brought him), and elements such as oriental carpets and landscape are also part of their vocabulary. In Lotto's *Married Couple,* portrayed waist-length (Prado), the sitters hold hands and a little Cupid motions as if to bring their heads close together; in the *Double Portrait* formerly in Berlin, a man sitting by a table covered with the usual oriental carpet holds a scroll bearing the words *Homo numquam,* while his wife places her right hand on his shoulder and holds a little dog in her left. Let us compare these couples with the Arnolfini portrait: this is not a question of comparing a simple object to a complex one of the same type, for the conception itself is different. After all, in Flemish religious scenes the saints were shown like people in well-defined surroundings (cf. Robert Campin's *Saint Barbara* and Rogier van der Weyden's *Annunciation*);[6] one can see that awareness of surroundings and their flavour was the stimulant that from the beginning caused Flemish and Dutch family groups to be depicted in their particular environments, whereas their Italian equivalents for a long time remained merely outlined against the neutral background of a generalized setting — even in cases like Bernardino Licinio's portrait of his brother's family (fig. 189), in which the bourgeois spirit reaches a no less complete and unmistakable expression than in the Biedermeier style.[7]

In the Foreword to the catalogue of a Scottish exhibition of conversation pieces[8] a division of these scenes into two categories

5 B. BERENSON, *The Italian Painters of the Renaissance* (Oxford: Clarendon Press, 1930), p. 33. 6 See M. PRAZ, *An Illustrated History of Furnishing* (New York: Braziller; London: Thames and Hudson, 1964), pp. 88-89. 7 Compare Licinio's group with that of Eduard Magnus' *Family of the Banker Martin von Magnus,* reproduced here in fig. 248. 8 *Scottish Groups and Conversation Pieces,* The Scottish National Portrait Gallery, 12th July to 16th September 1956 (The Arts Council, Scottish Committee).

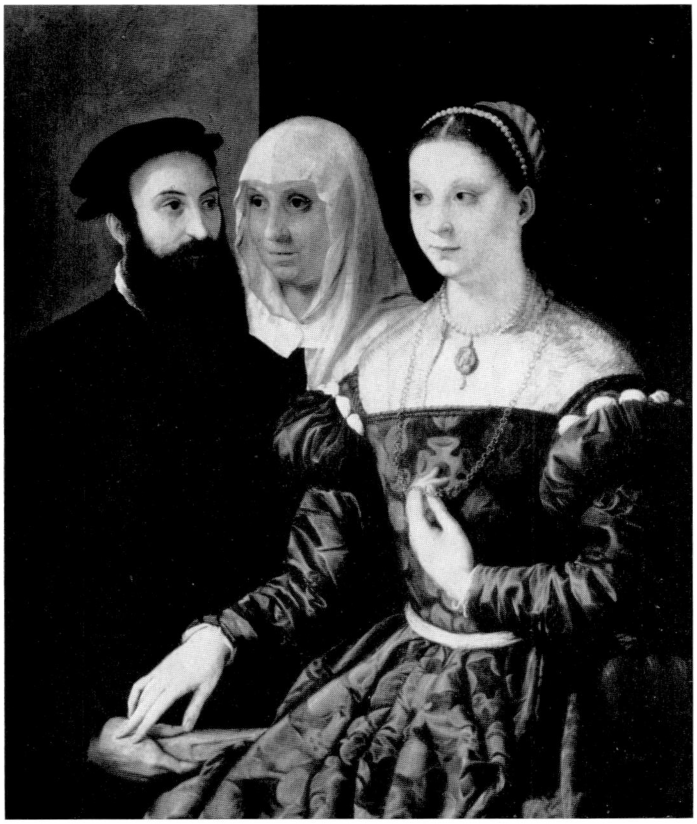

20

20 FRANCESCO SALVIATI (1510-1563), *A Man and Two Women.* New York, F. Kleinberger Galleries.

was proposed: group scenes, and conversation pieces proper. The conversation piece proper differs from the group scene in that it shows two or more people in their normal surroundings, busy with a social or domestic activity, whereas the group scene portrays two or more people posing in order to form a composition. This distinction is less satisfactory than at first appears. There are, in fact, groups which — though not really represented in identifiable surroundings — show some of the members busy at something or communicating among themselves (exchanging words, or delivering some object). The so-called *Theotocopuli Family* by a follower of El Greco depicts women spinning, embroidering, and sewing (fig. 193). Giuseppe Baldrighi's *Self-portrait with his Wife* shows the painter addressing his wife with a gesture, and some of the surrounding objects are visible (fig. 195). The Scottish painter Alexander Runciman (1736-1785) portrayed himself and John Brown (fig. 196) discussing a passage in Shakespeare's *Tempest* (John Brown [1752-1787] studied in Rome and belonged to Fuseli's circle; some of his spirited sketches of Roman women recall the manner of the Swiss painter). *The Painter and his Family* (fig. 197) by Friedrich Wilhelm Schäfer (c. 1800) represents several people, some of whom are talking to each other; a girl has stopped knitting and a boy fondles a dog. Are these domestic activities? In the portrait of *Lorenzo Mascheroni and his Friends* attributed to Andrea Appiani (fig. 198), we are faced with the usual sixteenth-century type of juxtaposed portraits; the simple gesture of shaking hands is hardly sufficient to classify the painting as a conversation piece. The same may be said of *The Family of John, First Marquess of Tweeddale* by Sir John Medina (1639-1710), who was born in Brussels of Spanish parents and settled in Scotland as a painter of historical scenes and portraits (fig. 201).[9] The group was painted in 1692-96, after the death of the Marquess' wife (in 1688), so that the wreath she holds has a symbolic significance. Two of the children, who had also died previously, are shown as angels in the sky. There are no links between the various figures; the painting is conceived as a collection of individual heads. In the *Group of Three Persons* which was shown at an exhibition at Palazzo Grassi in Venice, a lady has spread before her an engraving

9 On Sir John Medina and his method of work (he first prepared the figures without the heads, which he later added from real life, as the " primitive " American painters were to do), see the article by JOHN FLEMING, " Sir John Medina and his 'Postures' ", in *The Connoisseur*, CXLVIII, September 1961, pp. 23-25.

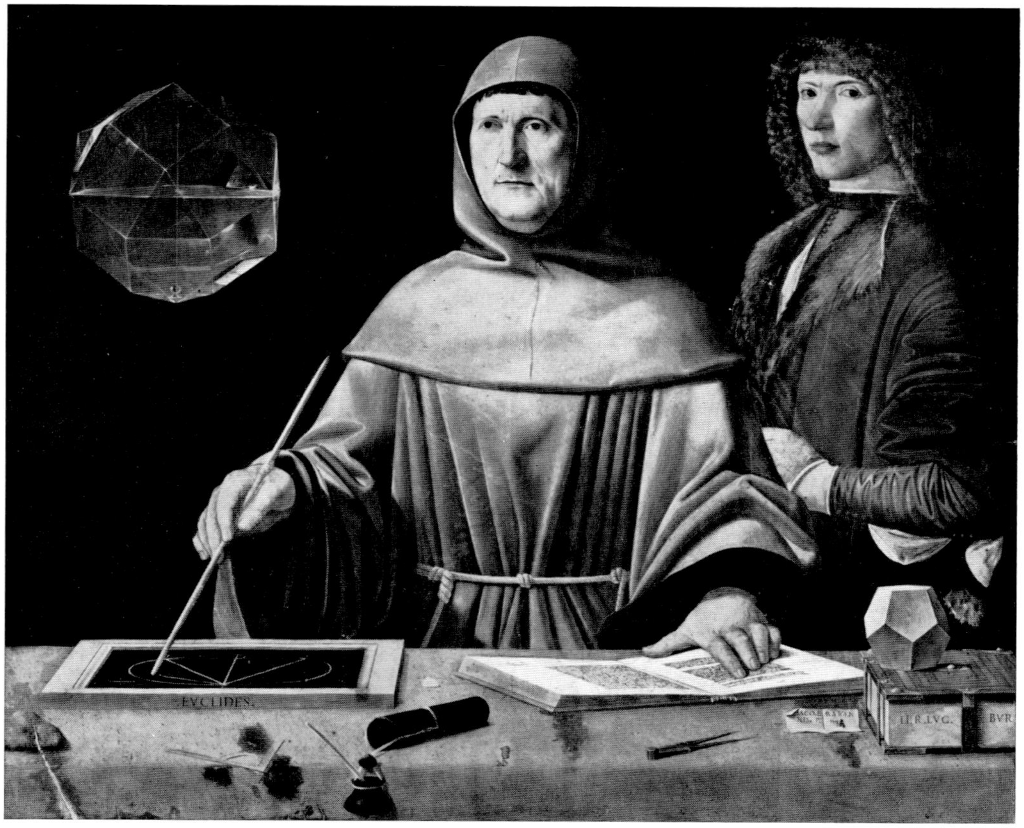

21

21 VENETIAN SCHOOL (signed *Iac. Bar.*), *Fra Luca Paciolo with a Bystander*. Naples, Museo di Capodimonte.

reproducing Canova's statue of *Religion* while a gentleman explains it to her (fig. 200). There is no indication of the surroundings, unless we consider the arm of the Empire chair and Canova's colossal head of Napoleon on the right as sufficient hints. In *The Family of L. De Brucker* by Josip Tominz (fig. 199), a little boy presents his mother with an apple, while with his other hand he squeezes his father's. Are the console-table, the Empire mirror, and the vase of flowers enough to create an environment? This and other paintings by Tominz (*The Moscon Family* [fig. 202], *The Buchler Family* [fig. 203], and *The Frussich Family* — the latter at the National Gallery in Ljubljana) still maintain the convention of the half-length portrait, usually with a decorative curtain. This type of conversation piece passed on to provincial portraiture, as in the *Portrait of an Elderly Woman and a Little Girl with Pets* (figs. 182 and 204) from the little Tuscan town of Montepulciano. The so-called *Family of Michel Gérard*, once attributed to David (Le Mans Museum),[10] should be called a group scene, but the girl playing the piano and the mantelpiece with a cup offer at least an indication of the surroundings.

However, keeping in mind the two prototypes of the conversation piece, the Arnolfini portrait and *The Family of Sir Thomas More*, we realize that the decisive factor is not so much that the sitters are engaged in a social or domestic activity, as it is the representation of the environment and the proportion of the sitters in relation to it. The conversation piece has an affinity with genre painting and with what is called in the Low Countries the *tableau de modes*, such as the *Company at their Meal* by Esaias van de Velde (fig. 207). The group scene belongs instead to the category of portraits. In the conversation piece the environment is depicted with an attention to detail no less scrupulous than we find practised in the portrayal of the sitters, and this gives to the picture a *Stimmung*, an intimate feeling which is not shared to an appreciable degree by the group scene, isolated or presented against a summarily indicated background as it is. And this is because, as we have repeatedly said, the family portrait developed simultaneously with the representation of interiors in the bourgeois Low Countries.

10 For the attribution, see M. BRIÈRE in *Bulletin de la Société de l'Art Français*, 1945-46, pp. 168-79, and D. COOPER in *The Burlington Magazine*, XC, 1948, p. 280.

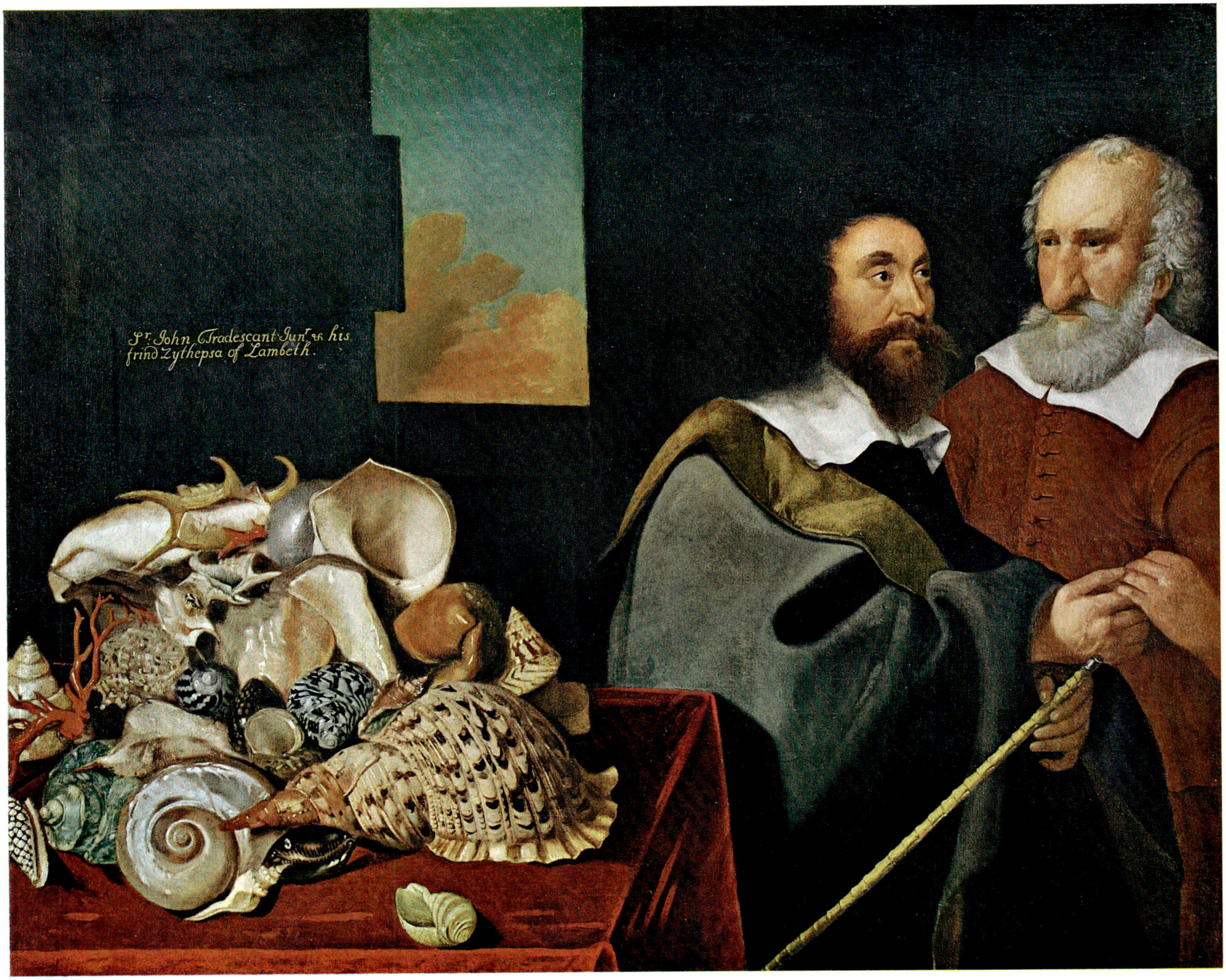

22

22 EMMANUEL (?) DE CRITZ (d. 1665), *John Tradescant Grasping the Hand of his Friend Zythepsa.* Oxford, Ashmolean Museum.

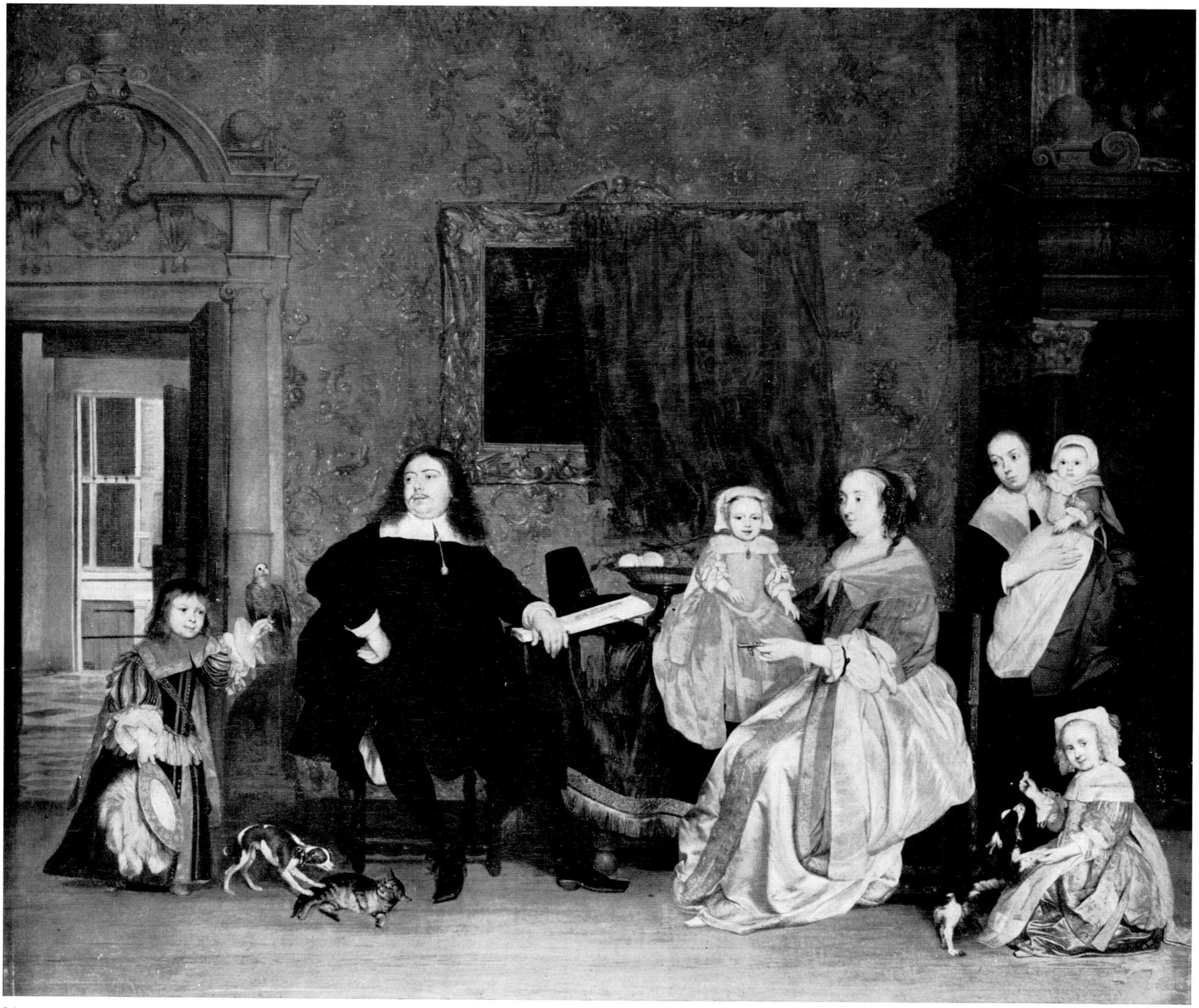

23

23 GABRIEL METSU (1629-1667), *The Family of the Merchant Geelvinck*. Formerly in Berlin, Kaiser Friedrich Museum (1931 catalogue, no. 792).

CHAPTER IV – THE INDOOR CONVERSATION PIECE

It would be unfair to the painter to say that the Arnolfini portrait anticipates the camera by many centuries; still, like an absent-minded photographer who lets a mirror reflect his apparatus hooded with its black cloth, van Eyck deliberately represents a diminutive self, in the act of painting the couple, in the convex mirror on the far wall. The harmonious peace communicated by the picture is that of the fleeting moment come to a standstill. The long sitting achieves the effect of a metaphysical snapshot. The impression is the same as the one which Virginia Woolf received from an episode in Jane Austen's *Mansfield Park:*

Here is nothing out of the way; it is midday in Northamptonshire; a dull young man is talking to a rather weakly young woman on the stairs as they go up to dress for dinner, with housemaids passing. But from triviality, from commonplace, their words become suddenly full of meaning, and the moment for both one of the most memorable in their lives. It fills itself; it shines; it glows; it hangs before us, deep, trembling, serene for a second; next the housemaid passes, and this drop, in which all the happiness of life has collected, gently subsides again to become part of the ebb and flow of ordinary existence.[1]

The presence of the Arnolfini married couple fascinates us and at the same time produces a vague uneasiness, as when we are facing uncannily lifelike wax figures, because their immobility is like that of the things which surround them: the bed and the big red-covered chair, the brass chandelier, the wooden shoes, the elegant pair of red boots, the oranges on the chest under the window. Still, these things throb as if into them had been transfused the life of the two sitters, which has stopped for a moment as if they were automata whose motor has wound down; the man has become motionless with his right arm raised and the hand in the act of blessing, and the woman's hand has remained palm upwards on the man's left hand. These hands are exquisite and delicate like a doll's hands screwed to a rudimentary structure hidden in the clothes. A strange transference has taken place; the objects have become invested with personality, the persons have become objects furnishing a room. One is reminded of the two lines of Keats' "Ode on a Grecian Urn": "Thou, silent form, dost tease us out of thought / As doth eternity".

1 *The Common Reader* (London, 1925), I, p. 78.

Such is the impression, exciting though somehow uncanny, left in us by van Eyck's painting. In the best conversation pieces of the English school we shall find something of this sensation, a mixture of magic and indefinable uneasiness.

Holbein's drawing has nothing so disturbing. While van Eyck's painting contains the quintessence of all the poetry of the conversation piece, Holbein's drawing fixes once and for all the paradigm of its prose, of its well-knit syntax. The two men sit in the middle, Sir Thomas and his elderly father, towards whom Margaret bends with an open book in her hand. Nearby, with hands folded on her lap, is young Elizabeth, and between the two men's heads appears the pretty figure of fifteen-year-old Anne. John pores over a book, next to an older man. Three more women sit in front, each with a book: Margaret Roper, Sir Thomas More's daughter, in the foreground, stares with vacant eyes while resting the book on her knees; behind her another woman is kneeling at a prie-dieu reading. The attitude of the young woman on the left of Margaret Roper is reminiscent of the *Lady with an Ermine* attributed to Leonardo.[2] The Gothic cupboard with its display of crockery, the clock, the view of another room through the open door at the back, and a lattice window on whose sill one sees pewter utensils form the background of this human conversation. If we compare it with the Gonzaga family in the Camera degli Sposi, we realize that the disposition of the sitters is not very different (there is also someone bending down next to the old Marquis — the secretary listening to instructions); but the atmosphere has changed, because instead of a vague background we have here a room in its precise details, and the furnishings produce the same effect as the substitution of a real background for the golden one in a holy picture, causing the saints to come down to earth among us.

The example set by van Eyck and Holbein had no immediate sequel. Quentin Massys (1465/6–1530) tries to combine sitters with their surroundings, as in the *Moneychanger with his Wife* at the Louvre, but both this painting and *The Legend of Saint Eligius and Saint Godeberta* by Petrus Christus (active at Bruges in 1442, died 1472-73), whose sitters are probably portraits, still present half-figures, as in the Italian groups of which we have been speaking; and the same may be said of Maarten van Heemskerck in the family group sitting at a laid table where, however, the background is not a room but the open sky (fig. 257). The convex mirror in the right corner of the goldsmith's desk, reflecting a street and two figures, evidently derives from the one in van Eyck's painting.

The progressive liberation of the traditional half-lengths of the group may be observed, as if in a tracking shot, in the paintings of banquets by Frans Floris (c. 1515-1570), Cornelius de Zeeuw (fl. c. 1563), and Frans Pourbus the Elder (1545-1581). Little by little the painter places himself further from the group and takes in whole figures and a larger section of the environment. In *The Wedding Feast of Joris Hoefnagel* by Pourbus (1571; fig. 205), the eye embraces the whole scene: the long table partly occupied by the virginals, partly laid with a tablecloth and dishes; two servants, an elderly man and a woman, carrying cheeses and artichokes; some of the guests sitting on the floor in front of the table, others standing behind, a few with musical instruments. They welcome the young couple as they enter the room.

This is not so much a conversation piece as one of those paintings of festivals and weddings which were to become so popular in Flanders, France, and Elizabethan England at the end of the sixteenth century. England, in fact, woke up to painting under Flemish influence, and a Flemish artist, or an English follower of the Flemish school, was the painter of the mediocre *Family of the Duke of Buckingham* (dated shortly before 1628; Hampton Court Palace). Of the large paintings of festivals, which are outside the scope of the more intimate type of the conversation piece, it is sufficient to mention the *Family Reunion* (1637; Amsterdam, Rijksmuseum) by Jan Miense Molenaer (c. 1610-1668). In the *Musical Entertainment of the van Loon Family*, of which more will be said further on, the number of people is reduced, but nevertheless the scene does not gain in privacy. Molenaer is closer to genre painting than to the intimate family gathering.

The representation of a family in its environment became the vogue both in the Spanish Low Countries and the United Provinces, which had become independent at the beginning of the seventeenth century. The conversation pieces by Gillis van Tilborch (born in Brussels in 1625, died c. 1678), Gonzales Coques (Antwerp 1614-1684), Gabriel Metsu (1629-1667), Adriaen van Ostade (1610-1684), and Pieter Codde (1599-1678) may serve as examples.

A table at one side consistently offers a resting place for the older sitters; children and pets provide a cheerful note. In Metsu's

2 See A. VENTURI, *Storia dell'arte italiana*, IX, i (Milan, 1901), pp. 98 ff.

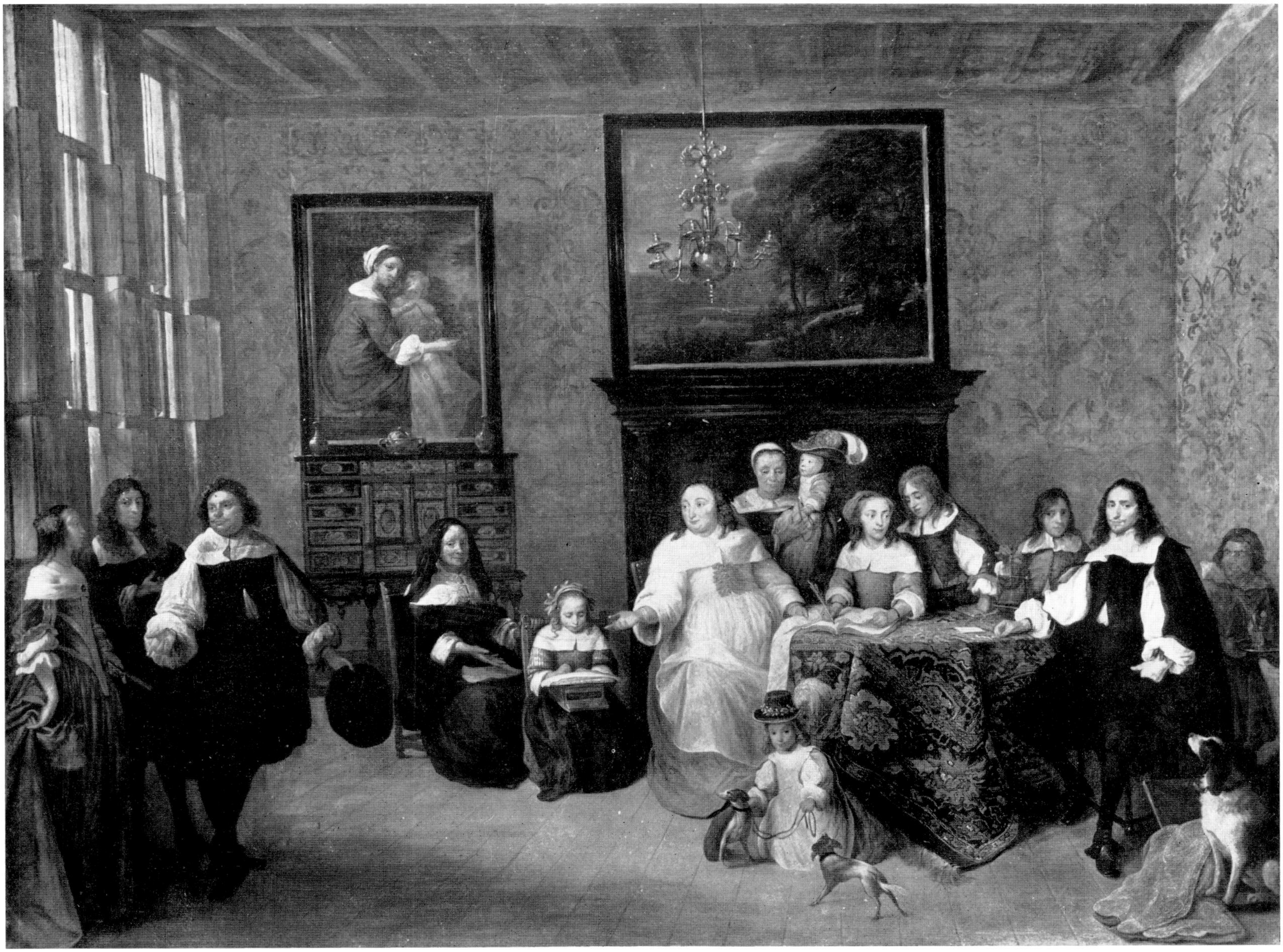

24

24 GILLIS (EGIDIUS) VAN TILBORCH (1625-c. 1678), *Portrait Group*. Rotterdam, Museum Boymans van Beuningen.

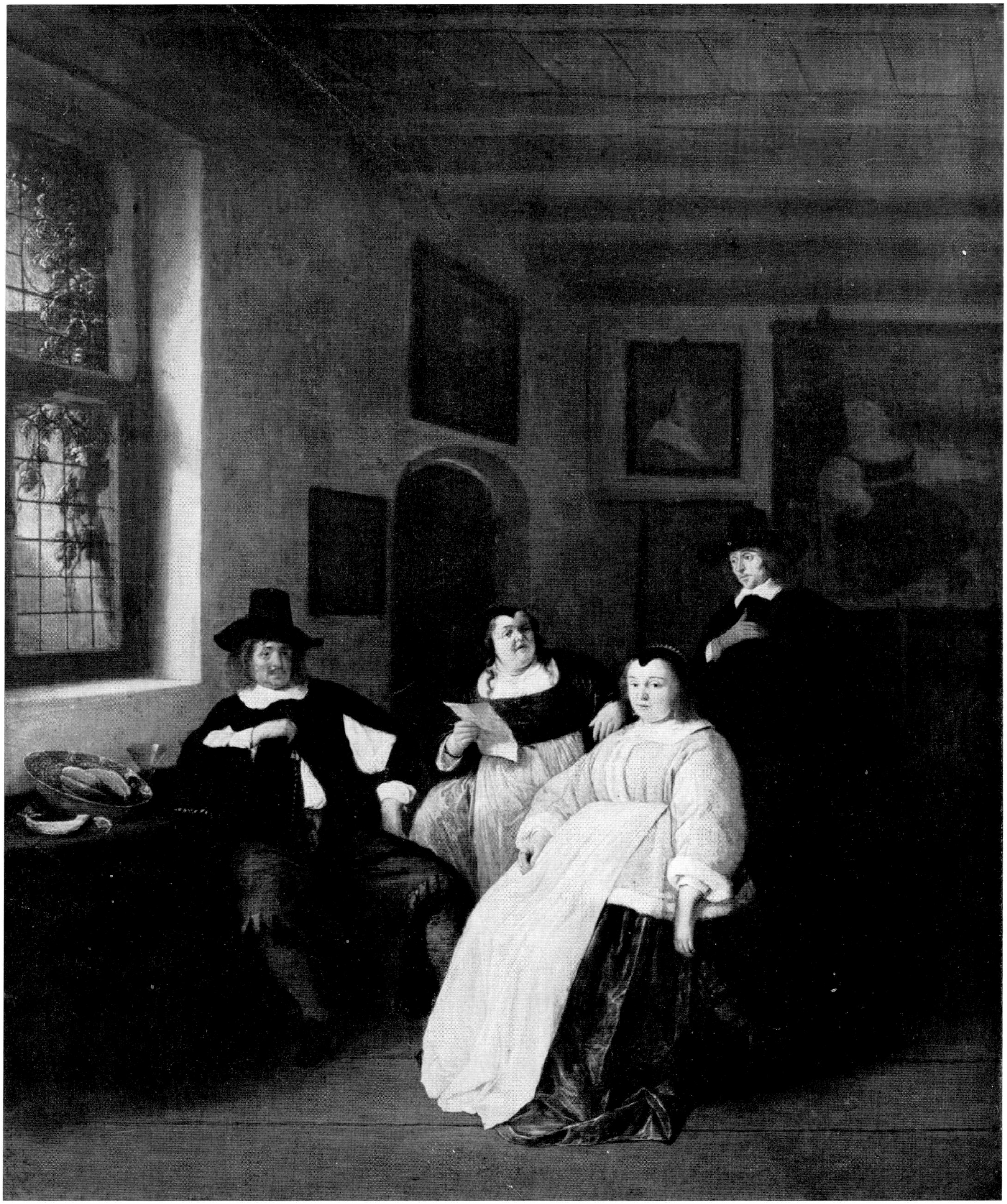

25

25 ADRIAEN JANSZ. VAN OSTADE (1610-1685), *The de Goyer Family*, 1650. The Hague, Bredius Museum.

painting of the *Family of the Merchant Geelvinck* (fig. 23) a boy in petticoats holds a parrot on the back of his hand as if it were a hawk, a little girl plays with a dog, and another dog, timid and aggressive at the same time, puts his forepaws on a spitting cat. In Gillis van Tilborch's painting (fig. 24) an elderly lady makes a gesture towards a group in the left corner, a young woman is writing what a young man suggests to her, a girl is embroidering, a child holds a dog by the leash, another dog looks at his master. Frequently, as in Adriaen van Ostade's conversation piece at the Louvre, the sumptuousness of the apartment, with paintings and Delft china, contrasts with the simplicity of the dresses, probably due to the fact that the family belonged to the Baptist sect. The sitters are portrayed without flattery; in the same way Hendrik de Goyer's wife, who appears reading a letter in van Ostade's painting at the Bredius Museum in the Hague (fig. 25), looks like a maidservant, and nobody would imagine that the other fat lady, Hendrik's sister-in-law, was a bluestocking celebrated in the verse of Vondel and Huygens, the greatest Dutch poets of the time. This painting is dated 1650. In 1656 a painter of far greater power, Velázquez, painted *Las Meninas*.

Velázquez, like van Ostade in the painting just mentioned, also portrayed himself together with his sitters, who are Philip IV and his wife Mariana, reflected in the mirror of the far wall — but the effect is the opposite of that of van Eyck's Arnolfini group, in which it is the painter who is reflected in the mirror.[3] But the complexity of Velázquez's composition is incomparably greater; the sitters are placed according to an "X" or Saint Andrew's cross pattern of which the pivot is the Infanta's face, to which the onlooker's eye is attracted and then led to what she is contemplating — the reflection in the distant mirror. Thus the centre is outside the painting and doubles its extent. The idea for this conversation piece may have come to the great Spanish painter from Flemish and Dutch examples; but looking at it after the others is like passing from a breakfast-room to a stately hall. There is a rustling of silks, an elegance in the movements of the maids of honour, who almost dance a pavan round the Infanta in the room painted by Velázquez; they are far removed from the padded corpulence of the middle-class sitters of van Ostade. It seems strange that Edwards, in his book on *Early Conversation Pieces*, should have left out Velázquez's name and that of Juan Bautista Martínez del Mazo, who between 1652 and 1658 painted his own family (fig. 206).

In the latter painting the children lack the vivacity we find in those of the Dutch paintings, for they look listless, too well behaved, as if bored by the sitting. Nevertheless del Mazo's group, arranged along the diagonal which crosses the picture, does not obey the conventions we have observed in Dutch conversation pieces, and the background, with the painter at work in his vast studio, is unusual. Here the table is not introduced as a support; covered with a velvet cloth and topped by a bust, it stands as a predella to the portrait of the sovereign.

Whereas in Dutch paintings bourgeois self-satisfaction is often tempered by severe, monotonous costumes, it flaunts itself cheerfully in the painting by the German Nicolaus Knüpfer (1640; fig. 208) in which he has portrayed himself in a relaxed attitude in the happy atmosphere of his family life. He is sitting like one of the merry boozers in genre paintings, and his wife, who holds up a naked child standing on the table, is a secular counterpart of the Virgin with the Child. The green trees seen outside the windows increase the idyllic character of the scene, and no doubt the sunlight will awake the song of the bird in the cage hanging in the window on the left.

An actual aristocratic magnificence (somehow contradicted by the *négligé* of the central figure) is displayed by the portrait of the *Family of the Cologne Banker Everhard Jabach* (fig. 209), director of the East India Company and Mazarin's agent and friend. Charles Lebrun painted him in his palace in the Rue Neuve Saint-Merry in about 1660. The structure is that of a Dutch family group, but in it breathes a Baroque air which is alien to the taste of the bourgeois of the United Provinces. The ceremonial curtain occupying the left corner of the painting, the opulent still-life formed by the bust of a warrior, a fragment of ancient marble, the globe, the open and closed volumes, and the drawing instruments, and the winning grace of the girl in silks on the right bear us to a higher plane than ordinary bourgeois comfort. This is the environment of an art lover, a collector, not merely a powerful financier. His collection, which was later purchased by Colbert for the Louvre (his old master drawings, which numbered more than five thousand, form the nucleus of the Cabinet des Dessins),[4] had been enriched with the spoils of that of Charles I, and tradition relates that Jabach returned to Paris from this sale at the head of a convoy of wagons laden with rich

3 See the subtle analysis of this painting in MICHEL FOUCAULT, *Les mots et les choses* (Paris: Gallimard, 1966), pp. 19 ff.

4 See FRANCIS HENRY TAYLOR, *The Taste of Angels: A History of Art-Collecting from Rameses to Napoleon* (London: Hamish Hamilton, 1948), pp. 237-38, 348-49.

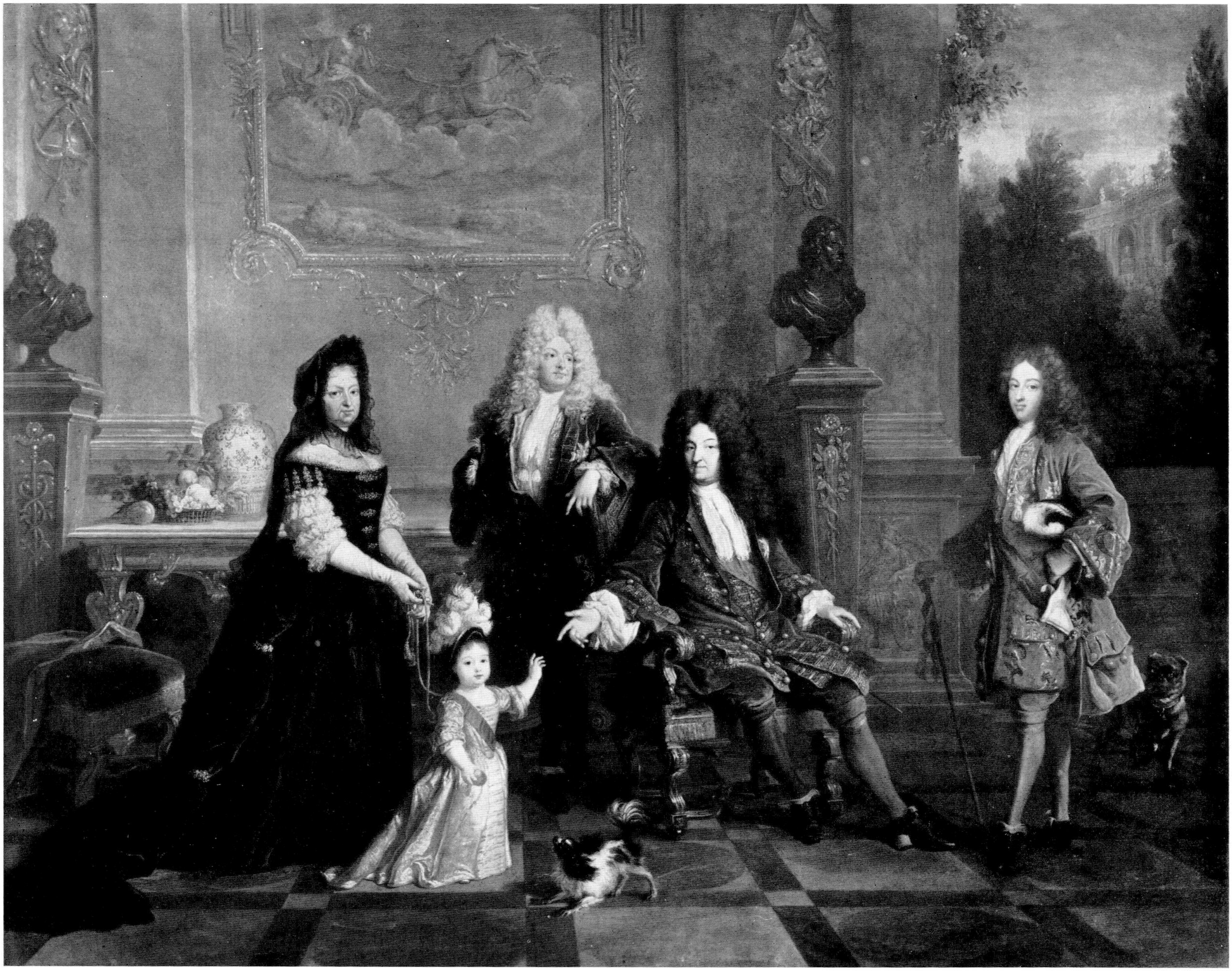

26

26 Nicolas de Largillière (1656-1746), *Louis XIV with the Grand Dauphin, the Duc de Bourgogne, the Infant Duc de Bretagne, and their Governess, Madame de Lévi-Ventadour*. London, Wallace Collection.

spoils, like a Roman conqueror at the head of a triumphal procession. Notice how in this painting the painter's own portrait is reflected in the mirror behind the warrior's bust while he is at work at his easel: a device reminiscent of the one used by van Eyck in the Arnolfini portrait.

The arrangement of a family group in an interior such as we have described is sometimes abandoned for a presentation very close to the subjects of genre painting. Thus the family group (once supposed to be that of the Leyden burgomaster, Johannes Meerman) by Pieter van Slingeland (1640?-1691; fig. 210) is inspired by Gérard Dou's small paintings, and one of the characteristics of genre painting is evident in the treatment of the dress of the young man on the right, which is said to have cost the painter a month's work; it needs a magnifying glass to be fully appreciated. By the minute execution of such accessories Slingeland secured a vast patronage among the prosperous middle class.

The *Family of Jacob Bierens* (1663) by Hendrik Sorgh (1611-1670) also shows the influence of genre and still-life painting (fig. 213). The family belonged to the Baptist sect; hence the simplicity of dress, and the inclusion of the maidservant among the members of the family. The furrier, a man of over forty, lifts a fish from the tray carried by the youngest of his children, Antony; his wife, Cornelia van Hoeck, peels an apple, the daughter plucks two pigeons and a snipe, while Abraham, the son, rather incongruously accompanies these domestic occupations on his bass viol. In the foreground is a still-life of various vessels, cabbages, artichokes, and fish. The only luxury in the room, which is in fact a kitchen, is the three paintings in the manner of van Goyen hanging on the end wall.

One is also reminded of still-life painting by the *Family of Eeuwout Prins* (1661), again by Sorgh (fig. 211). This is a family of notables, but provincial notables (Prins was the brother of one of the Rotterdam regents): hence the simplicity of dress and furnishings, which we feel here to be absolutely genuine (Dutch painters frequently represented interiors as wealthier than they actually were). Eeuwout Prins, who was the son of a brewer, looks from his office at his wife, who holds by the hand her younger daughter seated on a table, and gives the other a sweetmeat. The painting seems to anticipate some of Chardin's genre pictures (like the *Benedicite*).

The interior of *A Chemist's Shop* (1691; present location unknown), by a painter — perhaps Hastenbarg — whose signature is only partially visible, shows an important person (chemists were considered little less important than scientists), together with his wife (or mother) who sits behind a counter and a customer, among his bronze and stone mortars and the labelled china pots lined upon the shelves.

This survey of Dutch indoor conversation pieces of the seventeenth century may well be concluded with the *Unidentified Family* (1691) by Nicolaas Walraven van Haeften (c. 1663-1715; fig. 212). The subject must be a marriage contract. The future bride stands near her mother, and the grandmother offers her a rose. The young man, too, is accompanied by a widowed grandmother. The gentleman sitting on the right must be the father or a guardian, because the place he occupies would have been too conspicuous for a notary. The man behind, perhaps a servant, may have acted as witness. The mother, her coif adorned with a lace headdress (the *fontange*) and ribbons, is dressed in black and white, the aunt in grey, the bride in light blue, and the two grandmothers in black. With the servant in bluish-grey, the small bridegroom in light brown, and the gentleman in light blue sitting on a red upholstered chair, they form an agreeable harmony of colours. The table carpet is green with a red fringe. The men wear the type of necktie called the " Steinkerke " after the victory won in Belgium by the French over the English and their allies on August 3rd, 1692. This date would seem to contradict that of the painting (1691), but usually a historical name was given to a type of attire introduced at more or less the date of the event, so it is likely that the fashion existed even before the battle; the *cravate à la Steinkerke* had a negligent appearance that seemed to allude to the haste with which the French had had to dress when they were alerted. The furnishings do not give a precise indication of provenance; Staring[5] thinks that they may even be English and that the painter, like so many other Dutch artists, had gone to England — in which case the painting could figure among the incunabula of the English conversation piece.

The arrangement usual in Dutch conversation pieces may be noticed also in the large painting (127 × 160 cm.) by Nicolas de Largillière (1656-1746) representing *Louis XIV with the Grand Dauphin, the Duc de Bourgogne, the Infant Duc de Bretagne, and their*

5 STARING, *De Hollanders Thuis* (The Hague: Martinus Nijhoff, 1956), p. 100.

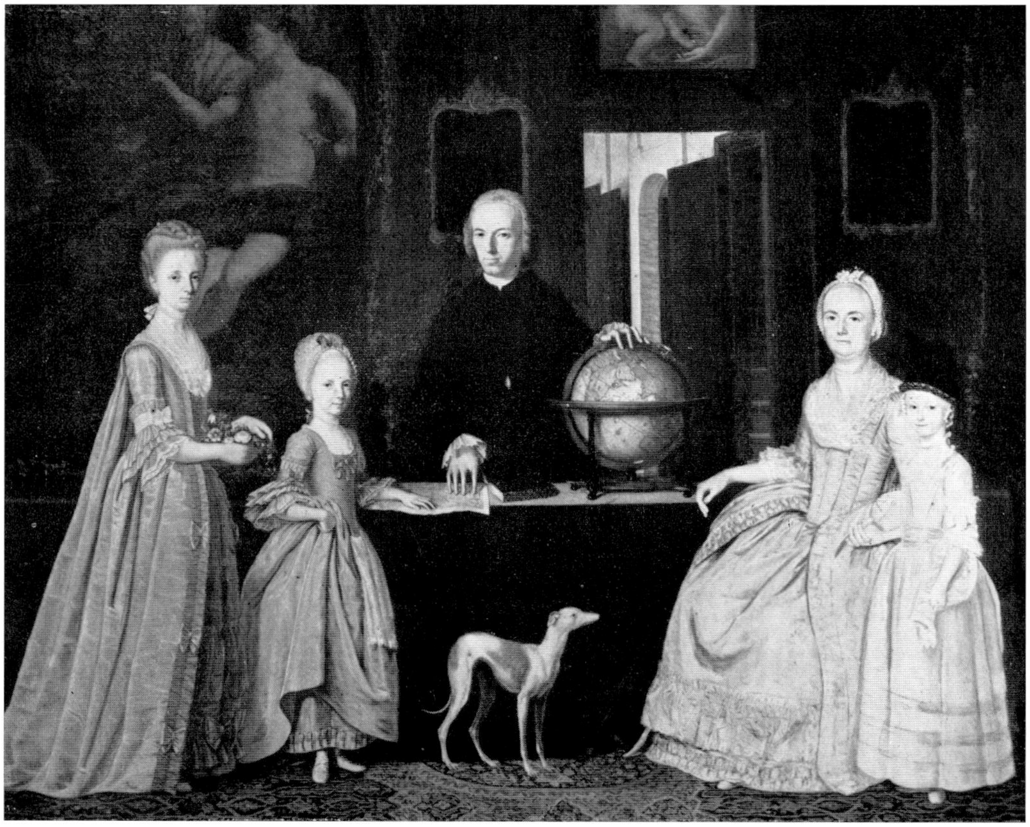

27

27 JORDANUS HOORN (1753-1833), *The Family of G. W. van Oosten de Bruyn*, 1775. Blaricum, collection of Dr. C. J. G. de Bruyn Kops.

Governess, Madame de Lévi-Ventadour (fig. 26) and may belong to the series of posthumous conversation pieces painted to commemorate various governesses of the royal family from Louis XIII to Louis XV.[6] But one can speak of an intimate atmosphere in this painting even less than in the one by Lebrun mentioned previously. The gesture of the Roi Soleil is more that of a sovereign showing a descendant to the people than of a relative who holds out his hand to a child, although the child's hand seems ready to catch it. As for the portrait of Monseigneur, his aspect of a corpulent and lazy man, lacking strength of character, as described by Saint-Simon (" le visage fort plein, mais sans aucune physionomie ") is evident even in a painting like this, which is intended more to flatter than to portray to the life.

In the *Unidentified Family* (1739; Amsterdam, Rijksmuseum) by Cornelis Troost (1697-1750), a variant on the usual scheme is attempted by presenting an asymmetrical background with the mother turning from the piano to show a passage in a musical score; but certainly the group is not caught unawares while engaged in its various occupations, for the eyes of all the members (except the lady's) look in our direction. The painter has been influenced by French models: by that time Hogarth had already painted conversation pieces in England, introducing several variants on the Dutch arrangements of indoor conversation pieces. Troost and other painters put new life into a genre that had been declining in Holland from the beginning of the new century. The traditional arrangement, however, persisted with some painters like Tibout Regters (1710-1768), who in *The Brak Family* (1752; Rijksmuseum) repeated the customary grouping with elderly sitters round the table and the father next to the mother, who has an infant sitting on her lap. This grouping keeps recurring throughout the century, as one may see in the paintings by Jordanus Hoorn and Louis-François-Gérard van der Puyl, which we mention here to document the persistence of a formula of composition in the Dutch school. The pronounced stiffness of Tibout Regters is not out of place in the representation of the Braks, a family of dissenters; the painter was very popular in such milieux for his specialization in family groups. Jan Brak,

6 See ÉMILE DACIER in *Bulletin de la Société de l'Art Français*, 1920, pp. 52-55; 1923, pp. 112-26.

28 JORDANUS HOORN (1753-1833), *The Family of the Painter's Parents*, 1775. Bilthoven, collection of Mevrouw Brouwer Nijhoff-Jordaan.

28

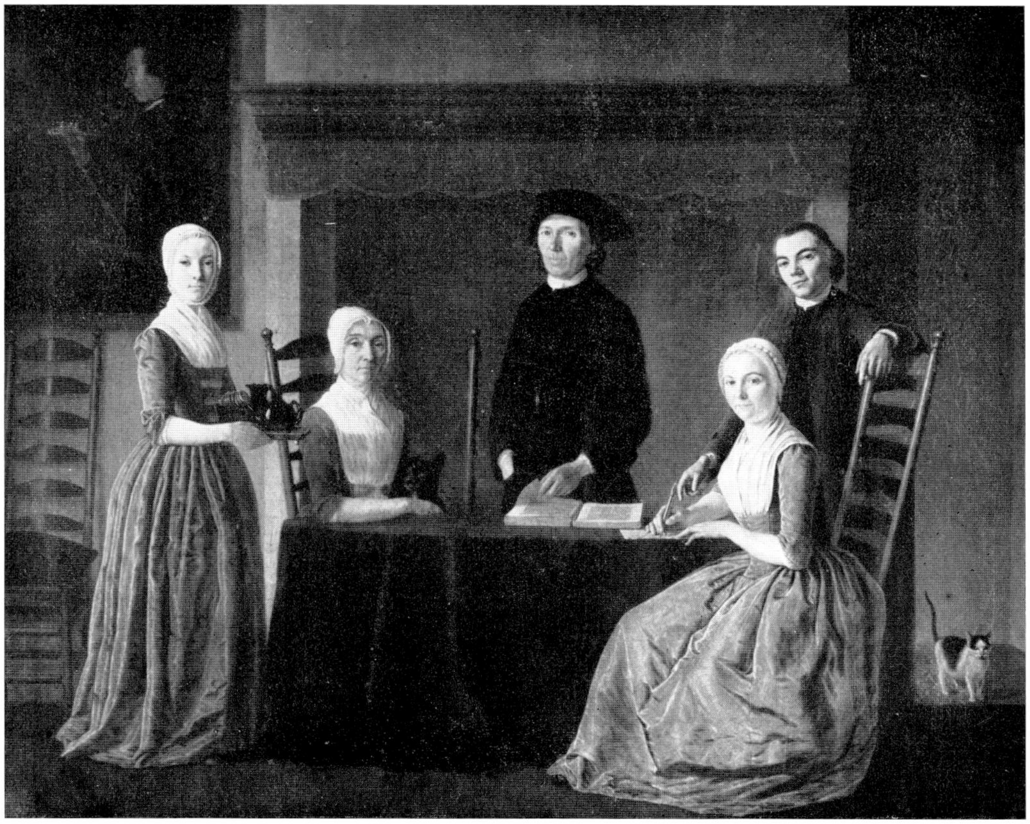

a Baptist minister, is reading the holy text to his relatives. The left section of the painting, which is austere and severe, forms an equilateral triangle. The right section is brighter and forms an " L " shape; it includes the young mother wearing a fichu of precious lace, and the husband, whose wig must have appeared old-fashioned in a period in which the fashion was to collect the hair in a net at the back. From his head there is a gradual downward progression to the centre of the painting where the little girl stands with her doll, which is the smallest and most extreme female figure of them all (one is reminded of Russian wooden dolls, one inside the other). The table is covered with a fine oriental carpet, but there is no light article of furniture in the whole room.

The grouping with a table and people sitting and standing for contrast is found in another painting with fewer sitters by Regters (fig. 216), the *Family of Jacob van Stamhorst* (1754), and the scheme is repeated in a picture attributed to Zoffany, *Charles Dibdin with his Second Wife and his Daughter*, where a difference of treatment is noticeable between the right side of the painting and the left (fig. 214).

In the *Family of G.W. van Oosten de Bruyn* (1775), Jordanus Hoorn (1753-1833) portrayed this preacher's son in his study (fig. 27); he was a man of letters and a scientist, author of Latin works on law and philosophy and of Latin poems and a life of Hadrianus Junius, and a collector, moreover, of Italian and Dutch paintings. Some of these paintings, probably Italian, hang on the walls. The composition is frontal and symmetrical: in the middle is the humanist, with one hand on the globe and the other on a plan either of Haarlem or his country house; at either side, contrasting with his severe figure, are his wife and daughters. The contrast is emphasized by the proximity of the tender hand of one of the younger daughters, placed on the plan, to the father's hand close by. The greyhound in the middle, against the dark background of the tablecloth, achieves an almost heraldic dignity. Equally symmetrical is the arrangement in another portrait by Hoorn (fig. 28), depicting the interior of a solid bourgeois house, that of the parents of the painter, who has portrayed himself here behind one of his sisters. The old father — wooden-looking, self-conscious of his hard-earned position in the world — and the elderly lady and the two girls, their heads in close-fitting lace caps, look in our direction almost with the fixity of animals surprised in a cage at the zoo; the mellow bronze tints cast on the scene an impression of deep tranquillity.

On the other hand, the group of the *Family of Nicolaas Hartingh* (1780) by Louis-François-Gérard van der Puyl (1750-1824) betrays an English influence (the painter lived in France and in England), especially in the view of the country house of this Leyden burgomaster (fig. 217). The composition no longer has a typical Dutch character, nor does the one by Tibout Regters executed about ten years after that of the above-mentioned Brak family, the *Family of Jan Carel van der Meulen* (c. 1760), which shows the influence of French fashions in the dress and furnishings (fig. 215). Van der Meulen, of a noble family, occupied the post of comptroller (equivalent to president) in the Amsterdamse Wisselbank. In this painting Regters seems to have retained of his former style only the predilection for a triangular or pyramidal arrangement of the sitters. The figure of the youth entering from the right is a motif which was found earlier in works by Hogarth (*Dudley Woodridge and Captain Holland*, a painting of 1730 in the Marshall Field collection, New York) and Joseph van Aken (*An English Family at Tea-time*, a painting in the National Gallery once attributed to Hogarth). The dog held on a leash on the left, leaping forward to be stroked by his master, is a motif also found in other conversation pieces — for instance in Desmarais's *Roncioni Family*.

Introduced by Dutch painters to the genre of conversation pieces,[7] England was not swept by it until the early eighteenth century. Even Hogarth succumbed to what he called " the epidemical distemper of the kingdom " in the field of art, and after his marriage with Sir James Thornhill's daughter in March, 1729, he began to paint small conversation pieces. Two years later he had all but abandoned this profitable branch of activity — which " though it afforded somewhat more scope for the fancy " proved almost as tedious to him as engraving — and was turning his attention to that " theatre in pictures " in which he was to produce his more memorable works: " I... wished to compose pictures on canvas similar to representations on the stage, and further hope that they will be tried by the same test, and criticized by the same criterion.... I have endeavoured to treat my subjects as a dramatic writer: my picture is my stage, and men and women my players, who by means of certain actions and gestures are to exhibit a dumb show ".[8]

One feels inclined to think that the conversation pieces paved the way to this dramatic style of painting, just as for Richardson the compilation of familiar letters on the principal occurrences of life paved the way to the epistolary novel. Sacheverell Sitwell, who by his volume *Conversation Pieces*[9] has the distinction (together with Williamson's essay[10] apropos of the 1930 Exhibition) of having made the first survey of this kind of painting, was carried by his enthusiasm for Hogarth to the point of saying that " the conversation piece owes its character and conception to the genius of Hogarth. He is the master of the school; the one or two exquisite Gainsboroughs, the tireless Devis, the ubiquitous Zoffany are but his pupils.... The lesson of realism through informality is to be found in nearly everything that Hogarth painted ".

It is one thing to say that Hogarth, the founder of the great tradition of English painting, marks an important stage in the history of the family portrait and another thing to attribute to him the invention of the genre. More judiciously than Sitwell, Edwards remarks:[11] " It is to their ' novelty ' that Hogarth attributed the success of his small ' Conversations ': he must not of course be understood to imply that until now such pictures had never been seen. He approached his sitters in a new way; and within a convention already established, revealed potentialities unexplored hitherto; but he had not introduced a new form of group portraiture ". Though there are Dutch forerunners and also, for the painting technique, French ones (Watteau, Mercier),[12] it remains difficult, Edwards remarks, to find proof that Hogarth's conversation pieces were influenced by the latter.

Let us try to see how Hogarth changed the approach to sitters in indoor conversation pieces. In Dutch portraits the subjects are usually placed as for a sitting. Consider, for instance, a painting like the Tilborch we have examined above. Although some of the people round the table on the right appear to be engaged in some occupation and the persons standing on the right are employed in a discussion, and although the connection between the two groups is secured by the glance of the matron sitting

7 For this period of initiation see RALPH EDWARDS, *Early Conversation Pictures, from the Middle Ages to about 1730* (London: Country Life Ltd., 1954). 8 JOHN IRELAND, *Hogarth Illustrated* (London: J.E.J. Boydell, 1791-98), III, 25-26. Notice also the influence of the prints of Peter Brueghel the Elder on Hogarth, particularly for the allusive and symbolic accessories (see for instance in Brueghel's *Alchemist* the empty purse of the alchemist's wife, emblematic of the vanity of the man's pursuit). 9 London: Batsford, 1936, p. 9. Reprint London: Batsford; New York: Schocken, 1969. 10 G.C. WILLIAMSON, *English Conversation*

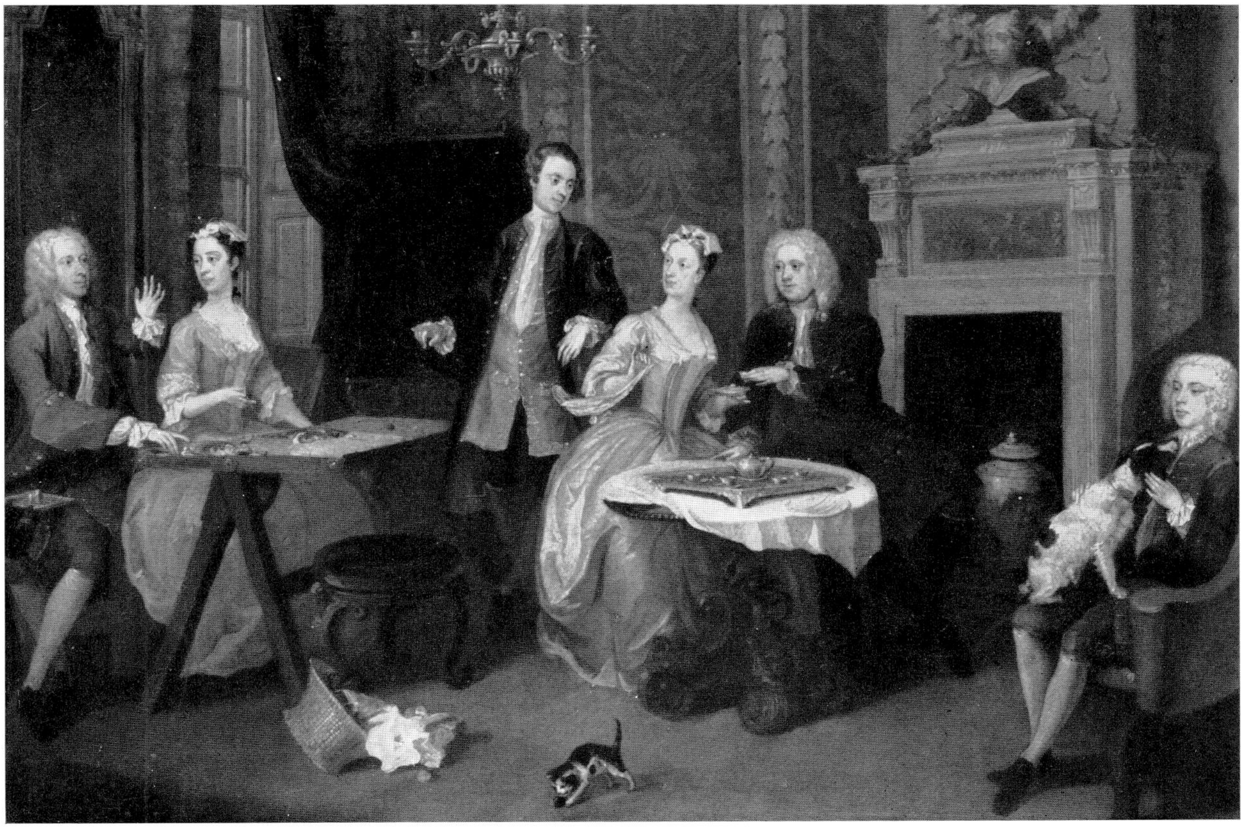

29 WILLIAM HOGARTH (1697-1764), *Family Reunion.* Washington, D.C., collection of Mr. and Mrs. Paul Mellon. 29

in the middle, the impression of the onlooker is that in reality all these people are sitting for us to form a *tableau vivant.* In Hogarth's *Wollaston Family* (1730; Leicester Art Gallery) almost none of the sitters looks in our direction. Those who are taking tea on the right fix their attention on various points, and the group on the left is really busy playing cards. A gesture of Mr. Wollaston in the centre — Edwards remarks — supplies " a sufficient if rather too obvious link between the two groups seated at cards and tea ". An identical arrangement occurs in the Mellon Collection conversation piece, in which there is a similar room of smaller size, and fewer people. On the left instead of the table there is an embroidery frame (fig. 29). Hogarth shows a predilection in these paintings for a frontal arrangement like a stage-setting, avoiding salient points in the fairly uniform line of the sitters.[13]

Hogarth tries on the other hand to present family reunions against irregular backgrounds formed by the angle of two walls, of which we usually see the end one and the one on the right side (as in *The Western Family* in the National Gallery of Ireland in Dublin), while a drapery on the left closes the scene both in *The Wollaston Family* and in *The Broken Fan*; in the latter (fig. 225) our eyes penetrate beyond an arch into a vast gallery. In *The Cholmondeley Family* (1732; fig. 30) a little Cupid actually draws the drapery on the left (just as in Lebrun's *Jabach Family*), and this drapery, with its counterpart on the right, forms almost a stage curtain: the theatre is already present in Hogarth's mind. When he combined an actual performance with a conversation piece, as in the *Scene from 'The Indian Emperor; or The Conquest of Mexico'*, through the meeting of the planes and the diagonal disposition of the spectators contrasting with the two couples of juvenile actors, he achieved an effect of depth and animation such as is hardly to be found in any other conversation piece ever painted (fig. 162). If the group of George, third Earl Cholmondeley, his wife, one of his sons, and a gentleman leaning against a screen is rather conventional (with the typical pyramidal arrange-

Pictures of the Eighteenth and Early Nineteenth Centuries (London: Batsford, 1931); the title of the catalogue runs: *Loan Exhibition of English Conversation Pieces in Aid of the Royal Northern Hospital at* 25 *Park Lane*, March 4th to 30th (inclusive) 1930. The catalogue is preceded by a brief introduction by Philip Sassoon, who promoted the exhibition. 11 *Early Conversation Pictures*, p. 63. 12 See F. ANTAL, "Hogarth and his Borrowings", in *The Art Bulletin*, XXIX, 1947, n. 1. 13 Similarly Gawen Hamilton, who in his conversation piece *The Earl of Strafford and his Family* (fig. 218) presents a scheme close to that of Hogarth's *Captain*

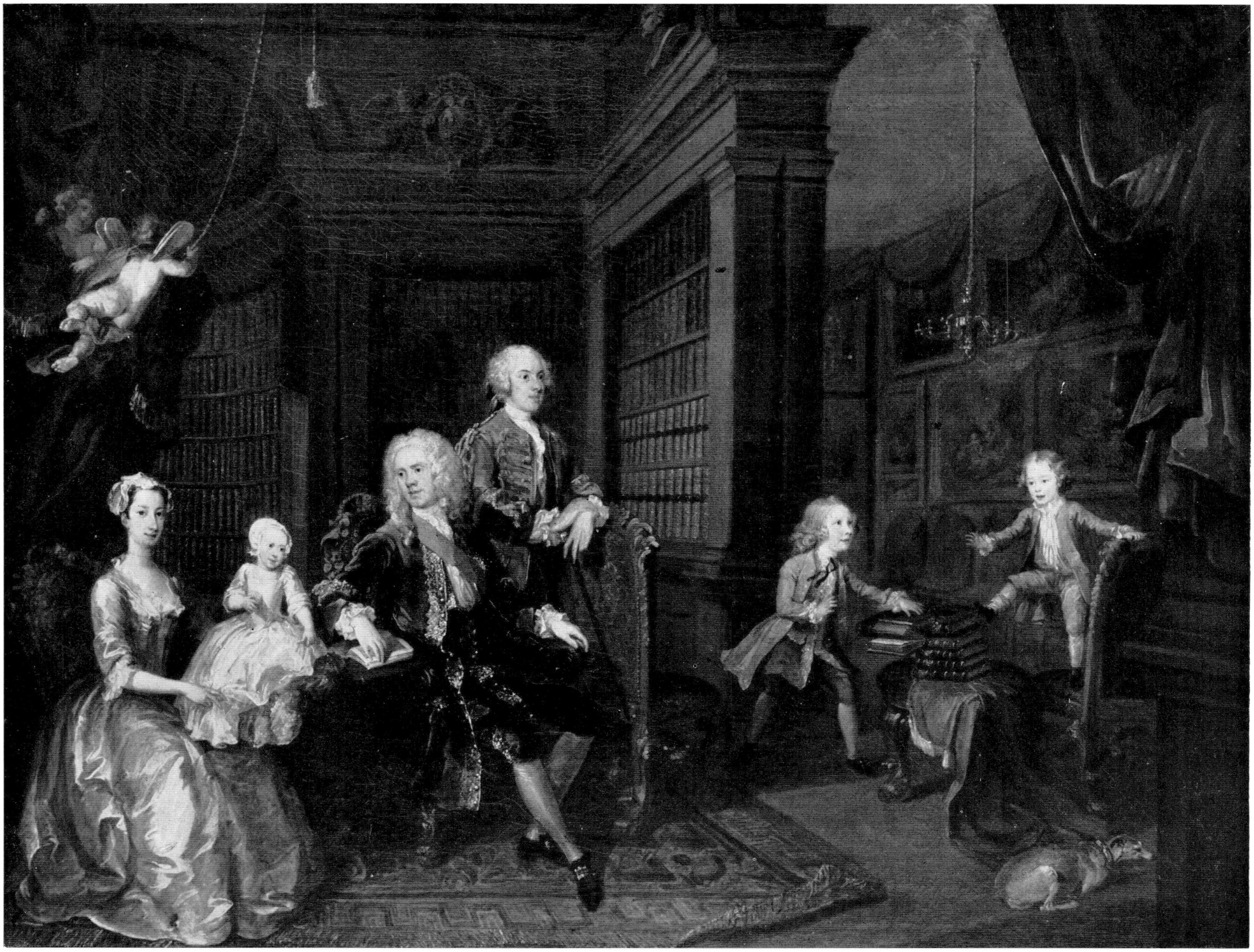

30

30 WILLIAM HOGARTH (1697-1764), *The Cholmondeley Family*, 1732. Houghton Hall (Norfolk), collection of the Marquess of Cholmondeley.

ment), the library wing projecting in the middle and the group of two children, one of whom is on the point of setting foot on a pile of books, create an unusual and playfully asymmetrical motif.

There was a growing tendency to assign tasks to the various sitters in order to avoid the rigidity of pose. This was the practice of Johann Zoffany, of whom we shall speak further on, and of almost all the painters of conversation pieces in the wake of Hogarth. Sometimes only a few of the sitters are involved and the movements are barely hinted at, as in John Hamilton Mortimer's (1741?-1779) *The Tyrwhitt Drake Family at Shardeloes*. The subjects are grouped rather conventionally against a wall that is parallel to the picture frame; this wall breaks off in the middle to give place to a landscape (fig. 219). One of the girls is embroidering, the gentleman in the centre holds a plan spread out on his knees, and the officer seated on the right holds a closed book. The two persons standing are the architects Robert and James Adam, and Shardeloes (in Buckinghamshire) was one of the earliest English country houses they built.[14]

In the group of *The Family of Don Carlo Barberini* (whose size, 140 by 200 centimetres, far exceeds that of the average conversation piece), the work of the otherwise unknown painter Prospero Mallerini (1802), the vocations of some members of the family are indicated by objects functioning as attributes: Maria, on the extreme left, draped like an antique statue, holds a quill, an obvious symbol of literary talent which was readily granted to young ladies in the Arcadian milieux; Teresa shows a drawing she has made after Raphael's *Fornarina*, a painting which at the time was in the Barberini collection; Antonio holds a violin and a bow; Francesco, the first-born, unfolds a plan of the palace and villa of Castelgandolfo, a seventeenth-century building he has drawn as a token of his (no matter if not original) talent for architecture. As for the vocation of the adolescent Benedetto, who sits with legs wide apart between Maria and Teresa, nobody could guess it from his tempting a fluffy white and brown dog with a dainty cake, unless the painter meant the act metaphorically, foreseeing for him the ecclesiastical career in which he was raised to the purple. The whole group of twelve people is distributed according to a rhythm of arsis and thesis; at the centre stands the head of the family, who vaguely reminds us of Goya's Charles IV, as Andrea Busiri Vici, who was the first to describe this painting, remarks (" Un singolare gruppo di Casa Barberini del 1802 ", in *L'Urbe* for May-June 1970). On the extreme right, a counterpart of the Arcadian shepherdess on the left, the group of the two sisters Caterina and Maria Lucrezia recalls the group of *The Two Sisters*, likewise embracing each other, sold as a painting by Elisabeth-Louise Vigée-Lebrun at the Sedelmeyer auction, Paris 1907, no. 250. The room, which cannot be identified with any existing in the Barberini palace, is probably imaginary, as in a number of Dutch conversation pieces: it shows in the centre of the back wall the portrait (a medallion in the style of the Louis XVI period) of the family's great ancestor, Pope Urban VIII (fig. 31).

The globe on which the sitter on the right rests his hand and the harpsichord played by the girl on the left help to give some appearance of animation to *The Putnam Family* (fig. 220) by an unknown painter (attributed to Arthur Devis). The Putnams emigrated to America from Sussex, and the landscape with a river and a ship on the right may allude to their expatriation. Perhaps the flowers of the festoon so languidly supported by the two standing girls are exotic, as are the flowers of the wreath the elderly lady holds on her knees and, of course, the parrot perched on the right hand of one of the girls. Has the wreath a symbolic meaning like the one of the Marchioness of Tweeddale in Sir John Medina's portrait we mentioned above?[15]

Again, in a painting by Thomas Patch (c. 1720-1782), who spent a great part of his life in Florence where he made engravings of the Brancacci Chapel frescoes, the far wall is taken up by a landscape, a view of the bridges on the Arno, which later belonged to the Holland House collection (fig. 221). The Duke of Roxburghe, a famous bibliophile, is talking to Patch, who is busy painting. Miss Tabitha Mendes, a wealthy Jewish dwarf, is seated and is waited on by a maidservant who is holding her lapdog. All the sitters are caricatures in the manner of Pier Leone Ghezzi, the well-known cartoonist who, among other things, had decorated a room in the Villa Falconieri at Frascati with portraits.[16] Sitwell says that some of Patch's conversation pieces " are without equal in the art ". But they may well be compared with *The Oyster Supper among Artists in Rome* by John Hamilton Mortimer (Washington, D.C., collection of Mr. and Mrs. Paul Mellon) and other caricaturists besides Ghezzi were not lacking in Italy. One should mention Gaspare Traversi (1725-1769), who in two conversation pieces shows members of Nea-

Woodes Rogers and his Family, with the chief person standing out at a distance from the others. (See below, Chapter VI, p. 117). 14 See ARTHUR T. BOLTON, *The Architecture of Robert and James Adam* (London: Country Life Ltd., 1922), 1, pp. 144 ff. 15 See p. 55. 16 On Thomas Patch, see F.J.B. WATSON, " Thomas Patch, Note on his Life, together with a Catalogue of his known Works ", *Walpole Society*, XXVIII, 1940. Patch must have known Ghezzi's work in Rome, and some of his sketches have been catalogued at the Uffizi under the name of Ghezzi (p. 26). On p. 24 are described the circumstances of the painting of which

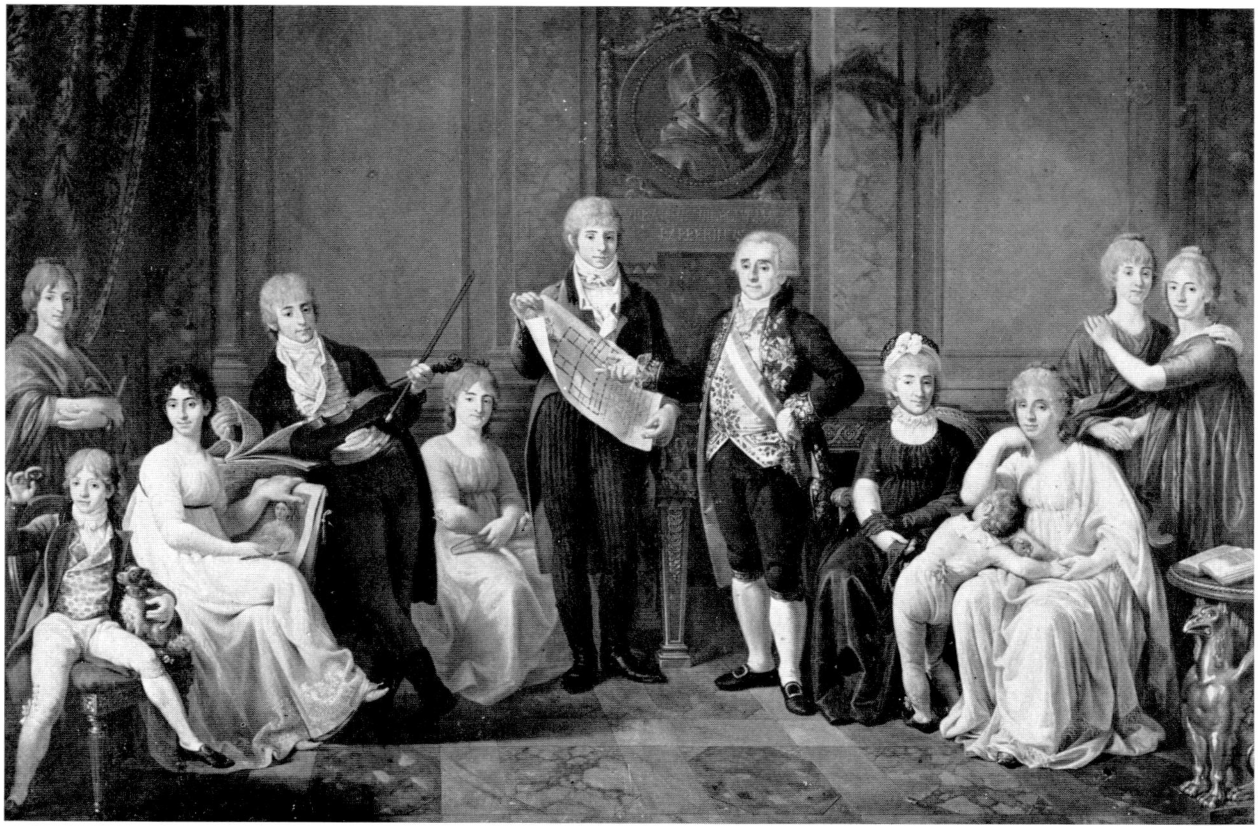

31

politan society (figs. 32, 33), portrayed with a realism verging on caricature, impersonating the various arts.[17] In the group of people playing cards and drinking coffee depicted by another Neapolitan, Giuseppe Bonito (1707-1789), caricature is limited to the maidservant, whereas an animation proper to genre painting prevails in the other sitters (fig. 222).

Conversation pieces were also made in silhouettes, enlivened by gestures and attitudes just as in paintings: for instance, Torond's silhouette in the Reresby Sitwell collection (Renishaw Hall, near Sheffield) and *The Grand Duchess Amalia with her Retinue in the Park at Weimar* (fig. 224). In the latter, regarding the lady sitting with her lapdog on the rustic seat (the one with the open parasol) and the other who, wearing a feathered hat, seems to emphasize by the movements of her closed fan the instructions she gives to a young woman, you would almost think that, were you only to turn round, you would see in the flesh the persons whose lively shadows confront your eyes. Look at the graceful family groups by Torond, a French artist who worked in England, and by the German, Anthing, who was employed at the Russian court and shared the disgrace of Marshal Suvarov. These silhouette artists knew how to give rhythm to the attitudes of the various people, so that the image, instead of presenting a monotonous row, charms like the cadence of a perfect line. Seated persons alternate with those standing, like the short and long syllables in a consummate prosody; grave, elderly persons are contrasted with vivacious shadows of children, some playing with dogs and some training little birds. The compact shadows of swelling petticoats counterbalance the delicate filigree of Chippendale tea-tables, with urns for that fashionable drink and all the elegant service. The animals' fur, the branches of potted plants, the plaiting of work-baskets, the jabots, and the curls and trinkets of headdresses are there, miraculously alive and fragile, so that you would think a single breath would be sufficient to disarrange them all.

An art of the court and polite society, sister of the miniature, the silhouette flourished in all its purity until the end of the eighteenth century, until the time when François Gonord — if tradition is not lying — cut silhouettes of the aristocratic victims of

we are speaking: the Duke of Roxburghe is supposed to be prevailing upon himself to propose to the wealthy but monstrous Portuguese dwarf, Miss Tabitha Mendes. 17 Such impersonations of the senses and the arts were then current. Thus Philip Mercier (1698-1760) represented the senses in genre pictures with groups of people (Mellon Collection); engravings were made of these.

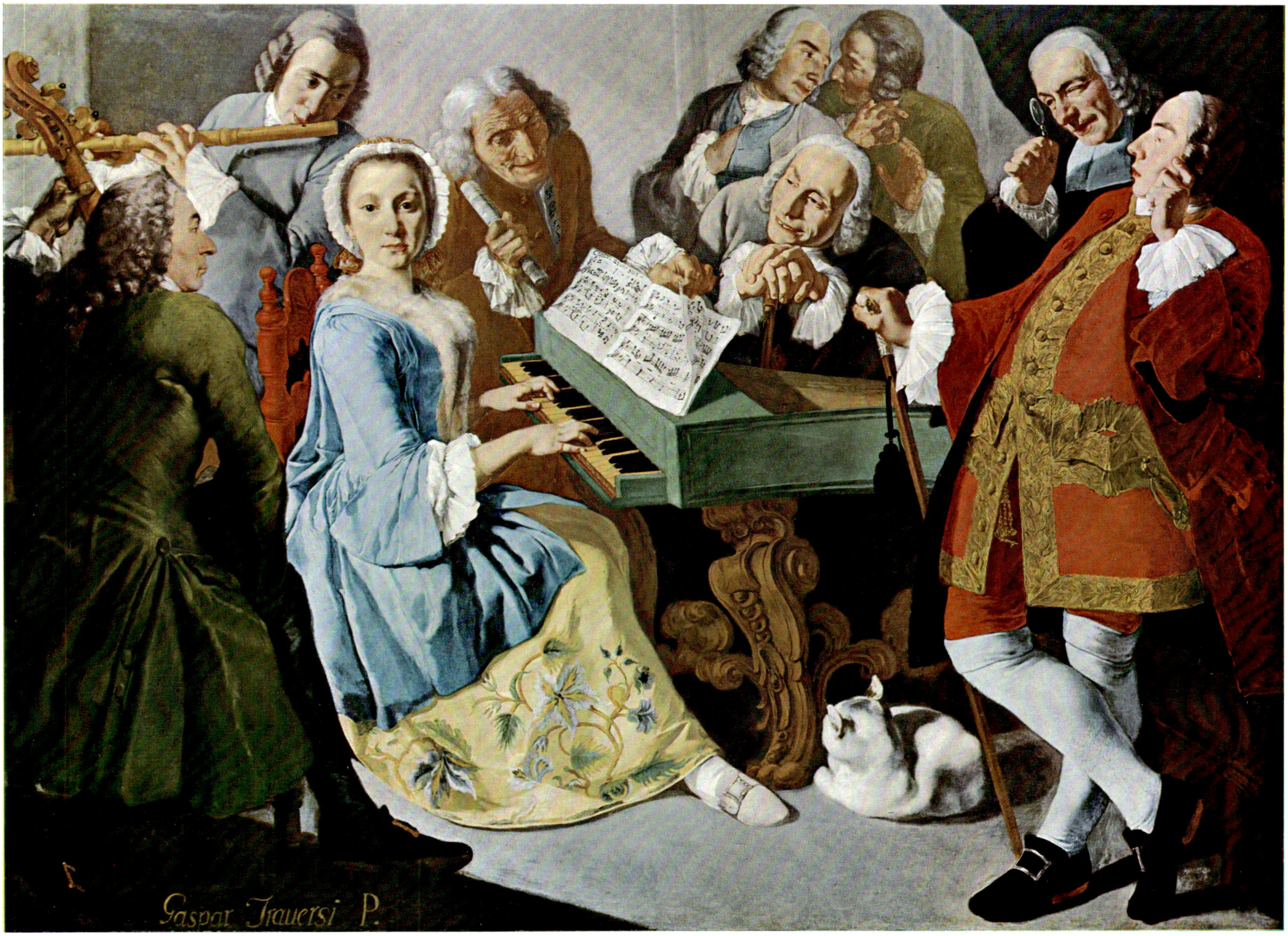

32

31 PROSPERO MALLERINI (fl. c. 1800), *The Family of Don Carlo Barberini*. Rome, Prince Augusto Barberini Collection. 32 GASPARE TRAVERSI (1725-1769), *The Arts: Music*. Kansas City (Missouri), William Rockhill Nelson Gallery of Art (Samuel H. Kress Collection).

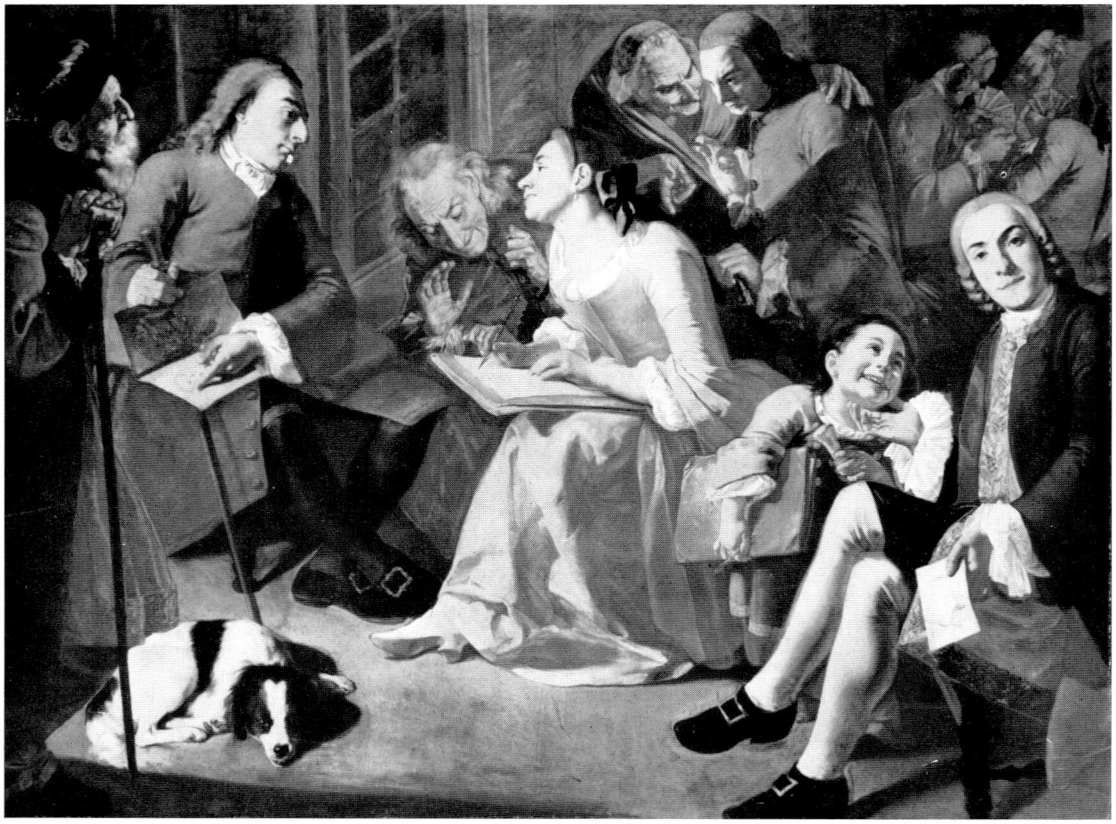

33

33 GASPARE TRAVERSI (1725-1769), *The Arts: Drawing*. Kansas City (Missouri), William Rockhill Nelson Gallery of Art (Samuel H. Kress Collection).

the Revolution while they were ascending the guillotine: black profiles suitable to the lugubrious occasion, which, conveniently reduced and set into the then-customary mourning rings, would perpetuate a tragic memory. Whether pasted on paper or painted on *églomisé* glass, whether encircled in pearls, amethysts, and turquoises or simply mounted in pinchbeck as in the bracelets that even Paris market women used to wear in about 1779, silhouettes remained immaculately black during the eighteenth century. Incomparable black of the profiles which adorn some services of Dresden, Meissen, Vienna, and Worcester china, contrasting with the whiteness of porcelain and the brilliant colours of the decorations! But from the beginning of the nineteenth century, makers of silhouettes began to " bronze " (i.e., to colour with flecks of gold) or to streak with white the body of the shadow; they sought cameo effects, or painted the officers' jackets in red; their attention ceased to be concentrated in the expressive outline. As in every decadent stage of art, they elaborated; they sought the complicated and the prodigious (profiles obtained in a single minute, with lightning speed of the scissors), and at the same time they relied more and more on mechanical processes — especially in America, where the silhouette enjoyed great favour during the nineteenth century.[18] Except in the work of a few (and among these Augustin Edouart excels), the silhouette thus lost its proper character of perpetuating the revealing, fleeting moment in an attitude and a profile, and was succeeded by a less exquisite and aristocratic art, more suited to the industrial and bourgeois century: i.e., photography.

In conversation pieces the harpsichord and needlework offered convenient pretexts to give a varied attitude to female sitters. Dogs, either jumping up or motionless, formed an attractive diversion; another was provided by children's games. The presence of a dog playing with a child is sufficient to give direction to the glances of the sitters, as in an anonymous English *Family Group* of the end of the eighteenth century, in which the only person who does not show any interest in the child and the dog is the pompous, almost grotesque clergyman who lays his right hand on his chest as if conscious of his own importance (fig. 35).

18 See E. NEVILL JACKSON, *Silhouette* (London: Methuen), 1938, and A. VAN LEER CARRICK, *A History of American Silhouettes* (Rutland, Vt.: Charles E. Tuttle, 1968).

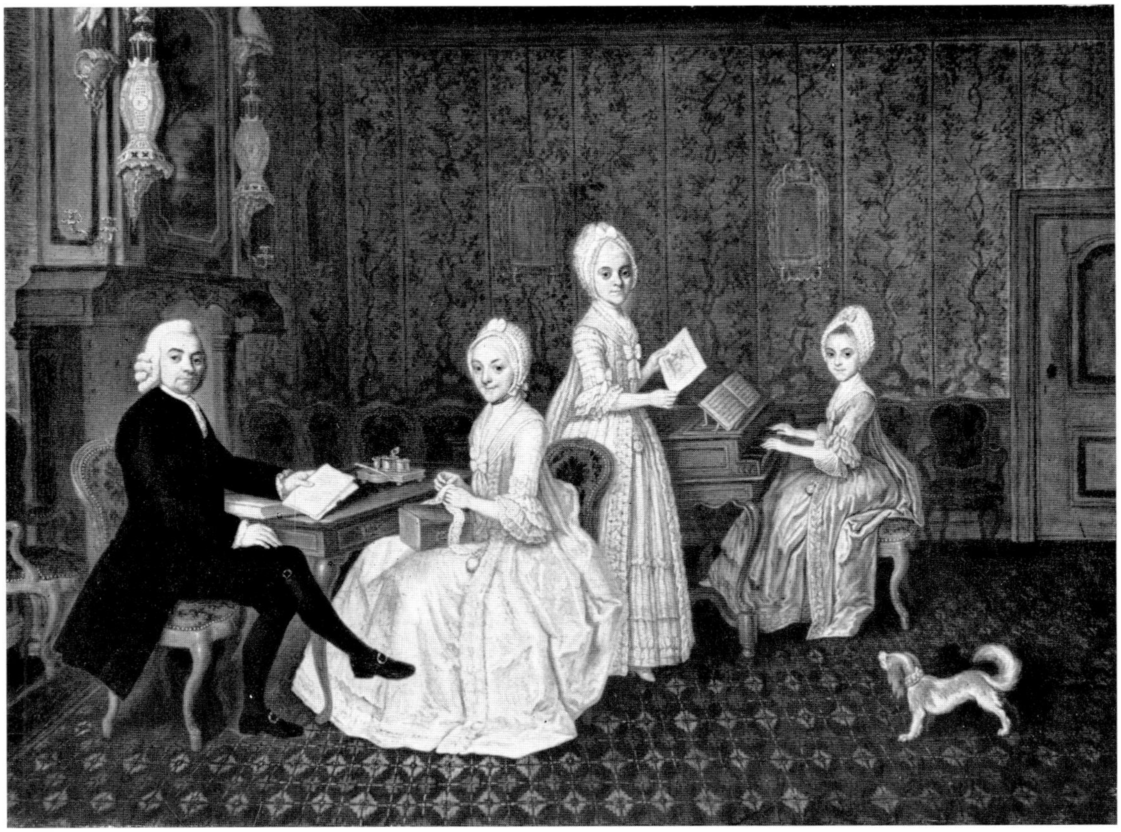

34 HIERONYMUS (GIROLAMO) LAPIS (1723-1798), *The Cornelis Verbrugge Family*, 1773. Houten, collection of Mevrouw C. H. Wttewaall-Cardinaal.

34

The harpsichord is perfectly justified in the portrait (fig. 223) by an unknown artist of about 1745 (not Philip Mercier, and not an English artist, though a family tradition attributes it to Hogarth) of the famous harpsichord-maker *Burckhardt Tschudi with his Wife and Two Children* (the property of Capt. Evelyn Broadwood, a descendant of John Broadwood, the founder of the well-known piano factory, who married Tschudi's daughter). But the girl at the harpsichord becomes a commonplace motif in conversation pieces, as in Jan Steen's *Van Goyen Family*, about which more will be said later; in Gillis van Tilborch's *Family Group* (Brussels, Musées Royaux des Beaux Arts); in François Duchatel's (1616-1694) *Jenssens Family* (Attre, De Meester de Heydonck Collection); in *The Cornelis Verbrugge Family* (1773) by Hieronymus Lapis (1723-1798), an Italian who had emigrated to Holland for religious reasons and had so thoroughly assimilated the Dutch manner as to be indistinguishable from Dutch painters (fig. 34); in Friedrich von Hetsch's *Family of the Building Superintendent R.F. Fischer* (1785; fig. 37); in F. Desmarais' *Roncioni Family* (fig. 226); in *Gustav Adolf Sparre with his Wife and Daughter*, a gouache by the Swedish painter Nicolas Lafrensen (Över Kloster); in C.V. Eckersberg's *M.L. Nathanson Family* (1818; fig. 38), in which there is also the motif of children taken to their parents; in the English *Family Group* (fig. 39) with a Clementi piano, painted by a *naïf* painter; in the so-called *Michel Gérard with his Children*, once attributed to David;[19] in *The Family of Lucien Bonaparte* (fig. 227) and in *The Stamaty Family* by Ingres (fig. 228); in Giuseppe Bezzuoli's *Niccolini Family* (fig. 229); in David Bles' *Family of Karel Enthoven* (1855; fig. 3); in a *Neapolitan Family* painted in 1819 (fig. 230); and in innumerable other conversation pieces. The harp player is much less frequent. We find her, for instance, in a painting by an unknown French painter of the eighteenth century of *Count Vaudeuil and his Family* (fig. 231) and in a watercolour by Oberlin, *The Musician G. Mazzinghi and his Family* (fig. 232): Mazzinghi organised concerts for George IV, and the greatest event of his life was his funeral, which was out of all proportion to his very modest capacities as a composer.[20]

19 See p. 56, and note 10 to chapter III of the present work.

20 William Beckford wrote on January 28, 1844: "... les funérailles de Monsieur le Comte Mazzinghi ancien disseminateur et compositeur (soi-disant) d'une immensité d'assez jolie musique. Ce brave seigneur a laissé des sommes très considérables pour fêter sa dépouille mortelle. Le spectacle était magnifique...." (J.W. OLIVER, *The Life of William Beckford*, London, 1932, pp. 328-29).

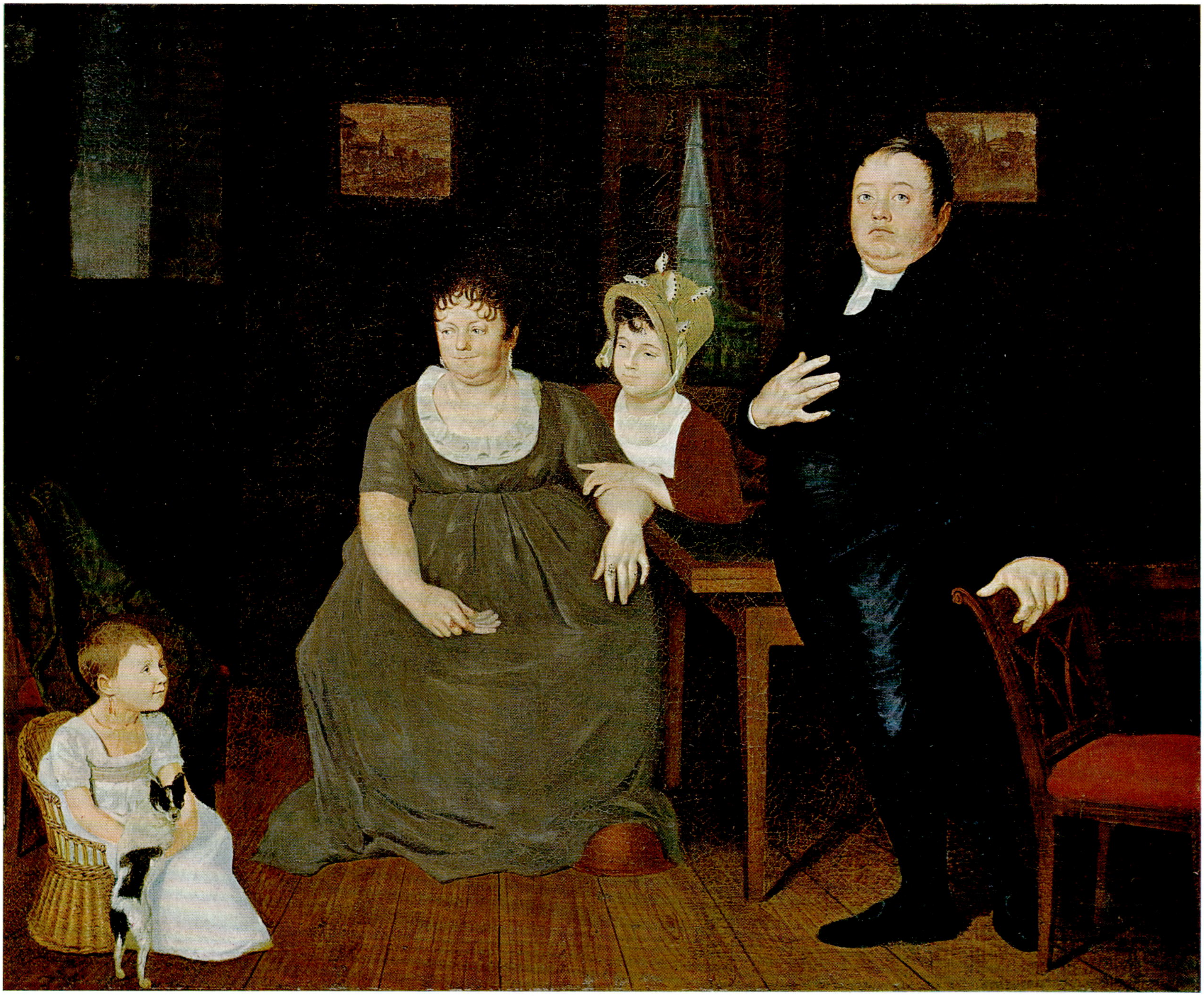

35

35 ENGLISH SCHOOL (end of the 18th century), *Family Group*. Rome, private collection. 36 ENGLISH SCHOOL (early 19th century), *Family Group*. Rome, private collection.

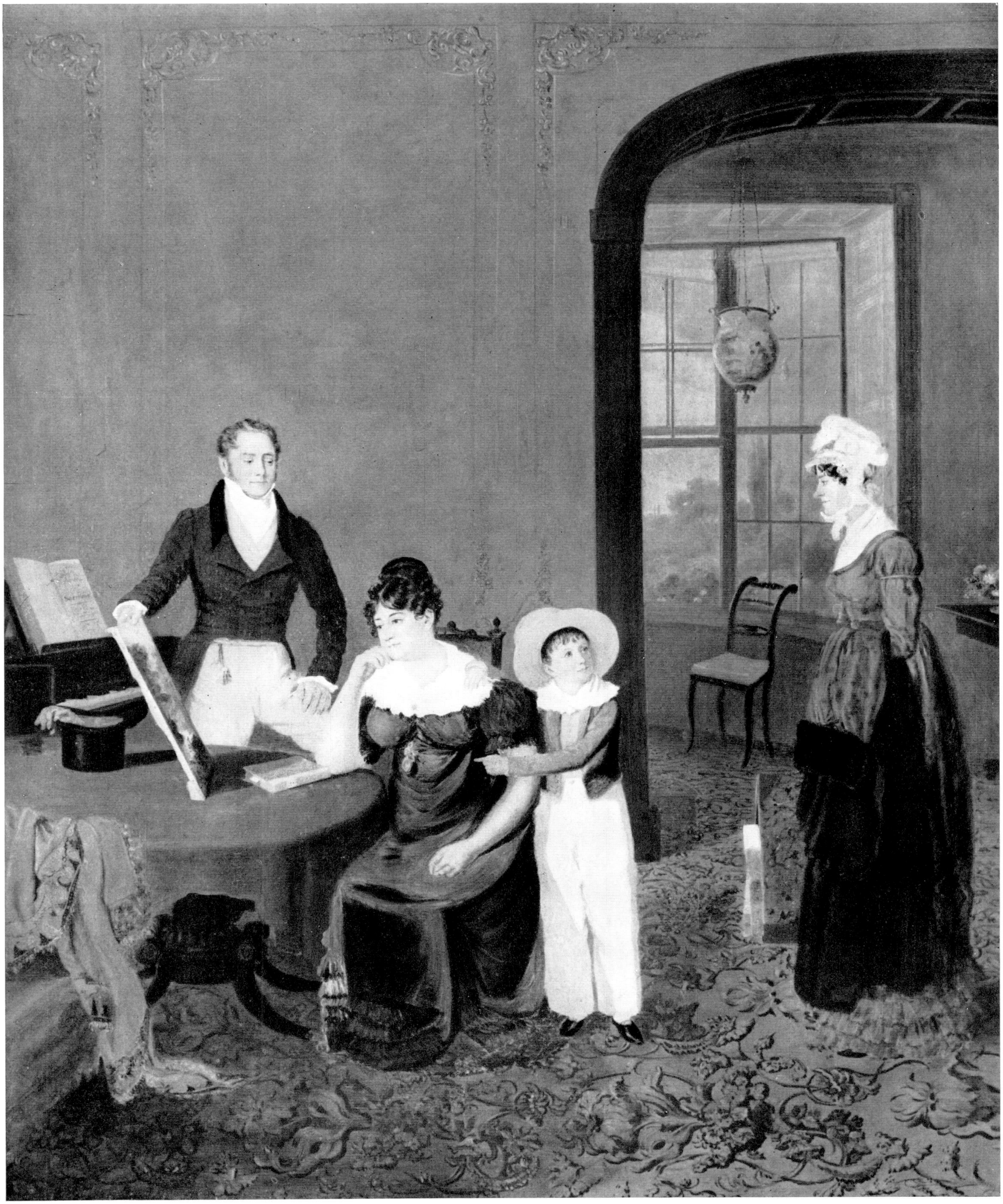

36

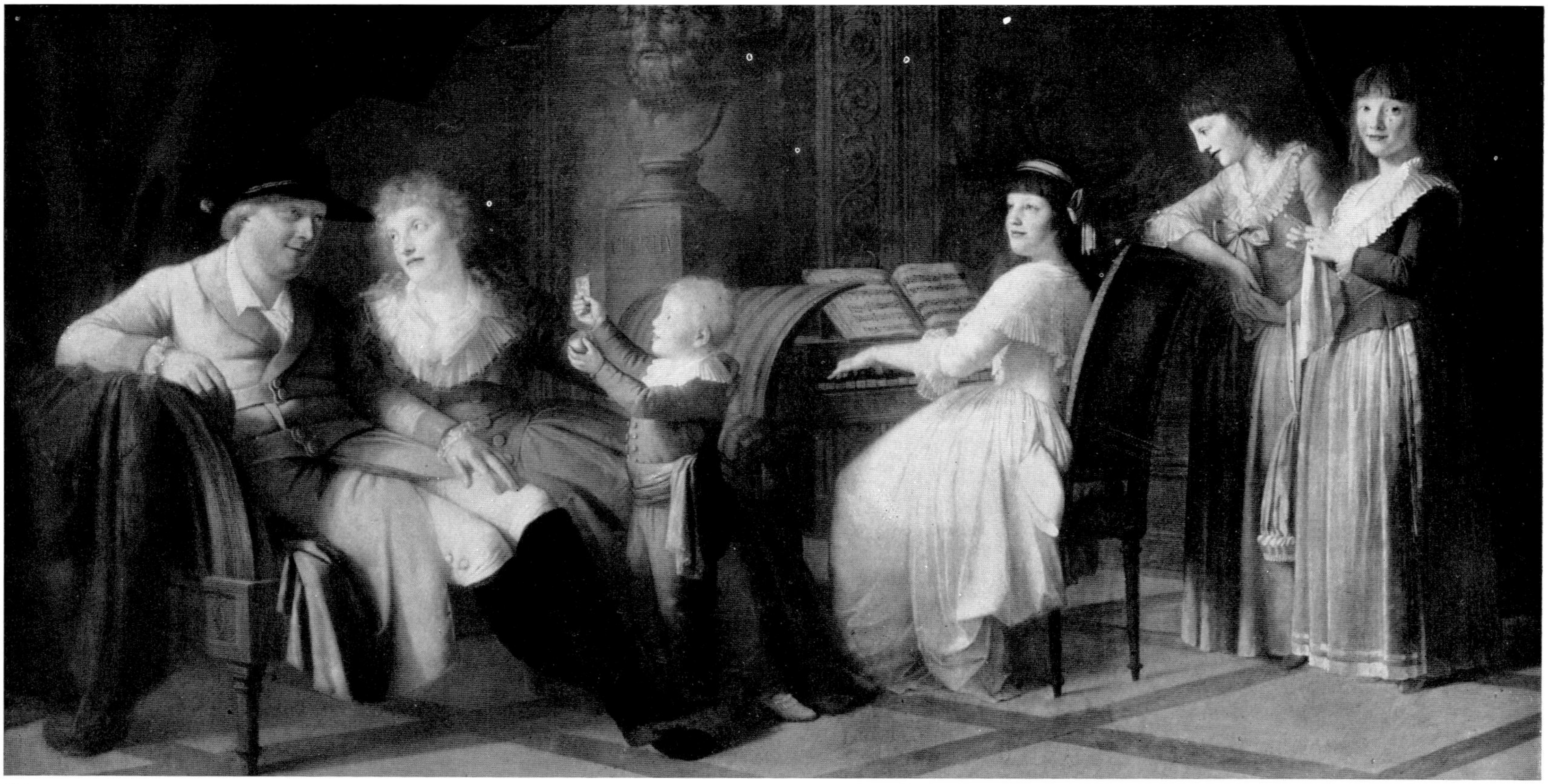

37

One is aware of the influence of Rousseau and the new sensibility on the conversation pieces of the second half of the eighteenth century. A greater relaxation appears in the poses and in the expressions of the faces, frequently beaming with the feelings of a " beautiful soul " (see the face of the pianist in von Hetsch's painting, where the costume à la Werther of the gentleman is also to be noticed); the tender charms of children now supply the motives of action, and at the same time the traditional devices, such as the showing of a paper or an object, become rarer. Their persistence is, however, witnessed by a number of pictures: Maria Theresia's children offering her souvenirs of their Italian tour in a painting by Friedrich Heinrich Füger (1776; Vienna, Österreichische Galerie des 19. Jahrhunderts); the artist's sister showing a picture to her brother Robert, the engraver, who is seated with a paper in his hand in front of Deidalsas' *Crouching Venus* in Nicolaas Muys' (1740-1808) painting of 1779 at the Boymans-van Beuningen Museum in Rotterdam; the artist showing a painting to his parents in William Dunlap's *Dunlap Family* (1788; fig. 235); the gentleman showing a picture with a landscape by moonlight to his fat, seated wife while a female relative approaches with a portfolio, in an anonymous English *Family Group* of about 1820 (fig. 36); or Wilhelm Bendz's *Michael Raffenberg Showing a Picture to his Mother and Sister* (1831; the property of the Artists' Association of Copenhagen). Or we have simply the homage of a subaltern, as in *Justice Heatly of the East India Company with his Sister* (painted in India by Zoffany between 1783 and 1789; fig. 233), to whom a servant or messenger makes a bow, while an Indian carrying a pipe stands at the back. Sentimentality brings the conversation piece near to genre painting. Greuze's adored mothers and tender fathers come to mind when we look at *The Poet Wieland in the Bosom of his Family* by Georg Melchior Kraus (1775; fig. 234). A little girl stands between his knees, and with his left hand he hugs another girl as with his right he presses the tiny hand of an infant the mother takes to him; behind the mother's skirts two more little girls watch the scene, one hugging a doll: this picture is the very emblem of the *bon ménage*, the idyllic return to nature of the human family.

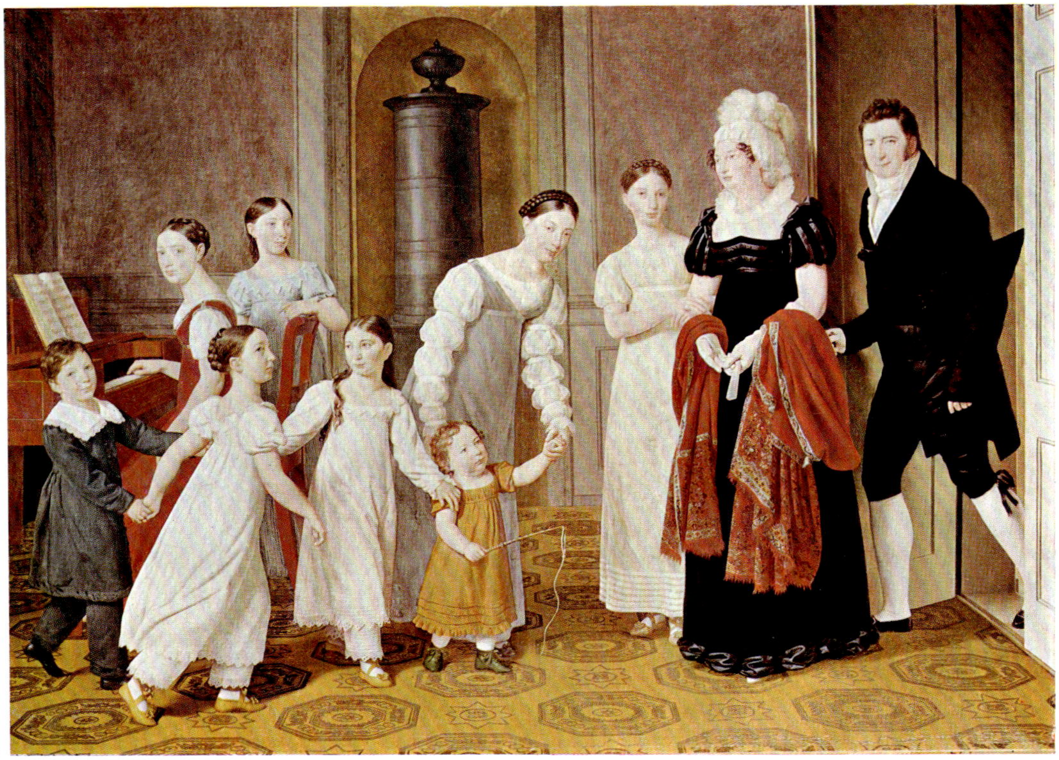

38

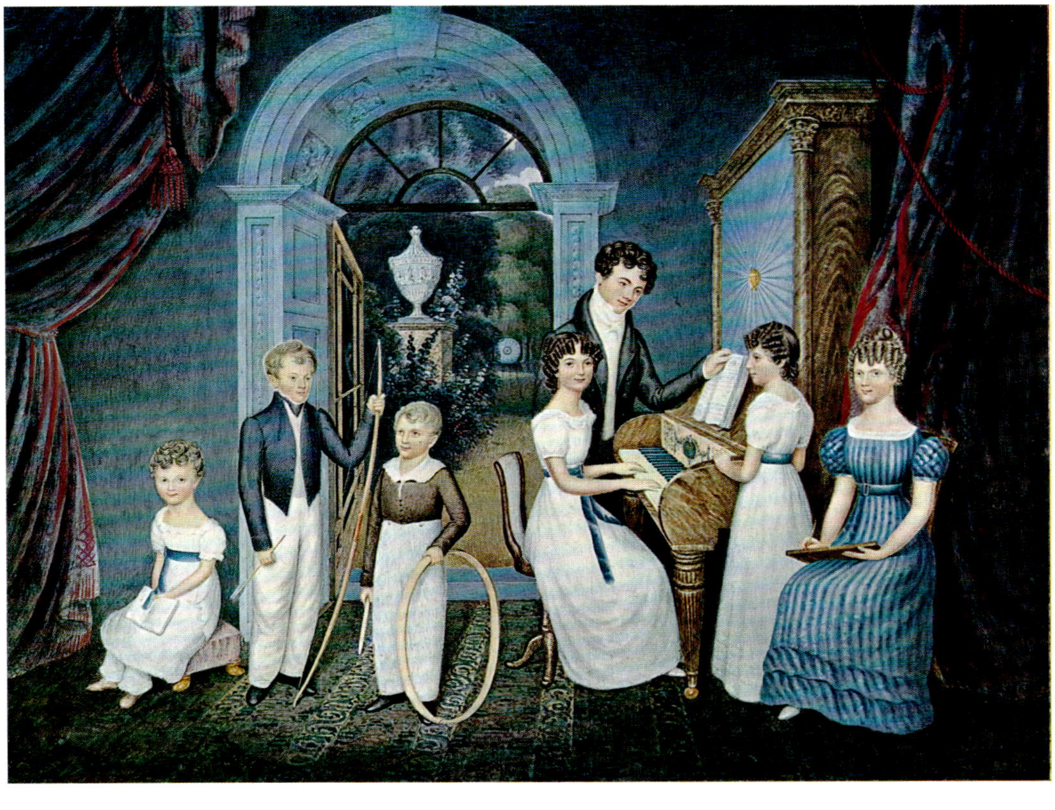

39

37 PHILIPP FRIEDRICH VON HETSCH (1758-1838), *The Family of the Building Superintendent R. F. Fischer*, c. 1785. Stuttgart, Staatsgalerie.
38 CHRISTOFFER VILLEM ECKERSBERG (1783-1853), *The M. L. Nathanson Family*, 1818. Copenhagen, Statens Museum for Kunst.
39 ENGLISH SCHOOL (early 19th century), *Family Group*. Rome, private collection.

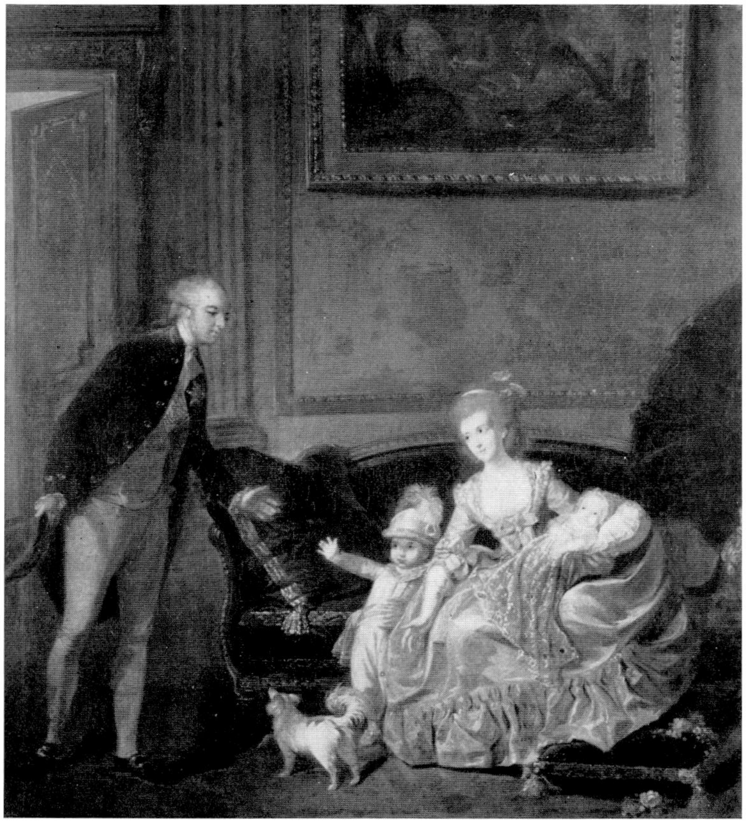

40

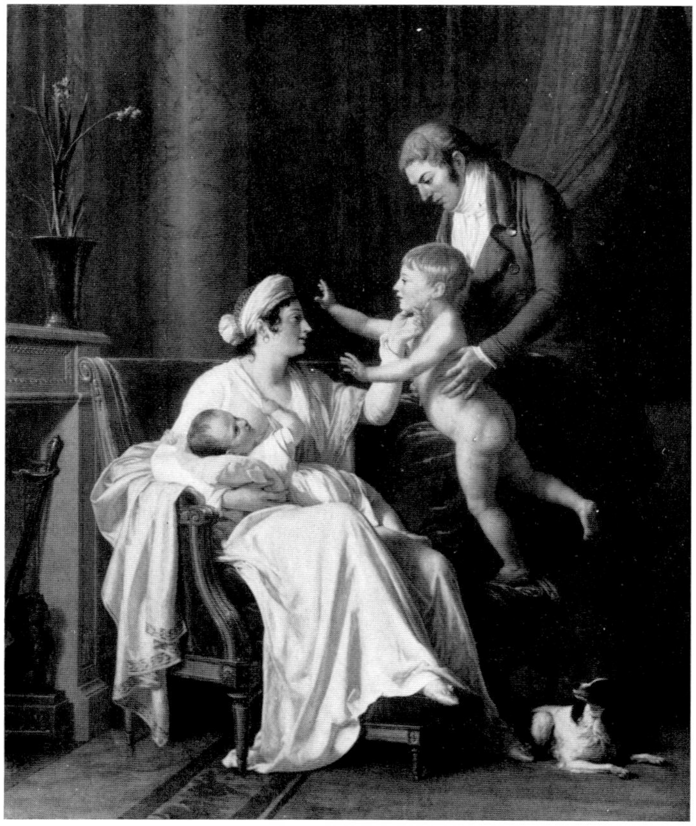

41

Joseph Reinhart presents a similar scene translated into neoclassical terms in *The Legran Family* of about 1800 (Basel, private collection). The affected gesture of the girl who hands the steaming cup to her father makes one think of the dancers of Herculaneum, while across their mother's knees the two children caress each other like little Jesus and St. John in Raphael's *Belvedere Madonna* or the *Madonna with the Goldfinch*. Recollection of the happy mothers and good fathers of sentimental novels and genre paintings suggested themes and poses to the painters of conversation pieces. *The Duke of Chartres Returning Home* by Charles Lepeintre (1735-1803; fig. 40) is greeted by a barking dog, as in the homecoming of the father of the family in Greuze and Fragonard. In a conversation piece by F. Desmarais (fig. 238) the grandchild runs to fondle his paralysed grandfather, as in a painting by Greuze. Many portrait paintings might easily be given a generic title, like J.F. Garneray's *Leçon de piano*. *The Roze Family* (fig. 42) by Marguerite Gérard partakes of the group portrait through the two elderly persons seated on the sofa and of genre painting through the gesture of the aunt who hands a sprig of cherries to her niece.[21] Many works by this artist give free rein to that rather saccharine *tendresse* which inspired the painters of this period.

In John Singleton Copley's (1737-1815) *Children of Francis Hart Sitwell* (1787; Renishaw Hall, Derbyshire, the property of Reresby Sitwell), one of the boys holds a pack of cards in his uplifted hand and is intent on building a house of them on the carpet; the other younger brother runs to embrace the elder one, and Mary holds a musical score on her knees. The picture is an image of domestic happiness, and if it is true that those who are dear to the gods die young, the gods must indeed have loved these young people, because none of them lived long: the eldest, Sitwell Sitwell, lived only forty-two years, from 1769 to 1811; the younger ones died, one in 1813 (Francis), the other (Herst) in 1803; as for Mary, she married Sir Charles Wake in 1790 and died the following year. In another Sitwell portrait (fig. 236), *Sir George Sitwell and his Family*, of about 1828 by John Partridge (1790-1872), the father, just returned from riding, caresses the infant in his wife's arms, and the two small children are fixed by

21 See M. PRAZ, *La Casa della Vita* (Milan: Mondadori, 1958), pp. 71 ff. (This part has been omitted in the English translation, *The House of Life*, London: Methuen, 1964.)

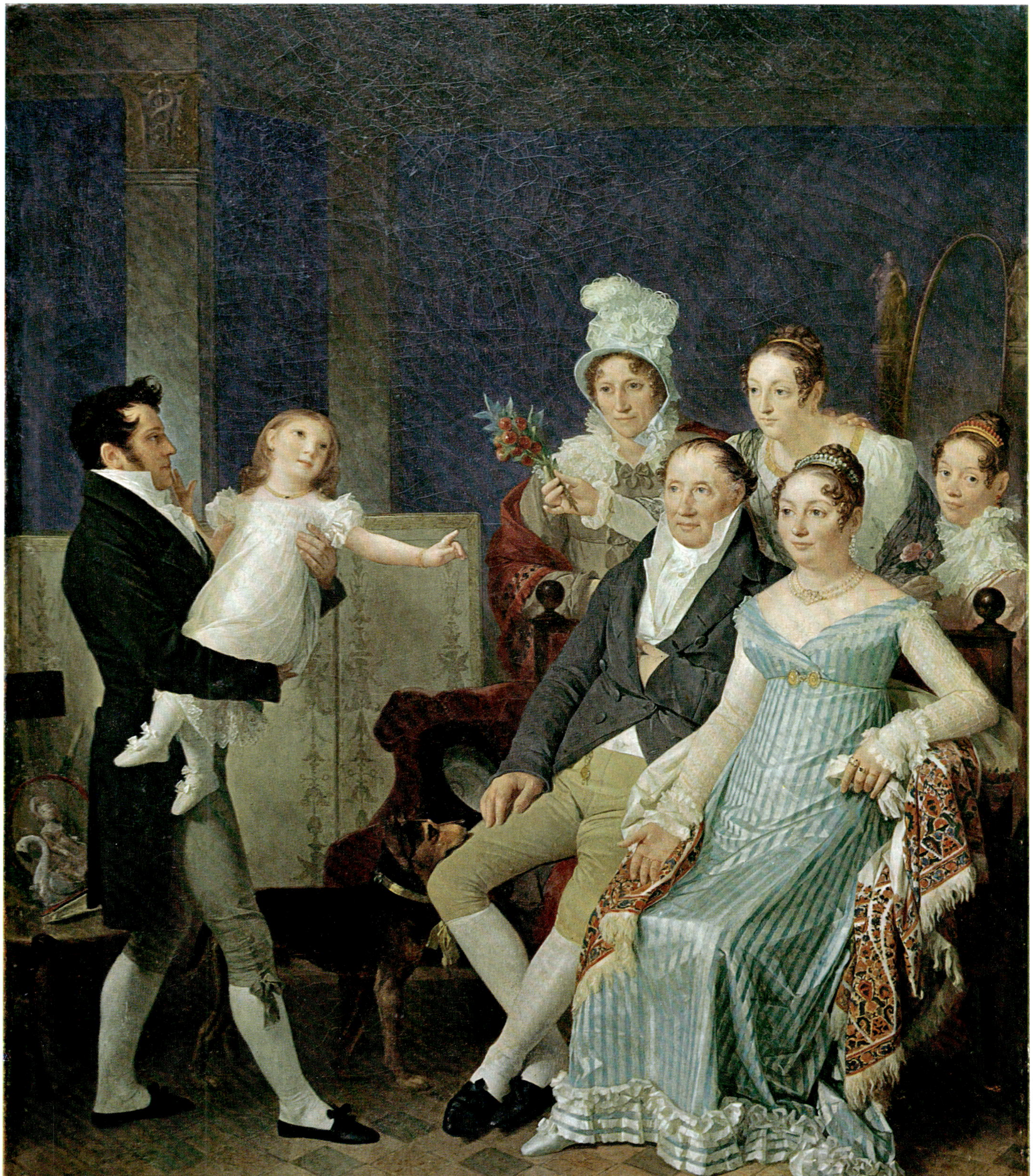

42

40 CHARLES LEPEINTRE (1735-1803), *The Duke of Chartres Returning Home*. Paris, private collection. 41 FRANÇOIS ANDRÉ VINCENT (1746-1816), *The Family of Boyer Fonfrède*. Versailles, Château de Versailles. 42 MARGUERITE GÉRARD (1761-1837), *The Roze Family*, 1816-7. Rome, private collection.

the painter in symmetrical attitudes romping round them. There is a similar pattern of children in motion in a painting by an unknown American artist of about 1800 (Washington, D.C., National Gallery of Art), *The Sargent Family*: with the two dark figures of the parents on the sides are contrasted a pair of children in light clothes in the middle of the picture, against a background formed by two Hepplewhite carved-back chairs. One of the children seizes her father's coat, the other holds a ball-on-a-string at which a little dog is jumping (fig. 48). Henry Edridge, in a watercolour of 1799, shows us two children tenderly pressing against their father (Victoria and Albert Museum). F.A.Vincent portrays Boyer Fonfrède holding a naked little boy stretching out his arms towards his mother, who is holding a baby (fig. 41); the faithful dog squats at the lady's feet. In Evariste Fragonard's painting, Napoleon is shown in the bosom of his family (fig. 237); he is fondling the King of Rome, whom he has just received from the arms of Madame de Montesquiou, while Marie-Louise, sitting opposite, contemplates the idyllic scene. To show sovereigns and illustrious people in the privacy of their domestic life was a favourite subject in a society imbued with the ideals of bourgeois enlightenment. For Louis-Philippe, Henri-Emmanuel-Félix Philippoteaux (1815-1884) took inspiration from a composition by Carmontelle and painted a retrospective portrait in the English manner, *Louis-Philippe, Duke of Orléans, in the Bosom of his Family* (French private collection).[22] Robert Thorburn (1815-1885) painted Wellington in his old age (1852) a little before his death, in the company of his grandchildren at Strathfieldsaye (Lord Gerald Wellesley Collection).

Children and domestic animals had already entered the scene of the conversation piece from the very first essays in that genre in seventeenth-century Holland (see Gabriel Metsu's *Family of the Merchant Geelvinck*, Gillis van Tilborch's *Family Group*, Lebrun's *Jabach Family*, Sorgh's *Family of Eeuwout Prins*, and even semi-official portraits like Largillière's *Louis XIV with the Grand Dauphin, etc.*). They are all but inevitable notes, harped on more and more in the Biedermeier period; like symbols of happy family life, they supply, moreover, that element of play which is necessary to counterbalance the gravity of the adult members of a group. See, for instance, how dull the sitters look, all in a row and staring straight at us, in *The Family of Joseph Moore* by Erastus Salisbury Field (1805-1900; fig. 239) painted in about 1830. They are all in their Sunday best, with Mrs. Moore in a starched collar; the smaller boy, instead of playing with his brothers, whittles a peg with his knife and actually looks as if he was sharpening the blade with murderous intent towards the onlookers. A grim sort of play, anyhow, but worse still in another American conversation piece, *Reverend John Atwood and his Family* by Henry F. Darby (1829-1897; fig. 49) of about 1870. The eight members of the family sit round a tapestry-covered Empire table, with solemn faces, engaged in reading four open Bibles — the very incarnation of Wordsworth's party in a parlour, " all silent " and, notwithstanding the devotional reading, " all damned ".[23] In this picture the children look almost as stern and forbidding as their elders. However, lacking as they are in the amenities of children and pets, these American conversation pieces display a Biedermeier characteristic in the minute rendering of the interiors.[24]

The bourgeois likes to be portrayed among the furnishings of his house, of which he is proud and which he complacently exhibits, especially if he is an art lover — even of modest pretensions like Jan de Bosch, painted in 1800 by Adriaan de Lelie (1755-1820) in his cabinet (fig. 241): he leans against the so-called juvenile bust of Marcus Aurelius, considered by him the gem of his collection. But even if he is not the owner of artistic treasures, the bourgeois is proud to show the happiness of his family life of which, as we have said, children and dogs are the symbols: see A. de Lelie's *Family of the Silversmith Adrianus Bonebakker* (1809; fig. 243), Abraham van Strij's *Family of Hendrik Weymans* (1816; fig. 240), F. Tolstoj's *Interior* (Leningrad, Russkij Musej), Louis-Pierre Spindler's *Interior of Lansdowne House* (fig. 245), Karl Begas the Elder's *Family of the Artist* (Cologne, Wallraf-Richartz-Museum), and so on.

While in some of these paintings one notices a few innovations in the grouping of the sitters, in others the traditional arrangement prevails. For instance, Pieter Christoffel Wonder's (1777-1852) *Family of Willem Jacob de Bruyn de Neve* (1813; fig. 242) presents no substantial innovation if we compare it with seventeenth-century conversation pieces by Pieter Codde or Gabriel Metsu. Sitters are arranged in half-circles, some very often standing with a table in their midst. The same can be said of Pietro Ayres' group of *The La Marmora Family* (1828; fig. 43). But Tolstoj's conversation piece, with women on either side of the

22 Reproduced in L. HAUTECOEUR, *Les peintres de la vie familiale* (Paris: Charpentier, 1945), p. 119. 23 WORDSWORTH, *Peter Bell*, II, ll. 516 ff. 24 See KATHARINE MORRISON MCCLINTON, "American Furniture in Family Portraits of the Eighteenth and Nineteenth Centuries", in *Apollo*, LXXXIX, 1969, pp. 226-29.

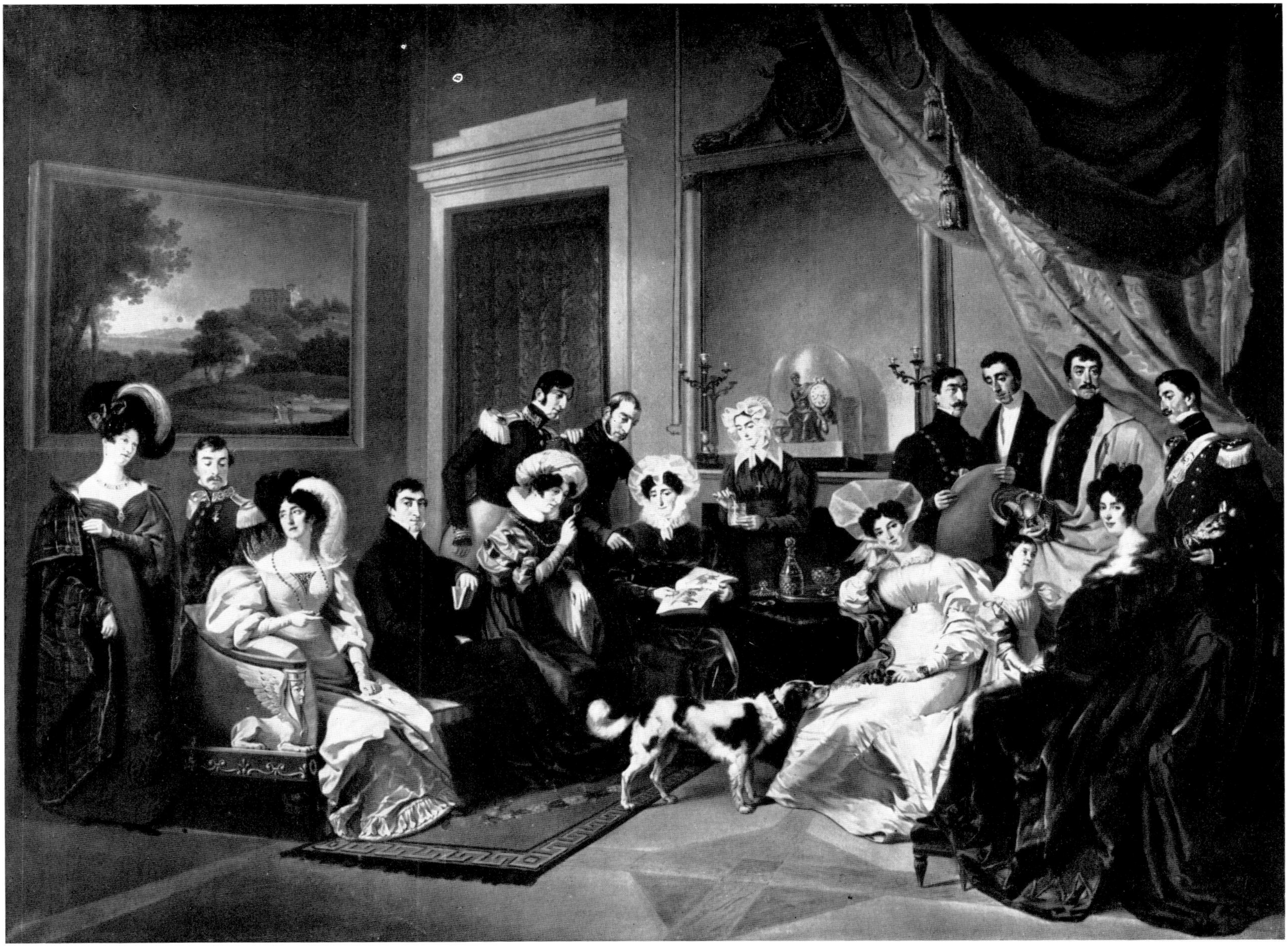

43

43 PIETRO AYRES (1794-1878), *The La Marmora Family*, 1828. Biella, La Marmora Collection.

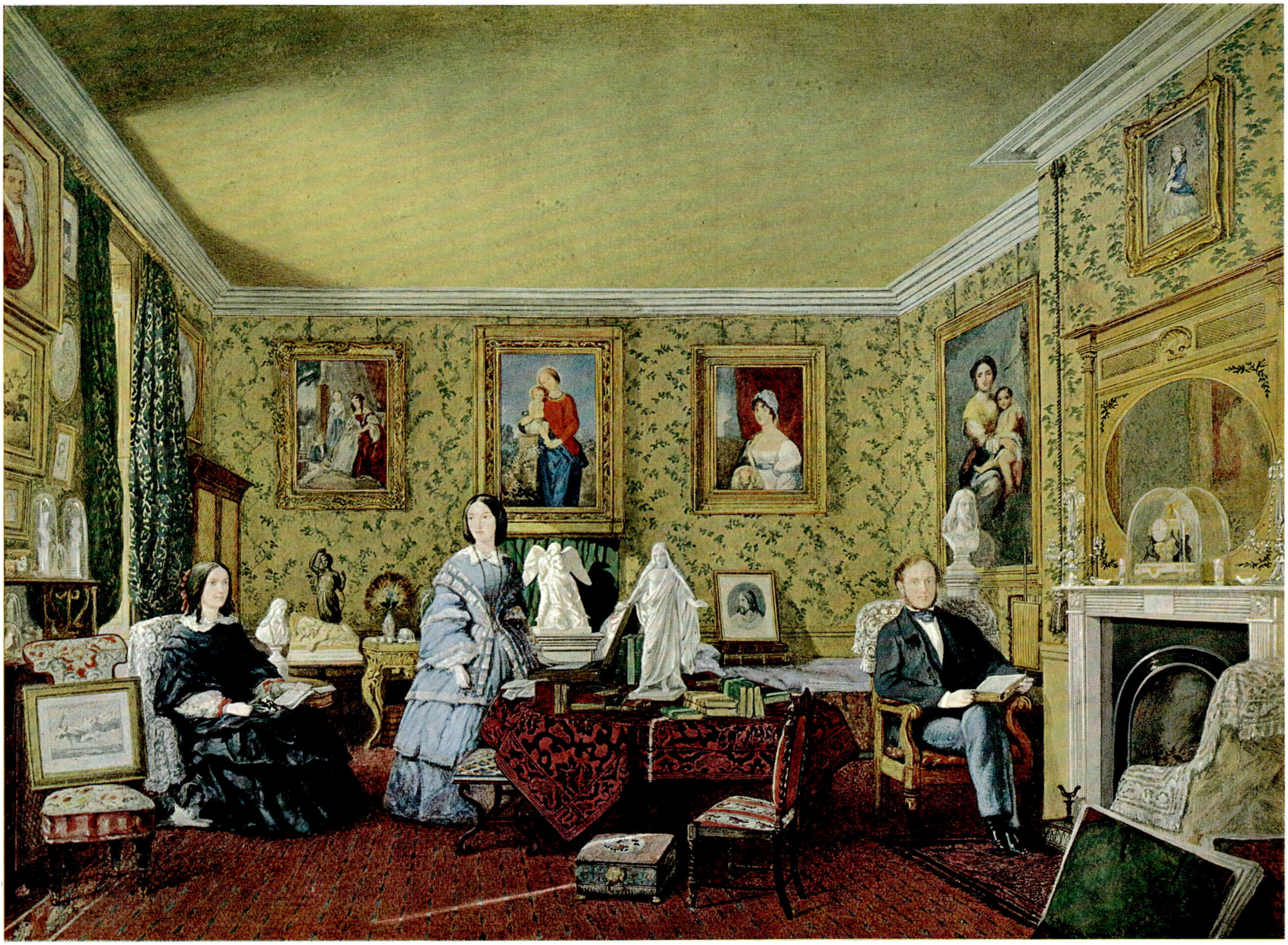

44

44 EDWARD HENRY WEHNERT (1813-1868), *The Drawing-room at Thirlestane House*, 1860. Rome, private collection.

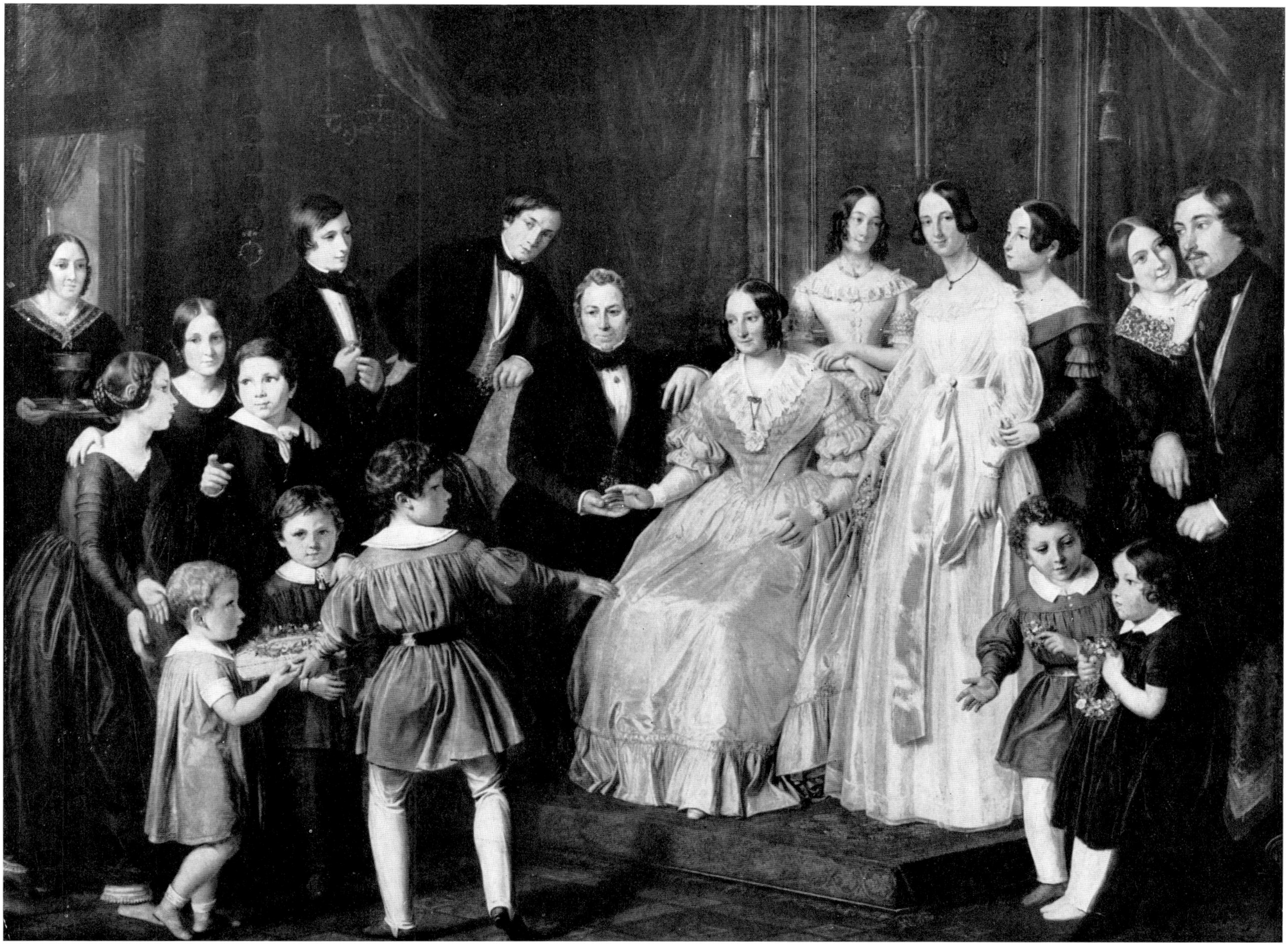

45

45 JOHANN BAPTIST BASTINÉ (1783-1844), *The Neuss Family*, 1842. Aachen, Städtisches Suermondt-Museum.

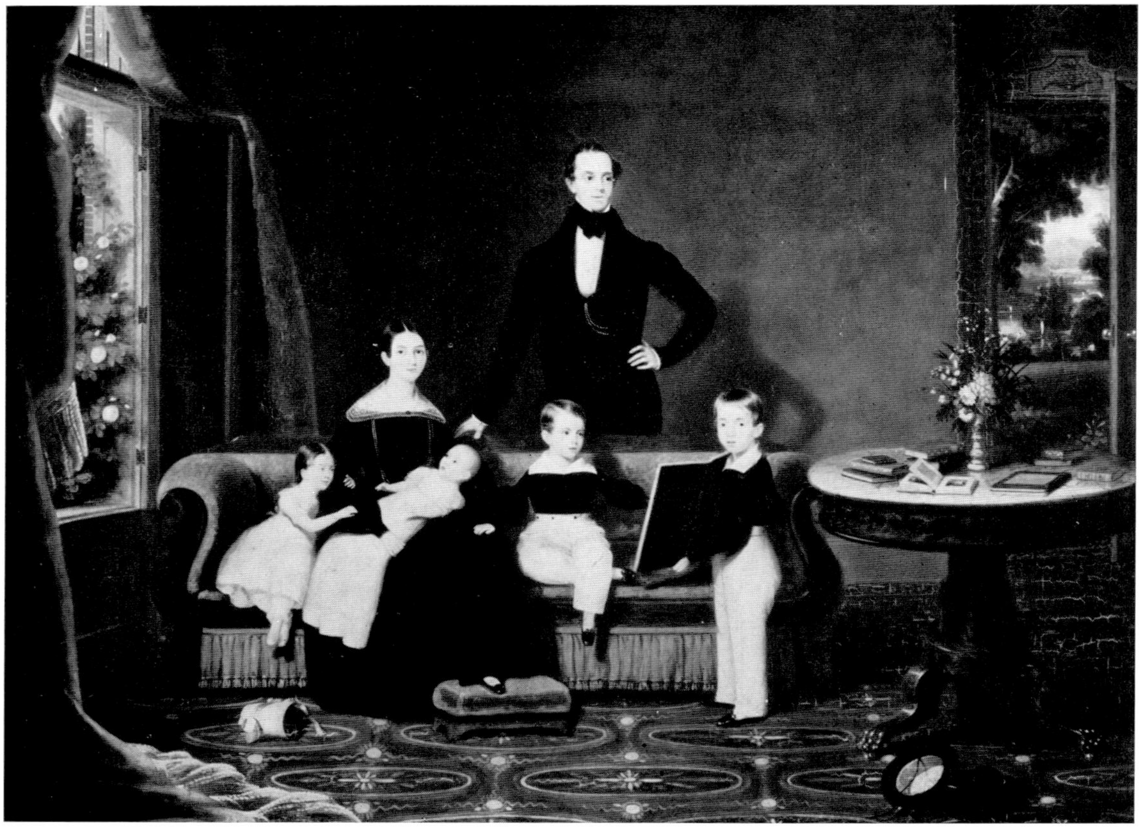

46

46 FREDERICK R. SPENCER (1806–1875), *Unidentified Family Group*, 1840. New York, Brooklyn Museum.

door, the child with toys in the middle, and the man at the writing-desk at the far end of the other room, has an unusual accent, although it still betrays the influence of Dutch genre painting. The painting by Spindler, with a view of a rotunda with statues beyond the arch at whose sides the sitters are grouped, is original enough. Begas' painting with its two groups, each of three persons, the two boys in contrasting attitudes in the centre — and particularly with that solemn pillar of the family, the gentleman with a pipe, against whom a girl leans affectionately — and with the Gothic pile seen through the window, has an atmosphere and a rhythm unlikely to be forgotten (the painter is the young man on the right, with paper and pencil). In *The Family of Parson Berduschek* (1842) by Maximilian Anton Piotrowski (formerly in East Berlin, Märkisches Museum, destroyed in the war; fig. 5), which shows us the parson and his wife in the centre going to church with devotional books in their hands, the church spire seen through the window contributes a sentimental feature to the harmony of the symmetrically arranged painting, with the central group standing and the children and the seated nurse at either side.[25]

The close intimacy of *The Family of Count Breunner-Enkevoirth* (1834) by Friedrich Amerling (Schloss Grafenegg, Austria) belongs to a sphere of art much superior to the conventional groupings of *The La Marmora Family* or *The Niccolini Family* by Giuseppe Bezzuoli (fig. 229), in which the dance of the children verges on caricature and the single groups do not succeed in forming a convincing whole. Johann Baptist Bastiné's horseshoe group of *The Neuss Family* (1842; fig. 45) shows a more developed sense of composition: the grandchildren are offering a wreath on a little cushion to their grandparents, who are celebrating their silver wedding anniversary; it looks like a bourgeois counterpart of the court painting we have mentioned by Friedrich Heinrich Füger, showing the children of Maria Theresia offering her souvenirs of their Italian journey.

The triangular or pyramidal group of a standing person and others sitting is a formula that recurs from the beginnings of the conversation piece. We find it in a small family composition of about 1845 which shows a standing figure, perhaps a musi-

25 These two paintings are reproduced in H. KRONBERGER-FRENTZEN, *Das deutsche Familienbildnis* (Leipzig: Johannes Asmus Verlag, 1940), pp. 58 and 74: Amerling's painting on p. 70, Bastiné's on p. 75.

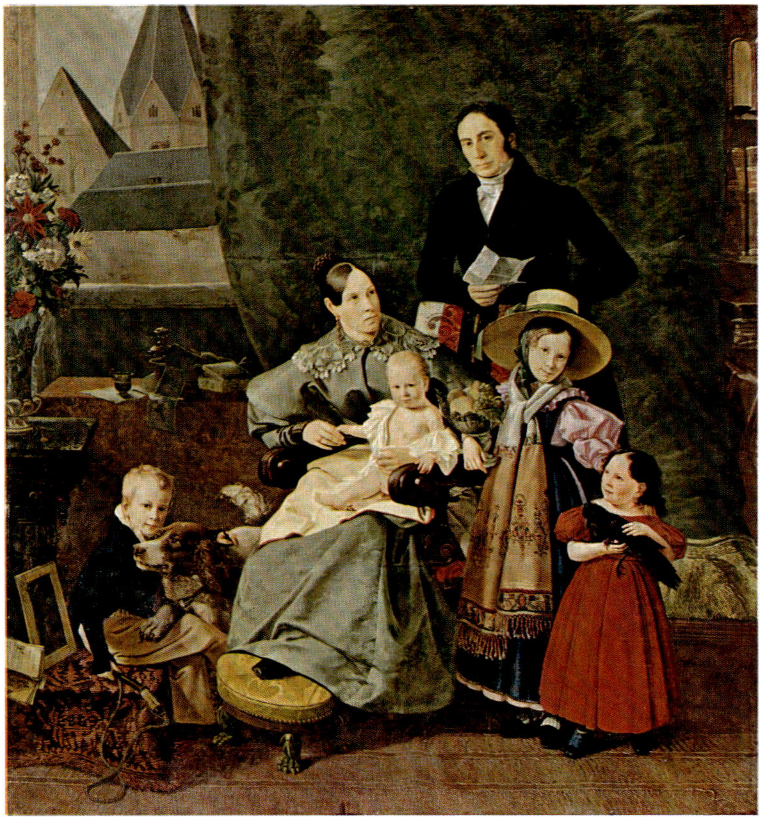

47

47 WILHELM KLEINENBROICH (1814-1895), *The Bernards Family*, 1837. Cologne, Wallraf-Richartz-Museum.

cian (decorated with an order of knighthood, near a piano), and two women: one, the wife, seated, and the other, the daughter, standing (fig. 244). In Wilhelm Kleinenbroich's *Bernards Family* (1837; fig. 47), where the paraphernalia of bourgeois domesticity — the workbox, the coffee-cup, the vase with flowers, the blackboard and the school books of the little boy, the whip with a roebuck-hoof handle, the dog stroked by one of the children and the raven by the other — are given full emphasis as perhaps never before in this kind of bourgeois painting. We find the triangular arrangement in some American conversation pieces. *The Hollingsworth Family* (c. 1840) by George Hollingsworth (1813-1882; fig. 51) has two triangular compositions on the right and left of a central standing couple: one is a group of two persons seated and one standing round a spinet; the other group includes the artist with his wife wearing a paisley shawl about her shoulders, seated, while one of their sons stands behind them and another sits on a footstool beckoning to a spaniel in the foreground. The latter is placed in front of the group around the spinet, thus linking the two sides of the composition. In an *Unidentified Family Group* by Frederick R. Spencer (1840; fig. 46) the straight line of the sofa accentuates the geometrical pattern. Other examples are Franz H. Heinrich's *The Ernest Fiedler Family* (1847: notice the motif of the child making a house of cards; fig. 247); David J. Bles' (1821-1899) *The August Belmont Family* (1854); John B. Whittaker's *The Lesson* (1869; fig. 246), a portrait of Mr. and Mrs. John Ewart Tousey with their children (a picture which is remarkable not only for the triangular composition stressed by the two children placed symmetrically at equal distances from the dog, to which the lesson is being given, but also for the characteristics of genre painting in the scene); and the almost photographic *Family Group* by an unknown artist (c. 1875; fig. 52), a watercolour portrait of two parallel groups in a parlour, one group shaped like an equilateral and the other like a scalene triangle. The triangle formed by one person standing in the middle flanked by a seated one at each side is also the dominant pattern of E.H. Wehnert's tempera of *The Drawing-room at Thirlestane House* (1860; fig. 44), which typifies the taste of the period for sacred art: one finds in it Thorvaldsen's Christ,

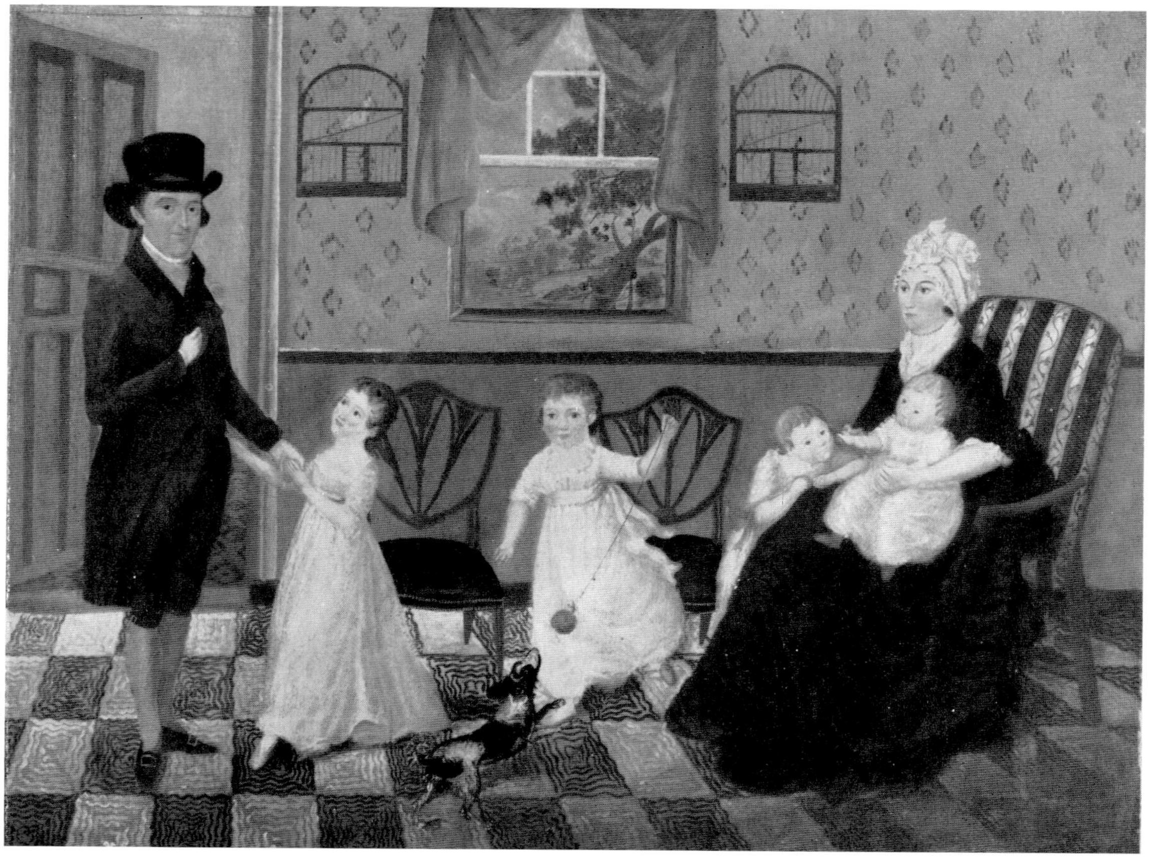

48

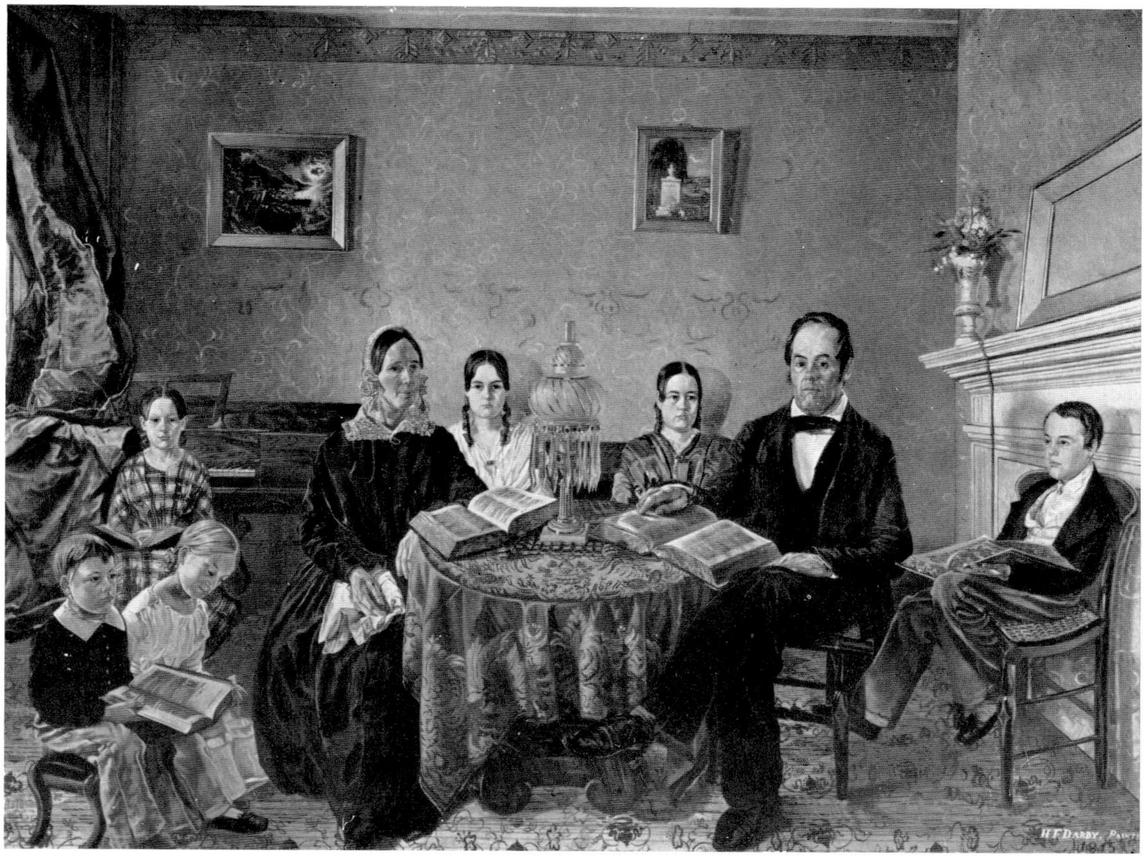

49

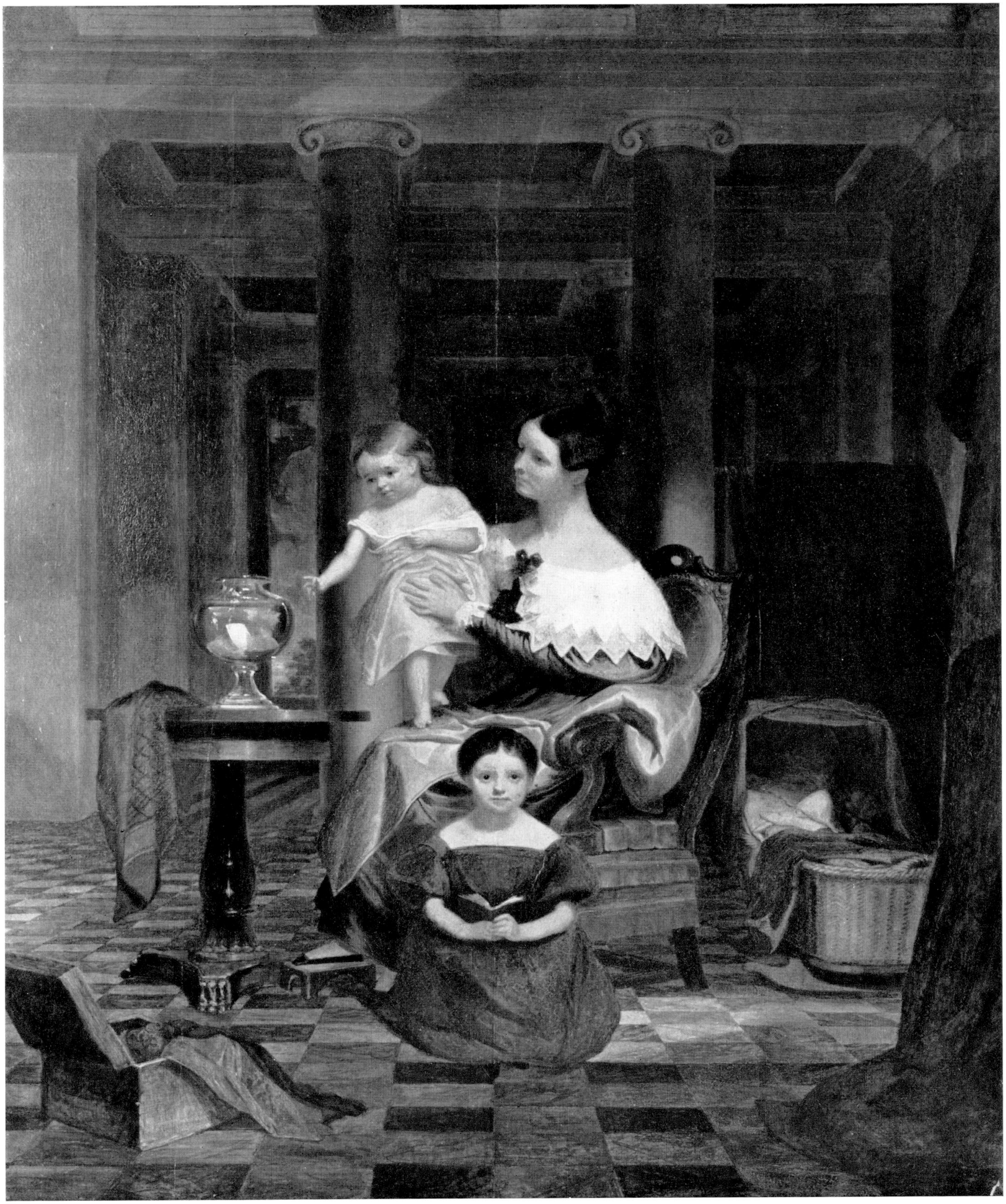

50

48 AMERICAN SCHOOL, *The Sargent Family*, c. 1800. Washington, D.C., National Gallery of Art. 49 HENRY F. DARBY (1829-1897), *Reverend John Atwood and his Family*, c. 1870. Boston, Museum of Fine Arts (M. and M. Karolik Collection). 50 SAMUEL F.B. MORSE (1791-1872), *The Goldfish Bowl*, 1835. New York, collection of Mrs. J. Wright Rumbough; photo courtesy of Mr. Louis Auchincloss.

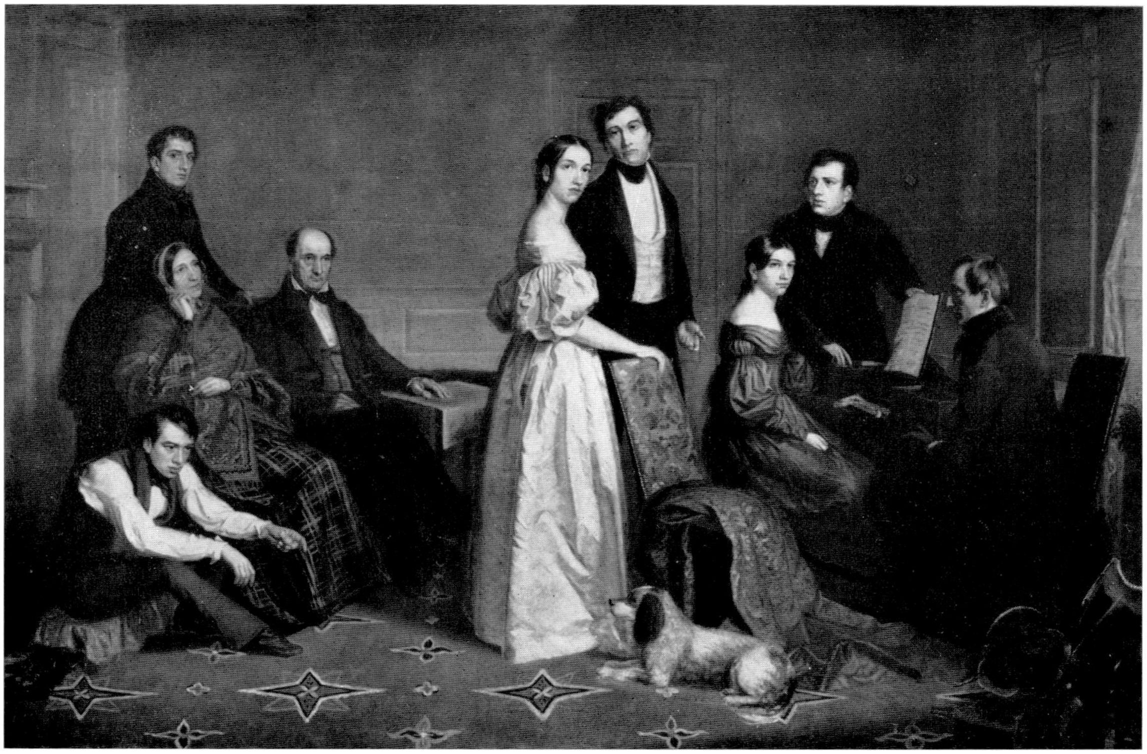

51

51 GEORGE HOLLINGSWORTH (1813-1882), *The Hollingsworth Family*, c. 1840. Boston, Museum of Fine Arts (M. and M. Karolik Collection).

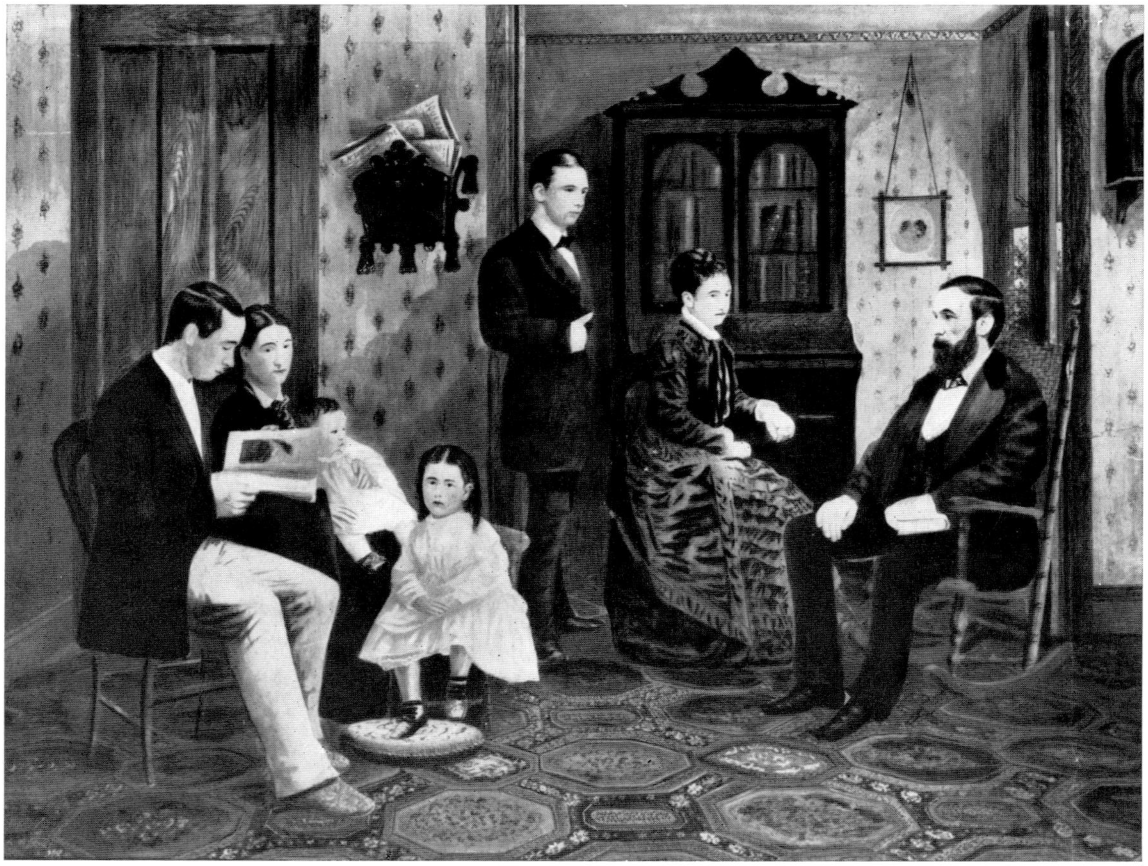

52

52 AMERICAN SCHOOL (19th century), *Family Group*, c. 1875. Dearborn (Michigan), Henry Ford Museum.

53 LUCIUS ROSSI (1846-1913), *The William Astor Family*, 1878. New York, collection of Mrs. W. Vincent Astor; photo courtesy of Mr. Louis Auchincloss.

53

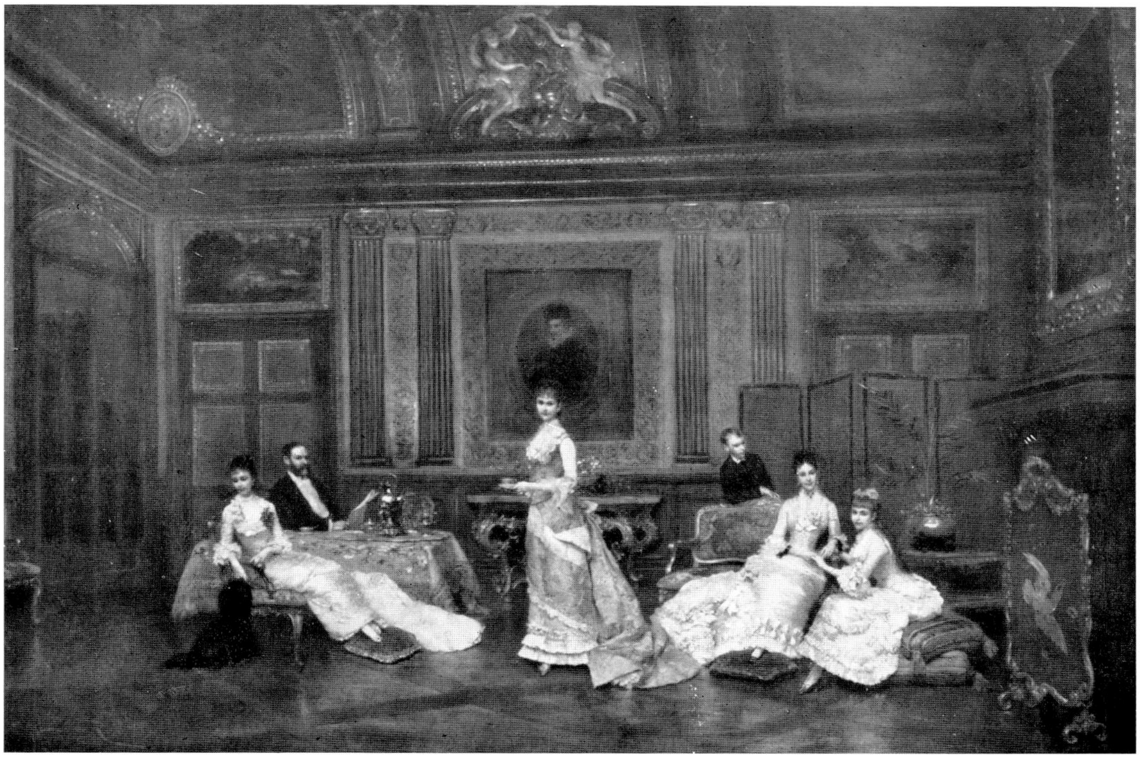

54 SEYMOUR J. GUY (1824-1910), *The William H. Vanderbilt Family*, 1873. Asheville (N.C.), Biltmore House and Gardens.

54

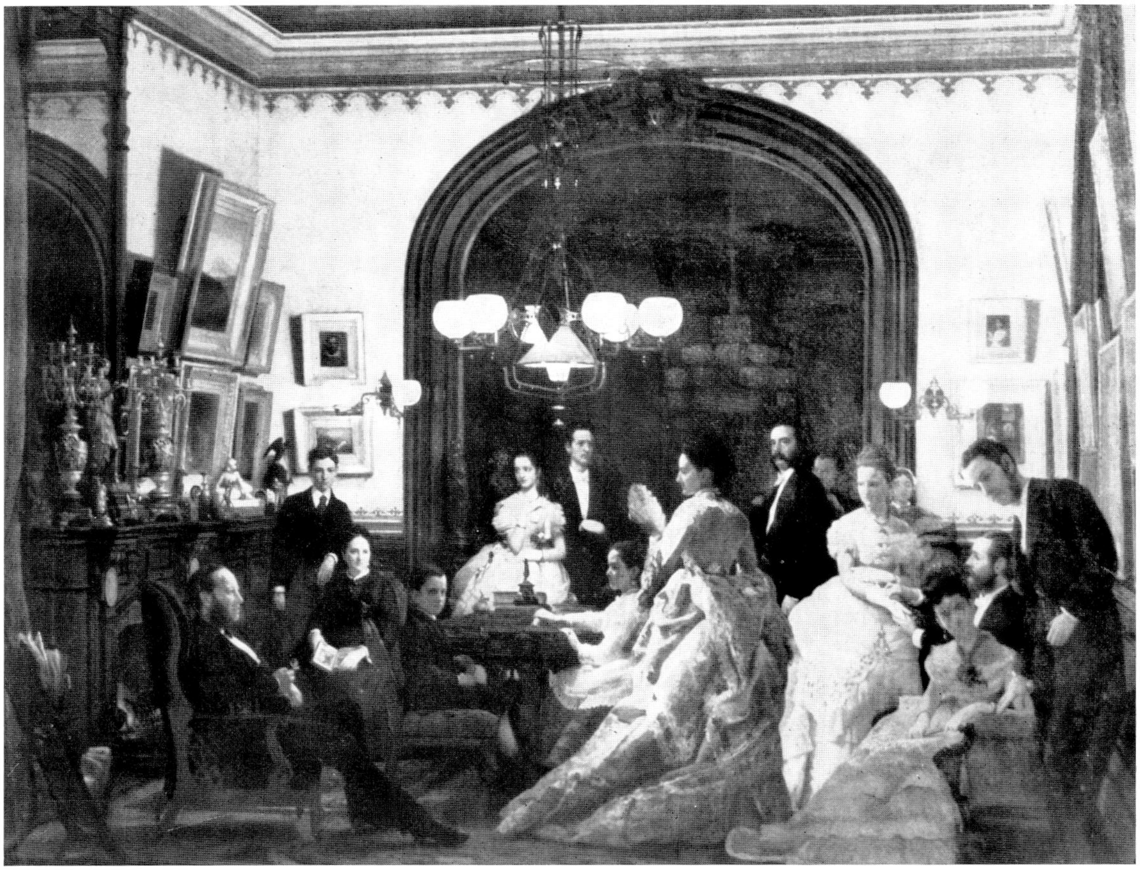

a Madonna by Murillo, Raphael's God the Father, etc. In *The Goldfish Bowl* (fig. 50) by the American Samuel F.B. Morse (1835),[26] an inverted triangle — formed by the mother with a child standing on her knees and stretching out an arm towards a fishbowl and the other girl with an open book in her hands at the foot of the armchair in which her mother is seated — is the elegant formula, set against two Ionic columns partitioning off the room. An inverted triangle also occurs in *The Family of the Banker von Magnus* (c. 1845) by Eduard Magnus (fig. 248). However, a certain novelty is imparted to David Bles's *Family of Karel Enthoven* (fig. 3) by the parallelogram-shaped grouping of the three adults, upon which is superimposed a triangle formed by the three luminous points of the children; the painting on the right side of the far wall represents, as we have already said in the Preface, the rolling-mill from which the family derived its prosperity.

The idea of including in a family group a picture allusive to the origin of the family's fortune was not new. We shall see[27] Dumont represent Madame Mercier, who had been the nurse of Louis XV, in the act of showing her relatives the portrait of the king who, as a sign of gratitude, had raised these middle-class people to the rank of gentlemen. And Louis-Léopold Boilly, in the group of *Louis Gohin and his Family* (1787; fig. 55), showed Louis Gohin, a wholesale merchant of colours and the inventor of Prussian blue, sitting near his desk, and on the left Gohin's daughter, Benjamine, arm-in-arm with her husband Henri-Jean-Baptiste Bouquillard, who points to a picture in which is painted the three-master that had brought him back from the Antilles, where he had made a fortune.[28]

A balanced symmetrical disposition also dominates *The William Astor Family* by Lucius Rossi (1878; fig. 53), with two scalene triangles whose vertex is formed in each case by a person dressed in black and the isosceles triangle of the lady in white in the centre: the sumptuous interior imitating a Louis XIV reception room is typical of the aesthetic ideals of the American tycoons of the period. Even in a modern conversation piece like Constant Le Breton's *Family Reunion* (fig. 251) the painter has succumbed to the appeal of the triangular composition.

We have stressed the geometry underlying these paintings because it results in evident patterns; but it is natural that the compositions which can escape such a reduction to geometrical figures should be rare. Sometimes, however, a painter seems to have been content to fix the image of a group as it presented itself to his eyes, as if in a snapshot. Karl Hümmel, in the watercolour drawing of Murat's widow, *Queen Caroline's Drawing-room at Frohsdorf* (fig. 252), appears to have reproduced the *conversazione* just as he found it, although it would be easy to inscribe the central group within an oval and the two on the sides in front within two triangles. This drawing illustrates the kind of gathering round a central table that Queen Hortense is presumed to have invented.[29]

There are paintings in which people seem to have been represented from life as in a photograph, or which are at least based on a more discreet geometrical structure, as for example in *The William H. Vanderbilt Family* (1873) by Seymour J. Guy (fig. 54) and in *The Alfrederick Smith Hatch Family* (1871) by Eastman Johnson (Metropolitan Museum of Art); whereas in the fairly recent *Edgar W. Garbisch Family* (1955) by John Koch (fig. 249) the triangular tyranny reappears in the two groups (in the one on the right, it should be noticed that the black servant is seen from the back, with a perhaps-involuntary racial discrimination).

The sentimental attitude was also gradually qualified in the course of the nineteenth century. The Biedermeier and Victorian climate was still favourable to that idyllic presentation of family life which had begun in the previous century, but the reaction against bourgeois ideals gained momentum in literary and artistic milieux: we need only mention Daumier and Flaubert. We have already quoted Thackeray in the Preface apropos of the involuntary irony of family groups. With naturalism, a more objective presentation of the family group prevailed, without the mawkish effusions which had become fashionable from the eighteenth century on; Degas' *Belelli Family* is typical in this respect.[30] Adolphe Félix Cals, in the portrait of *Count Doria and his Children in the Drawing-room at Orrouy* (fig. 250), also shows a more reserved approach, as Amerling had already done in the portrait mentioned above of Count Breunner-Enkevoirth. Even Giacomo Favretto's *The Guidini Family* (1873; fig. 253), although painted in a climate that soon afterwards was to produce Edmondo De Amicis' lachrymose *Cuore* (1886), retains of eighteenth-century tenderness only the dove in the little girl's hands, while the faces of her parents merely betray an affectionate participation.

26 See *Three Hundred Years of New York City Families, A Loan Exhibition of Conversation Pieces*, Wildenstein, 19 East 64th Street, New York, Jan. 12-Jan. 29, 1966.
27 See below, p. 211.
28 I owe these details to the courtesy of M. Serge Grandjean, keeper of the Département des Objets d'Art of the Louvre, whose family is related to the Gohins through the donor of this picture, Henri-Emile Perrin, uncle of Serge Grandjean's father.
29 See M. PRAZ, *An Illustrated History of Furnishing* (London: Thames and Hudson; New York: George Braziller, 1964), p. 197.
30 Reproduced in *An Illustrated History of Furnishing*, p. 330.

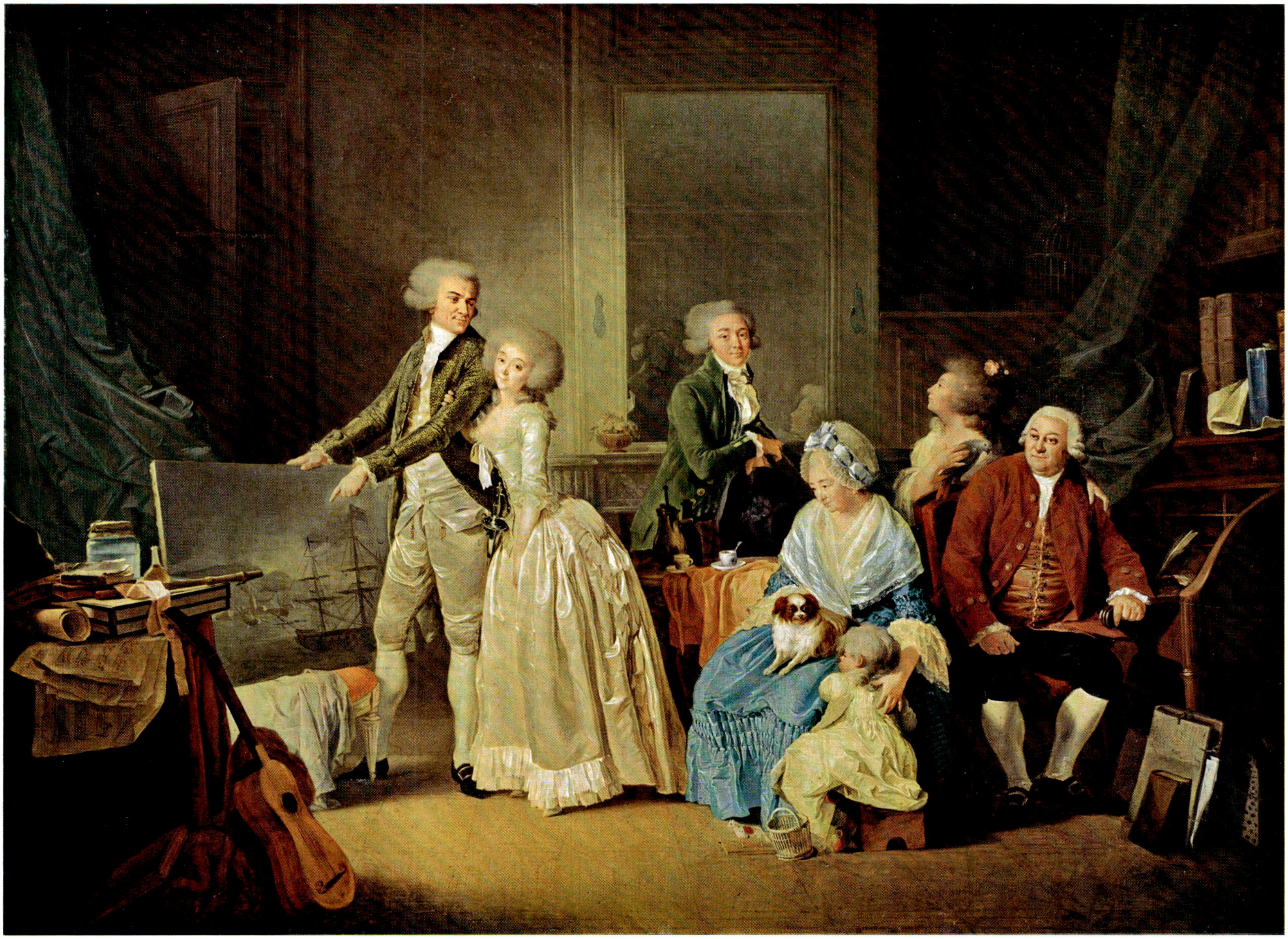

55

55 LOUIS-LÉOPOLD BOILLY (1761-1845), *Louis Gohin and his Family*, 1787. Paris, Musée des Arts Décoratifs.

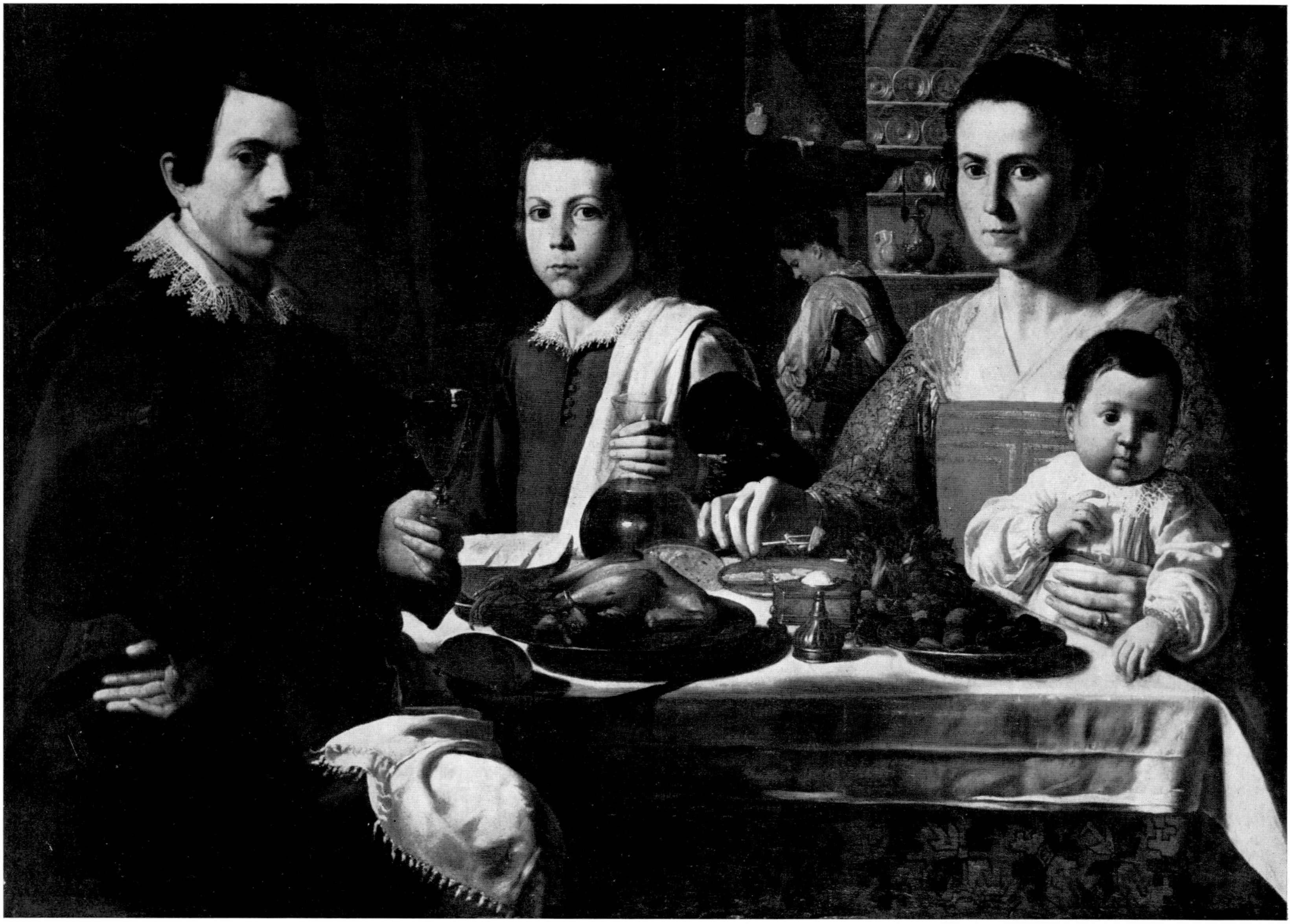

56

56 CARLO CERESA (1609-1679), *Family Group*. London, Sotheby's sale, 8 Dec. 1965.

CHAPTER V – THE CONVERSATION ROUND A TABLE

Vernon Lee, the unmarried English author who spent most of her life in Italy where she is chiefly remembered for her book on the Italian eighteenth century — which was greatly appreciated at the time — used to say: " From my friends' matrimonial adventures I avert my eyes and say: There goes something primaeval! "[1] One may smile at this sally of a woman whose chief fault was no doubt excessive cerebration, as all those who approached her could not help noticing; however, if not to this aspect of social life, a similar remark would be very pertinent to another. I mean men's custom of considering a meal as the best occasion to meet and entertain each other in a friendly way. Surely this habit of accompanying the words which come out of one's mouth with the food which enters it is very primaeval, though few would disapprove of Thackeray's warning: " RESPECT YOUR DINNER; idolize it, enjoy it properly.... All a man's senses are worthy of employment, and should be cultivated as a duty ".[2] Nevertheless, whereas the representation of sexual love does not stimulate our sense of humour (at least when the actors are not physically disagreeable), to catch a man, whether handsome or ugly, in the moment in which he conveys food to his mouth is a well-known trick of modern photo-reporters in order to obtain a degrading caricature without effort. One cannot therefore blame a lady who, in our time, brought a libel action against a foodstuff firm for having used for publicity purposes a photograph in which she appeared in the act of eating greedily.

Among the devices first employed by painters to represent a group was the placing of figures round a laid table, were it laid only with a fruit-basket. This was a means of establishing a natural relationship amongst them. Just as men first formed a circle in order to discuss some animal killed in a hunt, so, to bring their groups of people together, painters found out that their problem was solved by making them sit round a table. One of the earliest instances is the portrait of *The Three Children of Christian II of Denmark* (Hampton Court Palace) by Jan Gossaert, called Mabuse (c. 1472-1536), probably painted soon after the deposition of Christian in 1523, when he had retired to the Low Countries. Edwards says[3] that Mabuse, who went to Rome

1 PETER GUNN, *Vernon Lee, Violet Paget 1856-1935* (London: Oxford University Press, 1964), pp. 203-4. 2 GORDON N. RAY, *Thackeray, The Uses of Adversity* (London: Oxford University Press, 1955), p. 282. 3 *Early Conversation Pictures...* (London: Country Life Ltd., 1954), p. 20.

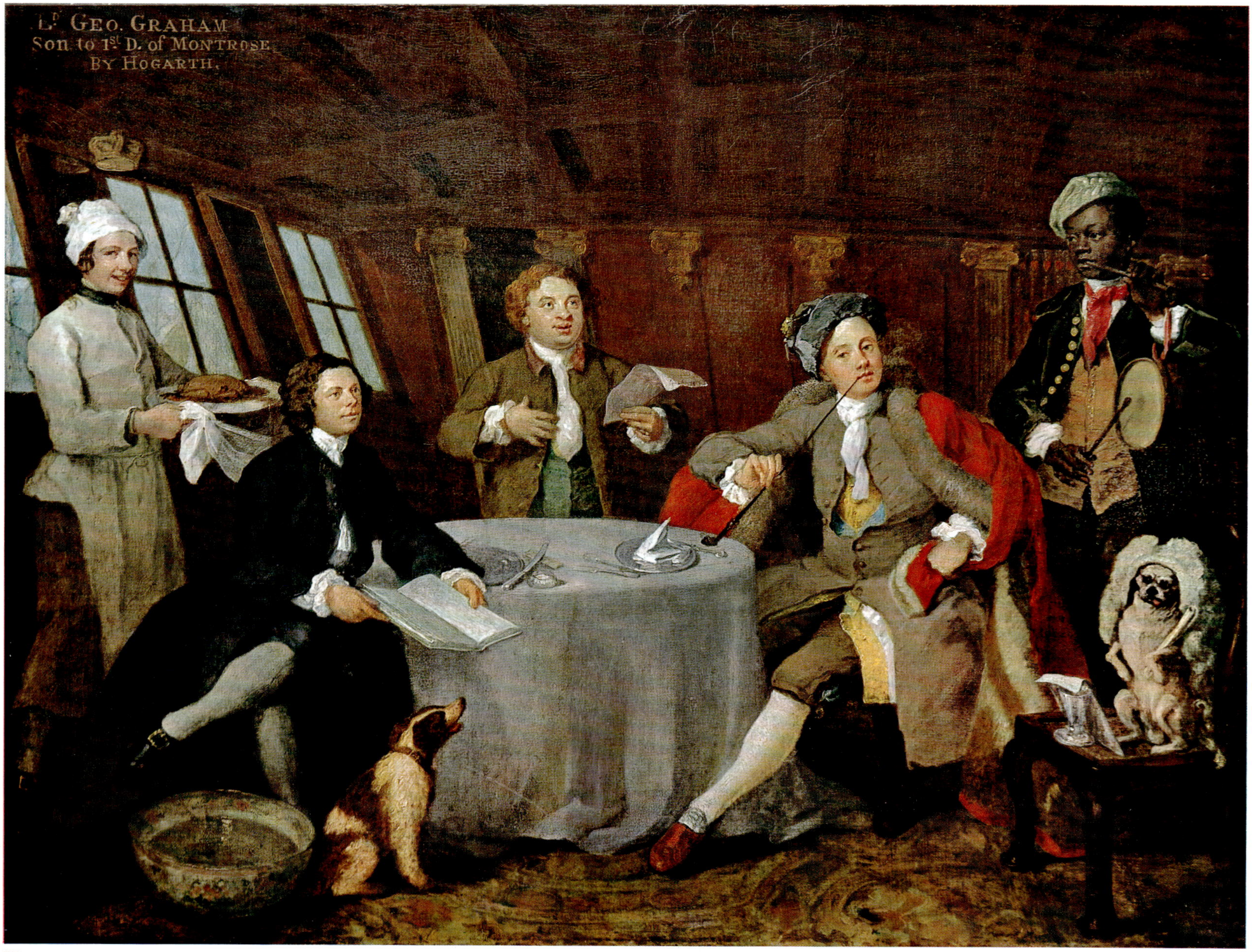

57

57 WILLIAM HOGARTH (1697-1764), *Lord George Graham in his Cabin*. Greenwich, National Maritime Museum.

in 1508 and learned much from the Italian masters, followed Italian precedent in representing the children of the King of Denmark around a table on which fruit for their refreshment is scattered. Indeed, a motif of the Venetian Quattrocento painters was to place an apple or a pomegranate (a symbol of the Passion) on the windowsill at which the Virgin shows herself with the Child Jesus, and Mabuse may have taken the idea from them. But we find actual tables with fruit-baskets or trays round which people are gathered only in Bernardino Licinio (c. 1498-1565; Hampton Court Palace), in Leandro Bassano (before 1582; fig. 254), in Scipione Pulzone's *Colonna Family* (1581: observe the typical fashion of stiff ruffs worn even by children; fig. 255),[4] and, outside Italy, in Cornelis Anthonisz. (or Teunissen)'s *Banquet of the Civic Guard* of 1533 (the 'Braspenningmaaltijd'; fig. 256). The latter is one of the early instances of portraits of corporations showing a juxtaposition of single portraits, as we have already noted in similar Italian groupings. We find a table also in Frans Floris' *Van Berchem Family* (1561), in which some of the sitters are playing musical instruments. Actual banquets, however, with various victuals, are depicted in Cornelis de Zeeuw's *Pierre de Moucheron and Isabeau de Gerbier with their Family* (1563; Amsterdam, Rijksmuseum), in which the laid table, though providing a link, by no means softens the stiffness of the attitudes, and in the *Family Group* by Maarten van Heemskerck (fig. 257), in which the attitude of the naked child in his mother's arms is a curious extrapolation from an Italian group of the Madonna and Child (Filippino Lippi). The other two children in the middle of the painting are taken from life with a truly astonishing realism, if one compares them with the stiffness of the sitters in the almost contemporary group by de Zeeuw or in another group of the same period (as shown by the date 1567 at the end of the Latin verse inserted between the parents) by Hans Eworth; here *William Brooke, Lord Cobham, and his Family* are shown round a laid table on which a parrot is pacing, while the child on the right holds a live monkey on a plate (fig. 260). In the *Family Group* attributed to Carlo Ceresa (1609-1679), the immobility of the sitters is of a different kind and resembles that of Louis Le Nain's peasants: they are no less a still-life than the victuals, the glass, and the decanter; serious and staring, they seem as if arrested and petrified in the fleeting moment (fig. 56).

A rather exceptional family group in the Italian tradition is that of *The Pellegrini Family* by Tintoretto, where eight life-size sitters are portrayed, some seated at a table, two standing motionless, and three moving from right to left (fig. 259). The latter, the young members of the family coming back from hunting, are bending with a symmetrical motion, and the three seated persons also make a symmetrical gesture, this almost ballet-like synchronization giving the painting a curious musical rhythm. But the most remarkable thing of all is the disposition of the group and the novelty of the device, from which the large proportions of the picture may distract our attention. If for one moment we imagine them reduced, as they are in our reproduction, we instantly see the affinity of our painting with outdoor scenes of banqueting such as were painted in the following century by David Teniers the Younger (1610-1690), who was alive to Dutch influence, and by Gillis van Tilborch, who made portraits in the spirit of genre painting. His *Family at Table* (once in the possession of Thomas Agnew & Sons), which was certainly modelled on Teniers' *Refreshment in the Open Air* (Louvre), like the Tintoretto shows a family seated at table on the left against a landscape, and a huntsman who approaches the family reunion. We find the same elements, but in a painting executed in a quite different style.[5] Portrait merges into genre painting with Tilborch, where the young huntsman on the right and the girl whom he invites with a gesture to taste the food belong altogether to genre painting.

Gerard Wigmana (1673-1741), in *A Colonial Family* (1697) painted before he went to Rome in 1700 to become a historical painter and acquire the reputation of a Frisian Raphael, represents (fig. 258) a family from the East Indies which had brought Asiatic servants with them, who are recognizable in the picture although they are dressed as Europeans. A Javanese page stands with a drinking-cup, and behind the lady's chair is a maidservant, perhaps an adopted illegitimate daughter; two more Asiatic maids are approaching behind the white servant, who is pouring wine. The inhabitants of the little town where they lived, perhaps Dokkum, must have been unaccustomed to Asiatic faces, because we see them peering with curiosity behind the window on the left. The seated persons are a white pair and a half-caste. Another Dutch painter, Jan Maurits Quinkhard (1688-1772), portrays a severe *Baptist Family* (1735; fig. 261) eating oysters and *An Orangist Family* (1746), the men smoking while, on the table, coffee is served, and from the painting over the mantlepiece William IV of Orange looks on approvingly (fig. 265).

4 See the remarks on this painting from the point of view of fashions in R. LEVI-PISETZKY, *Storia del costume in Italia*, III (Milan: Istituto Editoriale Italiano, 1966), plate 8. 5 That Tintoretto's painting should have appealed to Dutch taste is proved by the fact that it belonged to one of the few seventeenth-century Dutchmen who appreciated Italian painting, Jan Reynst, the son of Gerrit, governor of the Dutch Indies. He died in Venice in 1646, and twenty years later the

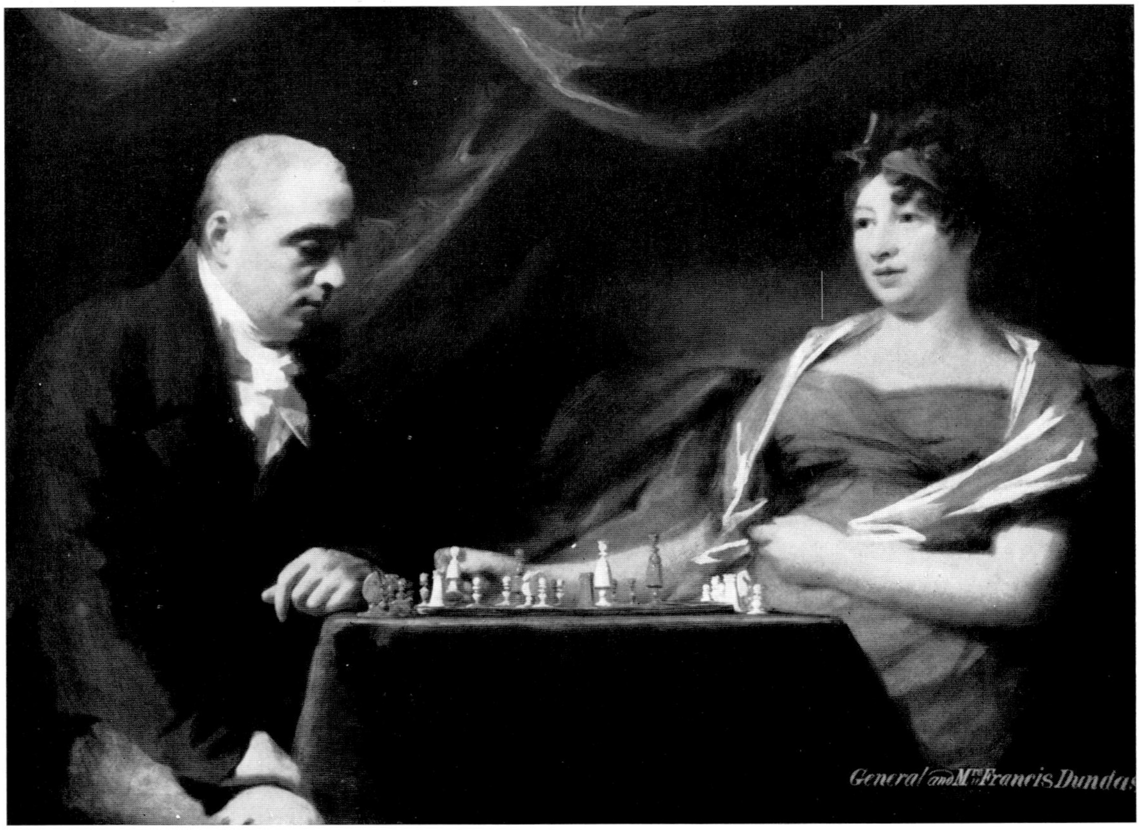

58

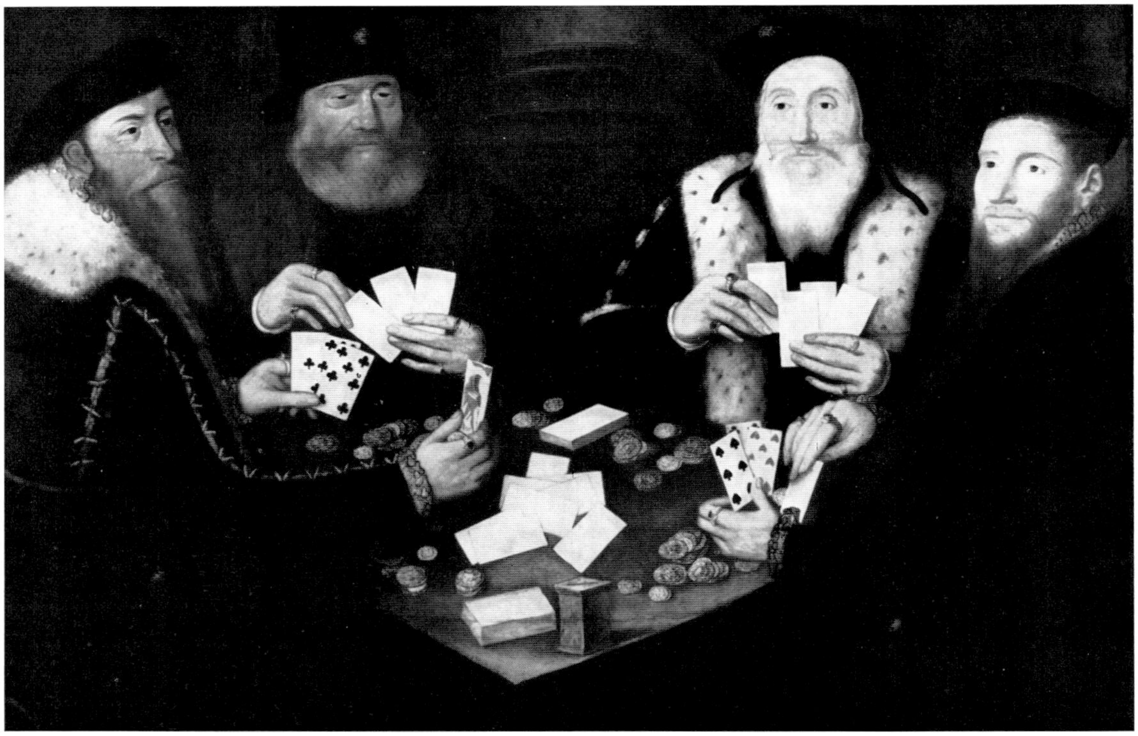

59

58 SIR HENRY RAEBURN (1756-1823), *General Francis Dundas and his Wife Playing Chess*. Arniston, Gorebridge (Midlothian), reproduced by courtesy of the Trustees of the late Lady Dundas and Miss Dundas of Arniston. 59 ANONYMOUS (16th century; copy after JOHN BETTES?), *Four Gentlemen of High Rank Playing Primero*. Manchester, Wythenshawe Hall (on loan from Lord Derby's collection).

60 JOHANN ZOFFANY (1734/5-1810), *The Dutton Family*. Farley Hill (Berkshire), Farley Hall Collection.

60
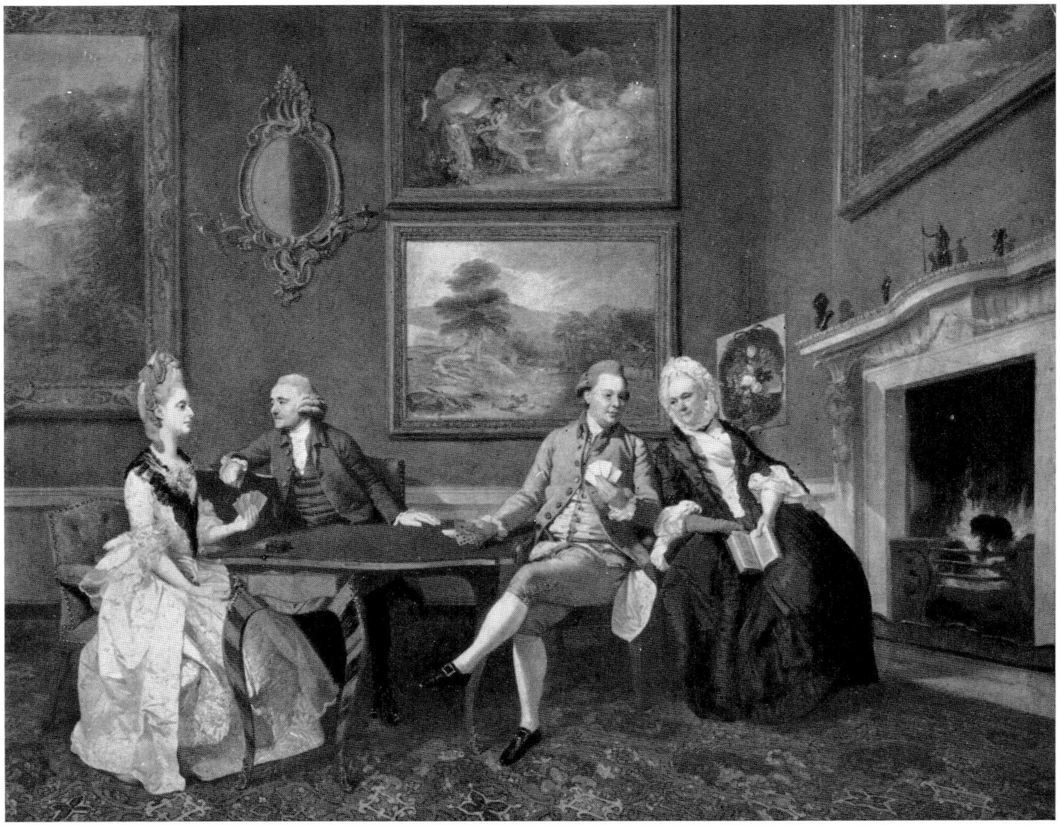

The French painter Robert Tournières (1667-1752), a follower of Dutch and Flemish masters who in 1717 became *peintre ordinaire du Roy*, in the painting at Versailles called *Le souper d'Auteuil* portrayed round a table three gentlemen who are believed to be the dramatists Crébillon père and C.R. Dufresny, and the king's doctor, Bodin.

The English conversation piece by Benjamin Ferrers, signed and dated 1720 (fig. 266), has the distinction of being the earliest English painting of the kind with full-length figures. A coat-of-arms on the wall combines the heraldic devices of the four gentlemen drinking: Sir Thomas Saunders Sebright, Member of Parliament for Hertford from 1715 to 1736 (who by marriage became the brother-in-law of Sir Francis Dashwood, the founder of the Hell Fire Club, whose rakish exploits anticipated those of the Marquis de Sade); Sir John Bland, M.P. for Lancashire in 1714; and two more unidentified persons. Under the coat-of-arms one reads " Youle all Say another Day what jolly brave Boys were we ". Merry England, but with a sinister touch if you think of the Hell Fire Club. Gawen Hamilton (1698-1737), a portrait painter who specialized in conversation pieces after Hogarth's success, obtaining much reputation and patronage in the last years of his life, shows a company of drinking gentlemen who, perhaps because of their family likeness, have been traditionally called *The Brothers Clarke of Swakeleys* (fig. 263). One wonders whether the somewhat pouting, disagreeable mouth (particularly that of the gentleman holding a letter) is a family characteristic or a mannerism of the painter, for we find it again in another of his paintings, *The Raikes Family*.[6] Although one of the earliest painters of conversation pieces in England, Hamilton had no originality of motifs; in another painting[7] belonging to this class, or rather to that of genre, with the vicar of the parish at the house of the infant squire, he places on the left the same figure of a butler bending over the wine-cooler we have seen in the picture we have just examined. Vertue makes him a rival of Hogarth (in fact, he shares certain compositional schemes with Hogarth),[8] perhaps in order to spite the latter, because Hamilton is much weaker both in design and colour. The only information Vertue gives about him is that he was a small man and that

painting was purchased by the painter Niccolò Renieri. See SIMONA SAVINI BRANCA, *Il collezionismo veneziano del Seicento* (Padua: Cedam, 1964), p. 100, and CARLO RIDOLFI, *Le Meraviglie dell'arte* (Venice, 1648), II, p. 55. 6 Reproduced in *Painting in England, 1700-1850*, Mr. and Mrs. Paul Mellon Collection, Virginia Museum of Fine Arts, 1963, plate no. 99. 7 Reproduced in SACHEVERELL SITWELL, *Conversation Pieces* (London: Batsford, 1936), ill. 82 and text on pp. 70-1. 8 See p. 69, footnote 13.

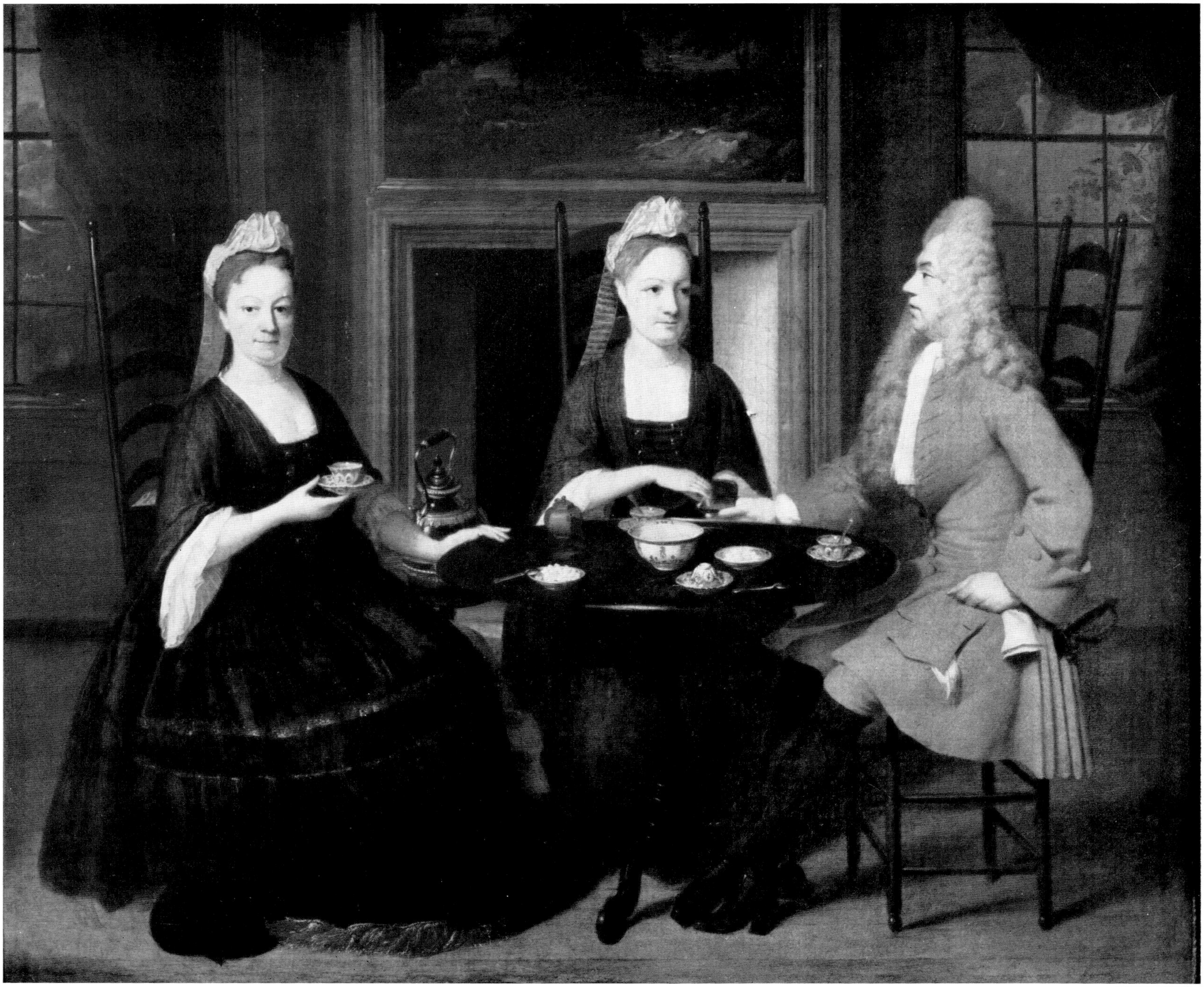

61

61 attr. to NICOLAAS VERKOLJE (1673-1746), *Two Ladies and a Gentleman at Tea*, c. 1715-20. London, Victoria and Albert Museum. 62 BALTHASAR DENNER (1685-1749), *The Duchess Elisabeth Sophie Marie of Braunschweig-Wolfenbüttel Taking Tea*. Hillerød, Nationalhistoriske Museum på Frederiksborg Slot. 63 WILLIAM HOGARTH (1697-1764), *The Strode Family*, 1738. London, Tate Gallery.

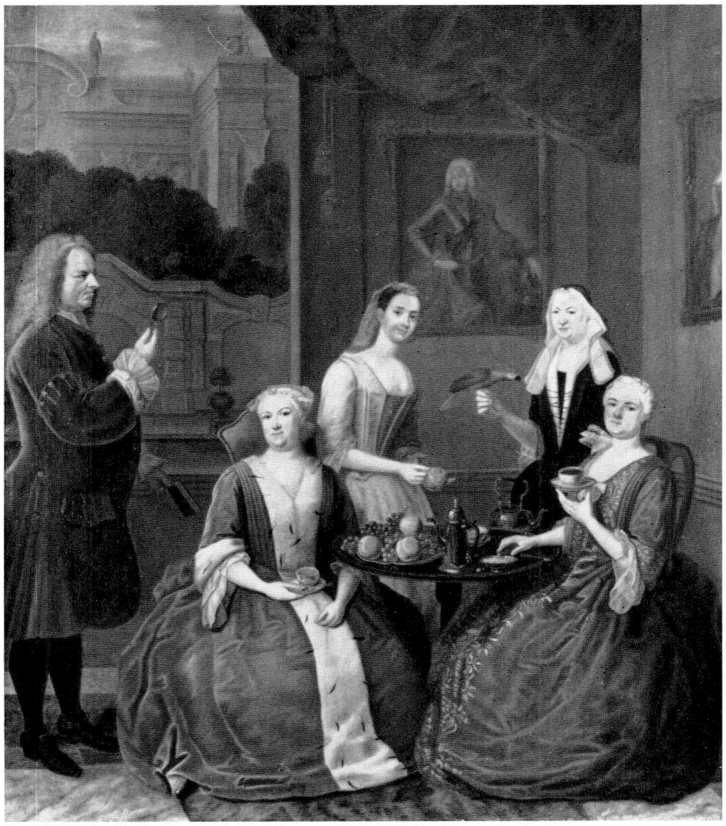

62

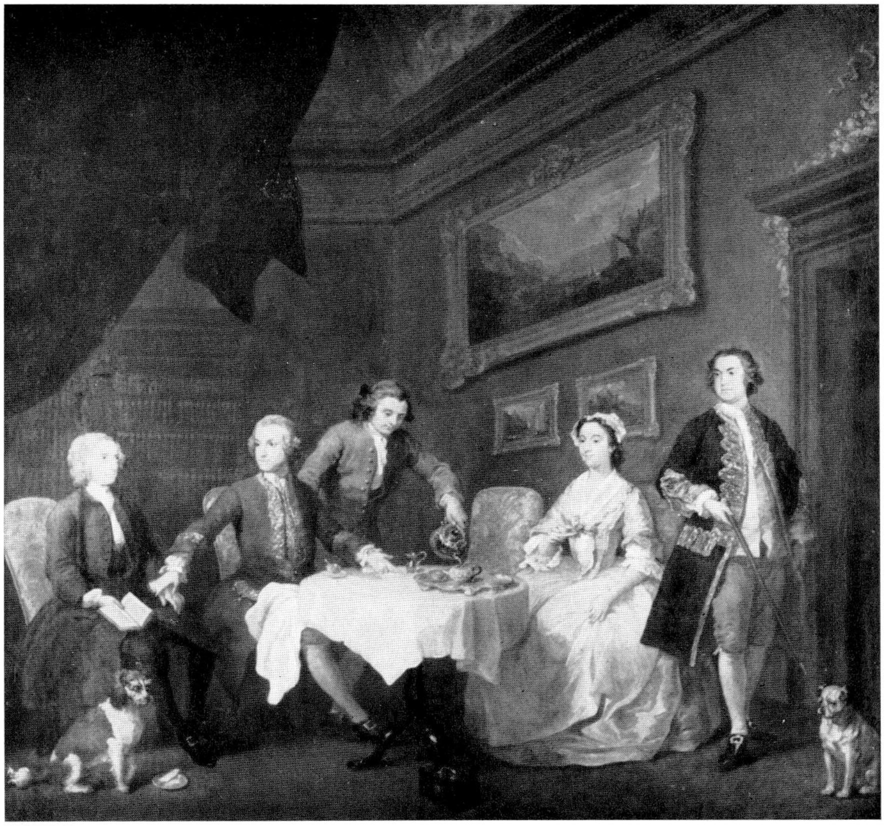

63

he died of a cold or fever caught in coming from a supper at an artists' club. He certainly had an unattractive appearance, as can be seen from his self-portrait inserted behind a group of card-players in another painting (Liverpool, Walker Art Gallery). A painting by Zoffany represents James Lennox Napier in the drawing-room of Sherborne Park in Gloucestershire; Napier, who took the name of Dutton from his mother's family (he is the second person from the left), is watching a card-game between his daughter Jane and the eldest son of his second wife, seated on the right with a book on her lap (fig. 60).

A card-game also provided the subject of one of the earliest English conversation pieces: four bearded persons are sitting round a table with cards in their hands (fig. 59). A tradition in the Falkland family, to whom the picture belonged at one time, described them as Lord Burghley and three of his friends. Another version of the painting (the property of Colonel W.A. Chester-Mason of Norcote House, Cirencester) shows variants in the cards held by the sitters on the right and left, and also in the coins and the cards on the table.[9] In both paintings (which are considered to be copies of a lost original) the untouched pack of cards bears lettering which in the second version mentioned above seems to identify the painter with a John Bettes, a portrait painter working during the reign of Henry VIII. We have already seen a chess game painted by Sofonisba Anguissola.[10] Sir Henry Raeburn (1756-1823), in the only known conversation piece by him (fig. 58), portrayed General Francis Dundas playing chess with his wife. General Sir John Murray, of whom we have spoken before,[11] also had himself portrayed playing chess with his goddaughter Ellen Adderley, by Pieter Christoffel Wonder (collection of Sir Victor Crutchley, Bridport).[12]

A Hogarth painting of 1730 (New York, Marshall Field Collection) shows Dudley Woodbridge, a lawyer, seated at a table in one of the rooms of the Middle Temple and drinking wine with Captain Holland; a servant holds a letter addressed to Woodbridge. But Hogarth's masterpiece in the treatment of this motif (people sitting and drinking or smoking round a table) is *Lord George Graham in his Cabin* (fig. 57). Since the nobleman, who was the son of the Duke of Montrose and at the time was a

9 EDWARDS, *Early Conversation Pictures*, p. 157. 10 See above, p. 51. 11 See above, p. 36. 12 See J.W. NIEMEIJER, " P.C. Wonder in England ", in *Bulletin van het Rijksmuseum*, 1965, no. 3.

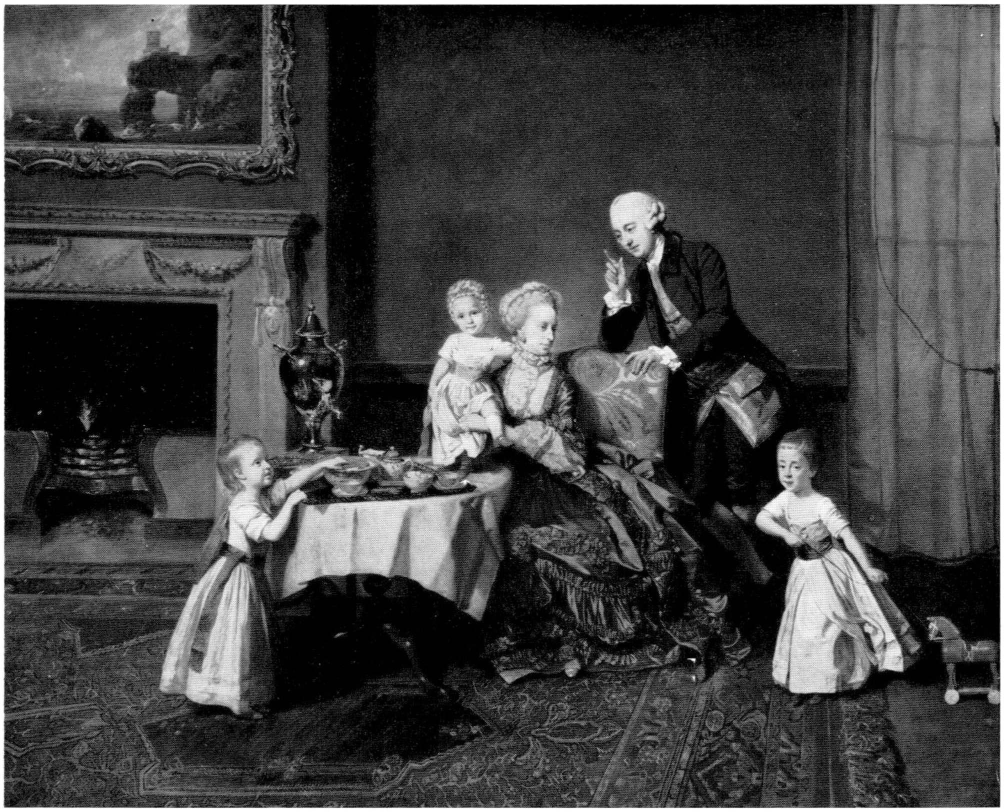

64

64 JOHANN ZOFFANY (1734/5-1810), *Lord Willoughby de Broke and his Family.* Woodley House, Kineton, collection of Lord Willoughby de Broke.

Captain in the Navy, is not in uniform, the painting should be dated before 1748 — the year in which uniforms were introduced in the Navy. He wears a smart red coat lined with fur, and, while a smiling servant brings in a roast chicken for a light meal, he smokes a long pipe and listens to a ballad read by a short, plump man; in the meantime, with the typical confusion of a Hogarthian *levée*, a black boy beats a drum, at whose rhythm a trained dog in a judge's wig and with a sheet of paper before it appears to play a part. Another, younger sitter — serious-looking and with an open book in his hands — for whom a place has been laid at the table, lifts his head attentively. The odd appearance of the cabin, with its slanting Corinthian pilasters and gilt capitals, and the sight of the white sails and blue sky through the windows imparts an unusual charm to this conversation piece.
Joseph Highmore (1692-1780), who illustrated the novels of Richardson — with whom he had an affinity of disposition — painted more family pieces than any of his contemporaries. Only one has been traced, however: *Mr. Oldham and his Friends* (Tate Gallery), probably painted soon after 1740. It shows us a group of boon companions who " seem to have stepped from the pages of Sterne rather than of Richardson ", as Waterhouse remarks,[13] with a robust, Hogarth-like characterization, but with a subtle play of facial expressions alien to the rude directness of that painter. Seated at a table, Oldham and his friends are smoking and drinking; although their faces are caught in a pause or a pose, the painting communicates — as few others do — the spirit of old England. The Scotsman John Thomas Seton (fl. between 1761 and 1806), in *William Fullerton and Captain Lowis Taking Wine* (1773), has also strongly characterized the faces of his sitters (fig. 264).
The most popular drink in eighteenth-century England — tea — provides the subject for a number of paintings which describe this very important occasion in the life of the period. The prototype, according to Edwards,[14] was provided by a " conversation " painted by the Dutchman Abraham Snaphaen (1651-1691), formerly in the collection of the Duke of Anhalt, in which five ladies are seated round a table of baroque design taking tea. Another early painting (fig. 61) representing a tea-party is also

13 E.K. WATERHOUSE, *Painting in Britain, 1530-1790*, Pelican History of Art, 2nd ed. (Harmondsworth and Baltimore: Penguin Books Ltd., 1962), p. 127.
14 *Early Conversation Pictures*, p. 42; he refers to pl. 196 of C.W.G. BIERMANN, *Deutsches Barock und Rokoko* (Darmstadt, 1914).

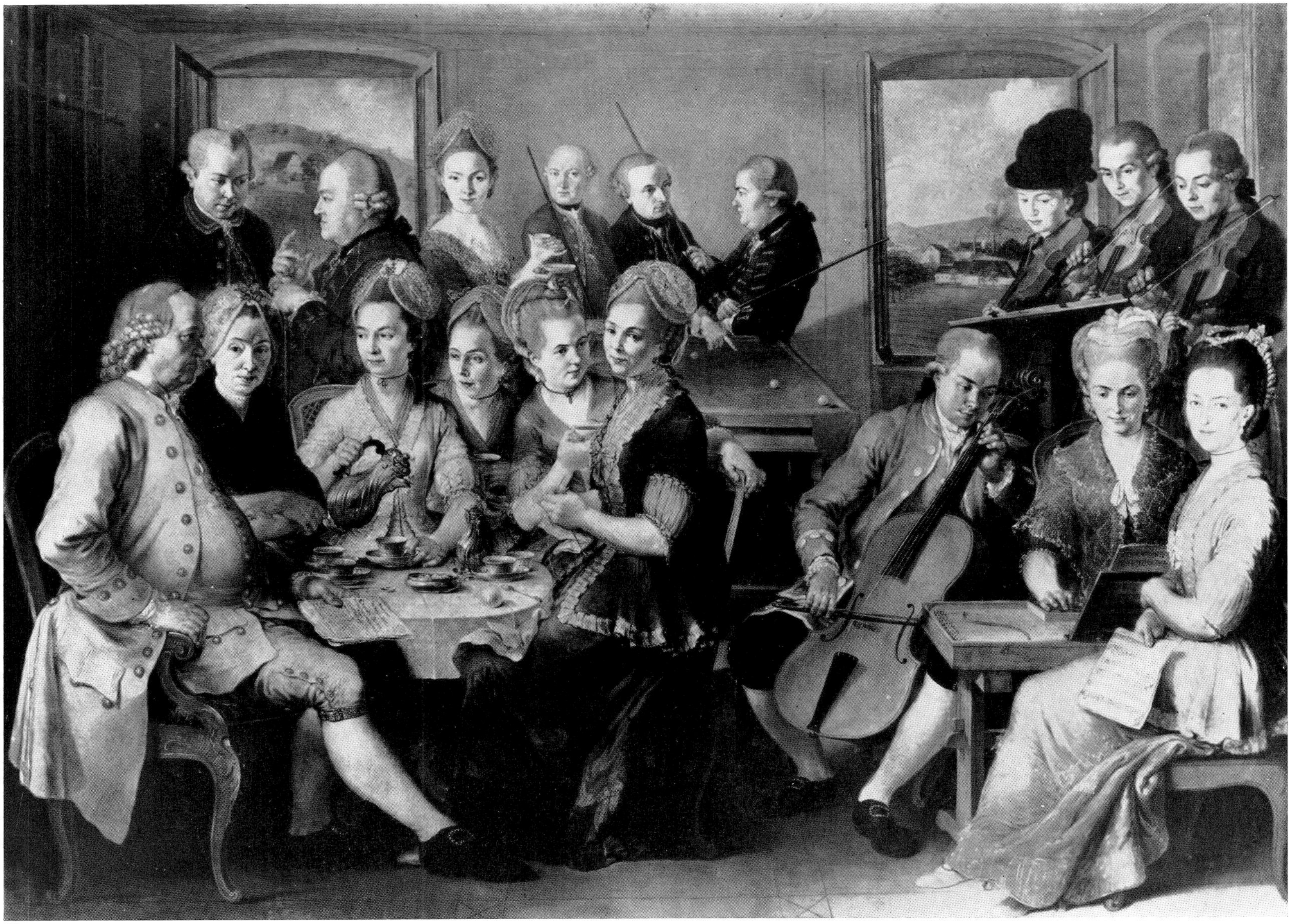

65

65 JANUARIUS ZICK (1732-1797), *The Remy Family at the Rasselsteiner Hütte*, 1776. Nuremberg, Germanisches Nationalmuseum.

by a Dutchman: *Two Ladies and a Gentleman at Tea* (c. 1715-20), which Staring has attributed to Nicolaas Verkolje (1673-1746), although it seems more akin to the manner Jan Maurits Quinkhard adopted at a later date than that of the painting.[15] A tradition which wrongly ascribed it to Hogarth gave the names of the sitters, two Flemish Huguenot misses of a family which had emigrated to England, to one of whom the gentleman on the right, a Captain Walker, her fiancé, is handing snuff. The furniture of the room has Dutch characteristics.

In *A Family Taking Tea* (fig. 262) by an unknown painter, we see a silver teapot, stand, and caddy in the style of 1705-6, and Chinese porcelain teacups and plate of the K'ang-hsi period (1622-1722).[16] The German Balthasar Denner (Hamburg 1685-Rostock 1749) painted the Duchess Elisabeth Sophie Marie of Braunschweig-Wolfenbüttel (1683-1767) taking tea (served with fruit) in the company of another lady. The two ladies are sitting in symmetrical attitudes, and bend their necks symmetrically in opposite directions. The elderly gentleman standing on the left holds a magnifying glass in his hand and looks almost disapprovingly in the direction of the old woman standing behind the two ladies and holding a parrot in her hand; the arm supporting the bird and the other holding the magnifying glass are also lifted in a symmetrical relationship. The two figures of the old woman and of the maidservant nearby carrying the teapot again present a symmetrical arrangement; and finally, the four female heads and the masculine one would, if joined by lines, form a pentagon (fig. 62).

In another *English Family Taking Tea*, attributed to Joseph van Aken (c. 1700-1749; London, National Gallery), all the accessories of the service are much in evidence as if for the illustration of a rite. In a family group by Hogarth (fig. 63), represented in a room with a foreshortening typical of the painter and a no-less-typical curtain on the left, we see Dr. Arthur Smith, who was Archbishop of Dublin from 1766 to 1772, taking tea with the Strode family. The scene is curiously flanked by two dogs, the one on the right like the mastiff Hogarth placed in his self-portrait. The idea of the two dogs attracted also the unknown painter who portrayed *The Carter Family* round the tea-table: another more conventional motif recurring in this painting is the young lady seated at the harpsichord on the right (fig. 67).

Johann Zoffany painted *Lord Willoughby de Broke and his Family* (fig. 64) taking tea in the breakfast-room at Compton Verney (the silver tea urn is still in the family's possession). The pyramidal composition of the group (the right section is particularly emphasized by the inclined posture of the father and the child pulling the red wooden horse) and the gestures of the children are typical of " conversations ", as we have had occasion to remark several times, but the painting, like all of Zoffany's, charms by its neatness and elegance. *The Remy Family at the Rasselsteiner Hütte* (fig. 65) by Januarius Zick (1732-1797) belongs more or less to the same period (1776). On the left some ladies and an elderly gentleman are drinking coffee, on the right a quintet is playing music, and at the back some people are playing billiards. The windows at the end, with a view of the countryside, relieve the impression of narrowness in the châlet room: one of them shows the family house, the other the ironworks belonging to this large bourgeois family.

In the Ruspoli palace at Vignanello there is a picture by an unknown artist bearing on the frame the title (in English) *The Family Breakfast* (fig. 66), commemorating a party which took place in the Ruspoli palace in Rome in the spring of 1807. Its companion piece, by the same hand — *The Walking of Children*, with a view of Vignanello — is in the Ruspoli palace in Rome (fig. 119). Evidently the two pictures are kept separate by the family in order to remind them of one place when they are in the other. An outline-drawing taken from the picture gives in English the names of the people sitting round the table: " Prince Francis Ruspoly [1752-1829], Princess Leopoldine Kewenüller [Kevenhüller] his wife [1764-1845], and their sons, Alexander, Prince of Cervetery the eldest [*sous-préfet* of Tivoli under the French government, he was so afflicted by the loss of his wife in 1821 that he embraced an ecclesiastical career], Sigismund, Knight of Malta and Officer in the Austrian Army, Camilus, Amélie, Leopold [who became a priest], Emmanuel, Bartholomew, Countess Mary Esterasy, wife of the Prince of Cervetery [Marianna Esterházy, who in 1805 was married to Alessandro], Hyacynthe their daughter, Hyacynthe Ruspoly, Sister of Prince [Francesco] Ruspoly married to the Prince Spada ". Entering from the door are Bartholomew, Bailiff of Malta (elected Grand Master of the Maltese Order, he refused the office because Malta was occupied by the English), and Laurence, a priest, later Knight of Malta. A tradition, perhaps originating from the manner in which these two relatives appear in the painting, relates that they

15 EDWARDS, *Early Conversation Pictures*, p. 147; STARING, *De Hollanders Thuis* (The Hague: Martinus Nijhoff, 1956), pp. 105-6. 16 EDWARDS, *Early Conversation Pictures*, p. 171.

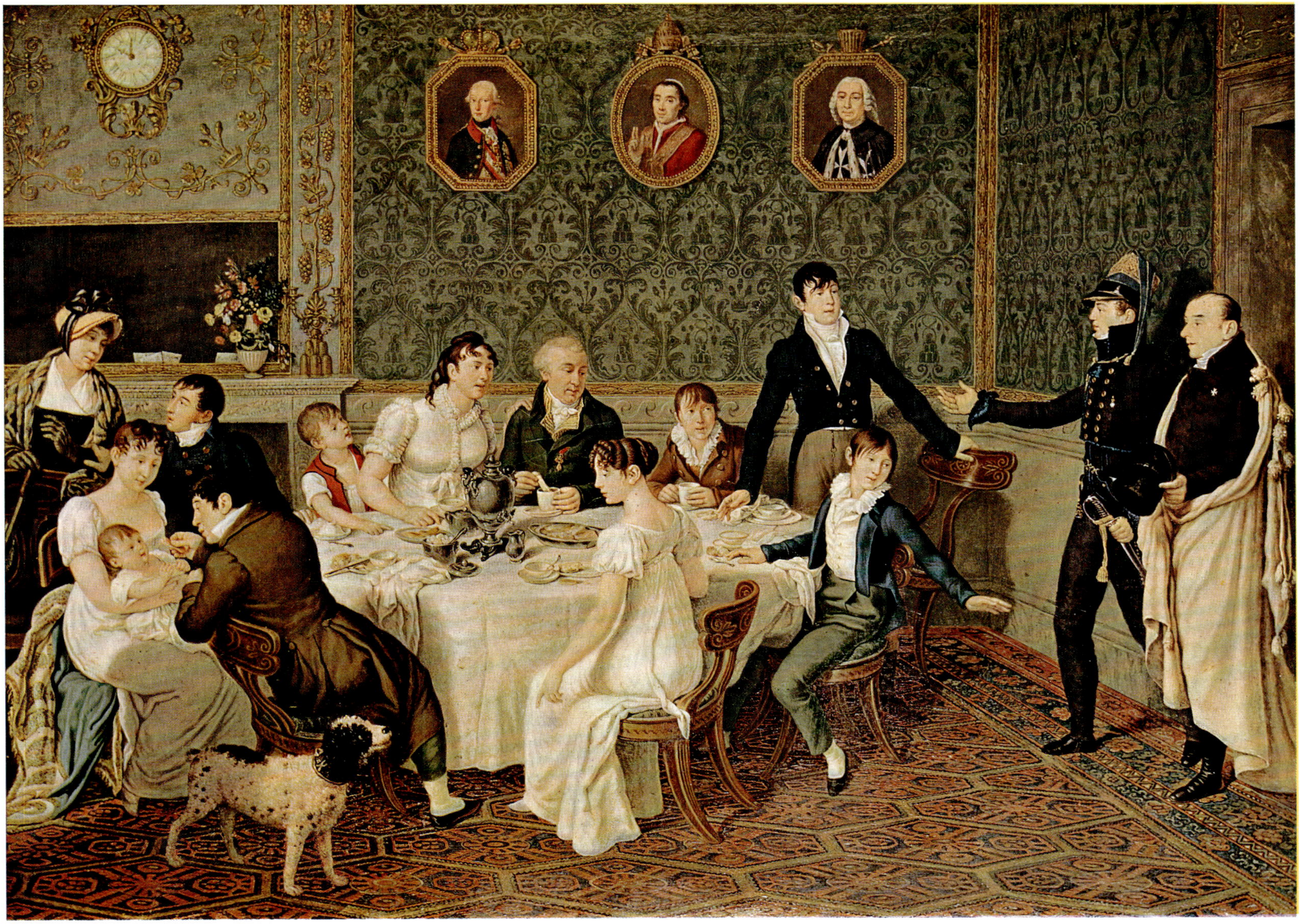

66

66 ANONYMOUS, *The Ruspoli Family at Breakfast* (“*The Family Breakfast*”). Vignanello, Palazzo Ruspoli, collection of Principe Ruspoli.

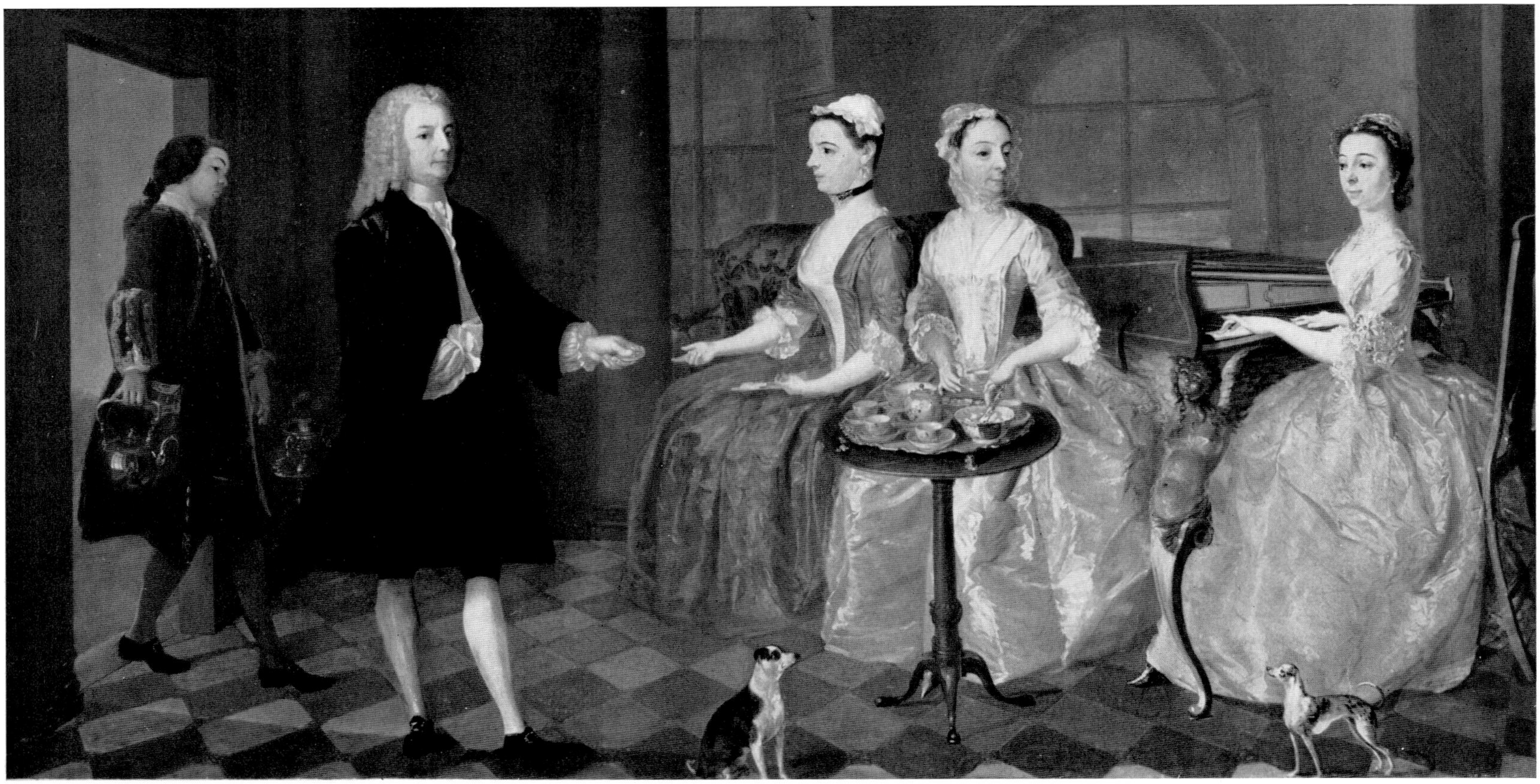

67

often came to scrounge a meal. The back wall is hung with portraits of Francis I of Austria, Pius VII, and the Grand Master of Malta (Emmanuel Rohan).

Tominz also painted a family, *The Moscon Family* (fig. 202), taking coffee. Georg Ludwig Vogel (1788-1879), a Swiss artist who was a member of the Nazarene coterie in Rome and who finally returned to Zurich in 1813, was the author of dull historical scenes. He portrayed himself and his family round a table under a pergola, with a view of a church and the town, quietly enjoying the hot, aromatic drink in a charming natural setting. The shadows of the trees and of the people on the wall make us guess the delights of the afternoon hour in mid-season (fig. 68). *The Family of the Berlin Gardener Mathieu*, painted in about 1820 by Louise Henry (1798-1839), has a more meditative atmosphere, as if the sitters were absorbed in a ritual (fig. 4). The daughter casually kneels in front of the maid to help her prepare the vegetables, the mother reads from a book, perhaps aloud — no doubt an edifying text, to judge from the pensive faces of the two young men on the right, one of them smoking a long pipe. The melon on the table, which is covered with an Indian cloth, acquires almost a liturgical significance; the magnolias and rhododendrons, and the large leaves of the banana tree, give the scene an exotic flavour which would strengthen the impression of a strange ritual were it not that beyond this almost tropical corner appear the spires and houses of Potsdam.

Sometimes the table was not even laid, but it still served as a centre where the sitters foregathered, as in the group of Sir John Murray with his aide-de-camp, Lady Murray, and Mrs. Crutchley, by P.C. Wonder (Sir Victor Crutchley Collection, Bridport).[17] Or it served as a support for a woman busy at embroidering; it is indeed surprising to find so few women embroidering in these paintings, in an epoch in which embroidery was one of the principal — if not the only — occupation of ladies. We find a table in a " conversation " with a mother and her two daughters (each with a booklet, perhaps of prayers, if we consider the late hour; the girls seem to be repeating a portion of it by heart): this is an English painting of about 1750, once attributed to

17 See the article cited on p. 101, footnote 12.

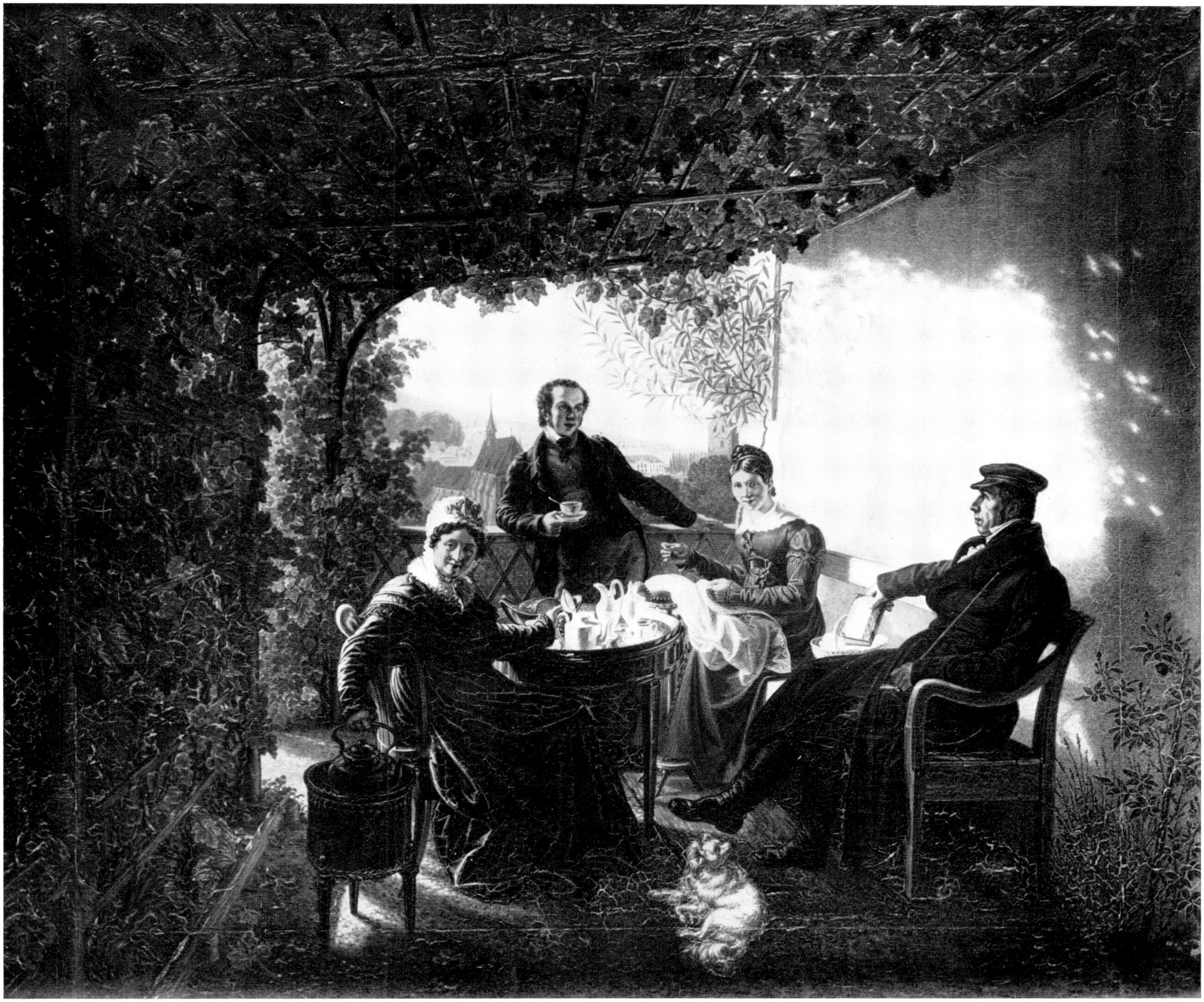

68

67 ENGLISH SCHOOL (18th century), *The Carter Family*, c. 1740. Washington, D.C., collection of Mr. and Mrs. Paul Mellon. 68 LUDWIG VOGEL (1788-1879), *The Painter's Family*. Zurich, Kunsthaus.

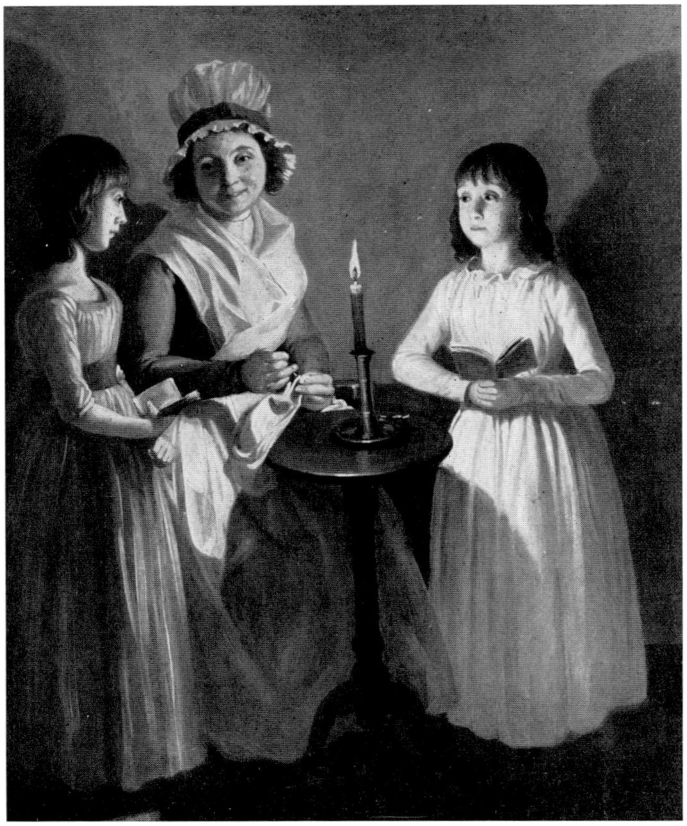

69

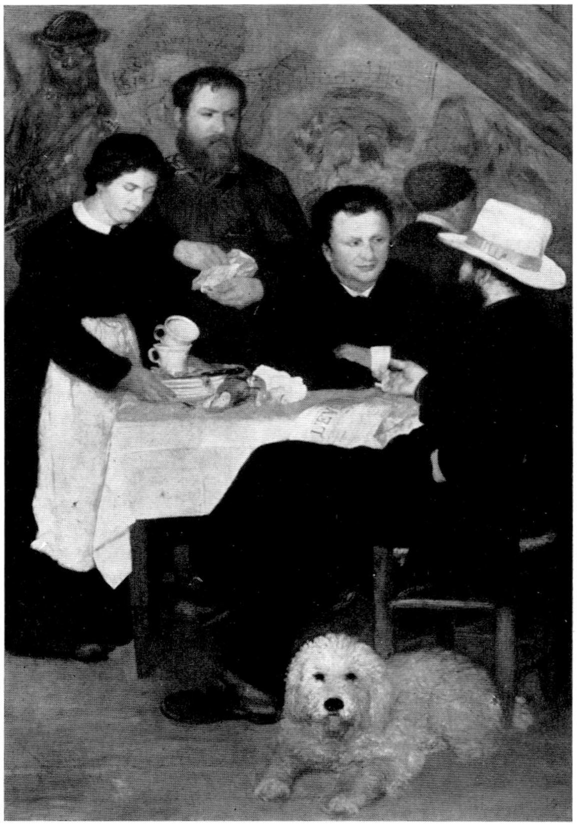

70

Raphael Smith (fig. 69). In another painting, attributed to John Downman (c. 1750-1824) or to Richard Cosway (1742-1821), Lady Jane Matthew leans her elbow on a table on which a workbox is placed; one of her daughters is embroidering, another is at the embroidery frame, while a third interrupts her reading as if lost in thought: there is an obvious family likeness in these far-from-beautiful women with goat-like profiles (fig. 71). Knitting and embroidering are, however, conspicuous in a curious set of drawings illustrating a manuscript once owned by Count Alessandro Verri (Rome, 1785): *Ozi ingegnosi del Caval.e Commendatore Andriani Capitano comandante in Perugia, e dal medesimo dedicati alle Dame, la immagine, vita e maniere delle quali egli descrive spesso nel presente volume* (the property of Countess Elisabetta Oddi Baglioni, Perugia). Twelve out of forty-five drawings — which form, according to the author, "an actual magic lantern of customs" of a "vegetating" provincial society — represent, not without humour, women of the Oddi family sewing, spinning, and embroidering.

The Family-Reunion Picnic (Newport, Rhode Island; private collection) painted in about 1850 by the American Jeremiah Pearson Hardy (1800-1888) commemorates a great institution in Maine life, described by Sarah Orne Jewett in *The Country of the Pointed Firs*. It may, however, only be a genre painting, as are the contemporary English paintings by W.P. Frith (*Derby Day*, *Ramsgate Sands*), although a family tradition locates this picnic on Sherman's Point at the entrance to Camden harbour on Penobscot Bay. The *Lincoln Family in 1861* by Francis B. Carpenter (The New York Historical Society) has an historical rather than an artistic interest: it appears as if the standing boy has been made to rise by the painter in order to form the traditional triangular composition.

A triangular scheme is also noticeable in *Le cabaret de la mère Anthony* by Pierre-Auguste Renoir, but certainly in this case it is a very secondary detail: the painter stands by a table at which the painters Sisley and Lecour are seated, while a waitress clears it (fig. 70).

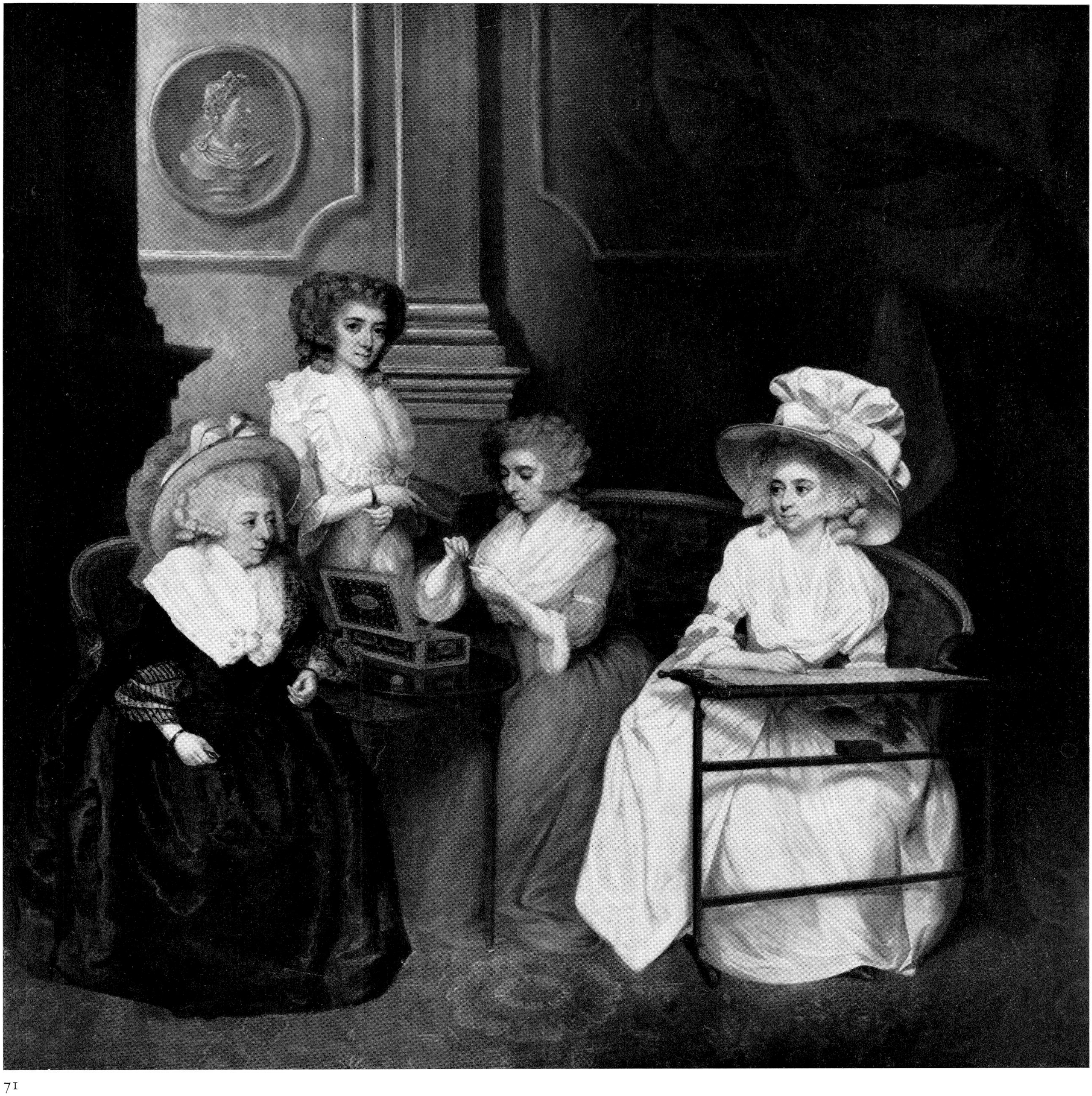

71

69 ENGLISH SCHOOL (formerly attr. to RAPHAEL SMITH), *A Woman Embroidering and her Two Daughters*, c. 1750. Washington, D.C., collection of Mr. and Mrs. Paul Mellon. 70 PIERRE-AUGUSTE RENOIR (1841-1919), *Le cabaret de la mère Anthony*, 1866. Stockholm, Nationalmuseum. 71 ENGLISH SCHOOL (formerly attr. to JOHN DOWNMAN [c. 1750-1824] or to RICHARD COSWAY [1742-1821]), *Lady Jane Matthew and her Daughters*, 1769. Washington, D.C., collection of Mr. and Mrs. Paul Mellon.

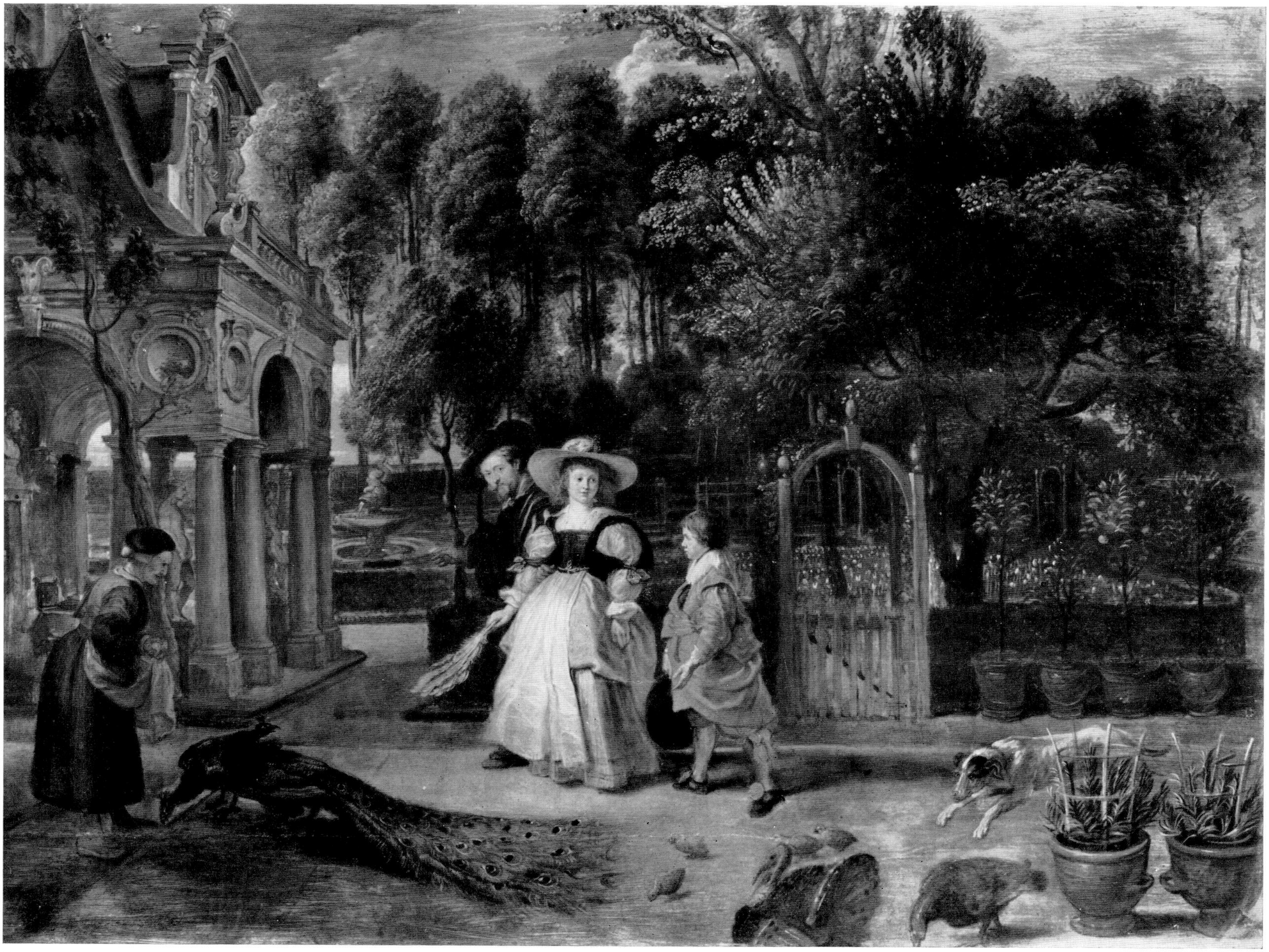

72

72 PETER PAUL RUBENS (1577-1640), *Self-portrait Walking with Hélène Fourment in their Garden*, 1630-1. Munich, Alte Pinakothek.

CHAPTER VI – THE FAMILY GROUP IN AN OUTDOOR SETTING

The family portrait with a garden for a background also has Flemish and Dutch origins. Frans Hals' portrait of a couple and Rubens' walk with Hélène Fourment in a garden (fig. 72) are the first essays in a kind of painting which was destined to be very popular, chiefly in England. One may attempt a classification within this very large category of conversation pieces according to the manner of representation of the group:

1. In front of a porch or balustrade.
2. In a courtyard or in the open air.
3. Against a screen of foliage or with a tree in the middle.
4. With a view of a country house.
5. With a view of a landscape.
6. In a boat.

And, finally, since a park is generally the favourite background for portraits of children:

7. Portraits of children.

Paintings representing a family in a boat are rare; those of the last section are, on the contrary, extremely numerous. This is not surprising, because from the earliest examples of this kind of painting much store was set by children, both for sentimental reasons and because of the picturesque qualities of their liveliness. Portraits of children became a conspicuous feature of eighteenth-century paintings in England, where, for the first time, special attention was paid to better methods of bringing up children, based on the conviction that what they needed most of all was fresh air, hygiene, and exercise.

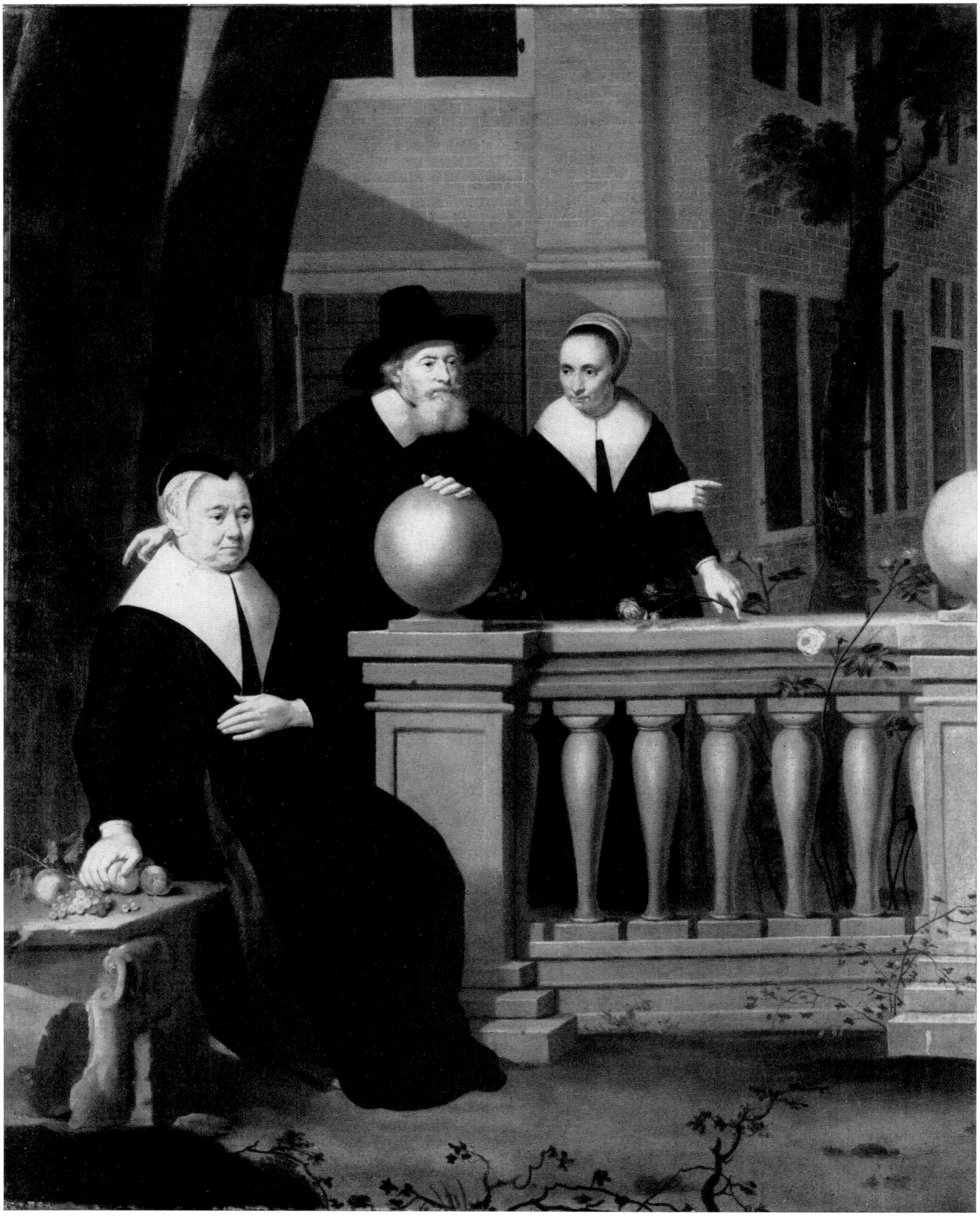
73

73 JAN VAN BYLERT (1603-1671), *Family Group*. London, National Gallery.

74 GONZALES COQUES (1614-1684), *The Verbiest Family*. London, Buckingham Palace, Royal Collections; copyright reserved.

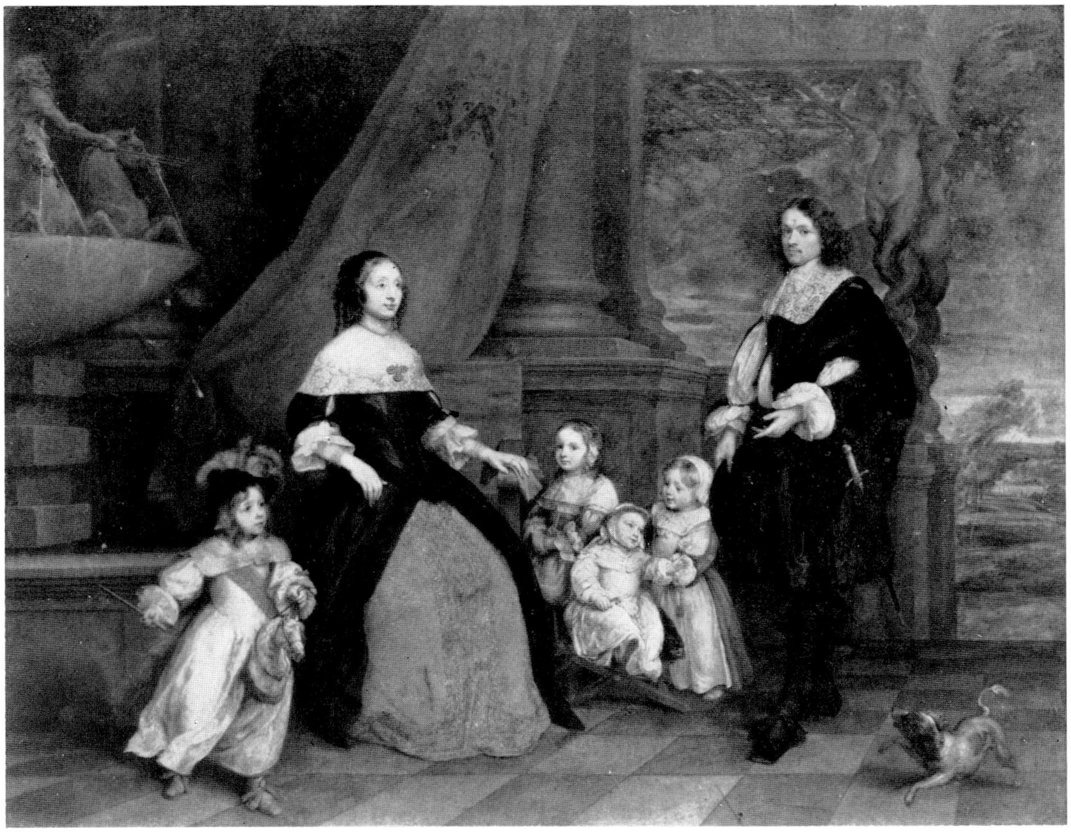

74

1. *In front of a porch or balustrade.*

Rubens was, if not the first, certainly among the earliest artists to represent a family against the colonnade of a country house with a view of a garden. In *The Family of Balthasar Gerbier* (a copy at Windsor Castle), the disposition of the family is reminiscent of that of the holy figures in paintings of the Venetian school (such as Titian's *Pesaro Madonna*). The mother with her child is seated on a step as on a throne towards which, instead of devotees, her other children are moving; behind her, her husband replaces St. Joseph in the holy families. In this case, one may truly say that the secular theme had developed from the sacred one, as had happened in drama.

Jan van Bylert's (1603-1671) *Family Group* (fig. 73) has a different character, directly inspired by real life and not borrowed from holy subjects. Its pedigree is that of genre painting. Instead of the ceremonial curtain of Rubens' painting, we have a tree-trunk; any reminiscence of the sacred scenes has vanished: the elderly lady seated on a bench does not in the least suggest an enthroned Madonna, and the two persons behind the balustrade are middle-class people such as one can run into at any corner. But the formal tradition with suggestions of holy pictures was to last for a long time. The curtain and columns reappear in *The Verbiest Family* by Gonzales Coques (fig. 74), as well as a monumental fountain. The same fountain occurs again in the group called *Le repos champêtre* by Coques (fig. 75), while the spiral columns and the baroque canopy are seen in the conventional background of the *Father with his Two Daughters* (fig. 267). And Jordaens painted a *Family Group* with life-size figures in a garden, at the foot of a fountain overshadowed by trees (fig. 76). We find the curtain and column again in John Singleton Copley's *Family of Sir William Pepperrell* (1778) (fig. 77). Although Lady Pepperrell had died in America in 1755, she is represented as alive in the painting; probably Copley's wife posed as a model for her. The group is composed like a traditional Holy Family,

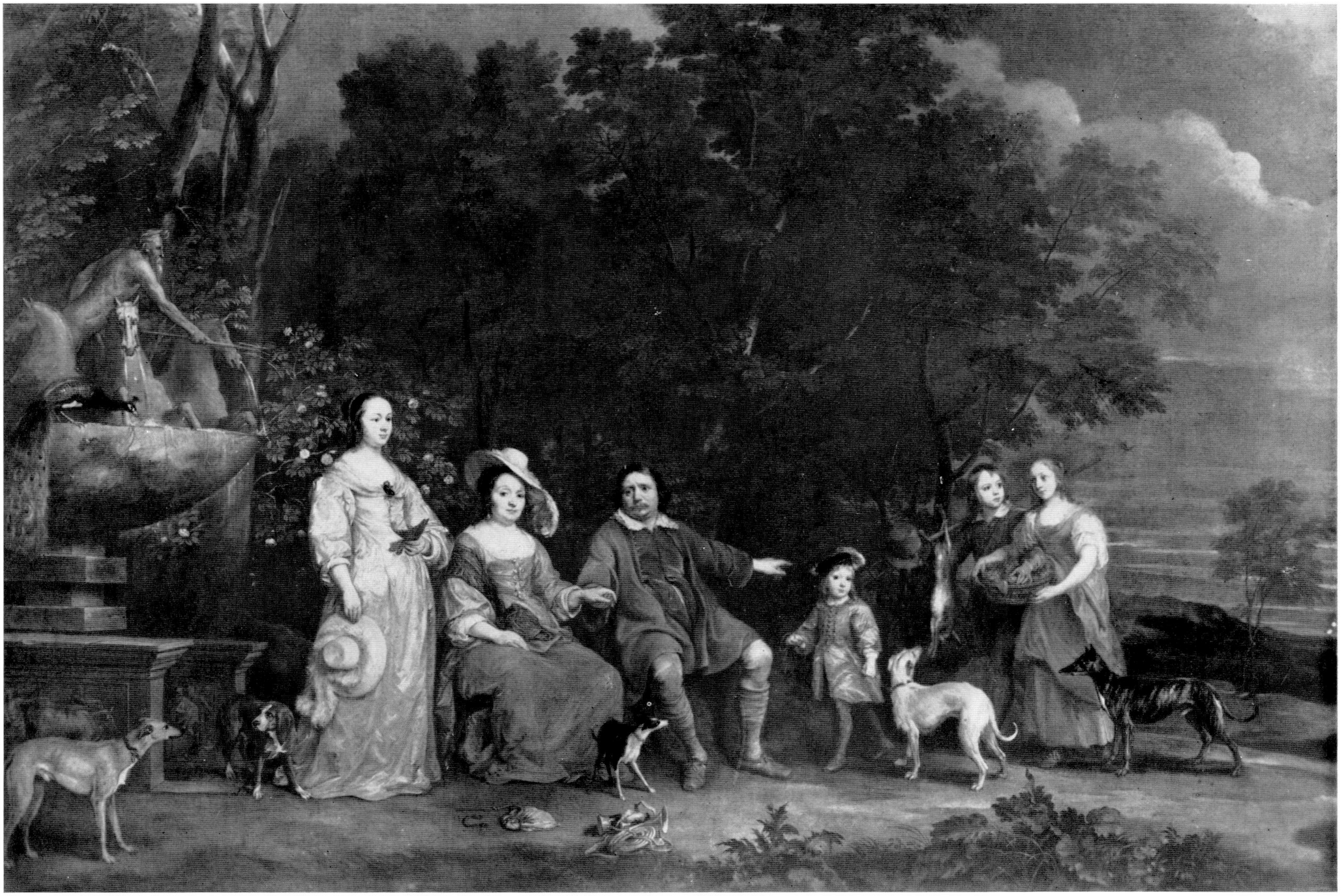

75

75 GONZALES COQUES (1614-1684), *A Family Group in a Landscape* ("*Le repos champêtre*"), 1647. London, Wallace Collection.
76 JACOB JORDAENS (1593-1678), *A Family Group in a Garden*. Madrid, Prado.

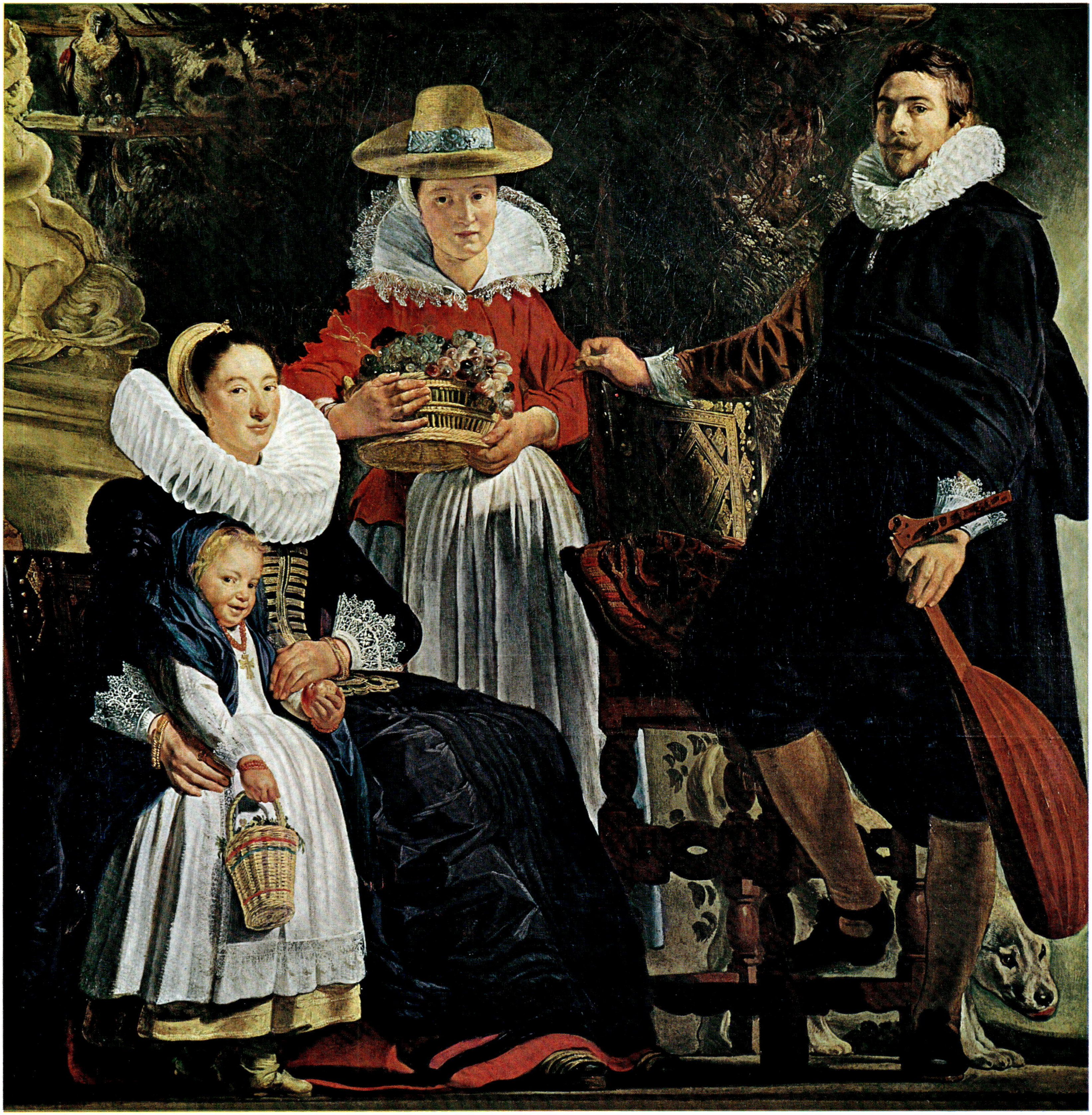
76

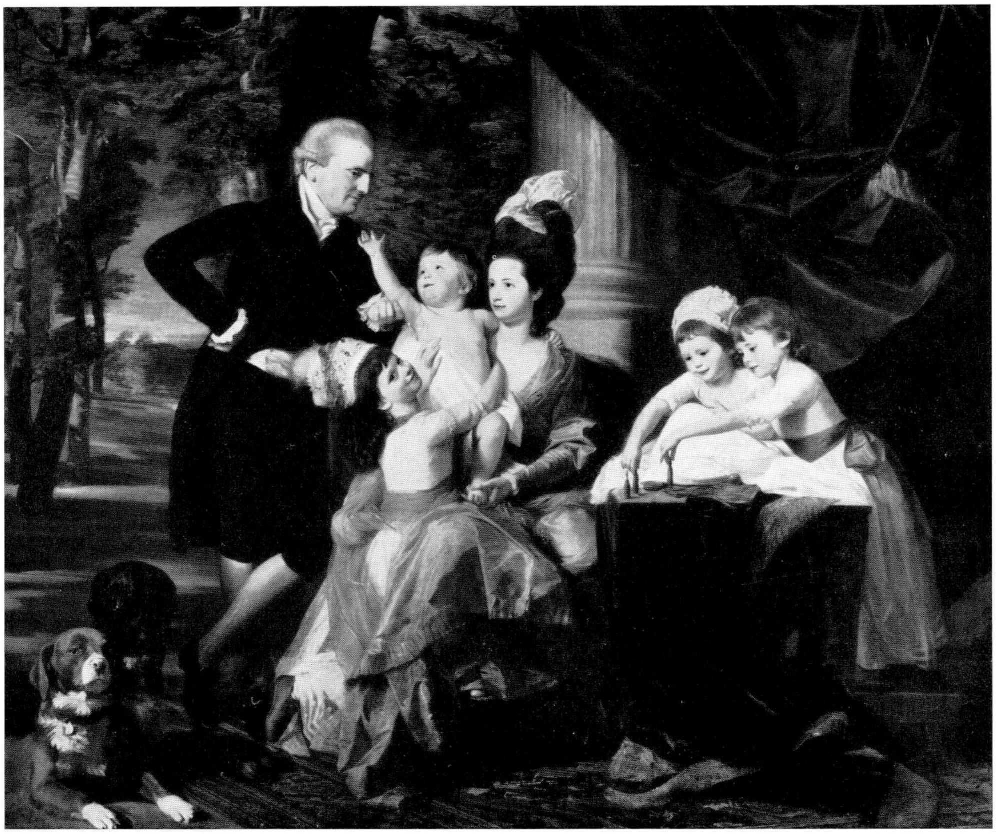

77

77 JOHN SINGLETON COPLEY (1738-1815), *The Family of Sir William Pepperrell*, 1778. Raleigh (N.C.), North Carolina Museum of Art.

78 JOHANN HEINRICH AUGUST TISCHBEIN (1722-1789), *The Ducal Family of Plöen-Holstein Taking Chocolate*. Hillerød, Nationalhistoriske Museum på Frederiksborg Slot.

with the eldest daughter in the role of little St. John. A fountain and caryatids appear in another family by Coques (London, National Gallery); here the children with their toys, the girl pushing a go-cart with the youngest child, the romping dogs, and the *puer mingens* or Manneken Pis darting his jet into the fountain basin add a gay note to the solemn scenery of the aristocratic park. In Coques' *Family on a Terrace* (Budapest, National Gallery), a canopy with gathered curtains overhangs a table covered with a Persian carpet, at which a cellist and an old gentleman are seated: a subordinate hands a letter to the gentleman and a group of women are sitting on the right near an organ, one of them holding a guitar; two figures are standing, a matron and a clergyman. These subjects are lined up against a background showing the façade of a country house, from which projects a porch, as in Rubens' *Walk*. There are columns, draperies, a balustrade, and a fountain in the distance in the *Visit* (fig. 268), in which Theodoor Boeyermans of Antwerp (1620-1678) portrayed the members of a patrician family receiving a Jesuit Father presented to them by another priest. Edwards justly remarks that this "is certainly a form of portraiture which is very closely related to the contemporary *tableaux de modes*".[1] Another follower of Van Dyck, Jacob van Oost the Elder (1601-1671), also shows a formal garden behind an architectural foreground (a flight of steps) in *A Family on a Terrace* (Bruges, Musée Communal des Beaux-Arts). Caspar Netscher (1635/6-1684) in a *Family Group* (Rotterdam, Boymans-van Beuningen Museum) places the classical triangular shape of family groups against the wing of a country house, with a fountain surmounted by a Cupid; a similar statue on the right is being wreathed with flowers by three children. In *The Grand Dauphin and his Family* (Louvre) Pierre Mignard (1612-1695) places the sitters in a baroque setting of furnishings, cushions, and ornate vases, with the usual column and a curtain supported by a putto. One has a glimpse of a formal park with tall urns like those of the park at Meudon; but the aristocratic character of the painting is somewhat relieved by the dog stretching towards his master to be stroked and by the little warrior armed with sword and spear on the right, preceded by a small barking dog. In 1694 Mignard painted

1 *Early Conversation Pictures* (London: Country Life Ltd., 1954), p. 39.

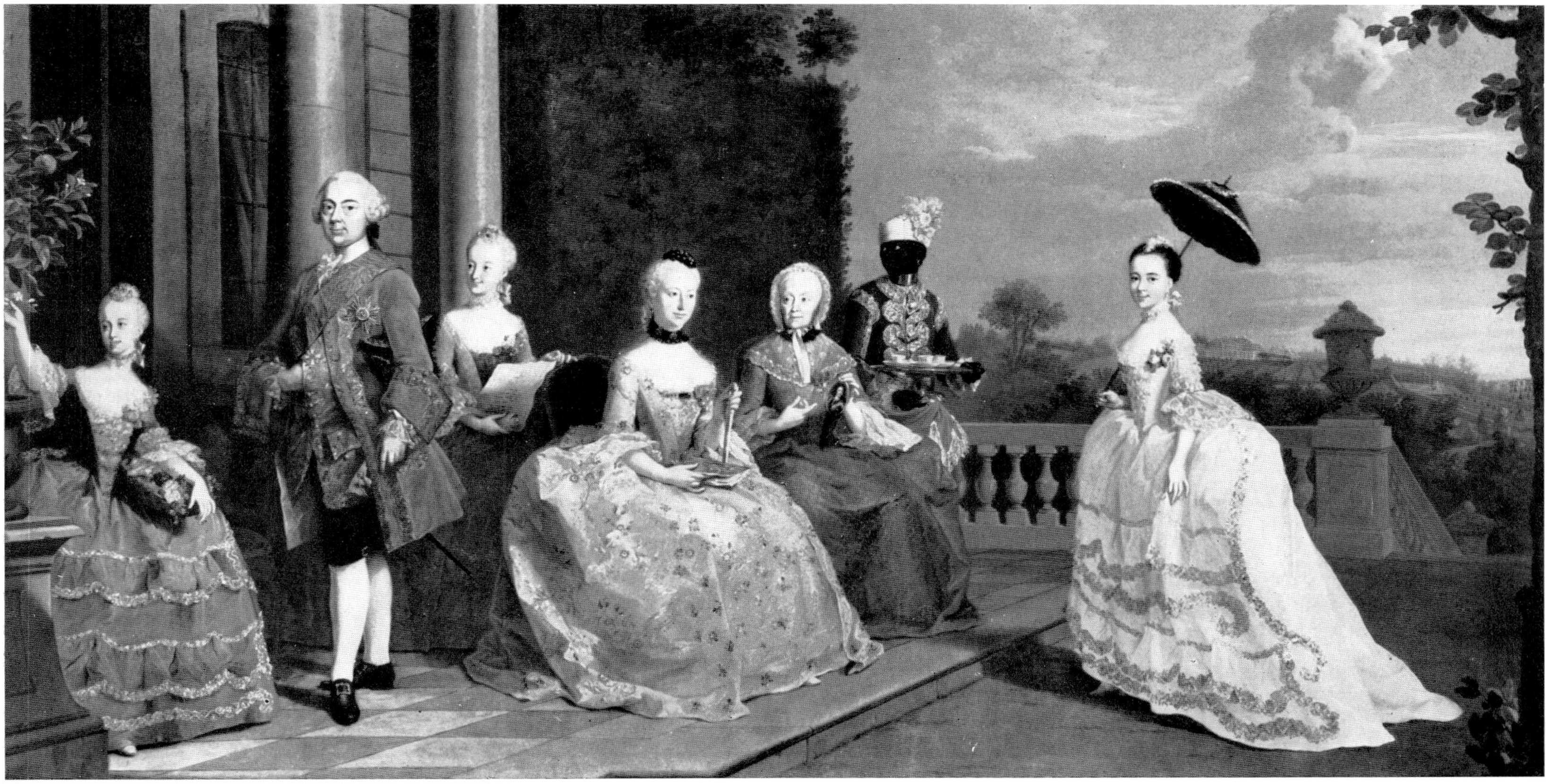

78

in a similar manner James II and Mary of Modena, exiles in France, at Saint-Germain; but of this lost picture only a reduced copy survives at Windsor Castle. Largillière adopts the traditional setting of columns, curtains, and arcades opening onto a park in order to present to us the *Boutin de Diencourt Family* (Musée des Beaux-Arts, Besançon) with, on the right, the usual triangular group and on the left the eldest children making music. One can see from this painting and from *A Family in a Garden* by Jan Josef Horemans the Elder (1682-1759) that the formal foreground of columns, statues of Cupid, and decorative urns, with the view of a garden (fig. 269), was adopted not only for patrician families (as by Johann Heinrich August Tischbein for the ducal family of Plöen-Holstein [fig. 78], with the dowager duchess showing the medallion of her late husband), but also for bourgeois families, with features appropriate to genre painting (such as the dog barking at a goat in Horemans' painting). Hogarth, in *Captain Woodes Rogers and his Family* (1729; Greenwich, National Maritime Museum), shows the circumnavigator of the world — hence the globe next to him — who rescued Alexander Selkirk (the prototype of Defoe's Robinson Crusoe) from the island of Juan Fernandez where he had been marooned for four years, close to a rampart adorned with a coat of arms. He is faced, against the background of a park, by his wife with a Pekinese and a maidservant carrying a dish of fruit; a river landscape with buildings (perhaps the Thames) stresses the motif of navigation; in that very year the captain sailed again to the Bahamas as Captain General and Governor. An unknown English painter of the eighteenth century in a *Family Group* once owned by Lady Hudson (present location unknown)[2] shows the usual triangular composition in a foreground formed by a tall pedestal, columns, draperies, and a balustrade with a view on a formal garden adorned with the statue of a gladiator. The children round the mother's swelling petticoat are like a brood of chickens surrounding a hen. Against the background of a colonnade in front of a landscape, John Smibert (1688-1751) commemorated (in a painting a small version of which is in the National Gallery of Ireland) George Berkeley's sojourn in Bermuda in 1729, in order to found "a universal college

2 Reproduced in SITWELL, *Conversation Pieces* (London: Batsford, 1936), ill. 25.

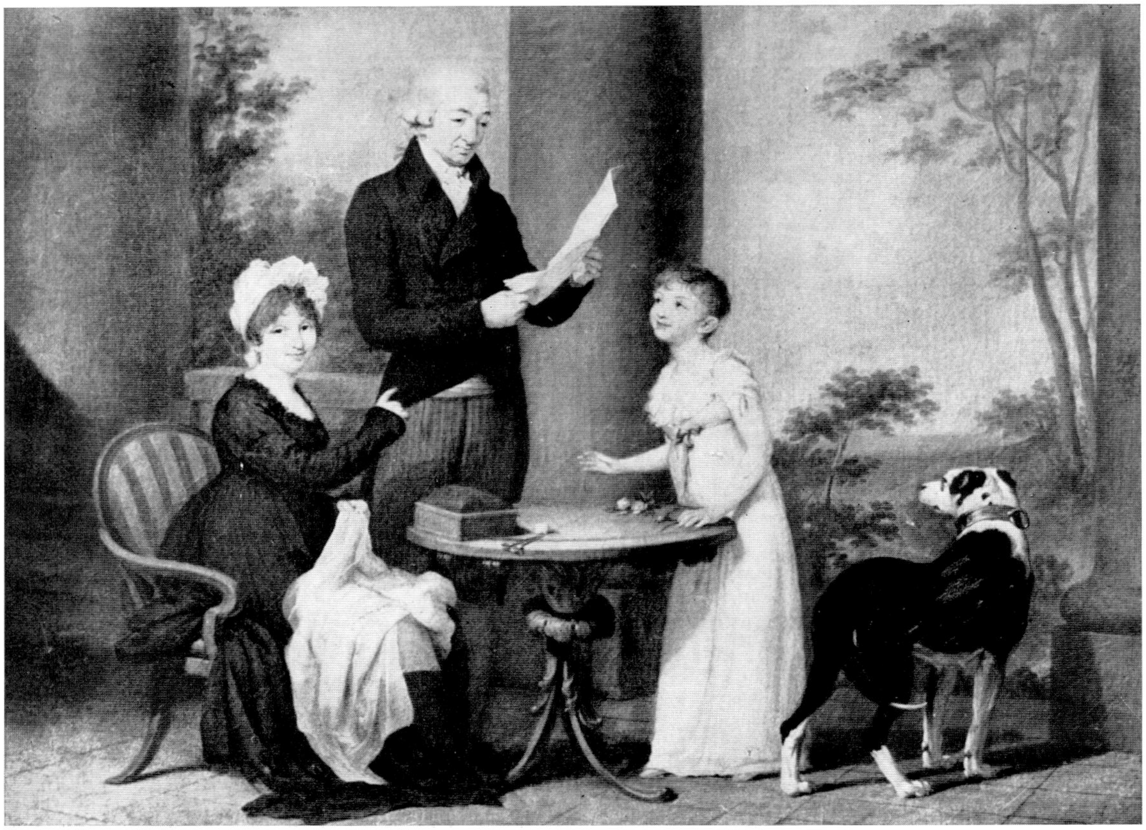

79

79 TEODORO MATTEINI (1754-1831), *Family Group in a Garden.* Present location unknown; formerly the property of Col. E. Francis Hutchinson.

80 FERDINAND VON RAYSKI (1806-1890), *The Schroeter Family on the Stairs of Bieberstein Castle*, c. 1850. Formerly in Dresden, Staatliche Gemäldegalerie; destroyed during the war.

of arts and sciences" for the Indians; we see him with his wife and friends, among whom is the painter on the extreme left. In 1772 William Joseph Williams — painting the portrait of *William Denning and his Family* (fig. 270) in the garden of their house in Wall Street, Manhattan — displays a tall pedestal with a vase in the foreground, as if to confer the dignity of an aristocratic park on that still unbelievably pastoral corner, with the river in the distance and a few village houses.

In 1778 Reynolds painted the most ambitious of his portraits, *The Marlborough Family* (The Duke of Marlborough Collection, Blenheim Palace), which Waterhouse calls "the most monumental achievement of British portraiture".[3] Here the archway, as formal as a triumphal arch, the draperies, the statue of the warrior with the Nike in his hand, and the twisted columns like those of the baldaquin in St. Peter's serve as a frame to a view of the park and a corner of Blenheim Palace. Historical, heroic painting, which then occupied the highest position in the hierarchy of art, is here applied to the conversation piece — which, however, remains such, notwithstanding the proportions of the picture. After this altogether monumental academy painting, we might envisage as faint echoes of a waning tradition Teodoro Matteini's *Family Group in a Garden* (fig. 79), with the columns of the portico of a country house; or J.A. Laurent's idyllic, mannered group of mother and daughters near the fountain in a garden, at the foot of stairs leading to an elegant neoclassical house (fig. 271); or *The Schroeter Family on the Stairs of Bieberstein Castle* by Ferdinand von Rayski (1806-1890), in which the family is coming down the stairs and the military tradition is being transmitted from father to son (fig. 80). Finally, in *Sunday Afternoon at the Artist's Home* by Theodor Hosemann (1807-1875), a painter who "knew his limits and did not overstep them, and was therefore a true Biedermeier"[4] (Berlin, Galerie Dr. Luz), the approaches to the house are not in the least monumental. The family is gathered in a humble arbour together with their friends; the women are seated at a table chattering, the men have started a game of bowls. Thus, on a minor, democratic note we may conclude our brief survey, which started from the thrones and the flights of steps of the *sacre conversazioni*.

3 *Painting in Britain, 1530-1790*, 2nd ed. (Harmondsworth and Baltimore: Penguin Books Ltd., 1962), p. 159.
4 PAUL WEIGLIN, *Berliner Biedermeier* (Bielefeld and Leipzig: Velhagen und Klasing, 1942), p. 76.

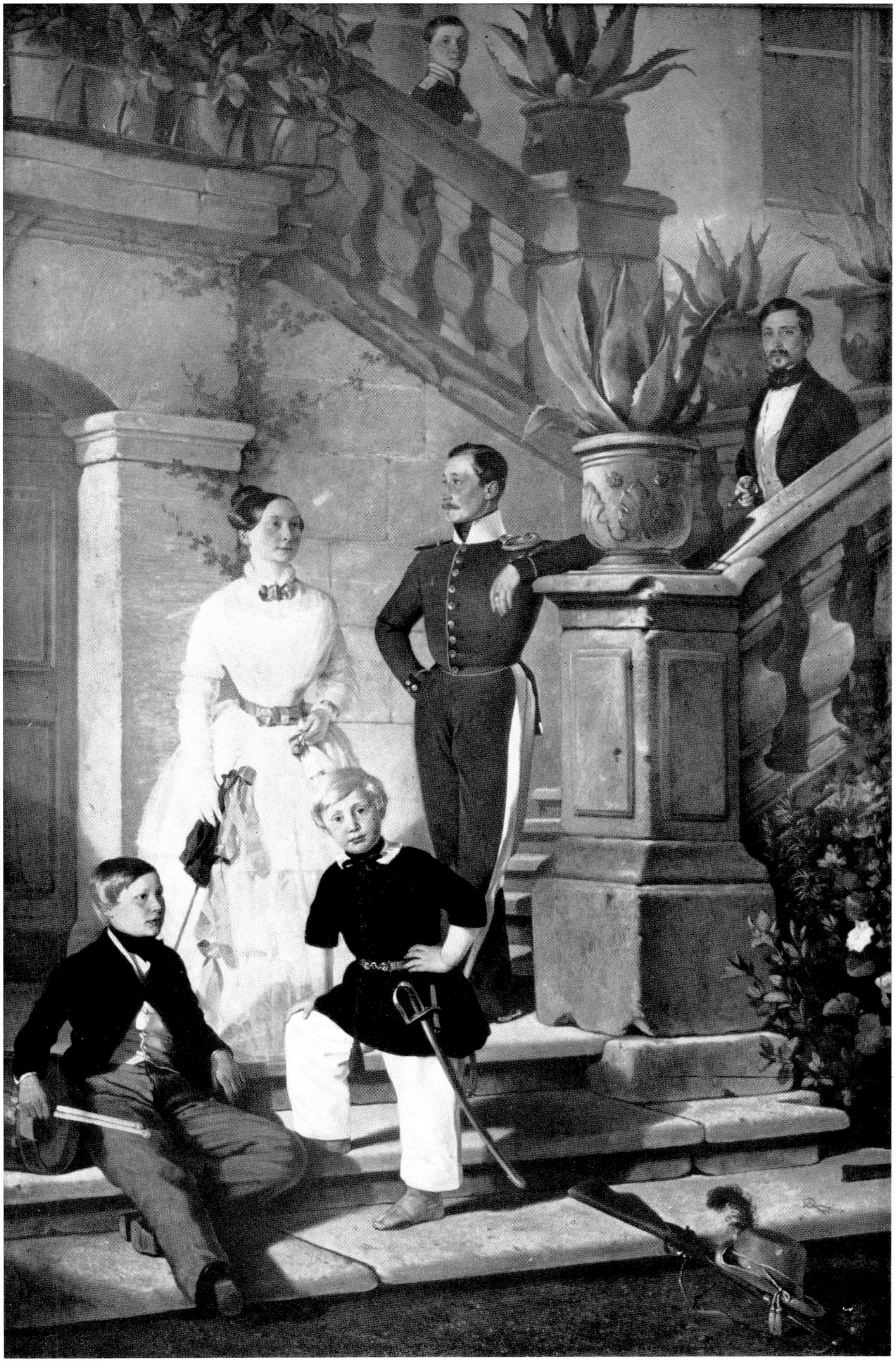

80

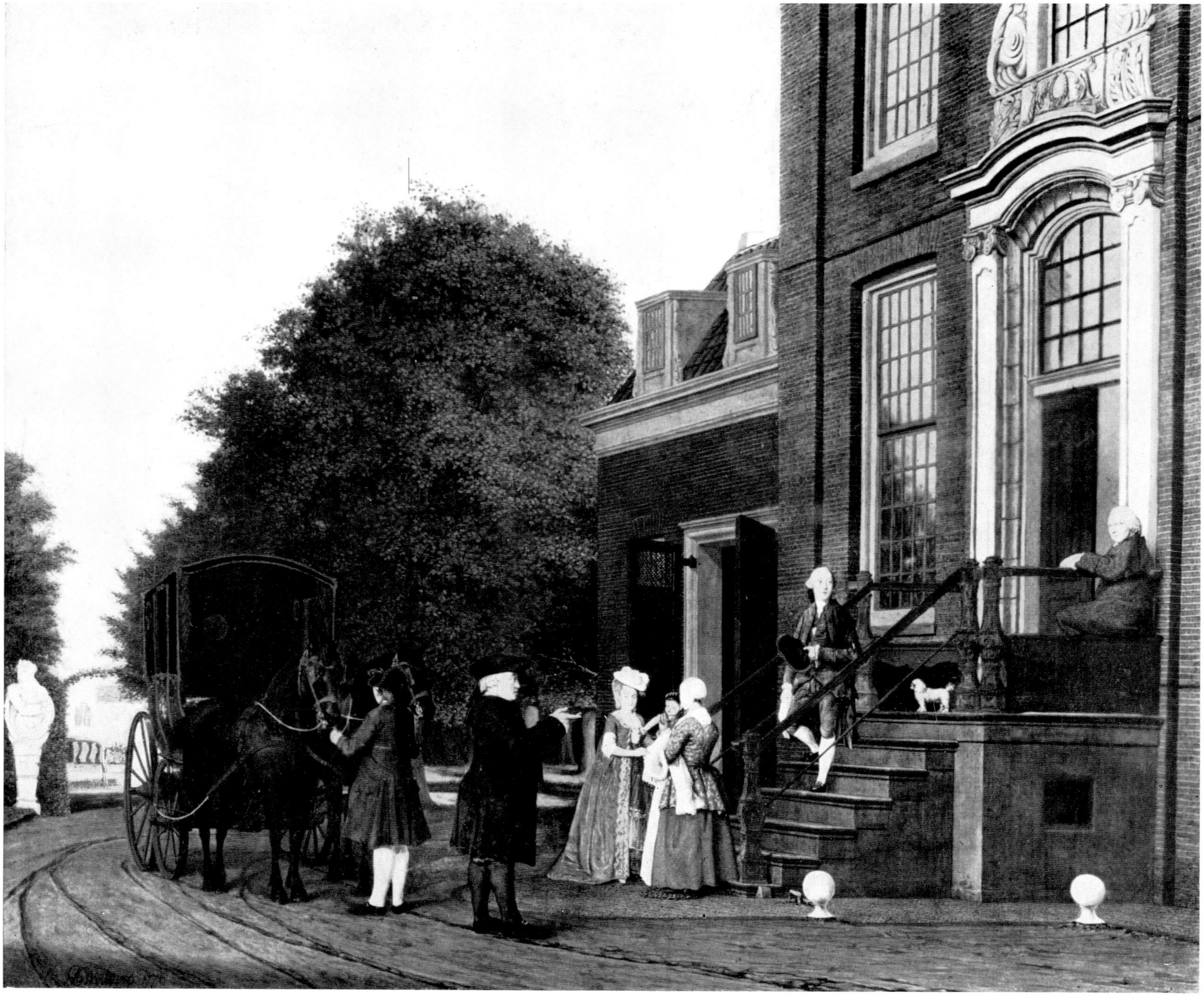

81

81 JAN GERARD WALDORP (1740-1808), *The Gildemeester Family at Frankendaal*, 1776. Present location unknown; photo Gemeentemusea, Amsterdam.

2. *In a courtyard or in the open air.*

The reader may have noticed that the last " conversation " we have described belongs rather to the category of those whose setting is a courtyard or the open air. The earliest composition of this kind is the celebrated one (fig. 82) of about 1660 by Pieter de Hooch (1629-1683). It has been suggested that the family is that of Willem van der Helm; the Nieuwe Kerke at Delft is seen in the background. Edwards[5] finds that this picture is inferior by far to the painter's other courtyard scenes because of the disturbing intersection of vertical lines by horizontals and because of the *pentimenti* (notably in the area where the old man is seated on the right), which make one think that de Hooch had not found his first attempt at assembling the sitters satisfactory. The present "T"-shaped disposition is a variant of the triangular pattern. This compositional scheme recurs a century later in the painting of the *Gildemeester Family* (fig. 81) at their Frankendaal country house by J.G. Waldorp.
Aelbert Cuyp's (1620-1691) *Family* (Amsterdam, Rijksmuseum) is a bourgeois counterpart of the patrician family group, such as we have found in Gonzales Coques. Instead of the park and the noble buildings, we have a decorous bourgeois house; instead of a smart equipage, a country cart. Rubens, in his famous *Self-portrait Walking with Hélène Fourment in their Garden* of about 1630-31, places his figures in a charming setting: the tails of the peacocks sweeping the ground provide an accompaniment to the pair's progress. The fountain, almost a musical symbol of the pleasantness of the park, is found again in the *Self-portrait with his Wife and their First-born* (Baronne Edouard de Rothschild Collection, Paris). In *The Park at Steen* (Vienna, Kunsthistorisches Museum; another version in the G. Dulière collection, Brussels), Rubens and his wife are no more than small figures lost in a vast landscape. In the same manner Adriaen van de Velde portrayed himself with his family in a landscape (Amsterdam, Rijksmuseum), and Jan van Belcamp (d. 1653) and Adriaen van Staelbent (1580-1662) showed Charles I and his court walking in Greenwich Park (Windsor Castle).
The first examples of open air " conversations " in England date from the end of the reign of Charles I. Another portrait (fig. 272) of a family walking out-of-doors is the one bearing the signature (discovered at the time of the work's restoration in 1910, but indecipherable now) of Bartholomeus van der Helst (1613-1670), whose composition is repeated in the Danish painter Johannes Senn's (1780-1871) *The Royal Family Walking* (about 1813; fig. 273), with Frederick VI, Queen Marie Sophie Frederika, and the Princesses Vilhelmina and Carolina. In the distance are the castle and church of Frederiksborg.[6]
In two " conversations " in the open air by Zoffany, also on riverbanks, we see in one the actor *David Garrick and his Wife Entertaining Dr. Johnson* in the garden of their country house on the Thames at Hampton (fig. 274); in the other (fig. 275), *Mr. and Mrs. Garrick at Shakespeare's Temple at Hampton* (also called " Pope's Villa ", which Robert Adam had built in the grounds of Garrick's country house in about 1756: in it stood Louis-François Roubiliac's statue of Shakespeare, now in the British Museum). These " conversations " were once in the possession of Garrick; a variant of the second (without the child and servant on the right) belonged to Horace Walpole and is now in America (New York, Wildenstein's; fig. 276). A painting by François Sablet (1745-1819) dating from the end of the eighteenth century represents *Princess Anna Maria Borghese (née Salviati) and her Sons Francesco and Camillo Walking in the Giardino del Lago at Villa Borghese* (fig. 83).
But the masterpiece of this kind of " conversation " is the portrait (fig. 277) of *The Painter's Parents with their Grandchildren* (1806) by Philipp Otto Runge (1777-1810). There is nothing conventional in this severe, almost surly pair of old people dressed in materials as hard as metal; solemnly taking a walk, they cross a sparse orchard and are considered with some misgiving by one of the grandchildren, who convulsively clutches a flower and who maybe a moment ago has given his grandmother the rose she holds in her left hand. One cannot suppose that she received it with a smiling face: one suspects that in the hands of such a formidable-looking woman any flower would soon wither. The house behind them looks like a prison wall; the free view of the water with its moored boats and of the sky (which is overcast by a black cloud) does nothing to dispel the sense of a cloistered and severe life communicated by the figures, the wall, and the toothed fence.
Gustave Courbet (1819-1877) instead has chosen a free horizon as a background for himself and the two persons who greet him in his famous *Bonjour, Monsieur Courbet* (1854; Montpellier, Musée Fabre).

5 *Early Conversation Pictures*, p. 37. 6 See J.B. HARTMANN, *København, Interiører og Prospekter, 1800-1860* (Copenhagen: Branner, 1948), ill. 6 and p. ii of the notes on the illustrations: " 'The august beloved family': thus it was called by Frederick VI, an absolute though bourgeois ruler who loved his subjects and brilliant uniforms and was a fop, though low in stature and unprepossessing ".

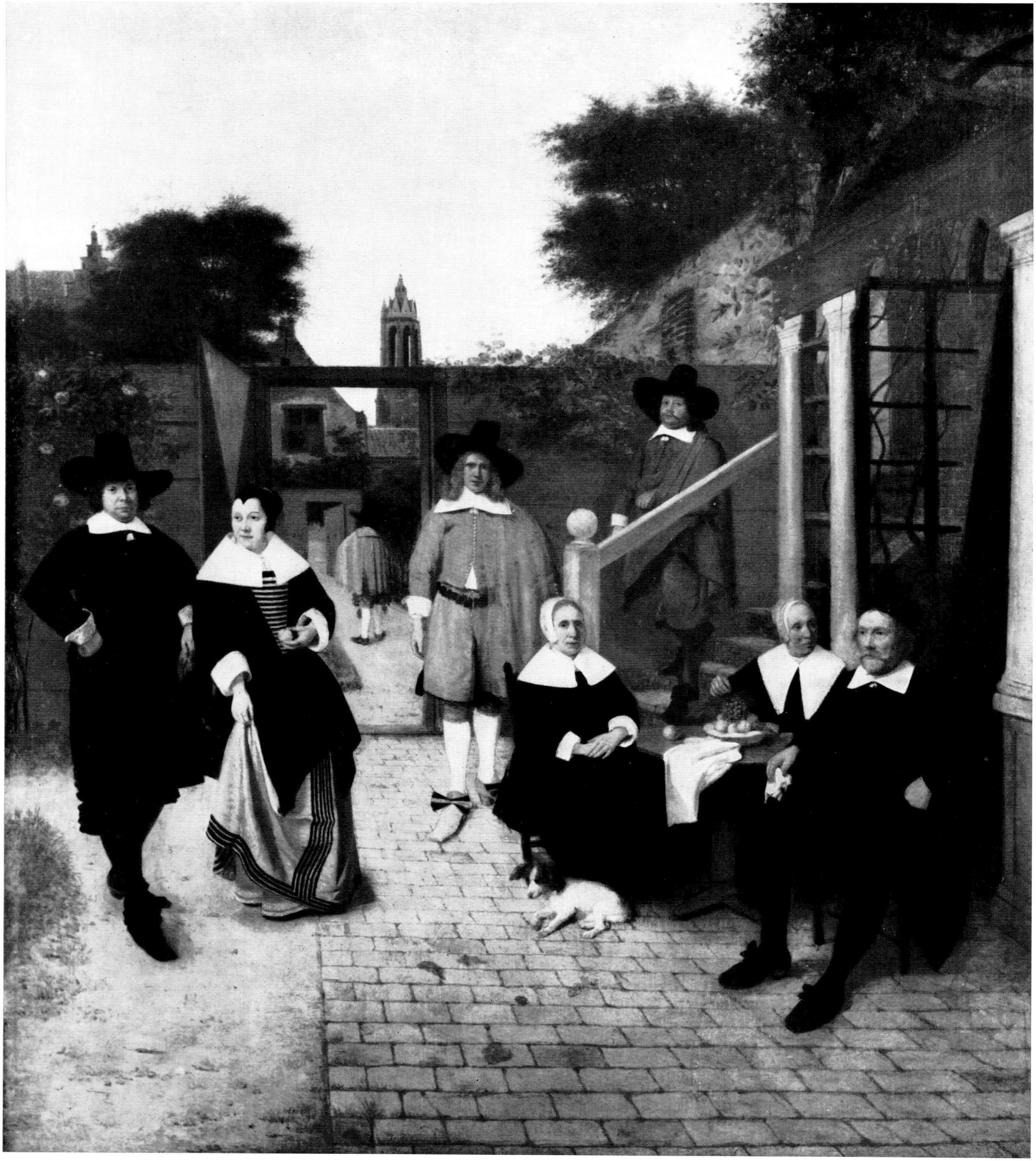

82

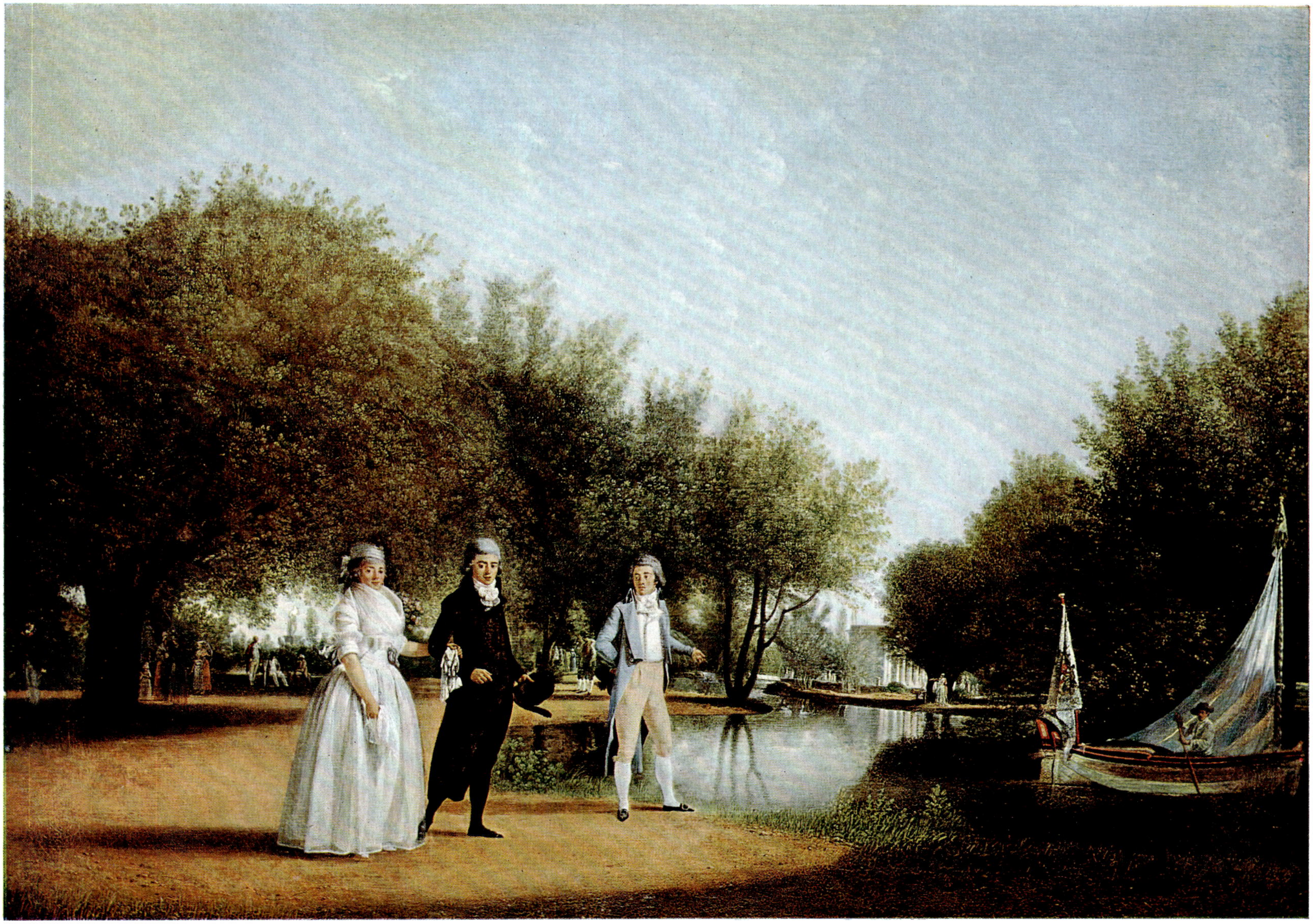

83

82 PIETER DE HOOCH (1629-1683), *Family in the Courtyard of a House*, c. 1660. Vienna, Akademie der bildenden Künste. 83 FRANÇOIS SABLET (1745-1819), *Princess Anna Maria Borghese and her Sons Francesco and Camillo Walking in the Giardino del Lago at Villa Borghese*. Rome, collection of Principe Giannangelo Borghese.

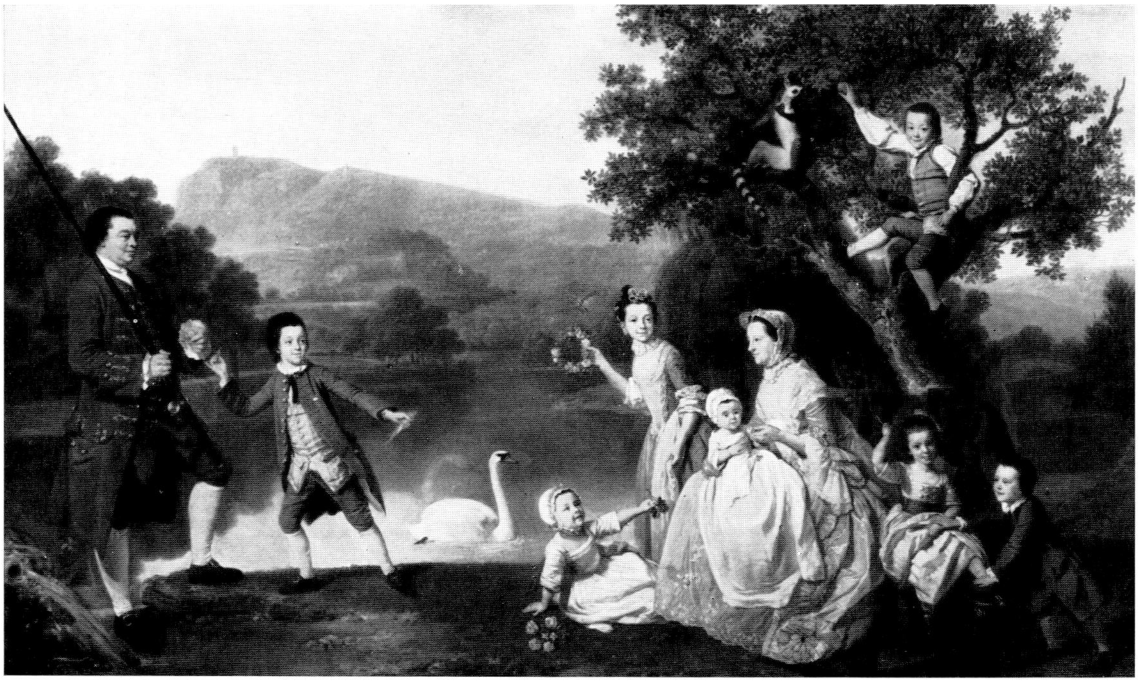

84

84 JOHANN ZOFFANY (1734/5-1810), *John, Third Duke of Atholl, and his Family on the Banks of the Tay at Dunkeld*, 1765-7. Blair Castle, Blair Atholl, collection of the Duke of Atholl.

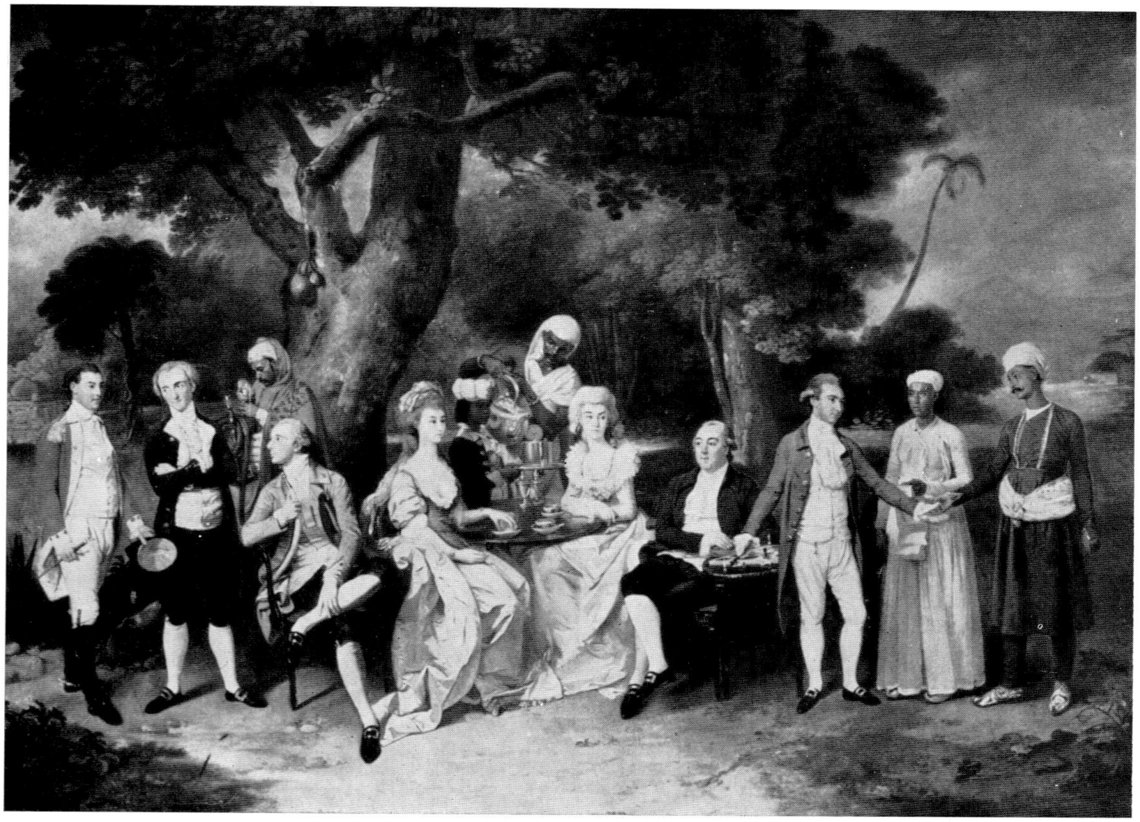

85

85 JOHANN ZOFFANY (1734/5-1810), *The Auriol Family*, 1783-9. Wilton House, Shenly (Hertfordshire), collection of R.H.N. Dashwood.

3. *Against a screen of foliage or with a tree in the middle.*

The most usual arrangement of a group in a park is against a clump of trees or round a single tree. Among the earliest painters to treat this motif was Frans Hals (1581/5-1666) with *The Family of Nicolas van Beresteyn* (Louvre) and *The Pair*, which, as we shall see, was the prototype of similar portraits by Gainsborough. The portrait of *Rubens with his First Wife Isabella Brant in the Honeysuckle Thicket* (1609; Munich, Alte Pinakothek) shows a similar arrangement, but with a very limited background. A cheerful animation throbs in Hals' group at the Louvre: a diminutive, familiar *kermesse*, almost a rout of romping children, as if Titian's *Worship of Venus* had been translated into a bourgeois idiom.

The motif was introduced into England by Sir Peter Lely (1618-1680), the Dutch painter who during the Restoration dominated the English scene as Van Dyck had dominated the Caroline period. His real name was van der Faes and he was born in Westphalia of Dutch parents. He knew how to group people with more skill than van Dyck, and his groups " are the forerunners of a kind of picture which was to remain fixed in the British tradition ".[7] The most famous of his " conversations " is the one wrongly called *The Artist and his Family* (fig. 278; London, Courtauld Institute Galleries). Waterhouse[8] denies that this is a portrait group and classes it rather with Lely's *Europa* at Chatsworth. Sitwell accepts the tradition according to which the bass-viol player is the artist himself, and his wife Ursula is represented on the right in four different attitudes. In any case, the painting offered a model of an open-air " conversation " with trees for a background. Moreover, at about the same period or a little earlier (c. 1658) Jan Mytens (1614-1670), who had taken refuge on the Continent after the execution of Charles I, painted Sir Charles Cotterell — a man of letters and courtier, sometime Master of Ceremonies to that king — with his family, also against a screen of foliage and a landscape (fig. 280). Another foreign painter who influenced the development of the English outdoor " conversation " in a park was Philip Mercier, the son of a French Huguenot, born in Berlin in 1689 (he died in London in 1760). According to Waterhouse,[9] it was perhaps Mercier who in about 1725-26 introduced into England the conversation piece with small-scale figures, to be followed by Dandridge, Hogarth, Charles Philips, and Gawen Hamilton. The small dimensions lessened the price of the painting; hence the popularity of this form of portraiture. Mercier worked in the wake of Watteau, and we shall mention him again further on. He influenced in his turn the Englishman Bartholomew Dandridge (b. 1691, still alive in 1754), who in this way echoed indirectly certain of Watteau's themes, such as the *Embarkation for Cythera*, of which he gives a provincial version in *The Price Family* (fig. 279). Here, together with Uvedale Price (a name destined to become famous through his namesake, Sir Uvedale Price, the author of the widely known *Essay on the Picturesque*, 1794) and his wife Anne (on the right), we see their son Robert (the last figure on the left) and members of the Greville and Rodd families. In another *Family Group in a Park* (fig. 283) of obvious French inspiration and ascribed to Dandridge, the scene is also on the bank of a river or canal, in which is mirrored a little girl reminiscent in style of the manner of Dandridge's contemporary, Nattier. Dandridge followed Poussin's method in his compositions: as Vertue reports, he first made little models of the sitters in order to study the play of light and shadow.

In the " conversations " of which we have just spoken we already find the features which Johann Zoffany (or Zauffelij; born in Frankfurt 1734-5, died 1810) was to develop triumphantly after 1760. Zoffany, in collaboration with Benjamin Wilson (1721-1788), had specialized in theatrical conversation pieces in which celebrated actors were represented in the roles in which they had particularly distinguished themselves; a genre, Waterhouse remarks, which bears witness to the progress in the social position of actors, " just as the conversation piece proper had appeared with the emergence of the prosperous middle classes ".[10] Having freed himself from dependence on Wilson in about 1762, Zoffany came to live in the house of David Garrick, for whom he painted several theatrical conversation pieces (Waterhouse thinks that Garrick himself promoted this kind of picture, as he had a good flair for publicity); but, while continuing to paint theatrical " conversations " until 1770, he devoted himself more and more to conversation pieces proper, taking advantage of the vogue prevailing under George III of having groups of children in small pictures, or family groups including children. Introduced to the King by Lord Bute, whose children he painted in two pictures which we shall see later, from about 1766 on he enjoyed the patronage of the sovereign who, being a

7 WATERHOUSE, *Painting in Britain*, p. 61. 8 Ibid., p. 62. 9 Ibid., p. 115. 10 Ibid., p. 217, and for the following dates, p. 219.

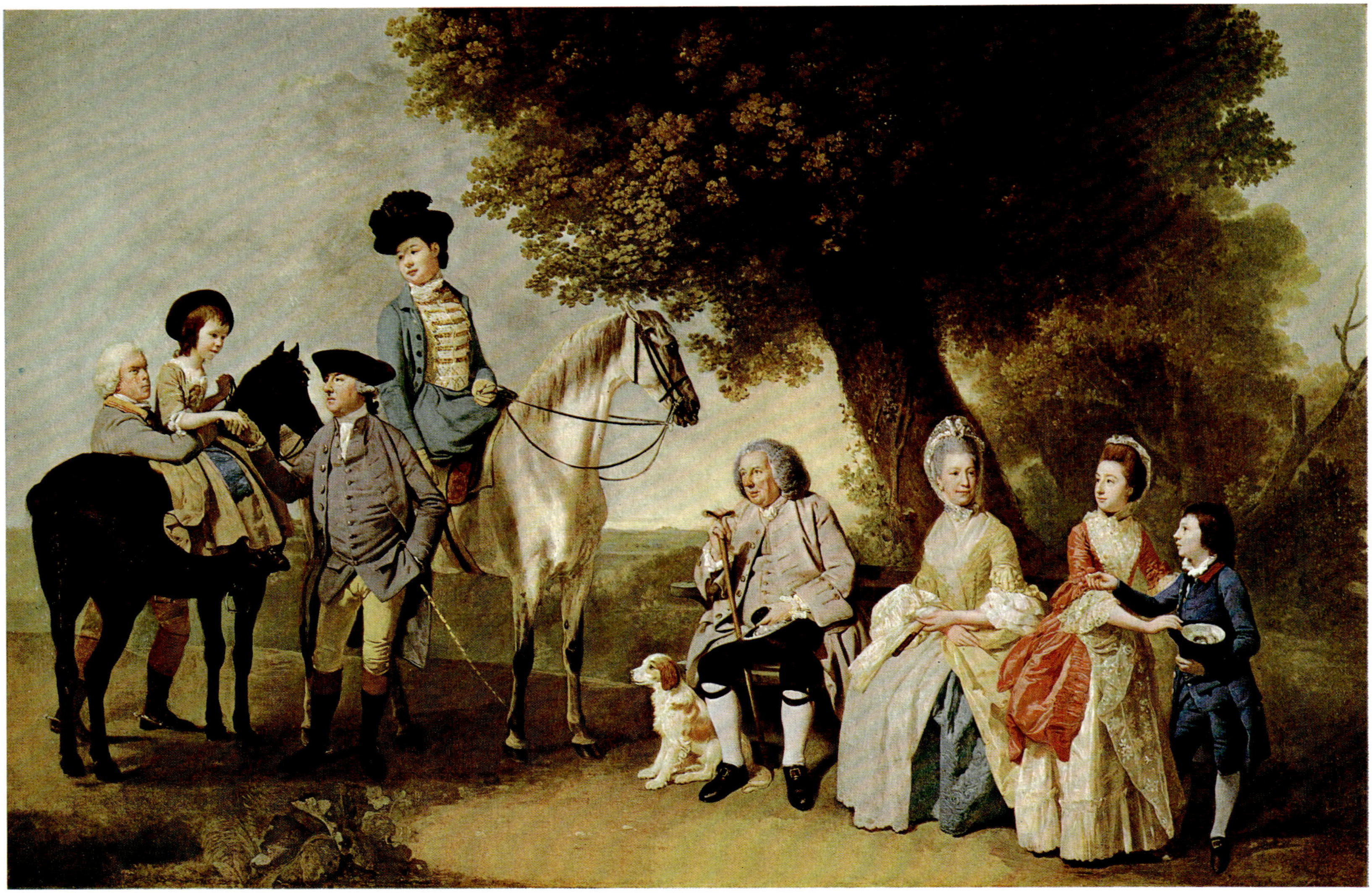

86

86 JOHANN ZOFFANY (1734/5-1810), *The Drummond Family*, c. 1765-9. Washington, D.C., collection of Mr. and Mrs. Paul Mellon.

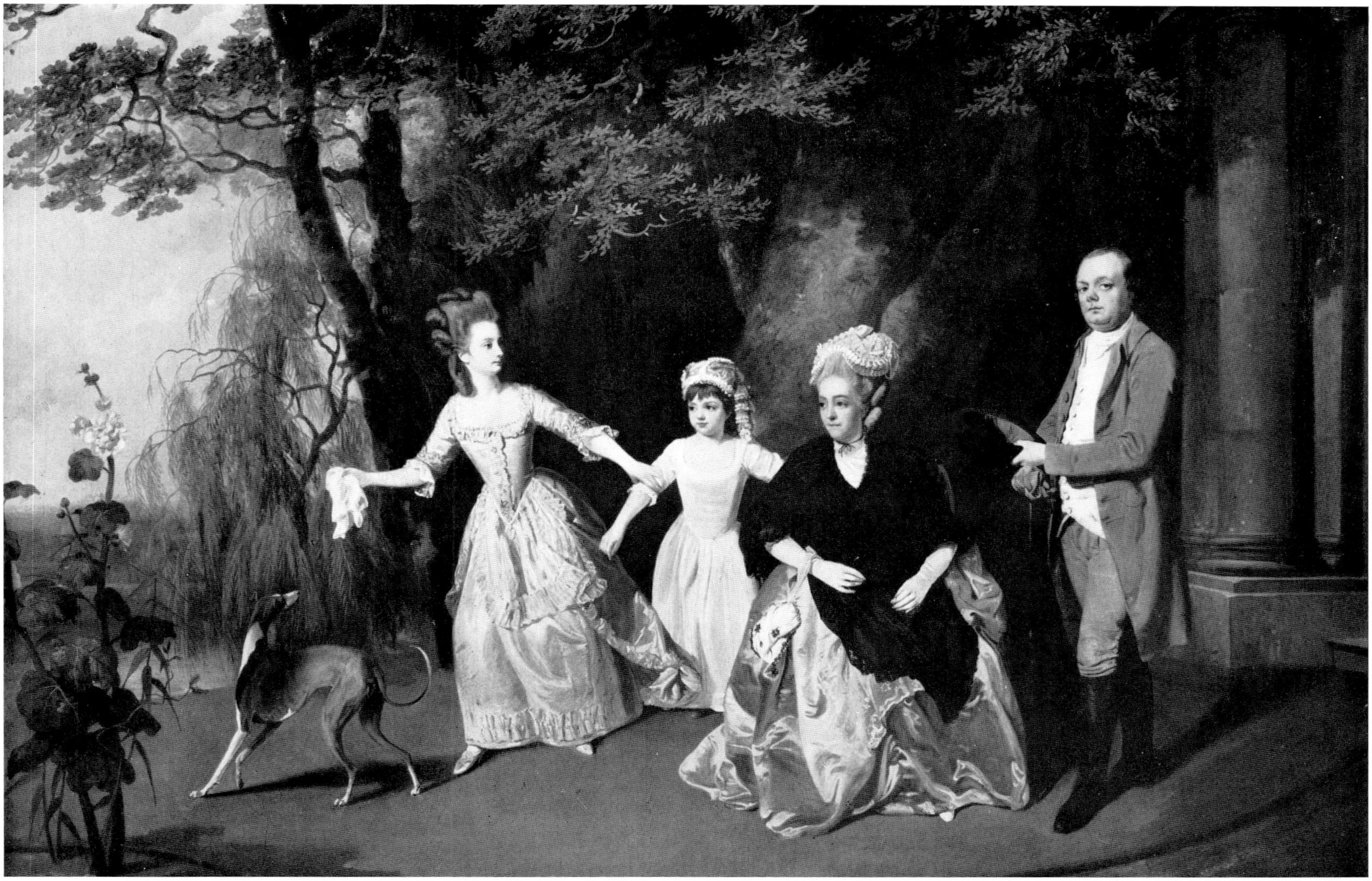

87

87 FRANCIS WHEATLEY (1747-1801), *The Wilkinson Family*. Detroit, Institute of Arts.

German, loved the painter's neatness and his taste for domestic scenes.

Zoffany, though a German and a Jew, has truly interpreted the quintessence of English domesticity. His family portraits no doubt breathe intimacy, but it is an intimacy which is strictly limited to the people portrayed in the paintings; it is not communicative and is far from inviting the outsider to join the group. Moreover, they breathe pride of race and caste and a vast satisfaction with the fine, smart, worldly things among which the subjects live. The scene is a noble room or luxuriant countryside. The room boasts precious furnishings, silver and a china tea service, oriental carpets of rare patterns; the countryside is an annex of the manor house, and the thoroughbred horses and dogs appear at the sides of their masters in these exclusive elysiums.

In his theatrical conversation pieces Zoffany had represented the scenes of a fictitious world — the world of the theatre — and Hogarth, in a picture which can be considered a forerunner of the type, had already shown a scene of *The Beggar's Opera* (1728-29). Zoffany, in these conversation pieces, displays before our eyes a world which is nearly as artificial in its daily ceremonial, almost a " Rich Man's Opera ". But instead of the pathos of melodrama, we have here restraint and reserve: so much reserve that often the furnishings are more expressive and expansive than the people, and we have, as Sitwell wittily remarks, " interiors of live objects and inanimate persons "; so much restraint that at times one has the impression that these magnificent gentlefolk have gathered round them all their precious things as for a funeral pyre. But one should not think of a monumental scene like Delacroix' *Mort de Sardanapale!* The appropriate element to consume in an exclusive hecatomb the fine worldly things owned by these English gentlefolk is not the roaring fire but the still water, the water of an aquarium.

And, indeed, we linger before these paintings as before the glass showcases of an aquarium: or rather before their photographs, because most of these family portraits are inaccessible unless one has had the chance of seeing a great number of them together at an exhibition such as the one which was held in Sir Philip Sassoon's house in London before the last war, in 1930. They nearly always belonged to the descendants of the people portrayed, who kept them jealously in the places where they were painted, so that the original of that very table or clock you saw in the picture was nearby in the room, materially present. This, however, belongs to the past; in our time, the English aristocracy having been ruined by death duties, their paintings have often been sold, and if they have not been purchased by museums it is difficult to establish their present locations.

Once scattered, for how long will one be able to meet the English type which is reproduced in these paintings, which is as representative of yesterday's England as the Beatles are of today's? The persons in these paintings have the stylized standoffishness of brilliantly coloured fish; the children of the family, fixed by the painter in playful and charming attitudes, present an image of small-fry frisking among motionless, stolid, full-grown fish. And the aquarium is lit by the sun of that century which never seemed to set, the sun of the Enlightenment. It has been arrested only for us, in these canvases; it is as if dancing automata, once wound down, had remained fixed forever in their essential poses, while the music which accompanied their antics continues to buzz in our ears.

This quality is evident in a painting like *The Minuet* by Zoffany (fig. 152), which we shall consider later, or in the *Phaeton and Pair* by Stubbs (London, National Gallery); but the same may be said of most of these conversation pieces, thanks to the neat precision of the painters of a school which, already detached from Watteau's fairy world, had as yet no presentiment of David and archaeological imitation. Their minute realism — Zoffany's in particular — was ennobled by a heraldic elegance which, penetrating beyond appearances, showed glimpses of the type, the perfect exemplar: the complete gentleman, the thoroughbred horse or dog, the perfectly planned park, the inimitably intimate room. It is a realism which reflects not so much life as the *douceur de vivre*. The hallmark which this kind of art has in common with the most exquisitely English products (furniture by famous eighteenth-century cabinetmakers; coaches; clothes and footwear by renowned firms) is quality.

The most perfect interpreter of this aristocratic society — it seems strange, but on the contrary it is very natural if one thinks of analogous cases, Proust for instance — was, as we have said before, a Bohemian Jew, who was also — as we might have expected — something of a snob and a megalomaniac in the manner of Lion Feuchtwanger's Jew, Süss, because he made his servants wear showy liveries, styled himself baron, and when he went to India assumed the title of "Sir". On the other hand, Hogarth, the initiator of conversation pieces in England, was — as we have said — too bourgeois, dramatic, and satirical to

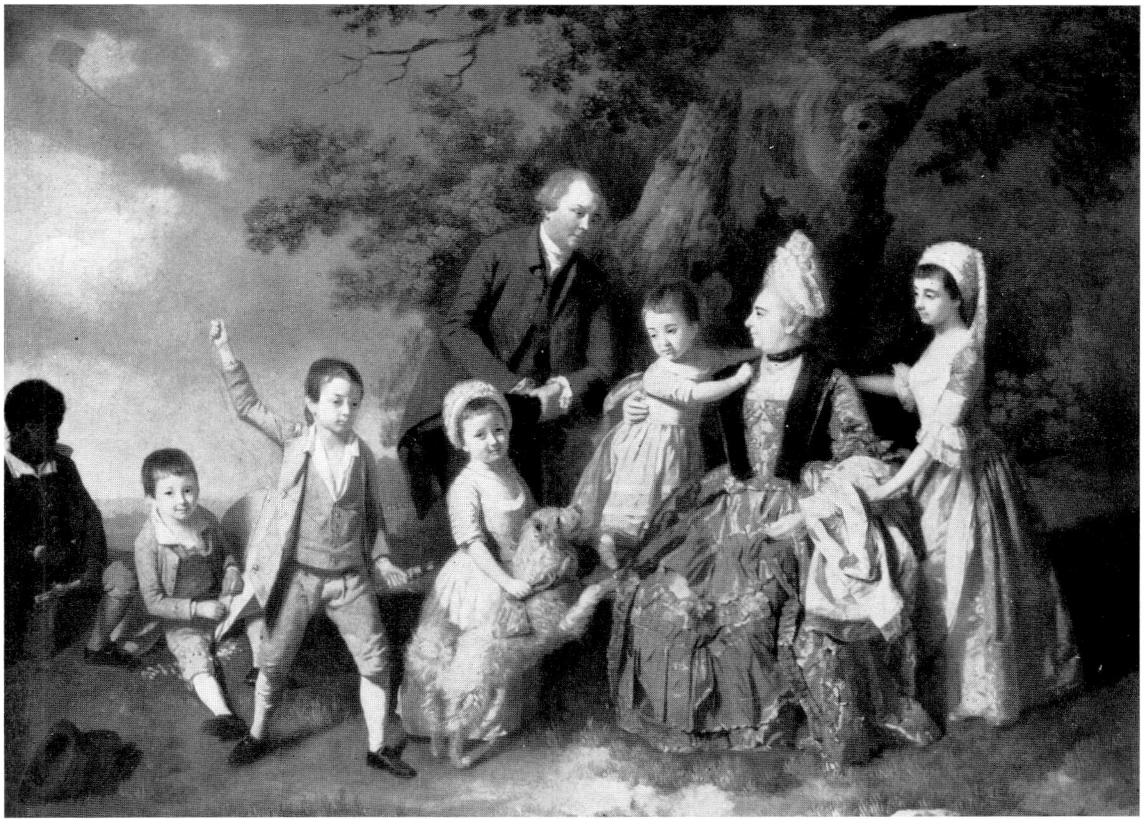

88 FRANCIS WHEATLEY (1747-1801), *A Family in a Landscape*. London, Tate Gallery.

88

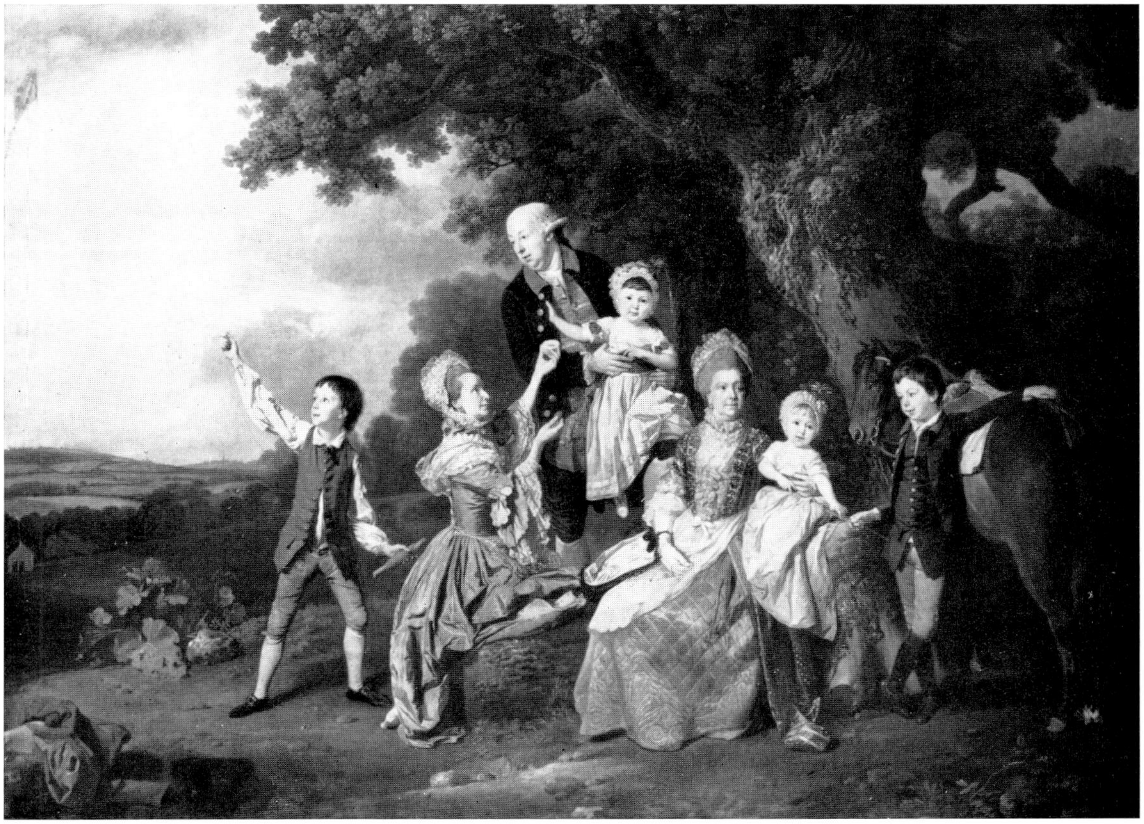

89 attr. to JOHANN ZOFFANY (1734/5-1810), *The Bradshaw Family*. London, Tate Gallery.

89

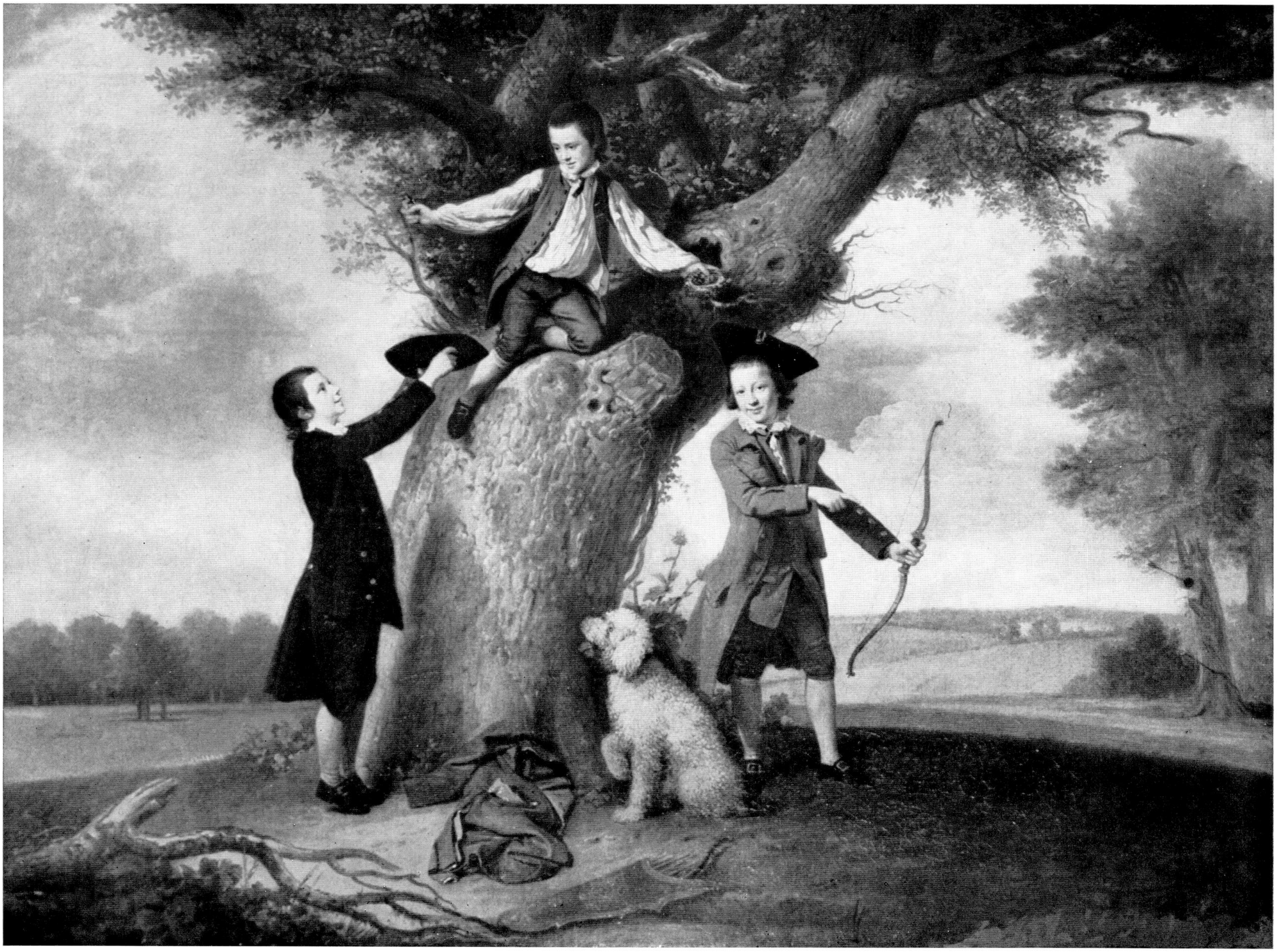

90

90 JOHANN ZOFFANY (1734/5-1810), *The Three Sons of John, Third Earl of Bute*. Mount Stuart, Rothesay (Isle of Bute), collection of Lord Bute.

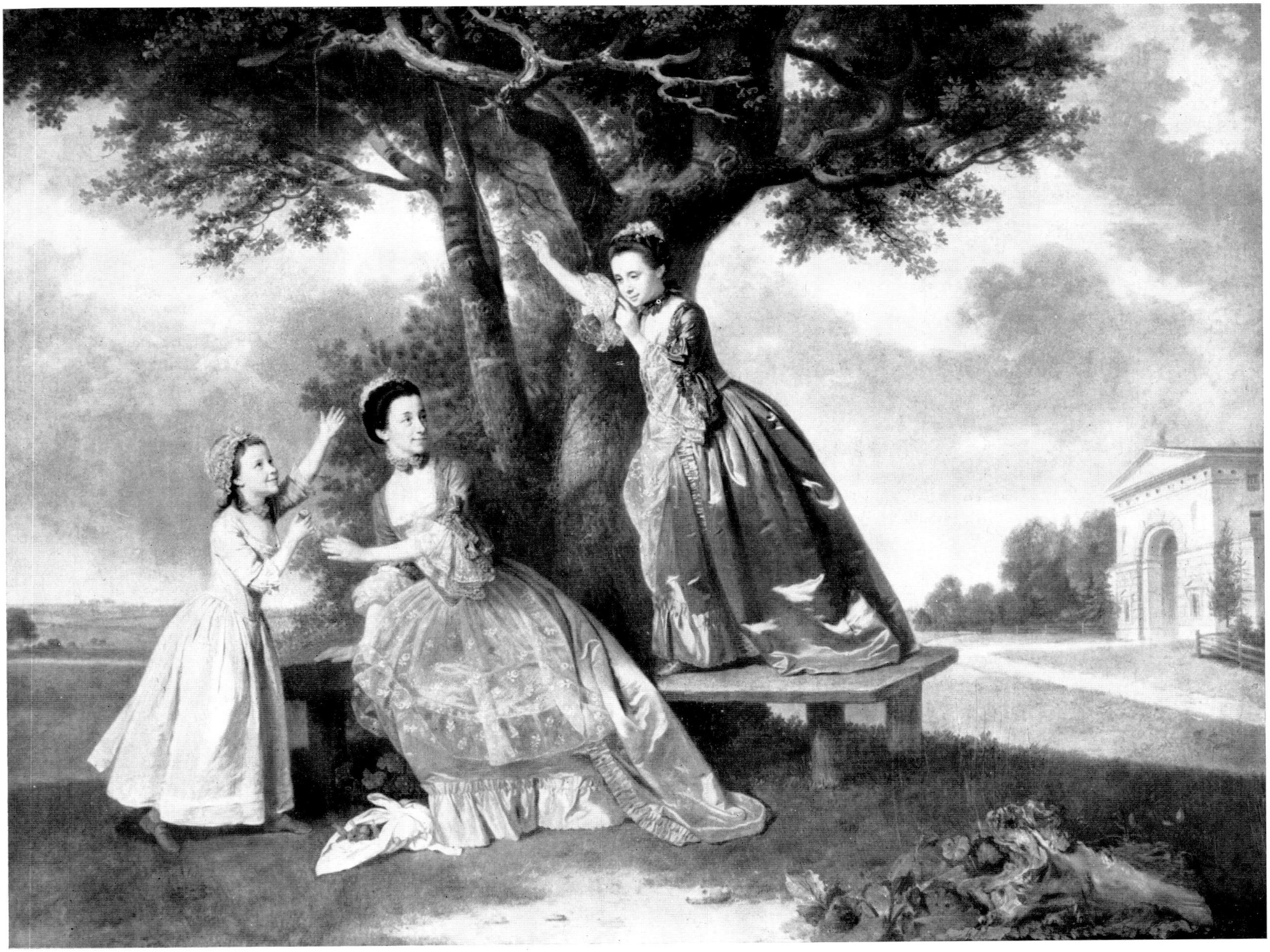

91

91 JOHANN ZOFFANY (1734/5-1810), *The Three Daughters of John, Third Earl of Bute*. Mount Stuart, Rothesay (Isle of Bute), collection of Lord Bute.

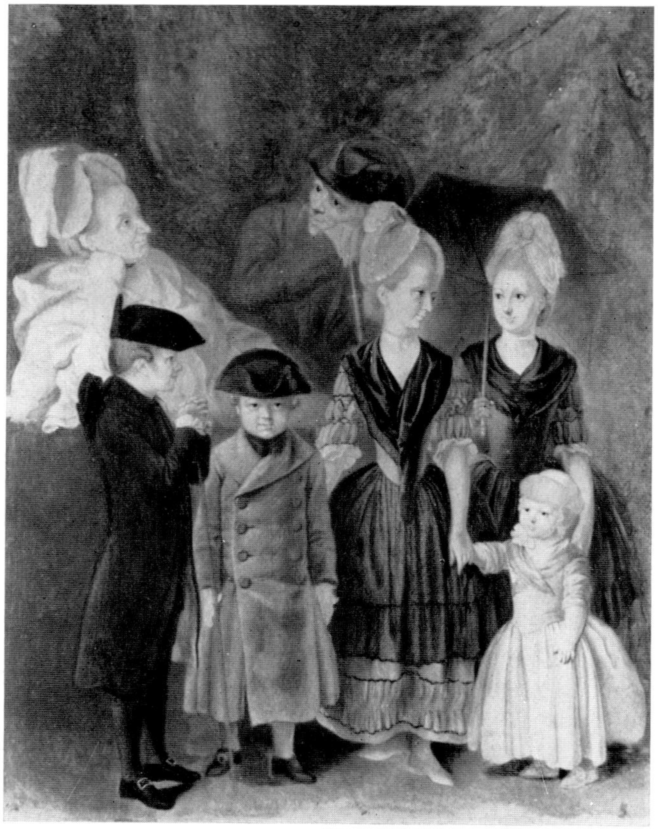

92

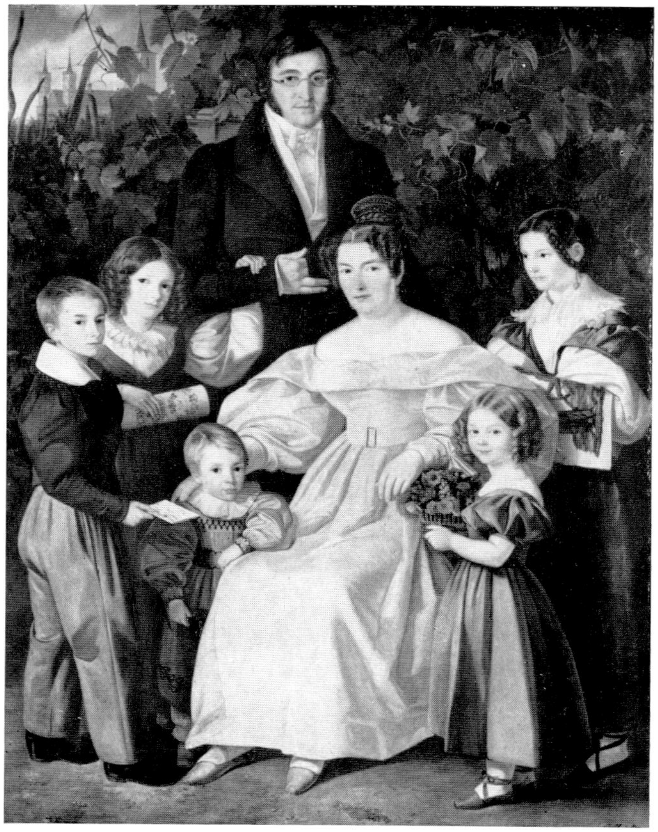

93

make a good painter of those human aquariums, family portraits. He lacked the indispensable impersonality, or, one could almost say, he was not sufficiently schizoid, whereas the feminine pliancy typical of many refined Jews could perfectly well mirror a social milieu without allowing it to disintegrate under the stress of individual reactions. In Hogarth we are aware of a power beyond the aristocratic world which he depicts; we are aware of Beer Street and Gin Lane, of Burns' " Jolly Beggars " and the French Revolution. But Zoffany paints an eternal present; he is only concerned with collecting in a single picture all the delightful things the subject may suggest. Zoffany's climate is well defined by a sentence in Jane Austen's *Emma* (vol. III, ch. xiv): " They sat down to tea — the same party round the same table — how often it had been collected! — and how often had her eyes fallen on the same shrubs in the lawn, and observed the same beautiful effect of the western sun!"

These people must have talked (we feel, looking at their " conversations ") as they would have danced: there was nothing clumsy about them, and they seem to move according to a secret rhythm, a rhythm of music, as in a very slow dance figure. The serving of tea is a ritual; even the teapot has a ritual name: it is the tea urn. Was theirs an artificial life? Or rather, does it not seem that the spirit of the open country enters the room from the luminous windows, pervades everything, and that there is after all no great difference between one of the beautiful plants in the park and one of these dignified persons?

Somebody, who had not necessarily read Carlyle, has said in our time: " Better to live one day as a lion than a hundred years as a sheep ". This opinion, in the light of romanticism, has been considered heroic; Jane Austen and her world did not think so. The eighteenth century, which loved an easy, long life, transmitted to us a civilization that man has so far been unable to surpass; our debased romantics, who believed they acted as supermen by choosing the one day of a lion's life, have at the most succeeded in destroying the traces of that civilization. The romantic age has said " Be like a lion! " through the mouths of all its prophets and thinkers. But the century of which Jane Austen has given us such a supreme portrait seems to say: " Be like a tree, that

92 DANIEL CHODOWIECKI (1726-1801), *The Painter with his Family in the Tiergarten*, 1772. East Berlin, Märkisches Museum.

93 SIMON MEISTER (1796-1844), *The Werbrunn Family*, 1834. Cologne, Wallraf-Richartz-Museum.

94 JANUARIUS ZICK (1730-1797), *A Father and Son and Mercury in a Garden*. Bonn, Rheinisches Landesmuseum.

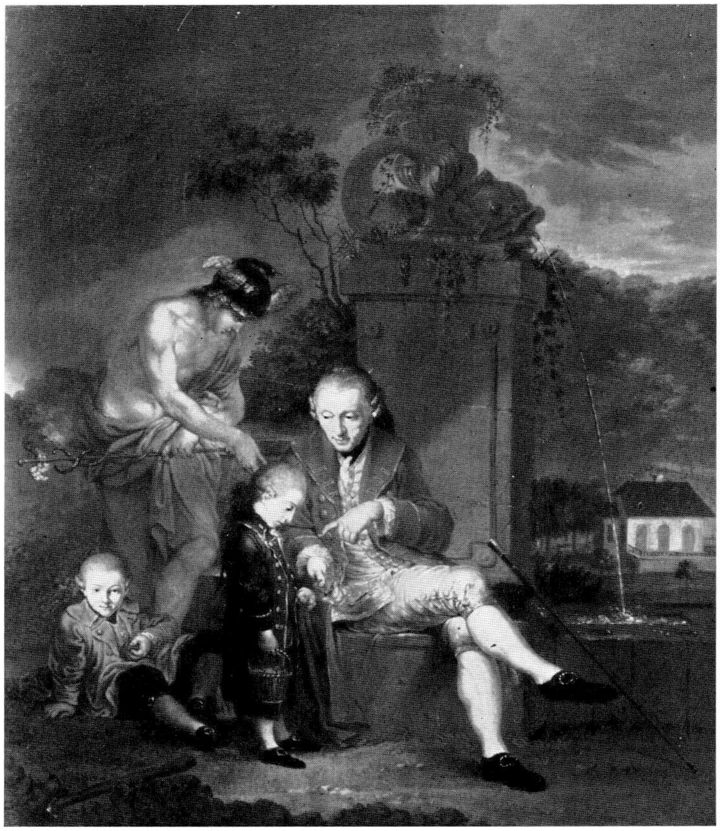

94

gives shelter, and is wise and generous ". A close sympathy linked men to trees, to beautiful local plants. It is therefore not surprising that most of the English conversation pieces take place in the open air, in the vicinity of age-old trees. In *The Family of Sir William Young* (Liverpool, Walker Art Gallery) we find sylvan scenery, and even a 'cellist at the centre like the one in the painting by Lely that is supposed to represent the artist's family. The figures are dressed in costumes of the van Dyck period, as if the painter intended to refer to Lely's group; Sir William, who was created Baronet in 1769, plays the violoncello and his wife a mandolin, while a Negro servant holds a little child on horseback in front of the elder brother. Sir William was for some time Governor of the islands of St. Vincent and Dominica.

Whereas in this " conversation " Zoffany appears to have been influenced by Sir Peter Lely, in *John, Third Duke of Atholl, and his Family on the Banks of the Tay at Dunkeld* (fig. 84) — one of the earliest he painted, dated 1765 — we seem to detect an echo of Dandridge's *Price Family:* here also is a river with swans, and the sitters form two groups like two juxtaposed triangles separated by a swan in the middle. To the movement of the woman alighting from the boat in Dandridge's painting corresponds that of the girl who bends forward holding a wreath in Zoffany's picture. Zoffany, who portrayed the Duke and the members of his family when they were in London, has placed on the right a leafy tree with a peasant boy and a marmoset in its branches; the landscape with the river Tay, Craig Venian hill, and Atholl Cairn was painted by Charles Stewart, who was at Blair Castle painting a series of landscapes for the Duke which form five panels in the dining-room. Grouped under an exotic tree with spheroidal fruits (perhaps a breadfruit tree) the members of the *Auriol Family* are attended by native servants in a " conversation " (fig. 85) Zoffany painted in India, where he remained for six years (from 1783 to 1789). There he also painted the group of *The Family of Major Palmer* (fig. 282); the unfinished condition of the painting makes the left portion seem almost to anticipate Gauguin (and not only because of the figure of the banana tree). Flanked by the two draped oriental figures like symmetrical columns, the group takes on the usual triangular shape, with the major at the top bending, together with the other persons near him, towards his wife — an Indian lady of princely caste. The sitters of *The Colmore Family* are also under a tree, with children on the mother's and grandmother's laps, and a bantam hen and chickens in the foreground (fig. 281); so too is *The Drummond Family* group, while nearby a girl prepares for a quiet ride, attended by a groom; she is accompanied by her elder sister, and her father speeds her on her way (fig. 86). At the foot of a tree and near a peristyle we see Francis Wheatley's (1747-1801) *Wilkinson Family* grouped (fig. 87): the delicate hollyhocks, the pale willow, the reddish greyhound, and the light blue sky overcast with soft clouds give to the left side of the painting a tender, idyllic flavour, not without a nostalgic touch when you think that today this Roehampton country house has been transformed into a convent. Francis Wheatley's compositions are very close to Zoffany's — to the point of hardly being distinguishable from them: thus his family group at the Tate Gallery (fig. 88), where we find a dog in the same posture as in *The Family of Sir William Young* and a Negro boy on the left; the affinity is evident if we compare it with *The Bradshaw Family* (fig. 89), unless this painting is also by Wheatley. Some Zoffany " conversations " are more animated and verge on genre painting: examples are *The Three Sons of John, Third Earl of Bute* (fig. 90), in which one of the boys has begun to climb a tree, and its companion piece, *The Three Daughters of the Earl of Bute* (fig. 91): in these paintings the two sexes are dealt with separately as in family groups in the early religious scenes. One of Zoffany's earliest "conversations" is *A Man and Two Boys, One with a Kite* (fig. 284). Sitwell, who in his volume does not stint the epithet " delightful ", here uses its synonym, " charming "; one cannot contradict him, because this painting is supremely elegant. The line formed by the right side of the boy and his outstretched arm echoes the one formed by the seated father, whose arm rests on his hip with the elbow turned out; the kite, cutting in between the two jagged lines, creates a counterpoint.

George Stubbs (1724-1806), of whom we shall have occasion to speak later, in a painting of 1780 places Josiah Wedgwood, the famous potter, on a bench under a tree on the right (nearby there is a black basalt vase on a table), with his wife. Of his seven children, four are mounted — thus offering Stubbs a means of parading his speciality as a painter of horses — and two are being dragged along in a go-cart by an older one: a motif which we shall find again and again (Miss Phoebe Wedgwood Collection, Cheadle). In a previous group, *Colonel Pocklington and his Sisters* (1769; fig. 95), Stubbs employs on the left the same tree as we find in another composition to be mentioned later. Indeed, this screen of foliage became a constant feature of the painter's work. The tree has the function of giving prominence to the sitters, just as the curtain had done in indoor "conversations".

Sometimes trees form a compact background, as in Chodowiecki's *The Painter with his Family in the Tiergarten* (1772: note in this painting the impression of detachment between children and adults, no one showing the least sign of affection towards the others; fig. 92), or in Simon Meister's (1796-1844) *Werbrunn Family*, with children carrying a letter and flowers to their mother for her birthday (fig. 93); or in Frank Stone's (1800-1859) *Samuel Rogers, the Hon. Mrs. Caroline Norton, and Mrs. Phipps* (c. 1845), where the banker-poet is in the company of two famous beauties, one of whom, Mrs. Norton (on the right), was considered " dangerous and formidable " — but not, presumably, for the octogenarian poet (London, National Portrait Gallery).

More frequently trees form a central reference point, whether or not accompanied by architectural elements, as in Angelica Kauffmann's *Family of Ferdinand I of Naples* (fig. 285), where motifs like the children's go-cart, the harp player, the dogs, and the wreaths recur, in a triangular composition, and all the sitters are idealised; and again in *A Colonial Louisiana Family* (fig. 286) by Marguerite Gérard (which is, however, a genre painting); in Michelangelo Grigoletti's (1801-1870) *Family Portrait* (the property of Ing. Carlo Occioni Bonaffons, Venice), which shows the persistence of the Italian tradition of half-length figures; and in the *Family in a Garden* by Frédéric Bazille, where the play of sentimental intercourse among the members of the group which prevailed in the first half of the nineteenth century has disappeared, while the triangular composition persists (fig. 291).

Occasionally, instead of the tree, a fountain is preferred — or else another architectural element in a garden, as in Januarius Zick's *Mother with Children* and *Father and Son with Mercury* (fig. 94), both dating from about 1770, the parents being of a rather didactic disposition. Sometimes there is even a little temple, as in Wendelin Moosbrugger's *Family of the Counsellor Joseph Barxel* (c. 1815; Konstanz, Rosgartenmuseum), in which the central group of children — especially the one who feeds the rabbits — has almost the characteristics of *naïf* art: this group is wedged in like a pillow between the triangular blocks of the adults.

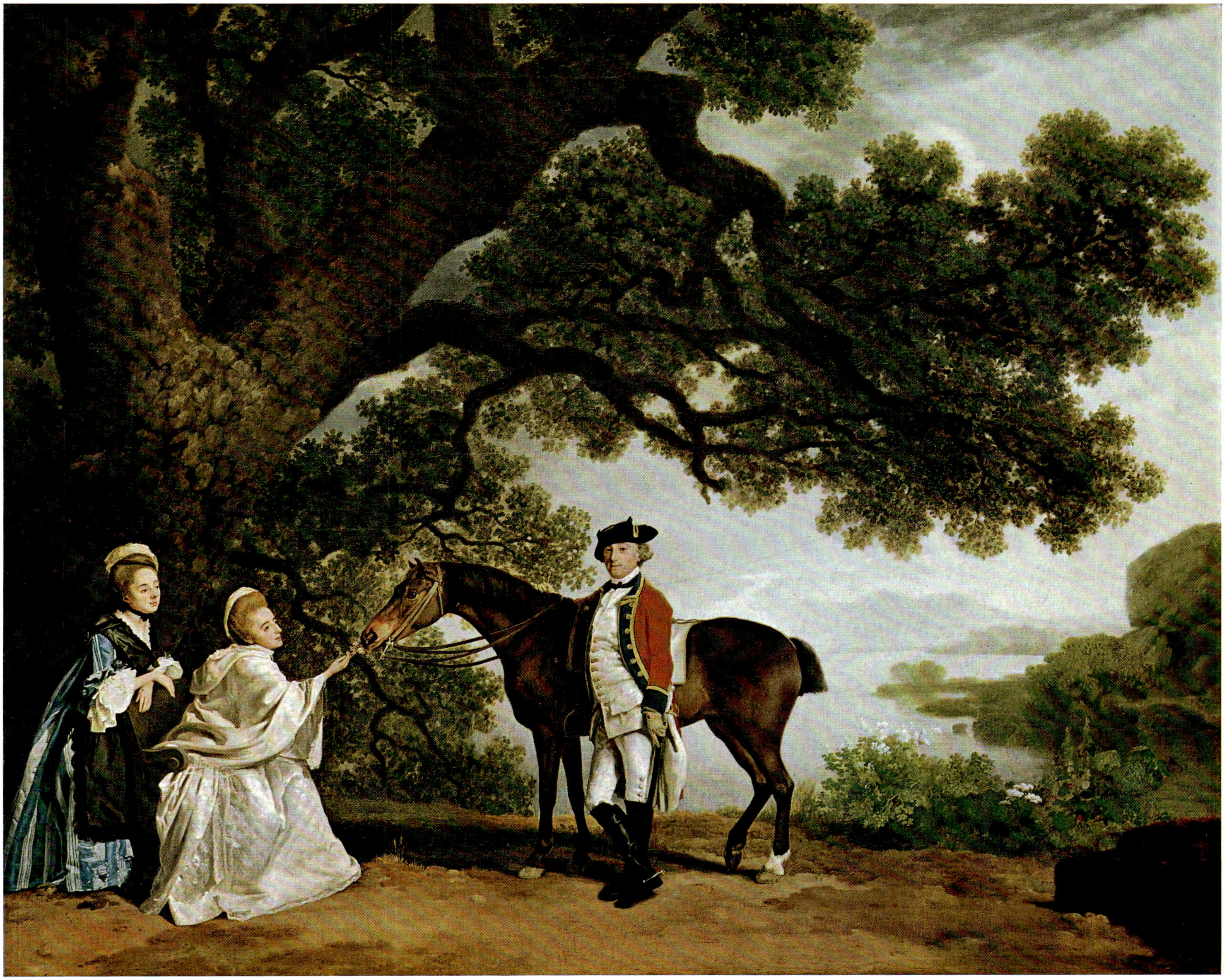

95

95 GEORGE STUBBS (1724-1806), *Colonel Pocklington and his Sisters*, 1769. Washington, D.C., National Gallery of Art.

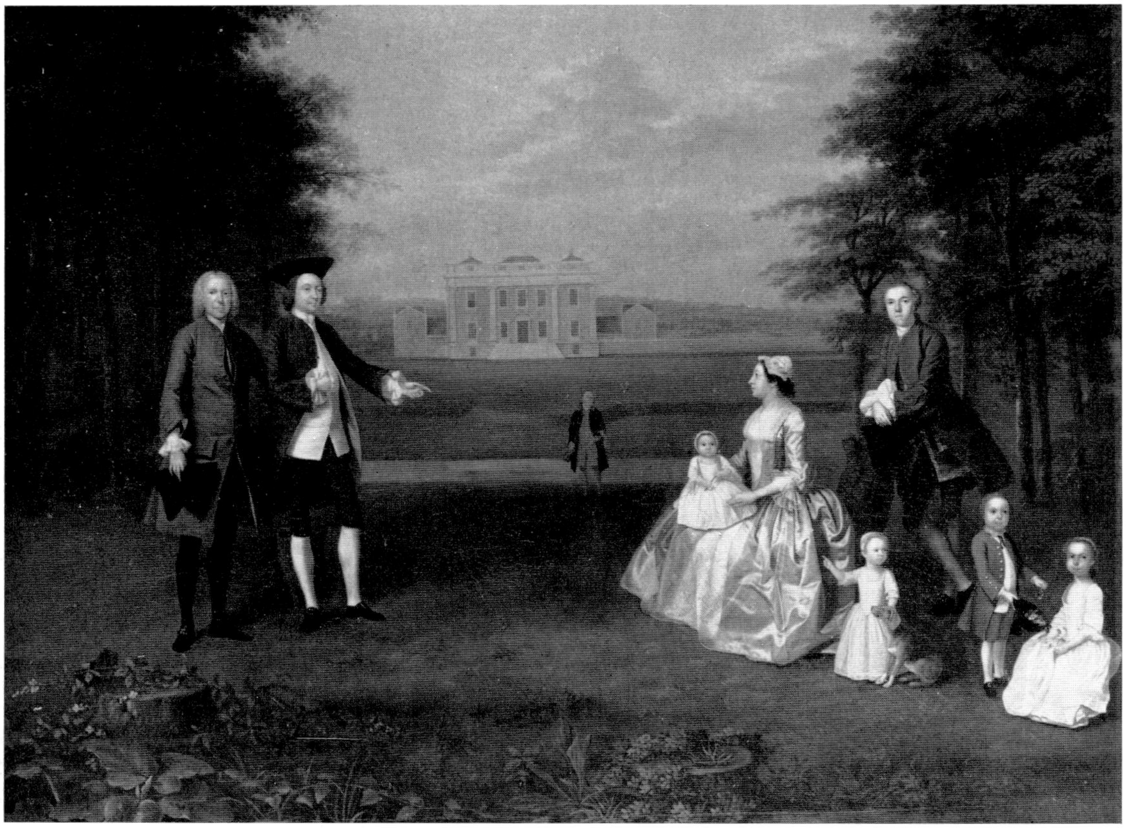

96

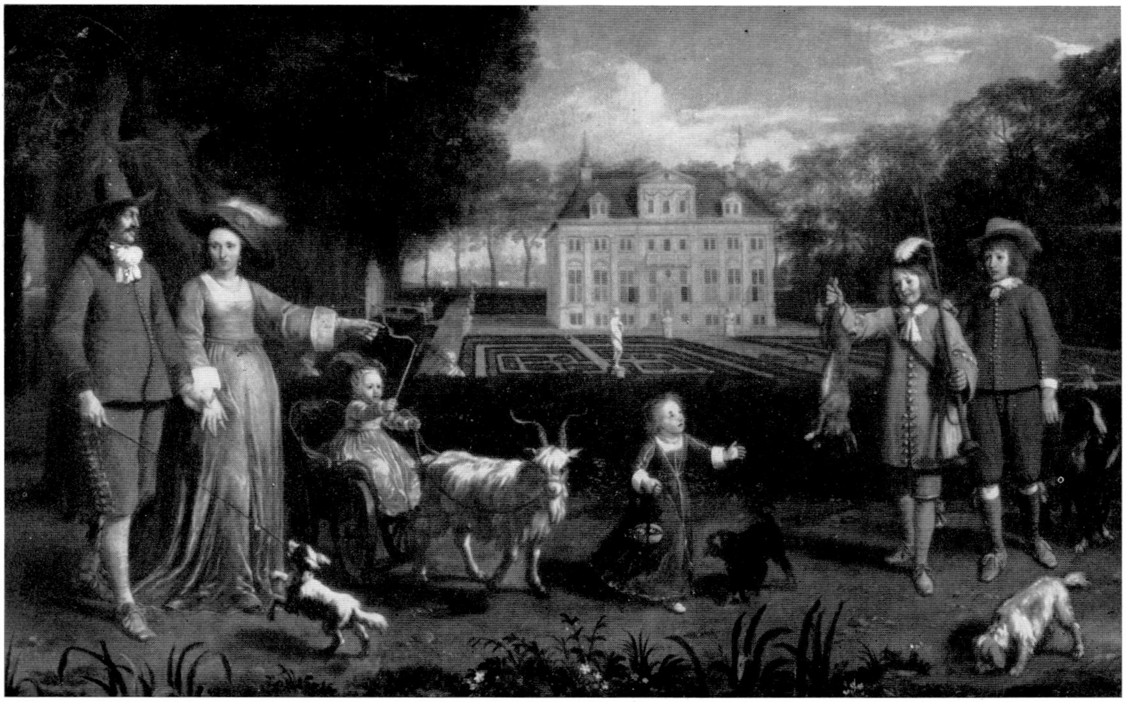

97

96 ARTHUR DEVIS (1711-1787), *The Family of Robert Atherton.* Washington, D.C., collection of Mr. and Mrs. Paul Mellon. 97 CORNELIS HOLSTEYN (1618-1658), *Reynier Pauw with his Wife Adriana and Four of their Children.* Christie's sale, 6 Nov. 1964; formerly the property of Mr. Reginald Leon. 98 DAVID ALLAN (1744-1796), *The Family of Sir John Halkett of Pitfirrane, Fourth Bart.*, 1781. Edinburgh, National Gallery of Scotland.

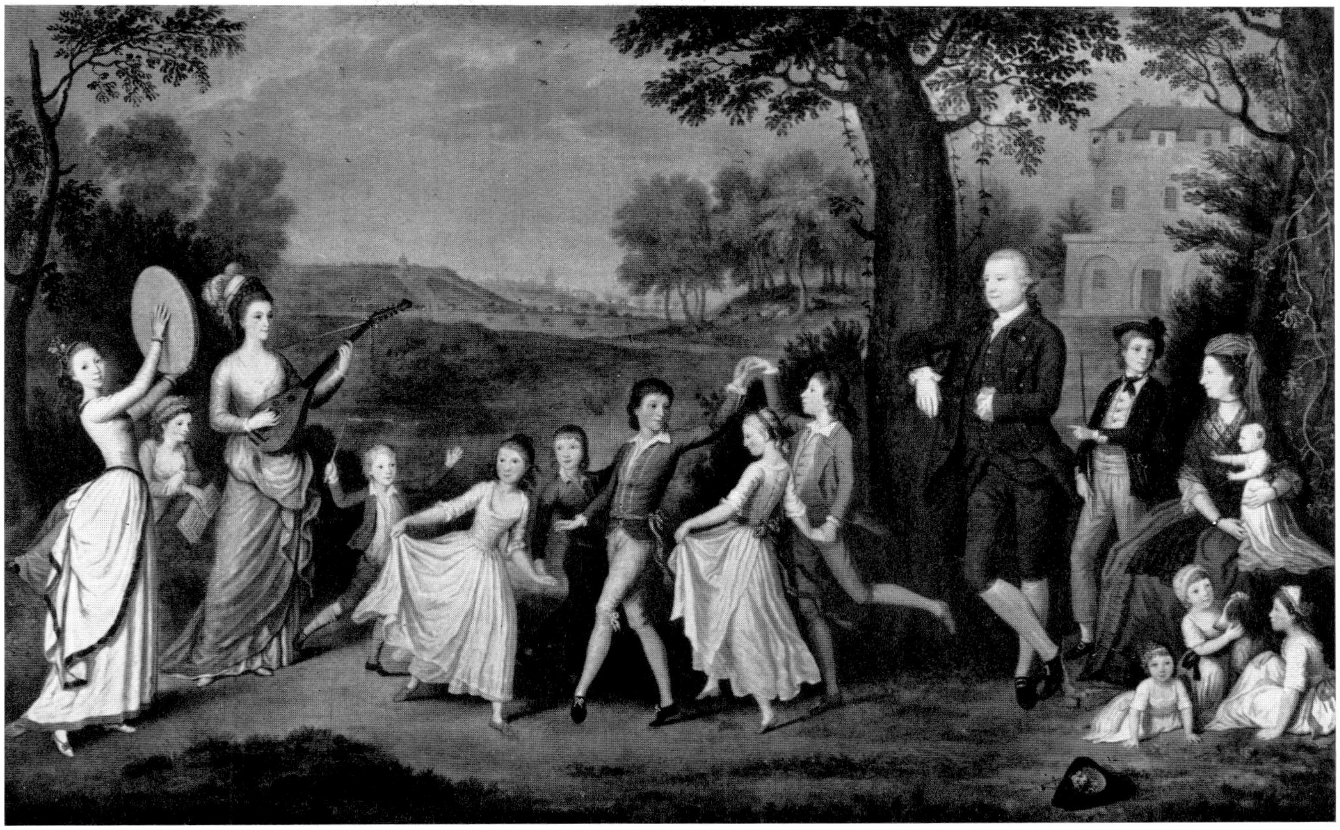

98

4. *With a view of a country house.*

Proprietorial pride or a device of the painter often meant that the architecture of the country house was included in a view of the garden. We have already seen how, in Rubens' *Walk*, the elegant colonnade of the porch of the building appears. Cornelis Holsteyn (1618-1658) in *Reynier Pauw with his Wife Adriana and Four of their Children* (fig. 97) places conspicuously in the background the Westwijck villa built in 1637 by Philips Vingboons, one of the most renowned Dutch architects of the seventeenth century (the villa is no longer extant). Pauw, the son of the famous burgomaster and ambassador, Adriaan Pauw, died in 1652. The composition is perfectly symmetrical: the lady's outstretched arm, vaguely pointing either to the young huntsman or to the formal garden, corresponds to the outstretched arm of her son on the opposite side, holding a hare he has just killed with his long stick. Between the two groups, one sees the motif of a child on a cart drawn by a goat and the lively figure of a little girl in long petticoats running with a basket, approached by a black dog symmetrically equidistant from the two dogs on the sides. In Jan Weenix's (1640-1719) *Sylbrand de Flines, his Second Wife Agnes Block, and his Daughters Anna and Elizabeth* (formerly in Mr. Reginald Leon's collection),[11] probably painted in the autumn of 1674 when Flines married Agnes Block, we see the buildings of the lady's villa: her wealth no doubt compensated for her lack of charm. Flines was a collector, and he holds a little statue in his hand; at his feet is shown a copy of Barocci's *Annunciation*, and the lady displays an ornithological plate.
Hendrik Danckerts (c. 1625-1679) painted *Charles II Being Presented with a Pineapple by Rose, the Royal Gardener* (fig. 319) with a view of Dorney House near Weybridge, which adjoined the royal demesne of Oatlands. In an unidentified *Family Group* by Pieter van Slingeland (Thomas Agnew & Sons)[12] the traditional triangular pattern, which we have seen in another painting by this artist, is shown against the background of a country house flanked by a pond and an avenue with statues; there is also the

11 Reproduced in EDWARDS, *Early Conversation Pictures*, fig. 41, p. 96. 12 Reproduced in EDWARDS, fig. 39, p. 94.

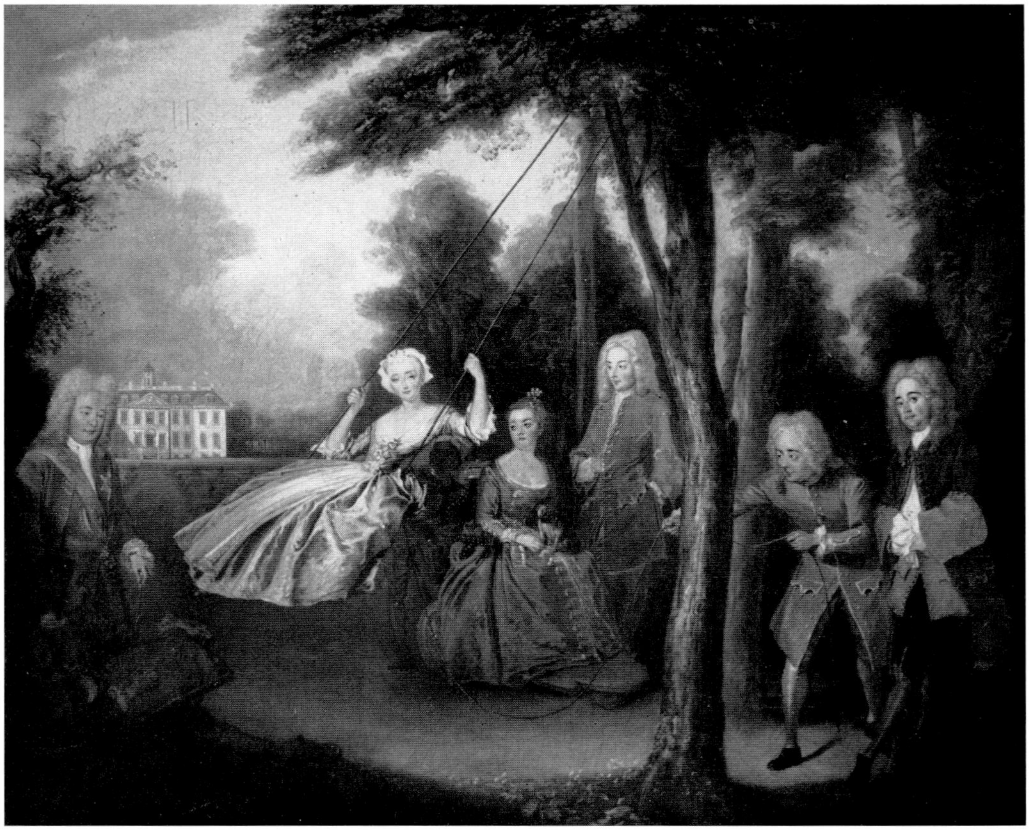

99

99 PHILIP MERCIER (1689-1760), *Viscount Tyrconnel with Members of his Family in the Grounds of Belton House*, c. 1725-6. Belton House, Grantham (Lincolnshire), collection of Lord Brownlow.

inevitable tree as a backdrop for the group. Philip Mercier's *Viscount Tyrconnel with Members of his Family in the Grounds of Belton House* (fig. 99) was probably painted in 1725-26. John Brownlow, Viscount Tyrconnel, created Knight of the Bath in 1725, is seen on the left with the star and ribbon of the order. Mr. Savile Cust holds the cord of the swing with Miss Darrel on it, and the last person on the right is Mr. William Brownlow, brother of the Viscount, who died in 1726. In the left hand corner we see the artist busy drawing the group. As we have said before,[13] Mercier tried to imitate his friend Watteau. In fact his own posture in the painting reminds one of his master, and the motif of the swing has a French flavour. Belton House is seen in the distance. In Arthur Devis' (1711-1787) *Family of Robert Atherton*, the sitters in the foreground are withdrawn to the sides in order to display a full view of the country house (fig. 96).

In a " conversation " of 1781 by David Allan (1744-1796), *The Family of Sir John Halkett of Pitfirrane, Fourth Bart.* (fig. 98), Pitfirrane House is seen in the background on the right, while in the foreground some of Sir John's fourteen children dance in a circle.[14] David Allan had studied under Gavin Hamilton and won a medal at the Academy of St. Luke in Rome in 1773 with his *Origin of Painting*; he had painted scenes of popular life in Rome and Naples, and in 1775 and the succeeding years he produced various versions of a conversation piece of Sir William and (the first) Lady Hamilton. In another painting by Allan, *The Family of John Francis, Seventh Earl of Mar* (fig. 101), one sees in the distance Alloa House, which was destroyed by fire in 1800. One of the children, who sits playing the xylophone, looks very quiet, and so does the girl kneeling by her mother; it appears that three of these children were blind. The eldest son was originally shown on a branch of the tree, but in consequence of a quarrel with him, the father instructed the painter to cut out his image and to replace him by the top hat. This is not the only case of the kind in conversation pieces.[15] It is a continuation of the ancient *damnatio memoriae*, of which there is a classical example in the Arch of the Argentarii in Rome where, in the scene of a sacrifice, the figures of Geta and Plautilla

13 P. 125. 14 For the motif of the children dancing, see above, p. 86, *The Niccolini Family*. 15 See p. 173.

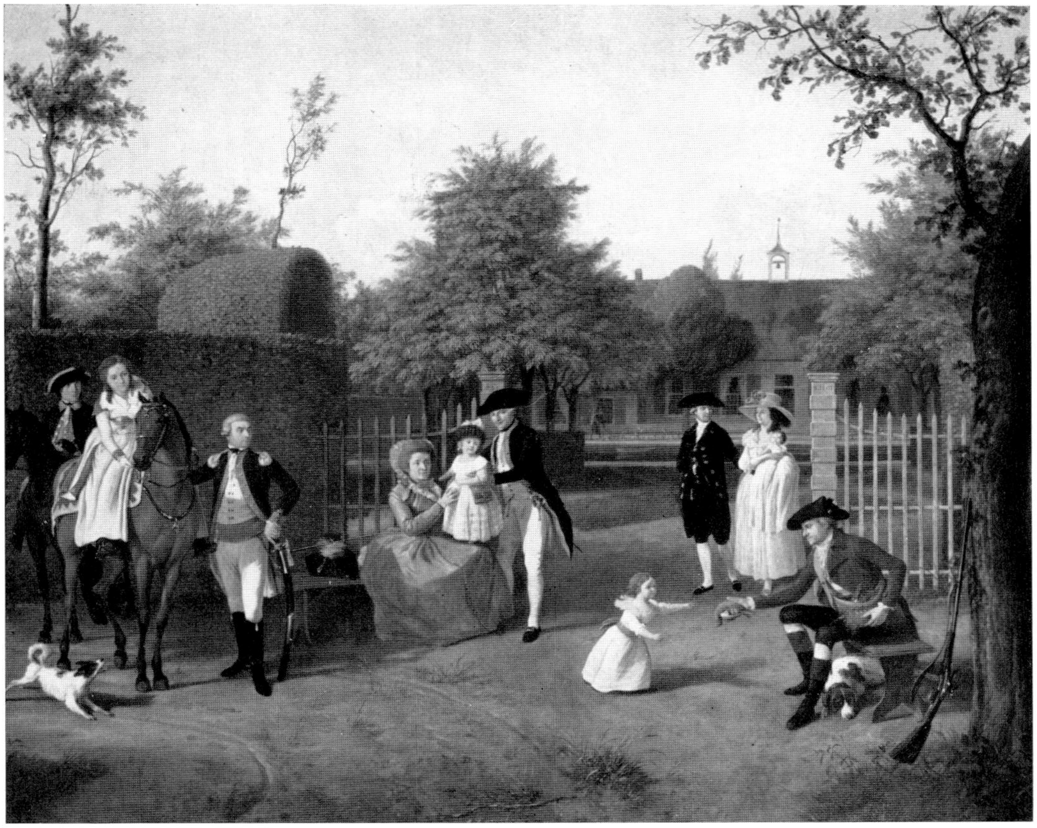

100 JACOBUS VRIJMOET (1756-?), *The van Breugel Family*, 1787. Lima (Peru), collection of señora Vera de Tudela; formerly the property of Mr. C. Baron van Breugel, Cannes.

100

were chiselled off by order of Caracalla. The same kind of composition (a family group in the foreground with children playing, a villa in the background) is seen in another painting by Allan, *The Family of Sir James Hunter Blair*, with Dunskey House. There is nothing of the magnificence of the English country house in the simple Dutch house, Rey's Hof, which Jacobus Vrijmoet has given as a background to the portrait of the *Van Breugel Family* (1787; fig. 100); it is believed that the painter portrayed himself in the figure of the jockey on the left. The animation of the little girl who runs towards her uncle Jan Festus van Breugel and of the pair passing through the enclosure contrasts with the two static groups on the left, which seem impatient to break away from the posture to which the painter has constrained them. This Dutch painting has a character of simplicity and domesticity which the English " conversations " with a country house background are far from possessing. An aristocratic character of a different style from the English one is apparent in Ferdinand Georg Waldmüller's *Family of the Legation Counsellor Theodor Ritter von Neuhaus*[16] in the garden of their villa, which is seen on the left at the top of a flight of stairs adorned with statues (fig. 102). The Cupid sculptured on the parapet of the stone bench, where the counsellor's wife Juliana is seated in her splendid white satin dress (an actual fashion plate for the year 1827, the date of the painting), seems the genius of the group, which is harmoniously composed in the usual triangular pattern with the blue jacket of the boy answering to the deeper blue tailcoat of his father and to the lovely dresses of the mother and the girl in pantalettes, who looks like an exquisite doll. The flowers the latter holds in her lap and those the little boy carries in the basket express the quintessence of this Biedermeier atmosphere. And as Vrijmoet's Dutch group with its modest bourgeois house contrasted with the aristocratic English groups, so Waldmüller's group may be compared with the *Hübner Family with Children and Grandchildren* (fig. 287) by Ferdinand Weiss (who died in Berlin in 1878): here the elderly gentleman explains something about the plant he holds in his left hand, while the grandchildren with the dog and the squirrel form a typical triangular composition on the right.

16 Colour plate in *Romantik und Realismus in Österreich, Gemälde und Zeichnungen aus der Sammlung Georg Schäfer, Schweinfurt* (Ausstellung in Schloss Laxenburg, 18 Mai - 14 Oktober 1968), pl. 234.

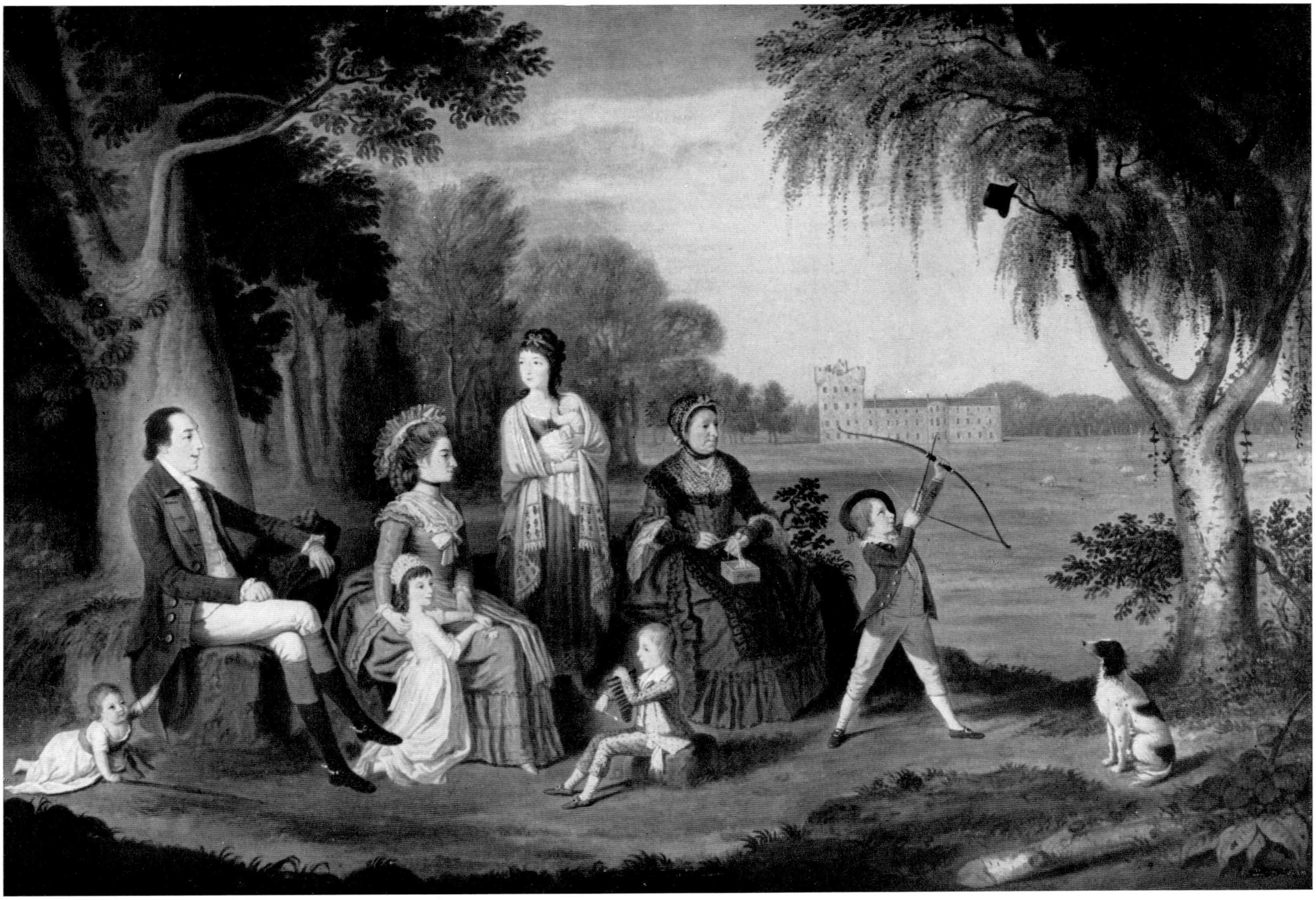

101

101 DAVID ALLAN (1744-1796), *The Family of John Francis, Seventh Earl of Mar*, 1783. Claremont House, Alloa (Clackmannanshire), collection of the Earl of Mar and Kellie. 102 FERDINAND GEORG WALDMÜLLER (1793-1865), *The Family of the Legation Counsellor Theodor Ritter von Neuhaus*, 1827. Schweinfurt, Georg Schäfer Collection.

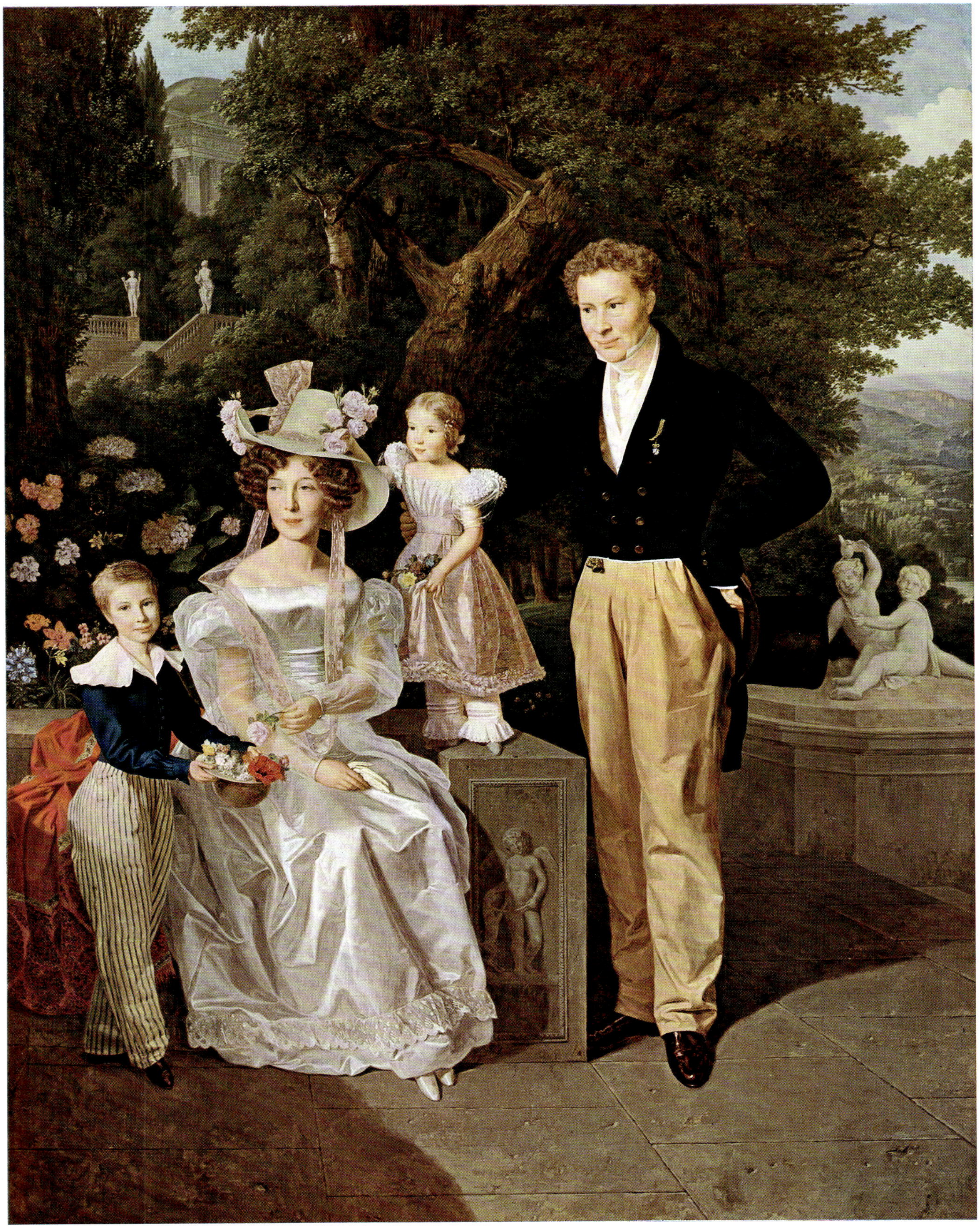
102

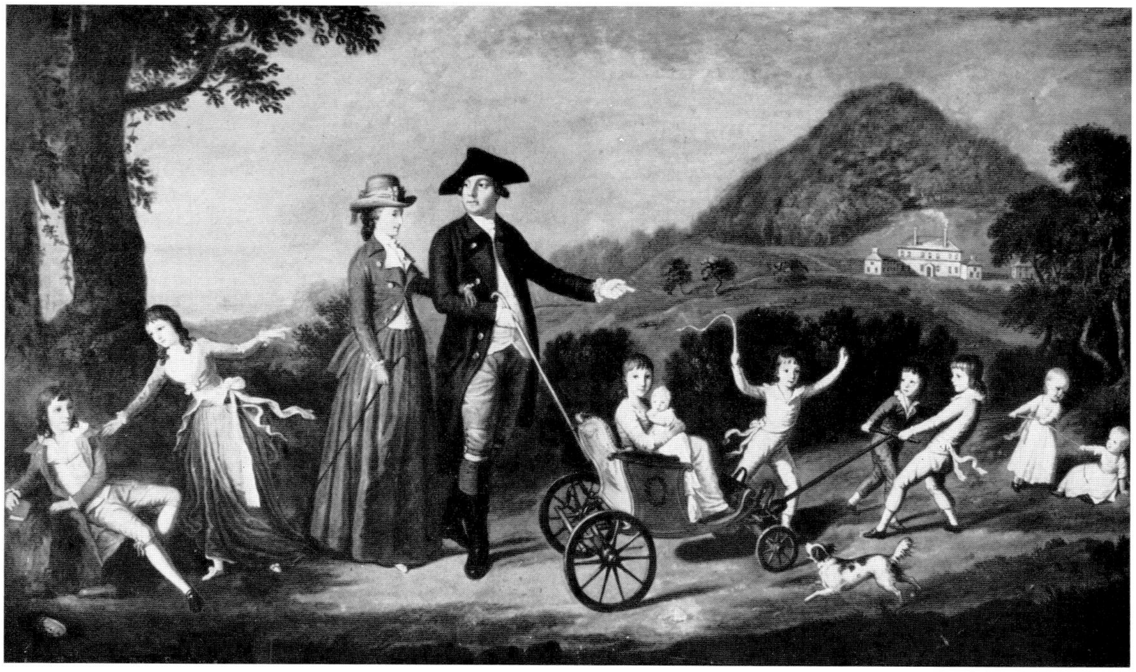

103

103 DAVID ALLAN (1744-1796), *The Family of Sir James Hunter Blair, First Bart.*, 1785. Blairquhan (Ayrshire), collection of J. Hunter Blair, Bart.

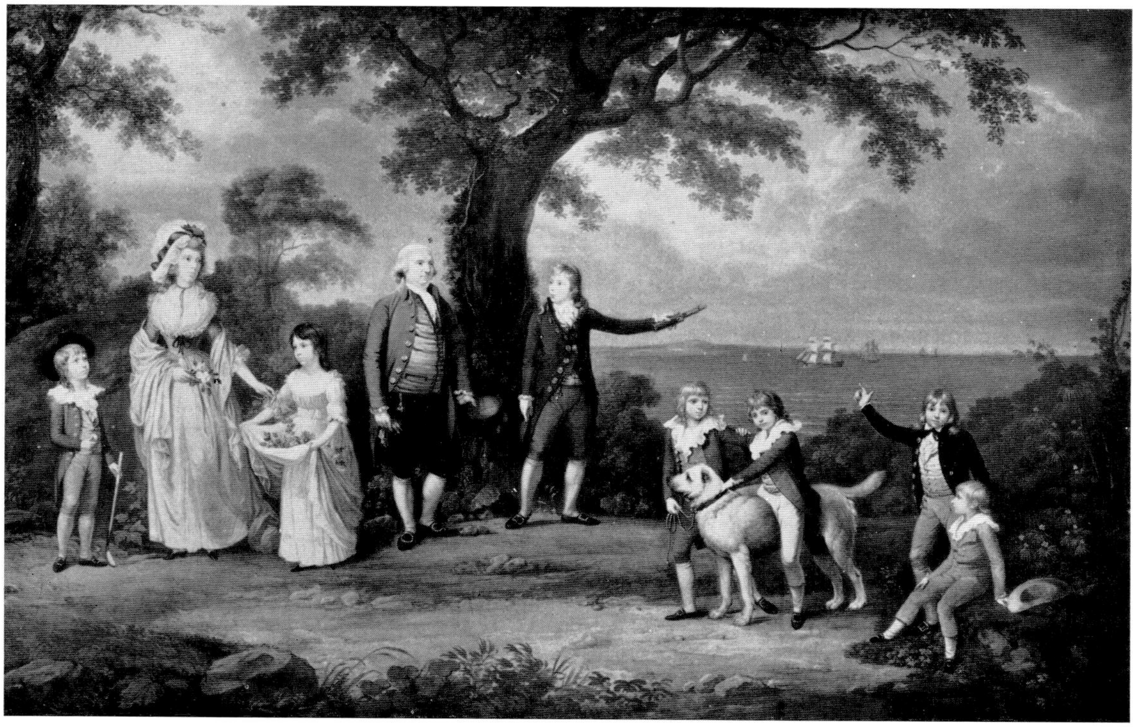

104

104 formerly attr. to JOHANN ZOFFANY (1734/5-1810), *The Drummond Family at Cadland.* Formerly in the collection of Mrs. Ionides; present location unknown.

5. *With a view of a landscape.*

In many open air " conversations " the background is formed by a vast landscape, as in Arthur Devis' *Sir Joshua Vanneck and his Family* (fig. 288), where Horace Walpole is the sitter on the right with an open book on his knees. The group is harmoniously disposed in a semicircle terminating in two benches. At the centre, one of the daughters focuses a small telescope in order to see the people and vehicles crossing the bridge more clearly. Behind the group is a bowling green with its wooden summer-house, and behind the trees the perpendicular tower of a church. In John Fearey's (1745/50-1788) *Family Group* (fig. 289) one sees the Greenwich cupolas, a bend of the Thames, and London in the distance; the group is gathered under a tree, and in the centre the animals of the park — a few deer and a goat — are grazing in the foreground. A view of a town near a river forms the background of the group of *Edward Rookes of Royds Hall* (near Bradford, Yorkshire) *with his First Wife and Three Daughters* by Arthur Devis (fig. 292); in *The Callis Family* by Benjamin Wilson (fig. 290) there is a seascape on the right with a castle and a ship, towards which one of the sitters seems to be pointing. In an unidentified group called *A Garden Party* (Tate Gallery) by Charles Philips (1708-1747) we see a vast extent of meadows and groves. The clergyman seated on the left holds in his hand a miniature portrait of his deceased wife, and occupies the lateral position which the painters of " conversations " generally give to ecclesiastics because of the dark colour of their clothes. In David Allan's *Family of Sir James Hunter Blair* (1785; fig. 103) we see the vast landscape of Blairquhan serving as a background to a kind of anthology of children's attitudes, as Waterhouse remarks,[17] and in particular to the motif of the go-cart, which we shall find many more times. In *The Drummond Family at Cadland* (fig. 104), wrongly attributed to Zoffany, we see — beyond the typical central tree we have already met several times, flanked here by Robert Drummond and one of his sons — the Solent and the Isle of Wight with some sailing ships, towards which the young man is about to direct a small telescope; another boy on the right — who already seems to wear the uniform of the Navy — indicates the ships and the sea as his vocation. The motifs of the large dog, ridden by another boy, and of the girl holding up the skirt of her dress to receive flowers recur in other " conversations ".

A Roman landscape (a view of the Campo Vaccino) appears in the *Portrait of the Duke of Hamilton with his Personal Doctor, John Moore, and the Latter's Son, Ensign John Moore* (the future hero of Corunna; fig. 293). Gavin Hamilton (1723-1798) is the painter. Douglas, eighth Duke of Hamilton, had begun his grand tour in 1772 and sojourned in Rome from about November 1775 to May 1776; the painting was finished in August of 1777. Nathaniel Dance (1734/5-1811 or 1816) places *Four Englishmen in Rome* (Sir James Grant; T. Robinson, later created Lord Grantham, seated; Mr. Mytton; and Mr. Wynne) against the background of the Colosseum (fig. 294). (There are two versions of the painting: one in the McFadden Collection, Philadelphia Museum of Art, and the other in the collection of the Countess of Seafield, Cullen, reproduced here. The painter must have made four replicas of the painting; one of them is attributed to Pompeo Batoni by Sitwell.) The Colosseum and the Arch of Constantine also form the background of *A Group of Englishmen in Rome*, a painting of the English school of about 1750 (Washington, D. C., collection of Mr. and Mrs. Paul Mellon). We see the Basilica of Maxentius in a painting by François Sablet representing a family near fragments of capitals and columns on the Palatine; the mother, seated, takes down her impressions in a notebook (Lausanne, Musée Cantonal des Beaux-Arts). In J.-B. Isabey's *A Family in about 1810* — a painting full of atmosphere — adults near a shrub (a poor substitute for the traditional screen of foliage) watch a couple of young people who prepare to dance to the strains of a violin; behind them a harbour appears, with a redoubt at its entrance (fig. 296).

A little girl is dancing to a guitar while her parents watch her, certainly with more enthusiasm than those of the preceding picture, in the *Family of Burgomaster Steder in Biberach* (1813; private collection, Biberach) by Johann Friedrich Dieterich (1787-1846); in the background is a view of the little town where this affectionate family, portrayed here without idealization but not without a touch of naive tenderness (see the infant on the right), led its tranquil life.[18] A hill town like those of central Italy forms the landscape of the luminous and somehow affected portrait of *Countess Maria Theresia von Fries with her Children* (1811) by Joseph Abel (1764-1818; fig. 295). The attractive lady holds an apple in her hand in an attitude which reminds one of that of Isaiah in the Sistine ceiling (a putto also emerges behind the shoulder of this prophet).

17 *Painting in Britain*, p. 204. 18 Reproduction in KRONBERGER-FRENTZEN, *Das deutsche Familienbildnis* (Leipzig: Johannes Asmus Verlag, 1940), p. 54.

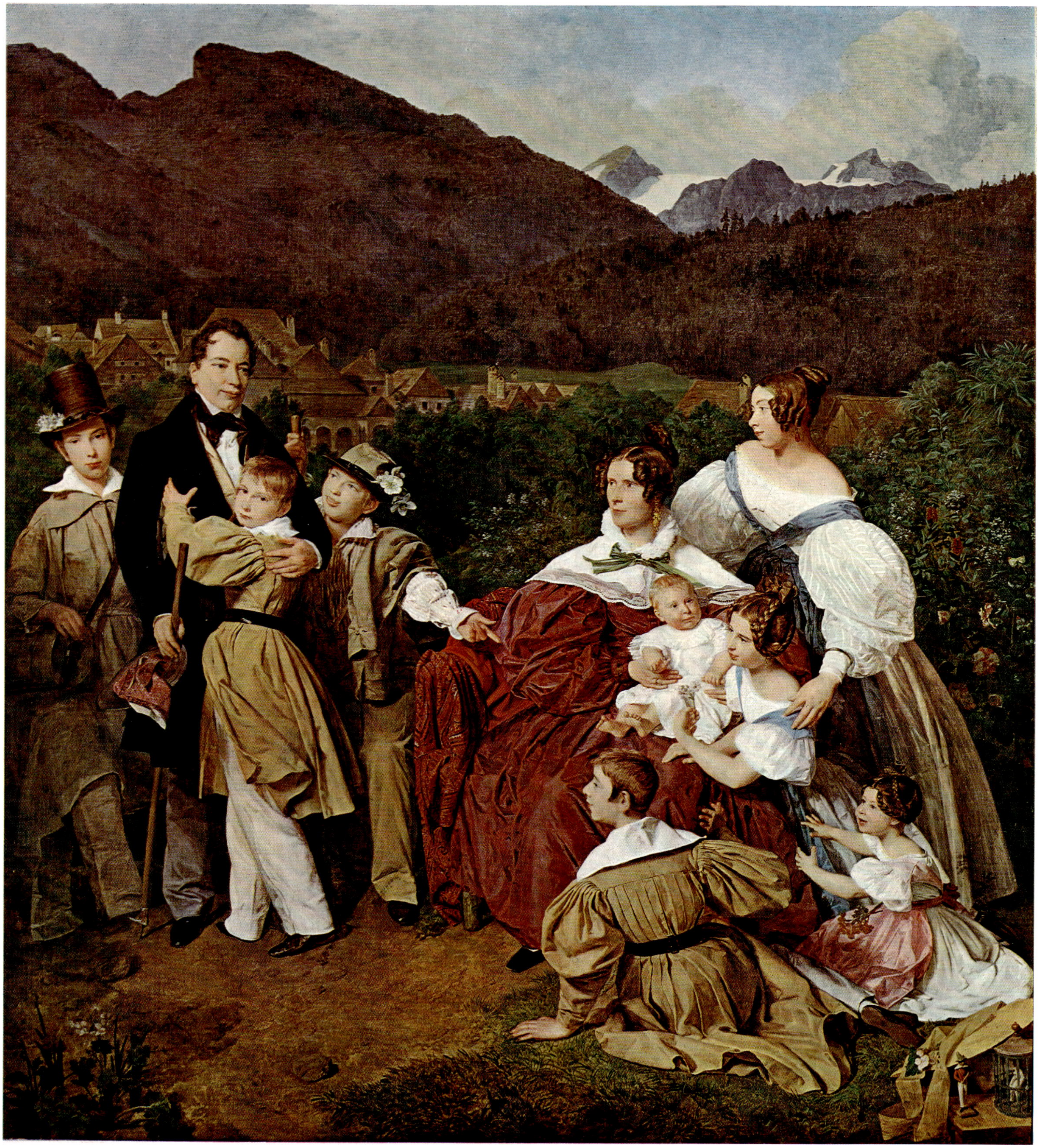

105

105 FERDINAND GEORG WALDMÜLLER (1793-1865), *Johann August Eltz and his Family at Ischl*, 1835. Vienna, Österreichische Galerie des 19. und 20. Jahrhunderts. 106 LOUIS-LÉOPOLD BOILLY (1761-1845), *The Second Madame Oberkampf with her Daughters*, 1803. Paris, Thierry Feray Collection.

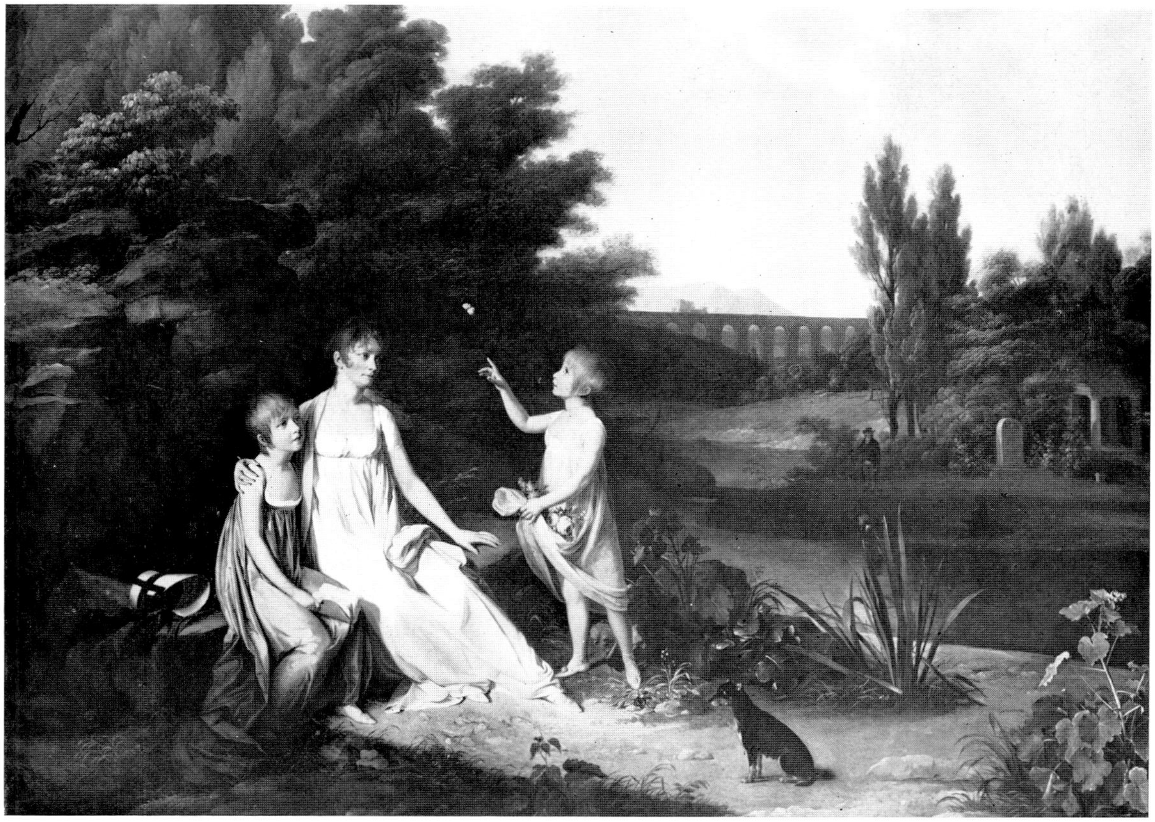

106

A similar affectation is noticeable in another neoclassical group, painted by Louis-Léopold Boilly for Christophe-Philippe Oberkampf, who had started in the Bièvre valley in 1760 the manufacture of the famous *toiles de Jouy* (printed cloth with patterns of various colours) which were so popular in household decoration in the latter part of the eighteenth and at the beginning of the nineteenth century. Of the two conversation pieces painted by Boilly in 1803, one represents Oberkampf talking to his son Alphonse, who had died the year before, while his daughter Julie (who in 1797 had married Louis Feray, one of the directors of the manufactory) is drawing on a piece of cardboard which rests on her knees, and Émile plays with a dog. Both Alphonse and Émile were sons of Oberkampf's second marriage to Elisabeth Massieu; Julie was the daughter of his first marriage to Marie-Louise Petineau (died 1782). The factory forms the background, and the printer, Rordorf, is seen spreading out the cloths. The second painting, a counterpart of the first (reproduced here, fig. 106), shows the second Madame Oberkampf with her two daughters, Émilie (born 1794, later Madame Jules Mallet), who points the forefinger of her right hand in the direction of a butterfly and with her left arm holds flowers in her lap, and Laure (later Madame James Mallet), who has stopped reading her book and leans tenderly against her romantically languorous mother, both staring vaguely ahead. This elegiac note is in tune with the view of " l'Élysée " of the family estate (Montcel): its tombs and the Temple de la Douleur across the river, built in memory of Alphonse. In the background, the aqueduct of Buc evokes in the Bièvre valley the landscapes of the Roman Campagna.

Gabriel von Max has instead placed his *Three Sisters Embroidering* (fig. 297) against an absolutely flat horizon: were it not for the Baroque pavilion whose corner one sees on the right, one would say that the painter deliberately intended to react against the picturesque landscape as a background. In Waldmüller's masterpiece, *Johann August Eltz and his Family at Ischl* (1835; fig. 105), the two groups — one of men, the other of women — are arranged like a frieze against the magnificent alpine scenery of mountain tops, glaciers, and forests. The romance of the mountains and of domestic life combine together to make of this painting one of the supreme expressions of the Biedermeier spirit.

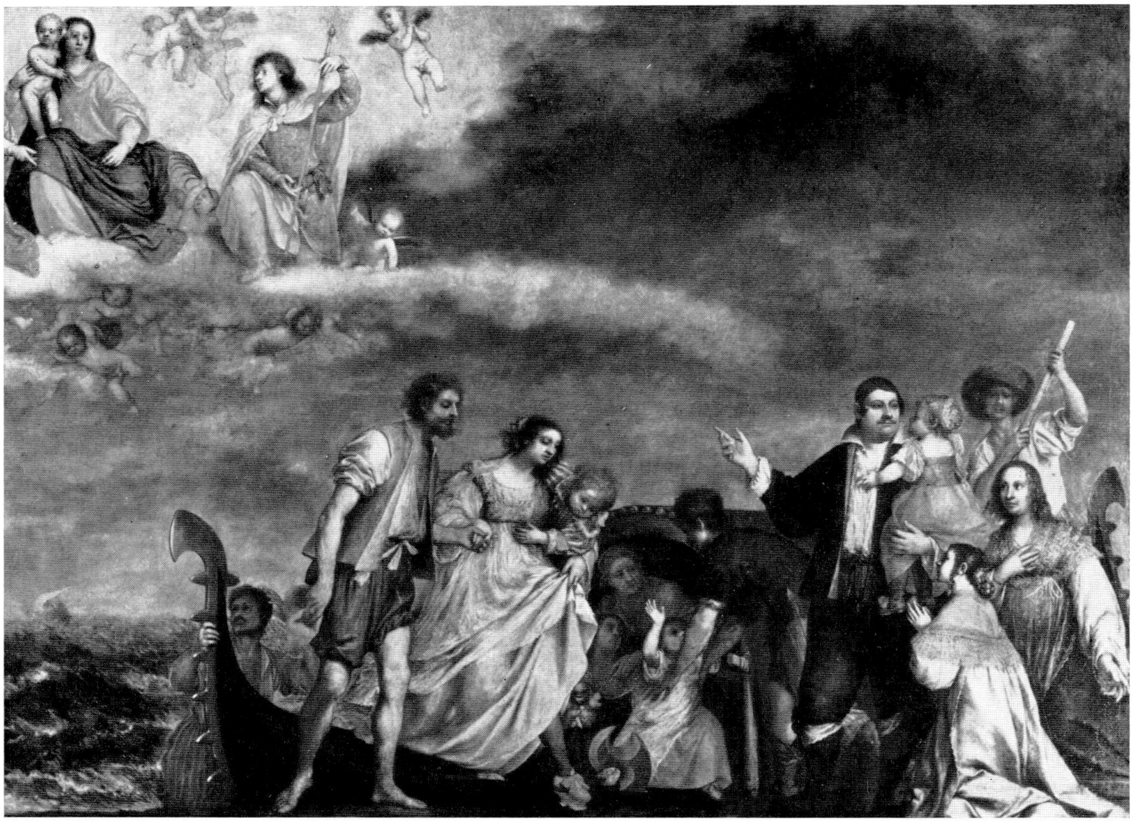

107

107 GIROLAMO FORABOSCO (1604/5-1679), *Miraculous Rescue from a Shipwreck* (detail). Malamocco, parish church.

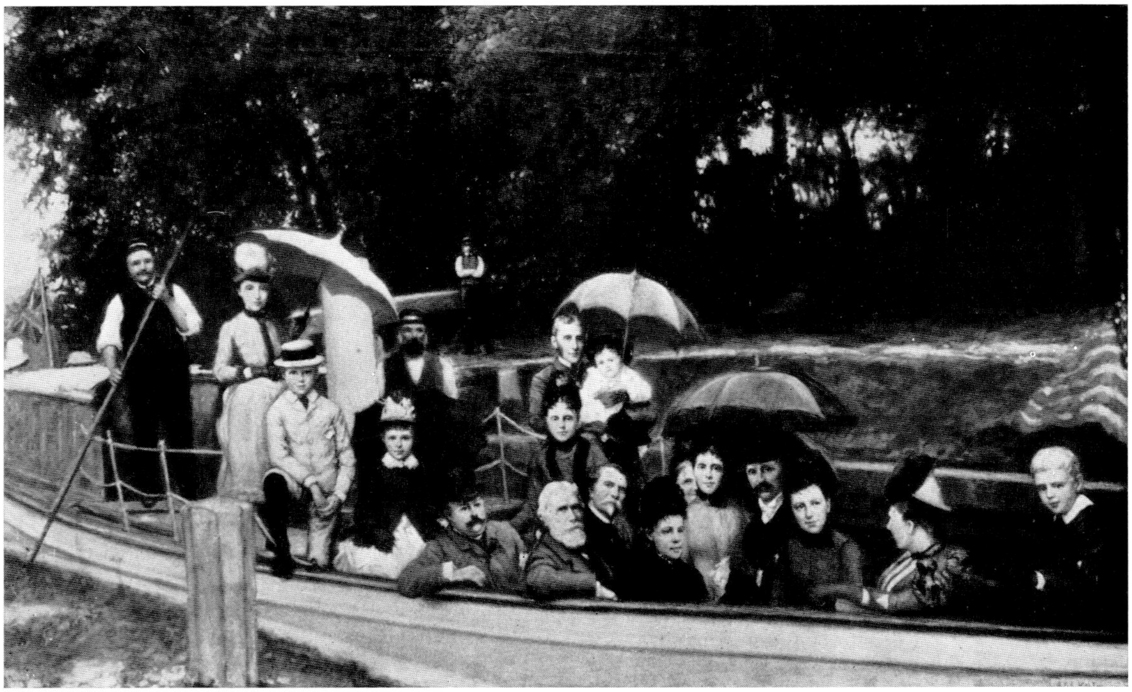

108

108 GEORGE PETER ALEXANDER HEALY (1808-1894), *Boating on the Thames: the Whitehouse Family and Friends*. New York, collection of Mrs. Sheldon Whitehouse.

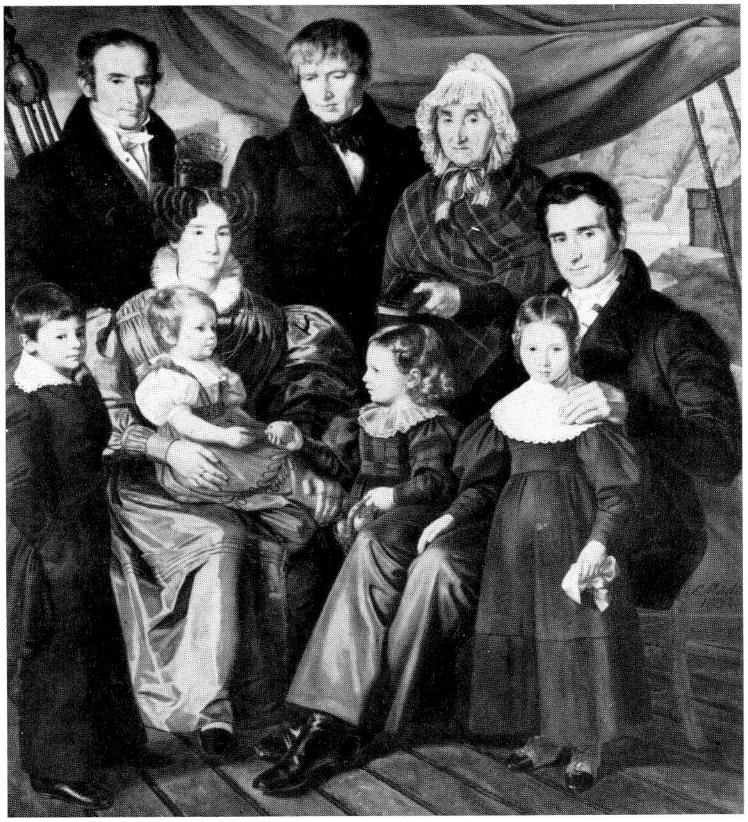

109

109 SIMON MEISTER (1796-1844), *The Tillmann Family*, 1832. Düsseldorf, Städtische Kunsthalle.

6. *In a boat.*

A few family groups in a boat offer a pleasant though very rare change from the type of open air " conversation " generally placed in a landscape. Of Zoffany's monumental *Musical Party on the Thames* we shall speak later. But both in this painting and in Simon Meister's *Tillmann Family* (1832; fig. 109), the nautical background is no more than hinted at. In the German picture, the sail has the function which the curtain had in indoor " conversations ", and the mast serves as a column; the block with the four ropes is the most characteristic feature, and over the heads of the figures one has a glimpse of the river scene and of the Rhine and the Ehrenbreitenstein shore. The faces of the adults are serious, almost sulky; no smile curls the lips even of the little girl offering an apple or of the infant who stretches his hand out to collect it. Eugène Devéria in his watercolour *The Boat* (once in the Alexis Rouart collection, Paris) has created instead a scene full of movement which might easily be taken for genre painting, if one did not know that it represents the family of Victor Hugo (fig. 298). " This boat ", Hautecœur remarks,[19] " makes one think of the one which was to capsize tragically at Villequier ", inspiring the poet to some moving passages, as well as sublime commonplaces culminating in: " Puisque ces choses sont, c'est qu'il faut qu'elles soient;/J'en conviens, j'en conviens ".[20] The rescue from a shipwreck is instead the subject of a picture (actually an *ex voto*) by the Paduan Girolamo Forabosco (1604/5-1679), in which the event naturally suggested the dramatic attitudes of the people portrayed (fig. 107). The American painter G.P.A. Healy produced in 1886 what is perhaps the most original of these " conversations " in a boat when he represented *Boating on the Thames: the Whitehouse Family and Friends* (fig. 108). The open umbrellas, the ladies' costumes, and the river atmosphere recall Tissot, of whose genre scenes we are reminded while looking at this boat which silently glides on the river between wooded banks.

19 *Les peintres de la vie familiale* (Paris: Charpentier, 1945), p. 120, where the painting is reproduced. See Hugo's poem " À Villequier " (1847) in *Les Contemplations*. Hugo's daughter, Léopoldine, was drowned in that accident. 20 A sketch of this painting, with fewer sitters, was on sale at the Galerie Roger Imbert in Paris in 1967. This is the version reproduced here, by courtesy of M. Imbert.

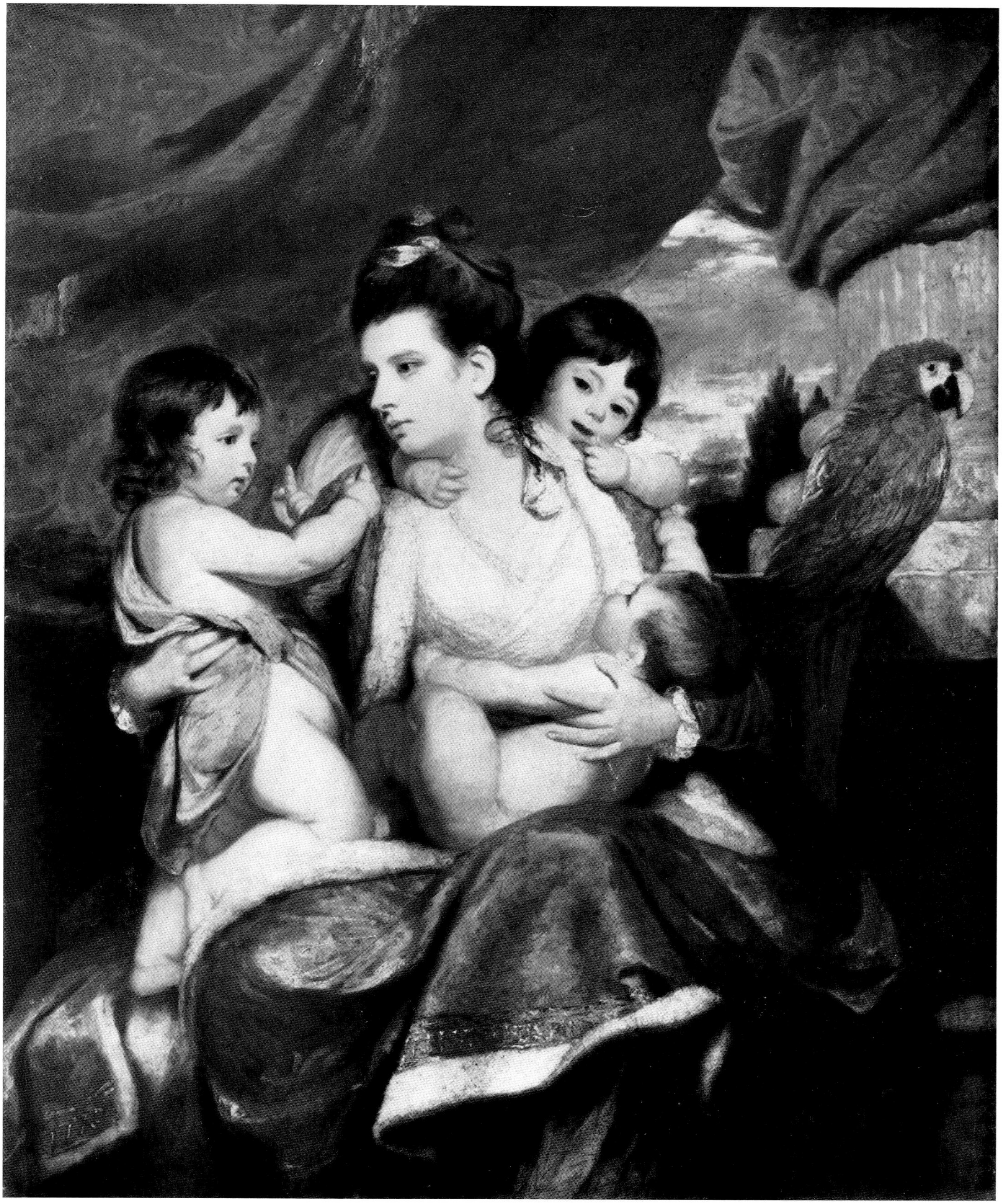

110

110 SIR JOSHUA REYNOLDS (1723-1792), *Lady Cockburn and her Children* ("*Cornelia and her Children*"), 1773. London, National Gallery. 111 JOHANN ZOFFANY (1734/5-1810), *The Lavie Children*. Washington, D.C., collection of Mr. and Mrs. Paul Mellon.

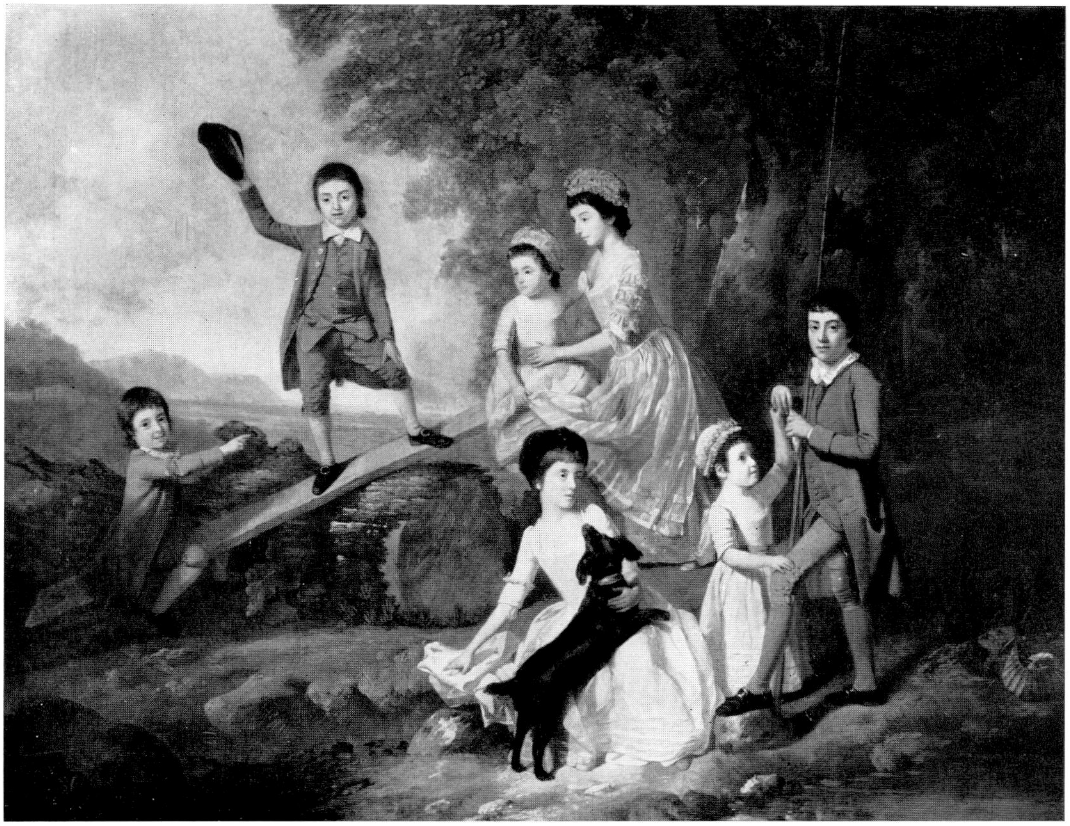

111

7. *Portraits of children.*

In many of the " conversations " we have examined so far we have seen that children played a large part, but there is a quantity of paintings in which they are the protagonists, chiefly in the eighteenth century — which has been defined as " the century of childhood "[21] — so as to form almost a section by itself deserving a monograph like Charles Moreau-Vauthier's *Les portraits de l'enfant*.[22] It is, however, true that subjects such as " children in art ", " the Madonna in art ", or " the nude " mean little, as they result in as many methods of treatment as there are artists, and it would be an unreasonable claim to deal with them as one would with the various ways of dressing a chicken. A literary genre, a kind of artistic composition such as the conversation piece, or a metrical form have an inner structure of which the artist has to take account; but a subject like those we have just mentioned is not an artifact by itself; it is, on the contrary, raw material to which the artist may fit whatever rules he chooses. We have already mentioned the triple portrait of *The Children of Christian II of Denmark* by Mabuse. Sofonisba Anguissola, who was one of the first painters in Italy to give an articulate form to the conversation piece, has left a *Portrait of Three Children* (Lord Methuen Collection), but each one of them sits by himself or herself, even more so than in Mabuse's portrait. There is, however, some sort of intercourse (though rather constrained) among the *Three Children of the House of Savoy* (Philip Emmanuel, Emmanuel Philibert, and Victor Amadeus) in the portrait by an unknown painter dating from the end of the sixteenth century (Turin, Royal Palace) and, less constrained though only slightly hinted at, among the children of the *Group* by Philippe de Champaigne (1602-1674; collection of the Marquise de Valori), between van Dyck's *William II Prince of Orange and his Fiancée, Princess Mary, Daughter of Charles I* (Amsterdam, Rijksmuseum), among the *Children of Charles I* by the same painter (at Windsor, Dresden, and in a different version in Turin), and between Rubens' sons Albert and Nicolas (Vaduz, Liechtenstein Gallery).

21 PHILIPPE MINGUET, *Esthétique du rococo* (Paris: Vrin, 1966), p. 243, footnote.

22 Paris: Hachette, n.d. (1906?).

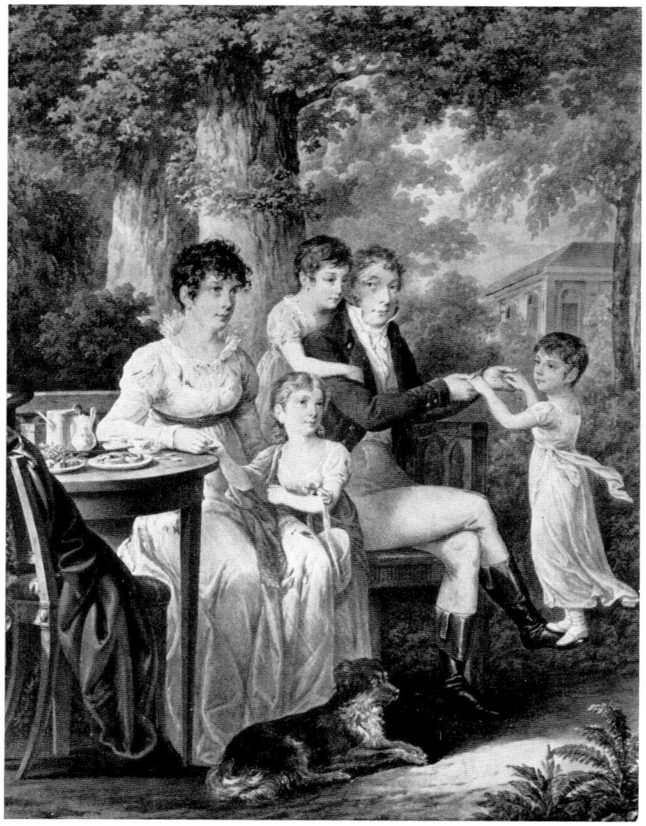

112

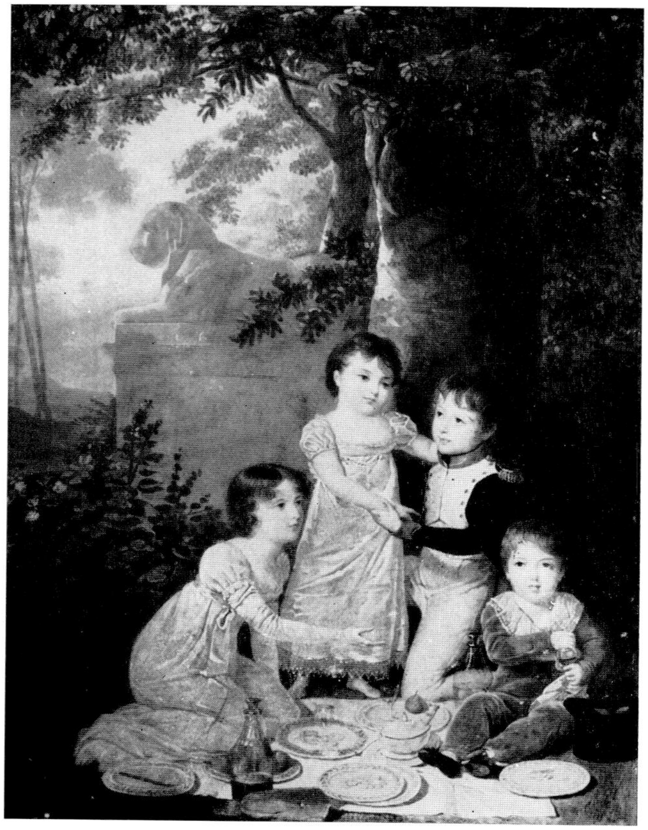

113

Jacob Huysmans (Houseman), a Flemish painter in England and a protégé of Queen Catherine of Braganza, who at a certain moment in the sixties of the seventeenth century looked as if he was going to rival Lely, painted *Four Children of John Coke of Melbourne* (fig. 299). Waterhouse[23] says of this picture that " no more Baroque group was painted in England ", and certainly for Baroque character the painting can compete with Pierre Mignard's *The Grand Dauphin and his Family* of which we have spoken, from which it borrowed the motifs of the boy with a spear and the hovering Cupid; the latter, in Huysmans' painting, stands for Francis, who died in infancy in 1680. Also, the lambs which recur in the portrait Huysmans made of Catherine of Braganza belong, like the cupids, to Mignard's Baroque iconography. In Huysmans' group, as in other groups of children of which we have spoken, we notice the triadic pattern. We find it also in *The Graham Children* (i.e., the children of Robert Bontine Cunningham Graham of Gartmore) by Hogarth (1742; London, National Gallery), where the girl who is dancing to the sound of a musical box, the handle of which is being turned by the boy, anticipates Zoffany's charming dancer,[24] and where the cat lying in wait for the caged bird adds a touch of genre painting. We find a triad also in Hogarth's *A Children's Party* (1730; fig. 300). These are probably the children of the first Earl of Pomfret, and this picture also has traits of genre painting (the dog upsetting the doll's furniture). The composition of Hogarth's painting is imitated by Zoffany in *The Lavie Children* (fig. 111), where again three groups are disposed ladder-wise: the child on the left beating the drum in Hogarth's painting corresponds in Zoffany's to the child sitting on the seesaw. There is a triad also in Barthélemy du Pan's *Children of Frederick, Prince of Wales* (1746; fig. 301), which Waterhouse[25] describes as " the first deliberately domestic royal portrait painted in England " and in which the archer on the right recalls a detail in Rubens' *Family of B. Gerbier*,[26] and again in *The Children of John and Elizabeth Mordaunt*, attributed to John Downman (c. 1750-1824; fig. 302).
Reynolds, in *Lady Cockburn and her Children* (1773; fig. 110), which bore the title *Cornelia and her Children*, introduces the group-

23 *Painting in Britain*, p. 65. 24 See above, p. 128 and p. 184. 25 *Painting in Britain*, p. 115. 26 See above, p. 113.

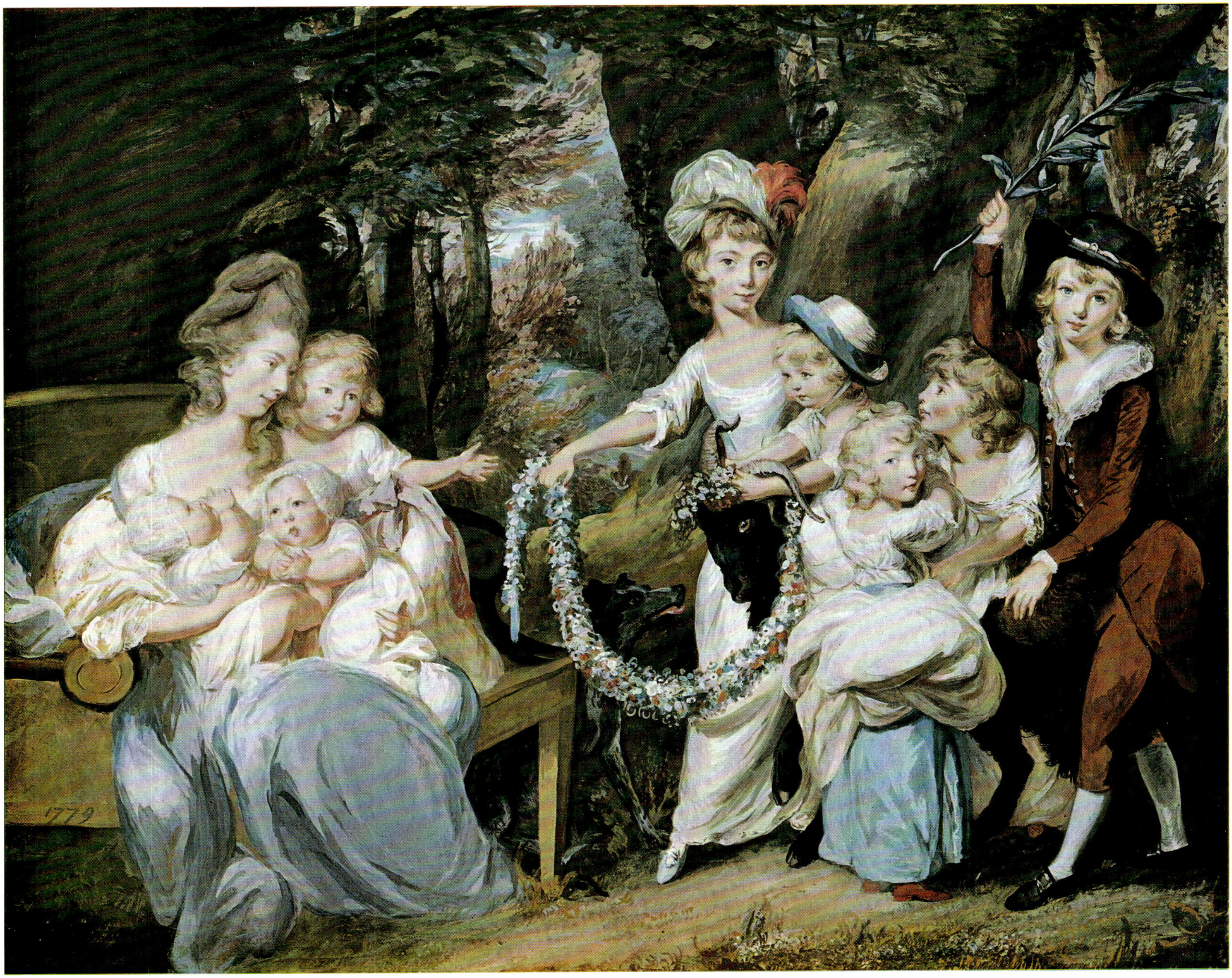

114

112 GEORG KININGER (1767-1831), *Prince Kaunitz's Family*, c. 1810. Schweinfurt, Georg Schäfer Collection. 113 JEAN-BAPTISTE ISABEY (1767-1855), *The Children of Murat Picnicking in the Wood*. Rome, Museo Napoleonico. 114 DANIEL GARDNER (1750-1805), *Mrs. Casamajor with Eight of her Twenty-two Children*. Washington, D.C., collection of Mr. and Mrs. Paul Mellon.

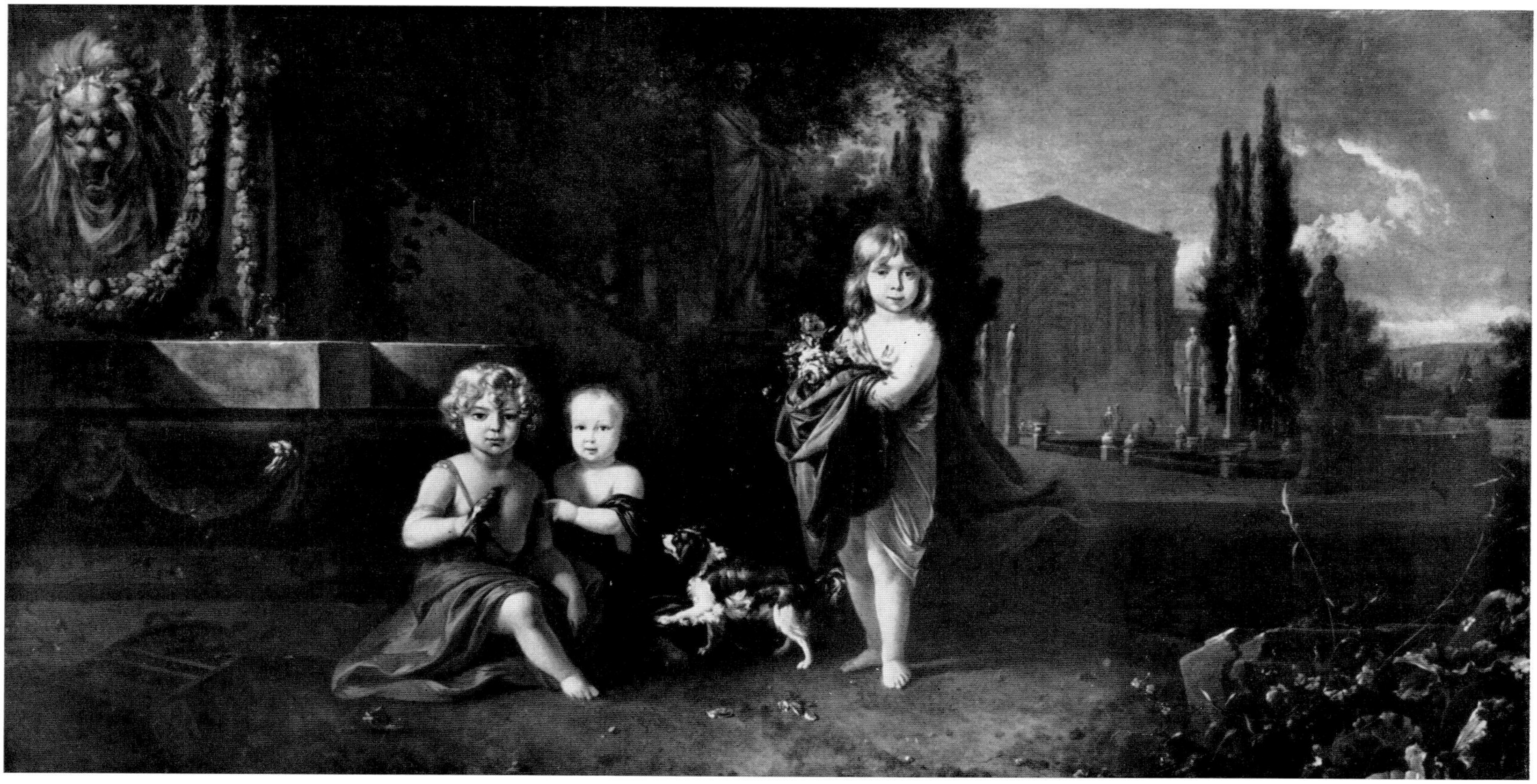

115

ing of children round their mother as in the symbol of Charity in the iconologies. We find a late version of it in Abel's painting:[27] " She shall hold on her left arm a child, whom she shall suckle, and two more shall be playing at her feet, one of them shall hold the right hand of the said figure ".[28] Also Daniel Gardner (1750-1805) in *Mrs. Casamajor with Eight of her Twenty-two Children* shows the prolific mother burdened with her offspring, while other more grown-up children mimic the Pompeian motif of the procession of little cupids, with one of them riding a wreathed goat (fig. 114). John Singleton Copley represents *The Three Younger Daughters of George III and Queen Charlotte* (Buckingham Palace) almost as in a dance figure, joined by the dogs; the parrots on the festoon at the top are a motif which we have found before in Reynolds.

Louis Ducis' (1773-1847) painting of *Napoleon with Murat's Children on the Terrace of Saint-Cloud* (Versailles Museum), Isabey's *The Children of Murat Picnicking in the Wood* (fig. 113), Chatillon's *The Children of Jérôme Bonaparte in the Garden* (Jérôme Napoléon with a bow, the Princess Mathilde, and little Napoléon Jérôme, later known as " Plon-Plon "; fig. 306), and F. Gérard's painting showing Marshall Lannes' wife going with her children down a flight of steps in a park (fig. 304) — all seem to show the desire of the élite of the Napoleonic period to compete with the English aristocracy in having themselves portrayed in moments of domestic privacy.

Children were usually shown in some animated posture, as a rule playing. The anonymous author of the portrait of *The Children of Francesco Caccia* (about 1776; the property of Count Federico Caccia Dominioni, Milan) represents them as they wreathe the youngest one; Nathaniel Dance, in the portrait of *The Sartorio Family* (about 1760) places in the centre of the painting the little figure, dressed in white and pink, of a fishing girl (Modena, Musei Civici); Zoffany portrays *The Three Children of Grand Duke Leopold of Tuscany*, the two girls dancing while the little boy plays a pocket-violin (Count Giovanni Treccani degli Alfieri Collection, Milan); Vincenz Georg Kininger (1767-1831), in the group of *Prince Kaunitz's Family* (c. 1810; fig. 112) seated under a

27 See above, p. 143. 28 CESARE RIPA, *Iconologia*, " Carità ".

115 JAN WEENIX (1640-1719), *Children in a Park*. Rome, property of Mssrs. C. and M. Sestieri.

116 OCTAVIUS OAKLEY (1800-1867), *Sir Reresby Sitwell with his Brother and Sister*, c. 1828. Renishaw Hall (Derbyshire), collection of Mr. Reresby Sitwell.

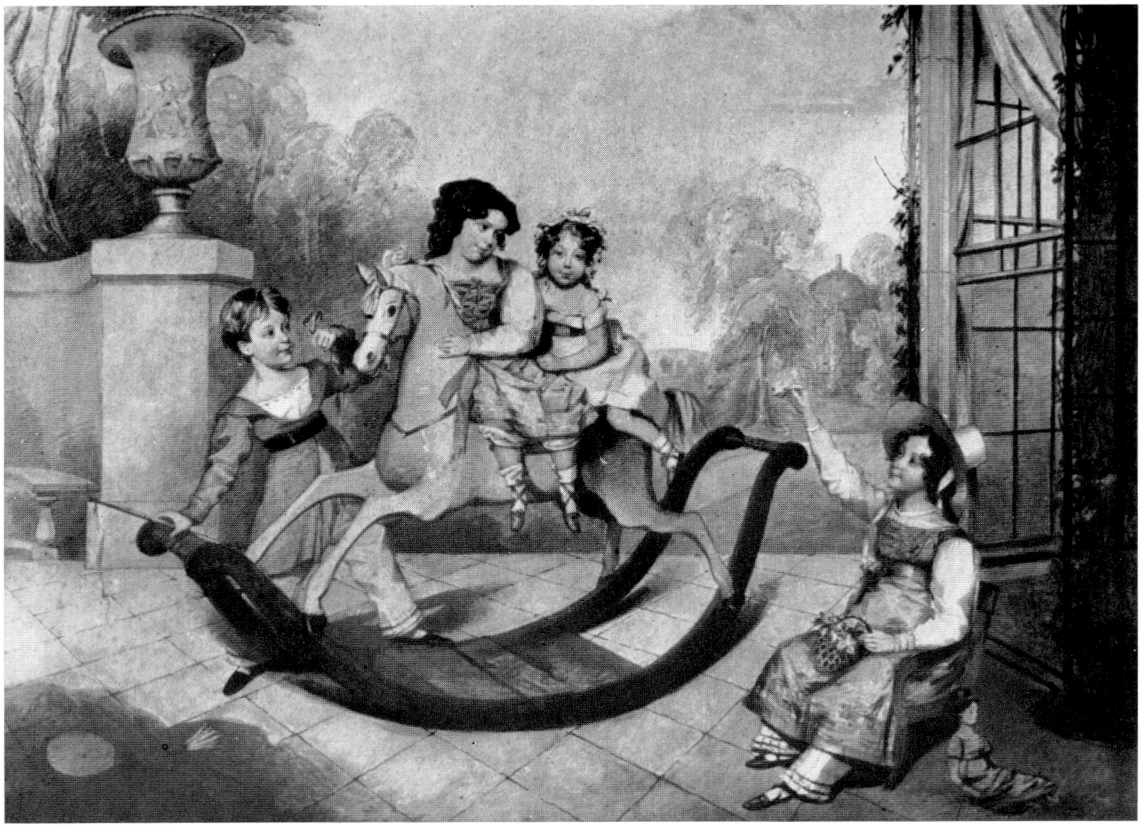

116

117 attr. to GEORGE WATSON (1767-1837), *The Children of Thomas Bruce, Seventh Earl of Elgin*, c. 1805. Broomhall, Dunfermline, collection of Lord Bruce.

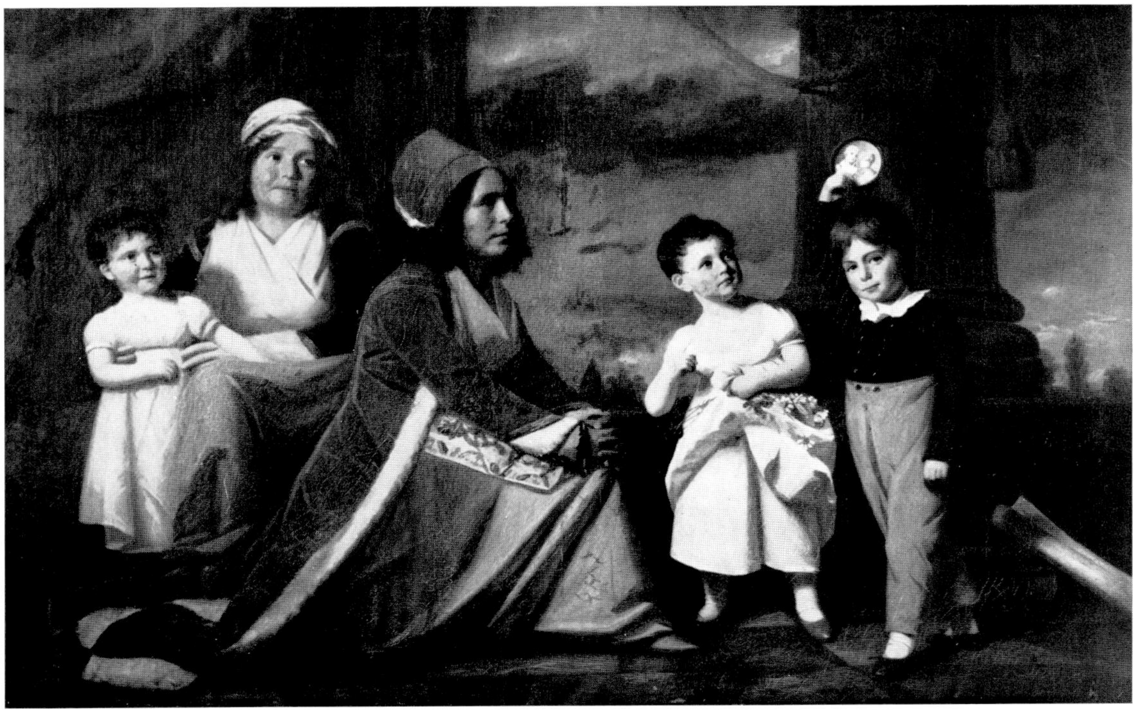

117

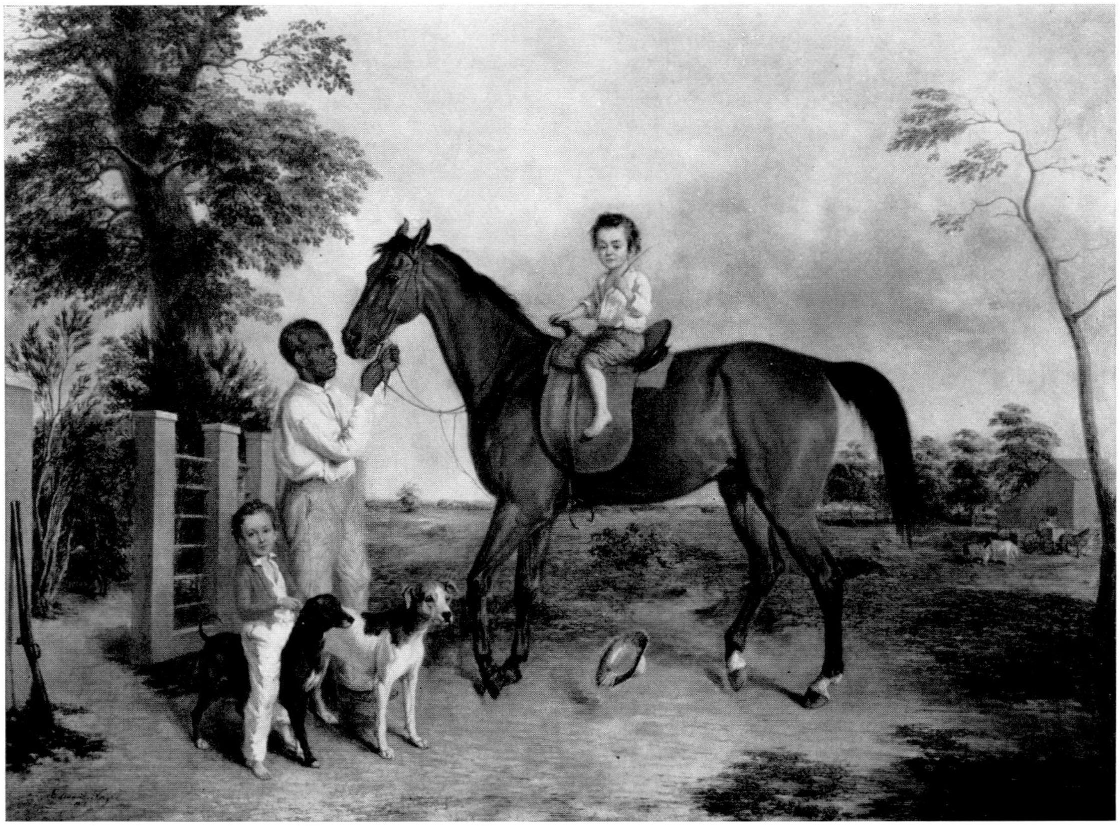

118 EDWARD TROYE (1808-1874), *The Children of a Southern Family*. New York, collection of Mr. E. J. Rousuck.

tree in the garden, shows the father in the act of rocking the youngest of his daughters on the tip of his boot; Daffinger represents Metternich's children busy round a caged bird (miniature in the possession of the Metternich family). The painter of *The Children of Thomas Bruce* (about 1805; perhaps by George Watson [1767-1837]) with two Greek nurses, who probably entered Lord Elgin's service when he was ambassador in Constantinople (1799-1803), shows us one of the children brandishing a miniature with the portraits of his parents, who at the time were Napoleon's prisoners in Paris: another child with her lap full of flowers is looking at the miniature and is about to make an affectionate gesture (fig. 116). A Swedish pupil of David, Per Krafft the Younger (1777-1863) portrayed in 1812 Lovisa Albertina Bohnstedt pushing the youngest of her children on a swing in a corner of a garden, with another child leaning against her and smiling at his brother (fig. 303). Johann Christoph Rincklake (1764-1813) in a *Family Portrait in the Schlossgarten of Tatenhausen* (the property of Count von Korff-Schmising, Münster) painted, in the setting of a garden with a view of a castle and a little statue of a Muse with a lyre, some boys on a pony, two girls carrying a small child on their joined hands, and more children round their father and mother.[29] In another of his paintings, *The Beierle Family* (the property of Friedrich Wirtensohn, Münster), the scene is a garden under a pergola, with children running about and tea being served on the table. Pietro Benvenuti painted *The Children of Prince Corsini* (1808) naked like classical putti, while a devoted dog patiently bears their weight (fig. 307). But Jan Weenix had already placed three half-naked children with a dog against one of his favourite backgrounds, a park at dusk adorned with sculpture, with a view of a villa (fig. 115).
Octavius Oakley (1800-1867), a local artist who worked chiefly in Derby and the country houses in the neighbourhood, in a watercolour of about 1828 portrays the Sitwell children on a rocking horse (fig. 117); one of *The Children of a Southern Family* (fig. 118) by the Swiss-American Edward Troye has, on the contrary, been hoisted onto a real horse: here the Negro slave is on much more familiar terms than in Zoffany's *Family of Sir William Young*.[30] The Dutch painter Georg van der Mijn (1723-

29 See the article by BURKHARD MEIER in *Cicerone*, 1913, pp. 821 ff. 30 See above, p. 133.

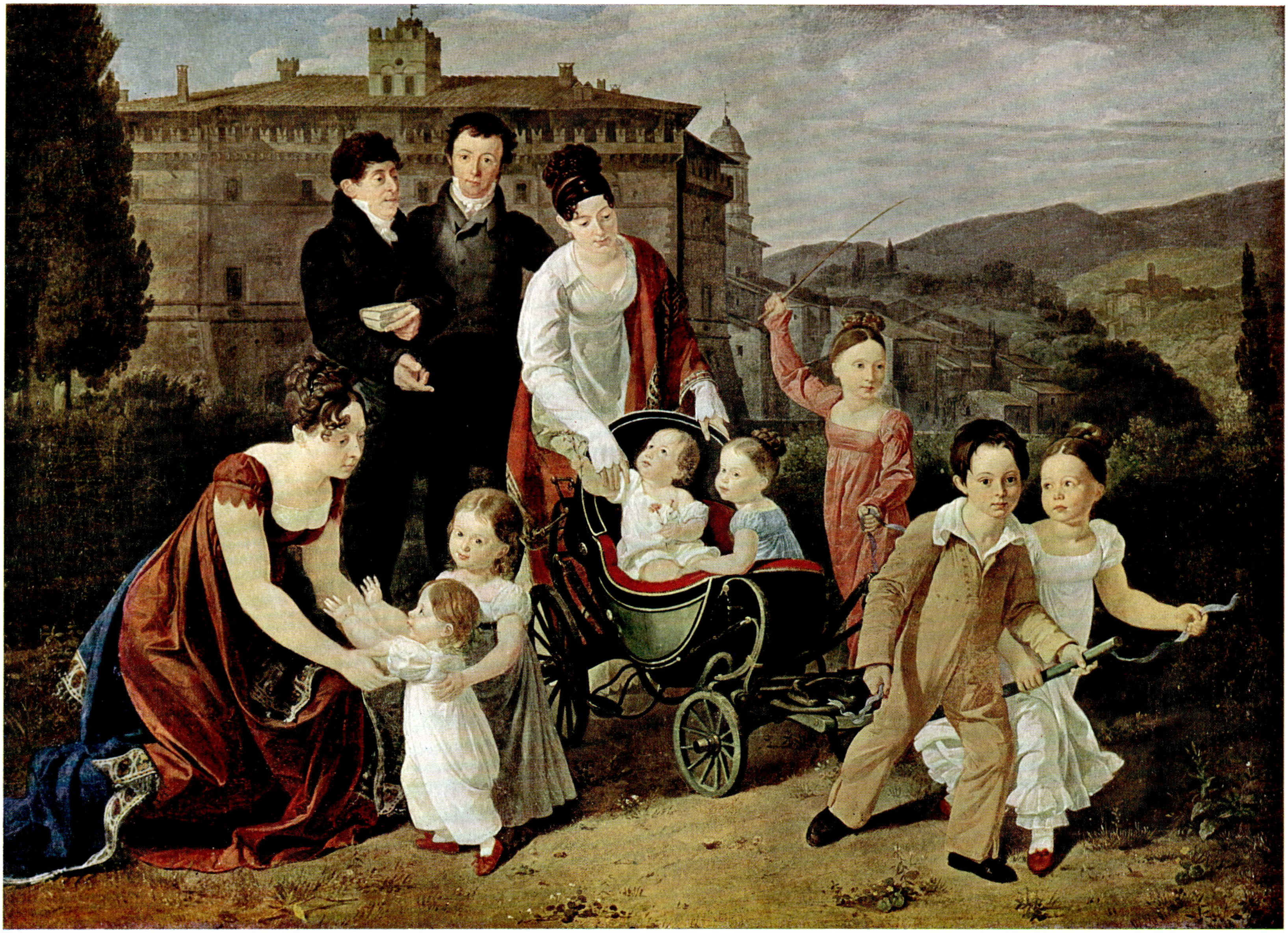

119

119 ANONYMOUS (19th century), *The Ruspoli Family in the Garden of Vignanello.* Rome, collection of Principe Ruspoli.

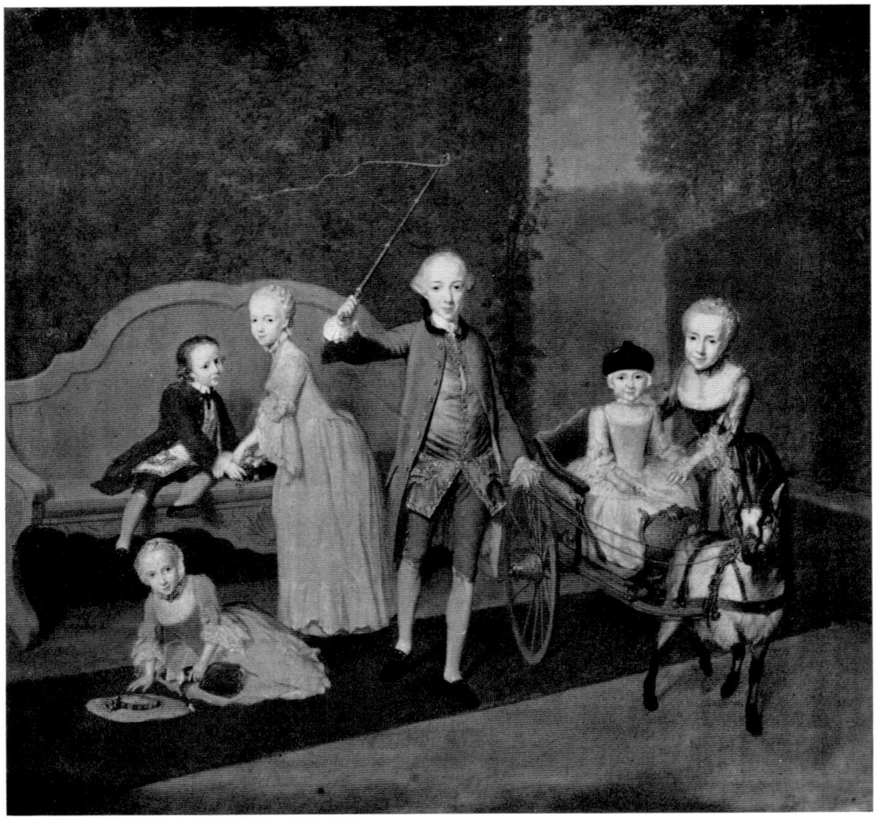

120

120 GEORGE VAN DER MIJN (1723-1763), *The van Sypesteyn Children.* Nieuw-Loosdrecht, Museum De Sypesteyn.

1763) introduces a go-cart drawn by a goat in the group of *The van Sypesteyn Children* (fig. 120); the Swiss Paul Melchior von Deschwanden (1811-1881), author of mediocre religious paintings in the spirit of the Nazarenes, also has represented in a drawing of 1842 *The Children of the Magistrate Dietrich Schindler* in a go-cart.[31] A much greater painter, Runge, in 1805 portrayed *The Hülsenbeck Children* (Hamburg, Kunsthalle) in an orchard, pushing the youngest in a go-cart: a suburban scene, whose realistic setting (a wooden fence and a modest house in the shadow of fir trees) surprisingly does not clash with the almost classical figures of the children. The same popular motif was taken up by the anonymous painter of *The Ruspoli Family in the Garden of Vignanello* (with the faulty English title *The Walking of Children*; fig. 119); by Giuseppe Tominz in a drawing in the Museo Provinciale di Palazzo Attems of Gorizia (fig. 305); and — at the end of the nineteenth century (1884) — by Francesco Gai in the *Princess Elisabetta Brancaccio with her Children Carlo, Maria Eleonora, and Marcantonio* (fig. 121); in the latter, the charming motif of the infant in the go-cart, pulled by his mother, is combined with that of the eldest child showing a butterfly he has captured to the other two, who make gestures of surprise and envy. There is a small carriage also in the group of *Rev. and Mrs. Henry Palmer with their Children* (1838), by John Ferneley (1781-1860; fig. 308); in the companion group, *Miss Heyrick with the Palmer Children* (fig. 122), a child is held by the governess on horseback and another leans on a donkey. The German Wilhelm Friedrich Herbig (1788-1861) drew inspiration from sacred compositions in portraying (in 1824) children clustering round their mother in *The Artist's Family* (fig. 310), thus giving a Nazarene version of the motif already treated by Reynolds, with wreaths and emblematic flowers like the rose and lily.

Three children, two of them in uniform, appear in a painting of a decidedly *naïf* flavour by Friedrich Weise, *The Puhlmann Children at Heiligensee, Potsdam* (c. 1830; fig. 123). Busy playing at soldiers, with a flag and a little gun, are the three children

31 See reproduction in *Schweizer Kleinmeister*, ed. WALTER HUGELSHOFER (Zurich: Fretz & Wasmuth Verlag), 1943, pl. 96.

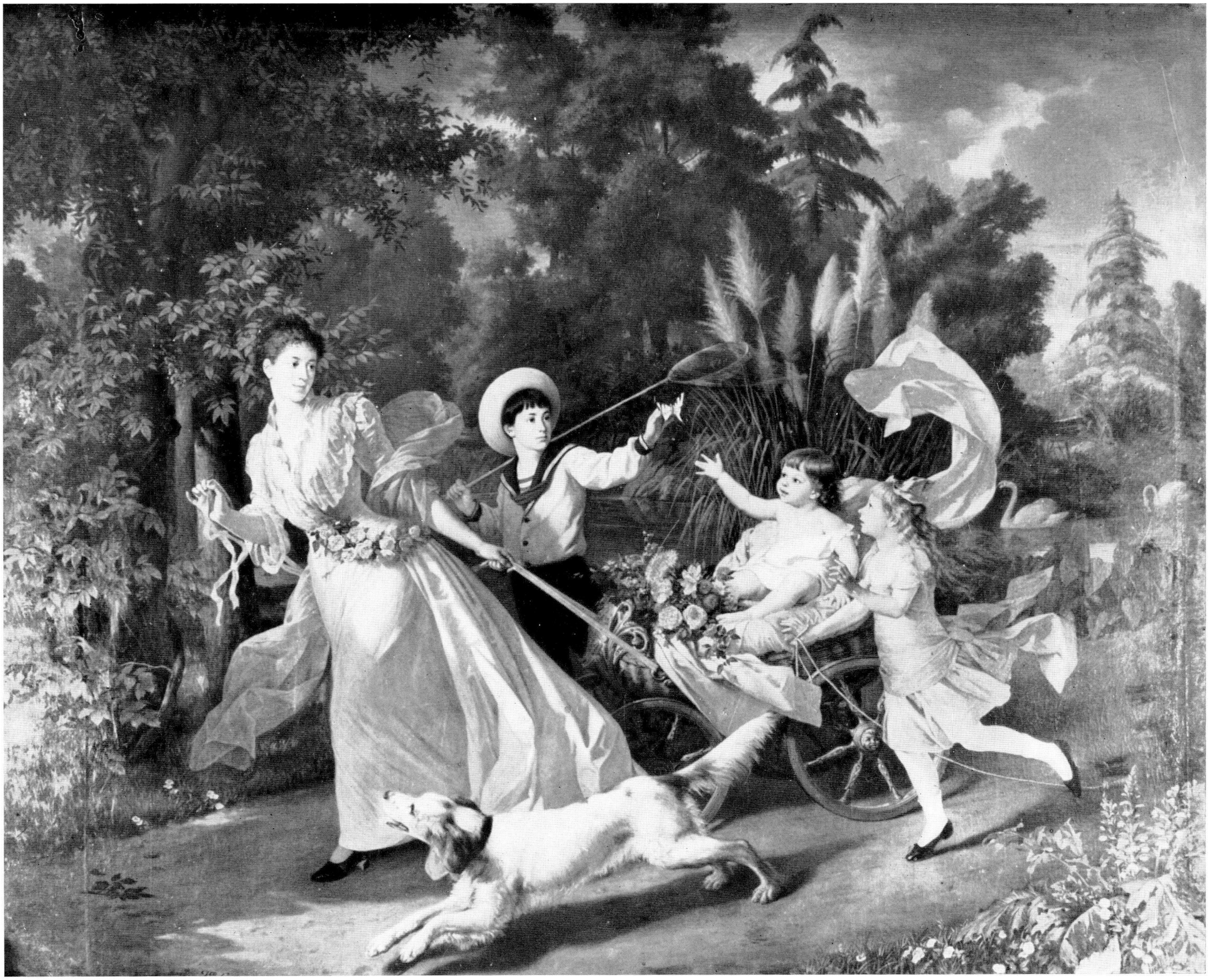

121

121 FRANCESCO GAI (1835-1917), *Princess Elisabetta Brancaccio with her Children*, 1884. Rome, Museo di Roma.

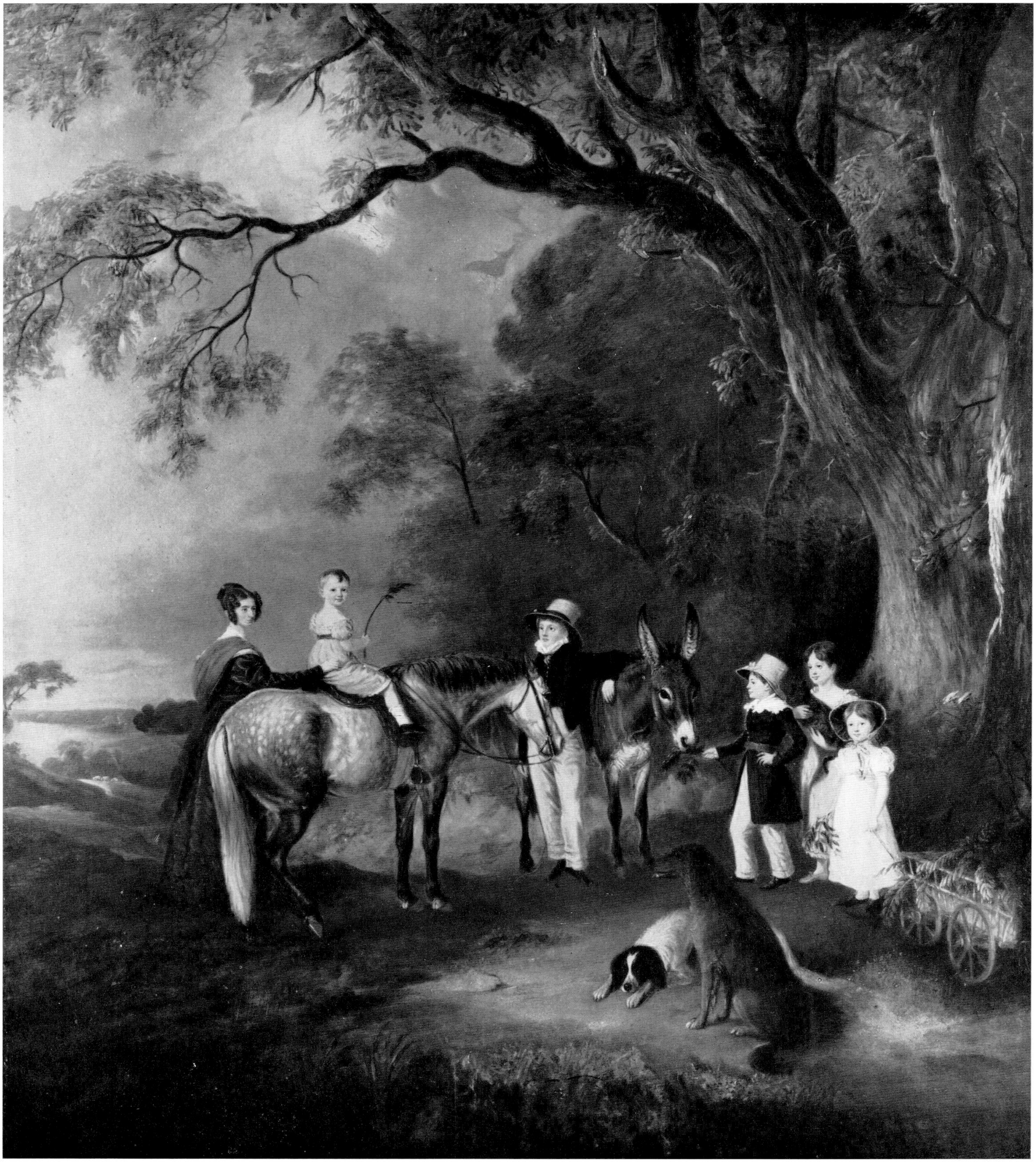

122

122 JOHN FERNELEY (1781-1860), *Miss Heyrick with the Palmer Children*, 1827. Washington, D.C., collection of Mr. and Mrs. Paul Mellon. 123 FRIEDRICH WEISE (1775-?), *The Puhlmann Children at Heiligensee, Potsdam*, c. 1830. Potsdam, Staatliche Bildergalerie. 124 ARTHUR DEVIS (1711-1787), *Emily and George Mason*. Washington, D.C., collection of Mr. and Mrs. Paul Mellon.

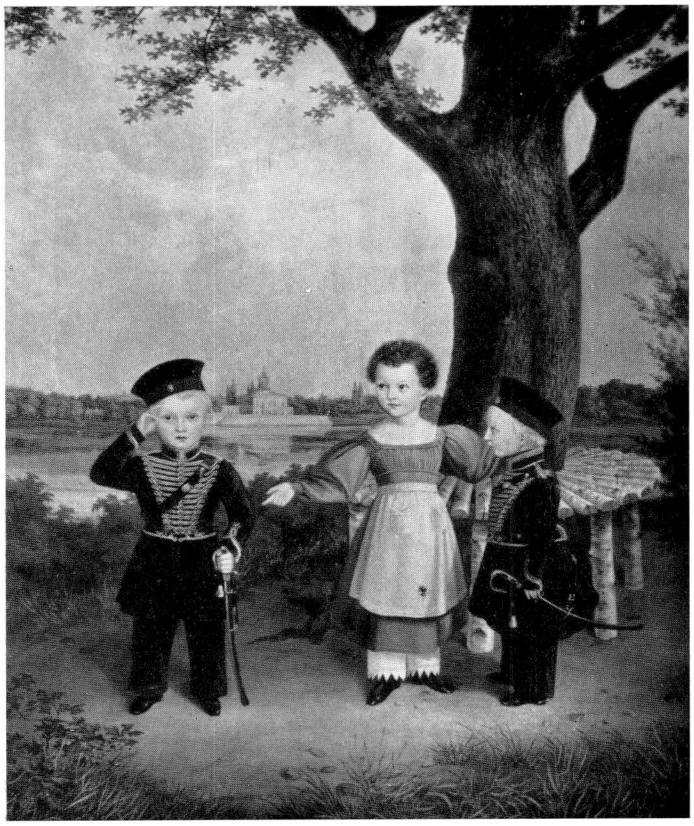

123

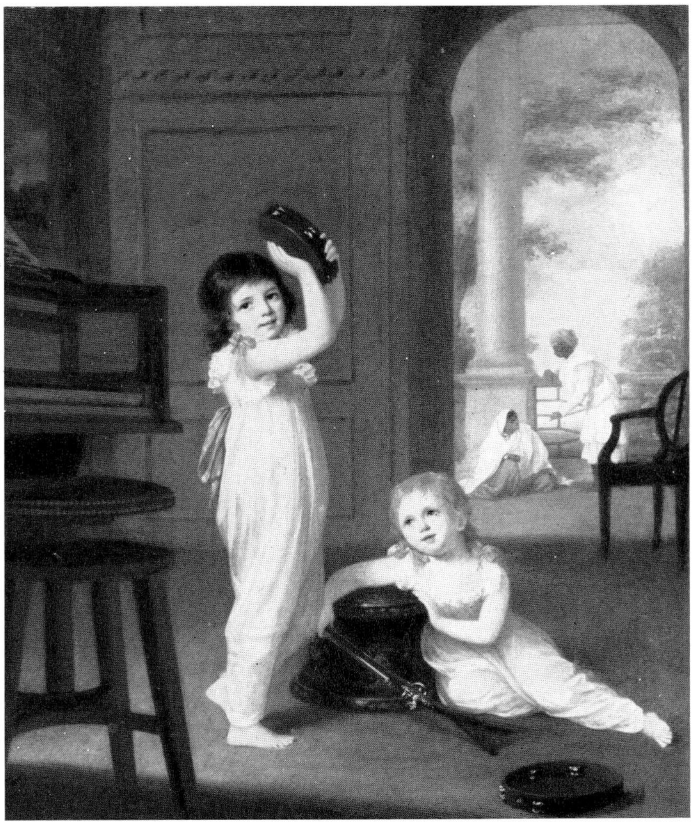

124

of the group (1848) by Johann Baptist Reiter (1813-1890), the creator of the " intimate portrait " of the late Viennese Biedermeier period; the parents are watching from behind a hedge. The manuscript dedication on the back of the painting has a decidedly Biedermeier flavour: "Beloved Camilla: in this painting you find again the children with whom your tender love has made me happy. Souvenir of March 13, 1848, from your faithful Fritz " (Georg Schäfer Collection, Schweinfurt).[32] The rifle hardly seems a suitable object in the hands of the little boy, indistinguishable in sex and dress from the little girl beating the tambourine, in the group of *Emily and George Mason* by Arthur Devis, in an Indian setting (two Indian servants are engaged in a discussion on the porch; fig. 124). The Danish painter Eckersberg shows the Holm children stooping to look at illustrations in a book, in a painting of tender nineteenth-century realism. Again we have a touch of the *naïf*, especially in the child who draws the toy cart, in the painting by Guillaume de Montval, *A.C. Gamel with his Children* (c. 1811; the property of the Gamel family, Denmark).[33] Danish nineteenth-century painters in particular showed great variety, and psychological insight as well, in dealing with the subject of children in their conversation pieces, especially Vilhelm Marstrand (1810-1873) in *The Waagepetersen Family* (1831; Copenhagen, Statens Museum for Kunst) — in which two boys stop playing skittles on the table in order to look in our direction, and the gentle face of one of them contrasts with the grimace of the caricature he is holding in his hand — and in another painting at the same museum which represents *The Artist's Wife and Children in the " Apartment of Famous Painters " in the Royal Academy of Fine Arts* (1861-62), where one of the boys, who has stopped leafing through his picture book, is staring into space as if rapt in a dream.[34] George Chinnery's sketch of *The Artist's Brother with his Children and their Chinese Nurse*, a triangular composition, is made attractive by the Scottish costume of one of the children and by the exotic nurse (fig. 309), who in the finished painting has been replaced by the mother (the view from the window is no longer the countryside, but a seascape; fig. 311).

32 Reproduced in colour in *Der frühe Realismus, 1800-1850, Gemälde und Zeichnungen aus der Sammlung Georg Schäfer, Schweinfurt* (Ausstellung im Germanischen Nationalmuseum, Nürnberg, 1967), pl. 220. 33 Reproduction in JØRGEN B. HARTMANN, *København, Interiører og Prospekter,* ill. 67. 34 These two paintings are reproduced in M. PRAZ, *An Illustrated History of Furnishing*, pp. 287, 331, together with many other Danish and Russian conversation pieces which are not repeated in the present volume.

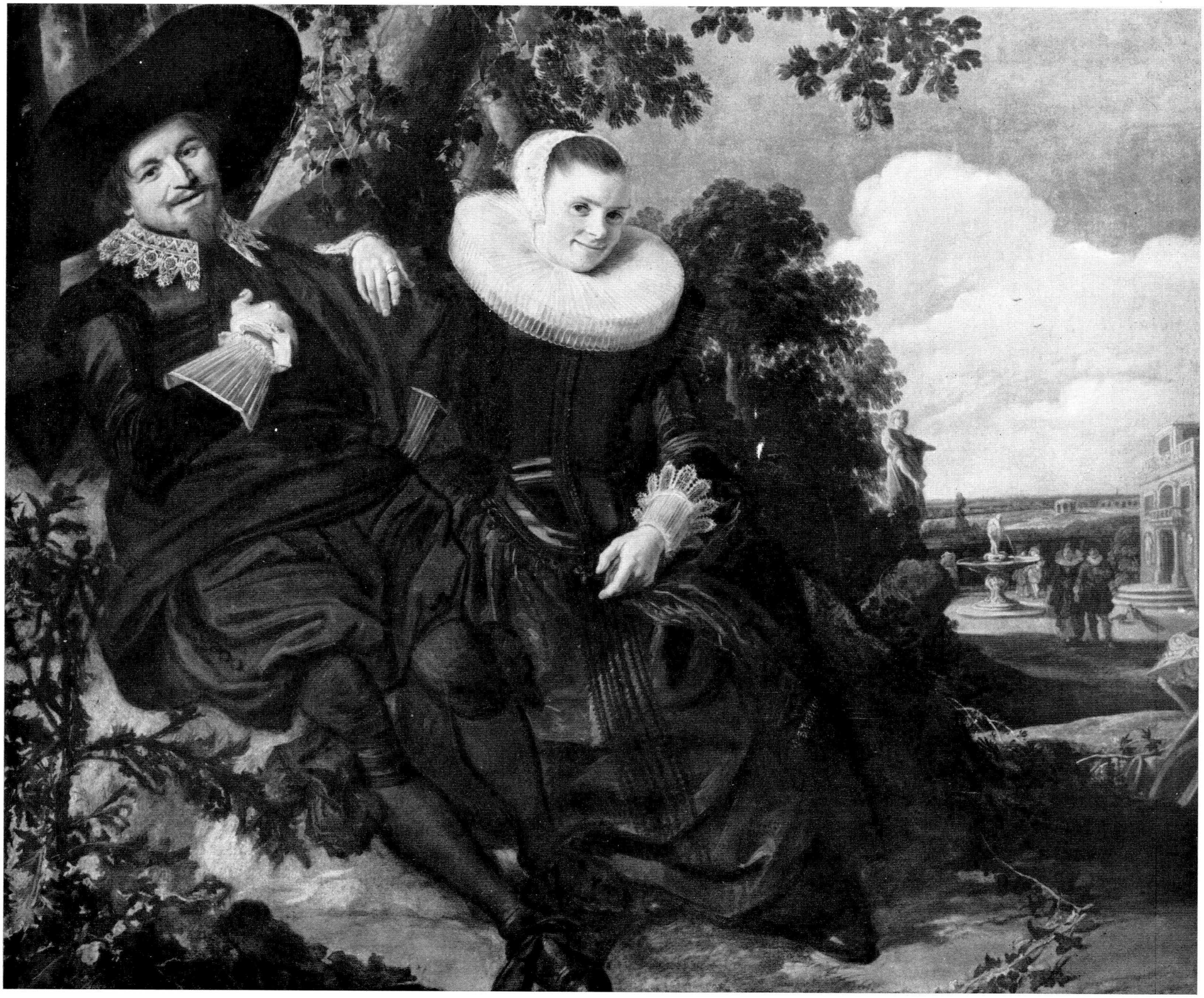

125

125 FRANS HALS (1581/5-1666), *A Couple in a Park*. Amsterdam, Rijksmuseum.

CHAPTER VII – THE COUPLE

Conversation pieces begin with a group of two people. As we have seen in Jan van Eyck's portrait of the Arnolfini couple, all the features of the genre are present: surroundings, intimacy, a significant gesture, small proportions. More tamely, they also begin in Italy with the waist-length double portrait. Many more examples of this could be added to those given already, such as the double portrait of Signorelli and another person, and others in no way different from the portraits which appear in sacred paintings — for instance, Ghirlandaio's in the Collegiata of San Gimignano, in the Sistine Chapel, and in the Sassetti Chapel in the church of Santa Trinita in Florence — were it not that they are detached from the sacred composition and presented by themselves.

The portrait of a couple of friends was established as a genre during the period of humanism, developed in the courts (the portrait of the prince with one of his household), and became widespread until it was limited to painters' circles during the nineteenth century. Among the best-known examples are the double portrait of young men by Giovanni Cariani (after a painting by Giorgione?) at the Louvre, one by Pontormo in the Cini Collection, the so-called *Ambassadors* (Jean de Dinteville and Georges de Selve) by Holbein at the National Gallery, London, and others mentioned by Harald Keller in his essay on this kind of portraiture.[1]

We are dealing here with the group of two persons as a somewhat separate category because its patterns of composition follow slightly different rules from those of the larger group, and because it introduces motifs which develop along different lines. The most striking of these motifs is the married couple portrayed in one corner of a landscape, almost as if the dawning cult of nature was replacing the sacred scene of the holy pictures of the Quattrocento in which the donor appeared in a corner. Interest in landscape started, in fact, in Italy with Annibale Carracci and Domenichino: see, for instance, the *Magdalen* by the former in the Doria Gallery, in which the saint is seated in a corner of a picture whose real subject is the calm, melancholy landscape

1 "Entstehung und Blütezeit des Freundschaftsbildes", in *Essays in the History of Art presented to Rudolf Wittkower* (London: Phaidon Press, 1967), pp. 161-73; see also K. LANKHEIT, *Das Freundschaftsbild der Romantik*, Heidelberger Kunstgeschichtliche Abhandlungen, ed. W. Paatz, n.f. 1 (Heidelberg, 1952).

of Latium, into which the state of mind of the penitent seems to be transfused and sublimated. Giorgione, too, presented beside a landscape and against a screen of foliage his *Three Philosophers* (Vienna, Kunsthistorisches Museum). In Frans Hals' *Couple in a Park* (fig. 125) the married pair is also portrayed against a background of foliage, in the corner of a garden seen on the right with its statues, fountains, and part of a building which resembles that in *Rubens Walking with Hélène Fourment*. Gerard Donck, who was active in the period 1627-40, again shows *Jan van Hensbeeck and his Wife Maria Koeck* beside a landscape (fig. 128); the arrangement of the composition resembles the scheme used by Pieter Codde[2] for a couple in an interior: one person is standing and the other sitting within the triangular design which, as we have seen, was so popular in paintings of groups. Another instance of portraits in a landscape is *Nathaniel Higginson, Governor of Madras, and his Family* by an unknown painter (Dr. J. Dellinger Barney Collection, Boston, Mass.), with Fort St. George on the left flying the English flag. The portrait was painted after Higginson had returned to England in 1700. Set once again in one corner of a landscape (the park of a country house), *The Lyttelton Family* (1748) by Arthur Devis shows a third person, as in the painting just described (fig. 313). In another painting, *Horace Walpole Presenting Kitty Clive with a Piece of Honeysuckle* (fig. 132), Devis has portrayed a standing gentleman and a seated lady beside a view of the Thames. Kitty Clive, an actress, was a great friend of Walpole; he presented her with a house at Strawberry Hill to which she retired in 1769, and the view in the picture was probably taken from it. The pattern of a standing man and a seated woman is also found in *Mr. and Mrs. Atherton*, an indoor " conversation " by Devis in which, with disarming naïveté, pictures in a dark room are clearly visible (fig. 312). According to Sitwell,[3] Arthur Devis — a pupil of the Antwerp painter Pieter Tillemans — deserves no less consideration than Pietro Longhi; his brightly coloured and somewhat wooden figures sometimes appear to have a *naïf* quality. Devis' talent was revealed by the 1930 exhibition of conversation pieces. Like all *naïfs*, he had a bag of tricks which he always used in his compositions: they are his trademark. Thus in *The van Harthals Family* (1749), we find the lady putting her hand on the tripod of a telescope directed towards a spacious background (fig. 133). The man using a tree trunk as a pulpit to declaim God knows what, attended by God knows whom, and the child in the centre leaning on a stick in the posture of the shepherd in Giorgione's *Tempesta* are figures enclosed each in his own isolation, just as in Giorgione's painting — with which, however, Devis' " conversation " has nothing else in common.

The pattern of the couple beside a landscape reached its full development with Thomas Gainsborough, whose masterpiece in this genre is the portrait of *Mr. and Mrs. Andrews* (fig. 131); Sitwell compares this painting for quality of inspiration to " a work of the Salzburg period of Mozart ".[4] This and other similar " conversations " were painted by Gainsborough before 1760 — i.e., before he was thirty-three (he was born in 1727) — and belong to the period when he lived in Ipswich. Afterwards he devoted himself to more profitable life-size pictures. Just as Ingres was to complain of having to cultivate the portrait for the sake of making money while his inclination (or so he thought) was for historical and mythological painting, so Gainsborough, in his letters, complained of having to paint portraits when what really interested him was landscape. Indeed, as Waterhouse has remarked: " Gainsborough is at his best with sitters who have almost no positive character and can be treated as arabesques with that lightness of manner and effect... ".[5] Not for nothing had he been a pupil of Gravelot and, through the latter's engravings, had become familiar with the work of Watteau. One might apply to the faces of his married couples what Siegfried Sassoon said of the typical English face: that it lacks expression, like a boot.[6] Gainsborough's landscapes were painted from memory (towards the end of his life he actually came to paint landscapes from little compositional models he made of pebbles, moss, etc.), and their foliage lacks the characterization you find in Constable, but the lyrical sense of landscape is rendered by Gainsborough in an inimitable way because his rare sensibility is alive to the play of light and shade, and it is in this that the expression of landscape lies. The expression which one misses in the faces is felt in the natural scenery. Gainsborough possessed, moreover, a powerful sense of the rhythm of line,[7] and the paintings which we are now discussing testify to it. It is chiefly this rhythm which gives us the impression of serene repose in the human beings represented in his conversation pieces.

Gainsborough depicts the delight of the landed gentleman in the countryside where he lives. These paintings are, therefore, a perfect mirror of eighteenth-century English society. They vary, however, in quality from the freshness of impression of *Mr. and Mrs. Andrews*, the *Unknown Gentleman and Lady* of the Dulwich College Picture Gallery, *John Joshua Kirby and Sarah Bull*,

2 See above, p. 60. 3 *Conversation Pieces* (London: Batsford, 1936), p. 49. 4 Ibid., p. 15. 5 *Painting in Britain*, 2nd ed. (Harmondsworth and Baltimore: Penguin Books, 1962), pp. 70-71. 6 In *Memoirs of a Fox-Hunting Man*. 7 Cf. *Painting in Britain*, p. 172.

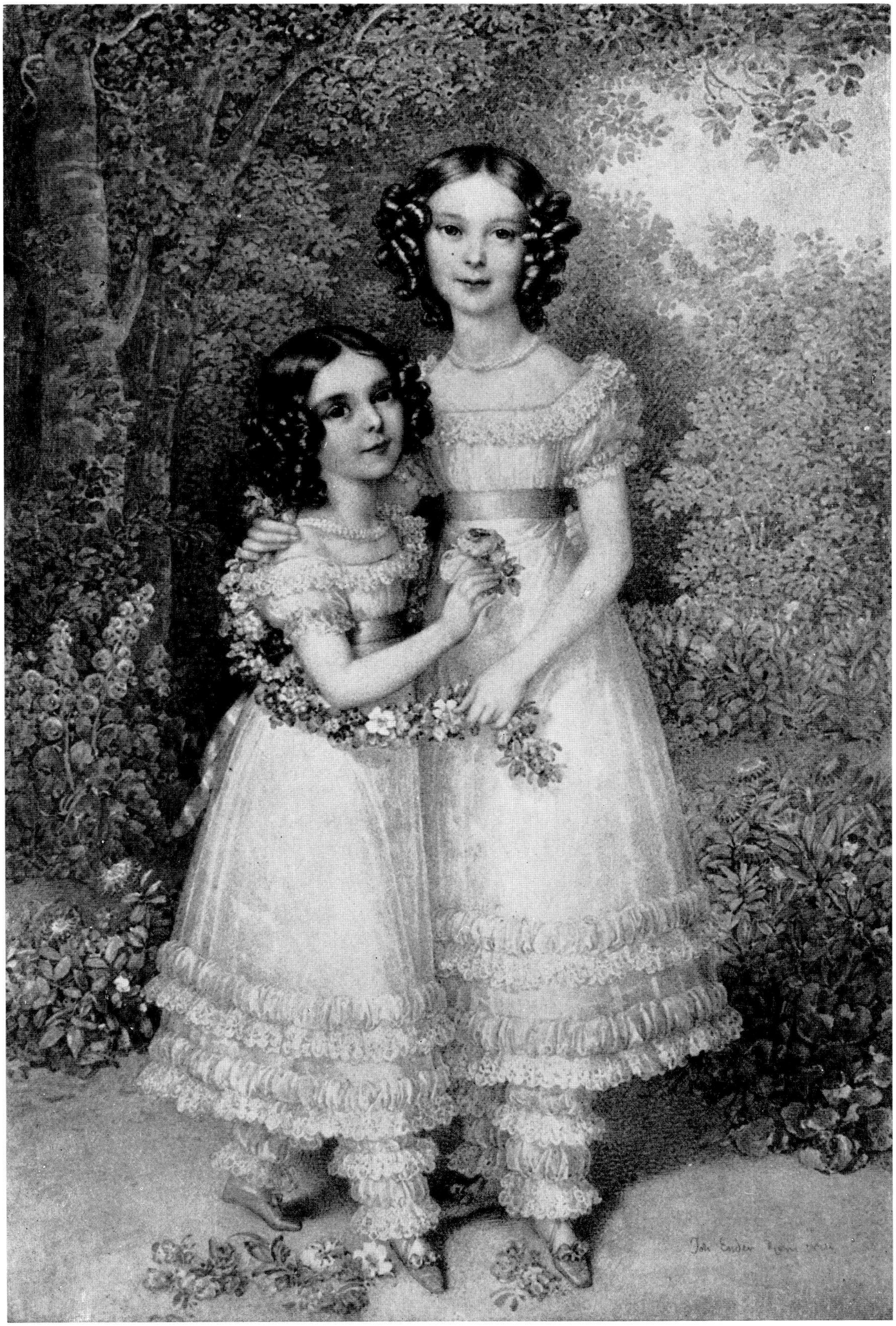

126

126 JOHANN NEPOMUK ENDER (1793-1854), *The Talbot Sisters*, 1824. Rome, private collection.

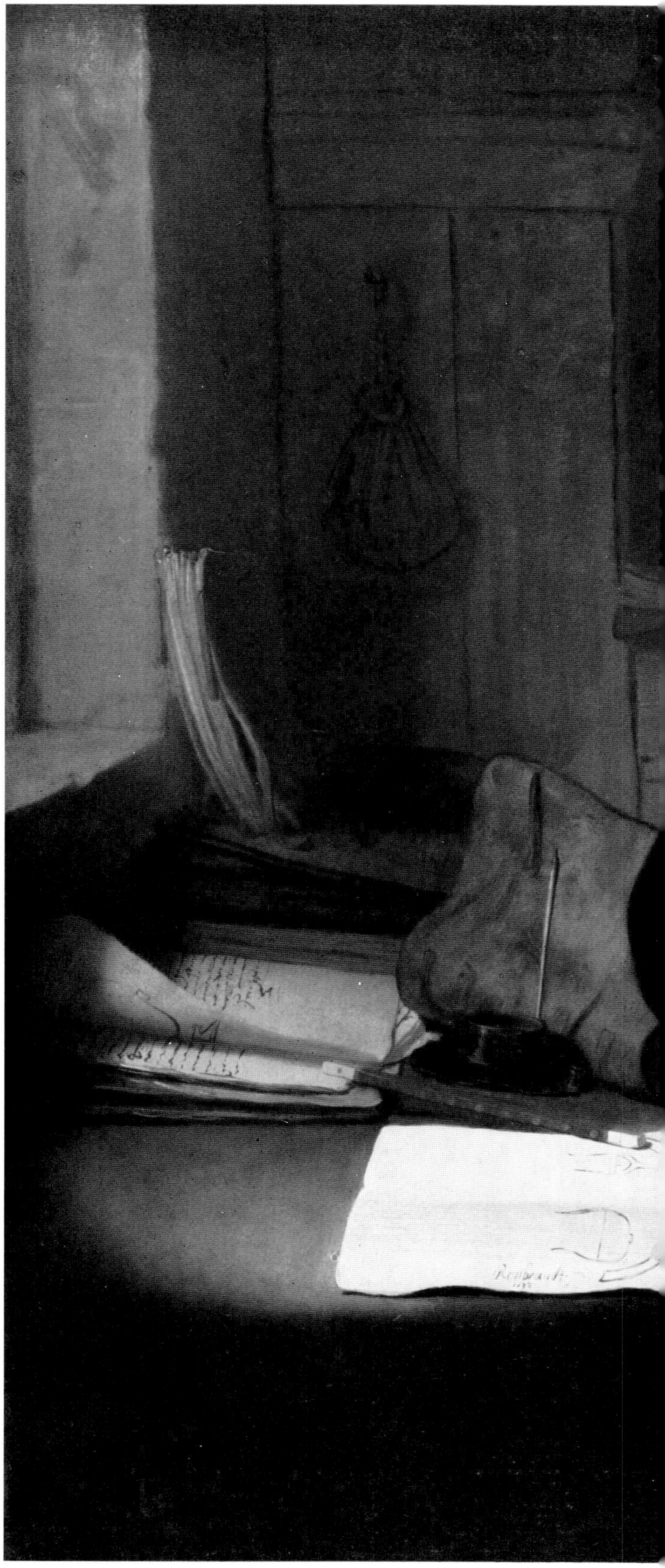

127

127 REMBRANDT VAN RIJN (1606-1669), *The Shipbuilder and his Wife*, 1633. London, Buckingham Palace, Royal Collections; copyright reserved.

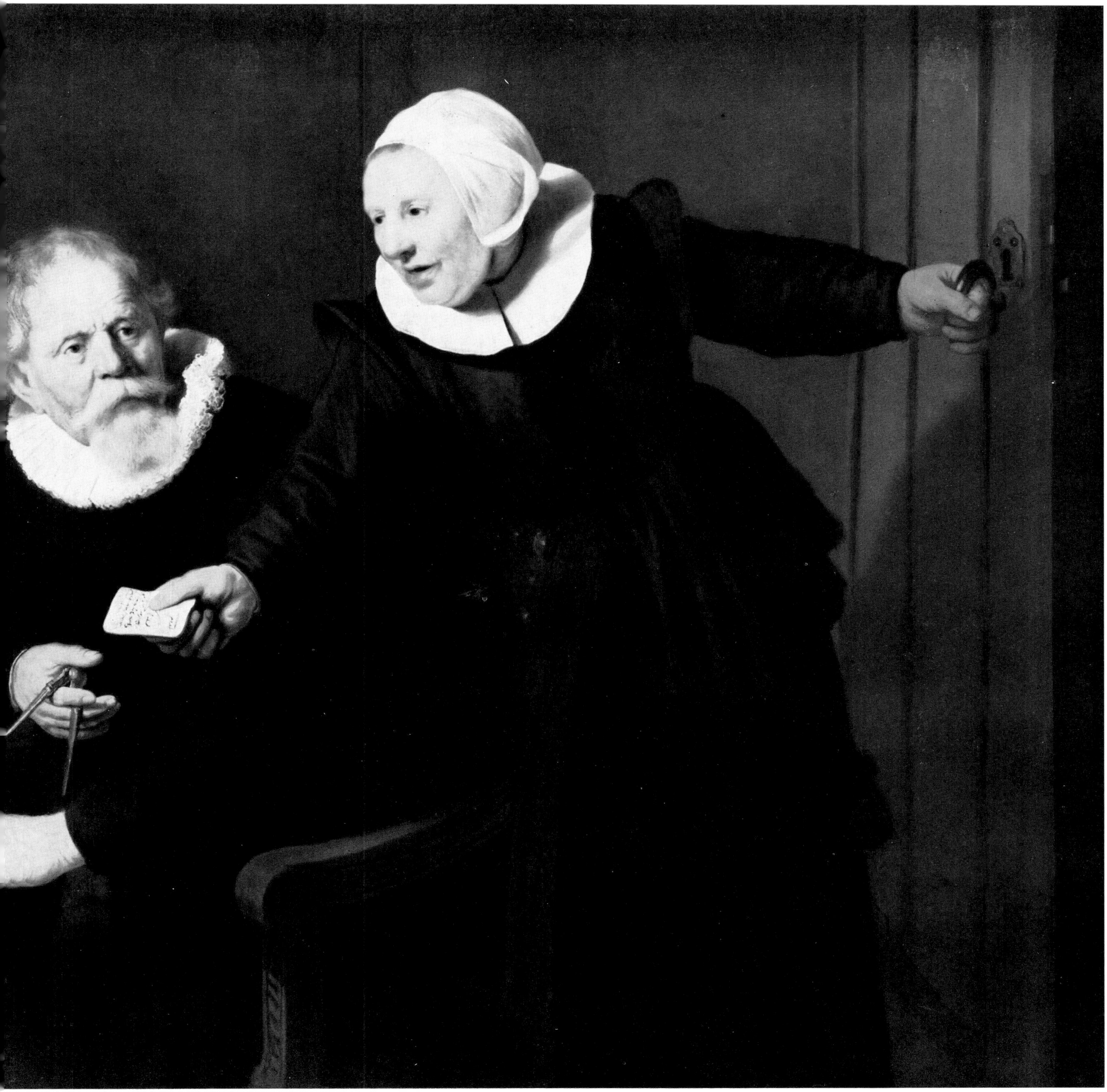

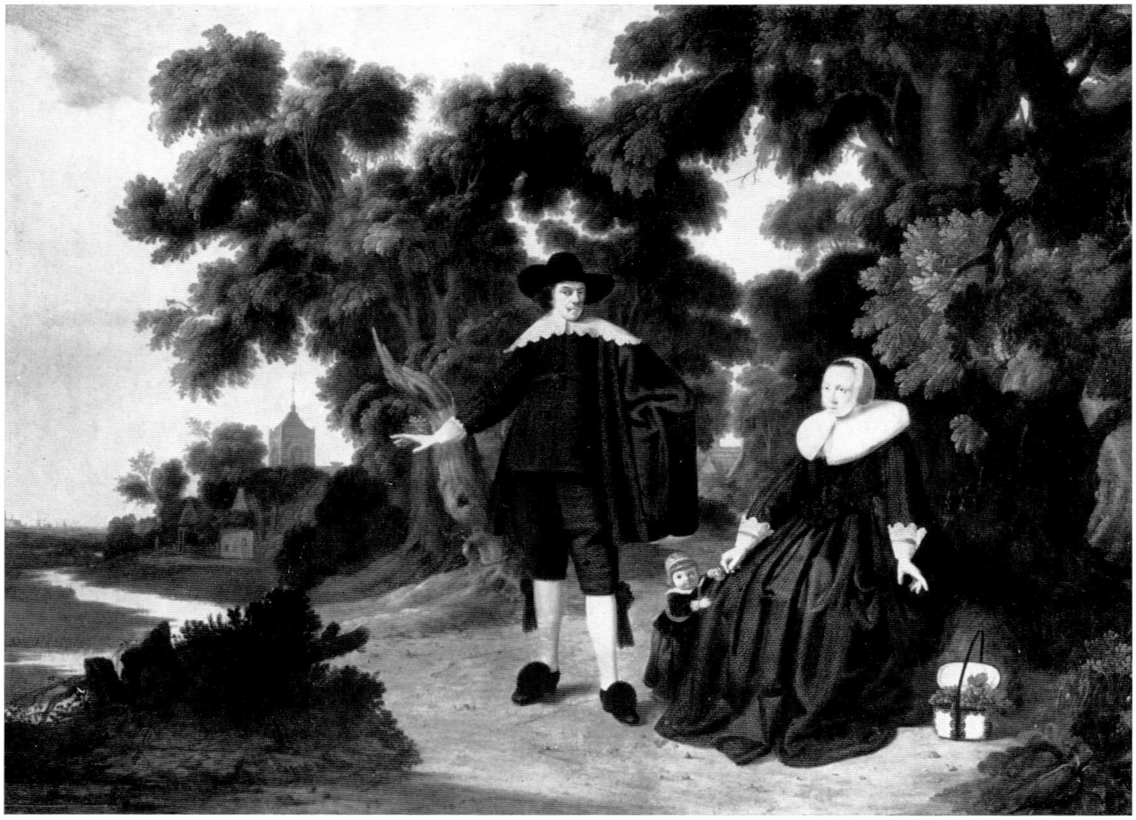

128

128 GERARD DONCK (c. 1610-1640), *Jan van Hensbeeck and his Wife Maria Koeck*. London, National Gallery.

his Wife at the National Portrait Gallery in London, *Richard Savage Lloyd with his Sister* (fig. 130), and *Mr. and Mrs. Brown of Trent Hall*— with its Flemish-type rural landscape (fig. 134) — to the almost mechanical formula, set in a conventional background, of *Heneage Lloyd and his Sister* in the Fitzwilliam Museum, Cambridge. Here the boy holds a bow in his hand and his sister an arrow, the attributes of an abstract, pastoral world presided over by Diana the Huntress. But there is nothing impersonal or generic in the midsummer landscape of *Mr. and Mrs. Andrews*. The wheat has been cut and lies in golden sheaves; beyond a white wooden gate the stubble-field gives way to pasture, flocks, and low forests; the sky is dappled by masses of bright and dark clouds; and such is the lyrical intensity of the landscape that a distant bellowing of cattle seems to echo in the memory of the onlooker. One feels that the moment is approaching when Keats will sing:

While barred clouds bloom the soft-dying day,
And touch the stubble-plains with rosy hue.

We find an arrangement similar to that of Gainsborough's groups in the portrait of an unidentified family by Johann Zoffany, where a girl brings to her mother, who is petrified in an impassive attitude, the ribbon which has fallen from her hat and been seized by a little lamb in its teeth (fig. 129). The father's gesture of pointing at the hat lying on the grass next to a wreath echoes the daughter's, but unlike Gainsborough's sitters they seem arrested in a pose as in a *tableau vivant*. The same arrangement of a group beside a landscape recurs in the *Family Portrait* (1825) by Albrecht Adam ([1786-1862]; Georg Schäfer Collection, Schweinfurt).[8] At the edge of a wood on the right a couple is holding hands, he in huntsman's garb, while a child shakes a grouse under the nose of a jumping dog. Munich is visible in the background on the left. An original variant of this motif, that of a lady seated on a horse and a gentleman dismounted with the trunk of a tree behind them, is to be found in *Mr. and*

8 See reproduction in *Der frühe Realismus in Deutschland, 1800-1850* (Ausstellung im Germanischen Nationalmuseum, Nürnberg, 1967).

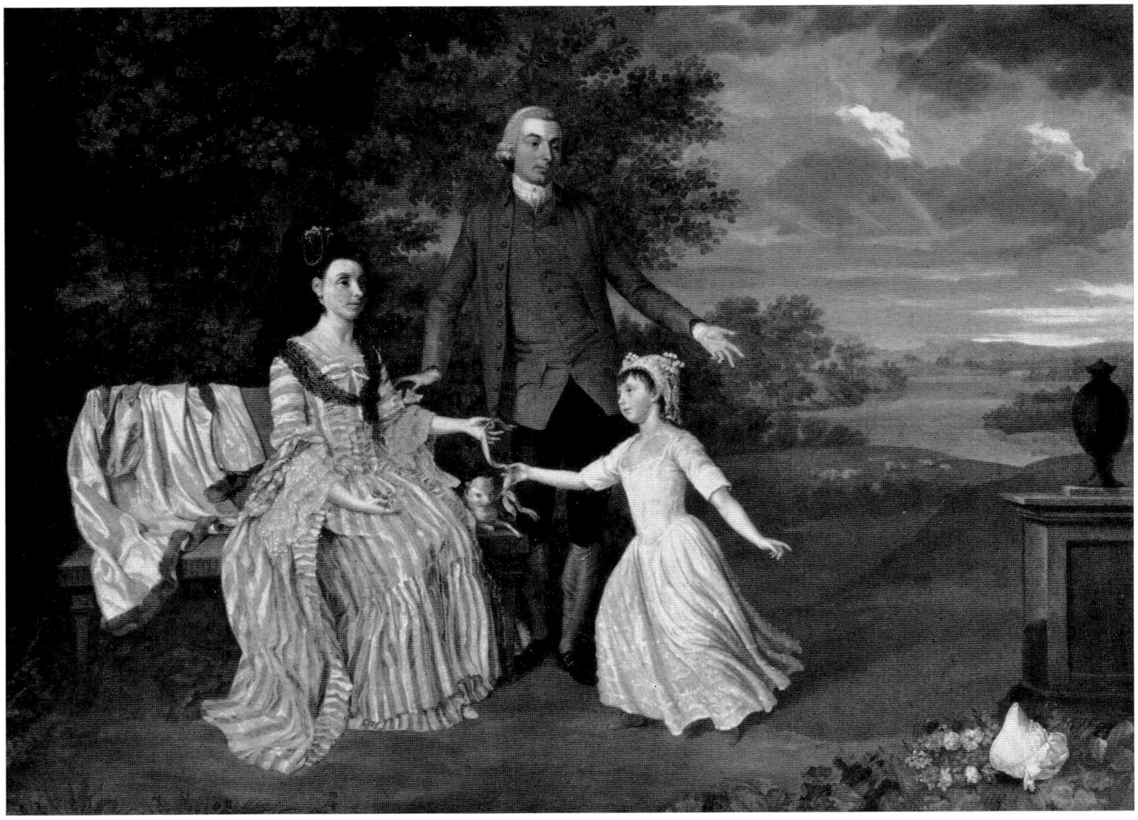

129 JOHANN ZOFFANY (1734/5-1810), *Family Group*. New York, Wildenstein Galleries.

129

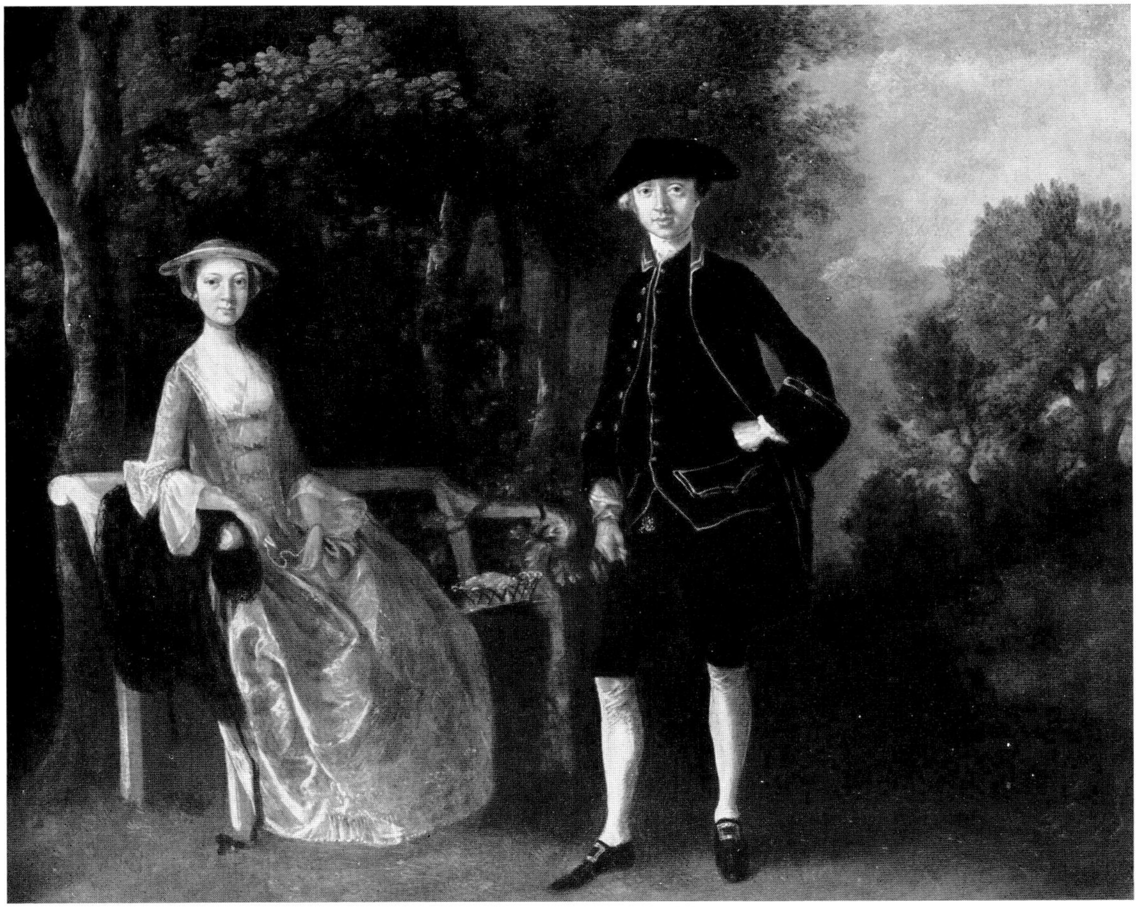

130 THOMAS GAINSBOROUGH (1727-1788), *Richard Savage Lloyd with his Sister*, c. 1750. Washington, D.C., collection of Mr. and Mrs. Paul Mellon.

130

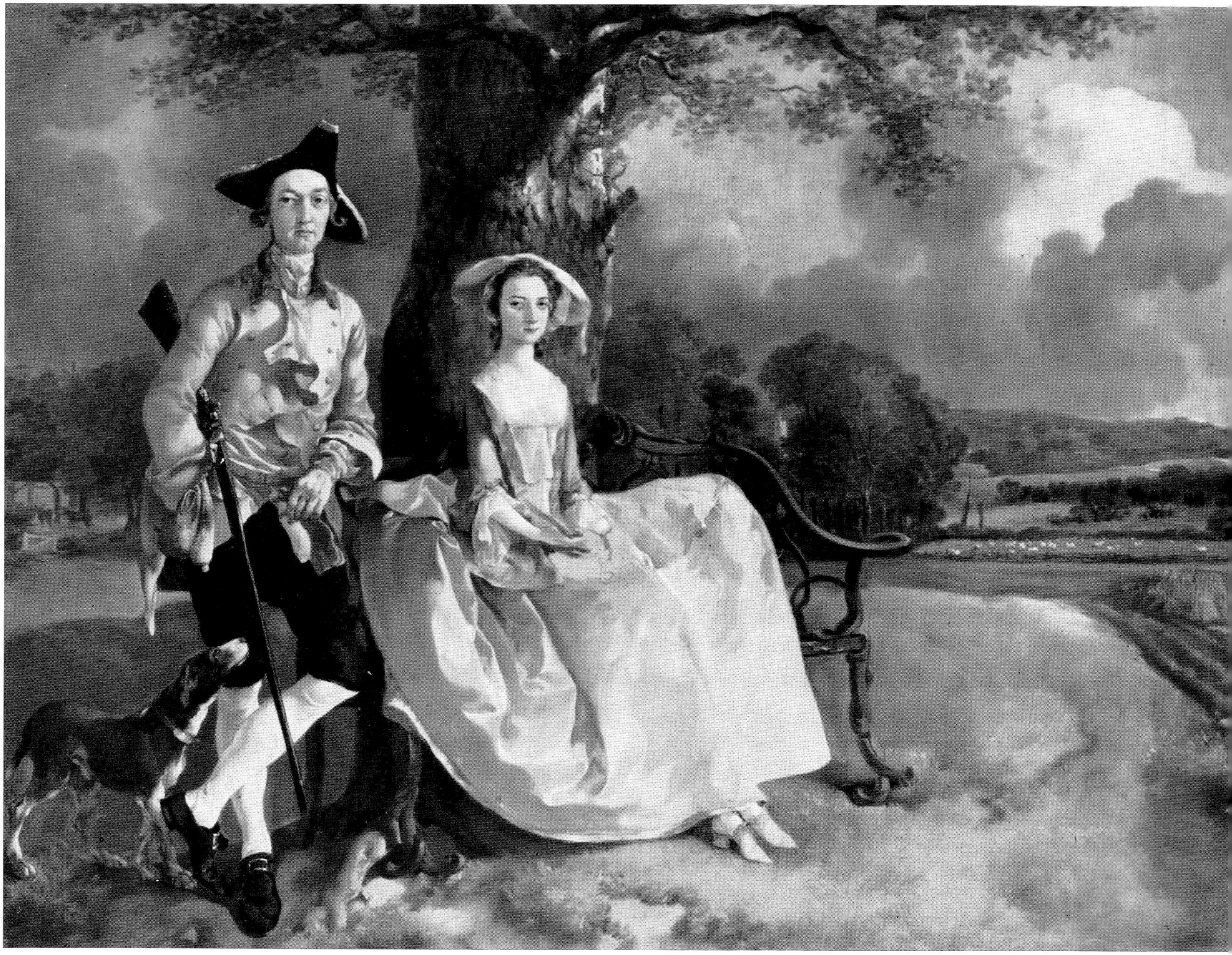

131 THOMAS GAINSBOROUGH (1727-1788), *Mr. and Mrs. Andrews*, c. 1755. London, National Gallery. 132 ARTHUR DEVIS (1711-1787), *Horace Walpole Presenting Kitty Clive with a Piece of Honeysuckle*. Wimpole (Cambridgeshire), collection of Mrs. George Bambridge. 133 ARTHUR DEVIS (1711-1787), *The van Harthals Family*, 1749. Upton House, Banbury (Oxfordshire), reproduced by courtesy of the Trustees of the Bearsted Collection.

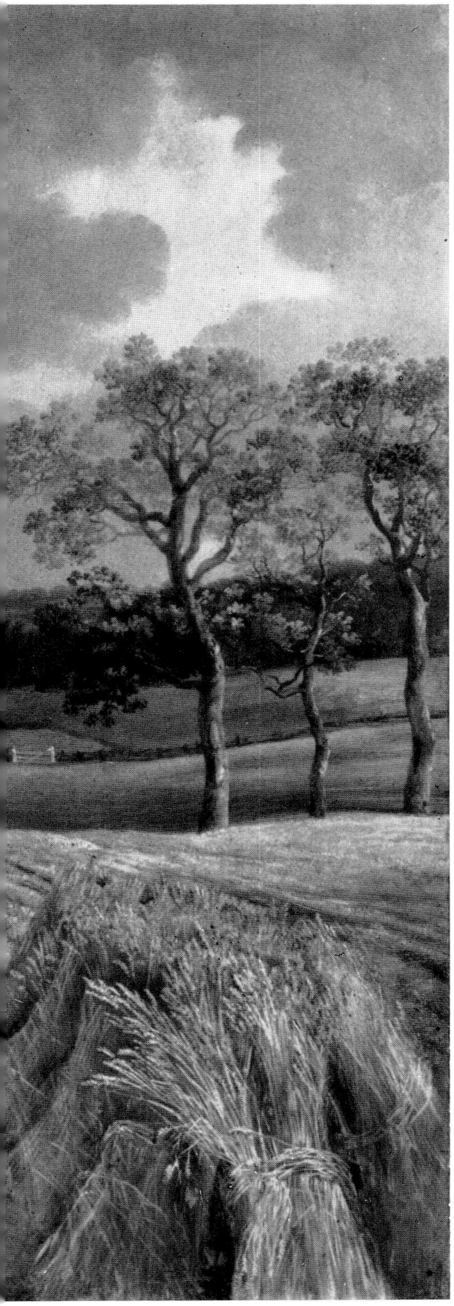

131

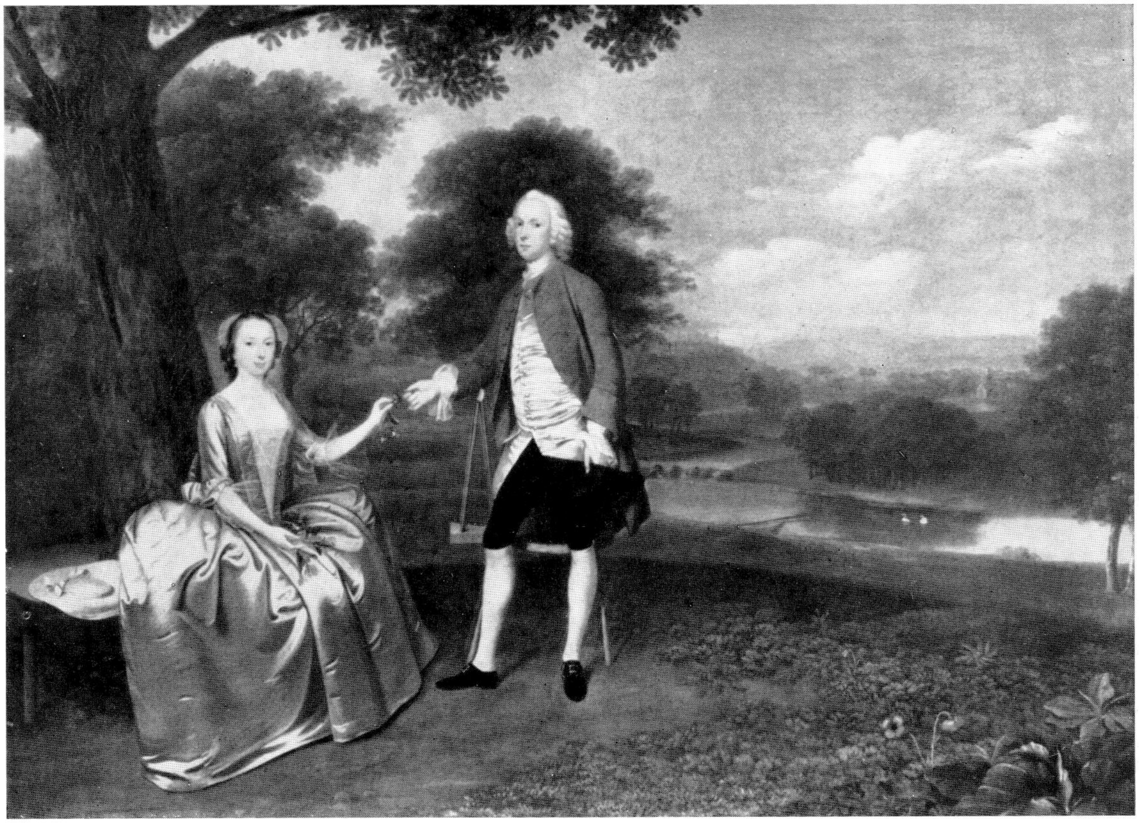

132

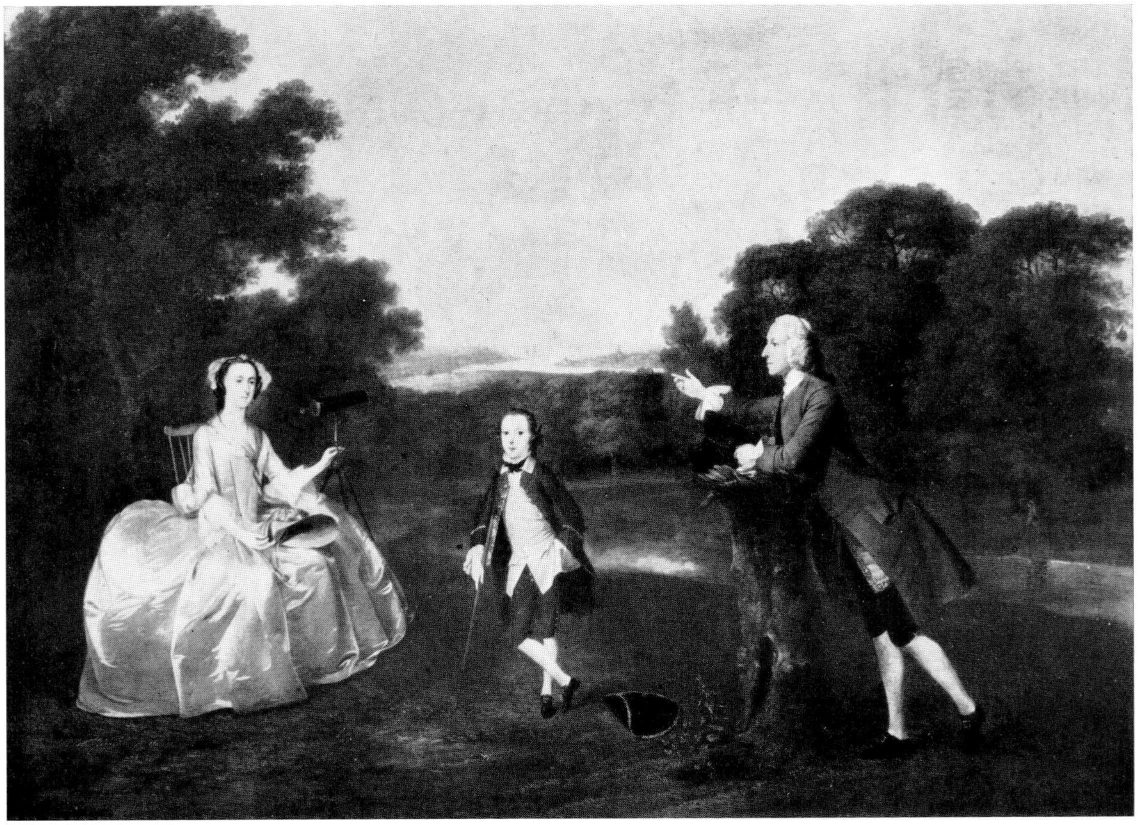

133

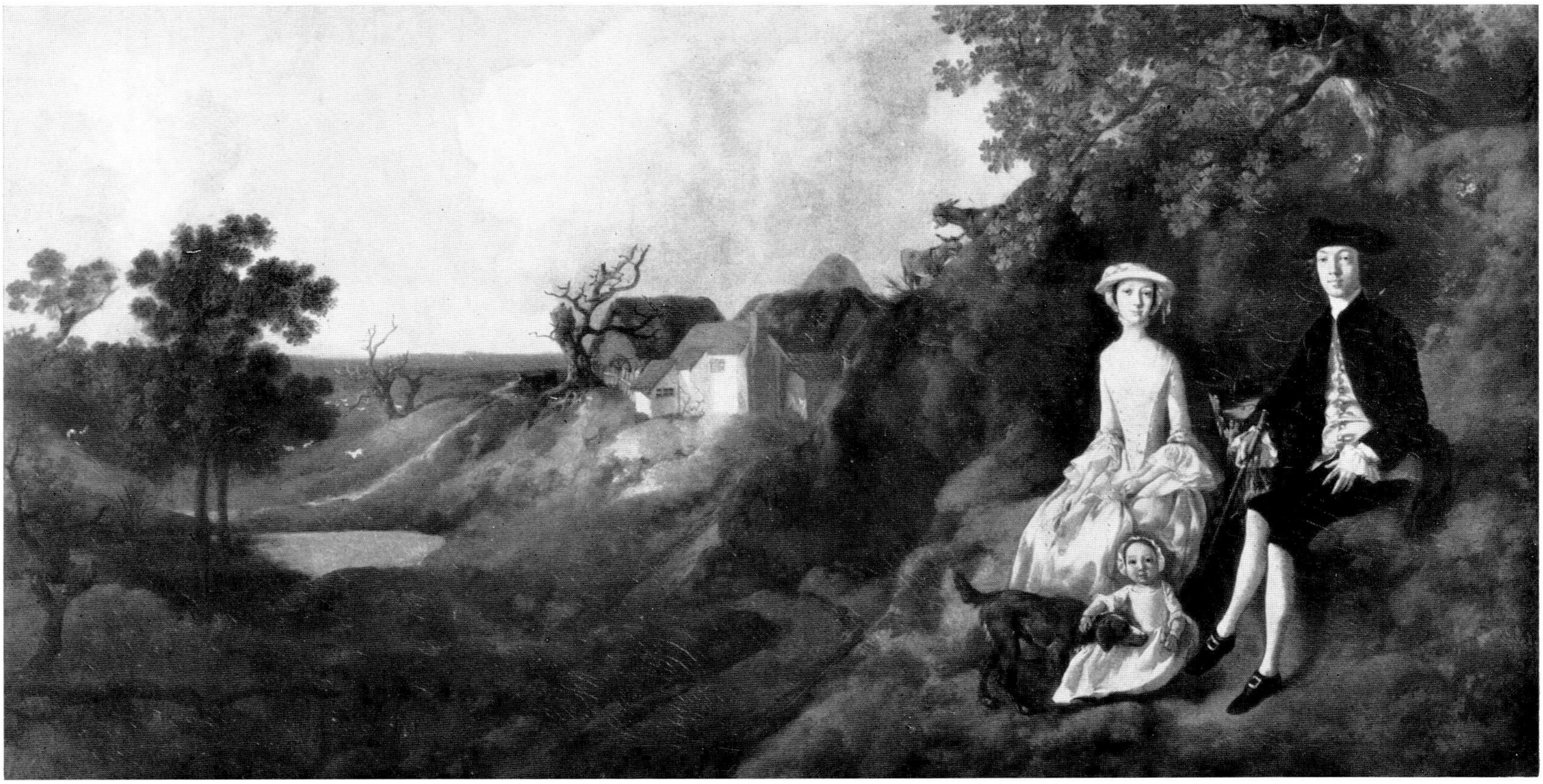

134

Mrs. Thomas Coltman by Joseph Wright of Derby (1734-1797), a painter famous for his effects of light and shade (fig. 135). Another motif of the " conversation " of two sitters is provided by a seated person being approached by a secretary or servant. This motif was known in sixteenth-century Italian portraiture — it is sufficient to mention Titian's *Paul III with his Nephew*, of which we have spoken already. Subsequently it is found in the portrait, dated 1627, of *Constantine Huygens with his Assistant* by Thomas de Keyser ([1596/7-1667]; National Gallery, London: Huygens was a Dutch humanist who was secretary to three stadtholders); in Rembrandt's *Portrait of a Shipbuilder and his Wife* of 1633 (Buckingham Palace; fig. 127);[9] and in Hogarth's portrait of Garrick seated at a table meditating on what to write, while his wife, Eva Maria Vogel — a Viennese dancer known as Mademoiselle Violette — approaches him as if to remove the pen from his hand (probably painted in 1757; fig. 316).
In 1773, John Singleton Copley painted *Mr. and Mrs. Mifflin* (Philadelphia, Historical Society of Pennsylvania), the man smiling as he interrupts his reading and the wife halting her embroidery to sit for the painter;[10] and in the nineteenth century Tominz represented a fiancé in the act of giving a ring to his betrothed (fig. 317). The American Nicholas Biddle Kittell (1822-1894) in *Mr. and Mrs. Charles Augustus Carter* (1845) shows the couple sitting near a table with the man's head higher than his wife's, so that it is located at one extremity of a line ending in the hem of the woman's skirt, thus forming the usual triangular structure (fig. 315).
Caspar Netscher (1635/6-1684), a German who had become a Dutch citizen — much patronized by the Dutch bourgeoisie and by ambassadors and known for his pictures of ladies dressed as nymphs and goddesses — painted *A Scholar at a Desk Delivering a Paper to a Young Man* (fig. 314). As in de Keyser's painting, all the objects on the desk — papers, books, and globes — are accurately represented and Netscher has added drapery in the corner, a conventional appurtenance of early " conversations ".
William Dobson (1611-1646), who was influenced by the Venetians and has left portraits of the period when Charles I and his

9 Rembrandt succeeds better than any other painter in dramatizing in a natural manner the attitudes of his sitters. See for instance the splendid family portrait at the Brunswick Museum, and the group of the Syndics (Rijksmuseum). 10 See J.D.PROWN, *John Singleton Copley* (Cambridge: Harvard University Press, 1966), I, p. 331.

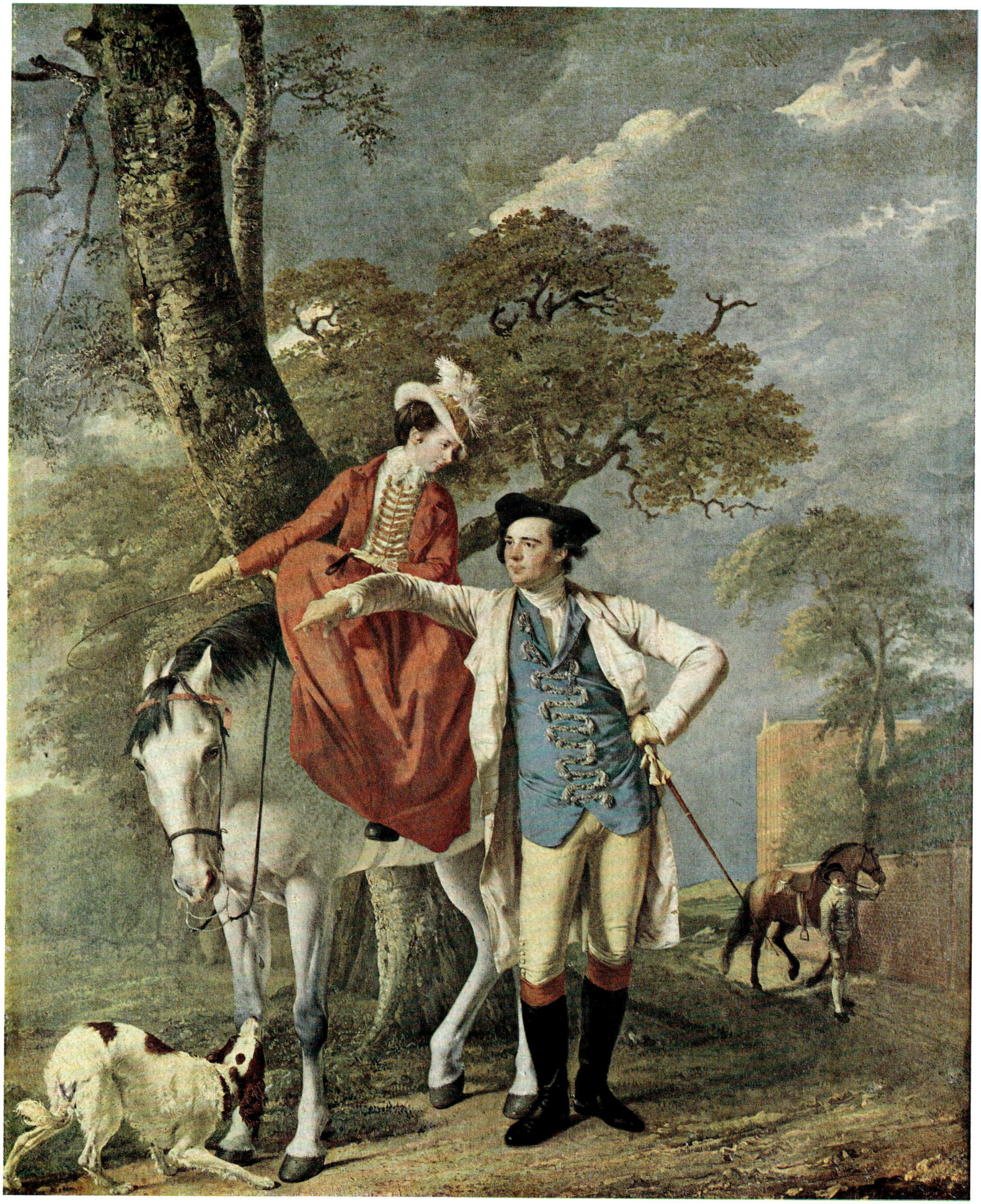

135

134 THOMAS GAINSBOROUGH (1727-1788), *Mr. and Mrs. Brown of Trent Hall.* Houghton Hall (Norfolk), collection of the Marquess of Cholmondeley.
135 JOSEPH WRIGHT OF DERBY (1734-1797), *Mr. and Mrs. Thomas Coltman*, c. 1773. Collection of Charles H. Rogers-Coltman.

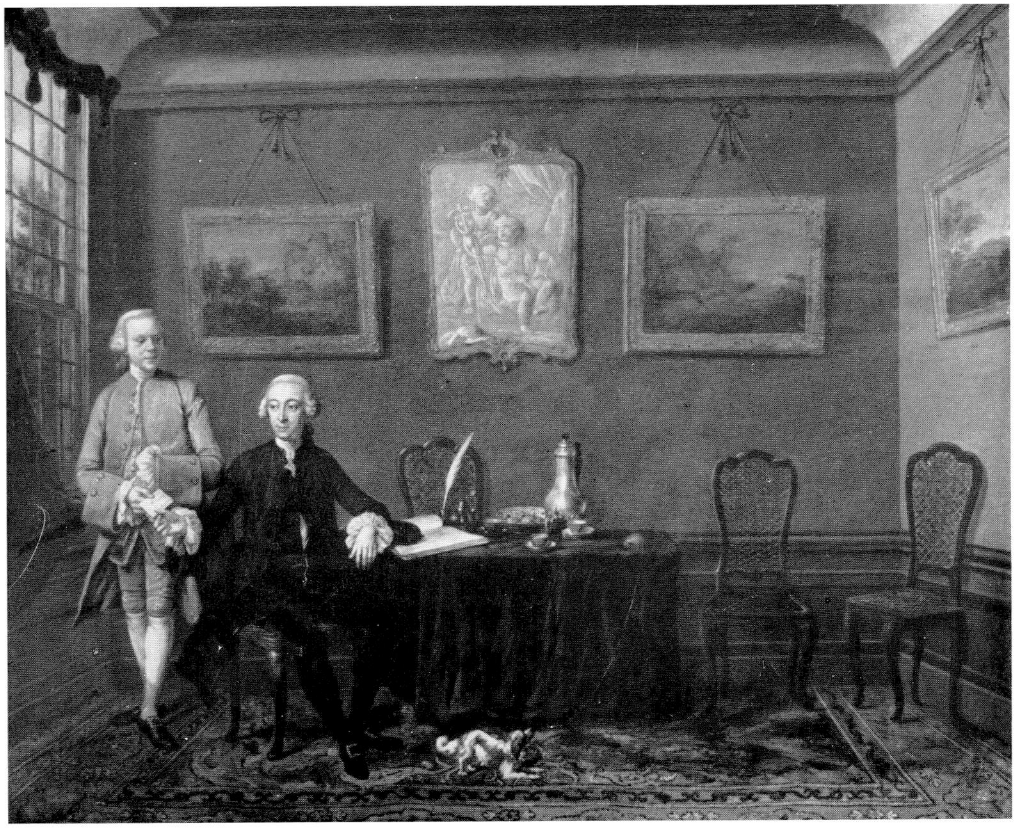

136

136 JULIUS QUINKHARD (1736-1776), *Paulus Determeyer Weslingh and his Accountant*, 1765. Amsterdam, Rotterdamsche Bankvereniging.

137 ANTON VON MARON (1733-1808), *Two Englishmen in front of the Arch of Constantine*. Rome, A. Busiri Vici Collection.

138 NATHANIEL DANCE (1735-1811), *The Violinist Nardini and his Impresario*. Rome, A. Busiri Vici Collection.

court resided in Oxford (1642-46), also represents one seated and two standing figures in *Prince Rupert, Colonel William Murray, and Colonel John Russell* (fig. 318) depicted in a setting of curtains and columns typical of the background of Italian portraits. Colonel Murray is dipping the cockade in a glass of wine as a pledge of success. Colonel Russell, who is seated, commanded a regiment and was wounded at Naseby. In an open-air scene by Hendrik Danckerts, of which we have already spoken (fig. 319), the royal gardener kneels in front of Charles II and presents him with the first pineapple grown in England.[11] In a painting of 1771 by Alexander Roslin (Stockholm, Nationalmuseum) there is a table with a globe and maps at which Gustavus III and Duke Karl of Södermanland are seated, with Duke Fredrik Adolf of Östergötland standing, again creating the conventional triangular pattern. Sir Ralph Abercromby converses with his secretary (or his son) in a painting by John Downman (National Gallery, London): a map of the town and bay of St. George at Grenada lies on the table and a map of the island of Carriacon hangs on the wall, both allusions to an expedition commanded by Sir Ralph against the French in the West Indies in 1795-96. Nathaniel Dance (1735-1811), a pupil of Hayman who formed his style mainly in Rome under the influence of Pompeo Batoni, has portrayed *The Violinist Nardini and his Impresario*, one standing, the other sitting (fig. 138); and using the same formula Anton von Maron (1733-1808) has represented *Two Englishmen in front of the Arch of Constantine* (fig. 137), and Francis Hayman (1708-1776) a couple, probably to be identified with *Margaret Tyers and her Husband* (fig. 324).
We again find a standing and a seated figure in *Paulus Determeyer Weslingh and his Accountant* (1765; fig. 136) by Julius Quinkhard (1736-1776), but here the relationship of scale between sitters and surroundings seems odd — and, indeed, a close study of the actual painting reveals that the two chairs on the right show clear signs of *pentimenti*, and there are two cups and a coffee-pot on that side of the table as well as a mysterious ball of wool with a little dog playing with its loose end. In fact, two more figures were originally seated on those chairs: the wife and daughter of Weslingh, whom he had had effaced[12] after a quarrel.

11 See above, p. 137. 12 For a similar case of *damnatio memoriae* see above, p. 138.

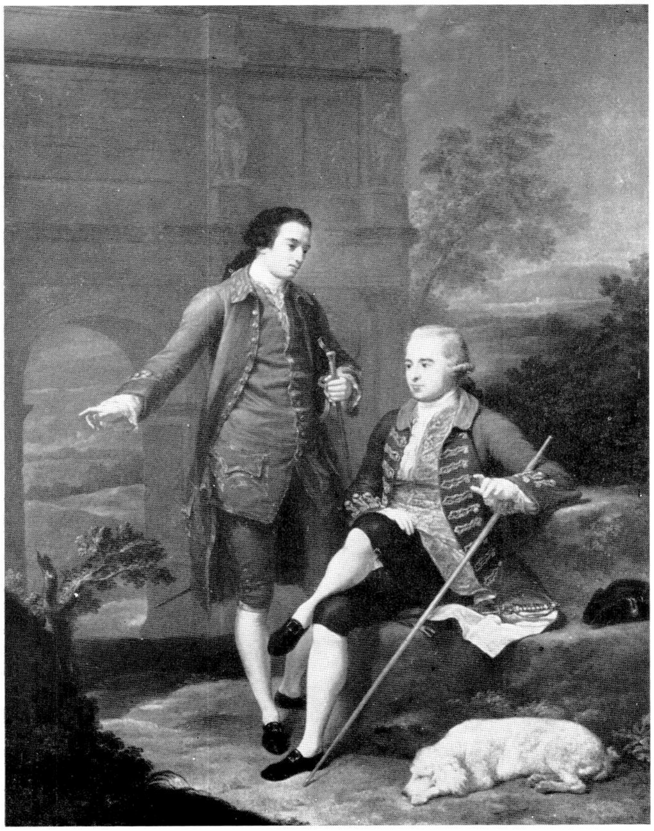
137

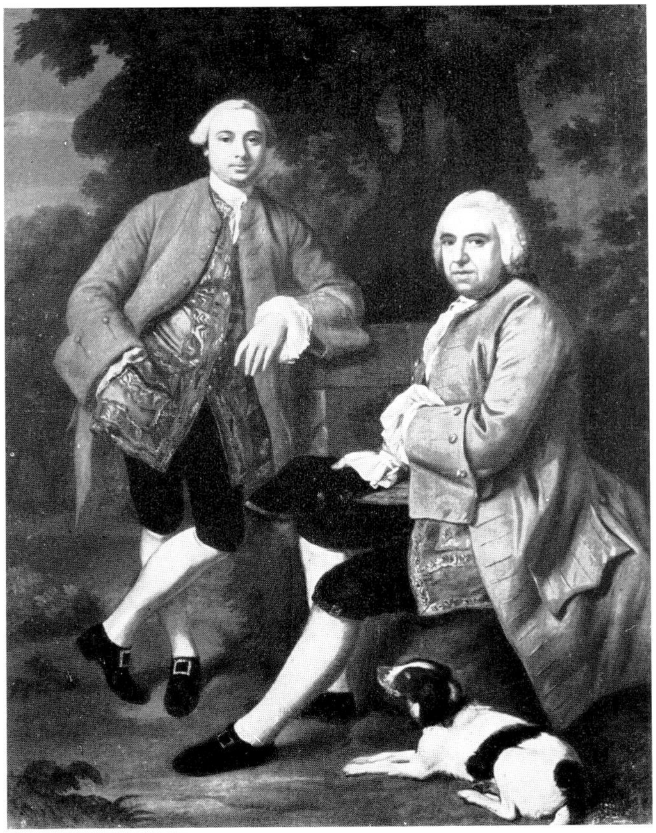
138

The daughter had annoyed her father because of a love affair and the mother had sided with the daughter, so he had thrown them both out of the house.
In these compositions one of the figures is usually seated (or kneeling), the other standing. This is not the case, however, in *Jeronimus Tonneman and his Son* (1736; fig. 323) by Cornelis Troost, in which the corpulent father and the smart son, who is playing the flute, both sit at a table. Staring also has a story concerning the persons in this painting, as of the Weslingh painting by Quinkhard, which dispels the apparent serenity of the moment. In the following year (1737) the son wounded his mistress who was pregnant by him and fled to the East Indies; the father, as one can see from the picture, was so greatly incommoded by the new fashion of French breeches which did not reach up to the waist that, following the advice of a magazine (the Dutch *Spectator*), he resolved to wear braces which, pressing on a tumour, caused an internal hemorrhage from which he died. *The Daughters of the Marshal Duke of Noailles* are both portrayed seated, one spinning and the other writing, by an anonymous painter in a picture in a French private collection which approaches genre painting, the title of which, Hautecœur remarks, could have been *The Afternoon Occupations*.[13]
The American couple, *Mr. and Mrs. Ralph Izard*, who commissioned John Singleton Copley to record their Grand Tour, are also both sitting at a table (fig. 321); the traditional drapery and the inevitable column frame a Roman landscape with the Colosseum and, nearer the foreground, a reduced version of the marble group known as *Orestes and Elektra* (then at the Villa Ludovisi, now in the Museo Nazionale delle Terme in Rome). Again, seated at the same table are *Mr. and Mrs. Knowles* in the nineteenth-century watercolour by the "primitive" Joseph H. Davis (Worcester Art Museum, Worcester, Mass.). The festoon with the portrait of President Jackson — a national hero — and the top hat equidistant from the two sitters stress the symmetry of the poses. Davis painted many portraits almost identical with this one. Apropos of one of them (*James and Sarah Tuttle*, at the

13 *Les peintres de la vie familiale* (Paris: Charpentier, 1945), p. 64.

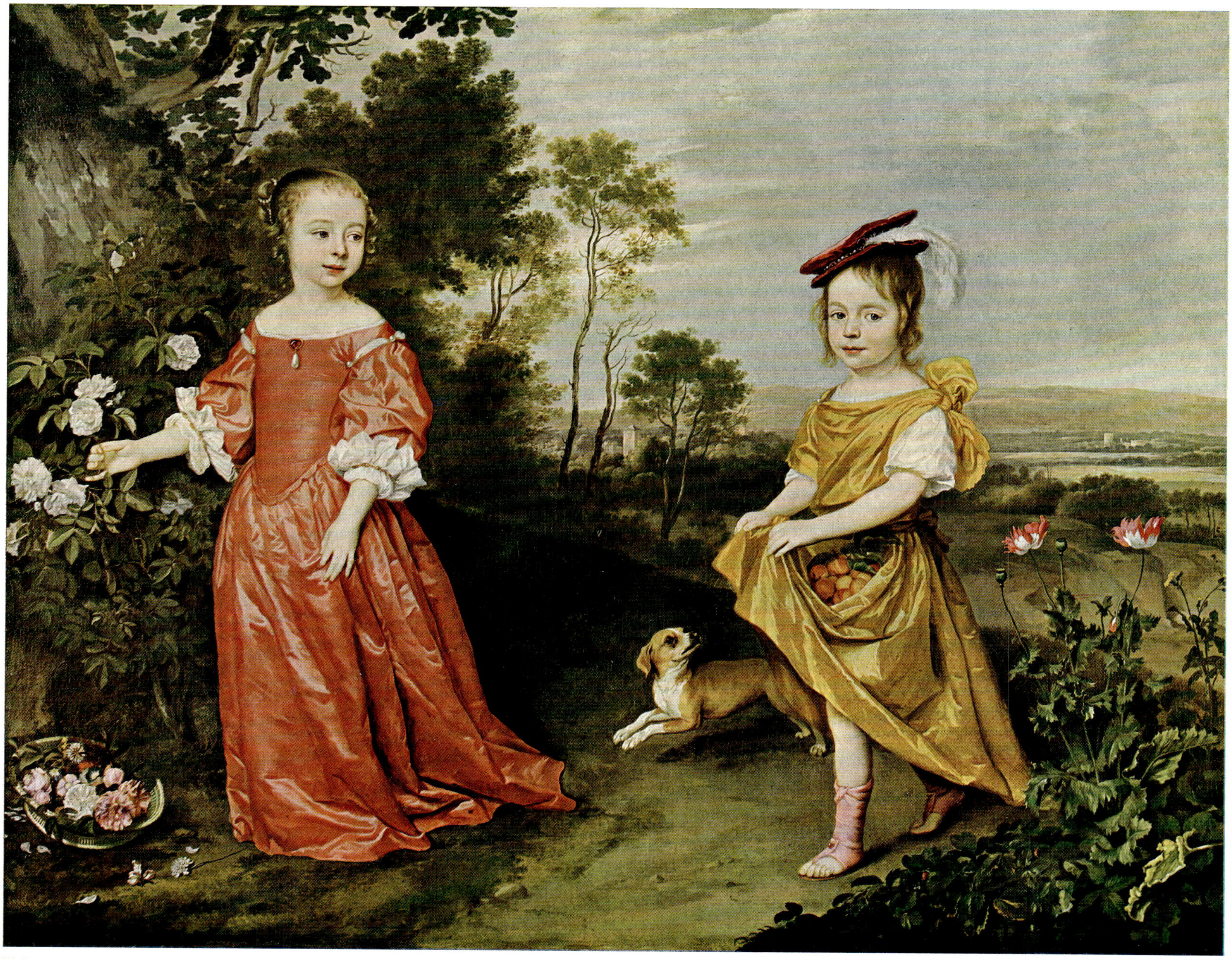

139

139 JAN MYTENS (1614-1670), *Two Children in a Landscape*. Godmersham Park, Canterbury (Kent), collection of Mr. and Mrs. Robert Tritton.

New York Historical Society), Katharine Morrison McClinton writes:

Many of the backgrounds of American nineteenth-century portraits were stock sets, like those seen in the quaint portraits of the primitive artist Joseph H. Davis. The portraits were stereotyped and there was very little, if any, individual likeness in the faces. Their interests and vocations were suggested by such accessories as a book, a bowl of fruit or flowers, or a picture on the wall. The setting was usually a small rectangular country-type table, with painted wood graining, turned legs and one centre drawer. On the table were a vase of flowers, a bowl of fruit, a book, a candlestick and a stove-pipe hat. The subjects, man and wife, or two women, sat on chairs at opposite ends of the table or stood facing each other. On the wall behind the table hung a banjo clock or a picture decorated with floral swags in the manner of the eighteenth century. A gaudy hand-sewn carpet of geometric design covered the floor beneath the table and chairs, and a cat was usually sitting under the table. This was a picture of a conventional type of interior of the period, but it was not any particular person's home. A water-colour of a similar type showing two women sitting on ladder backed chairs on opposite sides of a tripod candle-stand on which is a candlestick with a lighted candle is by Eunice Pinney. The draperies of the windows form a frame for the scene.[14]

These stereotyped American "conversations" represent an extreme case of compositional schemes, but as a rule artists adapted them fairly freely. Thus, for instance, Harmen Otten (born 1773) portrayed himself standing and reading a book of moral meditations (*Zedelijke Bespiegelingen*) near his wife, in a painting of 1810 (fig. 320) which gives a lively image of a modest Empire interior (the artist, his wife, and the fat little dog are perfectly enclosed in a scalene triangle); the dates of birth of husband and wife are framed on the wall.

We find other ways of posing two sitters in the portrait of *Pauline Borghese and the Baronne de Mathisse*, her lady companion, by René Berthon — of which two more or less identical versions exist, one in the Spalletti collection in Palazzo Rasponi at Ravenna (fig. 140) and the other in that of the Princes Metternich, formerly on loan to the California Palace of the Legion of Honor, San Francisco. The lady companion sits with her back turned to the onlooker. In *The Wife and Sister-in-law of the Artist* (East Berlin, Märkisches Museum) by Johann Erdmann Hummel (1769-1852), one of the young women is making a gesture in the direction of her relative, who is reading; the light of the oil lamp (Hummel was fond of light effects)[15] glimmers on their faces. In Louis-Pierre Spindler's *London Interior* (fig. 142) of about 1835, in which Lady Waterford and Lady Canning appear on the terrace of Carlton House with a view of Westminster Abbey and the Tower of London in the distance, only the features of the seated lady are visible as the other, at the balustrade, is turning her back; also turning their backs are the two Eckersberg daughters at the window at Charlottenborg (c. 1844), in their father's drawing at the Kopparsticksamlingen in Copenhagen. In the unidentified *Couple in front of a Window* (perhaps a genre painting) by Georg Friedrich Kersting (1785-1847) only the profile of the man is visible, whereas the face of the young woman is turned to the mountainous landscape (fig. 141).

A child led by the hand by one of his parents offers few possibilities of variation, as for example in *Lord Baltimore with a Child and a Negro Page* by Gerard Soest, a German who came to England before 1650 and died in 1680-81 (property of the State of Maryland), where a Negro raises the traditional curtain on the left. Compare this with François Gérard's *Portrait of Jean-Baptiste Isabey and his Daughter* (1795; Louvre); although the two paintings were independently conceived, the same scheme of composition has suggested itself naturally.[16] *Mevrouw van Walré-Kops* (1787) by Wybrand Hendriks (1744-1831; fig. 322), is almost a caricature in the clumsiness of the lady's figure; the hat placed askew makes her look like a clown. The worthy bourgeoise gives the little girl a toy she has produced out of a silver casket, while on the floor are a bucket and squirt to clean windows and a brush and sandbox to scrub the floors. Probably the mother is rewarding the little daughter, to whom she has taught the domestic virtue of cleanliness. Jan Carel Vierpeyl, a pupil of Jacob Peeters of Antwerp, represented in about 1697-98 Francis Hutchinson sitting at a desk near his daughter Anne, who is standing (Dublin, National Gallery of Ireland); he stops writing while his daughter points to the spinet. The furniture dates from the end of the seventeenth century and the costumes from about twenty years later. Hermanus Numan (1744-1820) depicted *Mevrouw van Collen-Mogge* (1776; Amsterdam, Rijksmuseum) embroidering a lace pillow and resting her feet on a foot-warmer; her little daughter, Johanna Ferdinanda, is about to

14 "American Furniture in Family Portraits of the Eighteenth and Nineteenth Centuries", in *Apollo*, LXXXIX, March, 1969. 15 See M. PRAZ, *An Illustrated History of Furnishing* (London: Thames and Hudson; New York: George Braziller, 1964), p. 293. 16 The former is reproduced by Waterhouse, *Painting in Britain*, pl. 60, and the latter, a very well known painting, in *La peinture au Musée du Louvre*, École française, XIXe siècle (Paris: Éditions des Musées Nationaux, 1959), II, fig. 915.

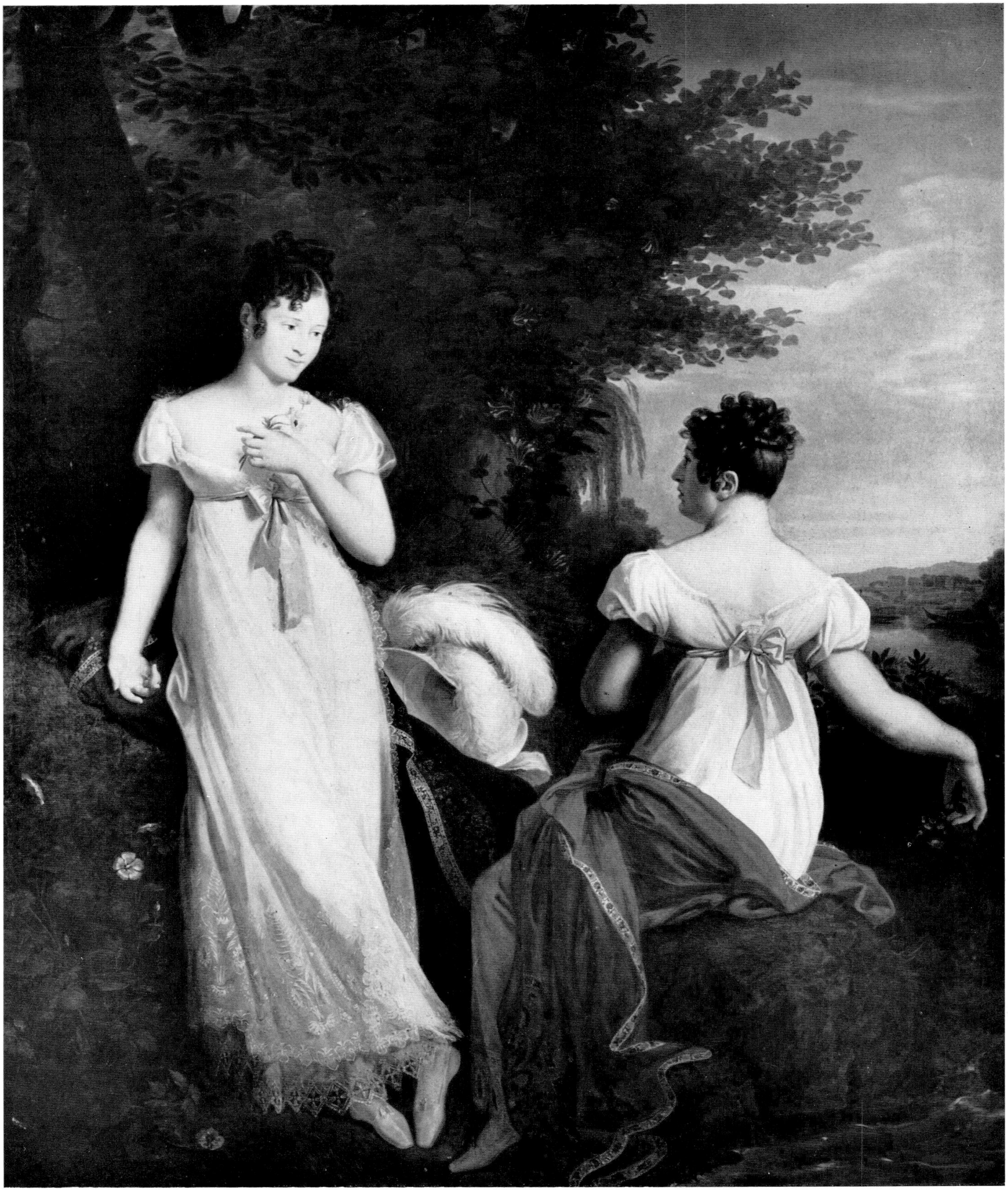

140

140 RENÉ THÉODORE BERTHON (1776-1859), *Pauline Borghese and the Baronne de Mathisse*. Ravenna, Spalletti Collection. 141 GEORG FRIEDRICH KERSTING (1785-1847), *A Couple in front of a Window*, 1817. Schweinfurt, Georg Schäfer Collection. 142 LOUIS-PIERRE SPINDLER (1800-1889), *London Interior*, c. 1835. Strasbourg, Musée Historique de la Ville de Strasbourg.

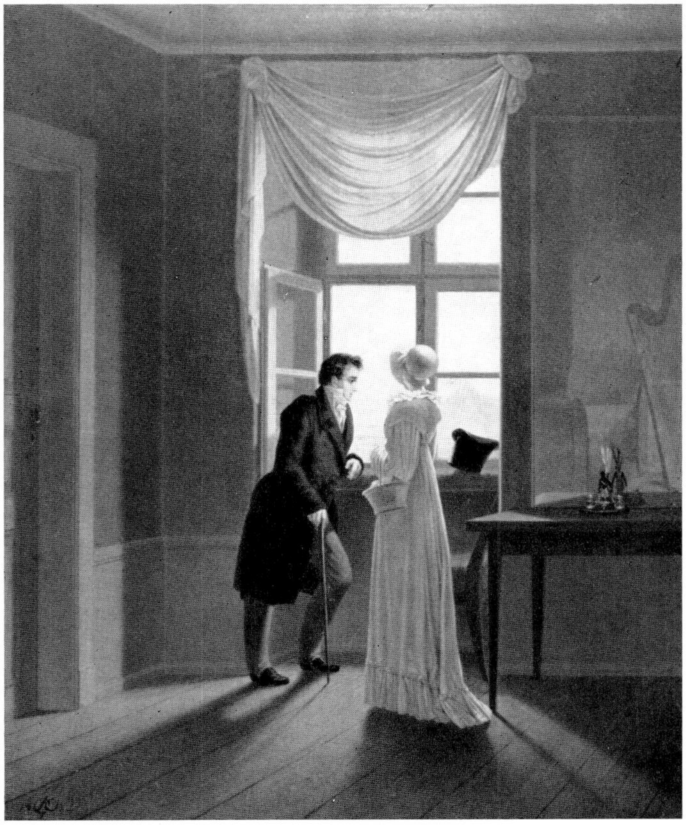
141

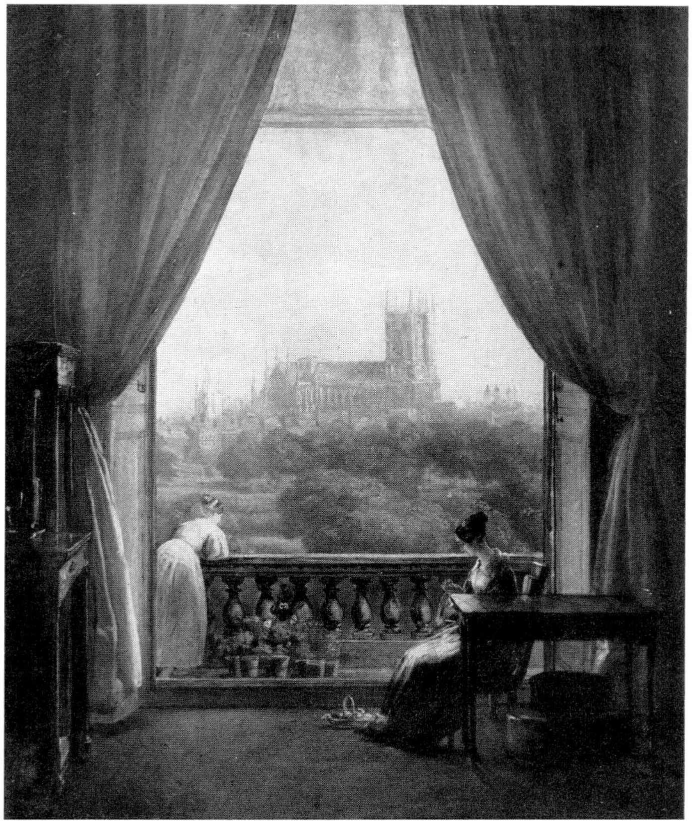
142

offer her a flower from a small basket. On the wall is a half-veiled portrait of the deceased husband.

Two children can be combined in extremely attractive postures, as may be seen in a number of portraits. The daughters of Cornelis de Vos, dressed in the elaborate costumes children were made to wear in those days, interrupt their snack for a moment to turn in our direction (Berlin, Staatliche Museen; the two little girls appear also in a family group by their father at the Musées Royaux, Brussels). The sons of Charles V, *Philip (II) and Don Juan of Austria* (a mediocre copy from an original perhaps by Titian; Tivoli, Villa d'Este) have flowers and fruit in their hands, but one also holds a sword; there is the usual background with a curtain and a column. The *Two Children in a Landscape* by Jan Mytens (fig. 139), a painting remarkable for its brilliant colours, shows one of the figures busy picking flowers to put in a basket and the other — in a curious, almost pastoral costume, wearing buskins — holds up her skirt full of fruit and is followed by a barking dog. *George III and his Brother, the Duke of York* (London, National Portrait Gallery) by Richard Wilson (1714-1782) are turning the leaves of an illustrated book. There is also a charming portrait of *The Talbot Sisters* — Gwendolen, who was to marry Prince Borghese and was lamented by all Rome at her premature death, and her sister, who married Prince Filippo Doria — portrayed in 1824 by the Viennese painter Johann Nepomuk Ender (1793-1854; fig. 126). The minute rendering of the foliage, the curls, the flowers, the frills of the petticoats and pantalettes, and the predominant pink and green colours make of this sugary picture a typical product of Biedermeier taste. The portrait of another pair of children, *Emily and George Mason*, by Arthur Devis — of which we have already spoken[17] — shows more animation.

A triplet, two components of which are pets — a dog and a parrot — is the subject of a painting by Louis-François-Gérard van der Puyl (fig. 325). This too is a " conversation " of sorts into which the lady introduces the notes of the piano, while the dog barks and the parrot croaks. It is a kind of Toy Symphony, like Haydn's.

17 See p. 159.

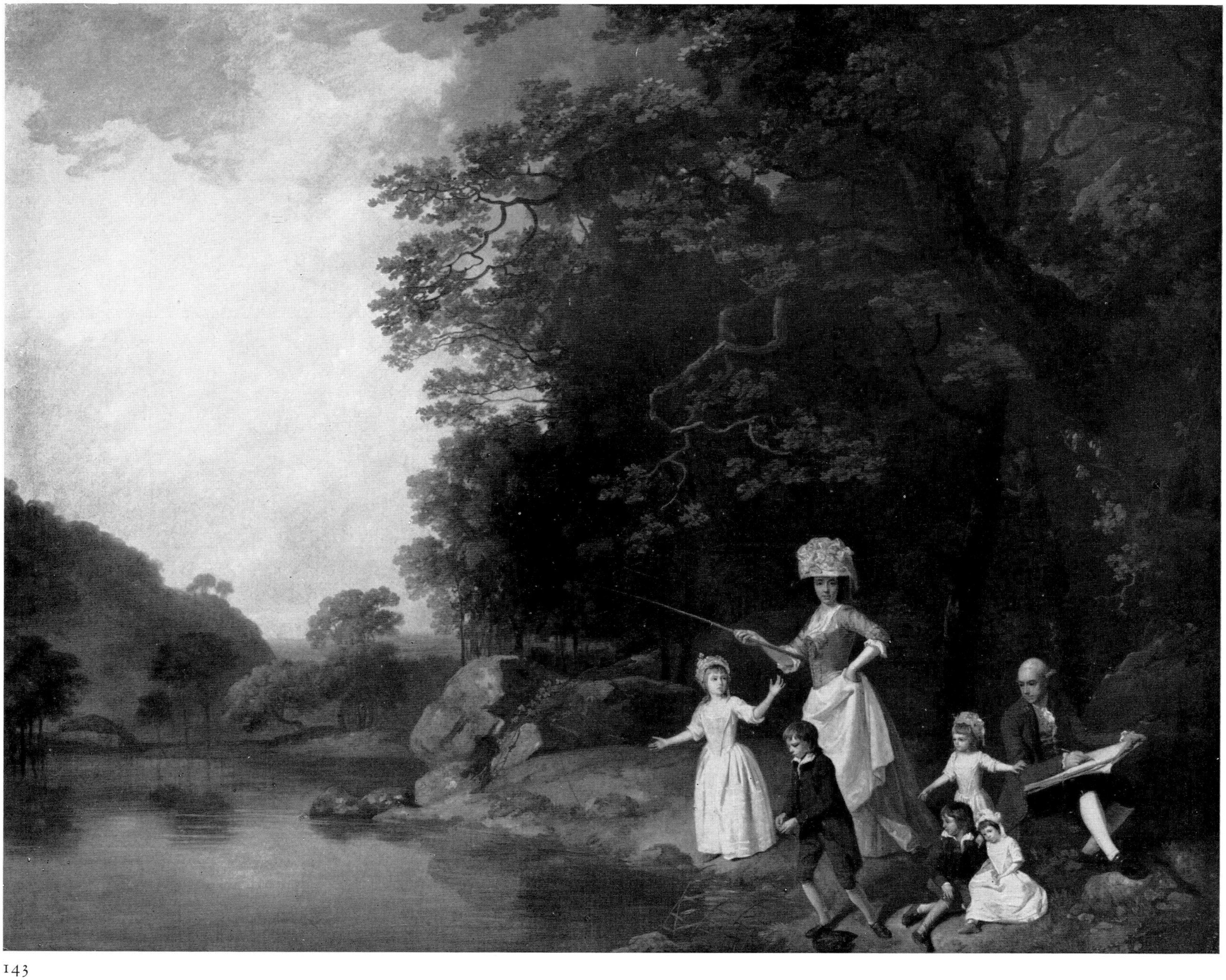

143

143 FRANCIS WHEATLEY (1747-1801), *The Browne Family*. Washington, D.C., collection of Mr. and Mrs. Paul Mellon.

CHAPTER VIII – SPORTING AND MUSICAL CONVERSATIONS, AND PAINTERS' FAMILY GROUPS

As one may imagine, it is in England that the " sporting " conversation piece had a passing vogue in the eighteenth century, just as the above-mentioned genre of theatrical conversation pieces remained confined to England. Joan Carlile (1606-1678/79) — an obscure lady artist whose husband, Lodowick, was a dramatist and Gentleman of the Privy Chamber of Charles I — at the beginning of 1654 moved to London to a house in Covent Garden, being " resolved then to use her skill for something more than empty fame ". Her painting *The Stag Hunt* (fig. 328) was probably done at Petersham Lodge, Richmond Park, where Sir Justinian Isham (the young man one sees in the group on the right) lived with her and her husband in 1649-50. The archer in the red " Maximilian " costume on the left, pointing to the stag he has killed with his cross-bow, is certainly Lodowick Carlile, who was a keen sportsman; the boy is his eldest son James, who inherited his father's passion for hunting and was later Sergeant of Hounds to James, Duke of York. Carlile's three daughters are among the young women who appear in the painting, and the artist herself may be the seated lady. Although the costumes are of a later period, the painting (whose composition resembles Aelbert Cuyp's *Family in a Rhineland Landscape* at the Budapest Museum) breathes a Shakespearian air, and looking at it a song from *As You Like It* (IV, ii, 11) comes to mind: " What shall he have that kill'd the deer? "
Hogarth painted a lady fishing in a river surrounded by woods (Dulwich College Picture Gallery), while a little girl tries to emulate her mother by holding the fishing rod. Another lady fishing, also assisted by a little girl, appears in a painting by Francis Wheatley, *The Browne Family* (fig. 143). A boy of *The Jeffreys Family* (fig. 326) by Hogarth is also busy fishing, while a child offers a duck to a little dog. In a painting attributed to John Singleton Copley we see a gentleman practising archery (fig. 144); the figures of the lady and the girl seem to have been added by another hand, for they are not connected with the figure of the archer. Francis Hayman — a second-rate artist in whose work every tradition that influenced English painting of the mid-eighteenth century met, and who was also a link between Hogarth and Gravelot and the early style of Gainsbo-

rough[1] — shows in *Thomas* (?), *Margaret, and Elizabeth Tyers* (fig. 147) a huntsman brandishing a pheasant he has killed. Arthur Devis painted another huntsman offering a pheasant to a seated couple (*John Ord and his Family*; fig. 329).

In *Thomas Mansel and his Half-brothers* (fig. 330) by Allan Ramsay, painted in about 1740, the girl's hand is on the grouse her twenty-one-year-old half-brother, Baron Mansel of Margam, has just shot with the fowling-piece he carries. In a lively scene by Giovanni Antonio Poch (1780-1842), *The Family of Count Carlo Melzi d'Eril* of 1827 (fig. 146), the return from the hunt is fêted by the family lined up on the near side of a gate and by friends (among whom are three ecclesiastics) beyond the gate, which opens onto a lawn; the painter has represented himself on the top of a wall, showing a scroll on which there is the image of a newborn baby with the words " Per l'avvenire " (" For the future "), an allusion to the child the prolific countess is expecting.

In eighteenth-century England there was a whole school of painters specializing in sporting scenes, and Sitwell compares this skill to the specialized pursuits of many noble families at the Japanese Court: for example, calligraphy, floral arrangement, football, poetry, sword-making, heraldry, wrestling, and divination.[2] John Wootton (1686?-1765) has the merit of initiating the series of conversation pieces on horseback with paintings such as *The Beauchamp and Rivers Families and Sir Nevil Hickman* (1749; fig. 331), in which the ladies' coach-and-six appears in the foreground, against a sweeping view over the estate. Lord Rivers has dismounted near his horse and the other gentlemen are on horseback, with the gamekeeper and the dogs adding a sporting flavour to the scene. George Stubbs (1724-1806) was foremost among sporting painters, and has become famous in our time because of his pictures of horses. His " conversations " have earned him a place not inferior to Zoffany's among the eighteenth-century minor masters; Waterhouse, though admitting that for Stubbs man was but one element in the animal kingdom — as he was interested in every kind of animal, but especially in horses (in this sense, the only artistic antecedent to which one can point is Aelbert Cuyp) — warns against classifying Stubbs among the sporting painters, for he possessed a more universal character. He must, though, have had a kind of mania for horses; for he could tolerate living for eighteen months among their carcasses in a remote Lincolnshire farmhouse near Horkstow, in order to study them in a series of drawings of astonishing scientific accuracy which he published with the title *The Anatomy of the Horse*.[3]

In the group of *The Melbourne and Milbanke Families* of about 1770 (fig. 333), Stubbs shows Lady Melbourne dressed in a rose-coloured silk skirt with a white wrap round her shoulders and sitting in a pony chaise near her father, Mr. John Milbanke. He is wearing a lavender-blue coat and stands with his hand on the neck of his horse, which is quietly grazing; Lord Melbourne, in a dark blue coat, buff waistcoat, and gold-laced tricorne hat, is astride a magnificent chestnut. The screen of foliage on the left — formed by an old, gnarled tree — throws its shade on the group, which is disposed in the shape of a T, the line of the two horsemen falling at right angles onto the pony chaise. We find the same scenery in *Colonel Pocklington with his Sisters*, of which we have spoken.[4] In *The Third Duke of Portland with his Brother, Lord Edward Bentinck* (fig. 148), the two horsemen halted near a fence in a clearing surrounded by woods represent the intensity of a moment of communion with nature. In *The Englington Brothers* (fig. 145) by Ben Marshall (1767-1835), another famous painter of horses, one is already aware of the peculiar flavour of English sporting life which was later to inspire Surtees' novels. The gold-laced, dark-blue liveries, proper to the county, and the yellow liveries of the jockeys stand out vividly against the gay landscape of Stubbs' *The Second Duke and Duchess of Richmond Watching Horses Exercising* (c. 1761-62); the group of jockeys in particular recalls certain iconographical patterns of the Persian miniaturists (fig. 149).

Stubbs' *Phaeton* in the London National Gallery, painted in 1787 — with its resplendent colours, the lively costumes of the human figures, and the superb carriage and horses — is one of those pictures in which the master has succeeded in seizing the spirit of a whole epoch: here we confront one aspect of an England which is now legendary. Another phaeton, driven by two ladies, crosses Phoenix Park in Dublin accompanied by the riding-party of Frederick Howard, fifth Earl of Carlisle (Lord Lieutenant of Ireland from 1780 to 1782), in a painting by Francis Wheatley (fig. 332), best known for his set of affected engravings of the *Cries of London* (the more valuable part of Wheatley's work has now [1970] been studied by Mary Webster).

Sir Edwin Landseer (1802-1873), the most acclaimed of Victorian painters but little appreciated nowadays, displays his speciality as a painter of animals and as a polished and sentimental recorder of the joys of family life in *The First Game-Bag* (fig. 327) of

1 Cf. WATERHOUSE, *Painting in Britain*, 2nd ed. (Harmondsworth and Baltimore: Penguin Books, 1962), pp. 135-36. On the group of the Tyers family, see JOHN E. RUCH, "A Hayman Portrait of Jonathan Tyers's Family", in *The Burlington Magazine*, CXII, August 1970, pp. 495-97. 2 *Conversation Pieces* (London: Batsford, 1936), p. 55. 3 *Painting in Britain*, p. 207. 4 See above, p. 134.

144 attr. to JOHN SINGLETON COPLEY (1738-1815), *A Gentleman Practising Archery, and his Family*. New York, collection of Mr. E. J. Rousuck.

overleaf:

145 BEN MARSHALL (1767-1835), *The Englington Brothers*. New York, collection of Mr. E. J. Rousuck.

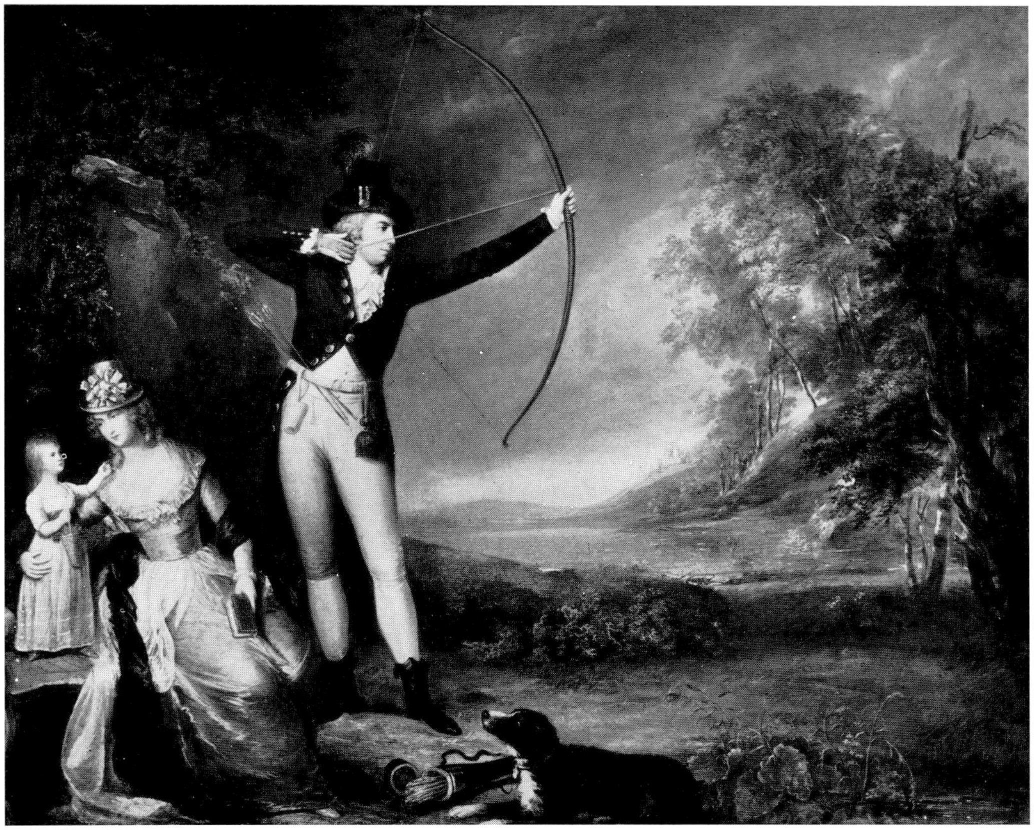

144

the son of Lord London. A hunting scene is also the subject of a painting by Wilhelm Leibl (1844-1900), in which the painter has portrayed himself with fowling-piece and dog, together with his friend Johann Sperl, who painted the landscape (fig. 334). Music played a great role in the entertainments of past centuries — and it was music played "live", not transmitted by mechanical means as nowadays. Compare a modern concert on television with one of the old-fashioned kind, in which the instrumentalists were rarely accomplished musicians but the participation of the audience was much more lively and stimulating.

We have already met several musicians in the "conversations" mentioned earlier. Frans Pourbus' *Wedding Feast of Joris Hoefnagel*[5] especially helps to conjure up the atmosphere. *The Family Reunion* by Antoine Le Nain (1588-1648), painted in 1642 (Louvre), reveals a very rudimentary skill in composing groups. A line of people are juxtaposed, not communicating with each other, like the multiple portraits of the sixteenth century; in the foreground is a lutanist and another ruddy-faced bourgeois sitting next to a woman who sings a song from the text in her hand. Her features are so minute compared with those of the men that she seems to belong to another race. Jan Miense Molenaer's *Entertainment of the van Loon Family* (1635) is a parable of the three ages of man: infancy, manhood, and old age (fig. 150). Old Aleyd van der Laen, significantly, has laid his hand on a skull, a gesture which, as Staring remarks, shows that he was dead when the picture was painted.[6] The young couples are his grandchildren, of the van Loon family: Nicolaas with his wife Emerentia van Veen, and his brother Pieter with his wife Anna van Forrest; the latter are playing a lute and a harpsichord. The setting is not an actual room but a stately apartment invented by the painter — as was often the case in these "conversations" in order to endow them with a more sumptuous character — the curtain on the right stressing the courtly quality. In another Molenaer painting of about 1640, *An Unidentified Family* (Haarlem, Frans Hals Museum), the musical instruments — lute, violin, theorbo, bass viol, and harpsichord — are in the centre of the scene; among the players a girl sings from a score, and the man with his hand on his chest is probably also playing a

5 See above, p. 60. 6 *De Hollanders Thuis* (The Hague: Martinus Nijhoff, 1956), p. 70.

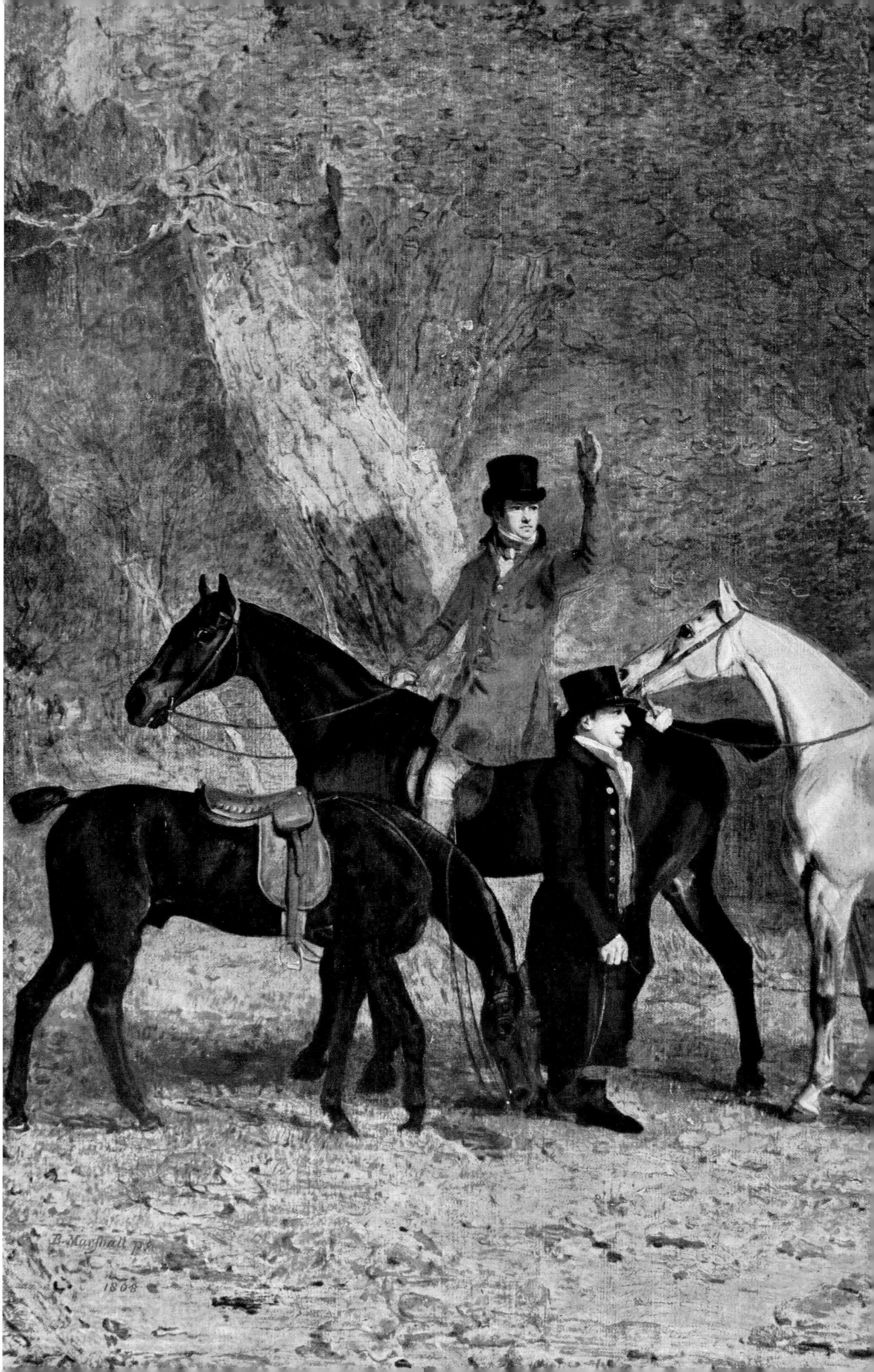
B. Marshall pt.
1808

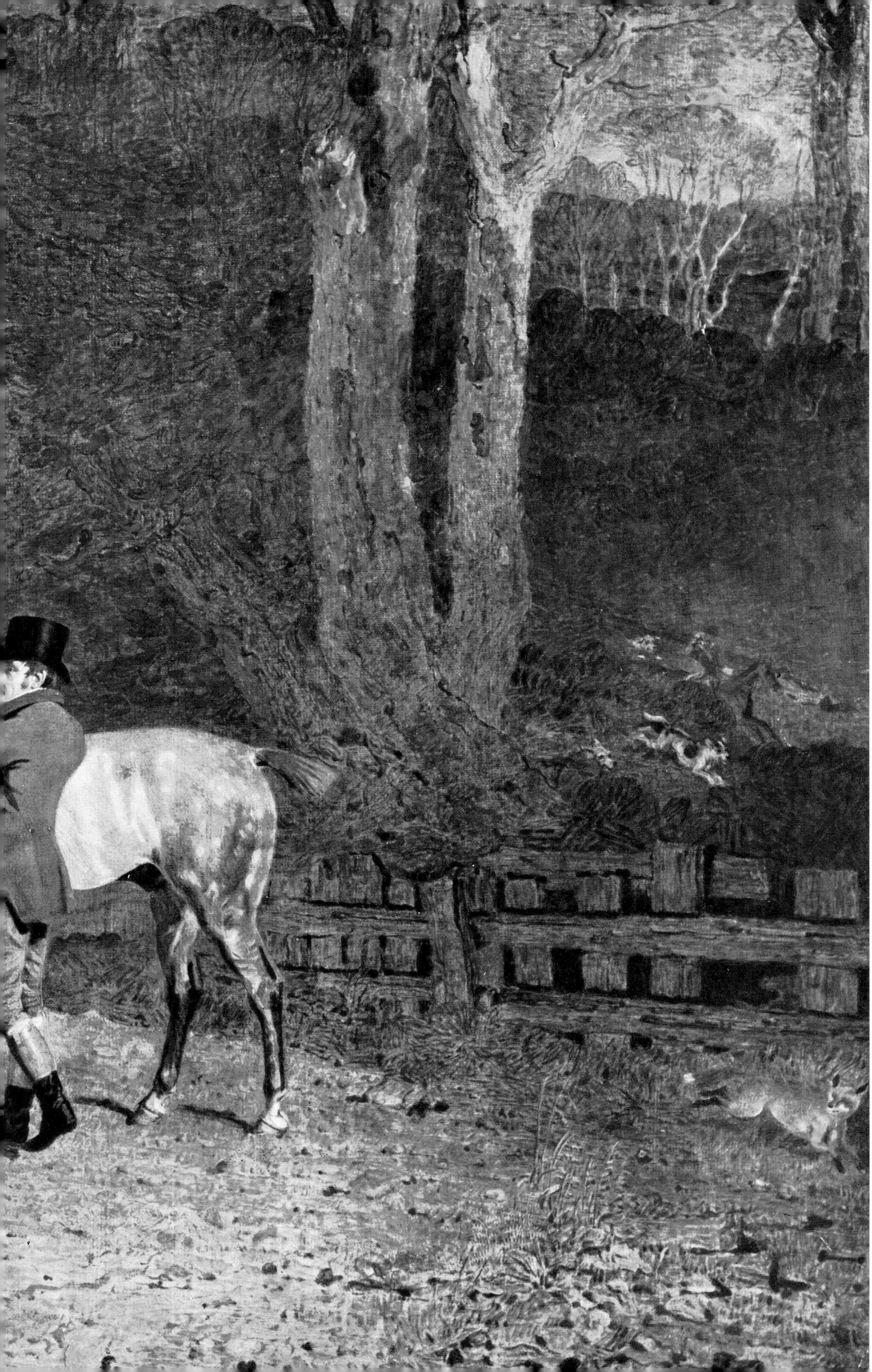

145

part. The figure of Justice in the bas-relief on the base of the pilaster hints perhaps at his office of *echevin*, or sheriff. That the sitters are members of an actual family and we are not looking at a mere genre scene (as some other features, such as the boy on the right blowing soap bubbles, might suggest) is proved by the portraits of ancestors on the wall and the small portrait held by one of the two elderly gentlemen behind the harpsichord. *A Family Making Music*, painted in about 1665 by Pieter de Hooch (fig. 151) in an interior with a view of other rooms, according to a formula frequently used by this painter, shows a seated lady singing from a book of songs and accompanied by flute, viol, and a little lute; a bass viol leans against a chair. The rich furnishings include a japanned casket between two azure pots on the top of a tall cabinet. Daniel Preisler (born in Prague in 1627, died in 1665) has portrayed himself playing the theorbo. The table round which the family is gathered and the naked child with an apple in his hand are features reminiscent of the tradition of Italian groups (fig. 336). Robert Tournières, a French artist whom we have already met, is perhaps the author of the early eighteenth-century painting showing *Michel de la Barre and Other Musicians* against a formal background of columns and curtains (London, National Gallery). The flautist and composer Michel de la Barre (1674-1743/4) is standing and turns the pages of a musical score; the person on the left, dressed with more refinement, is probably the rich patron who commissioned the painting. But this group is really outside the category of family portraits, as are the two groups attributed to Marco Ricci (1676-1729) representing the *Rehearsals of an Opera* (fig. 335, 337). Philip Mercier (1689-1760) in *A Music Party* (1733; London, National Portrait Gallery) presents Frederick Louis, Prince of Wales, eldest son of George II, making music with his sisters in the gardens of Kew Palace. There are also musical " conversations " with a great number of figures by Marcellus Laroon (1679-1772), but, as we said earlier, these can hardly be considered proper conversation pieces. Laroon painted a number of dinner parties, village weddings, *fêtes galantes*, and gallant " conversations " which belong to genre painting and thus do not concern us here.[7] In the field of musical parties Zoffany has also left exquisite compositions. *The Cowper and Gore Families* (fig. 338) has for its setting the Villa Palmieri near Florence;[8] it was painted for George Nassau Clavering, Earl Cowper (the gentleman standing in the picture), who had purchased the villa in 1765: the person playing the 'cello is Charles Gore, the prototype of the " travelled Englishman " in Goethe's *Wilhelm Meister*. In *A Musical Party on the Thames* (fig. 155) with the Sharp family (William Sharp was surgeon to King George III) on their pleasure barge at Fulham — which is seen in the background with the church and the Sharps' villa — one notices a serpent among the musical instruments. Walpole criticized the painting when it was first exhibited at the Royal Academy in 1781 by saying that " the figures are most natural, and highly finished, but a great want of keeping on the whole ". We must mention particularly the delicate *Mr. and Mrs. Blew and their Children* (fig. 339), with the children disposed in a half-circle between their father, who plays the flute, and their mother, who holds a book in her hand, and *The Minuet* (fig. 152), of which something has been said already,[9] with the fairy-like girl revolving slowly to the sound of the flute. With this painting we come very close to genre painting, and even closer with *The Piano Lesson* (fig. 153) by J.-F. Garneray, a painting whose elegance stands out if one compares it with Pietro Benvenuti's (1768-1844) *Princess Corsini and Signora Scotto* (fig. 340), and more so with *Rosmunda Pisaroni and her Husband*, wrongly attributed to F. Gérard (fig. 154). The *Family in a Garden* (fig. 341) by Teodoro Matteini, with musical instruments and two girls preparing to dance, is the counterpart of the other painting by the same artist which we have already described.[10] There is a touch of the *naïf* in the group of *The Children of Francis I of Naples* (fig. 342),[11] with its symmetrical and triangular disposition. *The Children of Dr. Archibald Bennie* (watercolour on ivory; fig. 343) by the Scottish artist John Faed (1819-1902) is suffused with Victorian sentimentality; the clergyman's daughters have just finished singing a song accompanied on the guitar, and the son, radiant as an archangel, has also interrupted reading a book of verse.

Painters frequently painted their own portraits when portraying their own family or a group of other people in their studio. The earliest example of this is the representation of St. Luke with the features of the contemporary painter, in the act of portraying the Virgin and Child — a motif frequently treated by Flemish painters such as Rogier van der Weyden (Munich, Alte Pinakothek), Dirk Bouts (Penrhyn Castle), Rueland Frühauf the Younger (Nuremberg, Germanisches Nationalmuseum), Mabuse (Vienna, Kunsthistorisches Museum), Lancelot Blondeel (Bruges, Musée Communal des Beaux-Arts), Heinrich Bornemann (Hamburg, Jacobikirche), and Herman Rode (Lübeck, Museen für Kunst und Kulturgeschichte). The most famous example

7 See above, p. 34. On Marcellus Laroon see the study by ROBERT RAINES, *Marcellus Laroon* (London: Routledge and Kegan Paul for The Paul Mellon Foundation for British Art, 1967). 8 For an account of the Villa Palmieri, see ENRICHETTA RITTER in *L'Oeil*, no. 133, January 1966, pp. 54-59. 9 See above, p. 128. 10 See above, p. 118. 11 See PRAZ, *An Illustrated History of Furnishing* (London: Thames and Hudson; New York: Braziller, 1964), p. 222. The

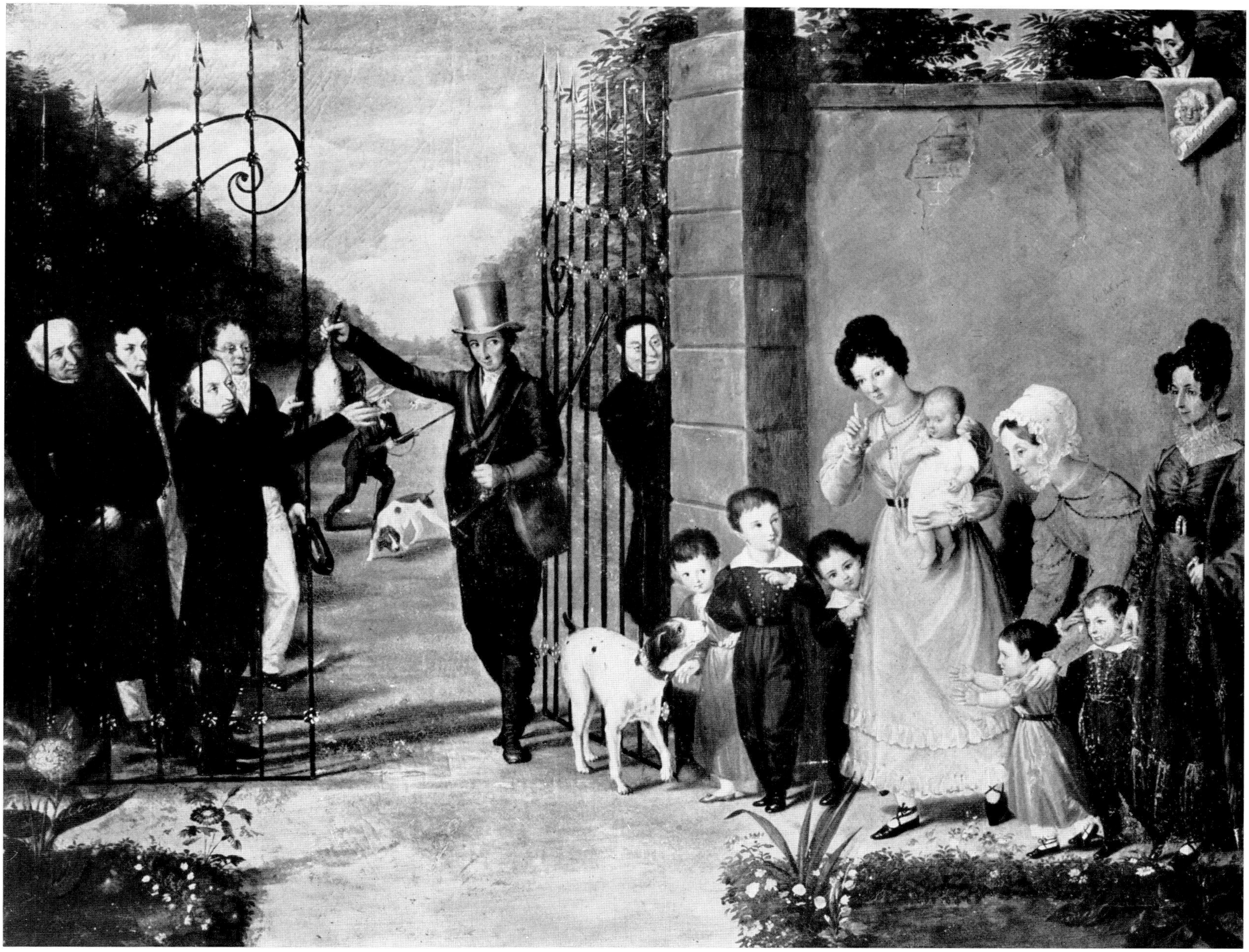

146

146 GIOVANNI ANTONIO POCH (1780-1842), *The Family of Count Carlo Melzi d'Eril*, 1827. Milan, collection of the Duke Lodovico Melzi d'Eril.

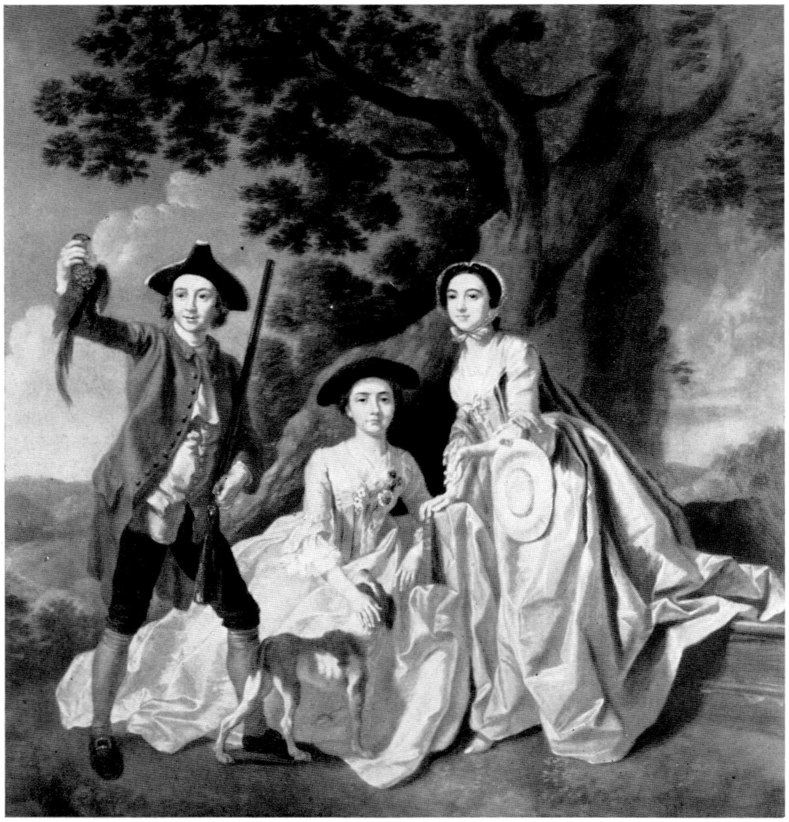

147 FRANCIS HAYMAN (1708-1776), *Thomas* (?), *Margaret, and Elizabeth Tyers.* Washington, D.C., collection of Mr. and Mrs. Paul Mellon.

147

of a painter working in his studio is Velázquez' *Las Meninas*, which we have already seen;[12] and Vermeer's well-known painting in the Kunsthistorisches Museum in Vienna may be added to this category.
Giuseppe Maria Crespi (1665-1747), in a small painting on copper (fig. 344) which he gave to the Grand Duke of Tuscany in 1708, portrays himself just as he has stopped working at the painting one sees on the easel in order to pull a child's go-cart; the mother and the other child, who is about to help his father, are happily smiling. This is a "conversation" which does not conform to the usual schemes, although even here one can trace a triangular pattern (upside down). In two paintings, one in Brussels, the other at the Louvre, Joos van Craesbeeck (c. 1605-1660) has portrayed himself at his easel — in one case facing the onlooker, in the other turning his back and surrounded by a merry company. Rembrandt portrayed himself (Glasgow Art Gallery) painting the nude figure of Hendrickje Stoffels and also drew himself correcting a pupil who is sketching a model. Molenaer is seen in the act of preparing the colours for a genre scene he is painting (Berlin, Staatliche Museen), and David Teniers the Younger shows himself painting a portrait in his studio in the presence of other persons (London, Sir William J. Farrer Collection). Also seen in their own studios with bystanders are Ferdinand van Apshoven (Dresden, Gemäldegalerie) and Giuseppe Nuvoloni (Milan, Brera), who is surrounded by members of his own family — some busy playing music (a harp-player is in the centre of the painting) and some engaged in talking. Other scenes of this type were done by Gerrit Adriaenszen Berckheyde (Leningrad, Hermitage); Frans Mieris, in two different paintings (Dresden, Gemäldegalerie); Michiel van Musscher (Swiss private collection, and in another painting at Hoevelaken, C.J.K. van Aals Collection); Largillière (Bremen, Kunsthalle, and in another painting at the Louvre, fig. 160); Giacomo Francesco Cipper (Hampton Court Palace); George de Marées (Munich, Alte Pinakothek); Justus Juncker (Cassel, Staatliche Gemäldegalerie); Charles van Loo (Versailles); Alexander Roslin (Stockholm, Nationalmuseum); J.H. Tischbein The Elder, with his first wife at the spinet (Berlin, Staatliche Museen);

statement that only the Count of Lecce is missing in this watercolour ought to be corrected; not only he, but six more children are missing. See my essay "10.000 Borboni", in *I Volti del Tempo* (Naples: E.S.I., 1964). 12 See above, p. 63.

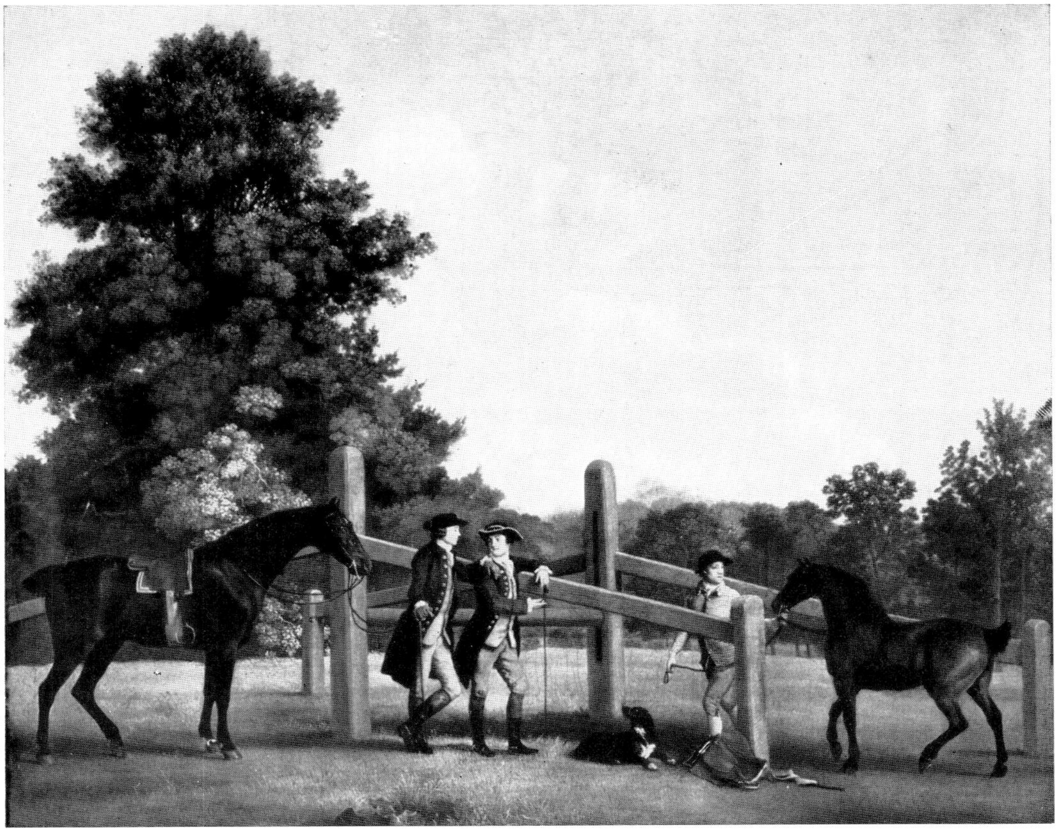

148

148 GEORGE STUBBS (1724-1806), *The Third Duke of Portland with his Brother, Lord Edward Bentinck.* Welbeck Abbey, collection of the Duke of Portland.

Adélaïde Labille-Guiard, with her pupils (Paris, once the property of Gimpel and Wildenstein); Julius Louis Asher (fig. 353); Friedrich Moosbrugger (Karlsruhe, Staatliche Kunsthalle);[13] J.-B. Isabey, at the easel painting the portrait of his first wife, who is sitting at his side (a picture once in the possession of Mme. Basily-Callimaki and reproduced by her in her monograph on the painter); and Felice Carena (Venice, 1954 Biennale).

Joachim Luhn (c. 1640-1717) in his *Self-portrait with his Family* (Brunswick, Herzog Anton Ulrich-Museum) has depicted himself (between 1670 and 1673) with the palette in his left hand in the act of laying his other hand on the shoulder of his wife, while near them are two of his in-laws, the Weiers. The painter's eyes wander outside the painting, not because he is looking at a mirror in order to paint his self-portrait, but as if he were meditating on life and the loneliness of every human being.[14] His father-in-law, in his turn, holds a skull in his hands, perhaps because he is aware of the imminent end of his life (this is the opinion of Frau Kronberger-Frentzen), for when the painter took his wife to his own home in 1673, her father was already dead. But from what we have seen in another painting,[15] the presence of the skull means that death had already occurred.

Watteau portrayed himself with his friend Julienne in a lost painting which survives in an engraving of 1727 by Tardieu and in a few preparatory studies. The tall, emaciated painter holds the palette in his hand and stands by an easel with one of his paintings on it while Julienne plays the bass viol. Cornelis Troost has portrayed himself at the easel making the portrait of a young couple in *An Unidentified Family* (Musée d'Ixelles, Brussels). The child in the high-chair with a trumpet in his hand also appears in the framed picture, leaning against a table behind which a Negro servant in silver-laced green livery pours chocolate. In *The Family of an Artist* (1746; Amsterdam, Rijksmuseum), Troost has represented a landscape painter indicating a painting with a rather naïve gesture, while his wife is drinking tea and one of the children points at a drawing in imitation of his father's gesture. Pietro Longhi in about 1750 also portrayed himself with his back turned, at the easel busily painting a young woman

13 Reproductions of all these paintings are to be found in *Fünfhundert Selbstporträts,* collected and introduced by LUDWIG GOLDSCHEIDER (Vienna: Phaidon Verlag, 1936). 14 The remark is made by KRONBERGER-FRENTZEN, *Das deutsche Familienbildnis* (Leipzig: Johannes Asmus Verlag, 1940), p. 17. 15 See above, p. 181.

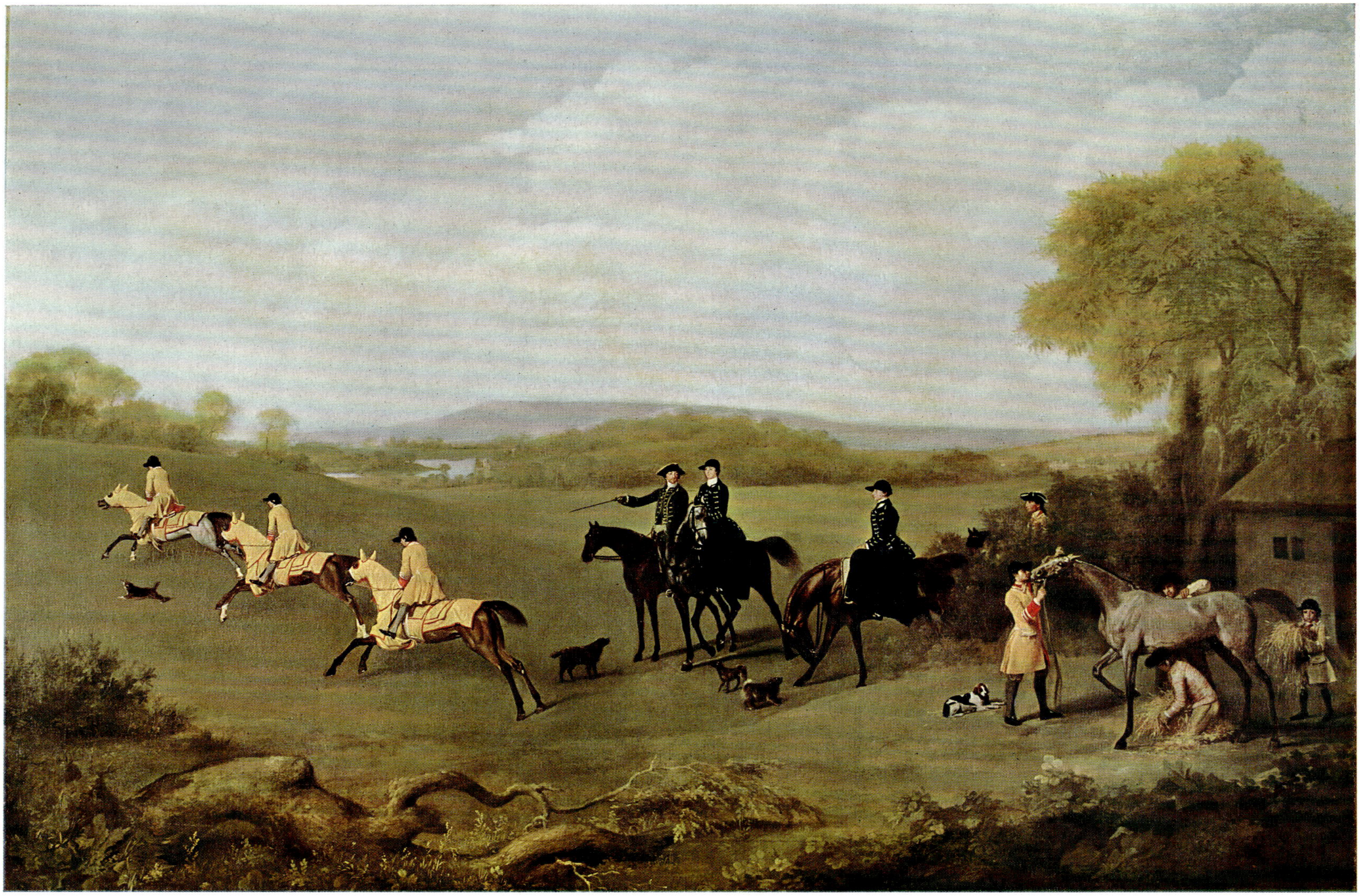

149

149 GEORGE STUBBS (1724-1806), *The Second Duke and Duchess of Richmond Watching Horses Exercising*, c. 1761-2. Goodwood, Chichester, collection of the Duke of Richmond and Gordon. 150 JAN MIENSE MOLENAER (1610-1668), *The Entertainment of the van Loon Family*, 1635. Property of Jonkheer M.N. van Loon; photo Rijksmuseum, Amsterdam.

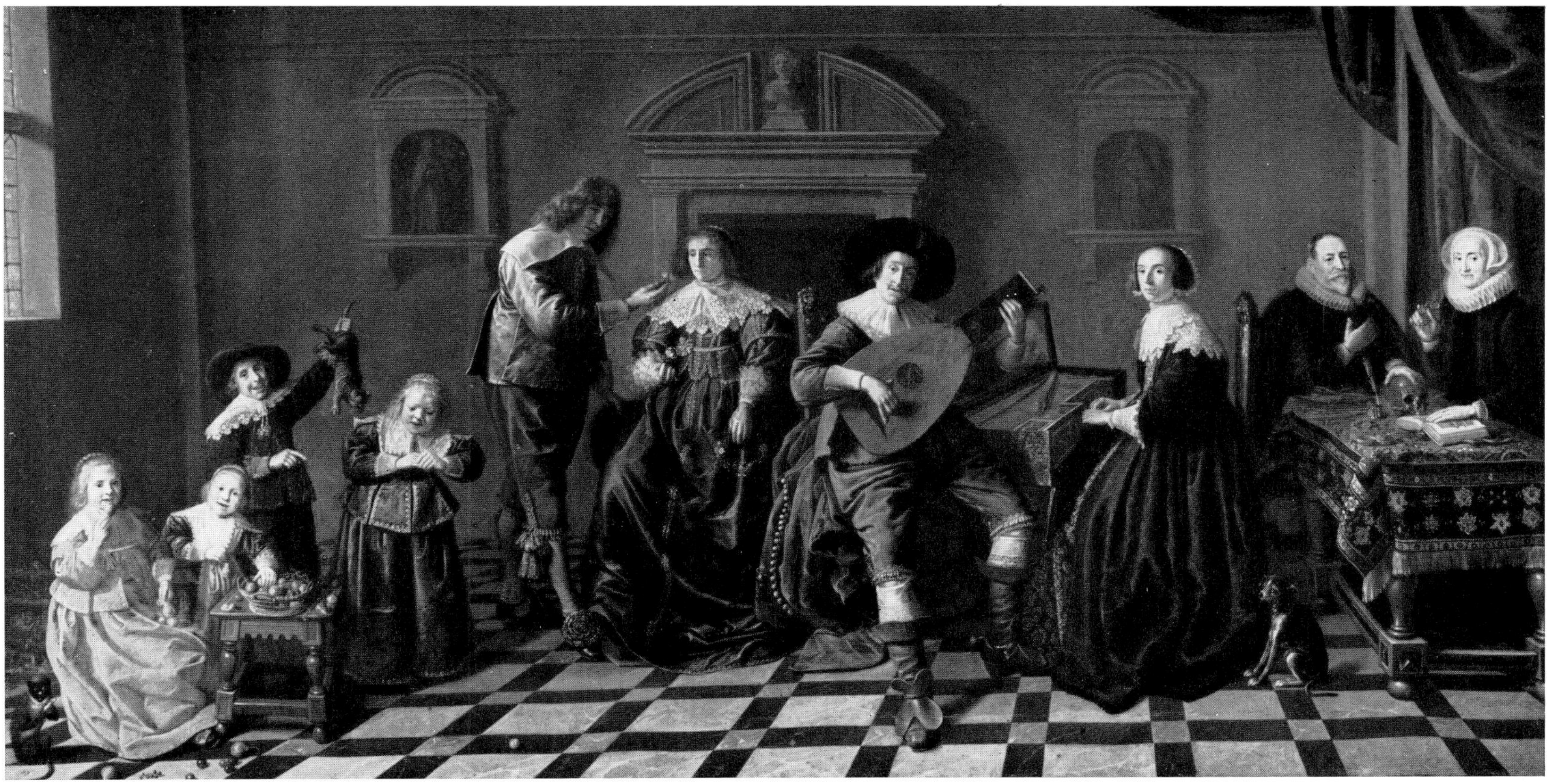

150

facing him and accompanied by a cavalier (Venice, Ca'Rezzonico).
Ubaldo Gandolfi, using a rather original device, turns in our direction (fig. 157) as if his sitter were on our side, whereas he is in fact seated almost next to the portrait and makes a gesture to indicate the painter. The vivacity of the two central figures is contrasted with the sulky expressions of the two old people at the edge of the picture.
Hayman represents *Sir Robert Walpole in the Artist's Studio* (London, National Portrait Gallery), and the son of the minister was perhaps thinking of this painting when he said that Hayman was " a strong mannerist, and easily distinguishable by the large noses and shambling legs of his figures ".[16] Vertue, apropos of Balthasar Denner — a Hamburg artist who resided in England from 1721 to 1728 — mentions a small " family piece " of the artist with his wife and children which he considers to be " very natural and well ", probably the one which is now in the Statens Museum for Kunst in Copenhagen.
Zoffany has portrayed himself, his children, and the old nurse Mrs. Ann Chase (fig. 345) with such a neat cleavage in the middle of the picture that posterity was unable to resist the temptation to divide it into two parts, which were sold separately (Christie's 23 July 1954 [fig. 346] and Sotheby's 20 January 1957 [fig. 348]). The painting presents a problem because Zoffany never had more than four children alive at the same time; perhaps the one in the arms of the nurse is a child who died in infancy, or perhaps he is a grandchild, since his daughter Cecilia married in 1799: but if this is the case the date of the painting would have to be advanced to the early years of the nineteenth century. The harp-player and the harpsichord-player are motifs common to paintings of the period. John Hamilton Mortimer (1741-1779) has portrayed himself shortly after 1760 closing his portfolio of drawings under the eyes of his master Joseph Wilton (fig. 347); a young man nearby holds in his hands a cast of Homer's head, which was perhaps the subject of the drawing. There is a similar composition in *Peter and James Romney* (fig. 161) by George Romney (1734-1802), in which Peter, sitting in front of the easel, demonstrates a Euclidean theorem. Peter studied art under

16 *Anecdotes of Painting in England* (London: Dodsley, 1782) IV, p. 124.

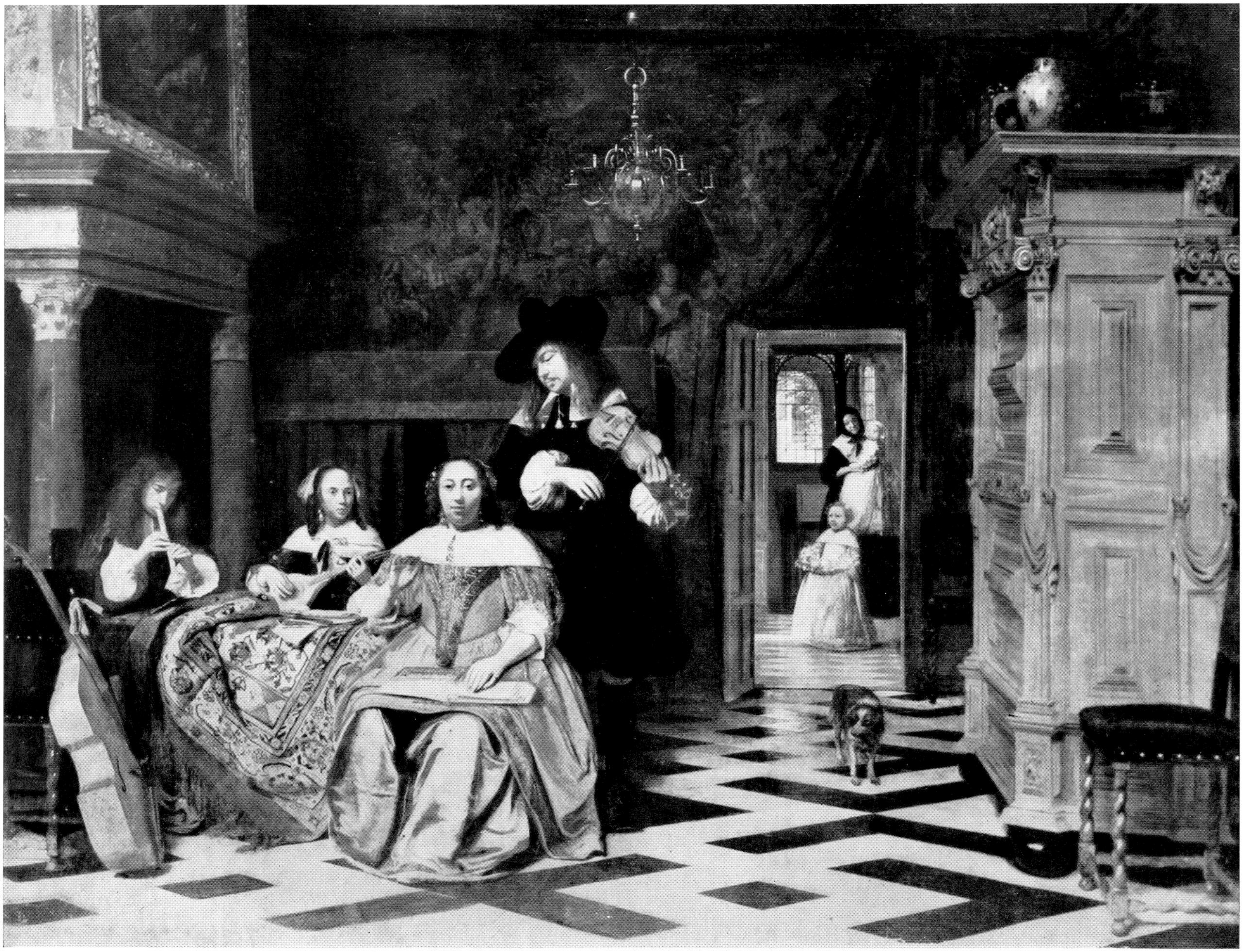

151

151 PIETER DE HOOCH (1629- after 1688), *A Family Making Music*, c. 1665. Cleveland, Museum of Art (Hanna Fund).

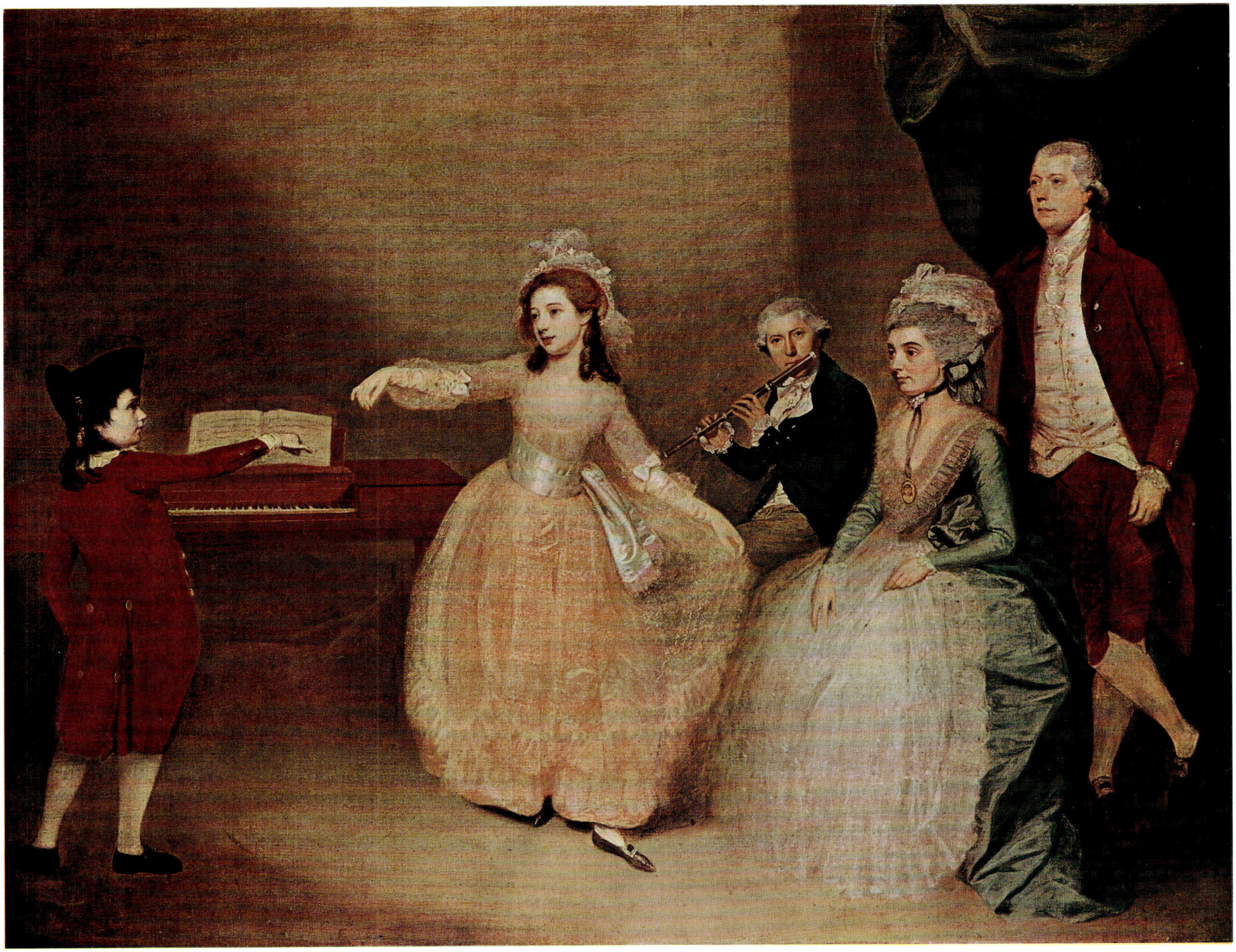

152

152 JOHANN ZOFFANY (1734/5-1810), *The Minuet*. Glasgow, Art Gallery and Museum.

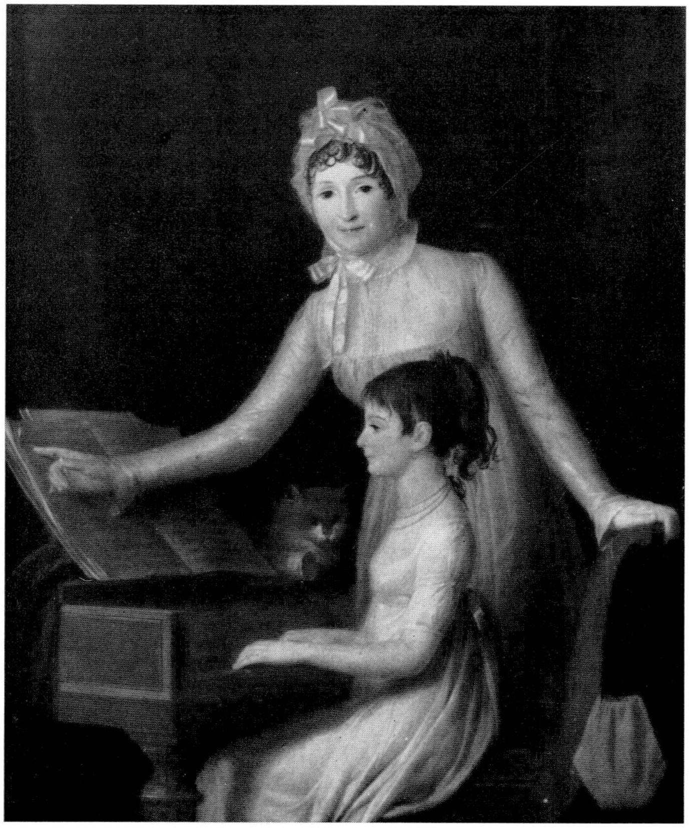
153

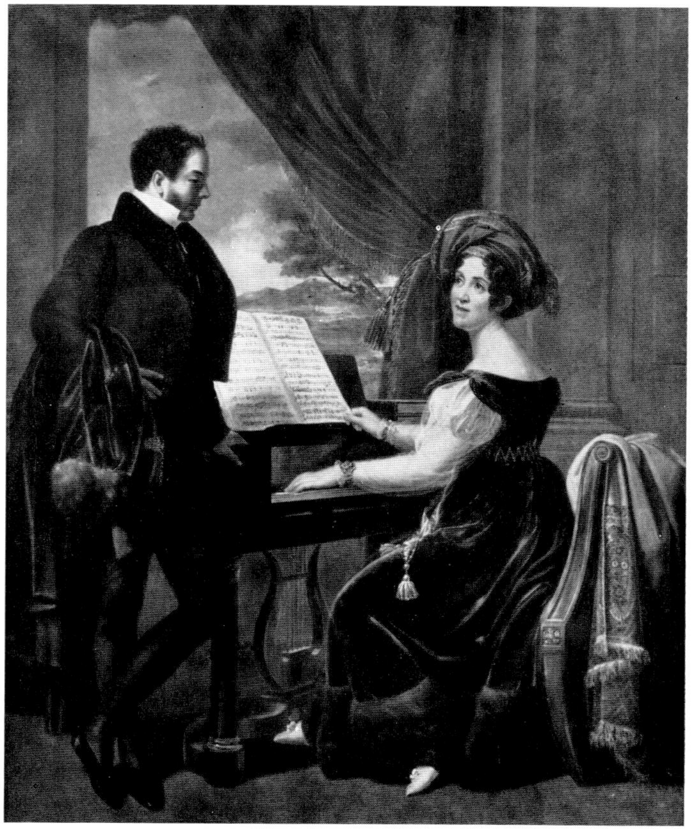
154

the guidance of his famous brother George and painted portraits at Cambridge and in northern England until his early death (he lived from 1741 to 1777).

With some originality, Franz Anton Leydensdorf (1722-1795) has given a theatrical turn to his *Self-portrait with his Family*. The painter appears in the frame as if at a window and makes a gesture while keeping his eyes on a board on which he is drawing; behind him is a canvas on an easel, and round him are three members of his family, one being his wife, who rubs her hands with satisfaction (fig. 158). A similar device occurs in an eighteenth-century painting perhaps by the same hand, in which a young artist indicates to an elderly virtuoso armed with a monocle a subject located beyond the picture-plane, near the observer (fig. 159).

We also find a certain originality in the disposition of the figures in *The Painter's Studio* (fig. 351) by Jean-Baptiste Lallemand (1716-1803). On the left, in front of a window, the painter is seated busily drawing, watched by a dog; an easel with a painting on it is placed between the table and the window. At the right of the window, facing a wall decorated with paintings and sculptures, the painter's wife sits drawing, her back turned to the onlooker — while nearby their little daughter is seated on a low chair, reading. The armour on the wall behind the painter is indicative of the growing interest in the Middle Ages. Moritz von Schwind (1804-1871) shows the Duchess of Orléans who, after climbing some scaffolding, has taken the brush from the painter's hand in order to paint the grass herself in one of the frescoes of the Wartburg; two members of her retinue are looking on (East Berlin, Nationalgalerie).

The Danish artist Jens Juel (1745-1802) portrayed himself with his wife sitting next to him studying the painting he is working on (Copenhagen, Statens Museum for Kunst); in a painting dated 1784 the Dutch painter Leendert Overbeek (1752-1815) depicts himself holding the palette in front of the easel on which he has just finished the portrait of his wife and son (fig. 156).

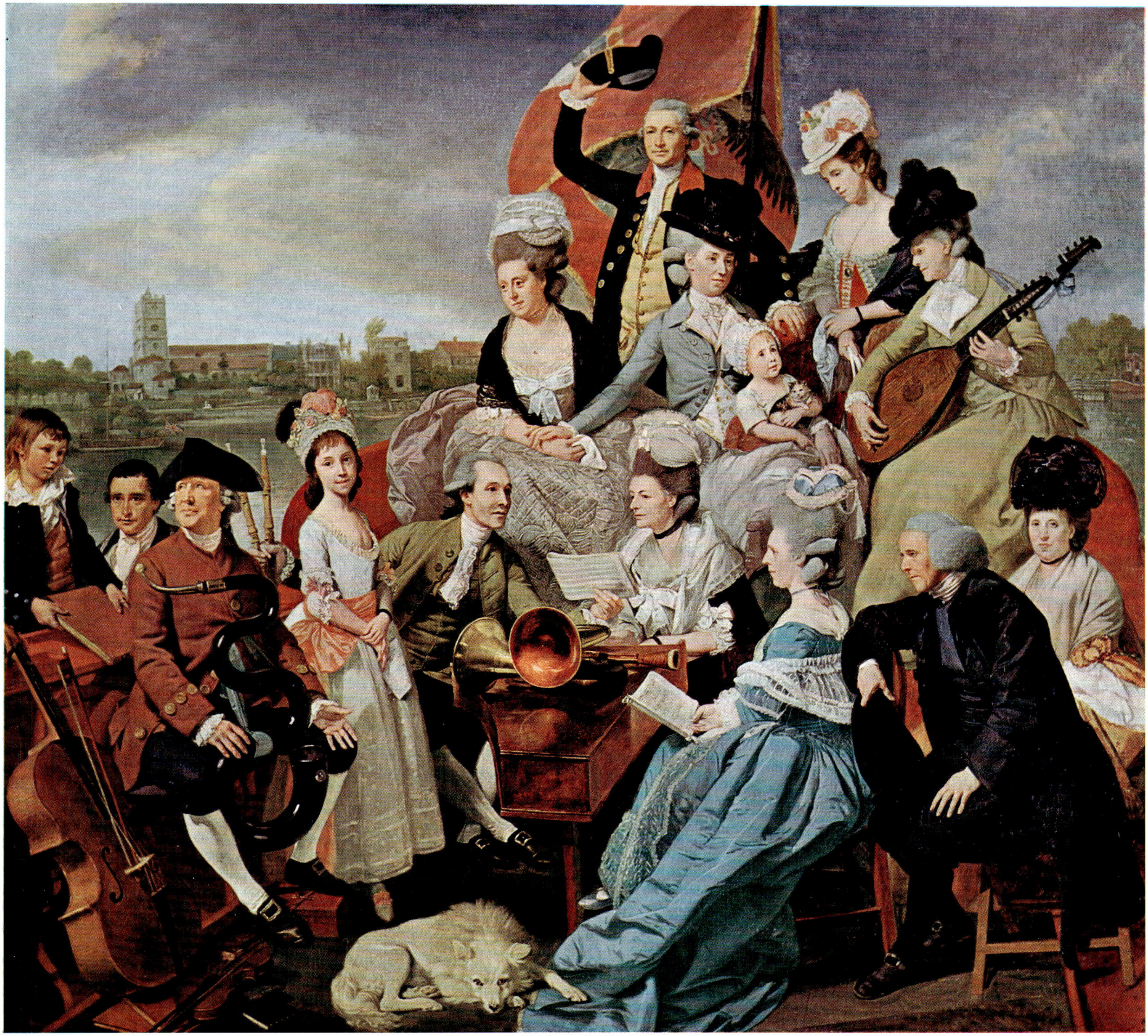

155

153 JEAN-FRANÇOIS GARNERAY (1755-1837), *The Piano Lesson*. Paris, collection of Mme Marguerite Semail; photo Studio Yves Hervochon, Paris. 154 attr. to FRANÇOIS GÉRARD (1770-1837), *Rosmunda Pisaroni and her Husband*. Piacenza, Anguissola Collection. 155 JOHANN ZOFFANY (1734/5-1810), *The Sharp Family* (*A Musical Party on the Thames*). Hardwick Court, Gloucester, collection of Miss O. Lloyd-Baker.

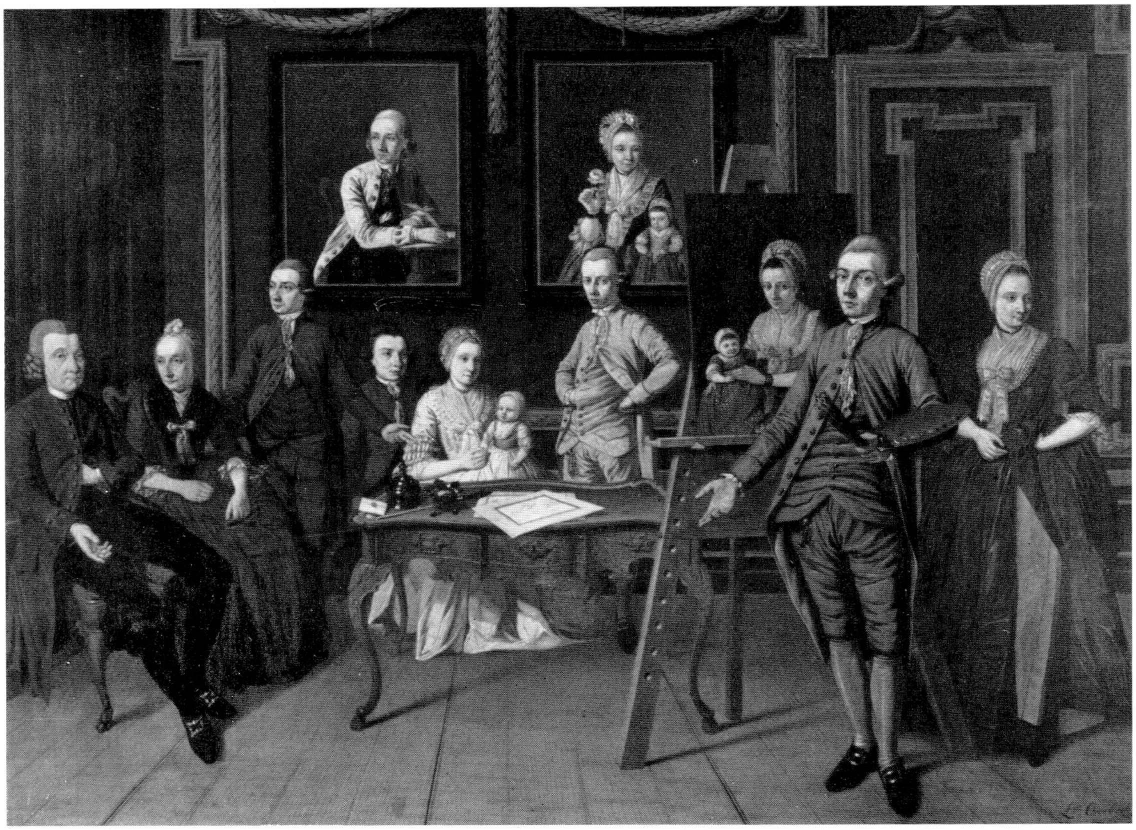

156

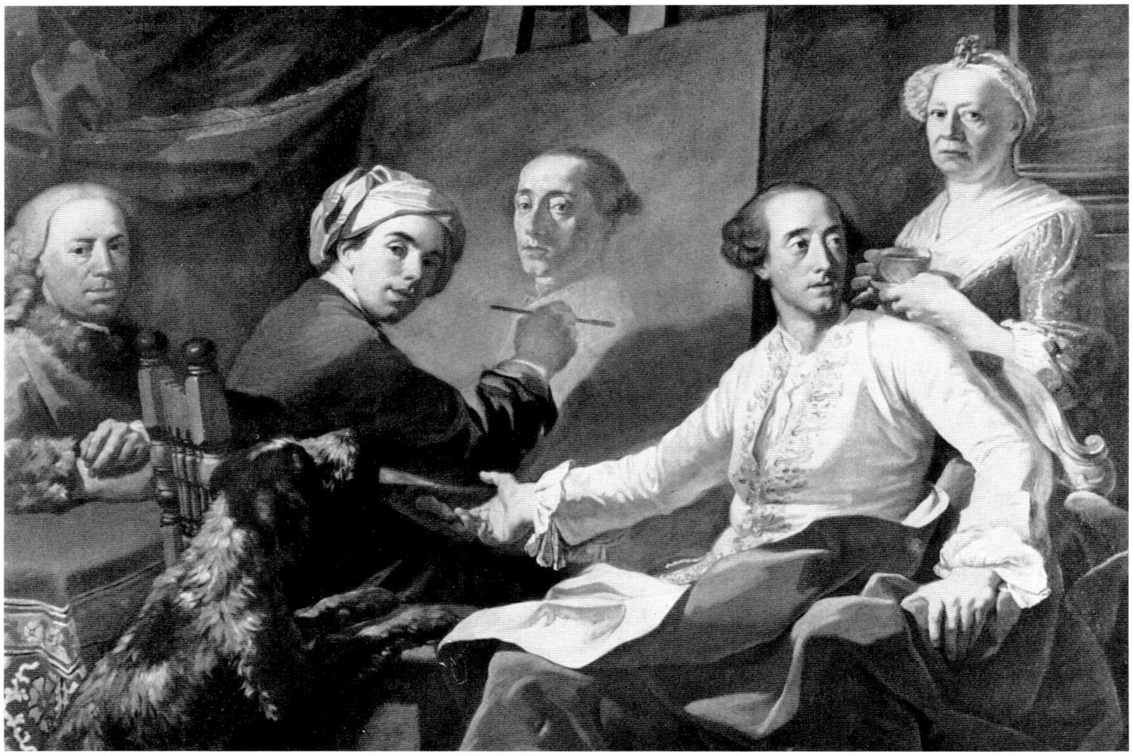

157

156 LEENDERT OVERBEEK (1752-1815), *The Overbeek Family*, 1784. Haarlem, collection of Mejuffrouw Agathe Overbeek.

157 UBALDO GANDOLFI (1728-1781), *The Painter at Work*. San Francisco, M. H. de Young Memorial Museum (Samuel H. Kress Collection).

158 FRANZ ANTON LEYDENSDORF (1722-1795), *Self-portrait with his Family*. Heidelberg, Kurpfälzisches Museum.

159 ANONYMOUS (18th century), *An Artist and a Virtuoso*. Present location unknown.

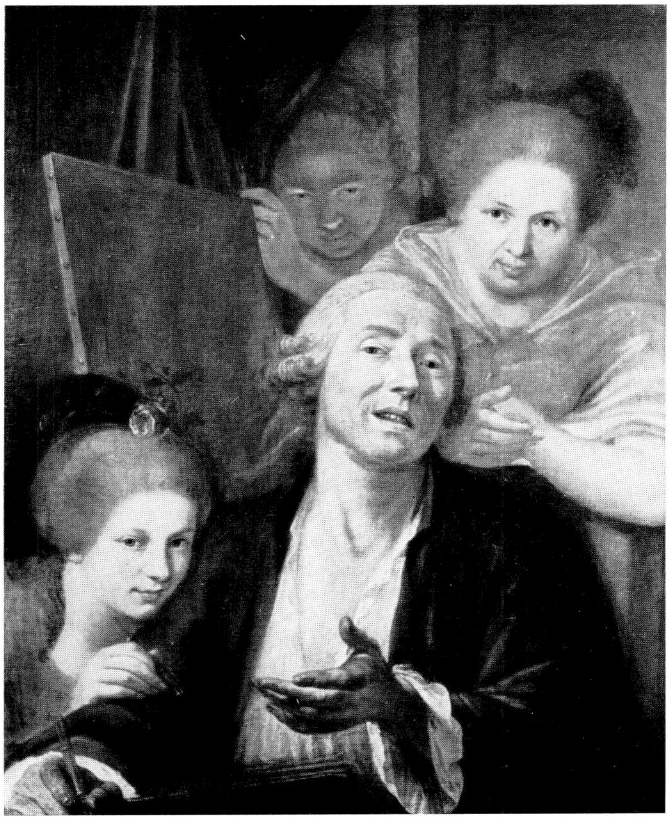

158

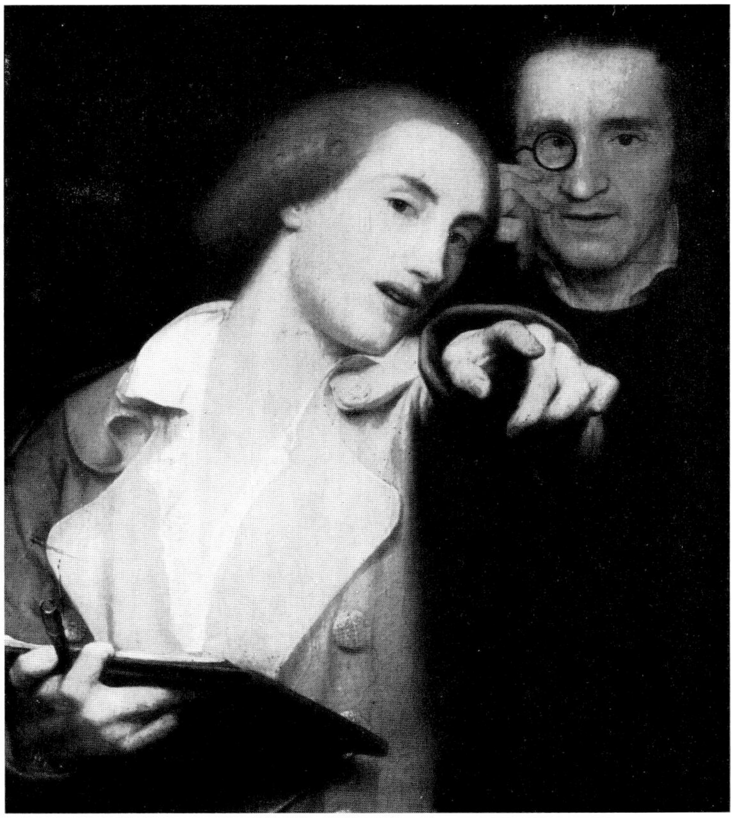

159

Other relatives are lined up behind — among them Lambert Overbeek, with his wife holding her son on her knees — while portraits of his daughter with his son-in-law and his grandson hang on the wall. The three mothers with their sons are deliberately placed symmetrically in the centre of the painting, but this achieves a rather surrealist and somehow grotesque effect. Near the painter is his unmarried sister. The furniture belongs to the middle of the century, but the Louis XVI decoration of the room is probably an invention. Hendrik Jan van Ameron (1777-1833) stops work on a picture on his easel in order to drink a cup of tea near his little son and wife, whose unprepossessing profile stands out against a dark background almost intentionally, as if to stress its ludicrous aspect (fig. 349).

Boilly takes us to *Houdon's Studio* (fig. 352) where Laplace sits for the sculptor in the presence of Madame Houdon and her daughters, a group as lovely as the Three Graces. Johann Friedrich August Tischbein (1750-1812) in *The Artist's Family* (1800; fig. 350) introduces his family in a kind of Bacchic procession, with a rosy putto riding piggyback; the group seems to overwhelm him as he is painting, and he is about to tickle the child's face with his brush. Johann Baptist Reiter (1813-1890) places a group of grave and thoughtful men in his studio, with an old man adjusting the strings of his violin conspicuous in the middle (fig. 354). The painter has stopped his work and, with palette and brush in his hands and a faraway look, has as stolid an appearance as the figure seated near the table with the refreshments.[17] Julius Louis Asher (1804-1878) is also about to interrupt his work in a painting of his studio dated 1828, as another artist, Porth, places his hand on his shoulder to suggest a correction (fig. 353). Jacques-Émile Blanche (1861-1942) in his *Portrait of the Painter Thaulow and his Family* (Paris, Musée d'Art Moderne) continues well into the beginning of our century the tradition of portraits of painters in their studios, with a composition which also harks back to the time-hallowed triangular pattern — the easel on one side has as its counterpart the group, which repeats the same geometrical motif.

17 The attribution of this painting to Josef Danhauser and the identification of the old violinist with Schubert by ANN TIZIA LEITICH, *Wiener Biedermeier* (Bielefeld and Leipzig, 1941), p. 3, are wrong. On Reiter see ERNA FELMAYER, "Johann Baptist Reiters Jugendentwicklung", in *Wiener Schriften*, Heft 5, 1957, p. 207.

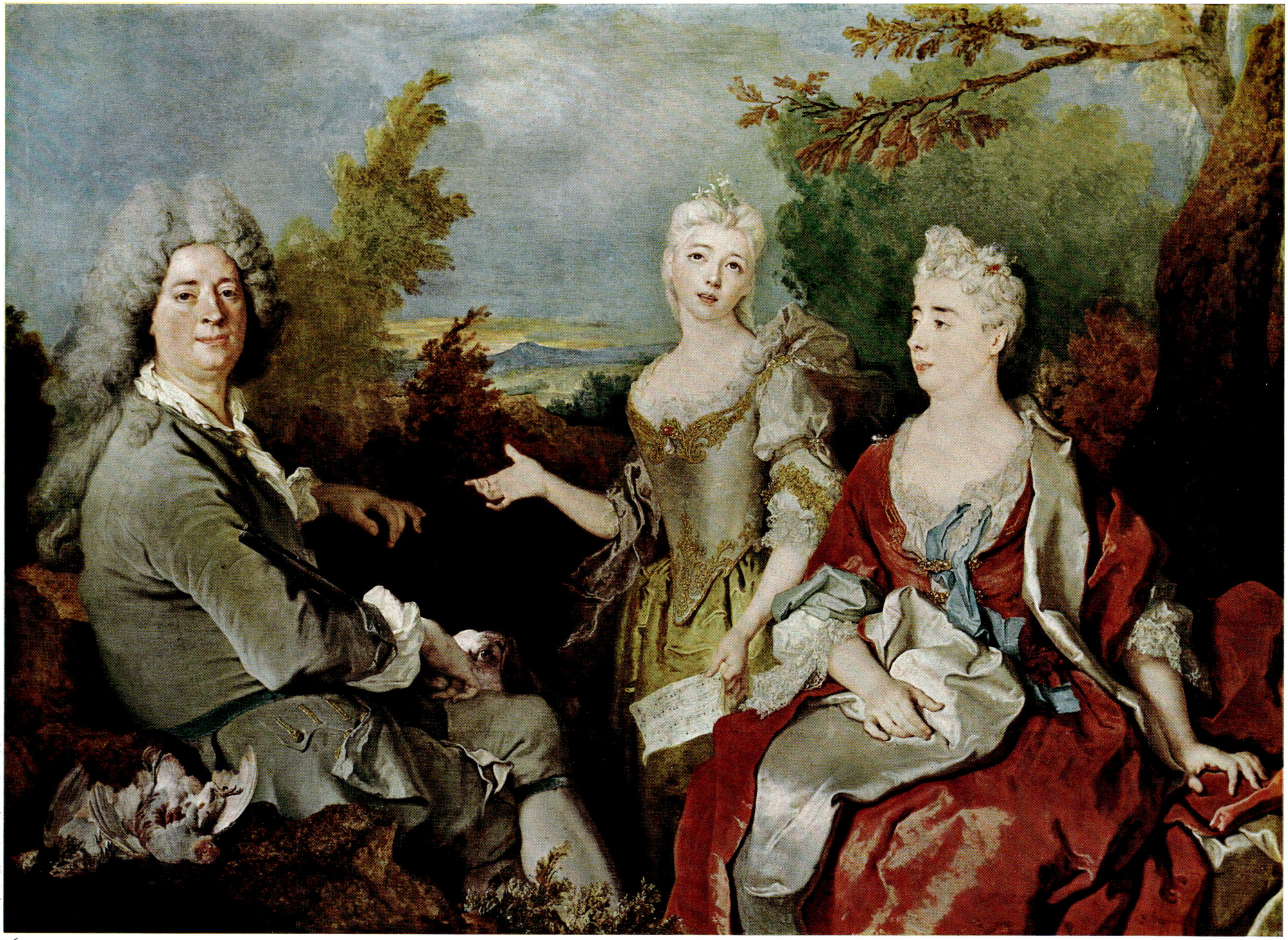

160

160 NICOLAS DE LARGILLIÈRE (1656-1746), *The Painter and his Family*. Paris, Louvre.

161 GEORGE ROMNEY (1734-1802), *Peter and James Romney*. Washington, D.C., collection of Mr. and Mrs. Paul Mellon.

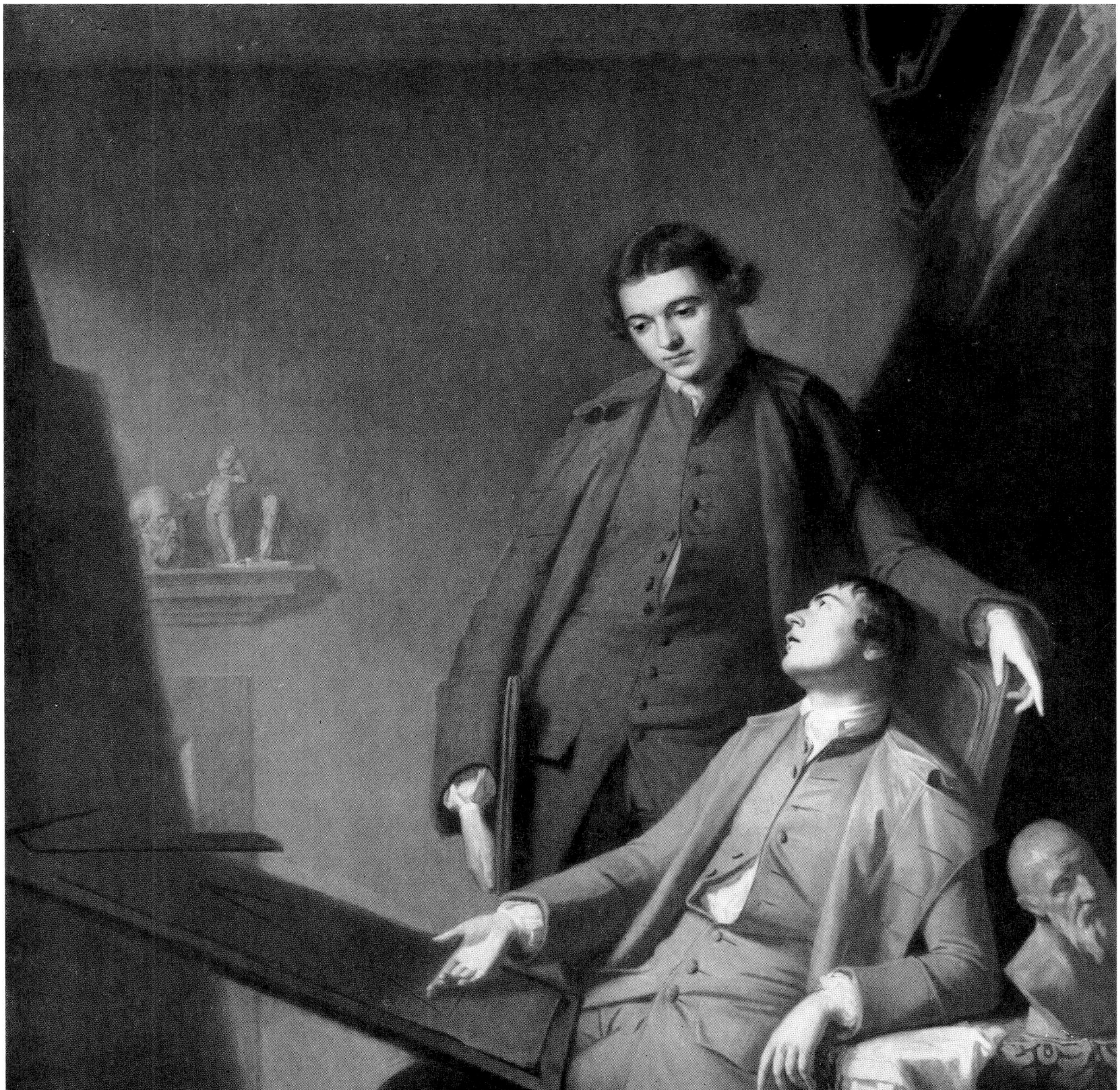

161

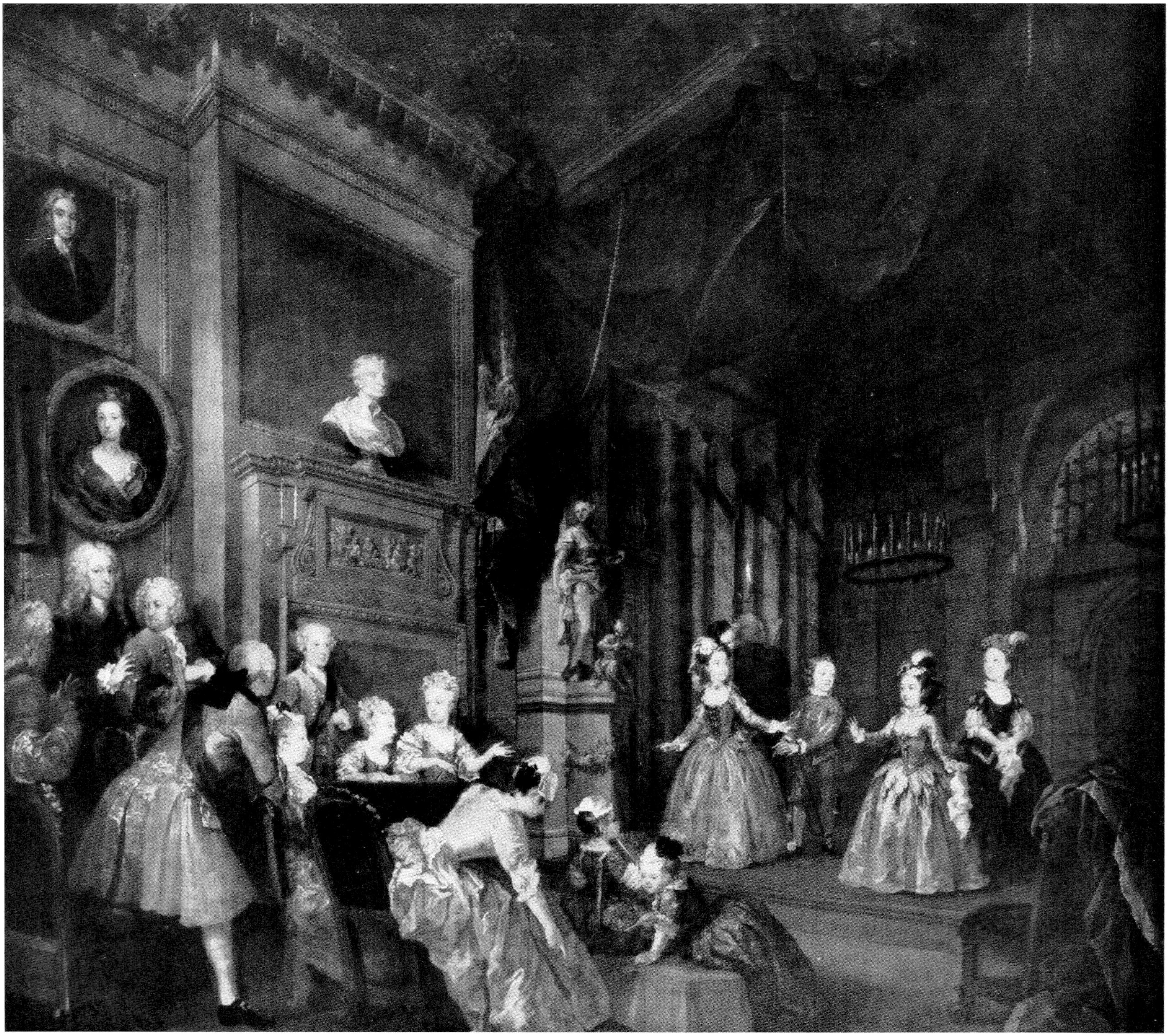

162

162 WILLIAM HOGARTH (1697-1764), *Scene from ' The Indian Emperor; or The Conquest of Mexico '*, 1731. Bishopfield House, Bawtry, Doncaster (Yorkshire), collection of Viscountess Galway.

CHAPTER IX – GROUPS IN PERIOD COSTUME AND ALLEGORICAL PORTRAITS

Portraits of Roman Emperors got up to look like deities are common. In this the Romans were merely following a Hellenistic tradition which continued well into the time of Canova, whose statue of Ferdinand IV — nicknamed "Re Nasone" because of his Bourbon nose — in the garb and with the attributes of Minerva verges on caricature. Private citizens, too, were transfigured in this way. At the Capitoline Museum there is a Roman couple of the period of Septimius Severus represented as Mars and Venus.

The representation of contemporary people dressed as figures in a *sacra conversazione* is abundantly documented. Some cases are very likely mere legends, like that of Raphael's *Deposition*, commissioned from the painter by Atalanta Baglioni and now in the Borghese Gallery, in which, according to a tradition, young Grifonetto is supposed to have posed for the figure who helps to carry Christ. It has been said that this " certainly is the closest to a real portrait ", whereas " in the other figures there is complete abstraction, and each of them is a symbol of a different way of expressing sorrow ".[1] Gabriele d'Annunzio alludes to the circumstances in one of his sonnets on Perugia (the fifth), where, after having borrowed from Matarazzo the chronicle of the murder of Astorre Baglioni and his companions, he concludes:

> Ma nella cerchia di quegli occhi intenti,
> Peroscia, è un divino testimonio:
> talun nomato Rafaele Sanzio.[2]

Some have seen *The Legend of St. Eligius and St. Godeberta* by Petrus Christus (Lehman Collection, New York) as the record of an engagement, but Friedländer[3] does not accept this interpretation; in his opinion, the couple is a purely ideal one and the painting was ordered by the Antwerp goldsmiths' guild. Jan van Scorel, in the triptych of Obervellach, portrayed Count

1 PAOLA DELLA PERGOLA, *Galleria Borghese* (Rome: Istituto Poligrafico dello Stato, 1959), II, p. 117. 2 " But in the circle of those intently gazing eyes, O Perugia, there was a divine witness, somebody called Raphael Sanzio ". 3 *Die altniederländische Malerei* (Berlin, 1924), p. 146. Eng. ed., *Early Netherlandish Painting* (Leiden: A.W. Sijthoff, 1967).

Frangipani with his wife and relatives in the garb of relatives of the Virgin. In a painting by Alessandro Allori in the Lancellotti Palace in Rome the holy persons are said to be portraits, and certain figures in the allegories by Jacopo Zucchi in the Studiolo of Francis I Medici in the Palazzo Vecchio in Florence are also supposed to be portraits, with that of Bianca Capello among them. Paolo Veronese in the *Marriage at Cana* (Madrid, Prado) showed Jesus among Venetians of the period who were certainly portraits (Madrazo affirms that the bald man with a black beard on the extreme right was the Vicentine painter, G.B. Maganza). Juan de la Pareja (c. 1610-1670) portrayed himself in a seventeenth-century interior with two ecclesiastics and two other people in costumes of the same period, at a table at which St. Matthew is sitting dressed as an Oriental and ready for Christ's summons (Madrid, Prado). In about 1481 Botticelli portrayed a lady, perhaps Caterina Sforza Riario, with the palm and the wheel, the attributes of St. Catherine (the painting is at Altenburg); and Girolamo Savoldo in about 1530 painted another lady with a dragon, the attribute of St. Margaret (Rome, Galleria Capitolina). Bronzino painted a portrait of Andrea Doria as Neptune, and the School of Fontainebleau portrayed Diane de Poitiers in the garb of the homonymous goddess. G.B. Caracciolo gave Saints Cosmas and Damian the features of two contemporary Neapolitan doctors (Berlin, Staatliche Museen; a copy is in the Prado), and Domenico Fetti, in a painting whose present location is unknown, seems to have given to an astronomer (Ptolemy?), represented in oriental costume and turban near a Mercator celestial globe, the features of Prince Paolo Spada, to whom the globe belonged. The two young men (his sons?) near him are dressed in costumes of the early seventeenth century.[4] Gonzales Coques represented a gentleman attended by members of his family in the act of distributing loaves, thus illustrating one of the Seven Acts of Mercy; and in 1671 Gillis van Tilborch painted a similar family group, with Henry Tichborne and his family distributing alms in front of their manor house, Tichborne Hall, a ceremony which was repeated every year.[5] Reynolds[6] and Mignard portrayed ladies of the aristocracy in the garb of mythological figures or Christian saints. Thus Mignard painted the portrait of the Marchioness of Seignelay as Thetis, of the Count of Toulouse as a sleeping Cupid, and of Madame de Maintenon as St. Francesca Romana, her patron saint. And Reynolds painted Mrs. Sheridan as St. Cecilia, Mrs. Blake as Juno, and both Mrs. Siddons and Mrs. Yates as the Tragic Muse. Following Reynolds' example, John Singleton Copley represented Mrs. Richard Crowninshield Derby in 1803-4 as St. Cecilia playing the harp; the lady appears in her usual dress, but on the left angels are listening from the clouds.[7]

Richard Steele in *The Tender Husband* (1705) had already ridiculed this fashion in a dialogue (Act IV, scene ii) between Captain Clerimont, who is dressed as a painter, and Biddy Tipkin (Mr. Tipkin's niece):

NIECE – Since there is room for fancy in a picture, I would be drawn like the amazon Thalestris, with a spear in my hand, and an helmet on a table before me. At a distance behind let there be a dwarf, holding by the bridle a milk-white palfrey.

CLERIMONT – Madam, the thought is full of spirit, and if you please, there shall be a Cupid stealing away your helmet, to show that love should have a part in all gallant actions.

NIECE – That circumstance may be very picturesque.

CLERIMONT – Here, madam, shall be your own picture, here the palfrey, and here the dwarf — the dwarf must be very little, or we shan't have room for him.

NIECE – A dwarf cannot be too little.

CLERIMONT – I'll make him a blackamoor to distinguish him from the other too powerful dwarf (*Sighs*) — the Cupid — I'll place that beauteous boy near you, 'twill look very natural — He'll certainly take you for his mother Venus.

NIECE – I leave these particulars to your own fancy.

Jan de Bray, in a portrait of his family (fig. 163), represents himself as Antony and his plain wife as Cleopatra detaching a pearl from her headdress to drop into the cup. The gesture but not the costume is Cleopatra's, as is the case in the portrait by an unknown painter of the Duchesse du Maine at Sceaux, in which the dissolution of the pearl is perhaps an allusion to the extravagant expenditure on sumptuous entertainments given there (the " Nuits de Sceaux ").

In 1746 Marco Benefial (1684-1764) portrayed *The Two Orsini Children as Apollo and Diana* (fig. 356) together with an allegorical figure and the Thunderer, riding an eagle, who from heaven transforms a group of shepherds into frogs (in the background on

4 A conjecture of the late Jacob Hess. 5 See F.-C. LEGRAND, *Les peintres flamands de genre au XVIe siècle* (Brussels: Éditions Meddens, 1963), pp. 99 and 164.

6 EDGAR WIND, "Humanitätsidee und heroisiertes Porträt in der englischen Kultur des 18. Jahrhunderts ", in *Vorträge der Bibliothek Warburg*, 1930-31, pp. 156-229.

7 See J.D. PROWN, *John Singleton Copley* (Cambridge: Harvard University Press, 1966), II, pl. 651.

163

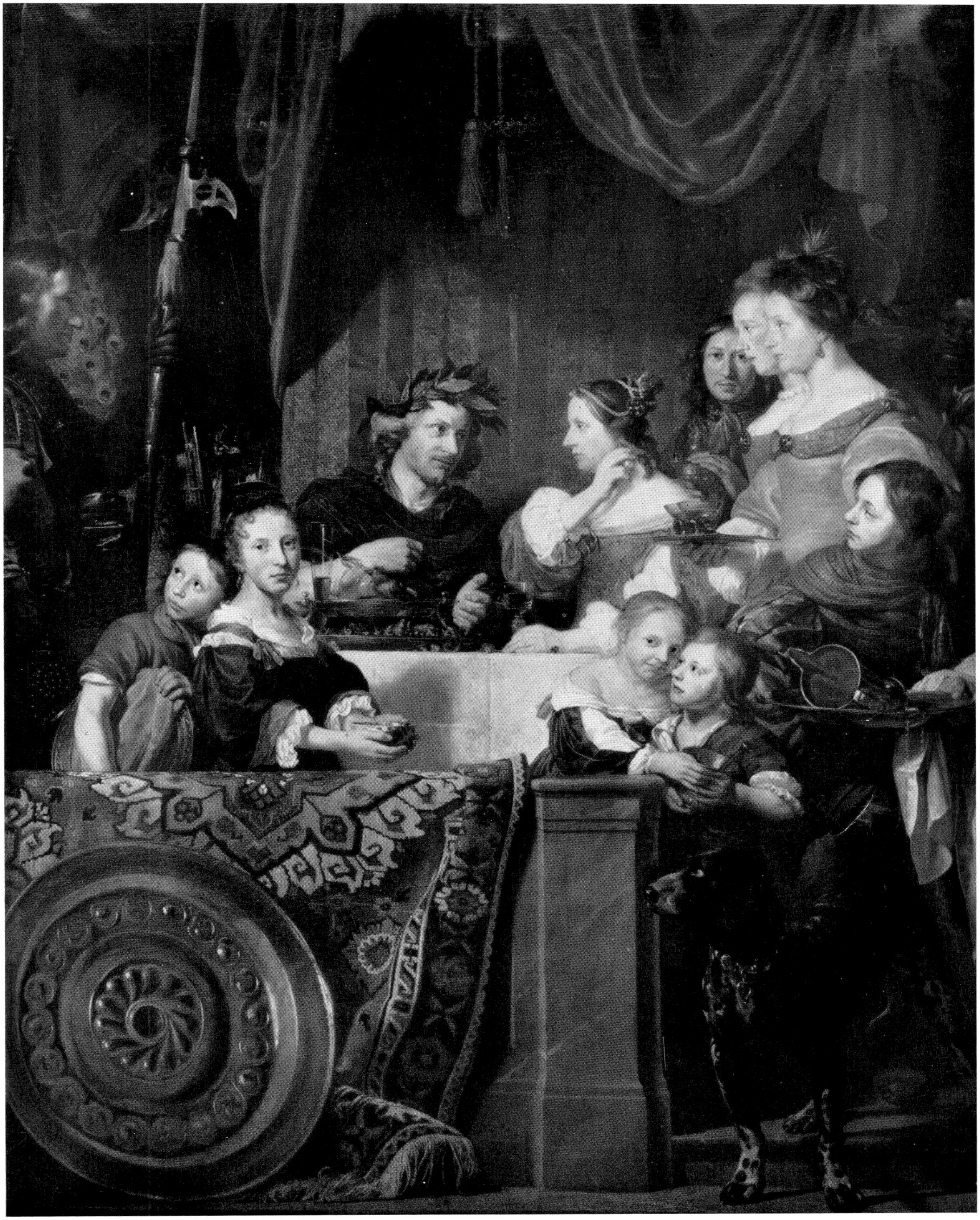

163 JAN DE BRAY (1627-1697), *The Banquet of Antony and Cleopatra* (*The Painter's Family as Antony and Cleopatra*), 1669. Manchester (New Hampshire), The Currier Gallery of Art; formerly in Nuremberg, Germanisches Nationalmuseum (Cat. ill. 400).

the left).[8] The same painter, in the group of *The Marefoschi Family* (1756), has represented (fig. 166) a priest preaching to a group of people, two of whom are dressed like Japanese, against a background of conventionally exotic scenery.[9]

William Hogarth, as we have seen,[10] represented a *Scene from 'The Indian Emperor; or The Conquest of Mexico'*, with children dressed as characters in Dryden's drama (fig. 162). Herman Doncker (c. 1620-1656) portrayed a family in pastoral costume holding shepherds' crooks among sheep and goats, against a background of wooded crags (fig. 165). Johann Conrad Seekatz (1719-1768) portrayed *The Goethe Family in Pastoral Costumes* (1762-63), in which Goethe's father with his wife and children appear in an Arcadian landscape with picturesque ruins (fig. 355). And we have seen how Zoffany painted members of *The Young Family* in costumes of the van Dyck period.[11] In a famous painting by David Wilkie, *The Family of Sir Walter Scott* (1817; fig. 167), the two daughters of the novelist appear as barefoot peasant girls carrying pails; and in *The Larkin Family* by John Downman, a watercolour made in about 1805 (Pierpont Morgan Library), the children are acting a scene from a play, while a girl in a turban adorned with a tall feather holds a mask in her hand. Sometimes the sitters were invested with an allegorical meaning without a change of costume. Thus Sebastiano Ceccarini (1702-1783) illustrates the five senses (fig. 164) in the actions of five children of a Roman patrician family.[12] Boilly painted *Danton's Second Wife, or 'Optics'*, in which the child looks through a magnifying glass with a mirror which reflects the prints shown to him by the lovely Louise Gély.

Oliver Goldsmith, in *The Vicar of Wakefield* (ch. xvi), has left us a witty satire of the " conversation " in allegorical costume, with which the unpractical clergyman who is the hero of the novel was persuaded to imitate the taste of the upper classes:

My wife and daughters happening to return a visit at neighbour Flamborough's, found that family had lately got their pictures drawn by a limner, who travelled the country, and took likenesses for fifteen shillings a head.[13] As this family and ours had long a sort of rivalry in point of taste, our spirit took the alarm at this stolen march upon us; and, notwithstanding all I could say, and I said much, it was resolved that we should have our pictures done too.

Having, therefore, engaged the limner — for what could I do? — our next deliberation was to show the superiority of our taste in the attitudes. As for our neighbour's family, there were seven of them, and they were drawn with seven oranges, — a thing quite out of taste, no variety in life, no composition in the world. We desired to have something in a brighter style; and, after many debates, at length came to a unanimous resolution of being drawn together, in one large historical family piece. This would be cheaper, since one frame would serve for all, and it would be infinitely more genteel; for all families of any taste were now drawn in the same manner. As we did not immediately recollect an historical subject to suit us, we were contented each with being drawn as independent historical figures. My wife desired to be represented as Venus, and the painter was desired not to be too frugal of his diamonds in her stomacher and hair. Her two little ones were to be as Cupids by her side; while I, in my gown and band, was to present her with my books on the Whistonian controversy.[14] Olivia would be drawn as an Amazon, sitting upon a bank of flowers, dressed in a green joseph, richly laced with gold, and a whip in her hand. Sophia was to be a shepherdess, with as many sheep as the painter could put in for nothing; and Moses was to be dressed out with a hat and white feather. Our taste so much pleased the Squire, that he insisted on being put in as one of the family, in the character of Alexander the Great, at Olivia's feet. This was considered by us all an indication of his desire to be introduced into the family, nor could we refuse his request. The painter was therefore set to work, and, as he wrought with assiduity and expedition, in less than four days the whole was completed. The piece was large, and, it must be owned, he did not spare his colours; for which my wife gave him great encomiums. We were all perfectly satisfied with his performance; but an unfortunate circumstance which had not occurred till the picture was finished, now struck us with dismay. It was so very large, that we had no place in the house to fix it. How we all came to disregard so material a point is inconceivable; but certain it is, we had been all greatly remiss. The picture, therefore, instead of gratifying our vanity, as we hoped, leaned, in a most mortifying manner, against the kitchen wall, where the canvas was stretched and painted, much too large to be got through any of the doors, and the jest of all our neighbours. One compared it to Robinson Crusoe's longboat, too large to be removed; another thought it more resembled a reel in a bottle; some wondered how it could be got out, but still more were amazed how it ever got in.

Goldsmith must have invented this plausible episode in order to ridicule similar mythological masquerades perpetrated by Reynolds and his followers, but one can be equally sure that another grotesque episode reported by the painter Philippe-Auguste Hennequin (1762-1833) is based on a personal experience.[15] An elderly gentlewoman had asked him to paint the portrait of

8 See the article by GIORGIO FALCIDIA, " Per un ritratto di Marco Benefial ", in *Bollettino dei Musei Comunali di Roma*, XI, 1964, nos. 1-4, pp. 19-33. 9 The painting is like a translation into a domestic masquerade of an earlier drawing representing a sermon of St. Francis Xavier in Japan. See ANTHONY M. CLARK, " Manners and Methods of Benefial ", in *Paragone*: Arte, XVII, September 1966, no. 199, p. 26. 10 See above, p. 69. 11 See above, p. 133. 12 See

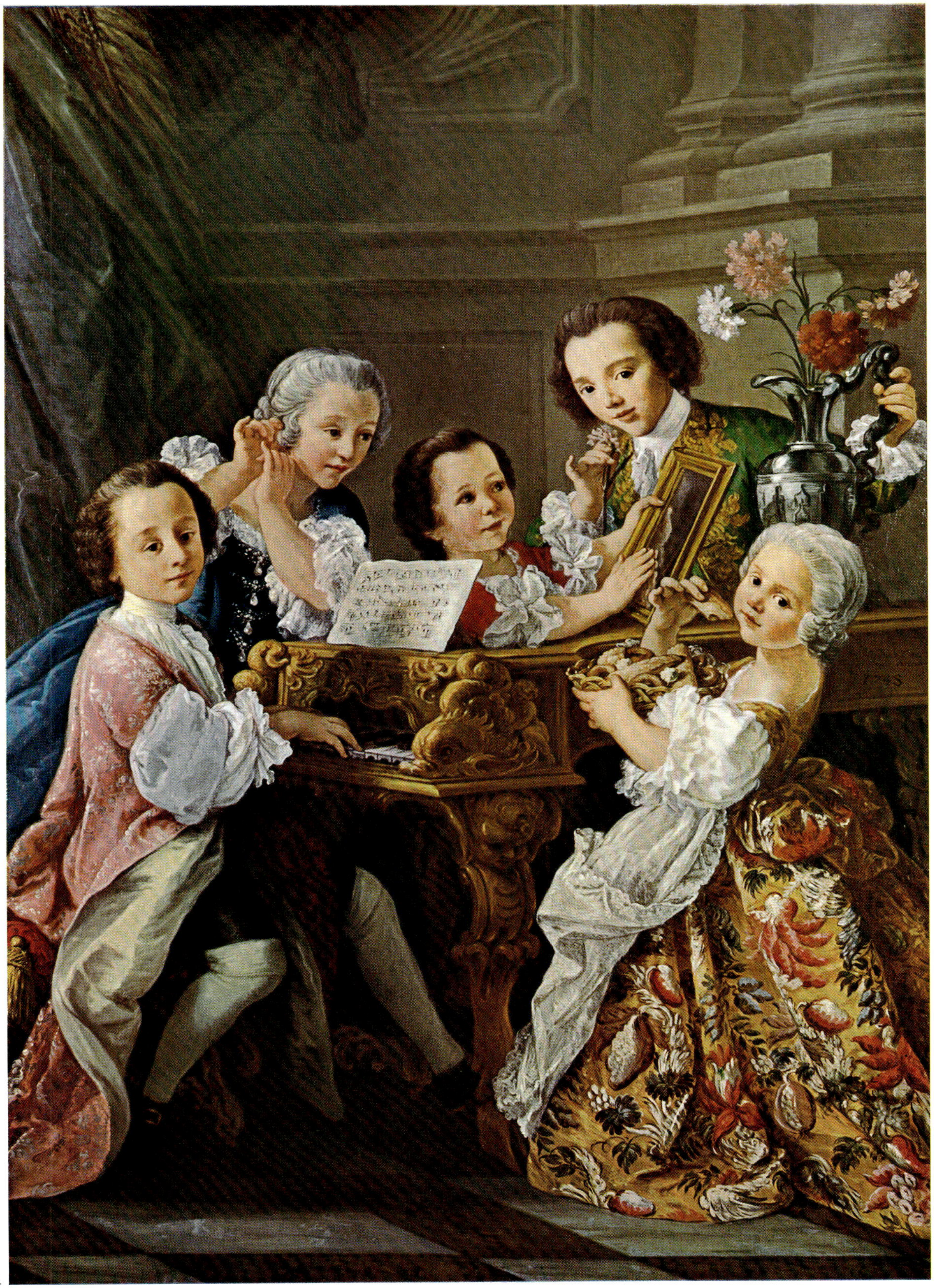

164

164 SEBASTIANO CECCARINI (1702-1783), *The Five Senses Symbolized in the Actions of Five Children of a Roman Patrician Family*, 1748. Present location unknown; formerly at the Pardo Gallery, Paris.

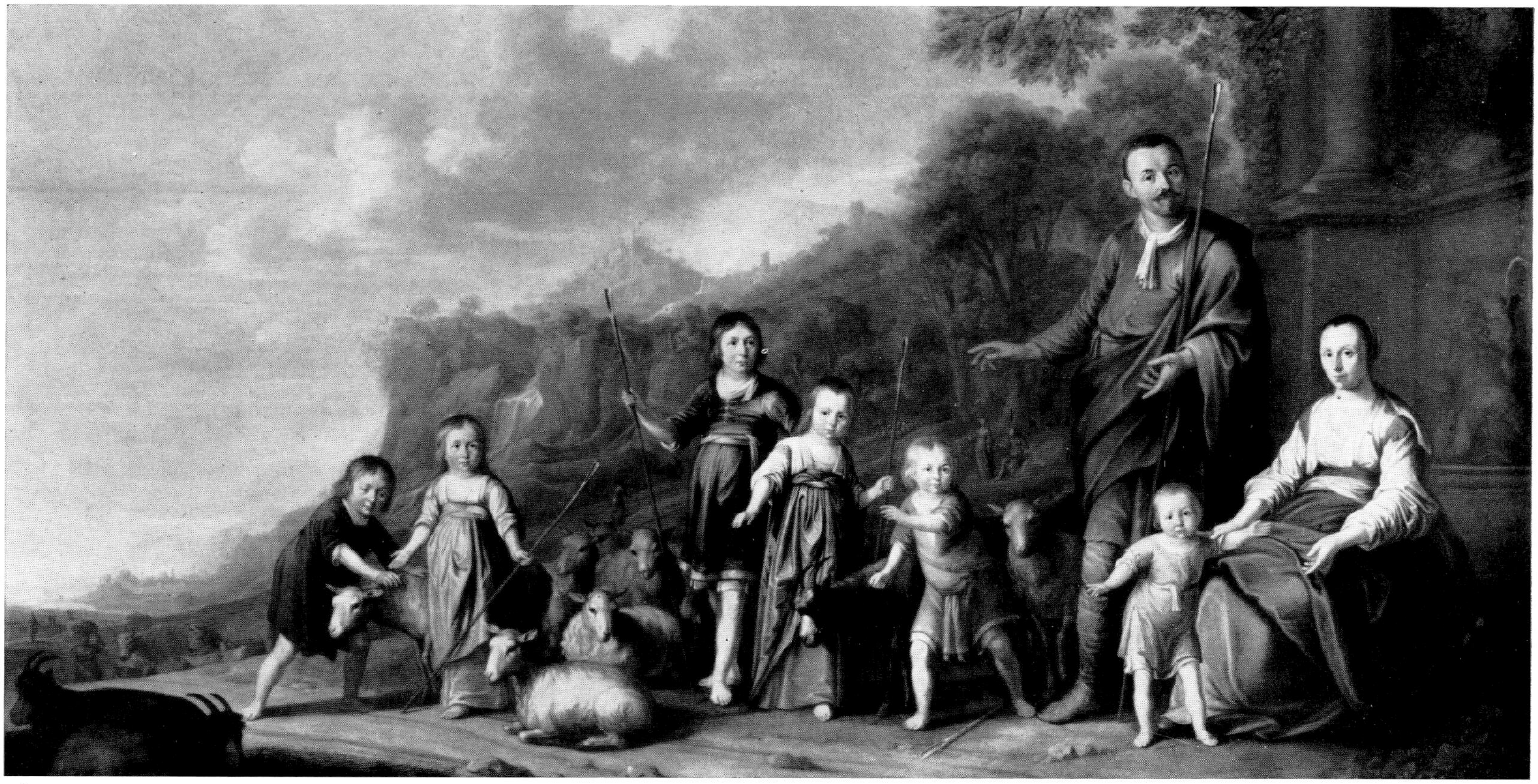

165

her family soon after 1790:

I placed my figures in the temple of Vesta, the grandmother seated in the foreground of the painting, watching the young couple; the girl's mother, whose tender gaze rested on her daughter, handed her over to the young man who received her in his arms and laid her at the foot of the altar of Hymen, who from a filmy cloud seemed to remove the virgin crown from the head of the bride and put the wreath of roses and myrtles in its place. Near this group, and standing on tiptoe in order to reach the top of the altar, Love blew out the lamp consecrated to the cult of Vesta. Some bas-reliefs suited to the temple and the chief subject formed part of the background.

They had agreed on a price of twelve hundred *livres*. When the picture was finished, the old lady was far from pleased with it:

I had noticed that she seemed to dislike the manner in which I had draped her silk robe: she thought she had to unburden herself at the last moment. I must explain that all the furniture and accessories of this composition were in the pure style of the antique, the only style which suited this composition; and since her portrait was in the foreground, I had arranged her robe on an armchair so that its folds should be pleasing to the eye, leaving a portion of the armchair exposed — something which increased the grace of the attitude. It was precisely this that gave rise to the following scene.
'Why', said she, 'have you so lifted my robe? I never tuck it up'. — 'Madam, this may be done in a painting without its being inconvenient or out of place: besides, it is more in the antique style'. At these last words, in which she saw an allusion to her age, she got up with an inconceivable vivacity, and from the height of her grandeur she rated me soundly, calling me impertinent and employing other more stinging epithets. Lost as I was in apologies, assuring her that I had not had the least intention of insulting her age and sex, to which I had always professed submission and respect, all was in vain. Nothing could appease her, and she ended by saying that this painting was not worth the agreed price and she would not pay for it before its value had been properly estimated. At these words my submissive be-

ANDREA BUSIRI VICI, "Ritratti di Sebastiano Ceccarini pittore fanese a Roma", in *Palatino*, s. 4, XII, 1968, no. 3, pp. 263-73; the painting has been reproduced here by courtesy of A. Busiri Vici. 13 The price of conversation pieces was calculated according to the number of sitters. Thus Zoffany's *A Musical Party on the Thames* (see p. 184 above), since it was full of sitters, cost eight hundred guineas. 14 A theological controversy. 15 *Mémoires* (Paris: Calmann-Lévy, 1933), pp. 135 ff.

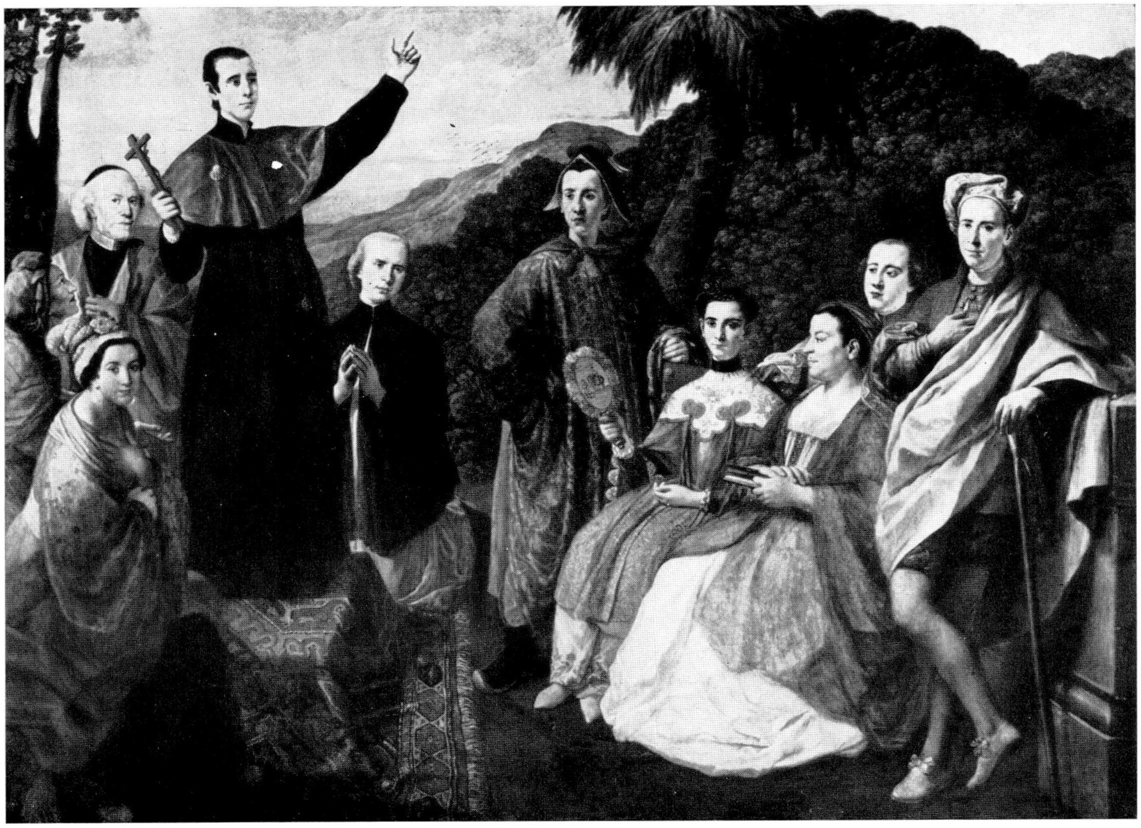

166

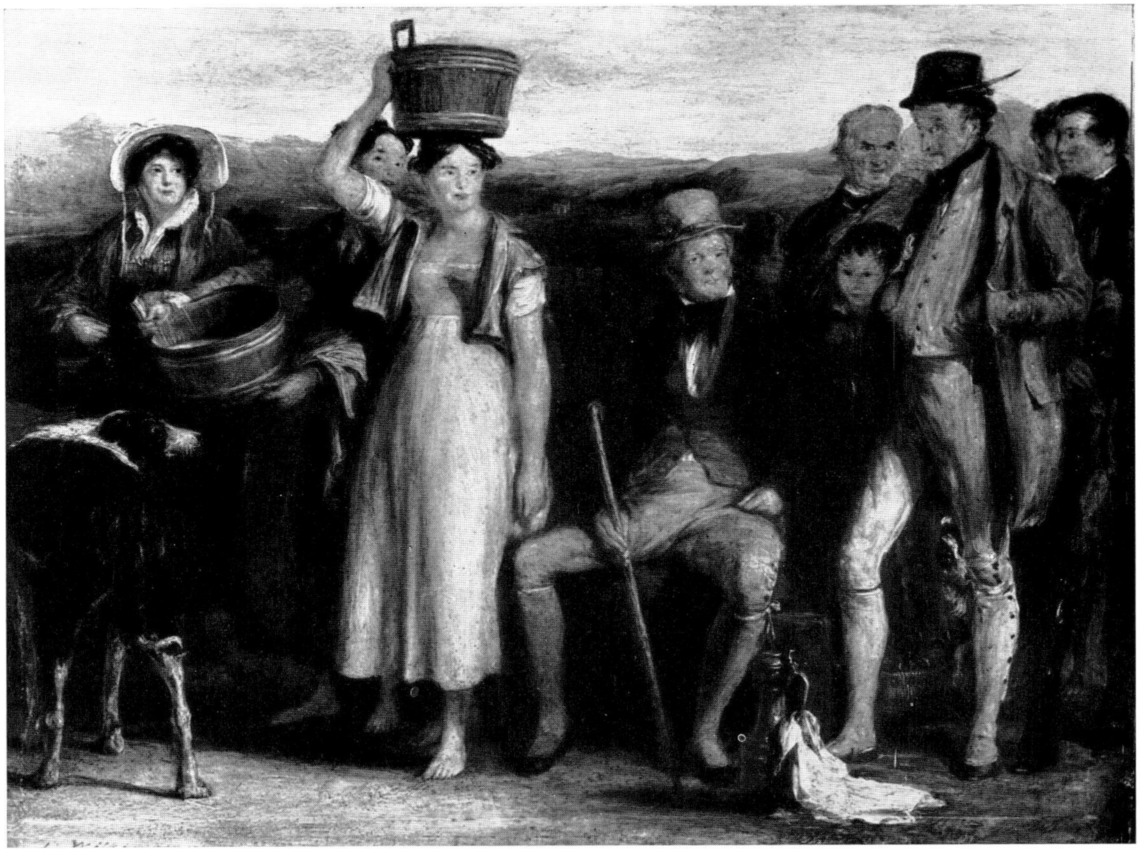

167

165 HERMAN DONCKER (c. 1620-1656), *A Family in Pastoral Costumes*, 1645. Koestler Gallery, London, June 1967; from the Frederick Müller sale, Berlin, Nov. 1903.

166 MARCO BENEFIAL (1684-1764), *The Marefoschi Family*, 1756. Rome, Palazzo Barberini, Galleria Nazionale d'Arte Antica.

167 SIR DAVID WILKIE (1785-1841), *The Abbotsford Family (The Family of Sir Walter Scott)*, 1817. Edinburgh, Scottish National Portrait Gallery.

haviour ceased; I assumed a dignified attitude, and without bitterness but in a very different intonation from that with which I had expressed myself at first, I assured her that I consented to the estimate provided she in her turn accepted the propositions I was going to make: ' You may, Madam, ask any artists you like to judge my work; I on my part shall not ask any. If these gentlemen estimate that it is not worth the sum I am claiming, I consent to accept the one they will fix. But if the experts estimate that it is worth more than one thousand two hundred, you'll give me the full amount, and I reserve the right to distribute the surplus to the poor'. Up to this point Madame D— had kept calm while listening to me; but her composure abandoned her altogether when I spoke of paying alms at her expense and, getting up with the resilience of a fifteen-year-old, she said: ' Is it then up to you, sir, to dictate to me acts of justice and generosity? ' Having said these words, she went out, got into her carriage, and I, not knowing what to think of this adventure, cursed my antique chair which had cost me such an outburst of anger, and retarded perhaps forever the payment for a work which was really not worth less than the price which had to be paid.

The controversy was settled before a justice of the peace; the arbitrators agreed about the perfect resemblance to the principal sitter, and the old lady consented to pay.
An even more dramatic case of a sitter in mythological garb is related in the *Mémoires* of the Duchesse d'Abrantès apropos of *Mademoiselle Lange as Danaë* by Anne-Louis Girodet-Trioson (1767-1824; fig. 168).[16]

I have known Girodet very well, and I was able to appreciate his wit, his talent, and all that made him a superior man; but he was passionate and hot-tempered. This very year 1800 saw him giving a proof of it, which might have tarnished his fine character. A lady celebrated for her beauty and her dramatic talent had caused him to make her portrait. The work once finished, she did not find it up to expectation, and wanted to take exception to certain points on which they had agreed. There was a discussion. Girodet was not yet in the wrong. He felt hurt. A thoroughly disobliging remark, which her husband was imprudent enough to utter, ended by making him utterly furious. He slashed the painting with a knife and sent it in this condition to Mme S—, telling her that she could dispose not only of the picture but also of the price destined to conclude the bargain, and that he was going to repay himself in his own fashion. If Girodet had not gone any farther, if the threat had been confined to giving a fright, all would have been well. But he went farther, and henceforth he was in the wrong.
The Salon was still open for a number of days. One cannot conceive the speed with which his brush was handled, but it is a fact that eight days at the most after the portrait had been returned, there appeared in the Salon of the Exhibition a painting of about two-and-a-half feet by four whose complicated subject would by itself have demanded much work. This painting was placed in the left corner by the door which nowadays leads to the second gallery of the modern Exhibition. As soon as it appeared, all the other paintings were deserted. People crammed the space in front of this one.
It represented the interior of a garret. In one of the corners there was a bed scantily covered with a straw mattress and a torn bedspread. On this mattress a young, pretty person was half lying down, her head adorned with peacock feathers, dressed only in a tunic of gauze which left a pair of rather fat legs exposed to view. She held the gauze up with both hands in order to receive a shower of gold coins which dropped through the roof of the garret. Near the bed was a lamp whose brilliant but treacherous light attracted a swarm of butterflies and fireflies and burned them. Under the bed one saw an enormous turkey stretching out one of its legs, which was ornamented by a fine wedding ring. In a very dark corner was an old woman in beggar's attire with a striking resemblance to a wretched old hag who begged for alms at the Porte d'Orléans — she was, it was rumoured, the mother of the subject of the slashed painting, who in turn bore a striking resemblance to the Danaë of the bedstead, before whom Vanity held up a mirror. There were also other allusions, such as a frog which swelled to bursting point and a number of droll things which I have forgotten since I saw this painting. I have spoken of it since to Girodet. He avowed that he felt some regret for having let himself be so carried away as to revenge himself in perhaps too drastic a manner. — ' But then she had greatly offended me! ', he would say.
I do not know whether it was because he relented, or whether the weight of repeated solicitations on the part of Danaë's friends had power to prevail upon Girodet. He has always avoided answering me on this point. The fact is that the wretched painting was exhibited only for a few days. It was removed, but not before the greedy crowd had had time to satisfy a malignant curiosity stimulated by an even more malignant intention.

Girodet, not content with the allegorical import of his *Danaë*, added four emblems in the spandrels of the frame which branded the subject of the painting as a loose and grasping female. If we reflect that the turkey impersonated the husband, and the old beggar — who, however, does not appear in the painting in its present state — the mother of the sitter, this picture may be considered the most satirical conversation piece that has ever been painted.

16 *Mémoires de Madame la Duchesse d'Abrantès* (Paris: Garnier, 1831-35), III, pp. 55 ff. The painting, formerly in the Wildenstein Gallery, has recently been purchased by the Minneapolis Institute of Arts. There is no trace of the old beggar in the painting. Either Girodet removed this detail, or else the Duchess, as is often the case in her writings, is inventing.

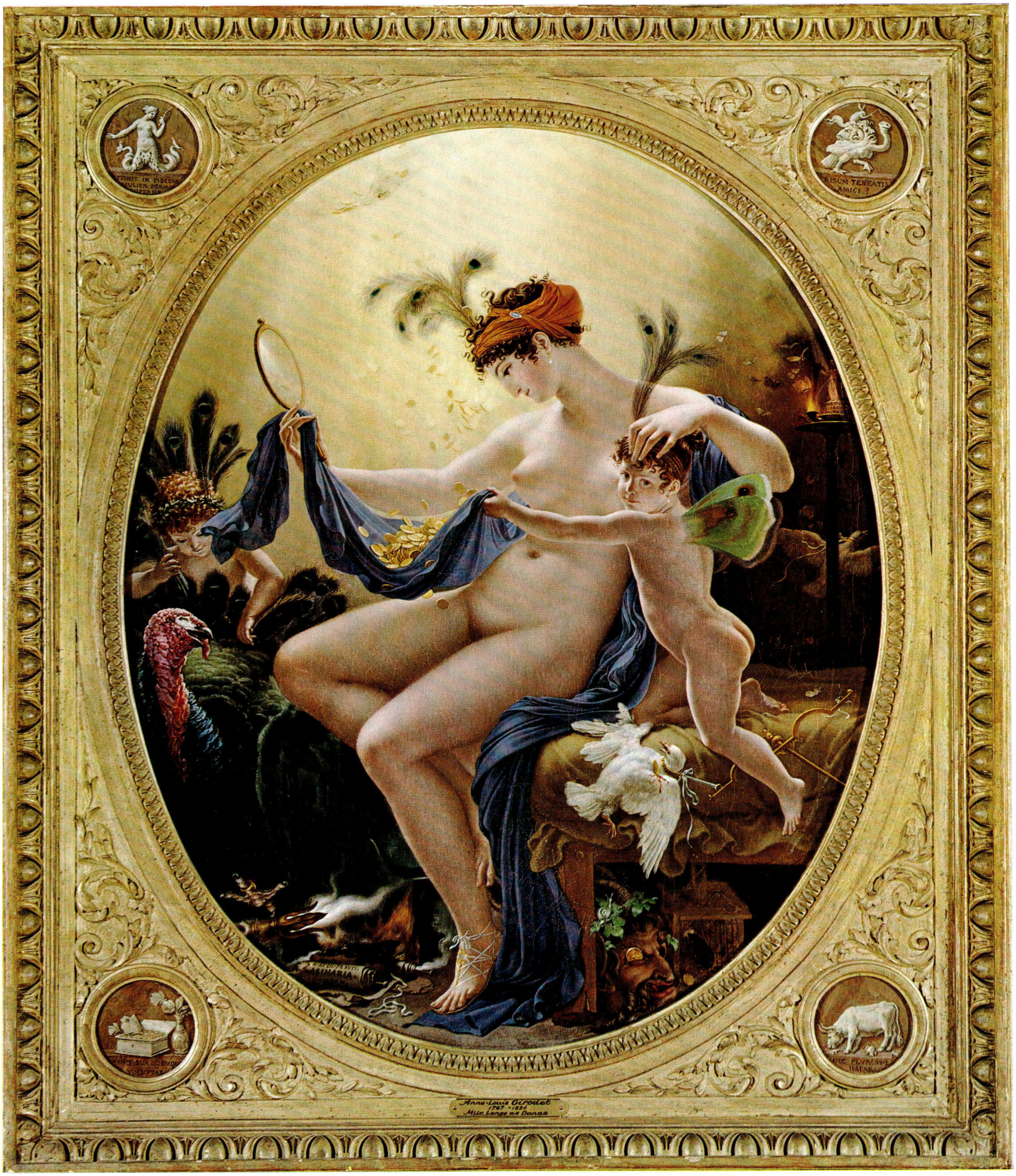

168

168 ANNE-LOUIS GIRODET-TRIOSON (1767-1824), *Mademoiselle Lange as Danaë*, 1799. Minneapolis (Minn.), Minneapolis Institute of Arts.

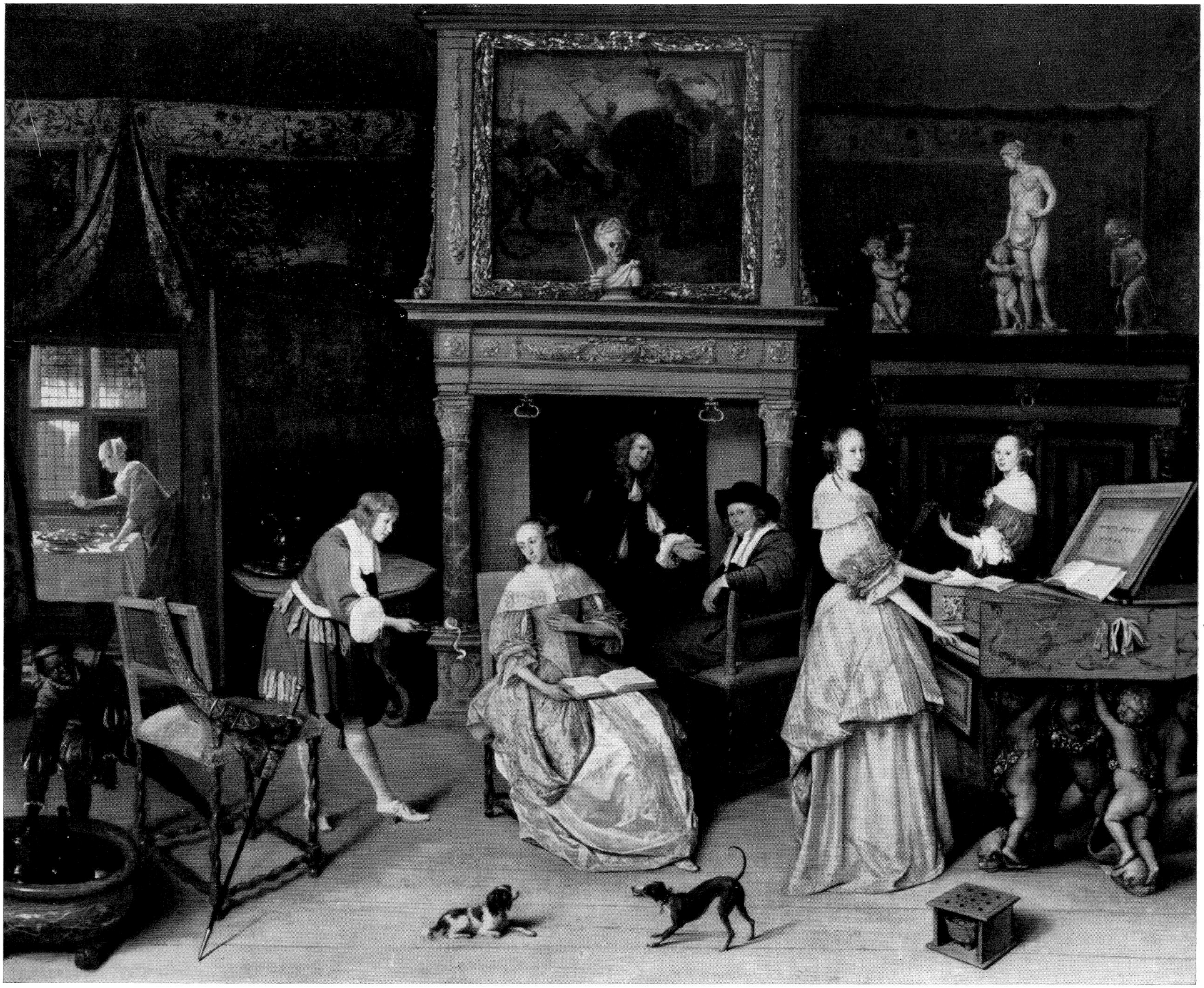

169

169 JAN STEEN (1626-1679), *The van Goyen Family and the Painter*, c. 1665. Paris-London, Heim Gallery.

CHAPTER X – MOURNING PICTURES AND PORTRAITS WITH A BUST

At the Capitoline Museum the statue of the so-called Barberini Brutus holds the effigies of the Penates, and at Villa Albani there is a similar statue of Lollius Alcamens who, seated, holds the bust of an ancestor. Walter Pater, in *Marius the Epicurean* (in the chapters " The Religion of Numa " and " White Nights "), has delicately recalled this Roman cult. In the northern Renaissance the deceased members of a family were frequently represented with the living. An extreme case is that of *The Funck Family* in Seftenau by Bernhard Strigel (c. 1460-1528), in which eight of the twelve children shown had already died and therefore appear in the picture clad in white.[1]
Various methods were resorted to in order to represent deceased persons in a family group. One was to make the hand of the person who appeared posthumously rest on a skull. We have already seen two instances of this (Molenaer's *Entertainment of the van Loon Family* and Joachim Luhn's *Self-portrait with his Family*).[2] Another example is provided in the *Family Group* (1583) by the vigorous Antwerp painter Adriaen Thomas Key (c. 1544-c. 1590; the property of Arthur Tooth & Sons), in which the head of the family has placed his hand on a skull, while the kneeling figure of a woman, perhaps his widow, gazes at him tenderly and lays one of her hands on his shoulder, the other on an hourglass.
In *The Gozzadini Family* (fig. 171) of 1584 by Lavinia Fontana (1552-1614), the senator Ulisse Gozzadini, whom we see seated on the left with one of his hands resting on his wife Ginevra's arm, had died in 1561, and his wife was also dead. It was their daughter Laodamia, seen here with a double string of pearls and two rings (one a diamond and one a ruby) who commissioned the painting. In another painting which we have already mentioned, *The Children of John Coke* by Huysmans,[3] little Francis — who died in infancy in 1680 — is represented as a hovering Cupid. In *The Family of John, First Marquess of Tweeddale*, the dead children are shown as cherubs,[4] and they had been so represented a few years earlier (in 1659) by Nicolaas Maes in a painting (North Carolina Museum of Art, Raleigh, N.C.) which portrays the family of the shipowner Cuyter near Dordrecht harbour,

1 Mentioned by KRONBERGER-FRENTZEN, *Das deutsche Familienbildnis* (Leipzig: Johannes Asmus Verlag, 1940), p. 9. 2 See above, p. 181 and p. 187. 3 See above, p. 150. 4 See above, p. 55.

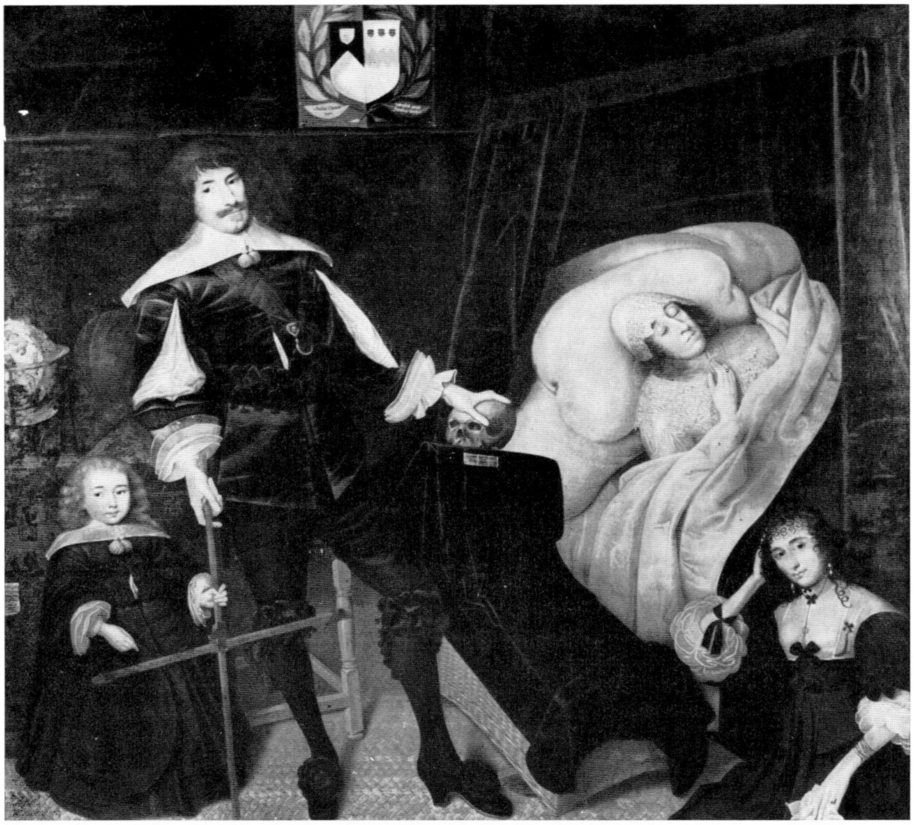

170

170 JOHN SOUCH (fl. 1616/7-1636), *Sir Thomas Aston at the Deathbed of his First Wife*, 1635. Manchester, City Art Gallery.

171 LAVINIA FONTANA (1552-1614), *The Gozzadini Family*, 1584. Bologna, Pinacoteca Nazionale.

172 CORNELIS TROOST (1697-1750), *Johanna Susanna Teding van Berckhout (represented posthumously) with her Three Sons*, 1723. Middelburgh, collection of Mr. T.A.J.W. Schorer.

where one of his ships is at anchor (notice the infant in the go-cart in the group of children),[5] and in *The van den Brandelaer Family* (1672-73), also of Dordrecht, where the orange shawl on the arm of the lady and the orange the man offers her are symbols of their belonging to the Orangist party (fig. 358).

In Jan Steen's *Van Goyen Family* (c. 1665; fig. 169), which we have already discussed,[6] there is a symbol of mortality in the bust of the skeleton armed with a spear and accompanied by the motto *Discite mori*, which can be read on the mantelpiece. In fact, Jan van Goyen — whom we see sitting nearby — had died ten years earlier in 1656, and of the three women represented — his widow, Steen's wife Margaretha van Goyen, and his sister-in-law Maria de Cleen — the latter had died in 1662-63.
The symbol of mortality in *Sir Thomas Aston at the Deathbed of his First Wife* (1635; fig. 170) by John Souch, a Chester painter active between 1616-17 and 1636, does not refer to the figure with his hand on the skull but to the woman lying on the bed. The sitters are not disposed according to a traditional iconographical pattern but as portraits from the life, except that the figure of the pensive woman in the corner is the portrait when she was alive of the person now lying on her deathbed. There is a similarity between the composition of this painting and that of *The Saltonstall Family* (c. 1637; fig. 360) by David des Granges, who was born in London in 1611 or 1613 and was still alive after 1670. He was a miniaturist who knew van Dyck's work well (see the second of the children on the left) but resolved this influence in a local, almost *naïf*, idiom. The painting, however, is concerned with the birth of one of the two youngest children of Sir Richard Saltonstall, and the woman lying on the bed is not dead but is Sir Richard's second wife, the mother of the child in the arms of the nurse.
Meesvrouw Teding van Berckhout with her Three Sons, whom we see in Cornelis Troost's painting, emerges from a stone parapet which looks rather like a tomb (fig. 172); in fact, the lady was dead, and the two cypresses we see in the distance have — at

5 See A. STARING, "Vier familiengroepen van Nicolaas Maes", in *Oud-Holland*, 1965, pp. 169-80. However, at the beginning of the nineteenth century the representation of children as angels had not necessarily this lugubrious meaning. J.-B. Isabey, for instance, portrayed himself with his wife and his brother Louis, also with his wife among the clouds, surrounded by cherubs' heads — their children — among whom one is only sketched: it was the child Louis and his wife were

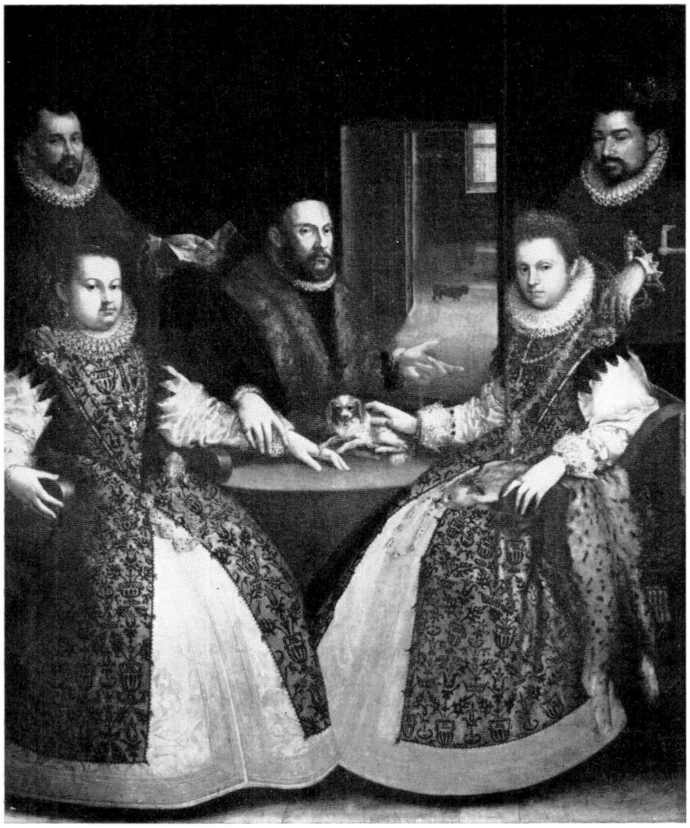

171

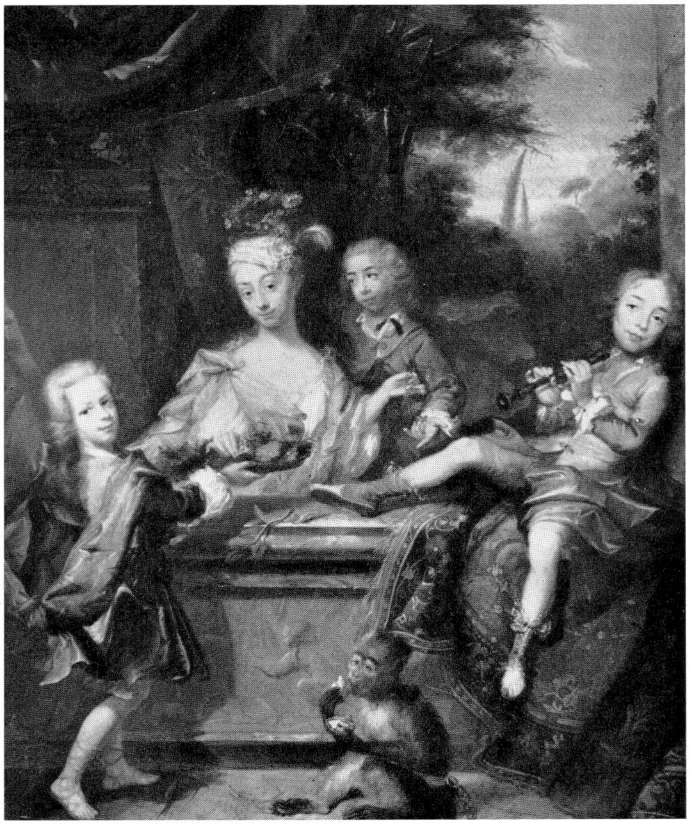

172

least for an Italian — a funereal association. Here the deceased is represented as still living, but by that date the dead were frequently shown in portraits. Thus in Gonzales Coques' *Father with his Two Daughters* (perhaps the painter himself and his daughters; fig. 267), which records a conventional setting with drapery and columns — fantastic spiral columns of a Rubensian character — the portrait of a deceased woman hangs high up on the left.

The representation of a dead person as a living one was to linger on with provincial or " primitive " artists like the American Edwin Romanzo Elmer (1850-1923) who, in an eerie picture of about 1889 (fig. 173), represented his own dead daughter with a lamb between a cat and a doll's pram on a lawn, while he and his wife are sitting at a table. The work has a visionary quality which makes one think of the children in Henry James's *Turn of the Screw*. Elmer painted from photographs, and if one compares his work with a photograph of Russell Harrison, President Harrison's son, taken in about 1890 with children on a lawn near the White House, the difference between the painting and the photograph is almost imperceptible — yet it exists in the deadly calm air which enfolds the sitters and the building in the painting.

There are a great number of " conversations " which emphasize portraits of the deceased; occasionally they may be sovereigns, as in Dumont's group *Madame Mercier and her Family* (Louvre), where the elderly fat lady in the centre shows her children an oval portrait of Louis XV, whose nurse she had been, while her husband, proud of his wife's rôle as wet-nurse to a king, indicates in his turn to his offspring the origin of their fortunes.[7]

An exceptional, though perhaps not unique, case is offered by the portrait of *The Countess of Forbach with her Children, Baron von Stein, and the Porter of the Castle Holding up the Portrait of the Duke of Zweibrücken-Birkenfeld* (fig. 177), painted in 1763-64 by Christian Mannlich (1741-1822).[8] In 1757 the Duke had made a morganatic marriage with the young dancer Marianne Camasse,

expecting. Mme. Basily-Callimaki in her work on Isabey (p. 28) thinks that this miniaturist was the first to start the new employment of this motif. 6 See above, p. 75. 7 This distinction allowed the men of that bourgeois family to wear a sword and to rank as gentlemen. 8 See G. and H. HAUCH, " Le Portrait de la Comtesse de Forbach par Christian de Mannlich ", in *Trois siècles d'art Alsacien* (1648-1948), Édition des Archives Alsaciennes d'Histoire de l'Art (Strasbourg-Paris: Librairie Istra, 1948), pp. 149-57.

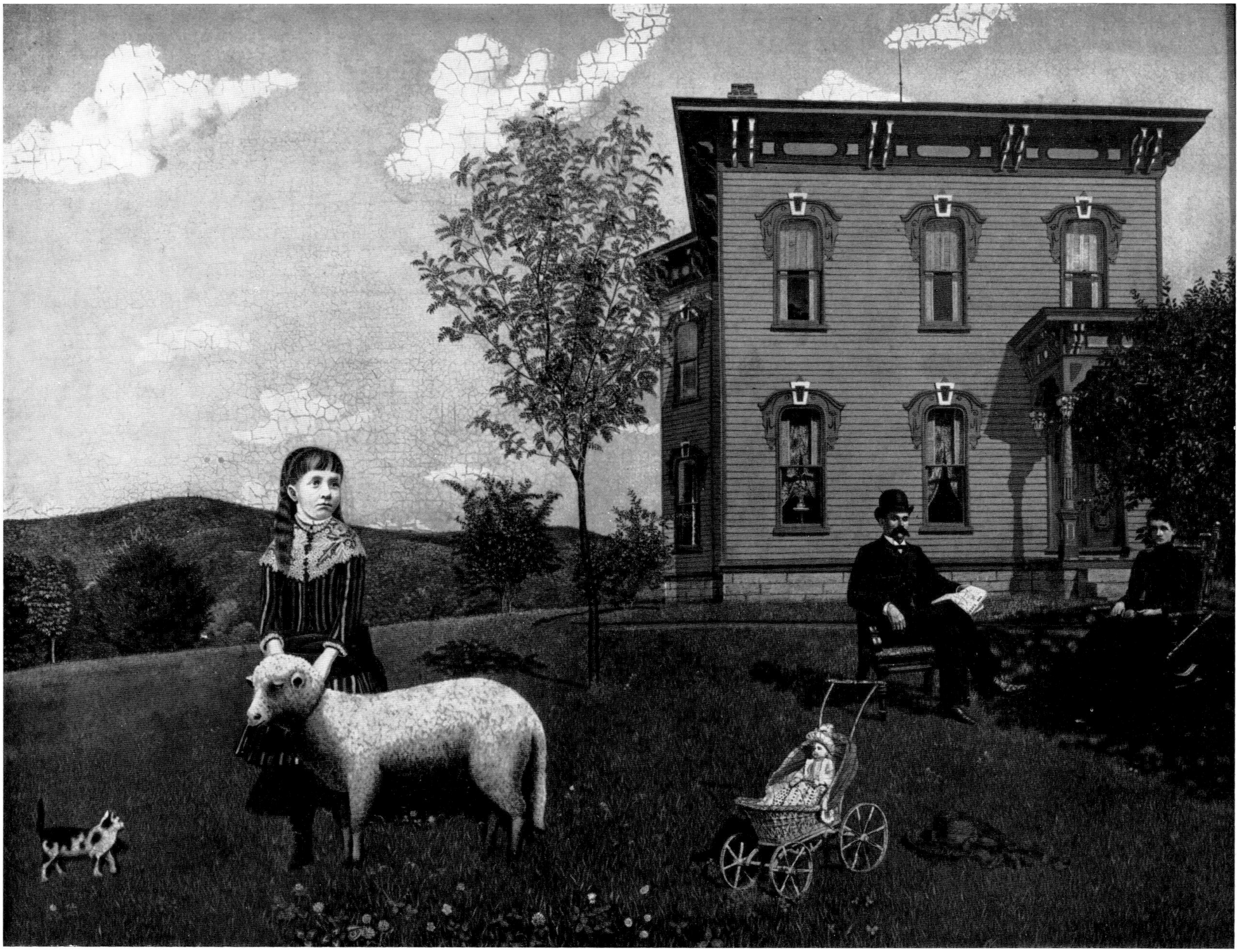

173

173 EDWIN ROMANZO ELMER (1850-1923), *The Painter, his Wife, and their Daughter (represented posthumously)*, c. 1889. Northampton (Mass.), Smith College Museum of Art.

for whom he had purchased the seigniory of Forbach. As she could not appear in an official picture with the same social standing as the Duke, he was therefore represented in effigy, in the painting held up by the porter of the *Schlösschen* of Zweibrücken, which had been appointed as the Countess's residence. The imitation of French taste was carried to such a point by the German sovereigns that at the Duke's express desire the painter gave the Countess the pose of the Marquise de Pompadour in Boucher's picture (1758; M. de Rothschild Collection).
At the Brera Gallery there is a portrait by Bernardino Licinio of *A Lady Showing her Husband's Portrait* which is one of the earliest instances known of this form of representing a deceased person. This painting, with *The Family of the Artist's Brother*[9] at the Borghese Gallery, of which we have already spoken, makes Licinio one of the forerunners of the conversation piece. The portrait of the dead father of the Duke of Buckingham appears in the background of the Vandyckian group of *The Villiers Family* (Hampton Court), painted shortly before the murder of the Duke in 1628; but Bernardino Licinio's formula is applied in the portrait painted by Jan Miel of the *Princess Maria di Borbone Showing the Portrait of her Deceased Consort Tommaso di Savoia Carignano* (Turin, Galleria Sabauda; the Prince had died in 1656). In a portrait by Johann Jacob Posner (fig. 357) we see Anna Maria de'Medici — the sister of Gian Gastone and widow of Johann Wilhelm, Elector Palatine — showing a portrait of her dead husband looking like one of those wax saints who lie under altars in crystal shrines. She was widowed in 1717, and it was said that her deceased husband, whom she nursed affectionately, had infected her with syphilis which he had caught through his dissolute habits.[10] In any event, she subsequently developed cancer of the breast which caused a fetid sore. The painting renders effectively the lugubrious surroundings of the widow, who apparently lived among black hangings and silver furniture.[11]

A number of Dutch paintings illustrate the custom of including portraits of deceased people in " conversations ". Tibout Regters' *Family of Jeronimus de Bosch* (1754) shows us the seventy-seven-year-old chemist and collector, Jeronimus de Bosch, sitting on the extreme left, with his son presenting a portrait of his dead mother (fig. 174). The only daughter, Elizabeth, is sitting in front. The door of the cupboard is decorated with an *Allegory of Painting* by Jacob de Wit, now in the Rijksmuseum, and a Chinese carpet with a rectangular pattern is spread on the floor. In a *Family Group* (1774) by Hendrik Pothoven (1728-1793) a portrait of the children's grandmother hangs between the windows (fig. 175). One sees from an open window a garden pavilion; the walls are hung with deep red Utrecht velvet and the Smyrna carpet is protected by a drugget. In *The Family of Pieter Cornelis Hasselaer* (1763; fig. 359), by George van der Mijn (1723-1763), one of the daughters shows her mother's portrait and the father appears in the middle of the painting — although in fact he was absent in India, where he made a brilliant career as a civil servant. (His likeness was taken from a portrait by Quinkhard.) The eldest son, standing by the table, holds a microscope in his hand. In the group of *Johann Maurits van Pabst with his Children* by Willem Joseph Laquy (1738-1798), the widower van Pabst shows his children the portrait of their dead mother, and one of the little girls opens her arms as if to go towards her (fig. 178). The *grisaille* on the mantelpiece is decorated with a symbol of mourning: a cupid weeping by an urn. In a painting by Nicolaus Guibal (1725-1784), *Count Leopold von Neipperg with his Family* of about 1760 (Schloss Schwaigern, private collection), three generations are represented: the grandparents in the paintings on the walls and over the mirror, the parents gathered round the fireplace, and the children with drum and doll at the edge of the picture, the whole as perfectly symmetrical as a genealogical tree. In a portrait by Adélaïde Labille-Guiard (fig. 176), the daughter of Louis XVI is represented in front of an elaborate easel on which rests an oval containing the bronze portraits of Louis XVI, Marie Antoinette, and the Dauphin.[12] The urn with her dead mother's ashes in the corner of a forest is embraced by one of the daughters of *Colonel J. J. Meyer of Zurich Portrayed with his Family* by Johannes Pfenniger (1749-1815).[13] (It is perhaps worth mentioning that the youngest of the children was destined to become the father of Konrad Ferdinand Meyer, the famous Swiss novelist.) In the portrait of the merchant *Karl Friedrich Kurtz with his Children* (1815; Biberach, private collection) by Johann Friedrich Dieterich, the dead mother is portrayed in a bust bearing a lengthy inscription, and the innocence of the little orphans finds an emblematic expression in the lamb which lowers its head to graze on a little plant. All of them have a tender, thoughtful air, even the toddler. But the category of portraits with a bust deserves more detailed treatment.

9 See above, p. 54. 10 G. PIERACCINI, *La Stirpe de' Medici di Cafaggiolo*, 2nd ed. (Florence: Vallecchi, 1947), II, part 2, p. 477. 11 HAROLD ACTON, *The Last Medici* (London: Methuen, 2nd ed. 1958), p. 319. 12 Between 1760 and 1765 Drouais painted Alexandre de Beauharnais at the age of eight showing the medallions of his father and his mother (Fitz-Henry Collection, no. 127 of the catalogue quoted below). Inspired by this painting, a miniaturist, Heinsius, represented the double portrait of François, Marquis de Beauharnais, Squadron-Commander and Governor of Martinique, and of his wife, Marie-Anne-Henriette Pivart

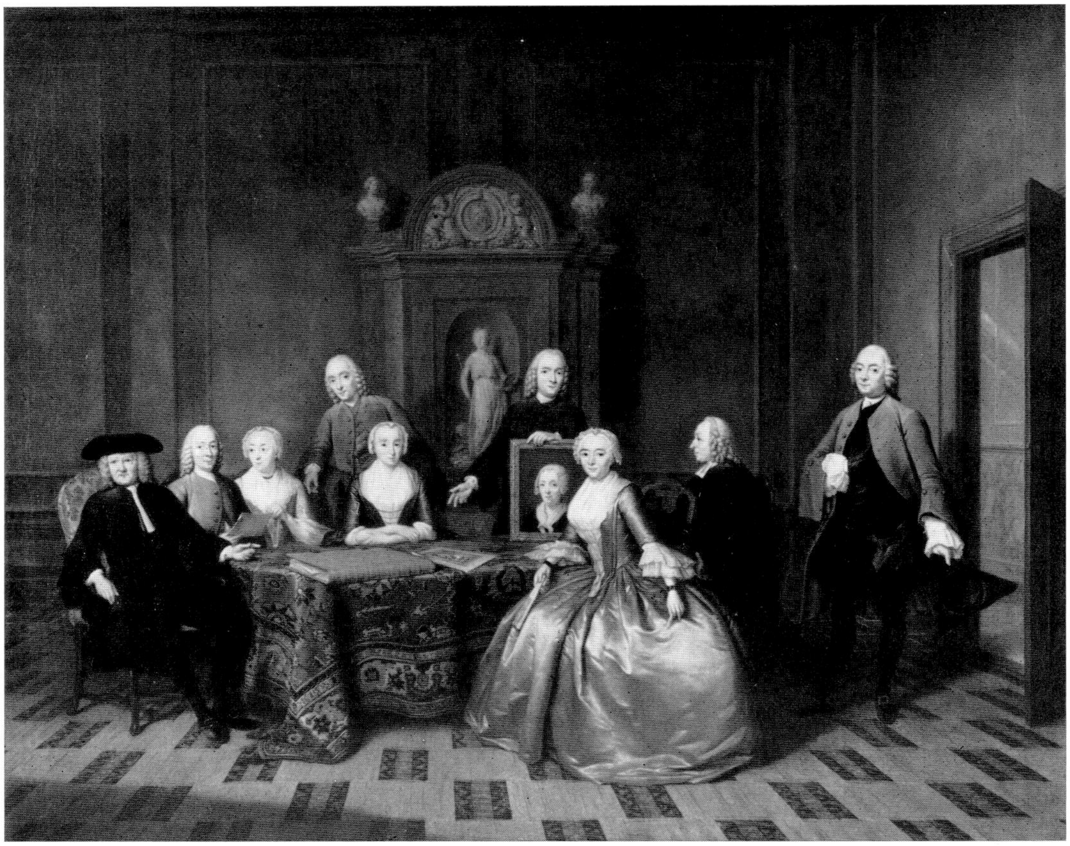

174

174 TIBOUT REGTERS (1710-1768), *The Family of Jeronimus de Bosch*, 1754. Goes, collection of Dr. J. M. van Daal.

These portraits of sitters near a bust with which they have a sentimental association go back to a humanistic tradition. Marsilio Ficino had a votive lamp burning in front of a bust of Plato. The idea developed in the late Venetian and Flemish Renaissance, and between the sixteenth and the eighteenth centuries the vogue for antique busts, and their prices, reached a climax unparalleled ever since.[14] We need only mention Rubens' so-called *Four Philosophers* (Florence, Pitti) with Seneca's bust (the sitters are Philippe Rubens, P. P. Rubens, Justus Lipsius, and Jan van Vouwen); the portrait of *Caspar Gevaerts*, also by Rubens, of about 1628-30 (fig. 361), with a bearded and toga'd bust; the *Burgomaster Rockox* by a follower of van Dyck, with a bust believed to be of Demosthenes (fig. 362); and Rembrandt's *Aristotle Contemplating a Bust of Homer* of 1653 (New York, Metropolitan Museum of Art). The motif was taken up by Sir Peter Lely in England in portraits of the period preceding the Restoration[15] and became a fashion with Neoclassicism.[16]

I have grouped these portraits with a bust together in my imagination, as did that character in Diderot's *Bijoux indiscrets* who " vit en rêve des bustes antiques, dont celui de Socrate ". But every time I return to visit the room in my brain that contains them, I feel the peculiar satisfaction of a collector, which may elicit a smile of compassion from most people. In Gainsborough's painting, Garrick embraces Shakespeare's bust; yet another actor, William Powell, had himself portrayed beside Shakespeare's bust by Benjamin Wilson (1721-1788), together with his wife and two daughters; he was in some measure a rival of Garrick, and during the absence of the latter on the Continent he acted by previous arrangement as his understudy, interpreting many of his characters with a success not anticipated by Garrick, whose return is said to have been hastened by Powell's triumph. There is a globe in front of the bust of Shakespeare, perhaps an allusion to the Globe Theatre (the painting is the property of the Trustees of the Garrick Club in London, but its bad condition does not permit an adequate reproduction). Reynolds portrays himself by

de Chastalets (they were the father and mother of Alexandre de Beauharnais, the husband of Joséphine Tascher de la Pagerie, later Empress of the French) shown by a person on the right, described as the "auteur du dessin, qui n'est pas Drouais ", according to the catalogue of *Miniatures, gouaches, estampes en couleur françaises et anglaises exposées à la Bibliothèque Nationale,* May 15 to October 15, 1906 (Librairie centrale des Beaux-Arts Émile Lévy). The miniature belongs to M. Fitz-Henry.

13 Reproduced in WALTER HUGELSHOFER, *Schweitzer Kleinmeister* (Zurich: Fritz & Wasmuth, 1943), pl. 63.

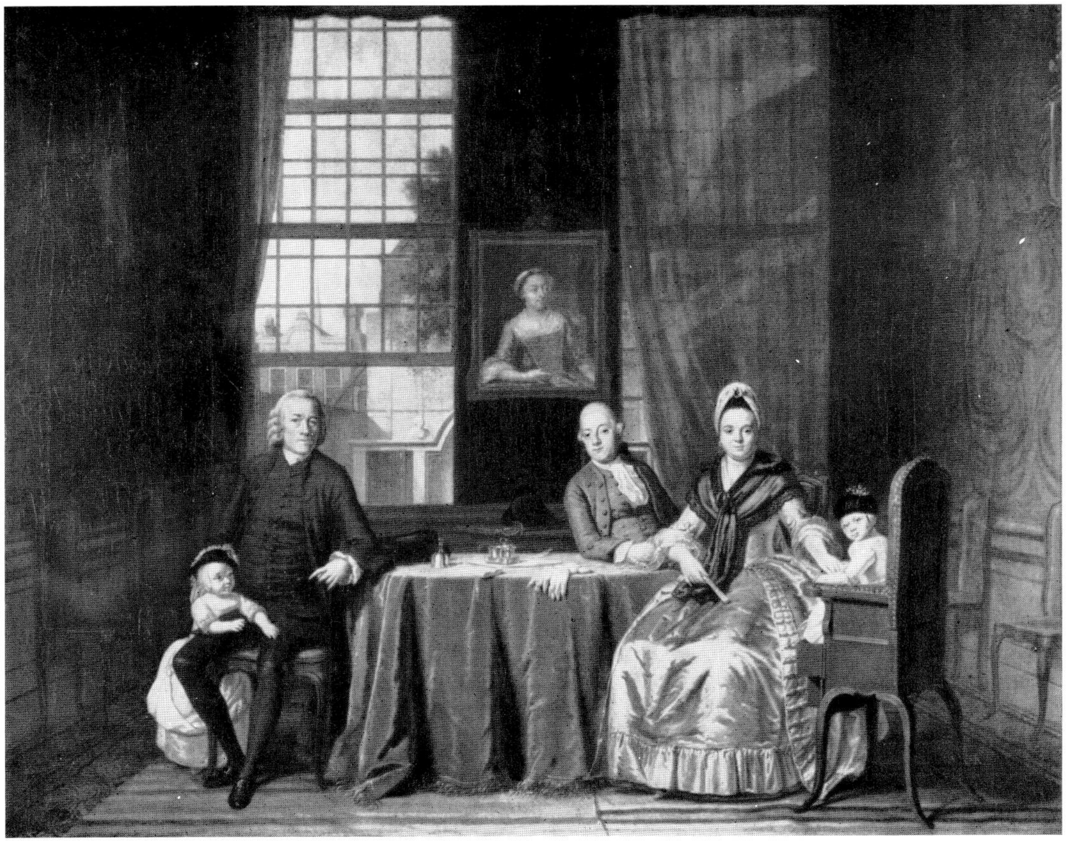

175 HENDRIK POTHOVEN (1728-1793), *Family Group*, 1774. Present location unknown; photo Gemeentemusea, Amsterdam.

175

the bust of Michelangelo, the artist who embodied for him the most sublime imagination (London, Royal Academy). In Ludowika von Simanowitz's portrait (Marbach, Schillerhaus), Schiller is sitting with his head romantically leaning sideways near the herm of a bearded bard, a Homer of the Epimenides type very widespread in the eighteenth century. Fuseli portrays himself in conversation with J. J. Bodmer, and between them is also a bust of Homer (fig. 364).

Jean-Claude Naigeon (1758-1832) painted himself with his family round a table in a garden while coffee was being served (fig. 372); on a wall there is the bust of Rousseau with the inscription *Vitam impendere vero* underneath.[17] The book the woman holds in her right hand is perhaps *Émile*. Henri-Pierre Danloux (1753-1809) represents the *Family of Mégret de Sérilly* (private collection), the husband tenderly clasping his wife round the waist while she uncovers the cradle containing her newborn baby. On the wall are the portrait of a woman and the bust of a man — the grandparents who watch the *heureuse famille* (fig. 366). Margaret of Austria, the " Madama " of the palace and the villa in Rome called after her and of Castel Madama near Tivoli, is portrayed near the bust of her father in a sixteenth-century painting in the Galleria at Parma usually attributed to Sebastiano del Piombo (fig. 365). In a painting of 1758 by Friedrich Georg Weitsch the young Princess Louise of Prussia and her sister crown the bust of Friedrich Wilhelm II; in a miniature painted on a china vase (Naples, Museo Nazionale di Capodimonte) the grandchildren of Ferdinand I of Naples surround his bust with a wreath. Ferdinand appears again by the bust of Maria Carolina in a small anonymous painting (Rome private collection; fig. 369), but the elegiac mood of the scene will hardly deceive those who have read the King's diary (see the edition by Umberto Caldara published in Naples in 1965), where the wife's fits of temper are the chief theme; she bullied him to such an extent that " he needed God's help to put up with her ". Nicolas Lafrensen the Younger in a painting of 1792 represents Gustavus Adolphus IV of Sweden burning incense in an *athénienne* before a statue of Hygieia and turning to the right towards the bust of his father Gustavus III, who was murdered in that very

14 See KENNETH CLARK, *Rembrandt and the Italian Renaissance* (London: Murray, 1966), p. 77 (Am. ed., New York: New York University Press, 1966). 15 WATERHOUSE, *Painting in Britain*, 2nd ed. (Harmondsworth and Baltimore: Penguin Books, 1962), p. 61. 16 Costanza Perticari, when she received letters from Niccolini, used to shut herself in a room with his bust; she was thus able to imagine she was listening to him in person as he told her things (see MARIA BORGESE, *Costanza Perticari* [Florence: Sansoni, 1941], p. 288). The fashion for portraits with a bust crossed the Atlantic; thus in the White House one may see a portrait

year (fig. 368). In 1807 C. F. von Breda painted Queen Fredrika of Sweden with her children Gustavus, Sophia, and Amalia near the bust of another son, Karl Gustavus, who had died two years before (this painting was once at Dresden, in the Residenzschloss; fig. 370).

Constance Mayer, the unfortunate mistress of the painter Prud'hon, exhibited a painting in the Salon of 1801 showing a father pointing out a bust of Raphael to his daughter — i.e., to Constance Mayer herself — and, in the words of the catalogue, " inviting her to take this famous painter as her model " (fig. 378). General Lasagni, a Roman bourgeois of the end of the eighteenth century, had himself portrayed in the plumed hat of the republican militia and a tricolour sash beside a bust of Brutus in a large miniature, the frame of which was decorated with the revolutionary emblems of the Phrygian cap and the lictor's fasces (Rome, private collection). Girodet in 1797 represented the commander of the brigade of the Santo Domingo police force, the Negro Jean-Baptiste Belley (later a deputy to the Convention and the Council of the Five Hundred) beside the bust of the Illuminist abbot François Raynal, who was among those who prophesied the future greatness of America (" The New World will rule the Old "; fig. 367).

In a hall decorated in the " antique " style with statues and busts, Gauffier sketched a lady in classical costume resting on a sofa, from which she points out an emperor's bust to her child (Montpellier, Musée Fabre); a similar painting by Gauffier, *A Mother Instructing her Son in the Virtues of his Ancestors*, is in the collection of Lt. Col. C. P. Brocklehurst, Macclesfield (Cheshire). Pauline, in Robert Lefèvre's painting, gracefully rests her sentitive white hand on a console bearing a massive bust of Napoleon at which she is gazing tenderly; and, in an exceptional reversal of relationships, in Gérard's portrait the bust of her great son dominates the seated figure of Laetitia. Teresa Pikler Monti, in Labbruzzi's mediocre picture, rests her elbow on a pedestal supporting her father's bust, with a weeping-willow in the background (fig. 371). The inscription reads: *Theresia parenti benemerentissimo*. Luigi Braschi had himself portrayed beside the bust of his uncle Pope Pius VI, who had created him Duke of Nemi; A. W. Narushkin was painted by Angelica Kauffmann near the bust of Catherine the Great.

The Countess of Tournon, with a gesture similar to that of Marie Louise in J. Franque's painting at Versailles, uncovers the cradle where her little son is resting in order to show him the bust of her deceased husband, former *préfet* of Rome, while from the window behind the conventional curtain one sees the dome of St. Peter's (Charles de Croix Collection, Château de Génelard, Saône et Loire). A plaster group at the Musée Marmottan in Paris, by Madame de Sermezy (1767-1850), represents Madame Dandignac showing her daughter her father's bust; on the base one reads the words: " *à la mémoire du meilleur des pères* ". In 1854 at the Ospedale Maggiore of Milan, Giuseppe Sogni painted Camilla Besozzi Figliodoni, Marchioness Lunati, showing the portrait of her husband (fig. 363). Gros painted the portrait of his wife near the bust of his master, David (Toulouse, Musée des Augustins), and that of the Countess of Lasalle standing near the bust of her husband, the general. The Duchess of Berry is represented in an anonymous engraving (after a painting by François Kinson, since destroyed, of which a copy exists at Versailles) with her little daughter Marie Louise stretching out her arms towards the bust of the Duke of Berry (fig. 180). Carlo Lodovico di Borbone Parma, Duke of Lucca, with his sister and his wife Teresa di Savoia (at the piano), is represented by an anonymous painter in a colonnaded hall; the child, who was later to become Carlo III of Parma, offers flowers to the bust of Maria Luisa di Borbone (fig. 373). The bust of the other Marie Louise, the French Empress and later Maria Luigia, Duchess of Parma, is being shown by an old and perhaps blind architect with lowered eyelids to his little granddaughter in a moving portrait by Giuseppe Molteni (1800-1867; fig. 181).

One of the Garnereys (either Auguste or Jean-François, but their styles are indistinguishable)[18] represented the family of the Crown Prince of the Two Sicilies (later Francesco I) on a terrace with a view of Vesuvius, near three busts: one of Ferdinand I, one of the Duchess of Berry, and one of Luisa-Carlotta-Maria-Isabella di Borbone, the wife of Francisco de Paola, Infante of Spain. The latter two have been decorated with flowers (fig. 179). General Carlo Filangieri, who distinguished himself in the service of Murat and reached the climax of his career under Ferdinando II, commissioned Natale Carta to paint him with his

of Franklin (by David Morton) reading beside a bust in the Green Room, and a portrait of the wife of President Martin van Buren (in office between 1837 and 1841) near the bust of her husband, painted by Henry Inman. 17 The motto added to a bust, as if to sum up its message, is uncommon. We find it, however, in De Chirico's self-portrait (Valdemari Collection) with Euripides' bust and the inscription: *Nulla sine tragoedia gloria*. 18 See PRAZ, *An Illustrated History of Furnishing* (London: Thames and Hudson; New York: Braziller, 1964), p. 70, note 25.

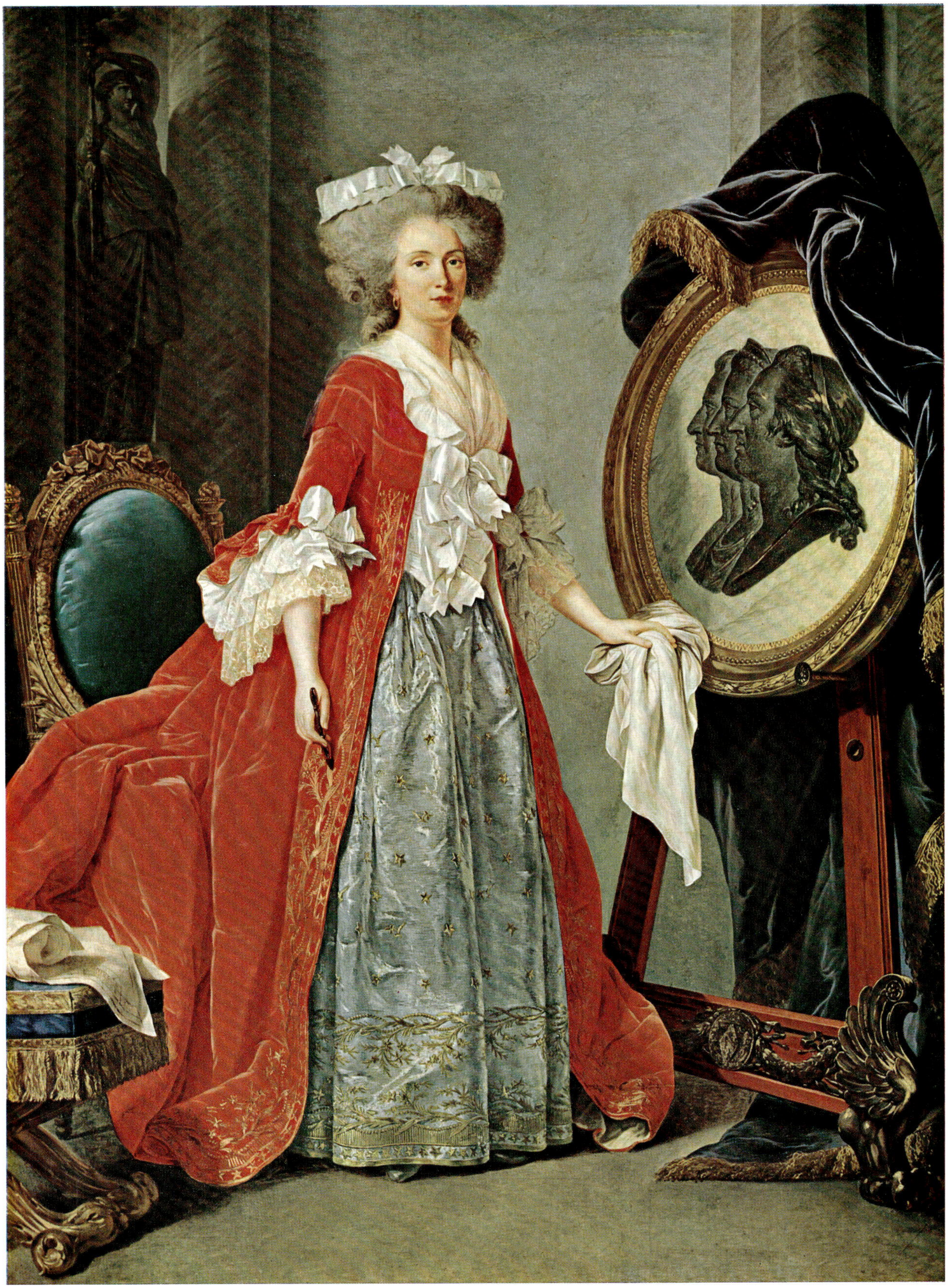

176

176 ADÉLAÏDE LABILLE-GUIARD (1749-1803), *Madame Adélaïde de France with the Portraits of Louis XVI, Marie Antoinette, and the Dauphin.* Phoenix (Ariz.), Art Museum.

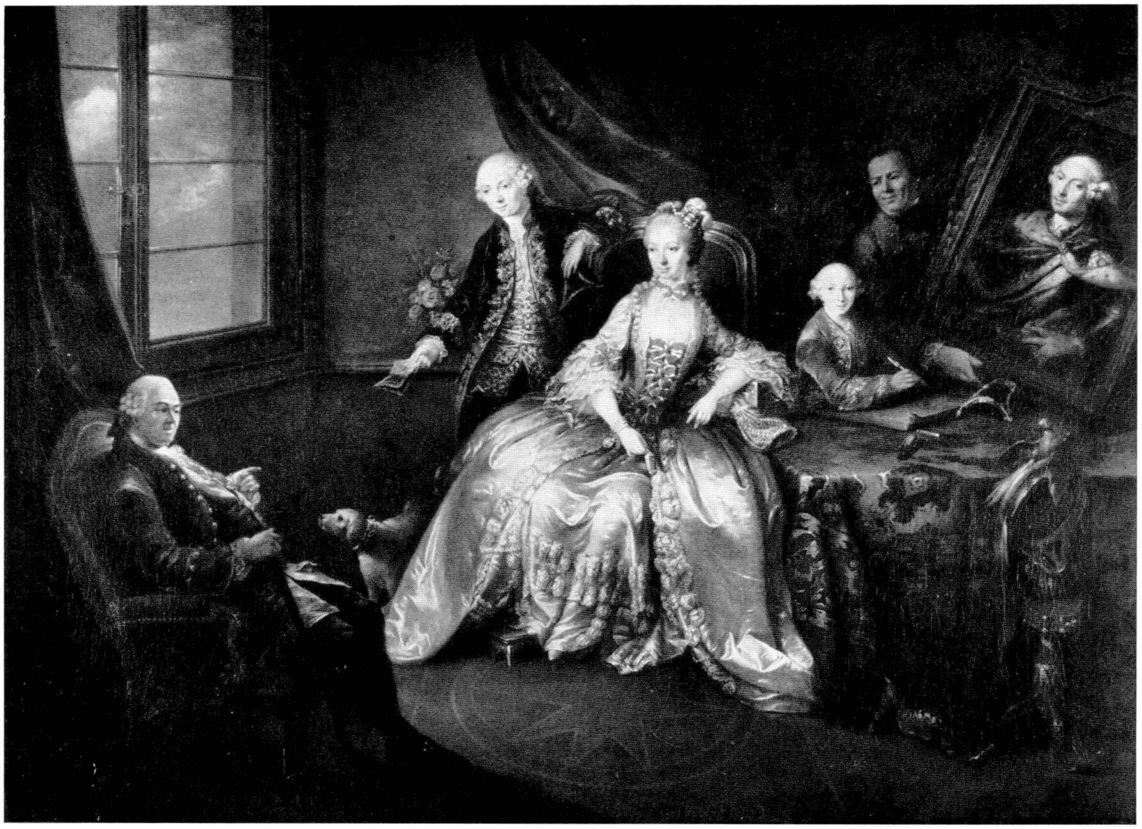

177 CHRISTIAN MANNLICH (1741-1822), *The Countess of Forbach with her Children, Baron von Stein, and the Porter of the Castle Holding up the Portrait of the Duke of Zweibrücken-Birkenfeld*, 1763-4. Paris, collection of Baron Élie de Rothschild.

wife, the Hungarian Carolina Fremdel, and their children near the tomb and the bust of the great Gaetano Filangieri: weeping-willows add to the churchyard atmosphere (fig. 374). The architect Luigi di Cambray-Digny had himself portrayed by Bezzuoli (a portrait once owned by Countess di Cambray-Digny and now in the collection of Prince Corsini, Florence) in a rather complex mimic action. Against a romantic setting of rocks among which a little waterfall roars, he indicates a large bust of his uncle, who fought for American independence with Lafayette and fortified and defended Charleston. The uncle had bequeathed the whole of his fortune to his nephew. The Count's little son points at the plan of the American fortress and looks at the bust; below there is a volume of the *Histoire de la révolution d'Amérique*.

But the most dramatic of this class of paintings is the portrait of *The Marquis Trophime-Gérard de Lally-Tollendal* (fig. 376) painted by Robin in 1779. The young Marquis, with a dramatic gesture, removes the black veil enfolding the bust of his father, the unfortunate Governor of Pondichéry, who was beheaded by order of the Paris Parliament and reinstated in 1778, thanks to the pleading of his son, who holds in his other hand a scroll with the words: " My father was not guilty ". The chains which surrounded a cuirass and a sword appear to be severed, and a sunbeam illuminates the pen which wrote the successful defence.[19] Although in the following case the object of attention is not a bust but a cameo, one might include in this section a portrait by Bronzino which remained a puzzle until recently (fig. 375). It shows a youth of melancholy mien, wearing a black jerkin which allows the impertinent upright codpiece to project from it, as was the fashion of the day[20] (it had been painted over until a recent restoration removed the additional touches). The young man holds in his hand a cameo whose subject he deliberately conceals with the forefinger of his right hand. The object he holds may appear to be a negligible accessory, but usually in such cases the image is visible: for example, in the fifteenth-century portrait by Botticelli of Giovanni di Cosimo de' Medici (Uffizi),

19 This painting, coming from a Swiss collection, was sold by the Kendl Galleries in New York at the auction of October 3 and 4, 1951 (see *The Connoisseur*, XXVIII, Dec. 1951, and *La Renaissance*, XII, 10, Oct. 1929, p. 487). 20 See ROSITA LEVI-PISETZKY, *Storia del costume in Italia*, III (Milan: Istituto Editoriale Italiano, 1966), p. 45.

178
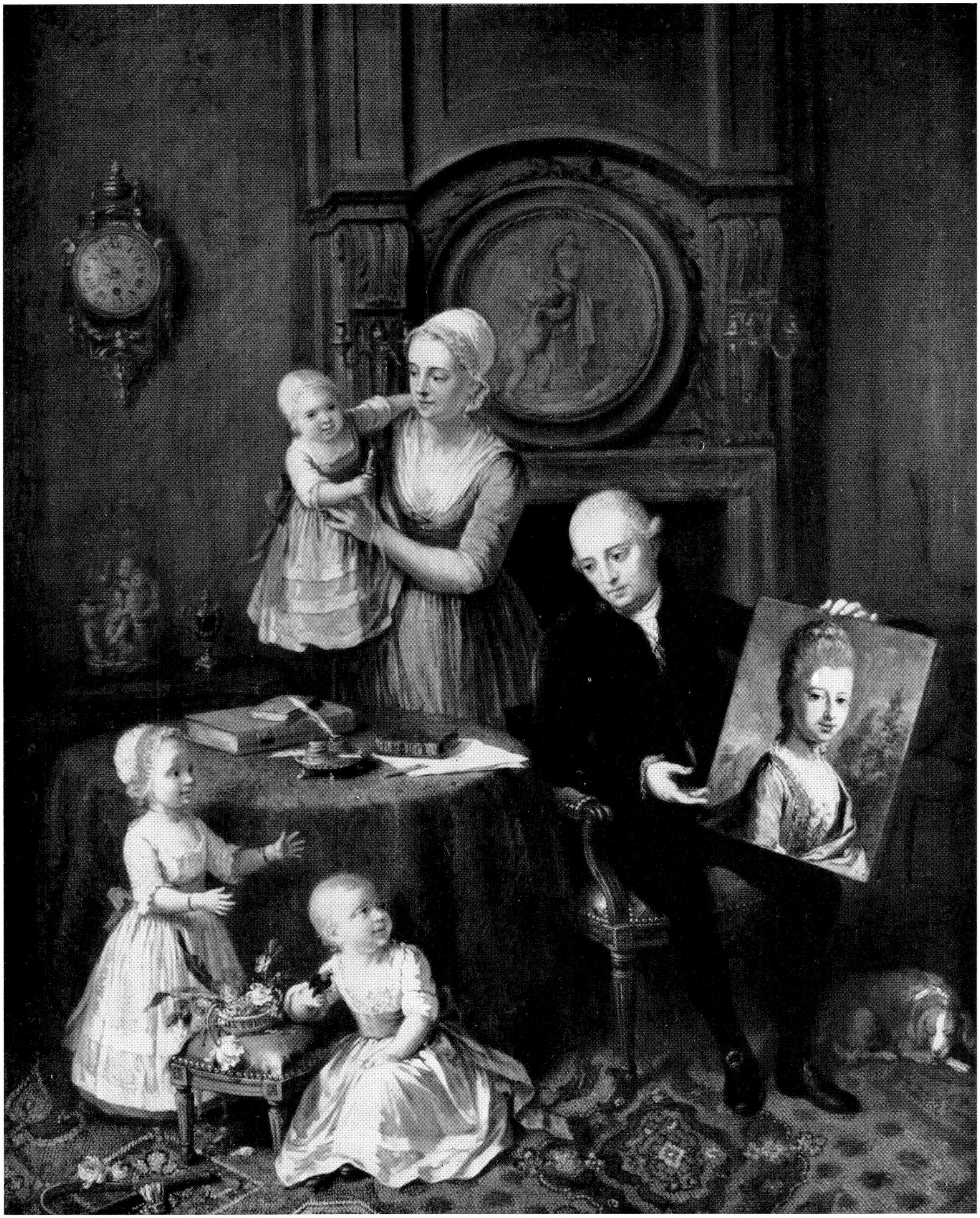

178 WILLEM JOSEPH LAQUY (1738-1798), *Johan Maurits van Pabst with his Children*, 1776-7. Collection of Jonkheer W.E. van Weede.

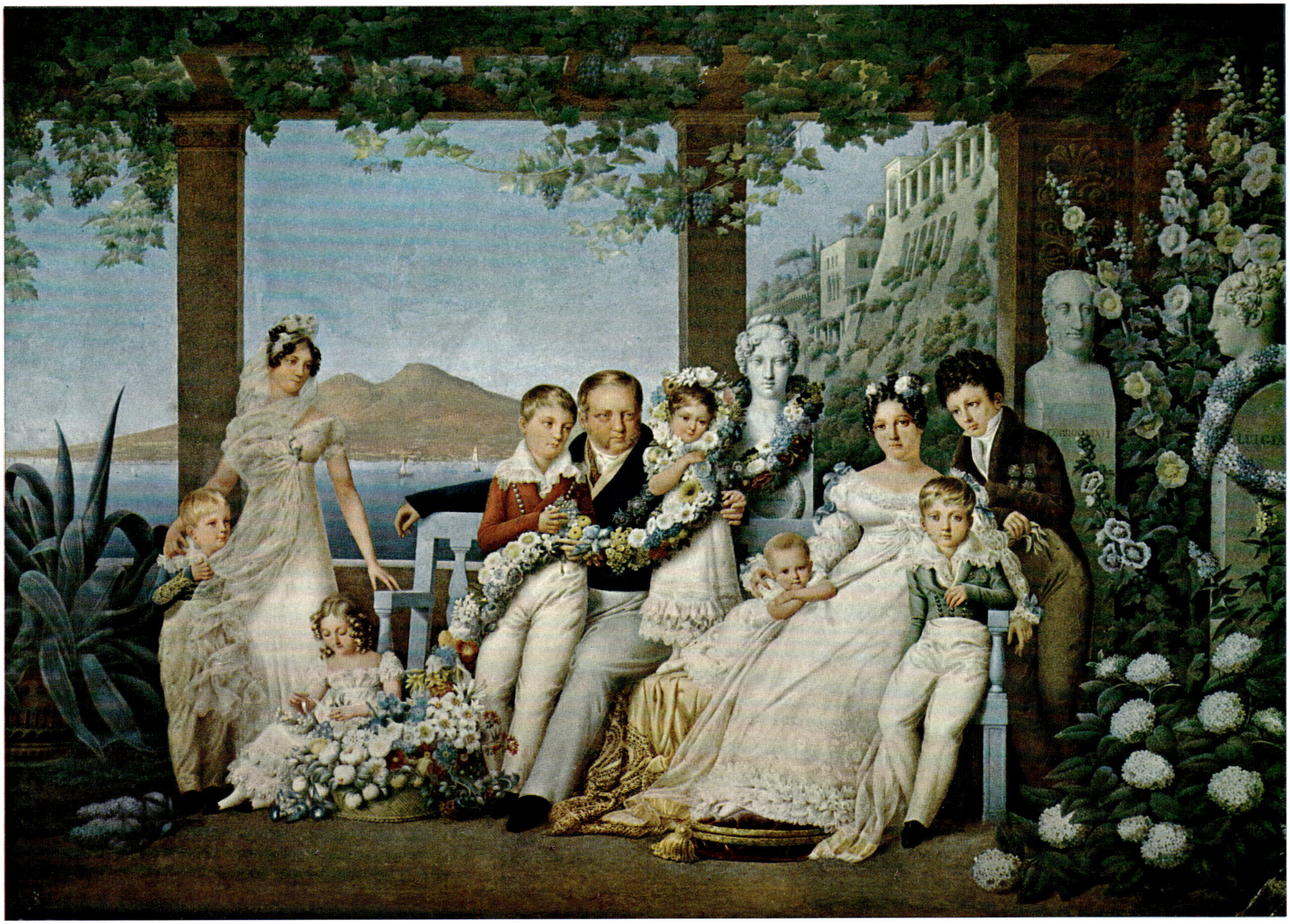

179

179 JEAN-FRANÇOIS GARNEREY (1755-1837) or AUGUSTE GARNEREY (1785-1824), *The Family of the Crown Prince of the Two Sicilies (later Francesco I)*. Brunnsee, Steyermark (Austria), collection of Count Lodovico Lucchesi-Palli.

who shows a medal bearing the effigy of his father, or in the seventeenth-century portrait by a follower of Sánchez Coello of the Infanta Isabella Clara Eugenia, who shows a cameo with the effigy of Philip II (fig. 379); or in the portrait miniature of the Empress Maria Ludovica (by Heinrich Friedrich Füger) showing a medallion with a portrait of the Emperor Leopold II (who died in 1792.[21]

However, the clue has been found by Luisa Becherucci[22] in an oval (in Palazzo Capponi in Florence) repeating Bronzino's portrait, with a few variations; it is among the farrago of historical and allegorical figures with which, in about 1585, Bernardino Poccetti filled the vaults and walls of the great hall by order of Lodovico Capponi, who wished thus to celebrate the deeds of his ancestors. The subject of Bronzino's portrait is Lodovico Capponi himself, whose manuscript biography written by the scholar Girolamo Muzio may be read in the Biblioteca Riccardiana. Lodovico, a handsome and valiant youth, had inspired love in one of the most outstanding young ladies of Florence, Maddalena Vettori, who — having lost her father — was very wealthy and was besieged by many young noblemen whose advances she had refused. To protect her against further importunities, her mother had had her shut up in a convent. Duke Cosimo I, in order to force the young woman to accept one of the matches he favoured, made her leave the convent and become one of the ladies-in-waiting to Duchess Eleonora. However, the girl withstood the many pressures on her, while Lodovico, opposed not only by the other suitors but by their friends and relatives as well, was avoided by everybody and " kept to himself, more in hope of the constancy of a young woman than in fear of the war waged against him by so many courtiers backed by the favour of the Duke ". He had rented a house in Piazza Santa Trinita with the sole purpose of seeing his beloved every time she went to church there with the Duchess. The latter and her adolescent daughter Maria at last took pity on them and pleaded with the Duke on their behalf until he relented, enjoining Capponi to prepare for the wedding within twenty-four hours. Helped by his friends, he succeeded in organizing a sumptuous feast and in decorating the house in Piazza Santa Trinita. At first Dr. Becherucci thought that Bronzino's portrait alluded to the period of thwarted passion, hence the concealment in the cameo of the supposed likeness of the girl to whom he was secretly betrothed. A further inspection, however, made her doubt this attractive explanation. The courtship took place between 1556 and 1559. Lodovico was born in 1533 and Maddalena in 1540, so that in 1556 the girl was sixteen and the young man twenty-three. Dr. Becherucci sees in Bronzino's portrait the likeness of an eighteen-year-old, so she thinks that the cameo alludes to one of those ephemeral love affairs in which Capponi was involved in his adolescence. (Bartolomeo Bartolini had warned Maddalena's mother that the young man used to "chase all the females he came across", and, more specifically, Muzio relates that he courted Leonora Soderini, wife of the jealous Matteino Strozzi.) Dr. Becherucci concludes: " Perhaps some similar passing sentimental affair offered Bronzino the hint to represent him as unwillingly diverted from the contemplation of a woman's portrait which his aristocratic hand is holding, while concealing the likeness with his finger ". But the estimate of a person's age is a matter of opinion, and although men in the sixteenth century aged sooner than nowadays, Bronzino's portrait might well be that of a twenty-three-year-old youth. In any case, the portrait mirrors a mute conversation between the young man and the portrait on the cameo — which, absorbed in his melancholy mood, he does not want to show us.

On the imaginary wall upon which I have grouped them, these " conversations " of living beings with marble busts make a curious show: hands that point, eyes that fix on adored images, allegorical attributes negligently laid on the floor. All this bespeaks a cult of which only a feeble memory lingers with us. What is the meaning of this rather rhetorical pantomime? Of this moral picture which admonishes and instructs? We do not see anything like it in modern homes, and nowadays we find such rhetoric astonishing. Yet it was as familiar a century ago as it was fifteen hundred years earlier. People who had themselves thus represented believed in Plutarch's heroes, and were not after all so far removed from the ancient Romans who kept wax busts of their ancestors in the most stately part of the house. The Romans had also had themselves portrayed near the images of their ancestors, as we have seen in the statues in the Capitoline Museum and at Villa Albani.

For those past generations, history merged into biography. It guided life by means of great ideal figures — ancestors, benefactors, masters — perennial presences, protective shades in whose ghostly company people imagined they lived. The deceased,

21 See E. LEISCHING, *Die Bildnis-Miniatur in Österreich* (Vienna: Artaria, 1907), catalogue no. 59, plate XIV. In the nineteenth century Tominz represented his father holding in plain view a snuff-box with a miniature of his first wife, Marianna Jancsig, mother of the painter (Ljubljana, National Gallery; fig. 377). 22 " Per un ritratto del Bronzino ", in *Studi in onore di Matteo Marangoni* (Florence: Vallecchi, 1957), pp. 202-9.

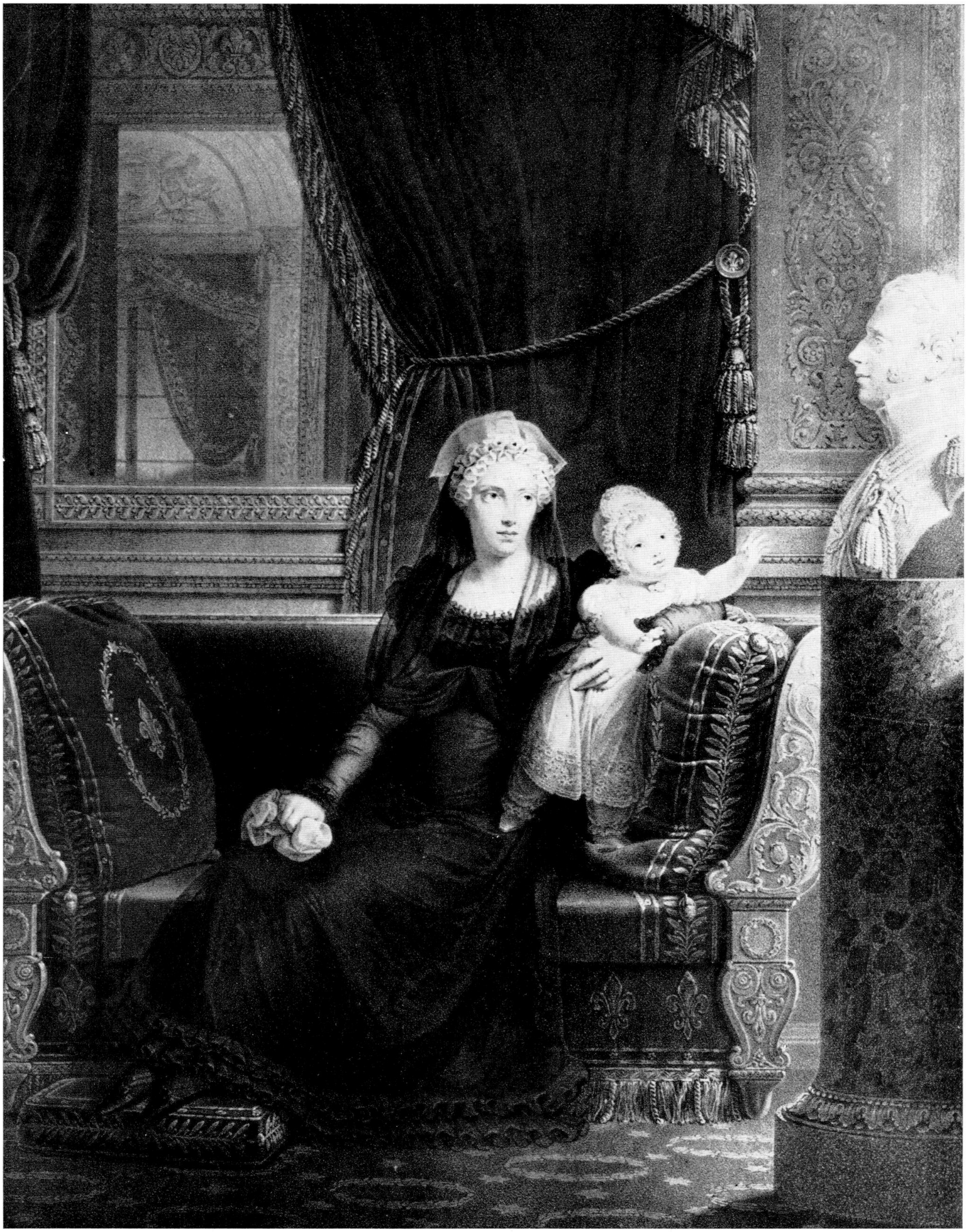

180

180 FRANÇOIS KINSON (1770-1839), *The Duchess of Berry and her Daughter Marie-Louise Stretching out her Arms towards the Bust of the Duke of Berry.* Engraving after a lost painting of which there is a copy at the Versailles museum; Rome, collection of Baronessa Galli Zugaro. 181 GIUSEPPE MOLTENI (1800-1867), *An Old Man Showing a Little Girl a Bust of the Duchess Marie Louise.* Parma, Galleria Nazionale.

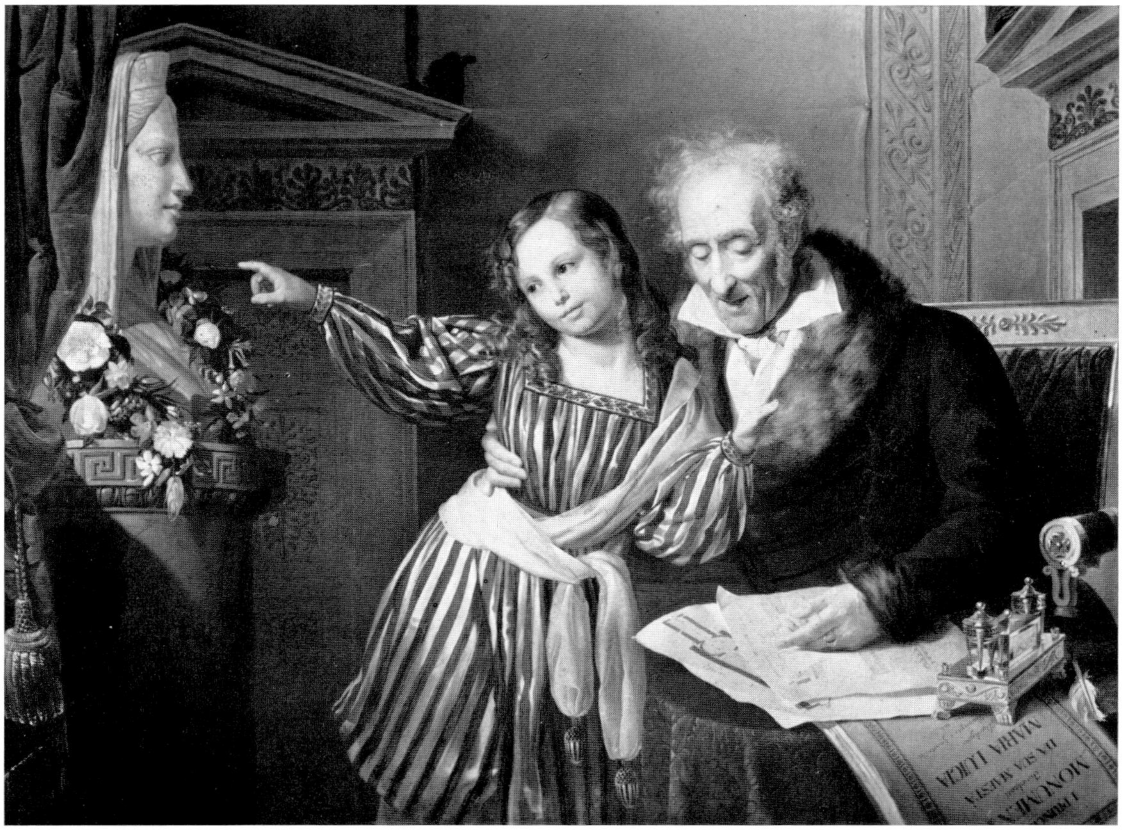

181

having taken on a legendary or divine significance, did not cease to exist, thanks to the memories of those living still, but in their turn they gave to the lives of the living the certainty of belonging to a tradition and provided a solid support in the perpetual stream of time. It was perhaps this, and not the mere imitation of a heroic Roman custom, that lay behind the cult of the tutelary effigy. These effigies were like splinters of ancient mountains transformed into human likenesses; they were things settled forever. Two lines of an Elizabethan dramatist who devoured Plutarch and Seneca perfectly embody the old attitude:[23]

Here like a Roman statue I will stand
Till death hath made me marble.

A theatrical attitude, no doubt; but when one thinks how exalted the idea of life as a theatre was in earlier generations, can one continue to smile at the emphatic gestures that recur in those paintings? In them pride of lineage and devotion to great minds have taken on forms that are eloquent, concrete, and corporeal. These people had refused to entrust life to the care of a capricious, momentary impulse; they let themselves be ruled by memory, a memory as sound and unshakeable as the marble of the busts to which they point. Life was made simpler in this way, and it was a simplicity we are sometimes disposed to envy. Such, then, is the language spoken by that wall on which, in my imagination, I have assembled so many portraits in this genre. Although at first the repetition of this immemorial gesture, so far removed from our modern habits of mind, may appear mechanical and even grotesque, yet one comes to regard it as being invested with an almost religious significance, like the opening of the arms of the priest when he pronounces the *Dominus vobiscum* of the divine service: "Be with us, tutelary spirit, assist us with thy example".

23 GEORGE CHAPMAN, *Bussy d'Ambois*, V, iv, 97-98.

Additional Works Cited in the Text

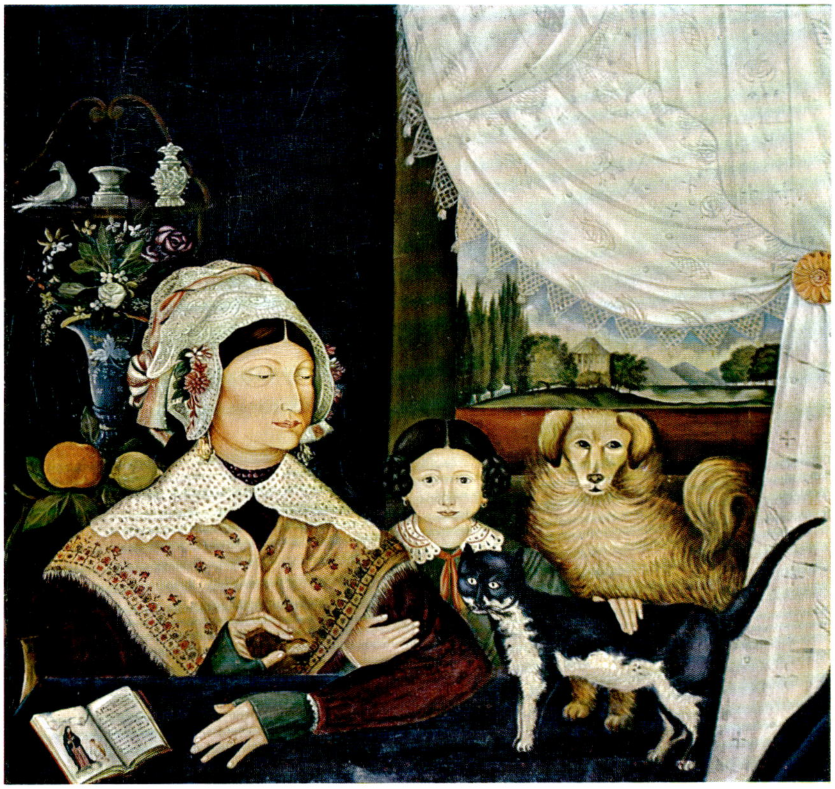

182

182 PROVINCIAL ITALIAN PAINTER (first half of the 19th century), *Portrait of an Elderly Woman and a little Girl with Pets.* Rome, private collection.

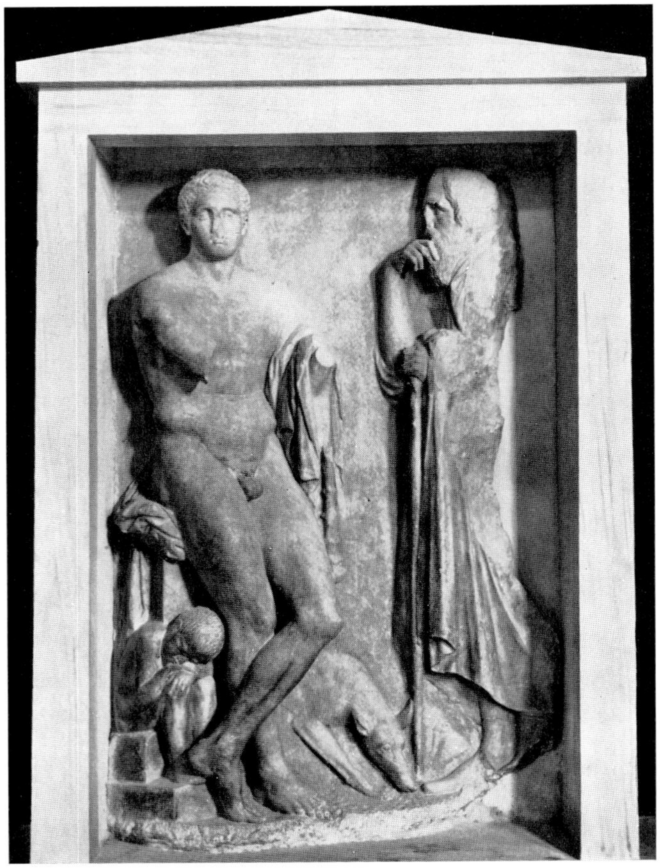

183

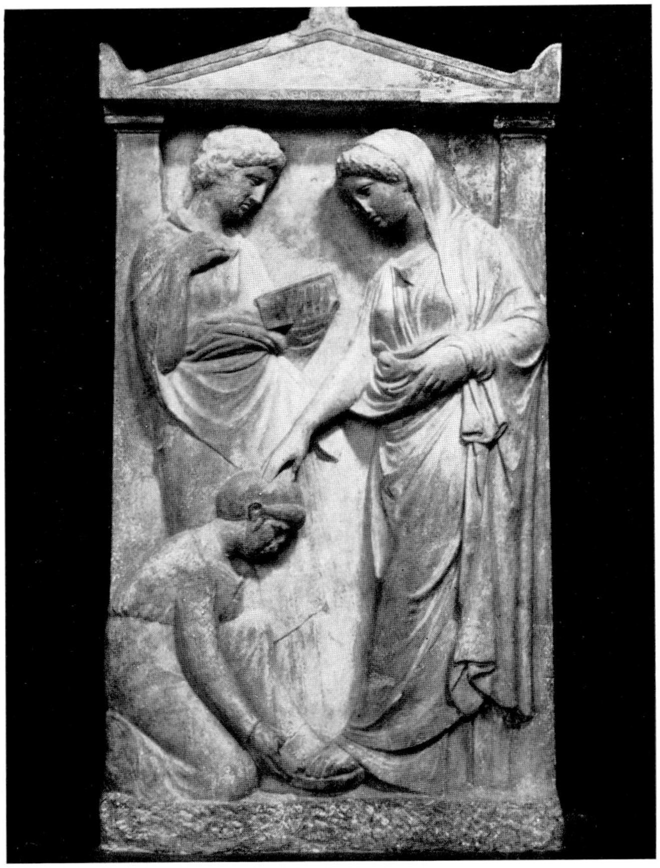

184

183 *Stele from the Ilissos.* Athens, National Archaeological Museum (see p. 39).

184 *Ameinokleia Stele.* Athens, National Archaeological Museum (see p. 39).

185 attr. to FILIPPINO LIPPI (c. 1457-1504), *A Master and a Disciple*. Denver (Colorado), Art Museum (Mrs. Simon Guggenheim Bequest) (see p. 46).

186 FLORENTINE SCHOOL (end of the 14th century), *Taddeo, Gaddo, and Agnolo Gaddi*, c. 1400. Florence, Soprintendenza alle Gallerie (see p. 46).

187 PAOLO VERONESE (1528-1588), *Family Group*. San Francisco, California Palace of the Legion of Honor (Gift of Mortimer Leventritt) (see p. 46).

188 attr. to GIROLAMO DA CARPI (1501-1556), *A Cardinal and a Gowned Gentleman*. London, National Gallery (see pp. 48 and 51).

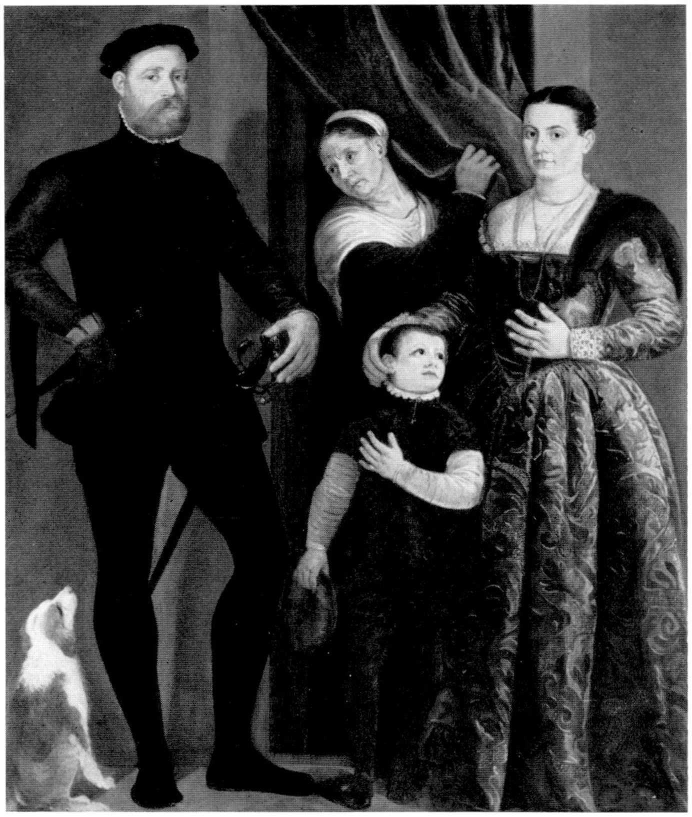

187

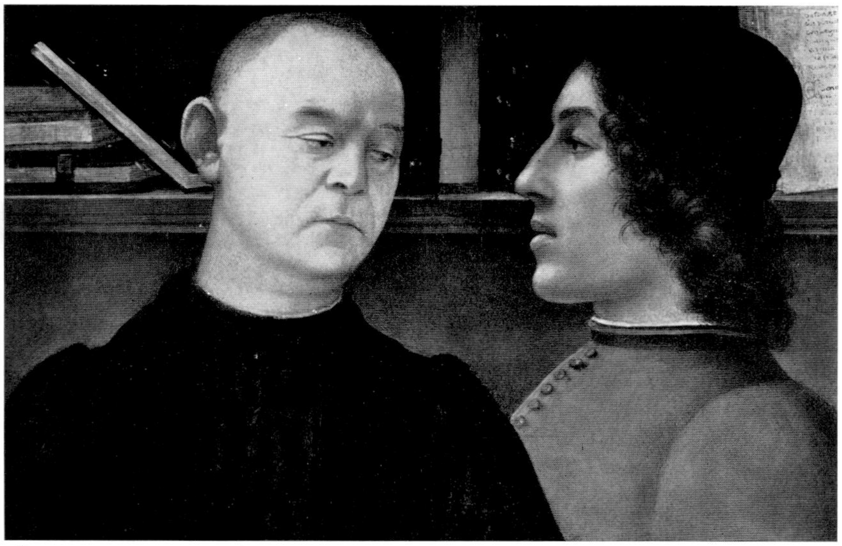

185

186

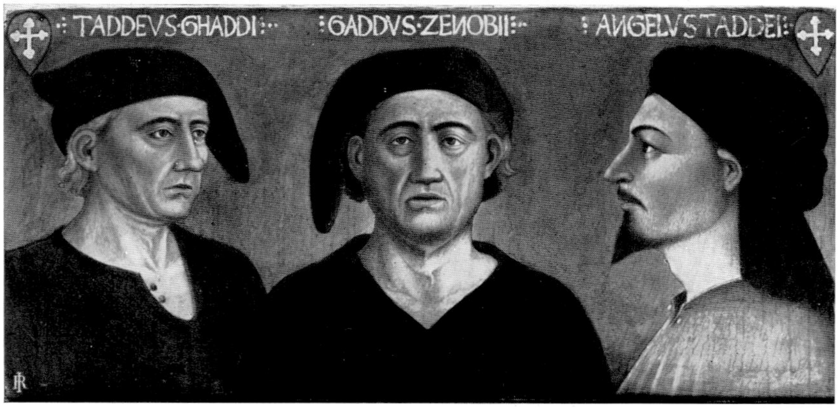

188

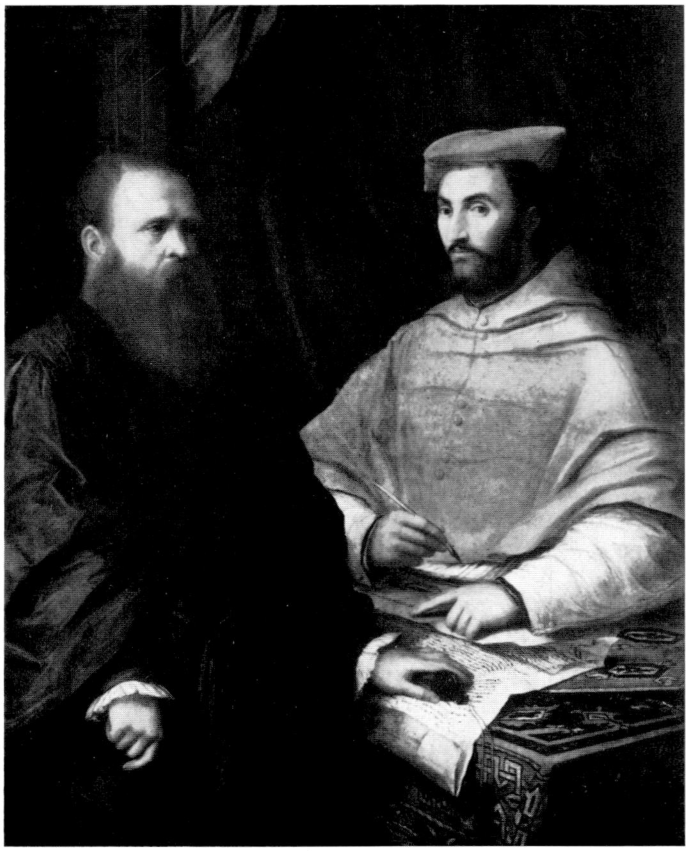

189 BERNARDINO LICINIO (c. 1498-1565), *The Painter's Brother and his Family*. Rome, Borghese Gallery (see p. 54).

190 SEBASTIANO DEL PIOMBO (1485-1547), *Cardinal Bandinello Sauli, his Secretary, and Two Geographers*. Washington, D. C., National Gallery of Art (Samuel H. Kress Collection) (see p. 51).

191 CORNELIUS JONSON (JOHNSON) (1593-1661), *Arthur, First Baron Capel, and his Family*. London, collection of Mr. Hugh Leggat (see pp. 51-54).

192 SOFONISBA ANGUISSOLA (c. 1528-c.1624), *Three Relatives*. Nivaagard Haage Collection (see p. 51).

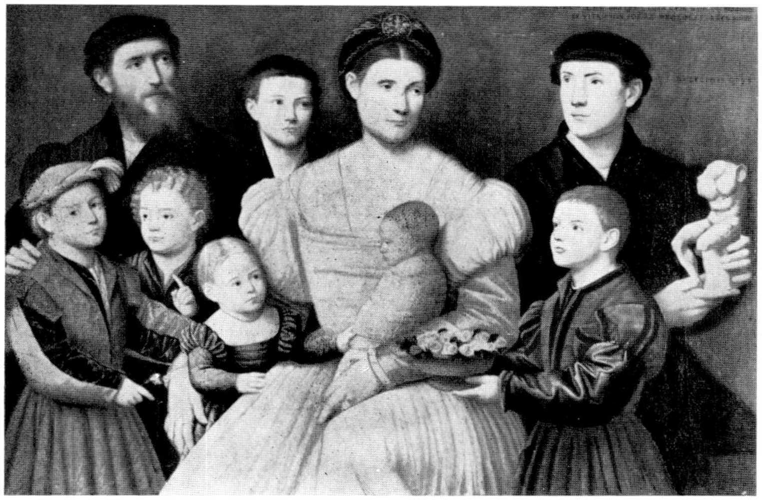

189

190

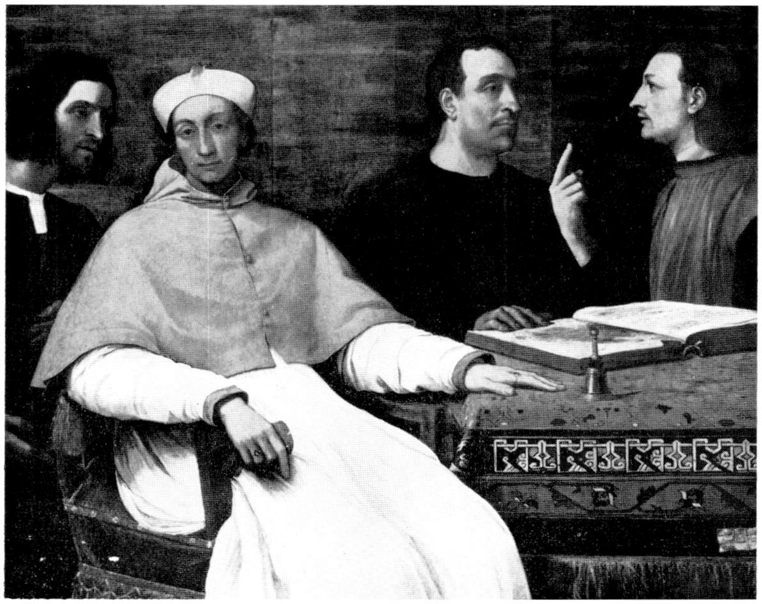

192

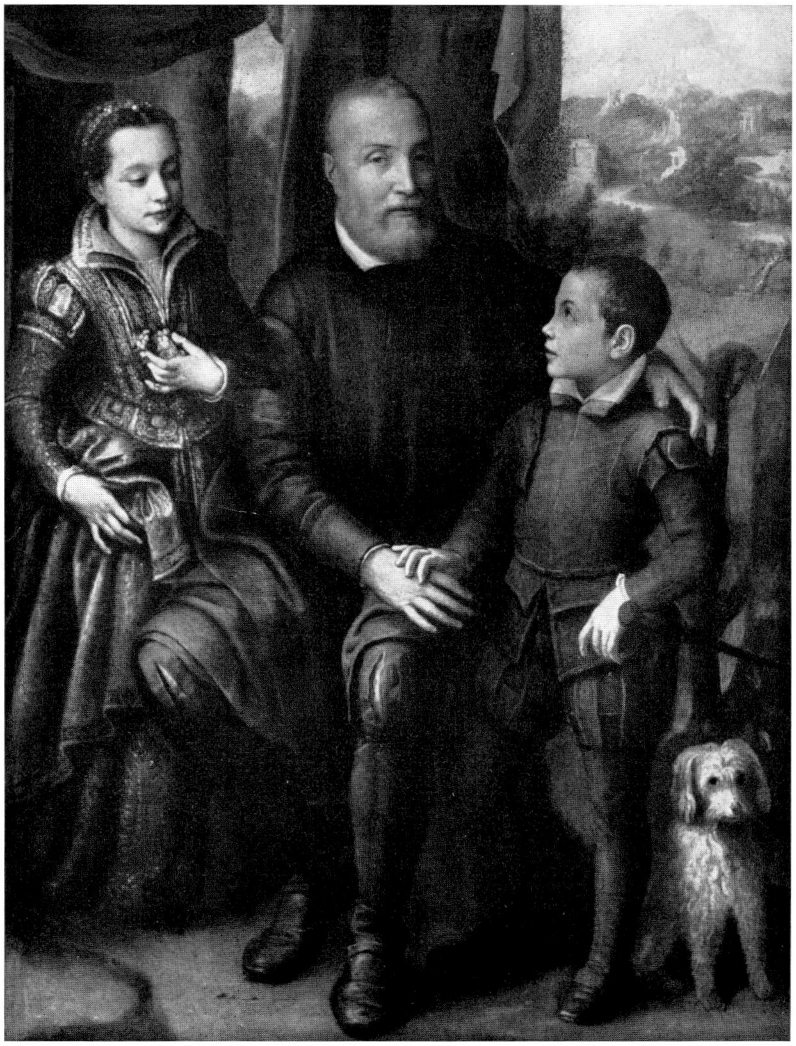

191

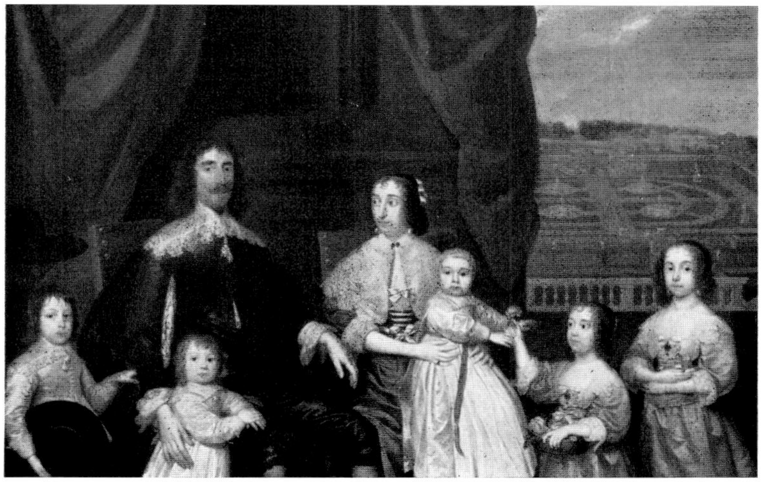

193 FOLLOWER OF EL GRECO, *The Theotocopuli Family* (?). London, Christie's sale, 1 July 1966 (see p. 55).

194 LORENZO LOTTO (1480-1556), *Family Group*, 1523 (Berenson's dating). London, National Gallery (see p. 54).

195 GIUSEPPE BALDRIGHI (1723-1802), *Self-portrait with his Wife*, c. 1760. Parma, Galleria Nazionale (see p. 55).

196 ALEXANDER RUNCIMAN (1736-1785), *Self-portrait with John Brown Discussing a Passage in Shakespeare's* Tempest. Edinburgh, Society of Antiquaries of Scotland (see p. 55).

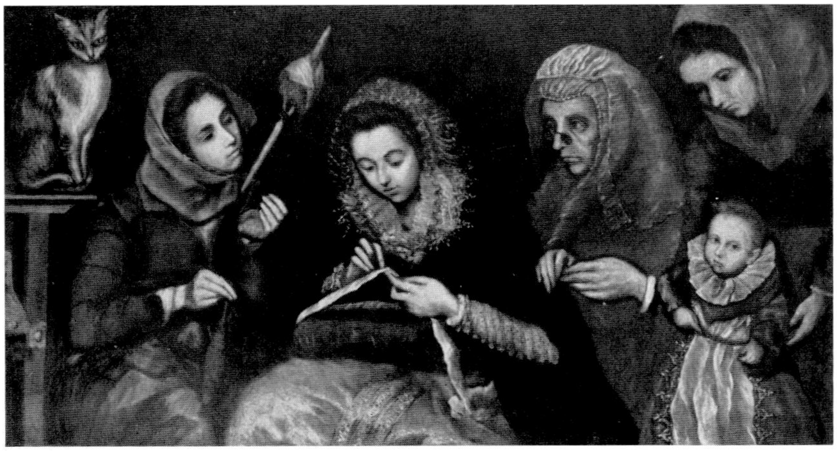

193

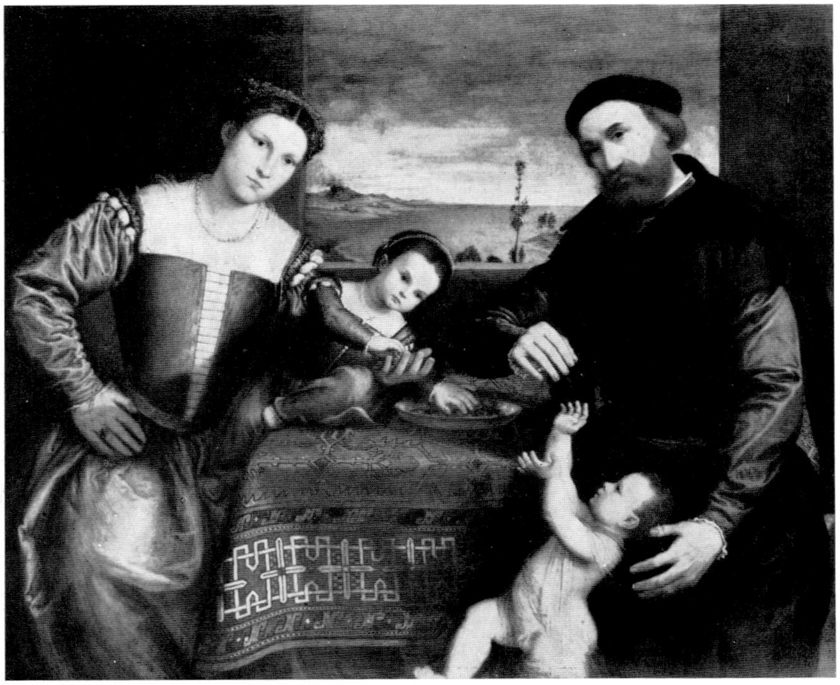

194

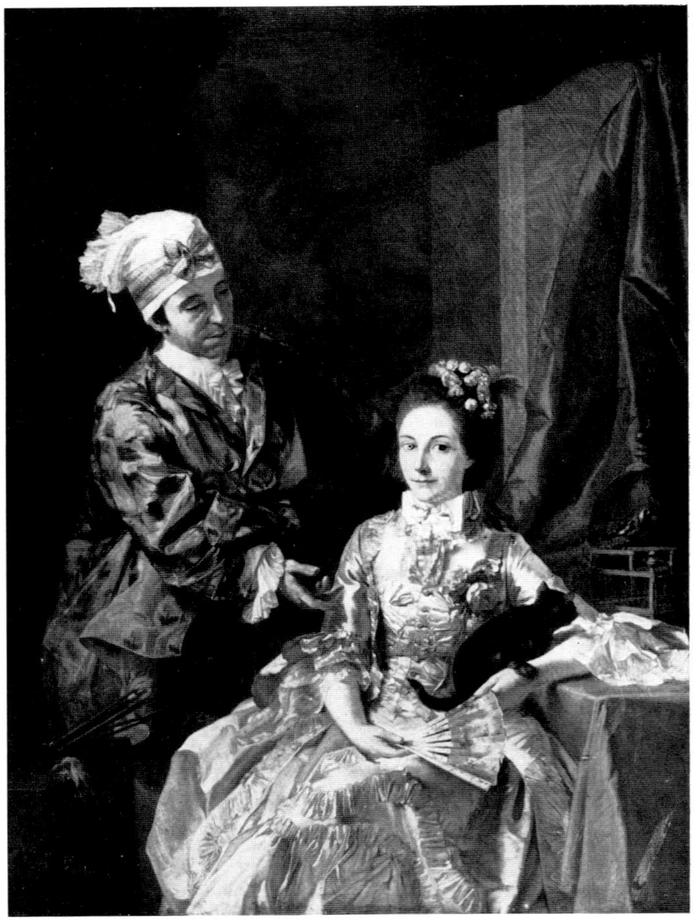

195

197 FRIEDRICH WILHELM SCHÄFER (c.1763-1807), *The Painter and his Family*, c. 1800. Frankfurt a.M., Städelsches Kunstinstitut (see p. 55).

198 attr. to ANDREA APPIANI (1754-1817), *Lorenzo Mascheroni and his Friends*. Bergamo, Accademia Carrara (see p. 55).

199 GIUSEPPE (JOSIP) TOMINZ (1796-1866), *The Family of L. De Brucker*. Trieste, Civico Museo Revoltella (see p. 56).

200 ITALIAN SCHOOL (19th century), *A Group of Three Persons*. Venice, Palazzo Grassi (exh. *Mostra del costume nel tempo*, 1951) (see pp. 55-56).

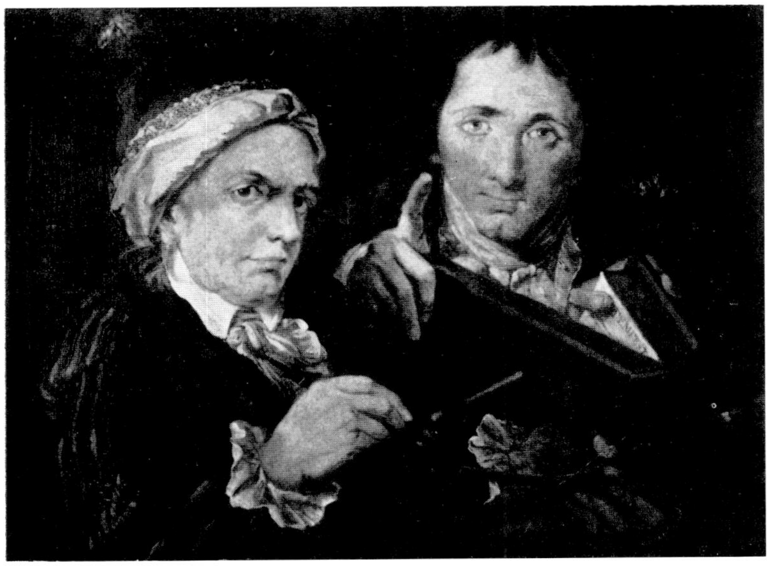

196

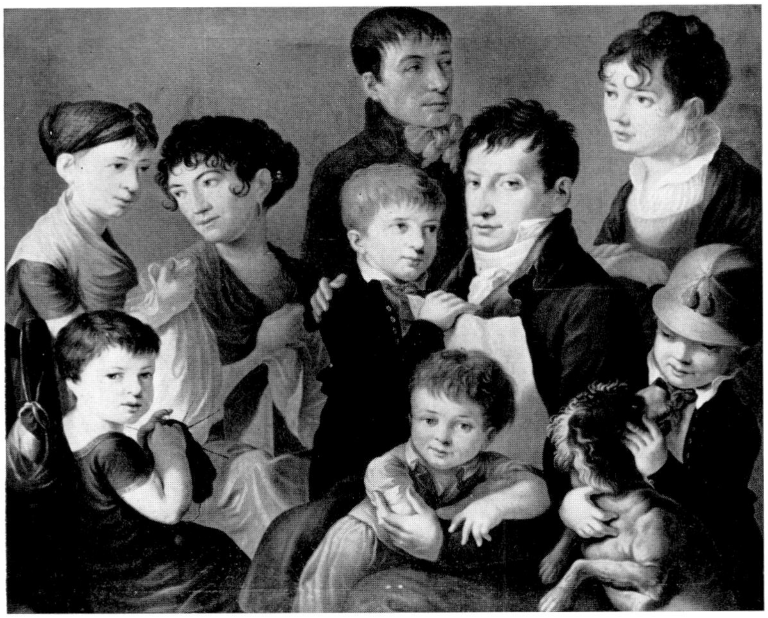

197

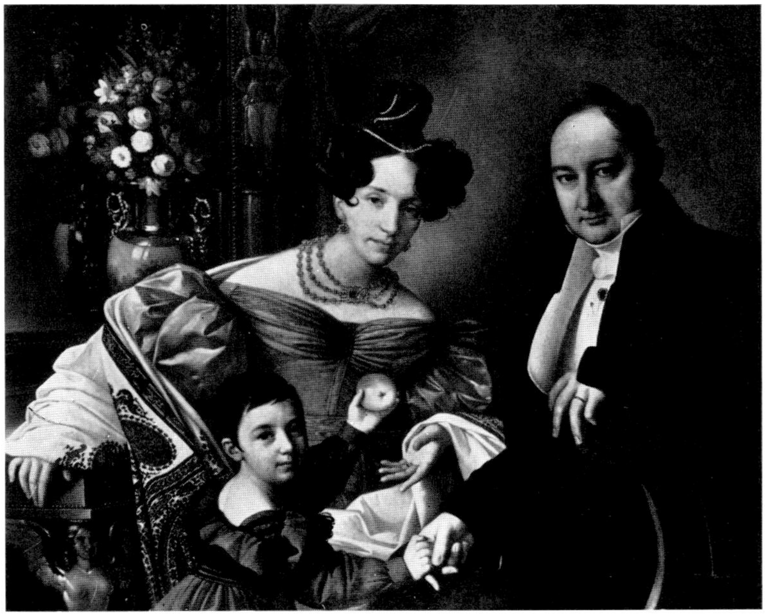

199

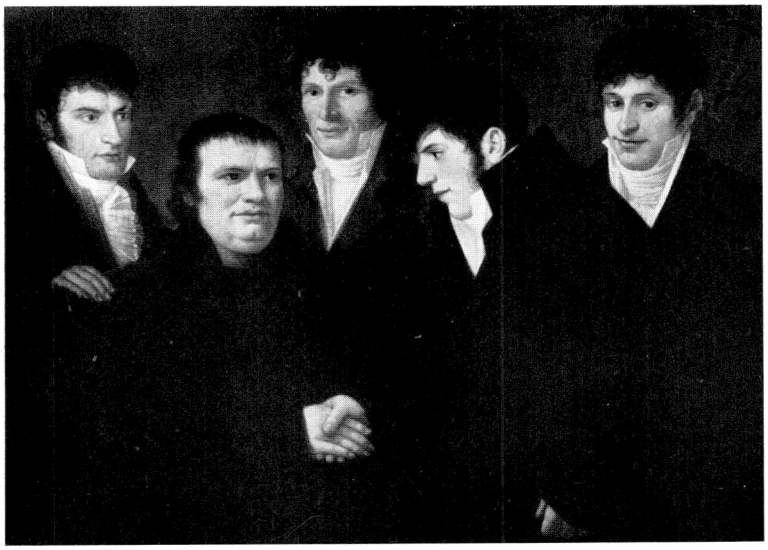

198

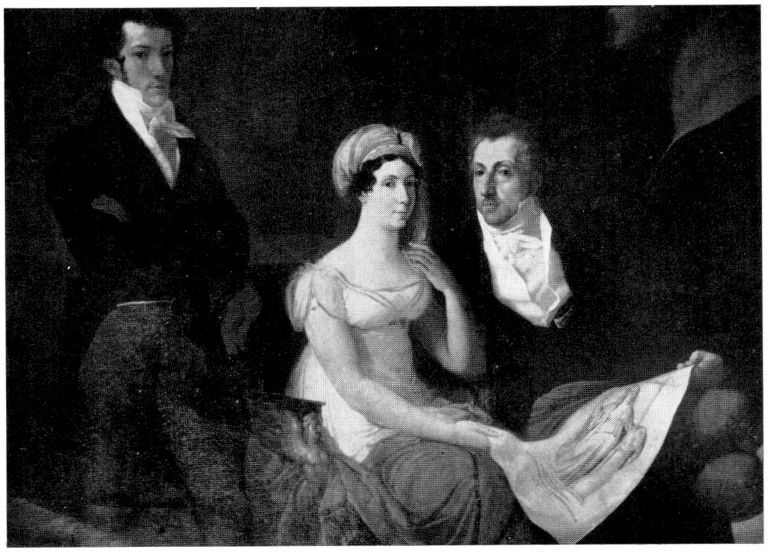

200

201 SIR JOHN MEDINA (1639-1710), *The Family of John, First Marquess of Tweeddale*, 1692-6. Yester, Gifford (East Lothian), collection of Peter W. Morris (see p. 55).

202 GIUSEPPE (JOSIP) TOMINZ (1796-1866), *The Moscon Family*, 1829. Ljubljana, National Gallery (see pp. 56 and 106).

203 GIUSEPPE (JOSIP) TOMINZ (1796-1866), *The Buchler Family*, 1829. Trieste, collection of A. Buchler (see p. 56).

204 PROVINCIAL ITALIAN PAINTER (first half of the 19th century), *Portrait of an Elderly Woman and a Little Girl with Pets*. Rome, private collection (see p. 56).

205 FRANS POURBUS THE ELDER (1545-1581), *The Wedding Feast of Joris Hoefnagel*, 1571. Brussels, Musées Royaux des Beaux Arts (see p. 60).

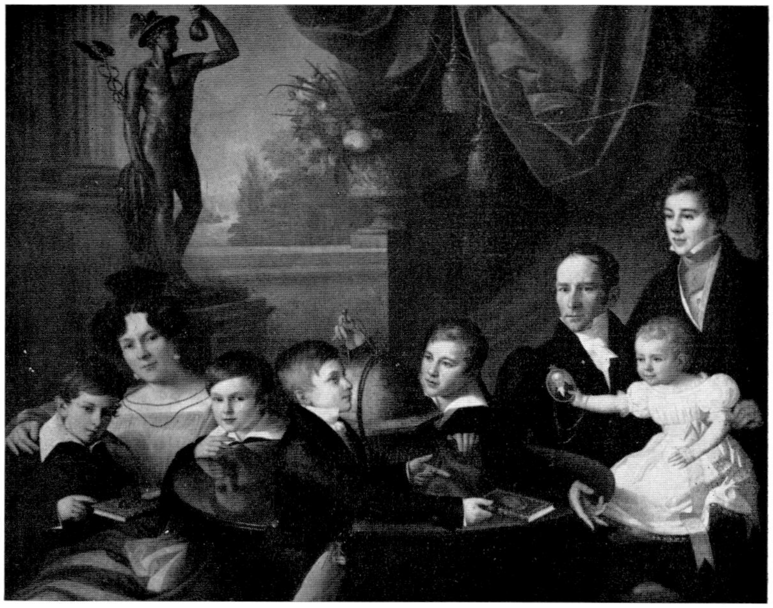

203

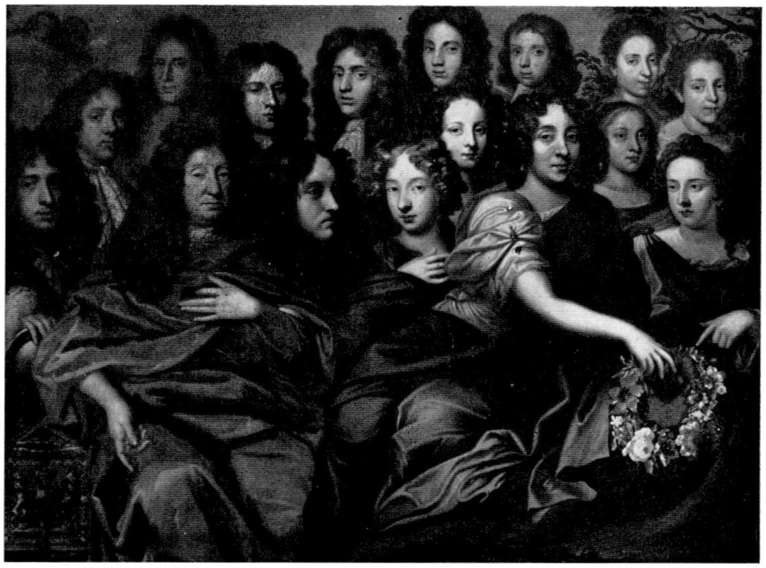

201

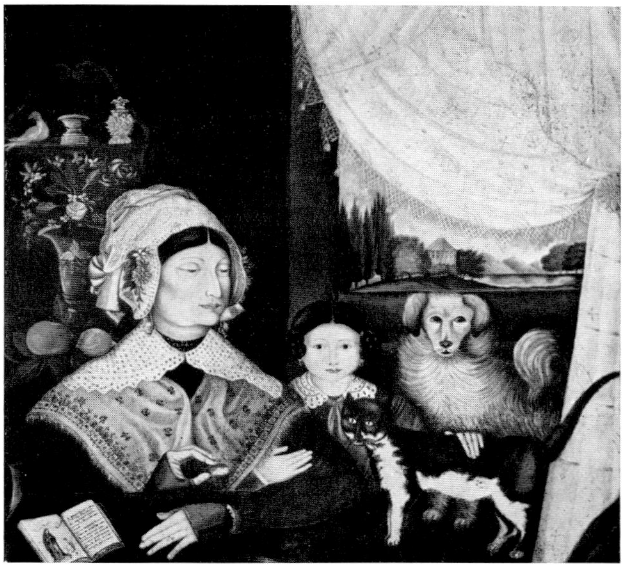

204

202

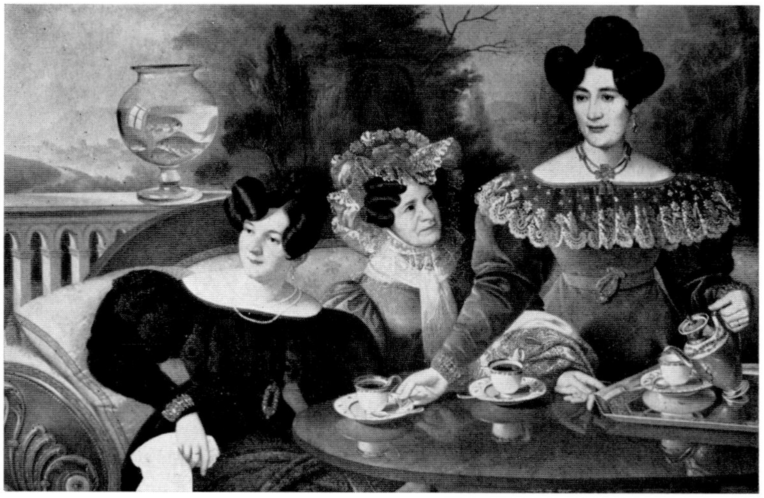

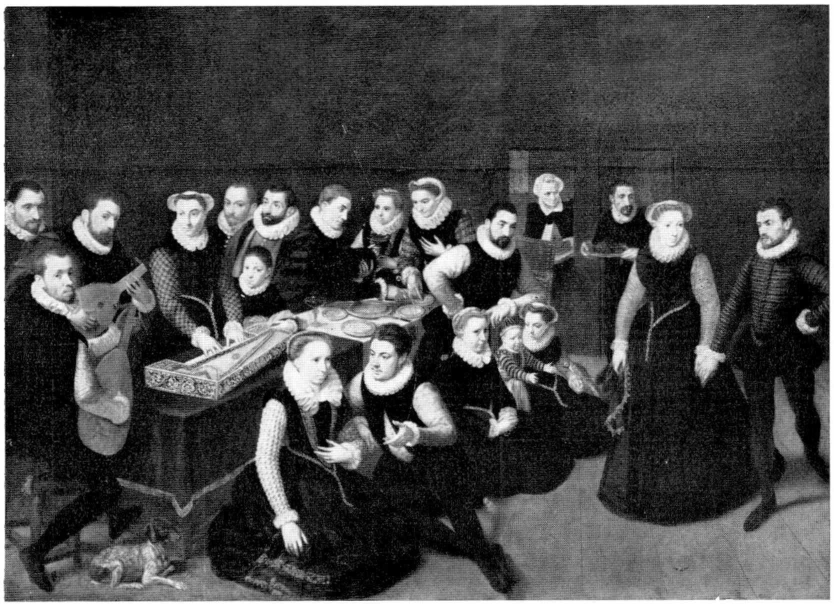

205

206

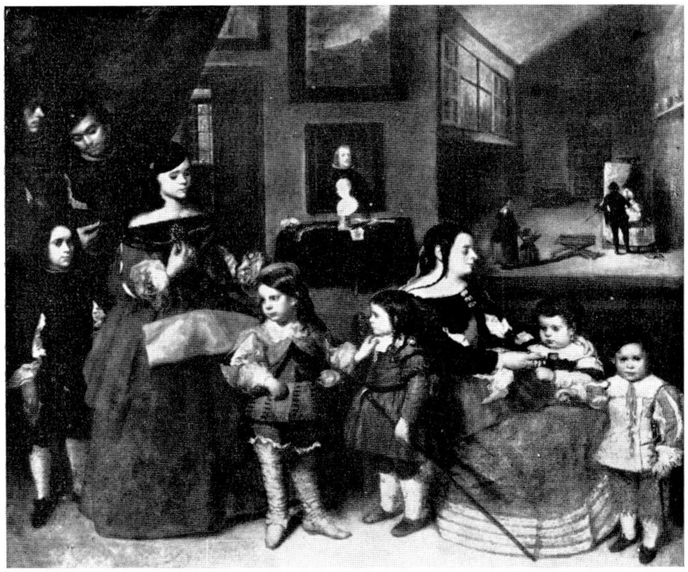

207

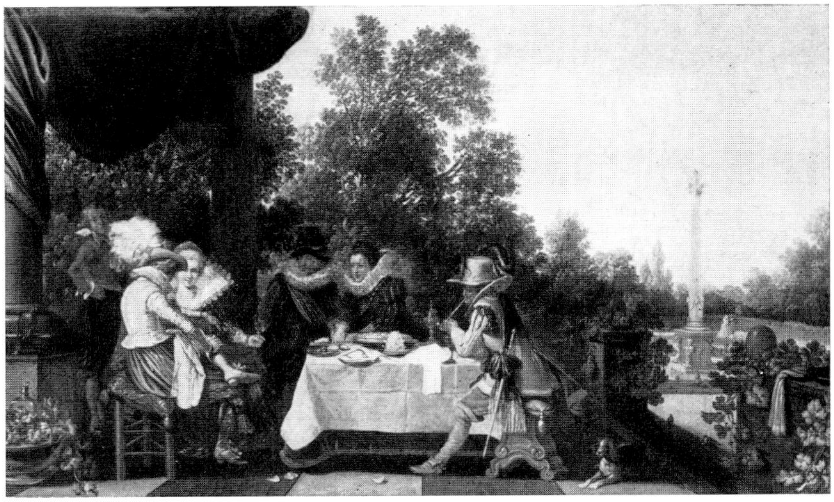

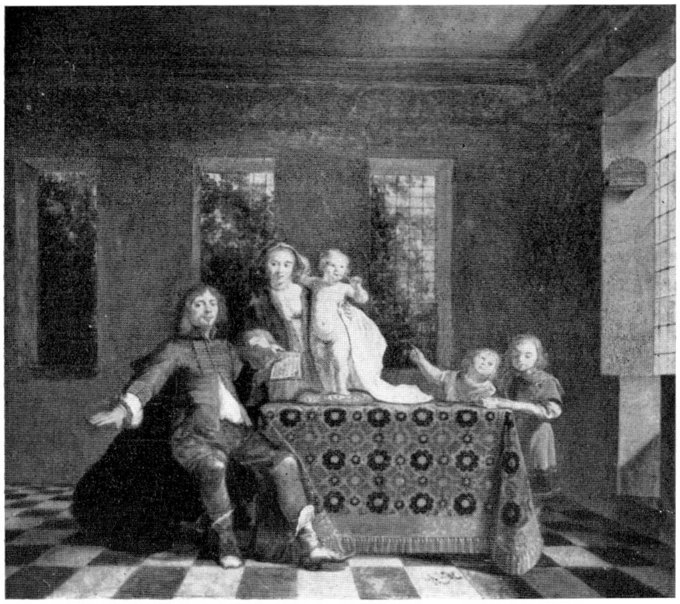

208

209

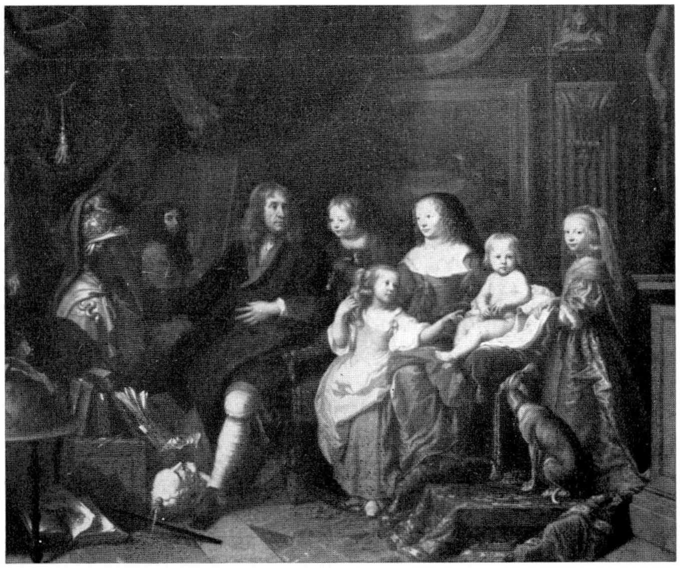

206 JUAN BAUTISTA MARTÍNEZ DEL MAZO (c.1612-1667), *The Painter's Family*, 1652-8. Vienna, Kunsthistorisches Museum (see p. 63).

207 ESAIAS VAN DE VELDE (1590/1-1630), *A Company at their Meal*. Berlin, Staatliche Museen (see p. 56).

208 NICOLAUS KNÜPFER (1603-1660), *The Painter and his Family*, 1640. Dresden, Staatliche Gemäldegalerie (see p. 63).

209 CHARLES LEBRUN (1619-1690), *The Family of the Cologne Banker Everhard Jabach*, c. 1660. Berlin, Staatliche Museen (formerly Kaiser Friedrich Museum) (see p. 63).

210 PIETER VAN SLINGELAND (1640?-1691), *Family Group*. Paris, Louvre (see p. 65).

211 HENDRIK SORGH (1611-1670), *The Family of Eeuwout Prins*, 1661. Brussels, collection of Jonkheer D. Prins van Westdorpe (see p. 65).

212 NICOLAAS WALRAVEN VAN HAEFTEN (c. 1663-1715), *Unidentified Family*, 1691. Easton Royal and London, collection of the heirs to the late Jonkheer F. I. van Haeften (see p. 65).

213 HENDRIK SORGH (1611-1670), *The Family of Jacob Bierens*, 1663. Wassenaar, collection of Mevrouw Bierens de Haan-van Riemsdijk (see p. 65).

214 attr. to JOHANN ZOFFANY (1734/5-1810), *Charles Dibdin with his Second Wife and his Daughter*. Formerly the property of Mr. E. J. Rousuck, New York (see p. 67).

215 TIBOUT REGTERS (1710-1768), *The Family of Jan Carel van der Meulen*, c. 1760. Rotterdam, collection of Mr. J. A. Grothe van Schellach (see p. 68).

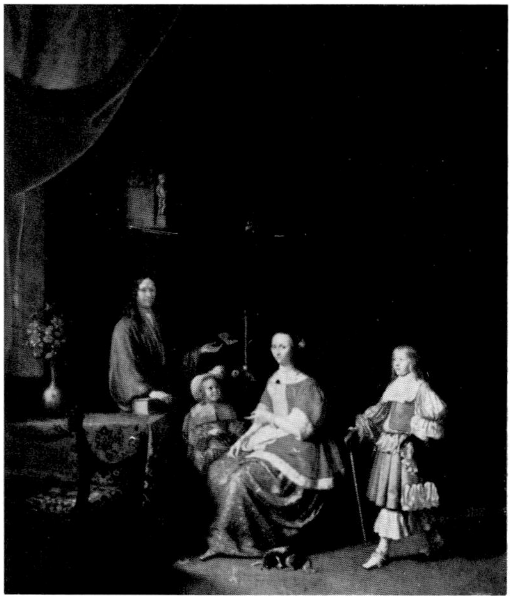

210

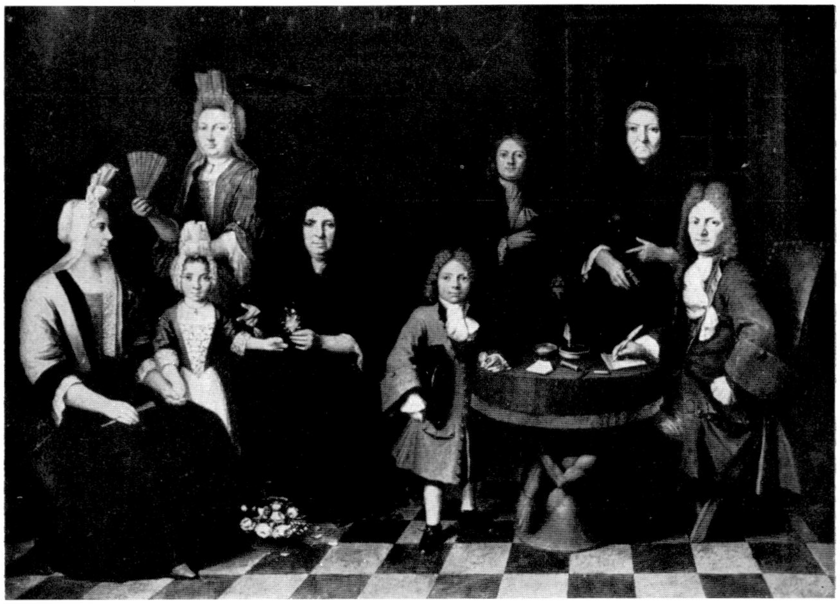

212

211

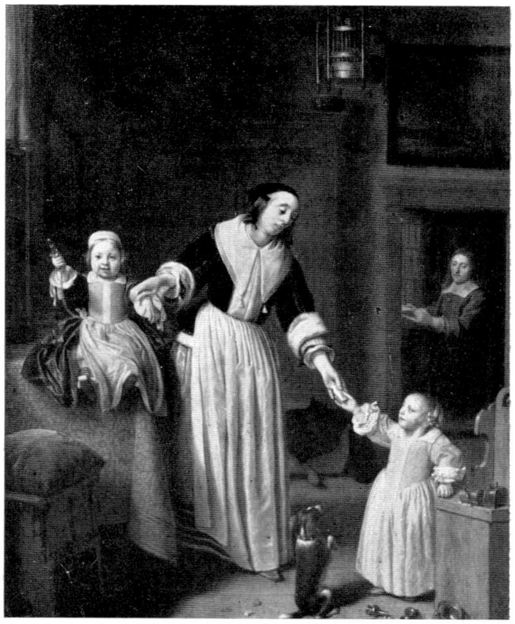

213

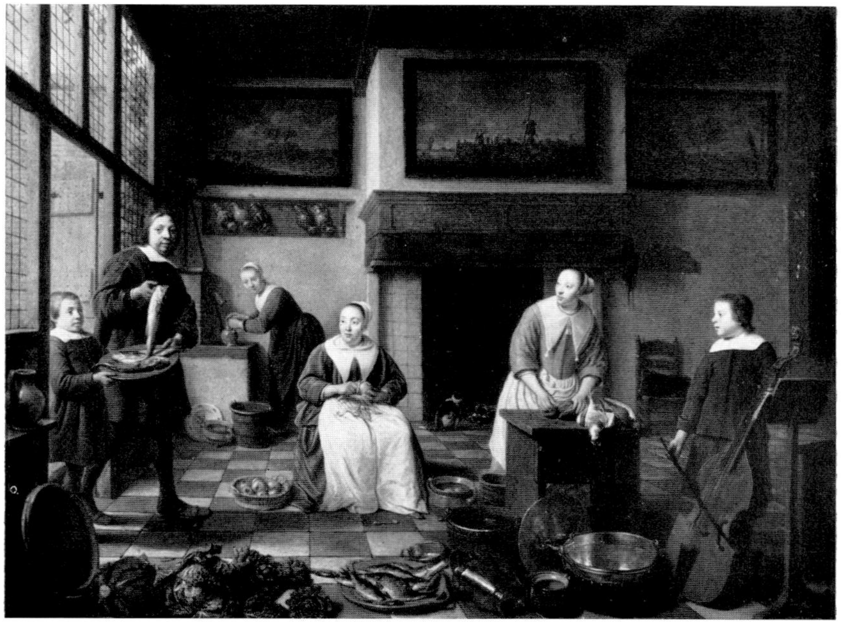

216 TIBOUT REGTERS (1710-1768), *The Family of Jacob van Stamhorst*, 1754. Aerdenhout, collection of the Misses Bierens de Haan (see p. 67).

217 LOUIS-FRANÇOIS-GÉRARD VAN DER PUYL (1750-1824), *The Family of Nicolaas Hartingh*, 1780. Rotterdam, collection of Mevrouw S. A. Verbrugge-Mees (see p. 68).

218 GAWEN HAMILTON (1698-1737), *The Earl of Strafford and his Family*. Ottawa, National Gallery of Canada (see p. 69, note).

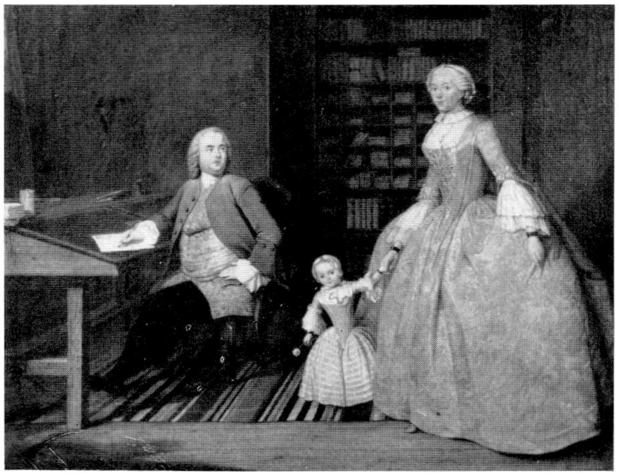

216

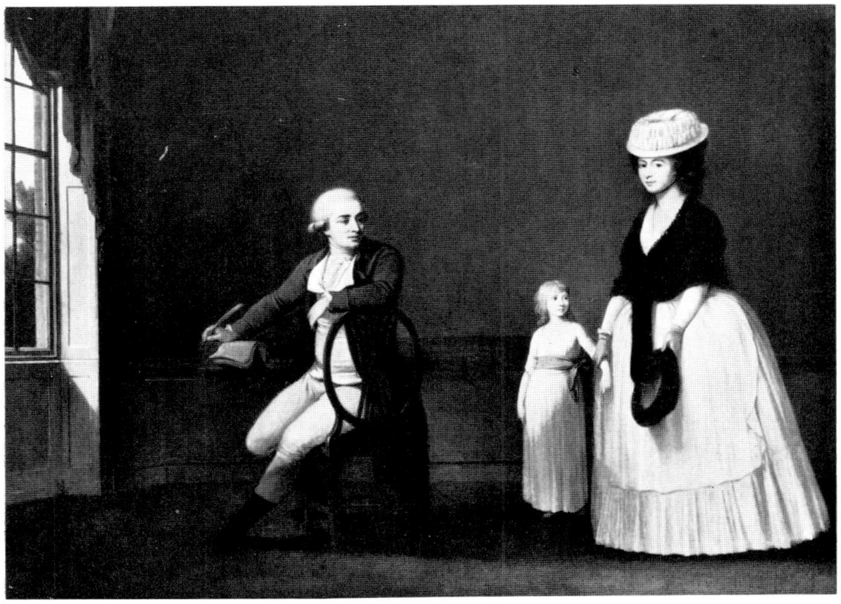

214

217

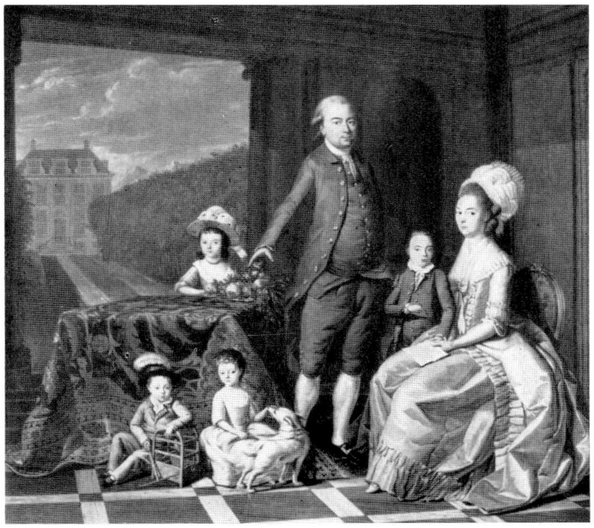

218

215

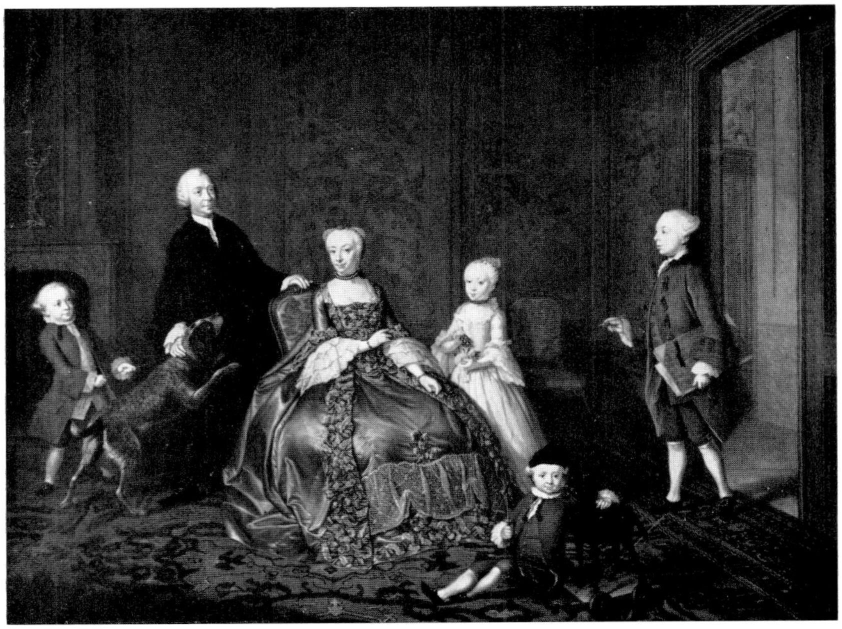

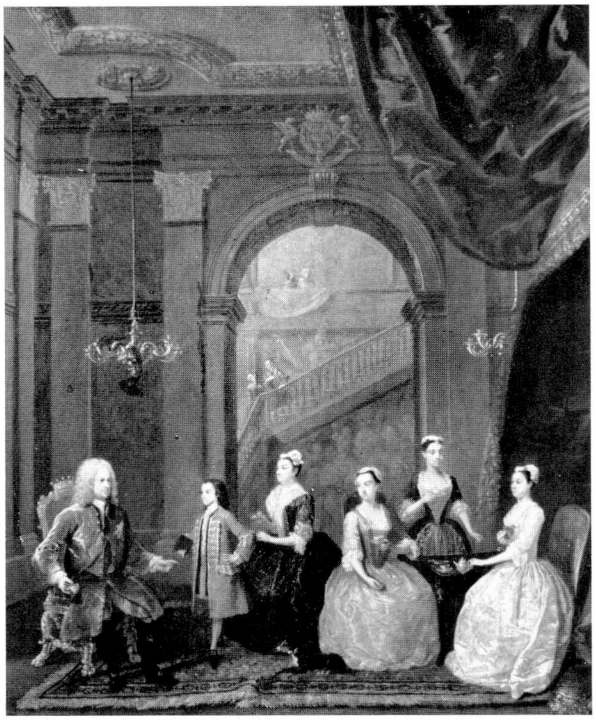

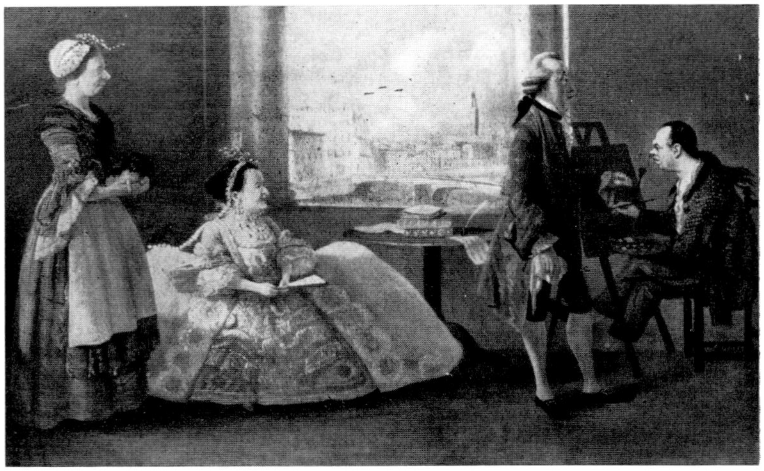

221

222

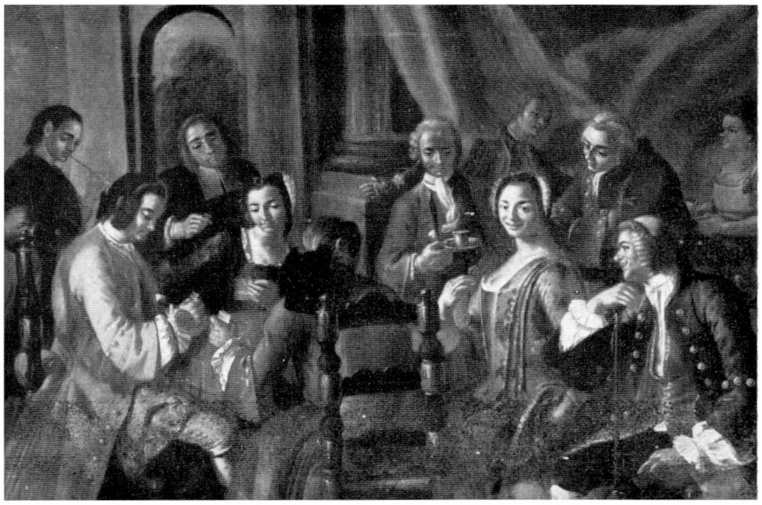

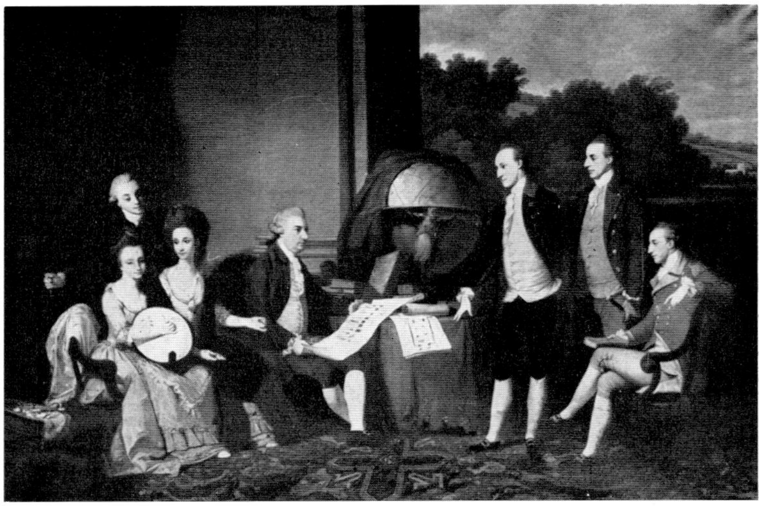

219

220

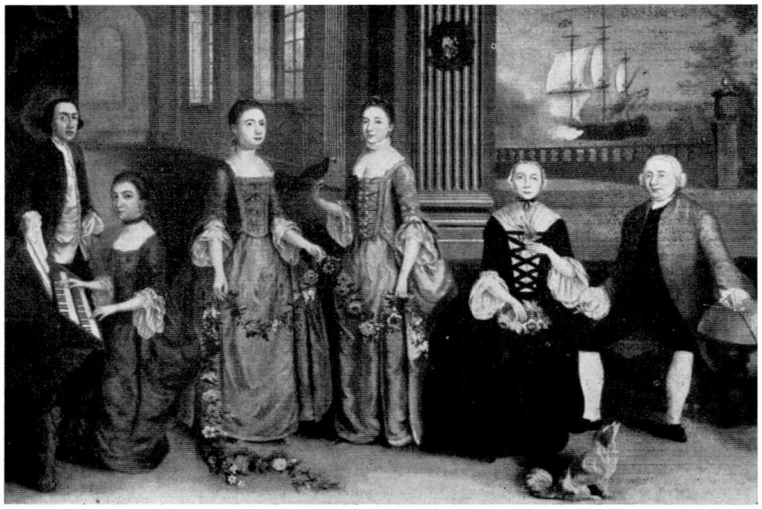

219 JOHN HAMILTON MORTIMER (c. 1741-1779), *The Tyrwhitt Drake Family at Shardeloes* (Buckinghamshire). Present location unknown; formerly the property of Captain T. Tyrwhitt Drake. Photo Witt Library, Courtauld Institute of Art (see p. 71).

220 ANONYMOUS (attr. to ARTHUR DEVIS), *The Putnam Family*. London, M. Knoedler & Co.; photo Witt Library, Courtauld Institute of Art (see p. 71).

221 THOMAS PATCH (c. 1720-1782), *The Duke of Roxburghe and Miss Mendes*, c. 1760. Bishopfield House, Bawtry, Doncaster (Yorkshire), collection of Viscountess Galway (see p. 71).

222 GIUSEPPE BONITO (1707-1789), *Family Group*. Present location unknown (see p. 72).

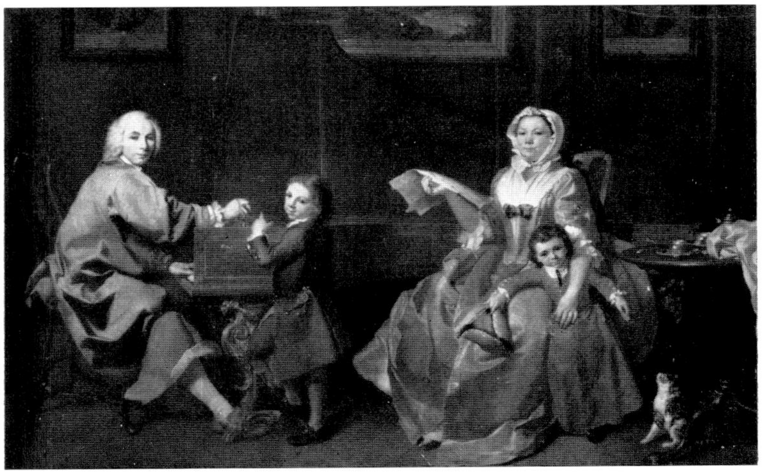

223

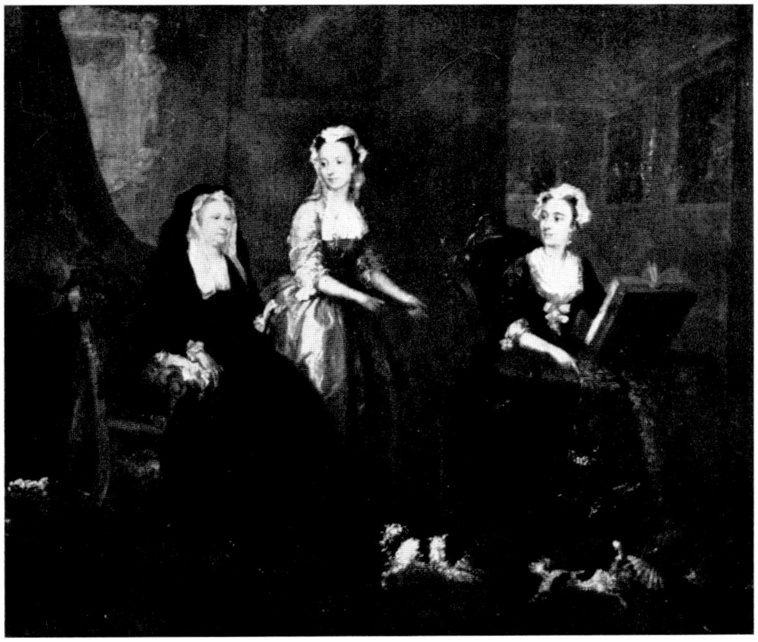

225

224

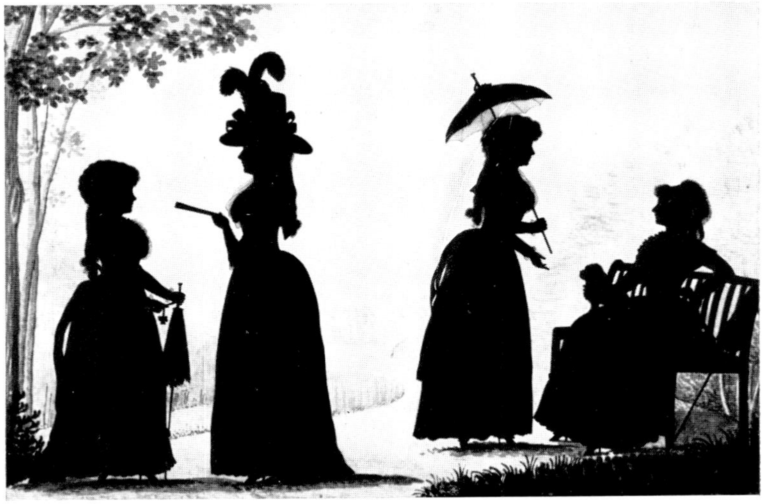

226

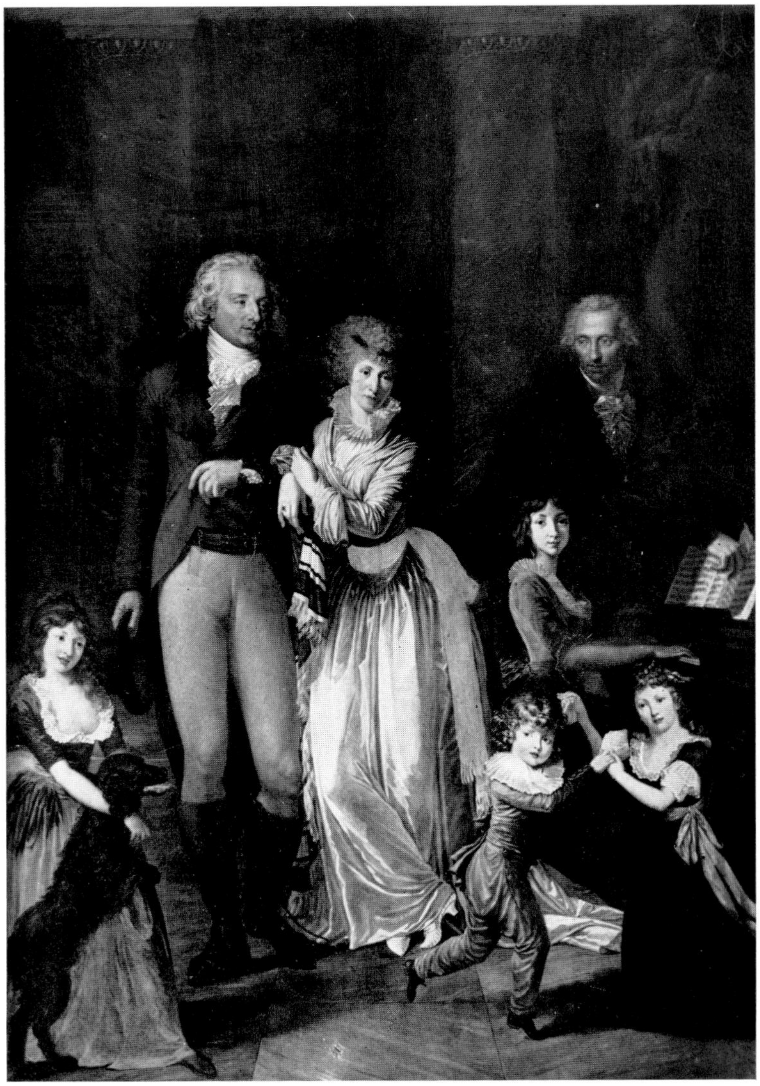

223 ANONYMOUS (attr. to HOGARTH), *Burckhardt Tschudi with his Wife and Two Children*, c. 1745. London, collection of Capt. Evelyn Broadwood, M. C. (see p. 75).
224 ANONYMOUS SILHOUETTE ARTIST (end of the 18th century), *The Grand Duchess Amalia* (1739-1807) *with her Retinue in the Park at Weimar*. Weimar, Goethe-National-museum (see p. 72).
225 WILLIAM HOGARTH (1697-1764), *The Broken Fan*. Formerly in the collection of Lord Northbrook (1936); photo Witt Library, Courtauld Institute of Art (see p. 69).
226 FRÉDÉRIC JEAN-BAPTISTE DESMARAIS (1756-1813), *The Roncioni Family*, 1797. Molina di Quosa (Pisa), Villa Roncioni (see p. 75).

227 JEAN-AUGUSTE-DOMINIQUE INGRES (1780-1867), *The Family of Lucien Bonaparte*, 1815. Cambridge (Mass.), Fogg Art Museum (see p. 75).

228 JEAN-AUGUSTE-DOMINIQUE INGRES (1780-1867), *The Stamaty Family*, 1818. Paris, Louvre (see p. 75).

229 GIUSEPPE BEZZUOLI (1784-1855), *The Niccolini Family*. Milan, art market (see pp. 75 and 86).

230 ANONYMOUS (early 19th century), *A Neapolitan Family*, 1819. Rome, private collection (see p. 75).

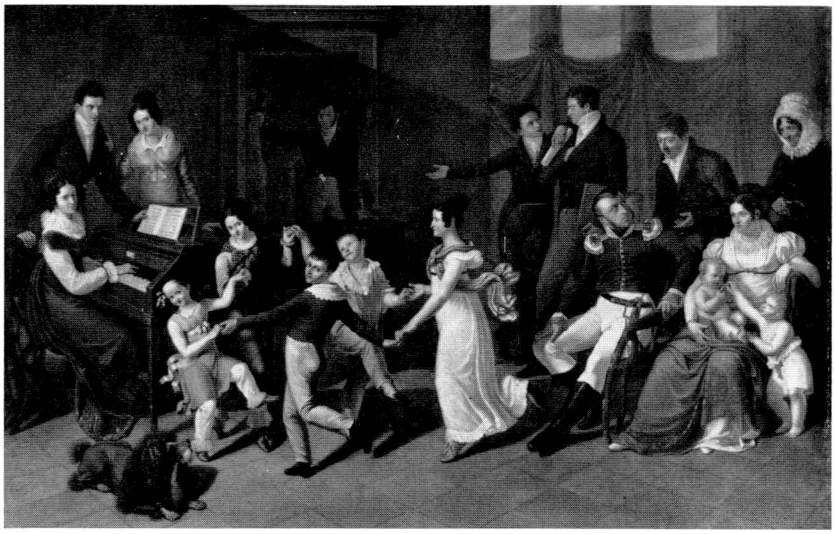

229

230

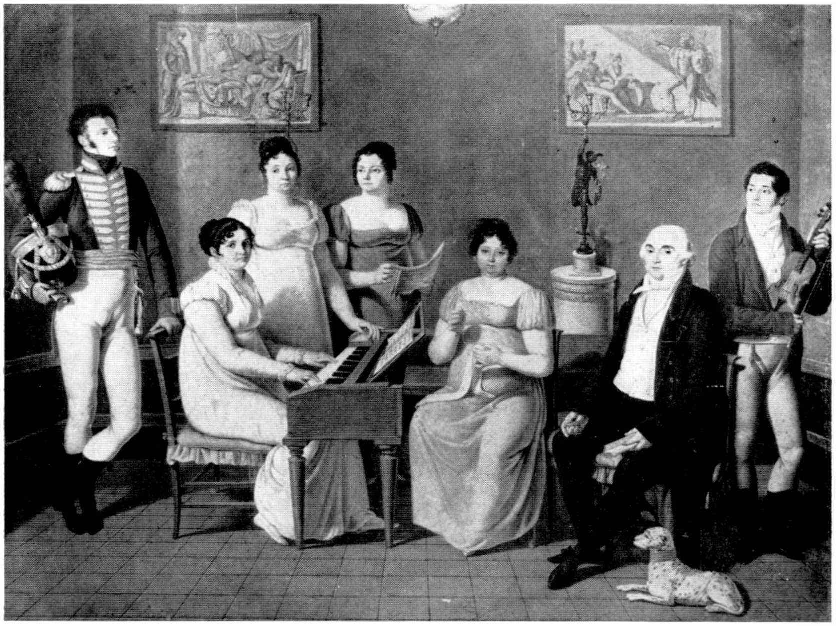

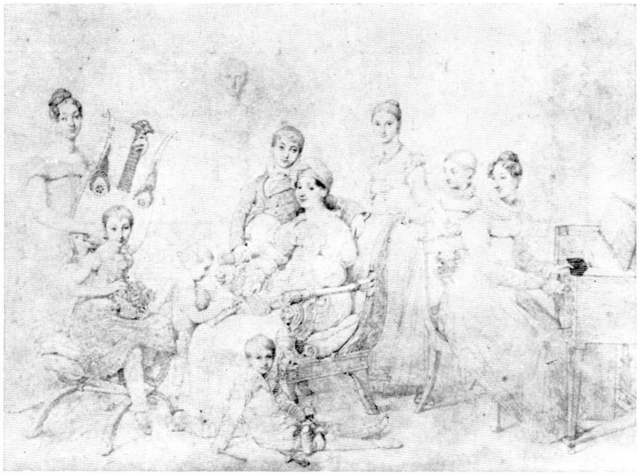

227

228

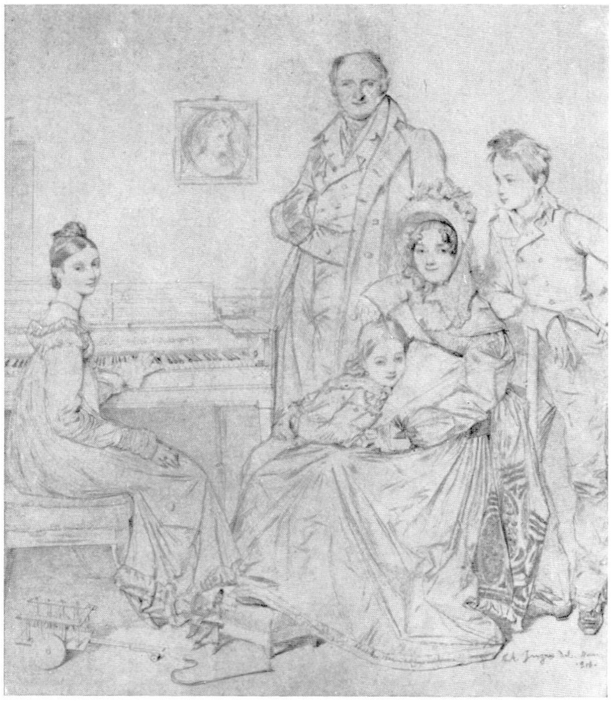

231

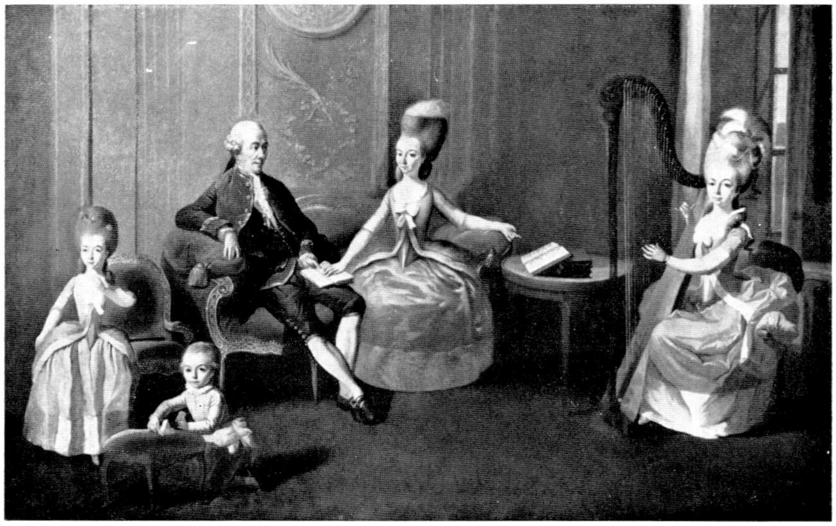

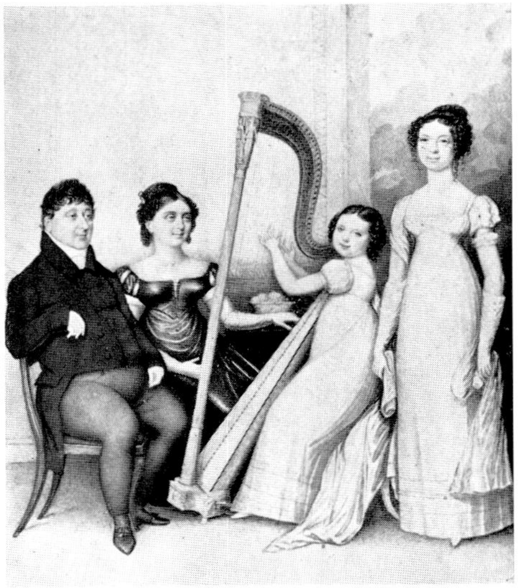

232

233

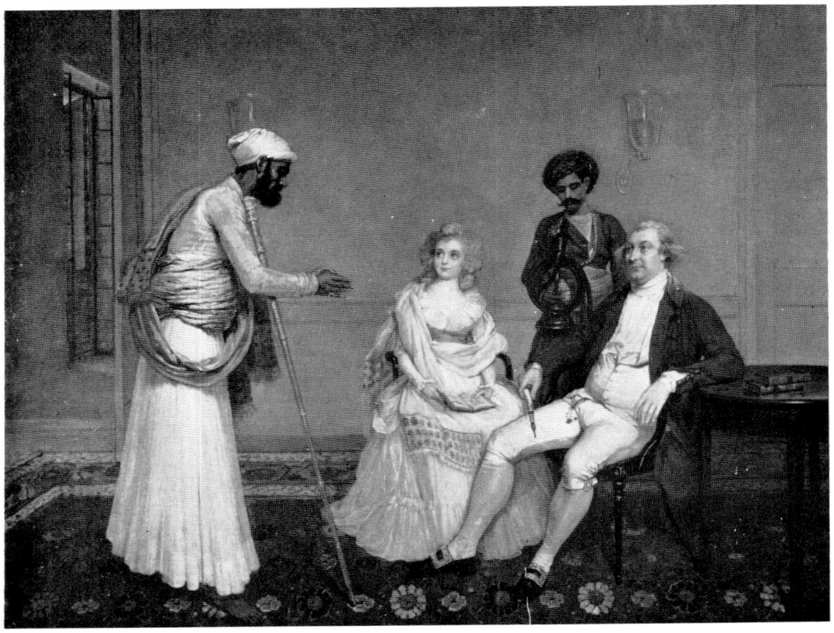

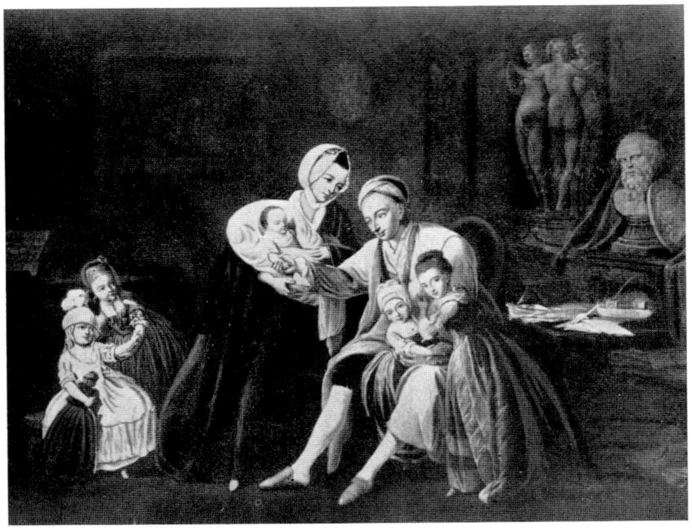

234

235

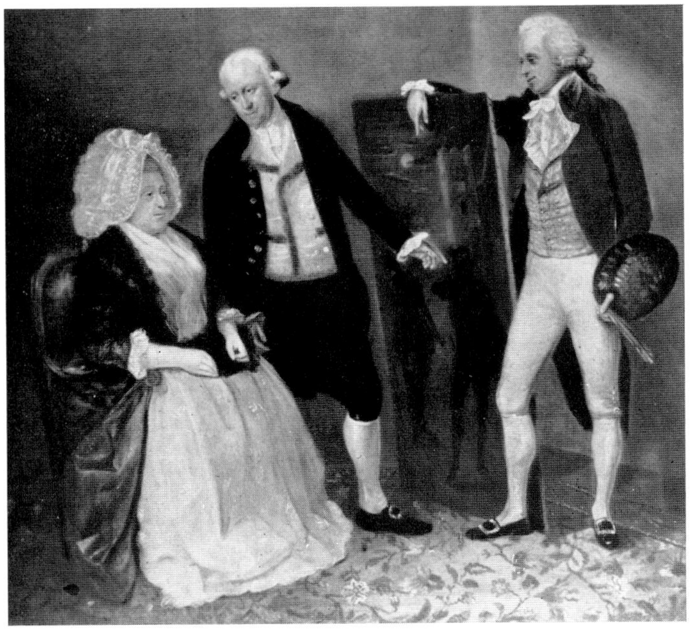

231 FRENCH SCHOOL (18th century), *Count Vaudeuil and his Family*. Paris, collection of M. Jacques Veysset (see p. 75).

232 MEMBER OF THE OBERLIN FAMILY (19th century), *The Musician G. Mazzinghi and his Family*. Rome, private collection (see p. 75).

233 JOHANN ZOFFANY (1734/5-1810), *Justice Heatly of the East India Company with his Sister*, 1783-9. Springfield (Mass.), Museum of Art (see p. 78).

234 GEORG MELCHIOR KRAUS (1737-1806), *The Poet Wieland in the Bosom of his Family*, c. 1775. Weimar, Landesbibliothek (see p. 78).

235 WILLIAM DUNLAP (1766-1839), *The Dunlap Family*, 1788. New York, New York Historical Society (see p. 78).

236 JOHN PARTRIDGE (1790-1872), *Sir George Sitwell and his Family*, c. 1828. Renishaw Hall (Derbyshire), collection of Mr. Reresby Sitwell (see p. 80).

237 ALEXANDRE-ÉVARISTE FRAGONARD (1783-1850), *Napoleon, Marie-Louise, and the King of Rome*. Paris, collection of Count Roger Walewski (see p. 82).

238 FRÉDÉRIC JEAN-BAPTISTE DESMARAIS (1756-1813), *Family Group*. Rome, private collection (see p. 80).

239 ERASTUS SALISBURY FIELD (1805-1900), *The Family of Joseph Moore*, c. 1830. Boston, Museum of Fine Arts (M. and M. Karolik Collection) (see p. 82).

240 ABRAHAM VAN STRIJ (1753-1826), *The Family of Hendrik Weymans*, 1816. Leersum, collection of Mevrouw S. Stratenus-van Brakel (see p. 82).

241 ADRIAAN DE LELIE (1755-1820), *Jan de Bosch in his Cabinet*, 1800. Amsterdam (?), property of the heirs of Mevrouw W. Cnoop Koopmans-Wolterbeek (see p. 82).

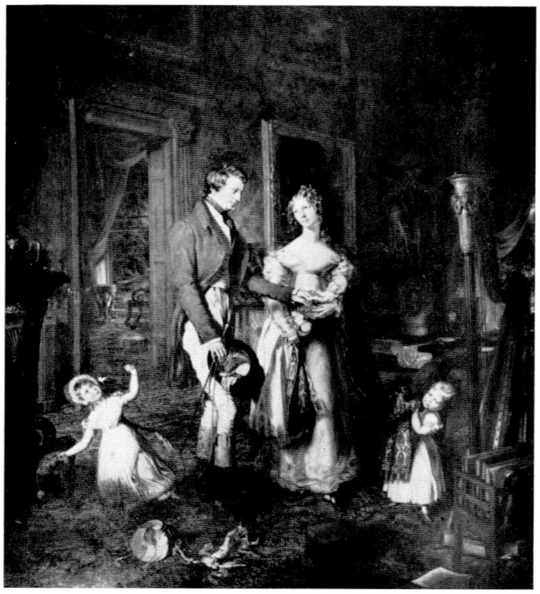

236

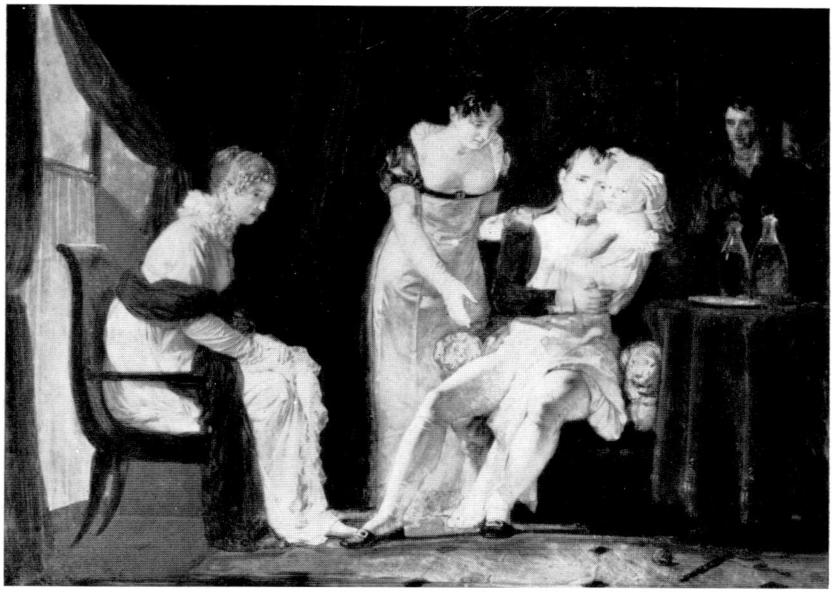

237

238

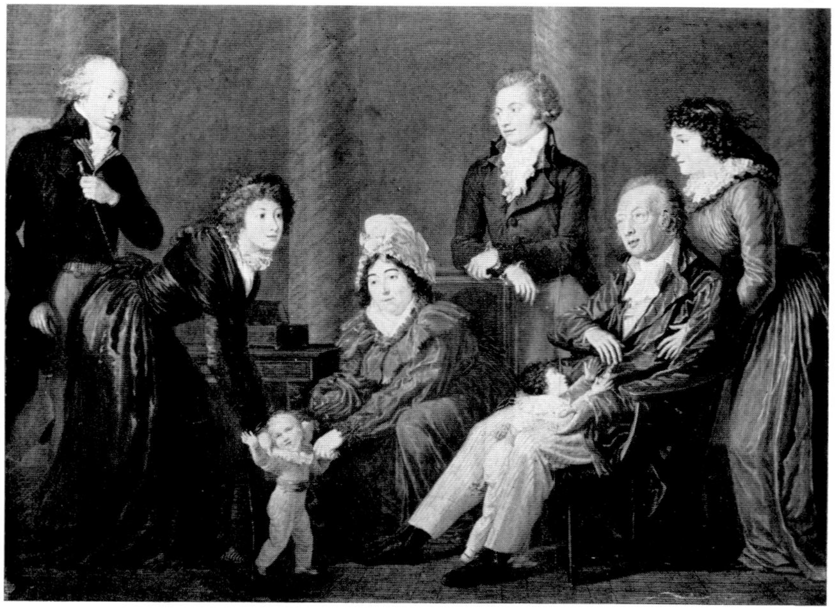

242 PIETER CHRISTOFFEL WONDER (1777-1852), *The Family of Willem Jacob de Bruyn de Neve*, 1813. Haarlem, collection of Mr. P. C. Vis (see p. 82).

243 ADRIAAN DE LELIE (1755-1820), *The Family of the Silversmith Adrianus Bonebakker*. Bussum, collection of W. C. Bonebakker (see p. 82).

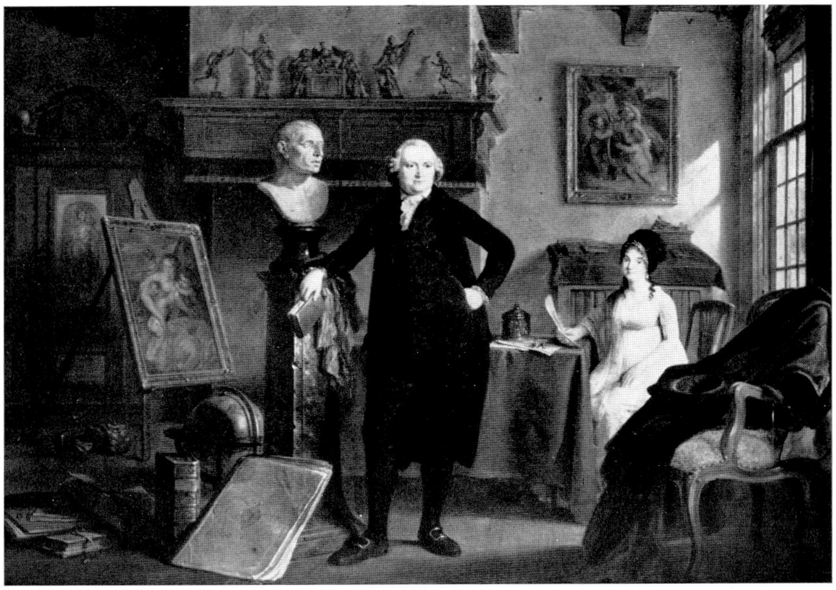

241

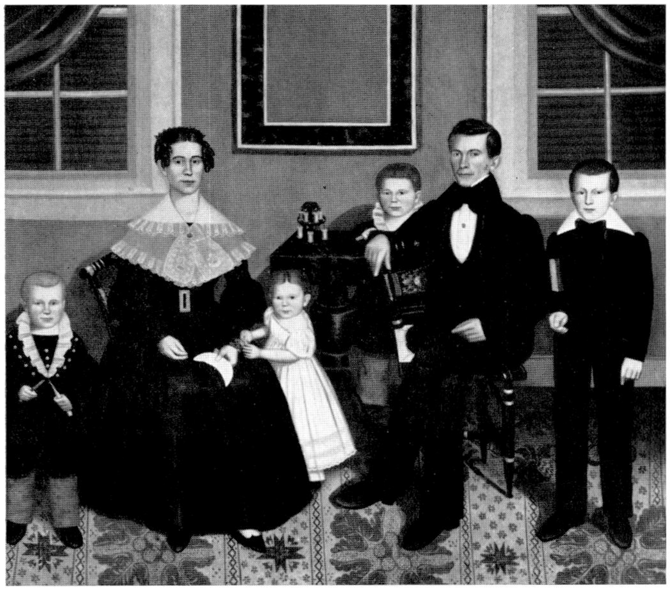

239

240

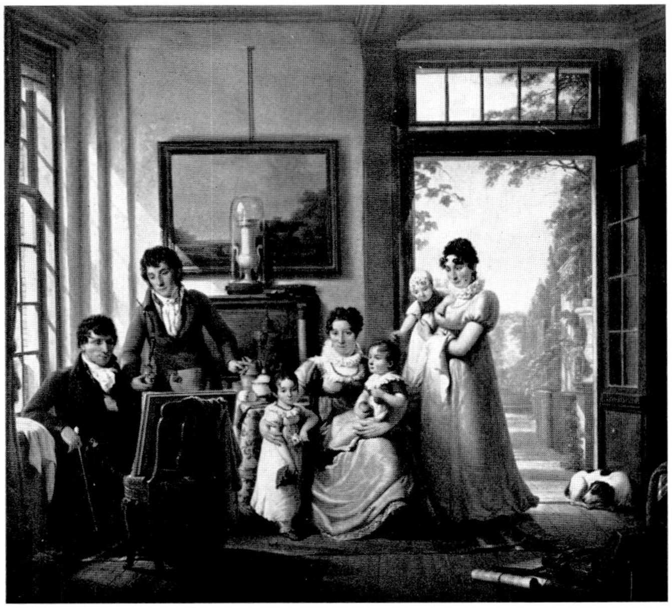

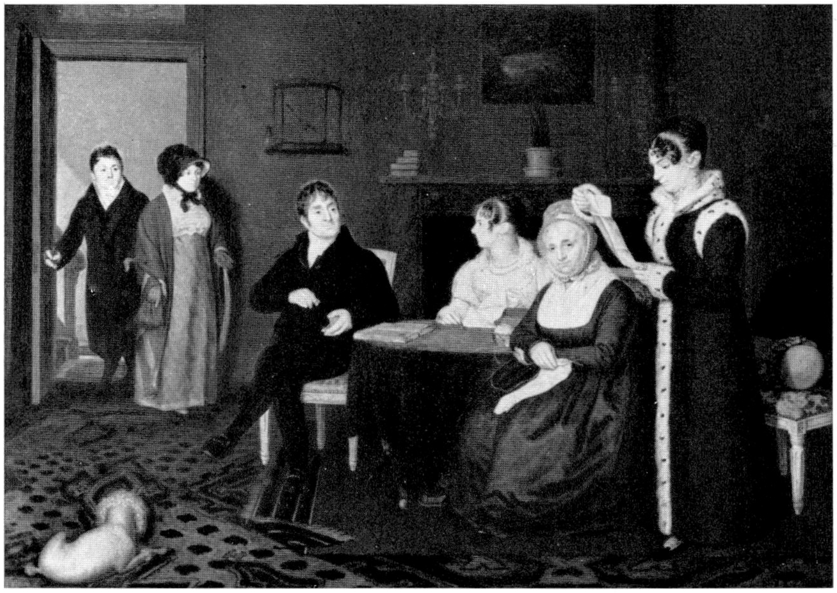

242

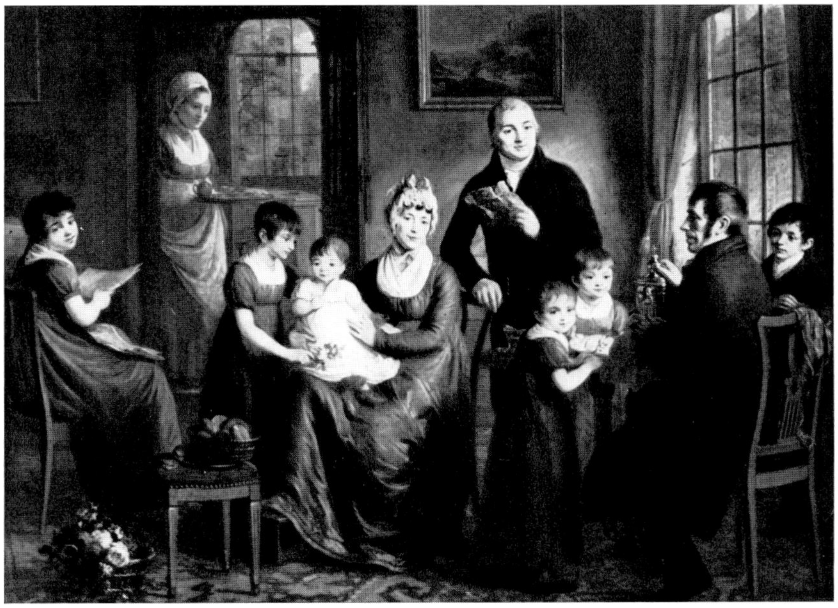

243

244 ITALIAN SCHOOL (monogram AF), *Family Portrait*, c. 1845. Rome, private collection (see pp. 86-87).

245 LOUIS-PIERRE SPINDLER (1800-1889), *Interior of Lansdowne House*. Rome, private collection (see p. 82).

246 JOHN B. WHITTAKER (1836/7-?), *The Lesson (Mr. and Mrs. John Ewart Tousey and their Children)*, 1869. New York (?), collection of Mrs. Paul E. Vernon (see p. 87).

248 EDUARD MAGNUS (1799-1872), *The Family of the Banker von Magnus*, c. 1845. Berlin, private collection (see p. 92).

249 JOHN KOCH (1910-), *The Edgar W. Garbisch Family*, 1955. Palm Beach (Florida), collection of Mrs. Edgar W. Garbisch (see p. 92).

250 ADOLPHE FÉLIX CALS (1810-1880), *Count Doria and his Children in the Drawing-room at Orrouy*. Present location unknown; photo courtesy of the Galerie Charpentier, Paris (see p. 92).

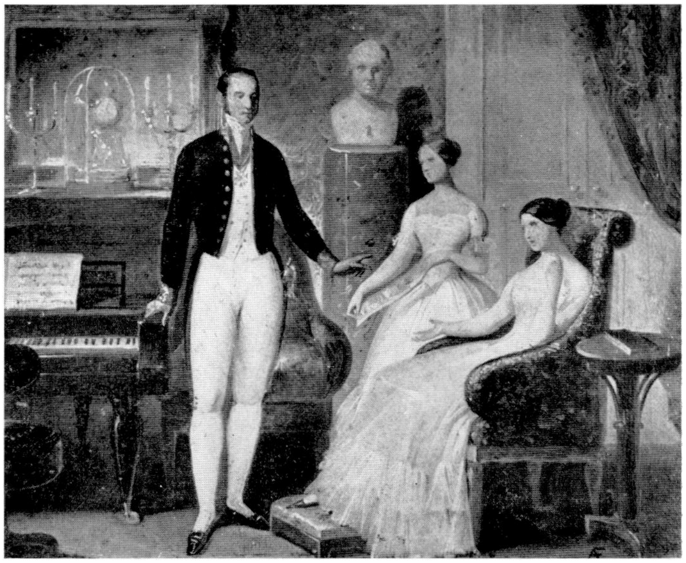

244

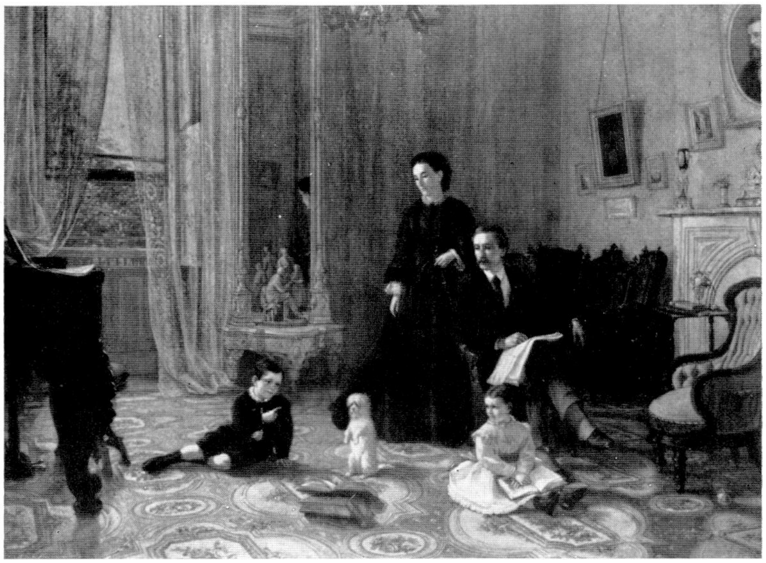

246

245

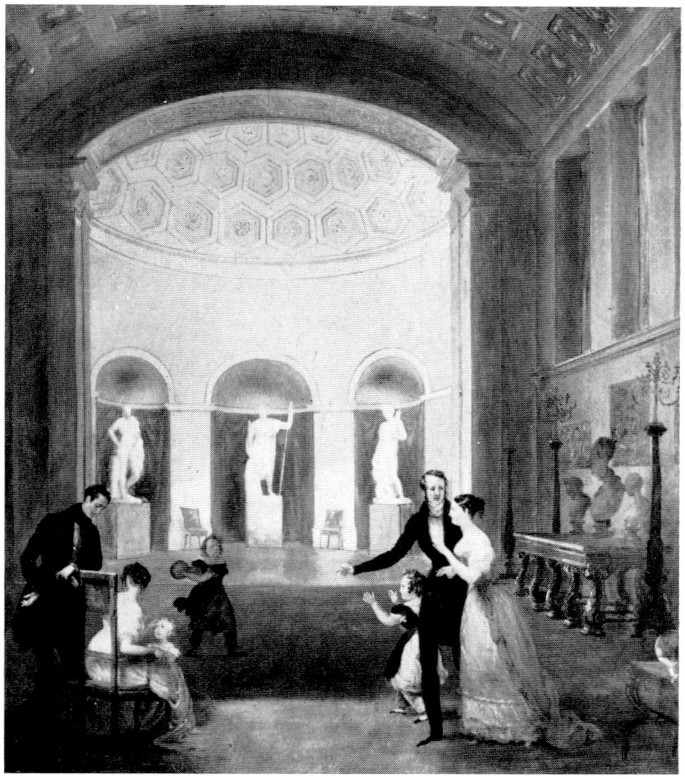

247

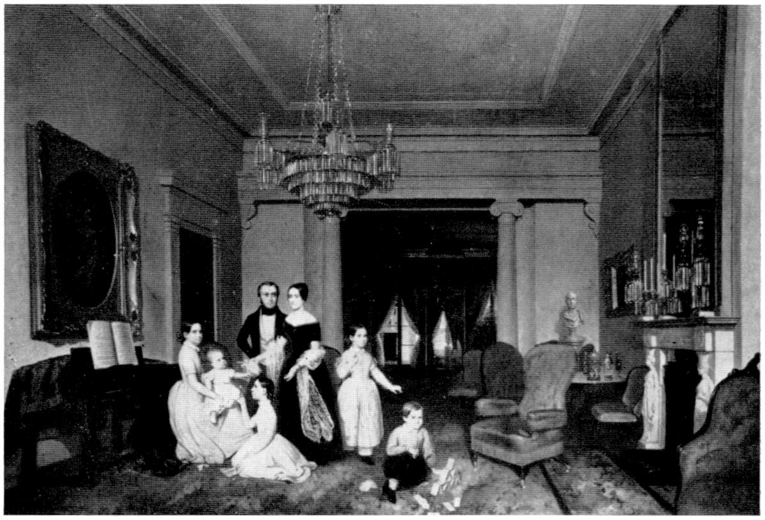

247 FRANZ H. HEINRICH (fl. c. 1845-1855), *The Ernest Fiedler Family*, 1847. New York, collection of Mrs. William L. Rich (see p. 87).

251 CONSTANT LE BRETON (1895-?), *Family Reunion*. Present location unknown; photo courtesy of the Galerie Charpentier, Paris (see p. 92).

252 KARL HÜMMEL (1769-1840), *Queen Caroline's Drawing-room at Frohsdorf*. Rome, Spalletti-Trivelli Collection (see p. 92).

253 GIACOMO FAVRETTO (1849-1887), *The Guidini Family*, 1873. Venice, private collection (see p. 92).

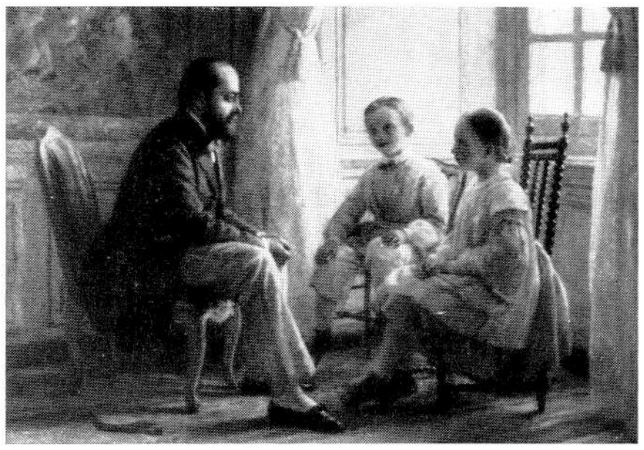

250

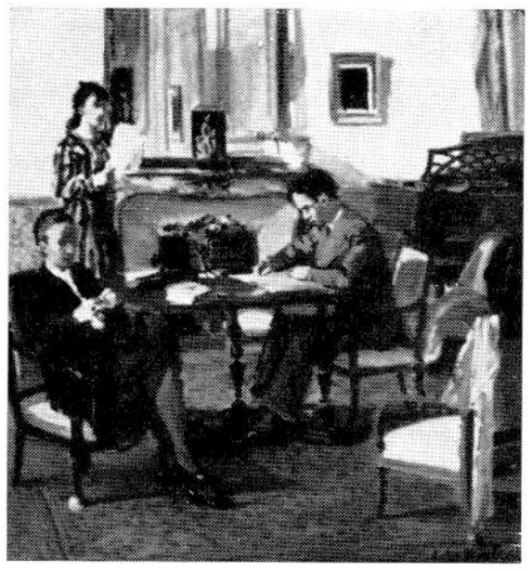

251

252

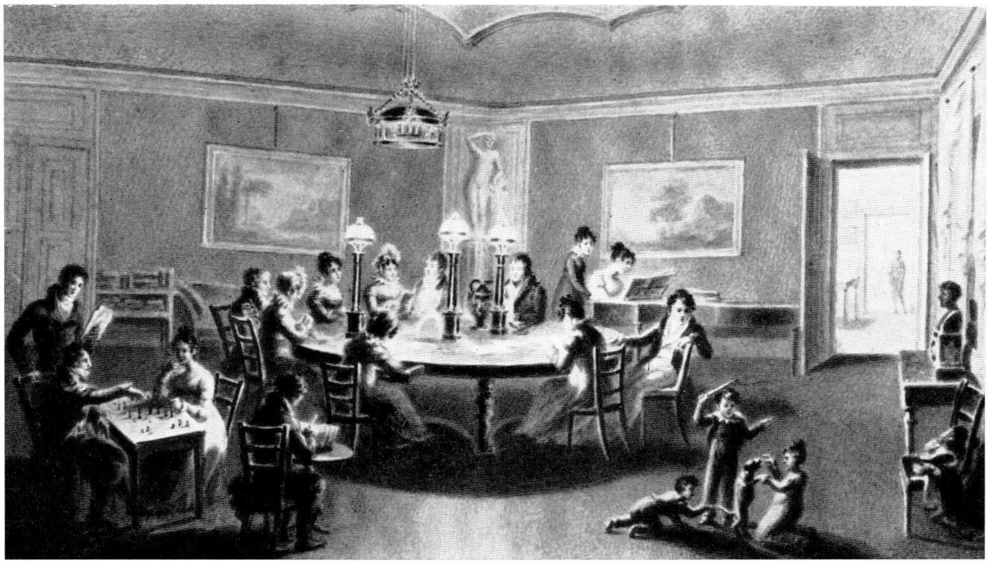

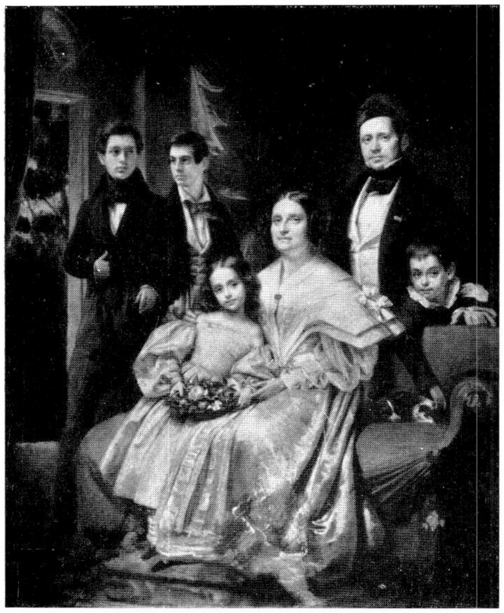

248

249

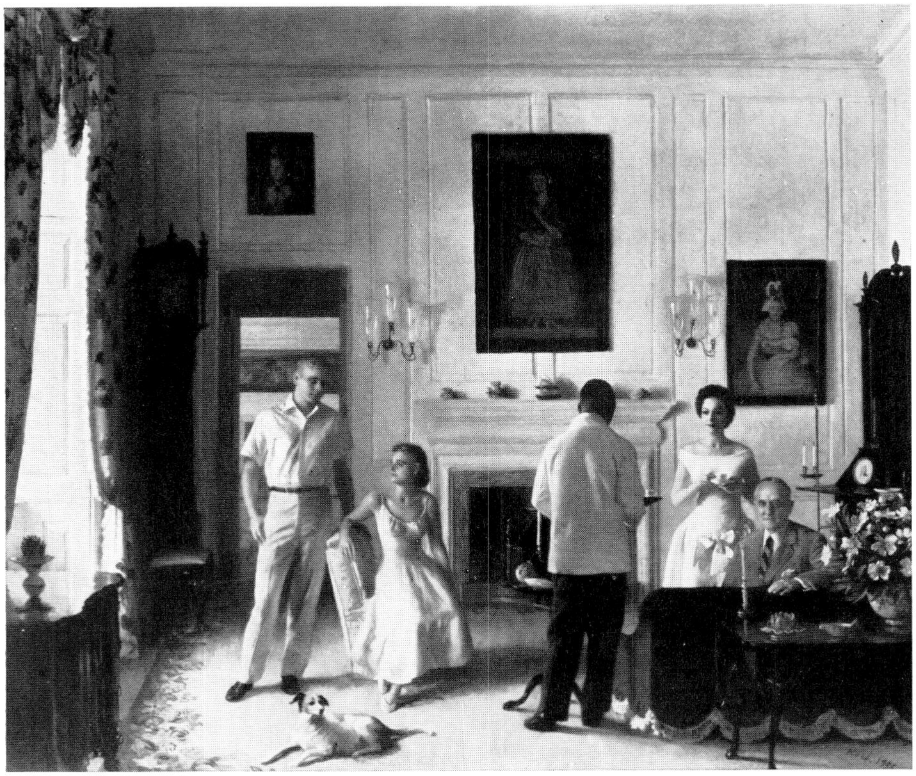

253

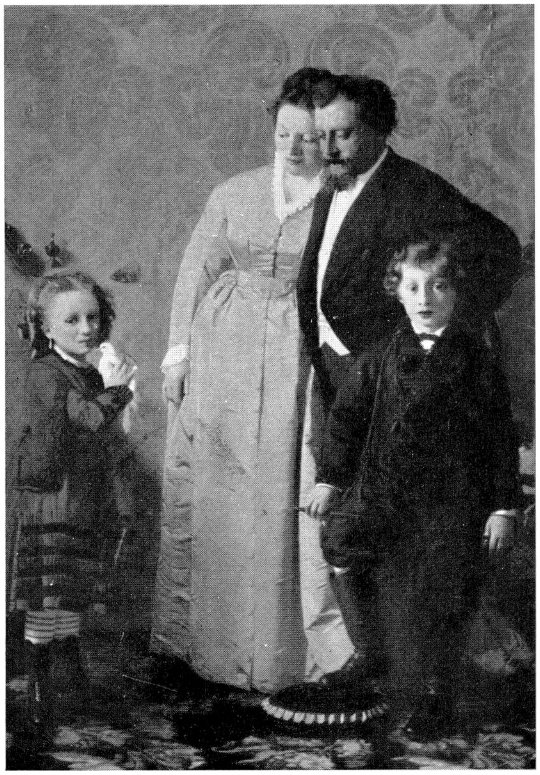

254 LEANDRO BASSANO (1557-1622), *Family Group*, before 1582. Florence, Uffizi (see p. 97).

255 SCIPIONE PULZONE (before 1550-1598), *The Colonna Family*, 1581. Rome, Colonna Gallery (see p. 97).

256 CORNELIS ANTHONISZ. (or TEUNISSEN) (c. 1499- c. 1557), *Banquet of the Civic Guard (the 'Braspenningmaaltijd')*, 1533. Amsterdam, Rijksmuseum (see p. 97).

257 MAARTEN VAN HEEMSKERCK (1498-1574), *Family Group*. Cassel, Museum (see pp. 60 and 97).

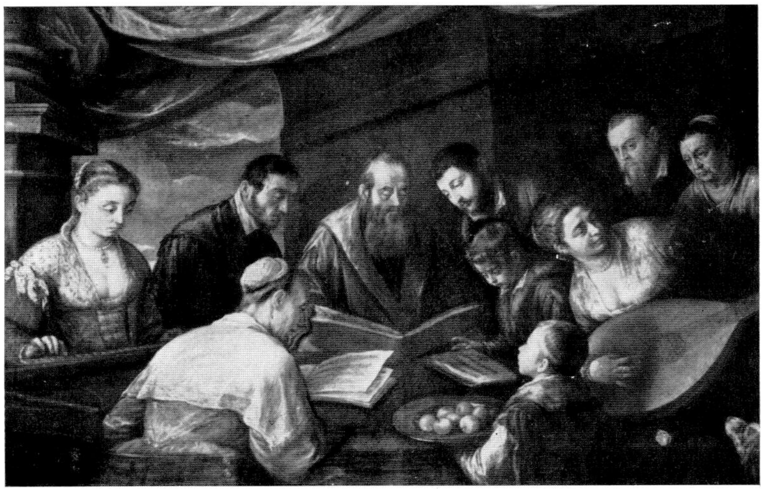

254

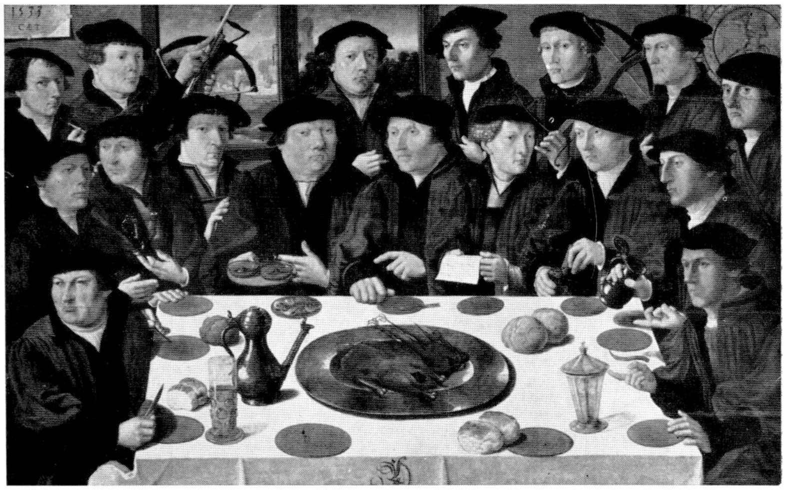

256

255

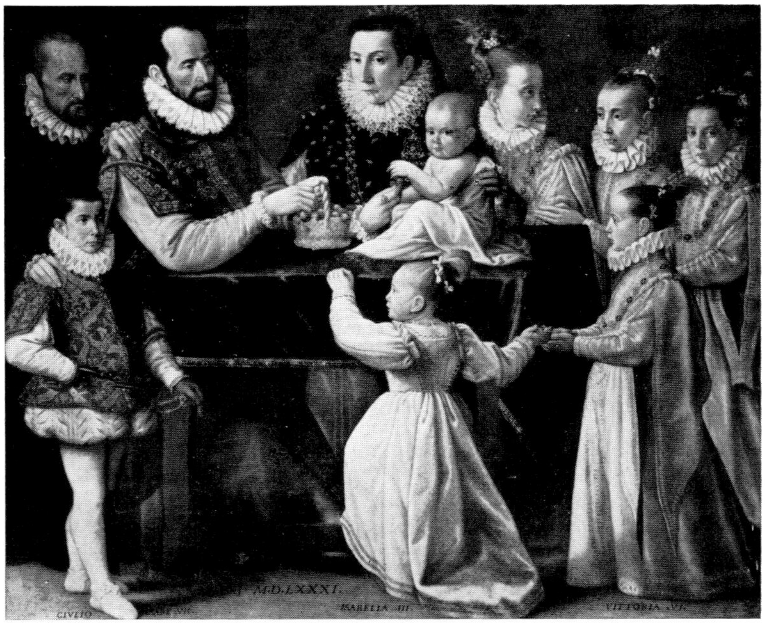

257

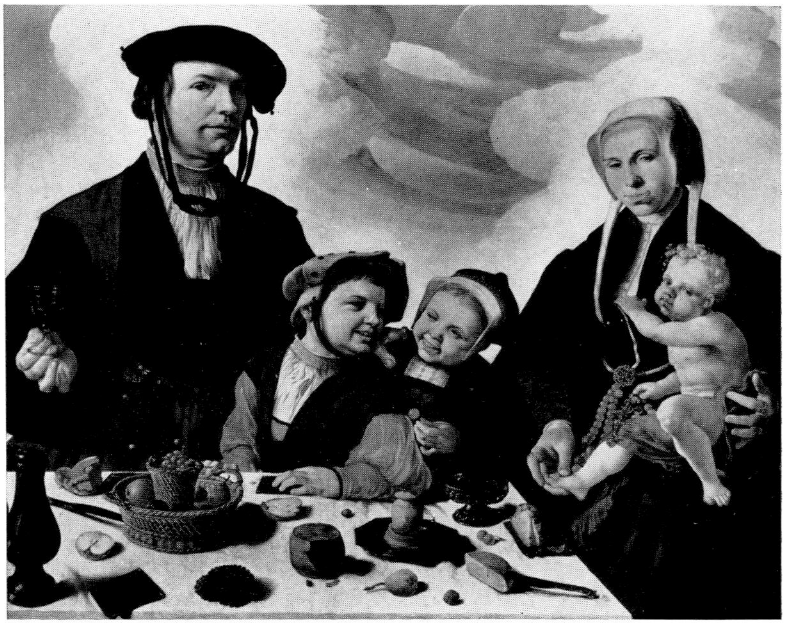

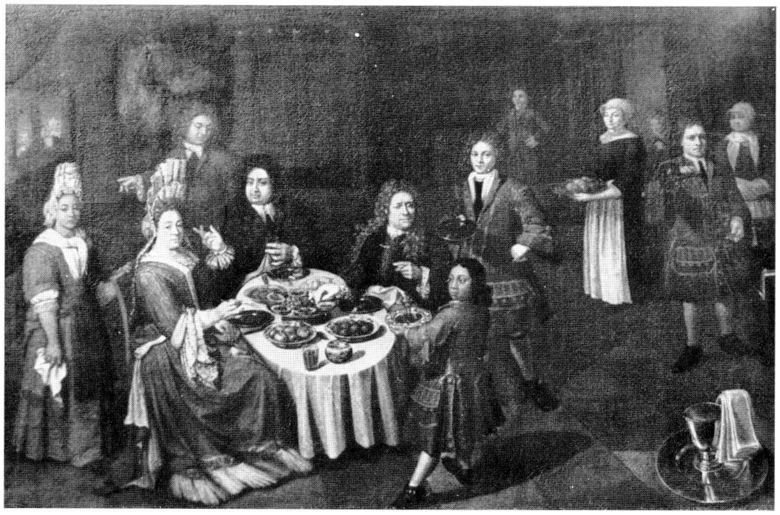

258

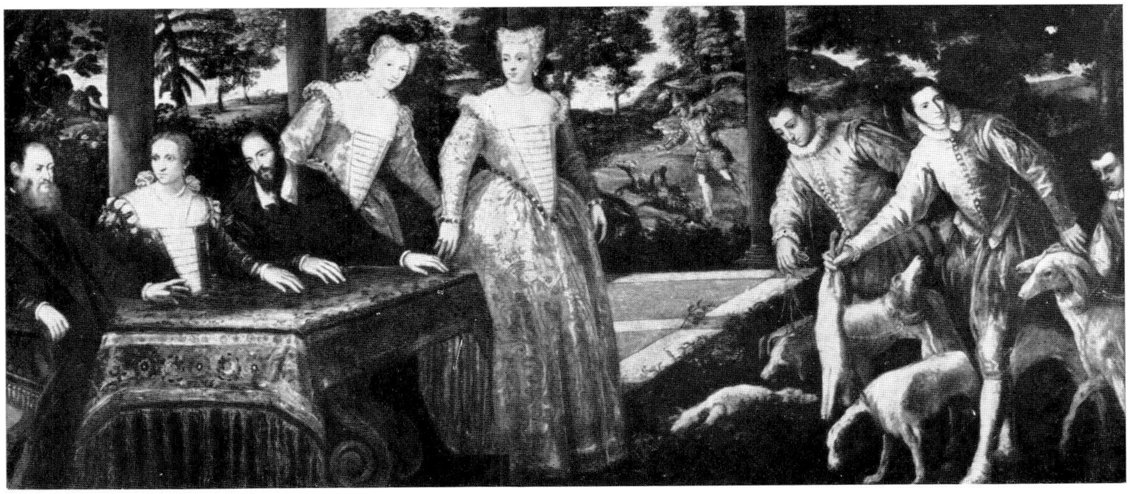

259

260

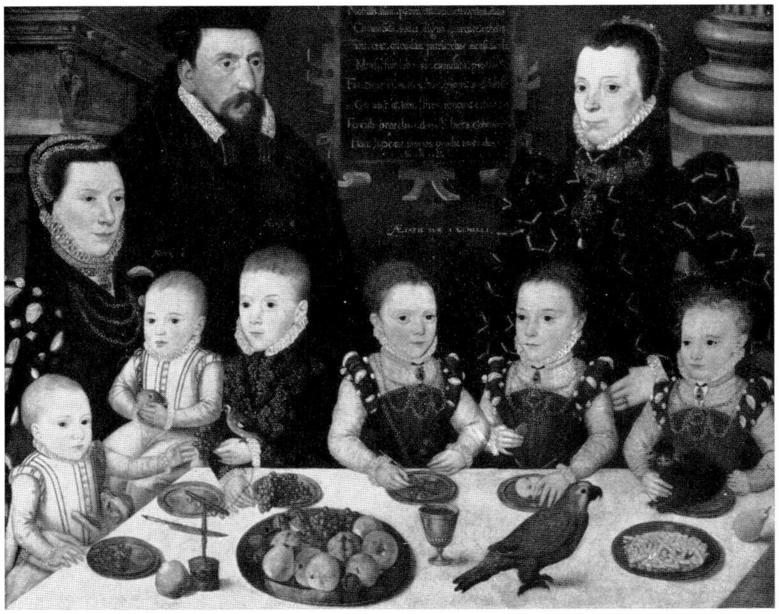

258 GERARD WIGMANA (1673-1741), *A Colonial Family*, 1697. Dokkum, Raadhuis (see p. 97).

259 TINTORETTO (1519-1594), *The Pellegrini Family*. Florence, collection of Marchese Niccolò Antinori (see p. 97).

260 HANS EWORTH (EWOUTS) (second half of the 16th century), *William Brooke, Lord Cobham, and his Family*, 1567. Longleat (Wiltshire), collection of the Marquess of Bath (see p. 97).

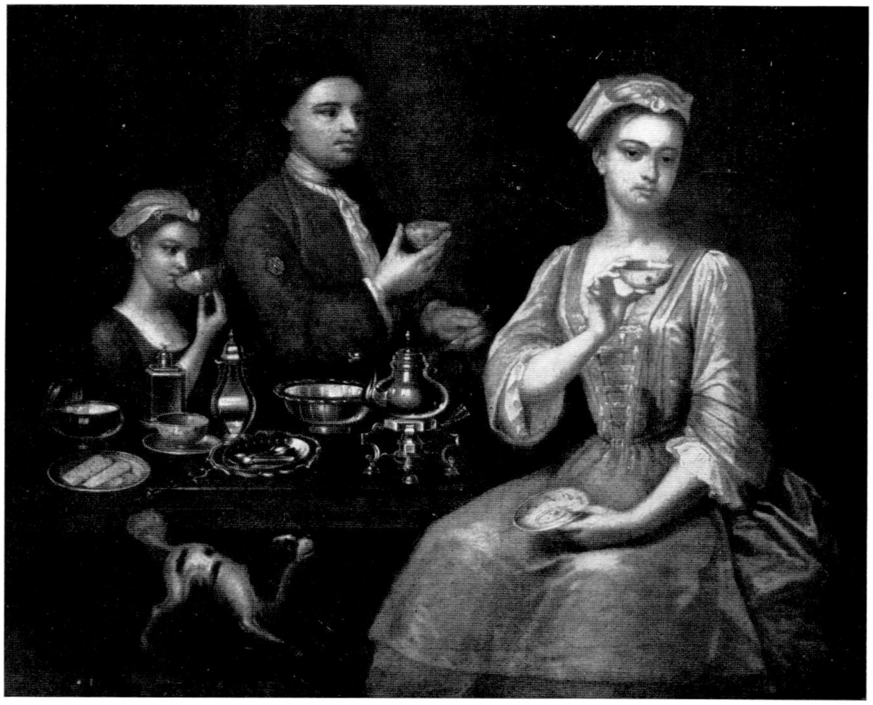

262

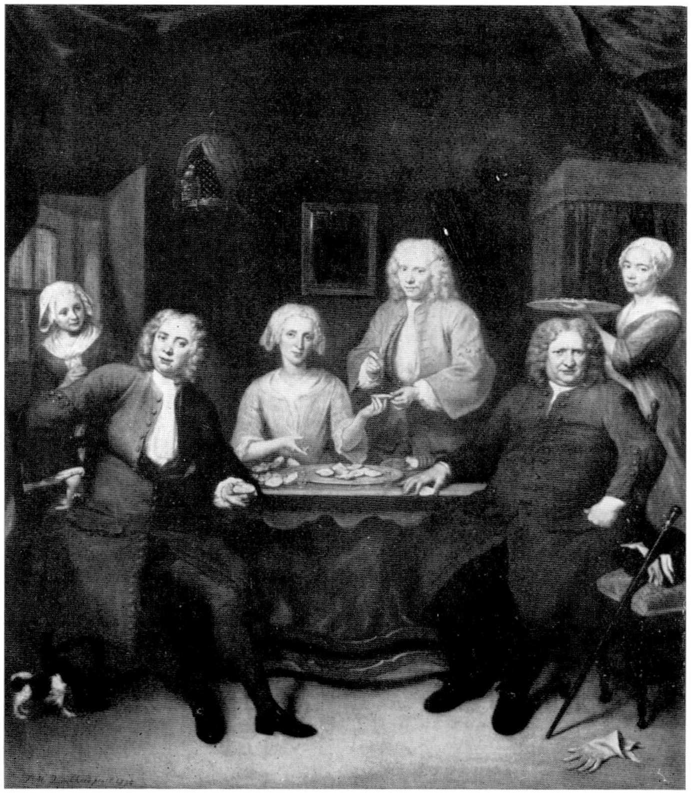

261

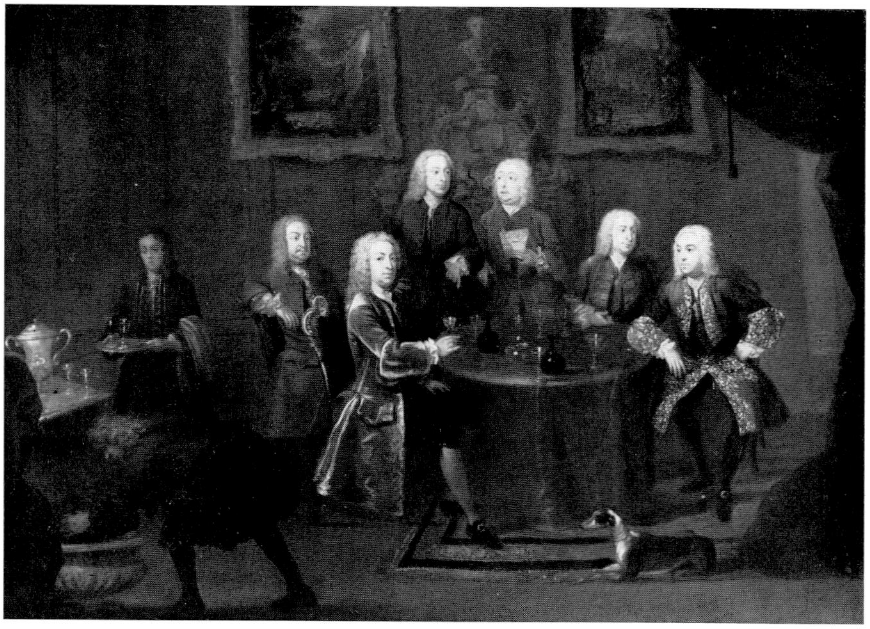

263

261 JAN MAURITS QUINKHARD (1688-1772), *A Baptist Family*, 1735. Vorden, collection of Dr. A. Staring (see p. 97).

262 ANONYMOUS (first half of the 18th century), *A Family Taking Tea*. London, Victoria and Albert Museum (see p. 104).

263 GAWEN HAMILTON (1698-1737), *The Brothers Clarke of Swakeleys and Friends*, c. 1730. Washington, D. C., collection of Mr. and Mrs. Paul Mellon (see p. 99).

264 JOHN THOMAS SETON (fl. 1761-1806), *William Fullerton and Captain Lowis Taking Wine*, 1773. Edinburgh, National Gallery of Scotland (see p. 102).

265 JAN MAURITS QUINKHARD (1688-1772), *An Orangist Family*, 1746. England, private collection (see p. 97).

266 BENJAMIN FERRERS (d. 1732), *Sir Thomas Saunders Sebright, Bart., Sir John Bland, Bart., and Two Other Gentlemen Smoking and Drinking*. Godmersham Park, Canterbury (Kent), collection of Mr. and Mrs. Robert Tritton (see p. 99).

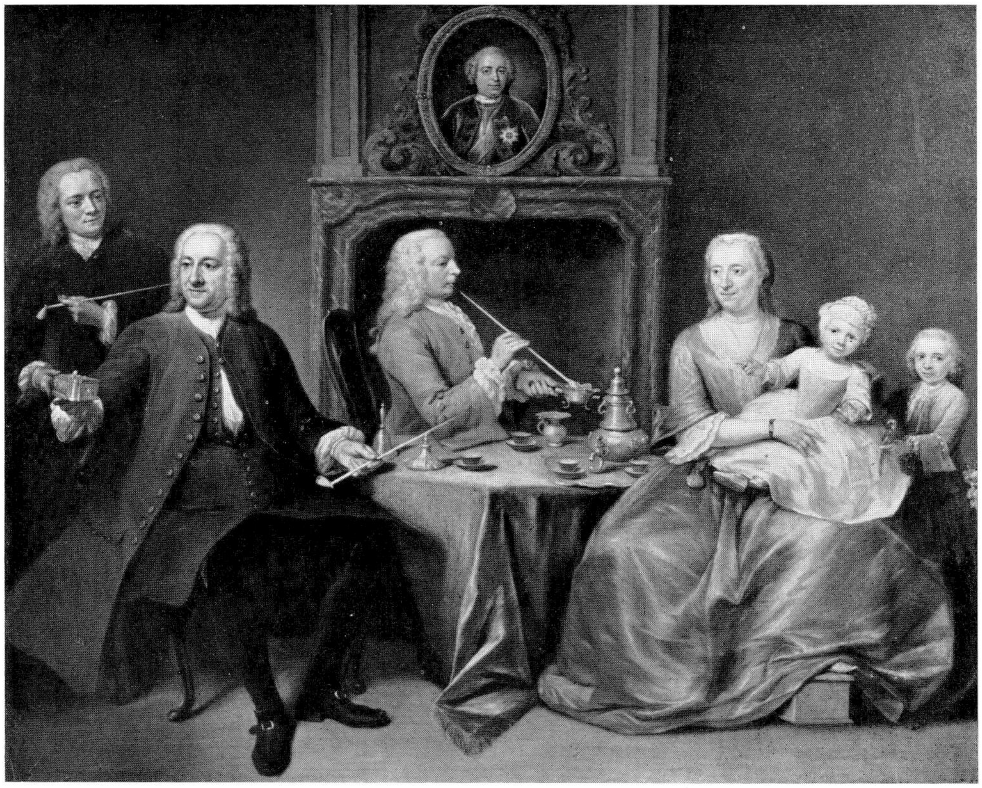

265

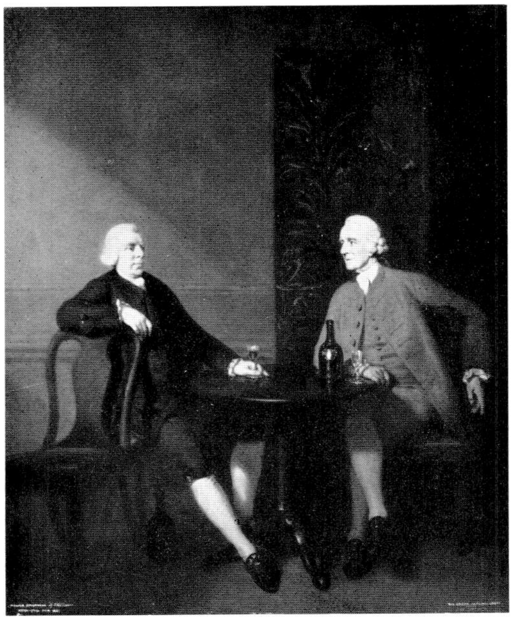

264

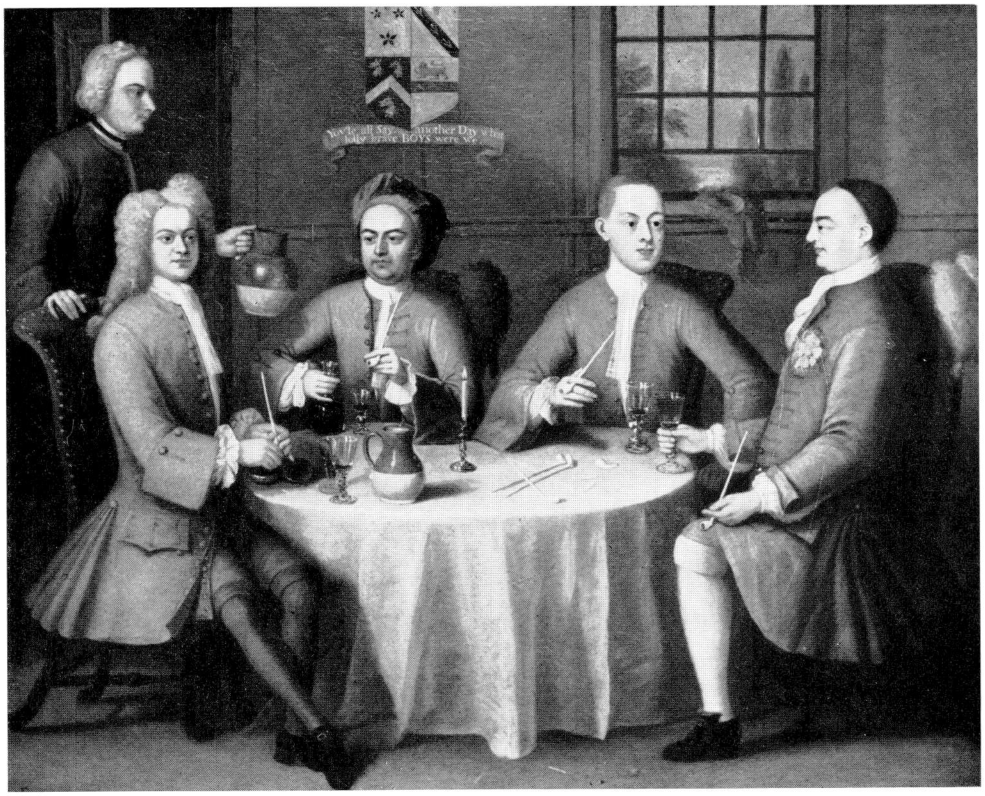

266

267 GONZALES COQUES (1614-1684), *A Father with his Two Daughters.* London, Wallace Collection (see pp. 113 and 211).

268 THEODOOR BOEYERMANS (1620-1678), *The Visit.* Antwerp, Musée Royal des Beaux Arts (see p. 116).

269 JAN JOSEF HOREMANS THE ELDER (1682-1759), *A Family in a Garden*, 1720. London, Christie's sale, 12 July 1957 (see p. 117).

270 WILLIAM JOSEPH WILLIAMS (1759-1823), *William Denning and his Family*, 1772. Bedford (N. Y.), collection of Mr. W. Denning Harvey (see p. 118).

271 JEAN-ANTOINE LAURENT (1763-1833), *Mother and Daughters in a Garden.* Paris, Louvre (see p. 118).

272 BARTHOLOMEUS VAN DER HELST (1613-1670), *A Family Group.* Wareham, collection of Major J.R.O'B. Warde (see p. 121).

273 JOHANNES SENN (1780-1871), *The Danish Royal Family Walking,* c. 1813. Copenhagen, Rosenborg Palace (see p. 121).

274 JOHANN ZOFFANY (1734/5-1810), *David Garrick and his Wife Entertaining Dr. Johnson.* Lambton Castle, collection of the Earl of Durham (see p. 121).

275 JOHANN ZOFFANY (1734/5-1810), *Mr. and Mrs. Garrick at Shakespeare's Temple at Hampton.* Lambton Castle, collection of the Earl of Durham (see p. 121).

276 JOHANN ZOFFANY (1734/5-1810), *Mr. and Mrs. Garrick at Shakespeare's Temple at Hampton* (a variant of the preceding picture). Photo courtesy of Wildenstein Galleries, New York (see p. 121).

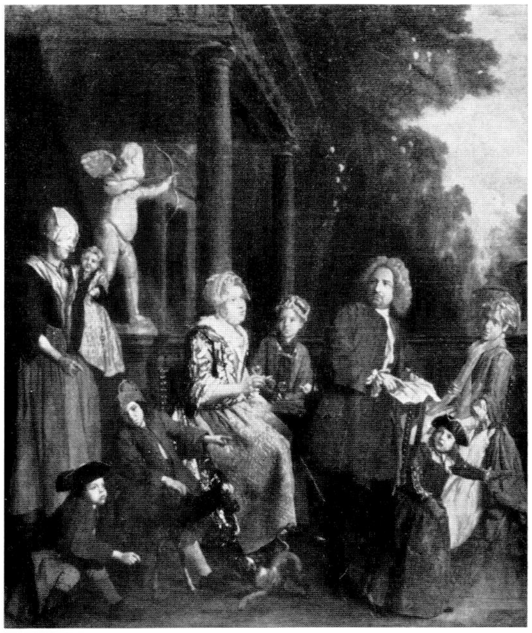

269

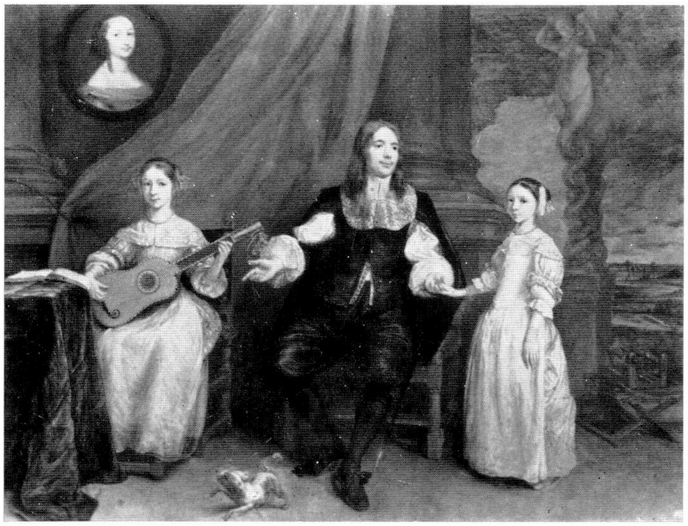

267

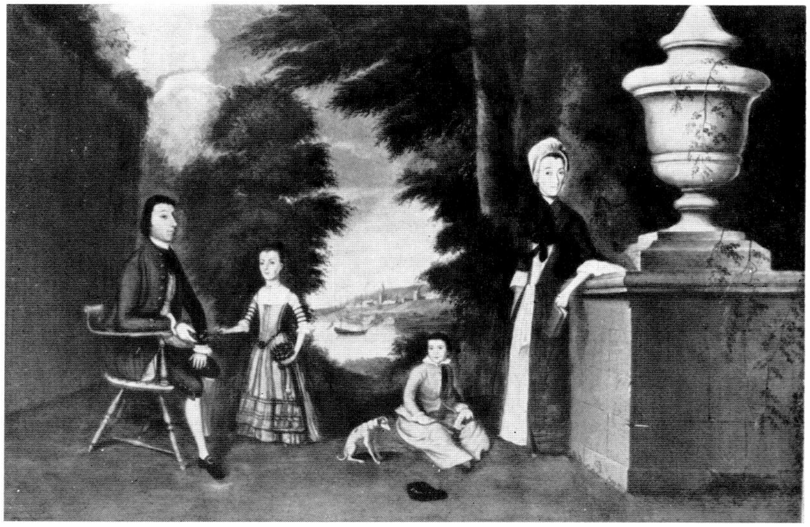

270

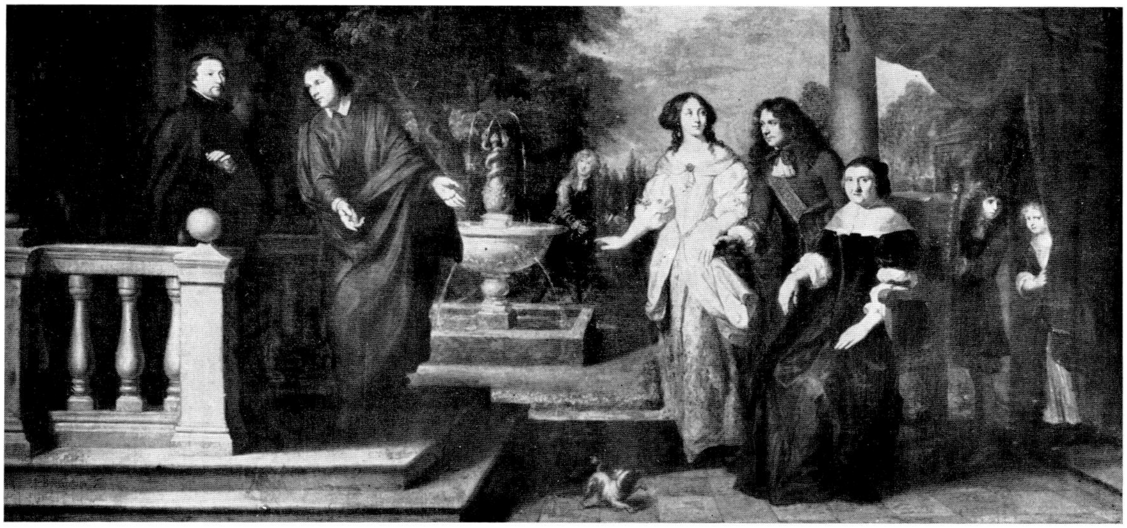

268

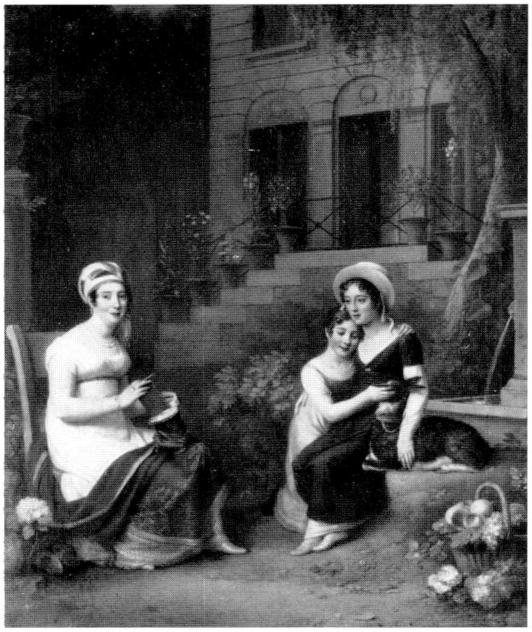

271

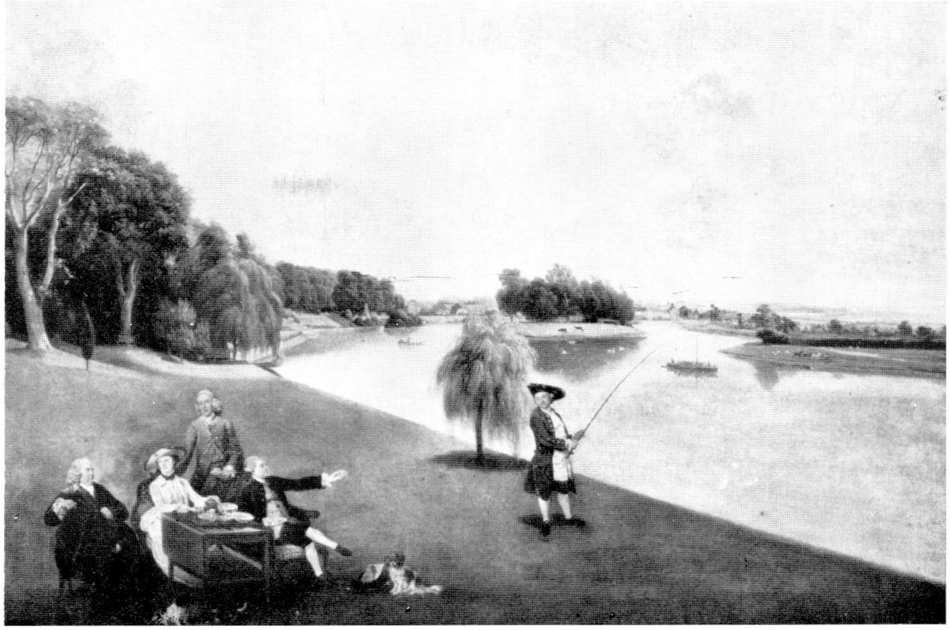

274

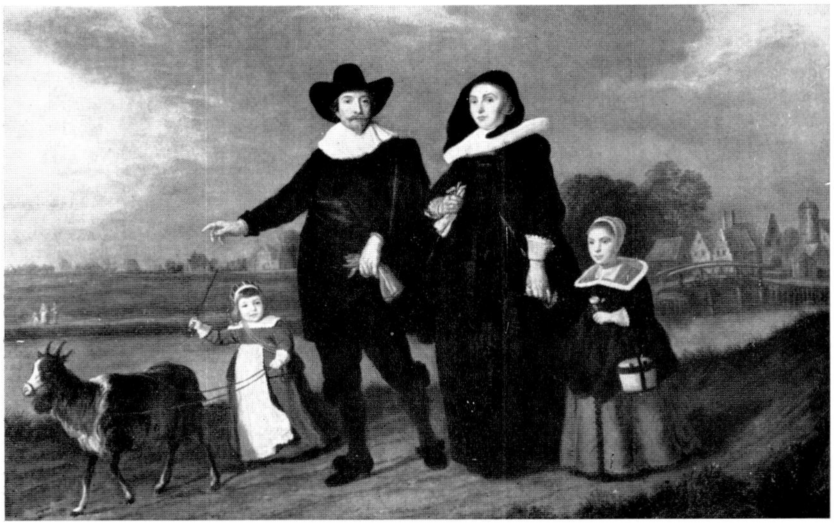

272

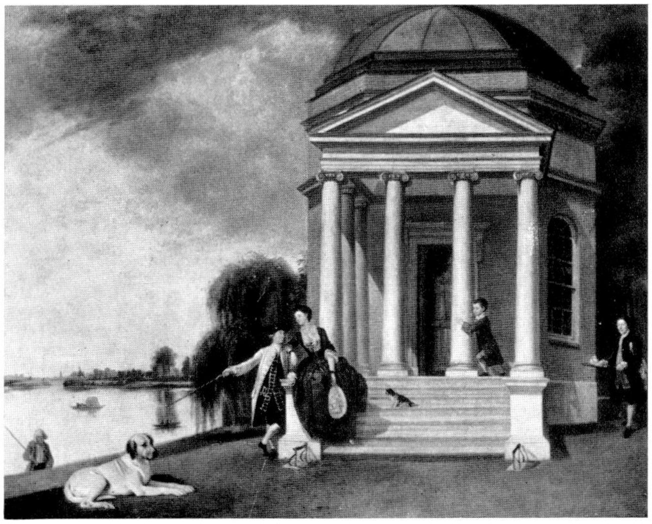

275

273

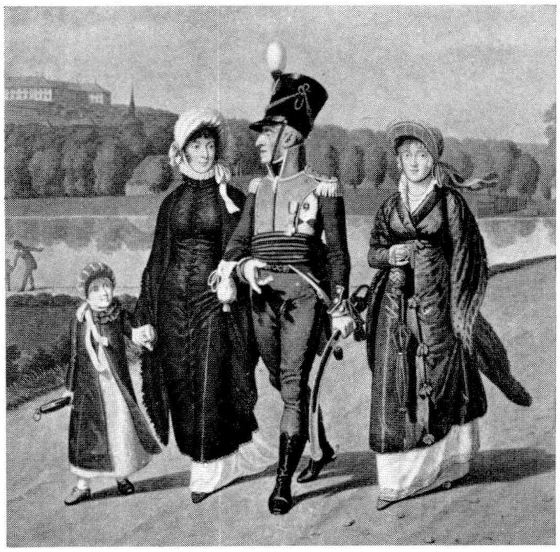

276

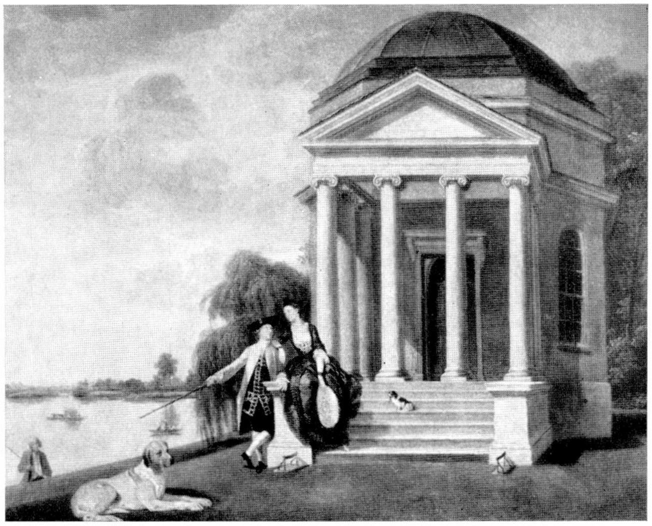

277 PHILIPP OTTO RUNGE (1777-1810), *The Painter's Parents with their Grandchildren*, 1806. Hamburg, Kunsthalle (see p. 121).

279 BARTHOLOMEW DANDRIDGE (1691-after 1754), *The Price Family*. New York, Metropolitan Museum of Art (see p. 125).

280 JAN MYTENS (1614-1670), *The Cotterell Family*, c. 1658. Fredericton, New Brunswick (Canada), Beaverbrook Art Gallery (see p. 125).

281 JOHANN ZOFFANY (1734/5-1810), *The Colmore Family*. Houghton Hall, Norfolk, collection of the Marquess of Cholmondeley (see p. 134).

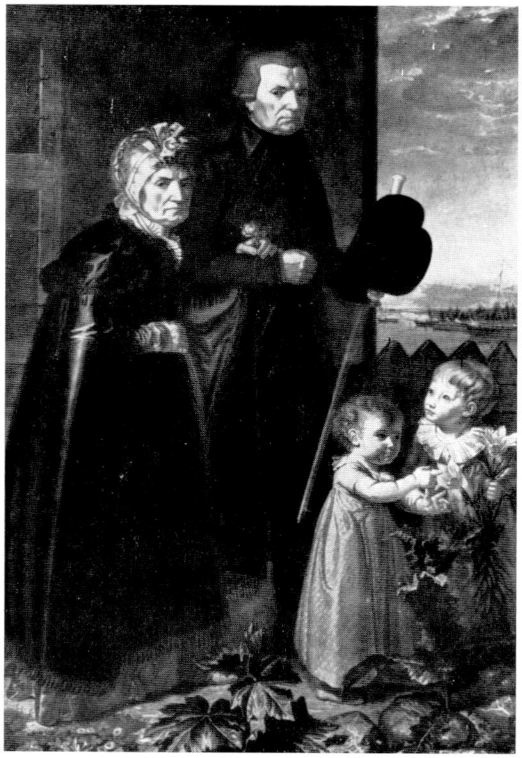

277

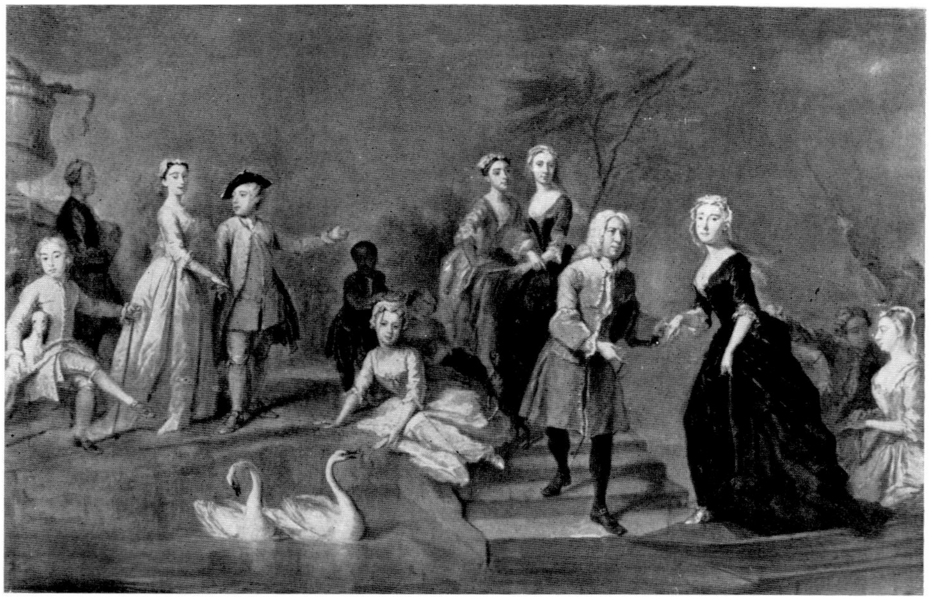

279

278

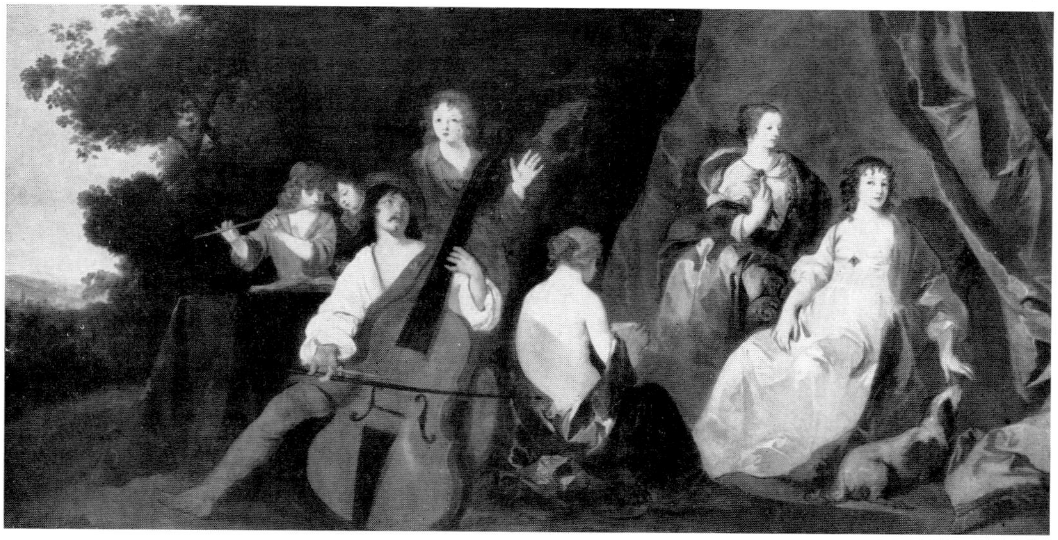

278 SIR PETER LELY (1618-1680), *The Artist and his Family* (so-called). London, Courtauld Institute Galleries (see p. 125).

282 JOHANN ZOFFANY (1734/5-1810), *The Family of Major Palmer*, 1783-9. London, India Office Records Collection; reproduced with the permission of the Secretary of State for Commonwealth Relations (see pp. 133-34).

283 attr. to BARTHOLOMEW DANDRIDGE (1691-after 1754), *Family Group in a Park*. Washington, D.C., collection of Mr. and Mrs. Paul Mellon (see p. 125).

284 JOHANN ZOFFANY (1734/5-1810), *A Man and Two Boys, One with a Kite*. Hatfield House, Hatfield (Hertfordshire), collection of the Marquess of Salisbury (see p. 134).

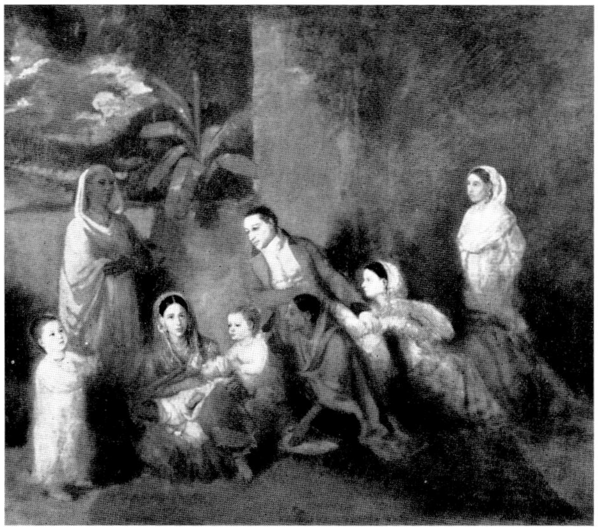

282

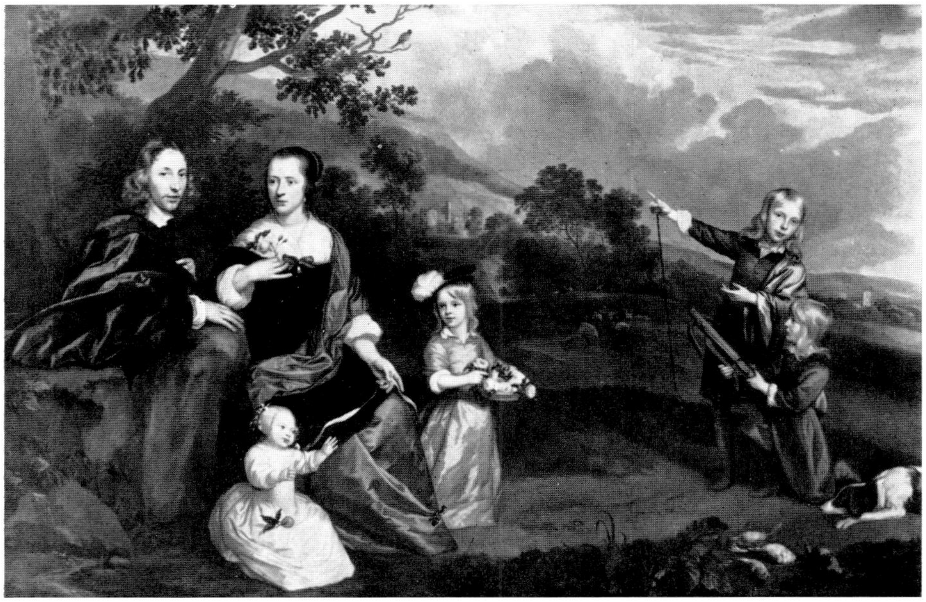

280

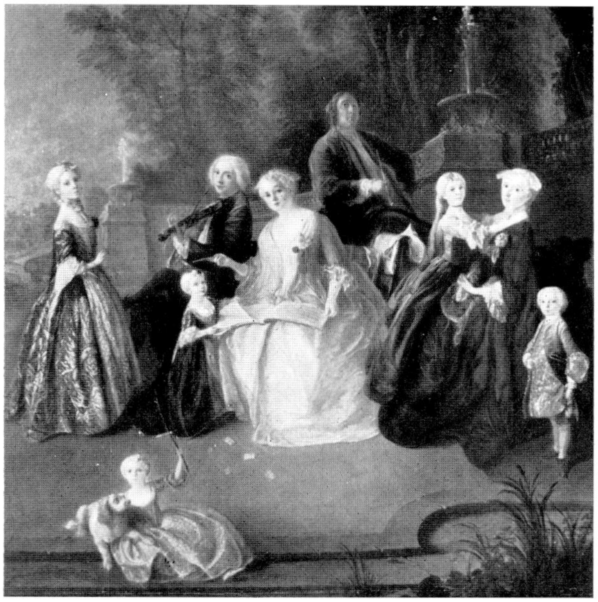

283

281

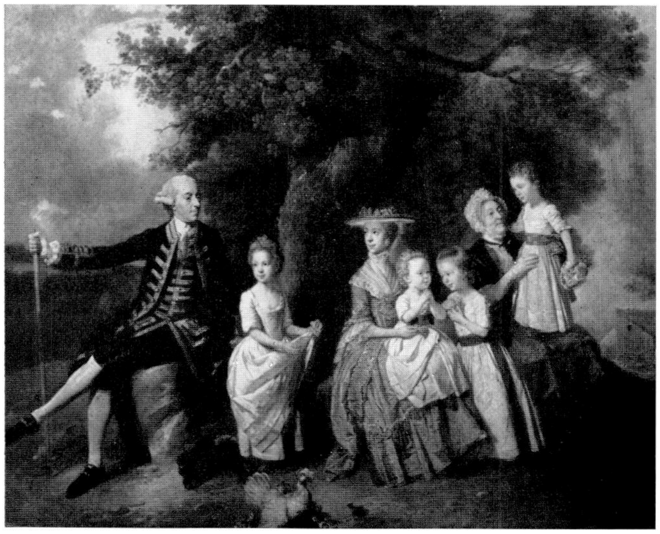

284

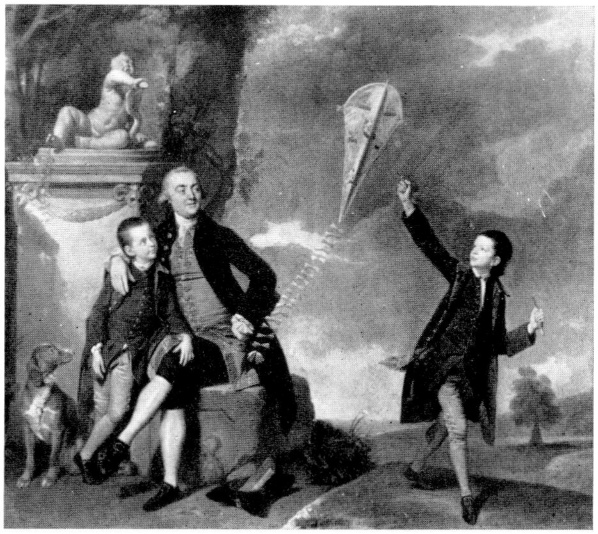

285 ANGELICA KAUFFMANN (1741-1807), *The Family of Ferdinand I of Naples.* Naples, Museo di Capodimonte (see p. 134).

286 MARGUERITE GÉRARD (1761-1837), *A Colonial Louisiana Family.* New York, Wildenstein Galleries (see p. 134).

287 FERDINAND WEISS (d. 1878), *The Hübner Family with Children and Grandchildren.* Berlin, Staatliche Museen; photo Käte Gläser Archives (see p. 139).

288 ARTHUR DEVIS (1711-1787), *Sir Joshua Vanneck and his Family,* 1752. "Clayton", Pittsburgh (Pa.), collection of Miss Helen Clay Frick; photo Frick Art Reference Library (see p. 143).

289 JOHN FEAREY (1745/50-1788), *Family Group with a View of Greenwich,* 1775. Washington, D.C., collection of Mr. and Mrs. Paul Mellon (see p. 143).

290 BENJAMIN WILSON (1721-1788), *The Callis Family.* New York, Wildenstein Galleries (see p. 143).

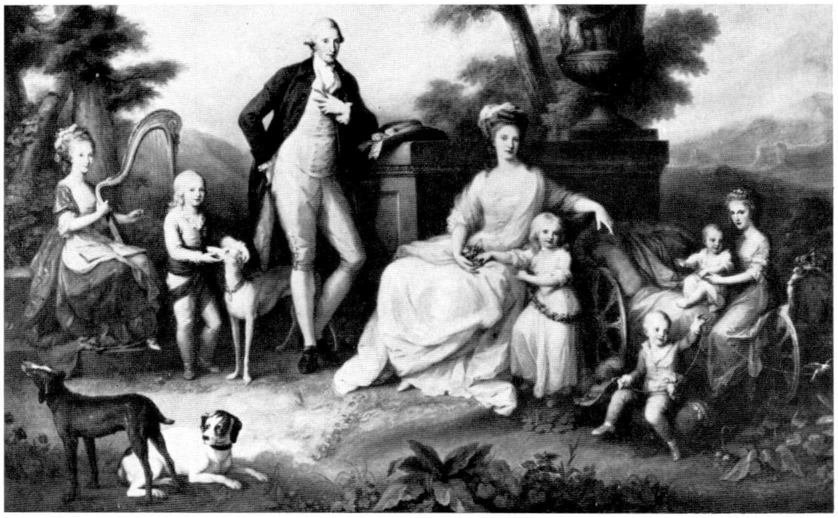
285

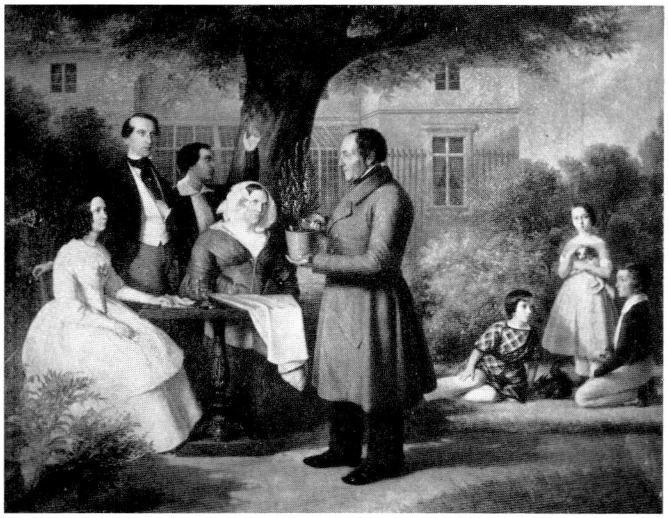
287

286

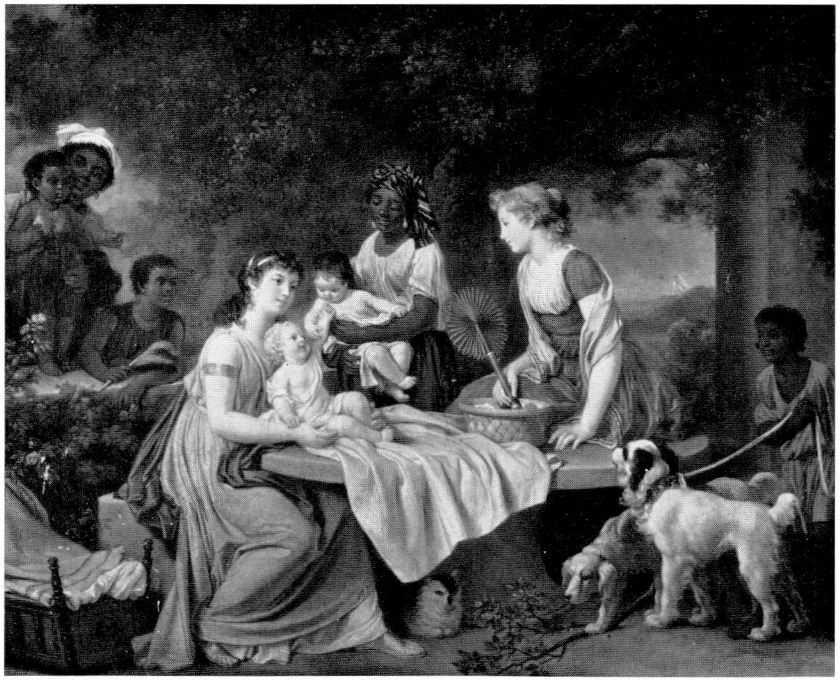

288

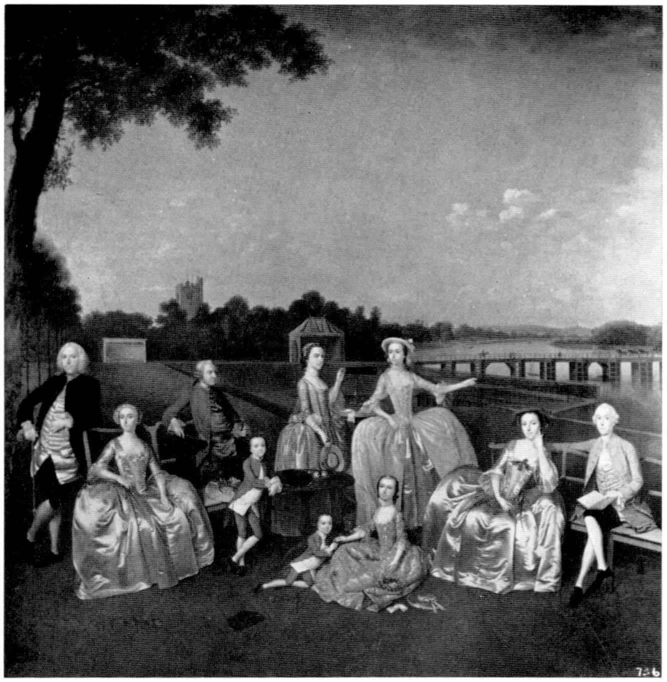

291 JEAN FRÉDÉRIC BAZILLE (1841-1870), *Family in a Garden*, 1867. Paris, Louvre (see p. 134).

292 ARTHUR DEVIS (1711-1787), *Edward Rookes of Royds Hall with his First Wife and Three Daughters*. Cottesbrooke Hall, Northampton, collection of the Hon. Mrs. Macdonald-Buchanan (see p. 143).

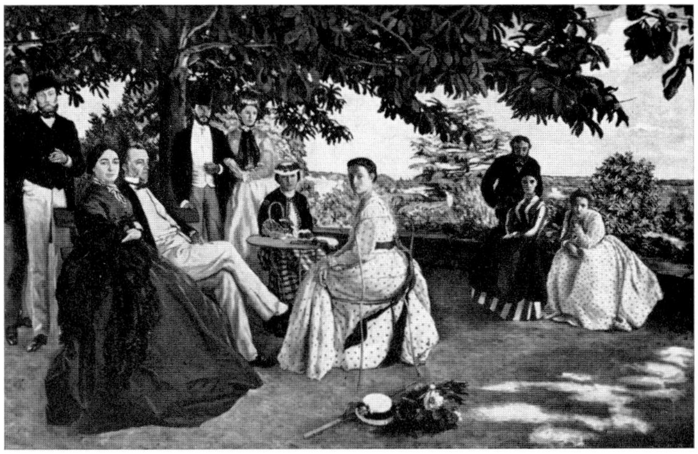

291

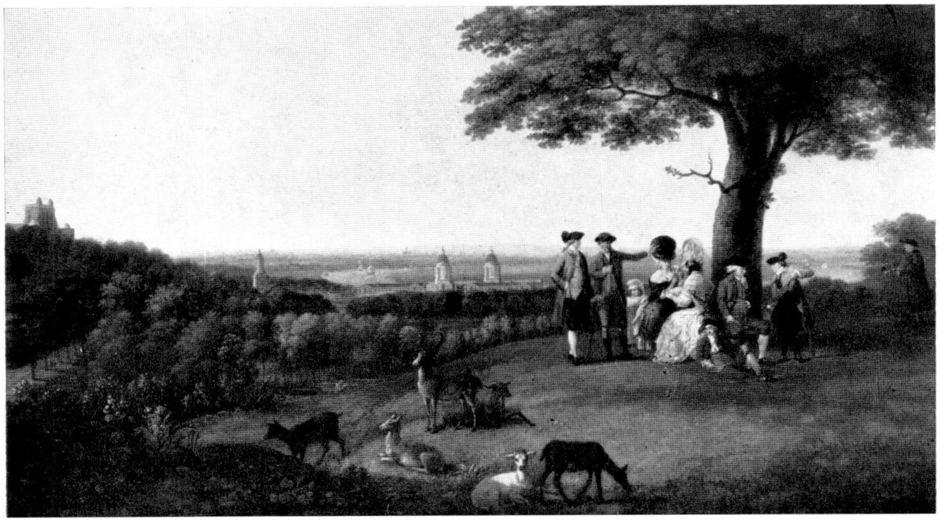

289

290

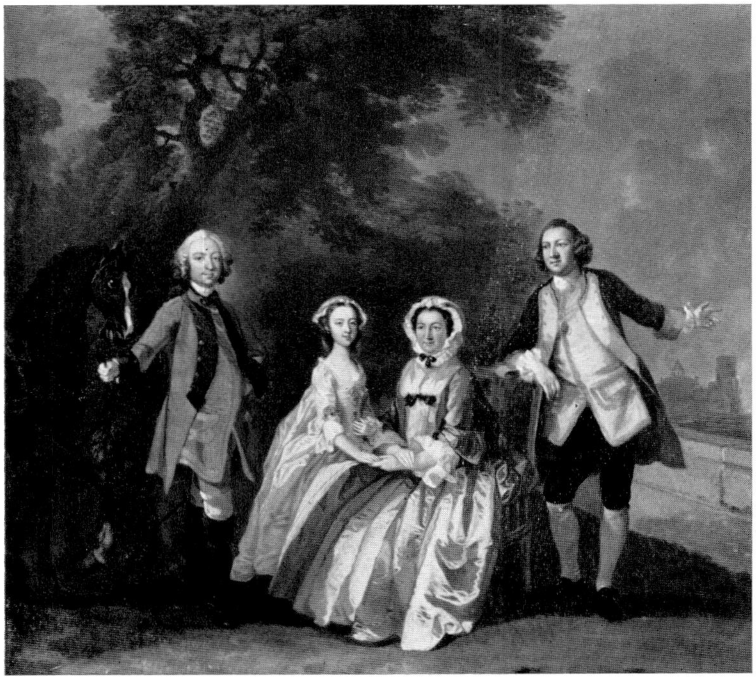

292

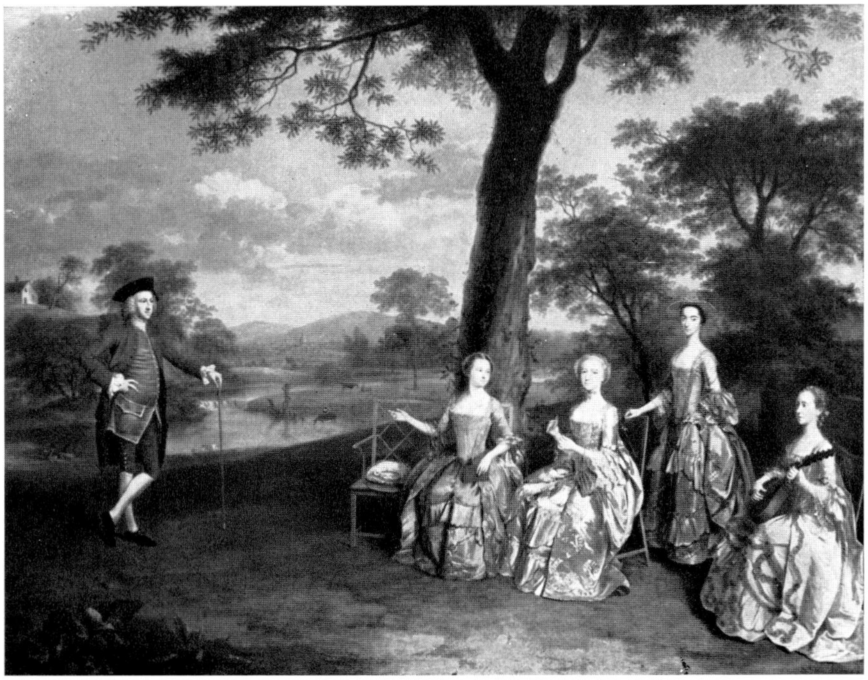

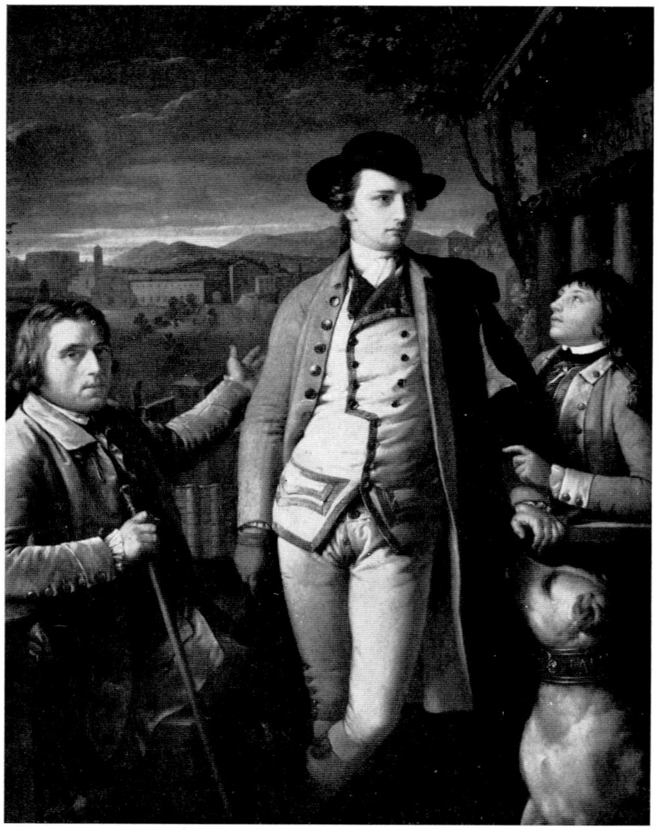

293

293 GAVIN HAMILTON (1723-1798), *The Duke of Hamilton with his Personal Doctor, John Moore, and the Latter's Son, Ensign John Moore*. Lennoxlove, collection of the Duke of Hamilton (see p. 143).

294 NATHANIEL DANCE (1734/5-1811 or 1816), *Four Englishmen in Rome*. Cullen, collection of the Countess of Seafield (see p. 143).

295 JOSEPH ABEL (1764-1818), *Countess Maria Theresia von Fries with her Children*, 1811. Nuremberg, Germanisches Nationalmuseum (see p. 143).

296 JEAN-BAPTISTE ISABEY (1767-1855), *A Family in about 1810*. Paris, collection of M. Jacques Veysset (see p. 143).

297 GABRIEL CORNELIUS VON MAX (1810-1915), *Three Sisters Embroidering*. Berlin, Nationalgalerie (see p. 145).

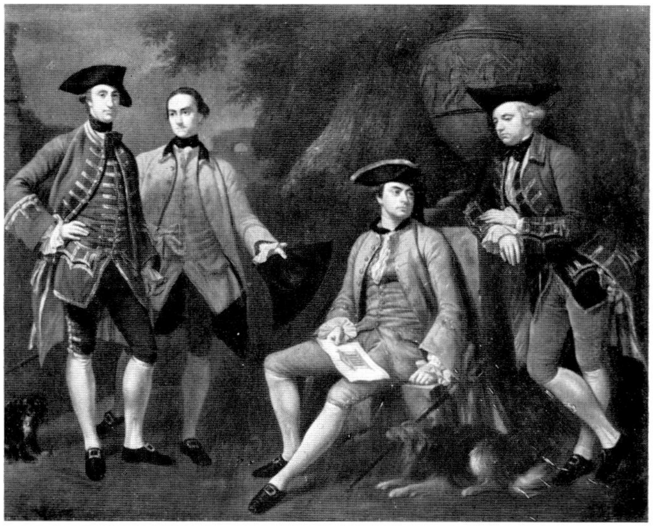

294

295

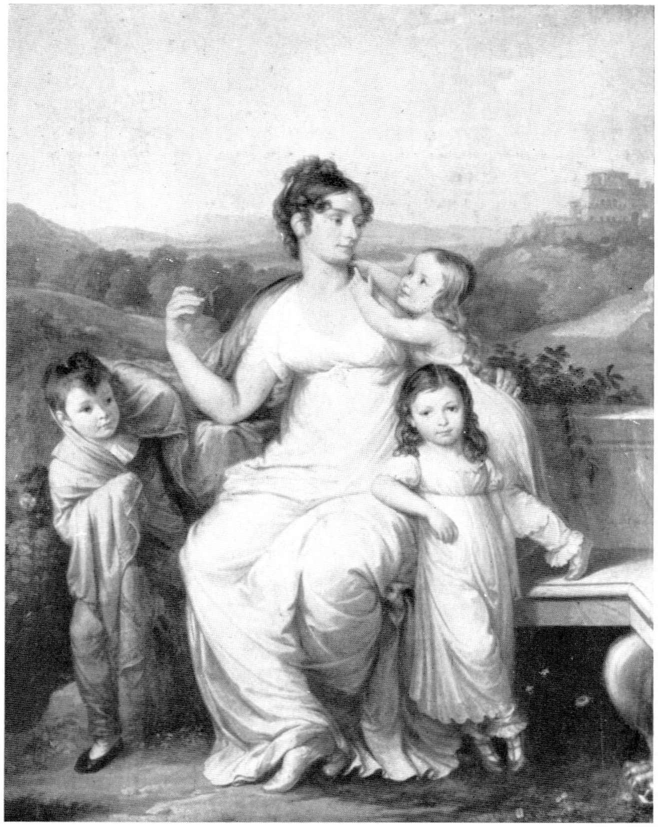

296

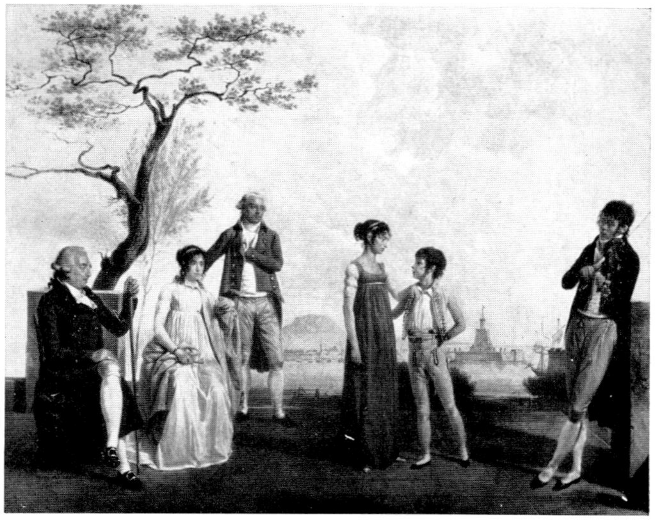

298 EUGÈNE DEVÉRIA (1805-1865), *The Boat* (sketch). Paris, collection of M. Roger Imbert (see p. 147).

299 JACOB HUYSMANS (HOUSEMAN) (d. 1696), *Four Children of John Coke of Melbourne.* Melbourne Hall, Derby, collection of the Marquess of Lothian (see p. 150).

300 WILLIAM HOGARTH (1697-1764), *A Children's Party*, 1730. London, at M. Knoedler & Co. in 1954; photo Witt Library, Courtauld Institute of Art (see p. 150).

301 BARTHÉLEMY DU PAN (1712-1763), *The Children of Frederick, Prince of Wales*, 1746. Windsor Castle, Royal Collections; copyright reserved (see p. 150).

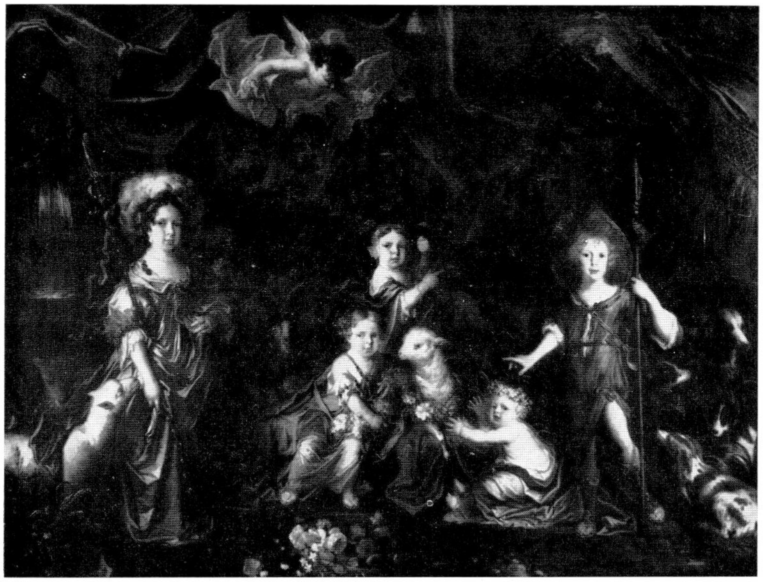

299

300

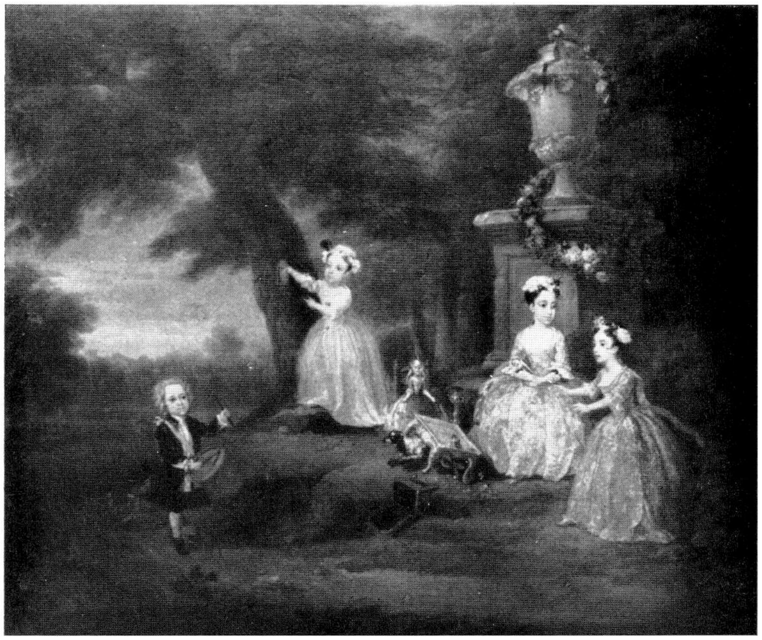

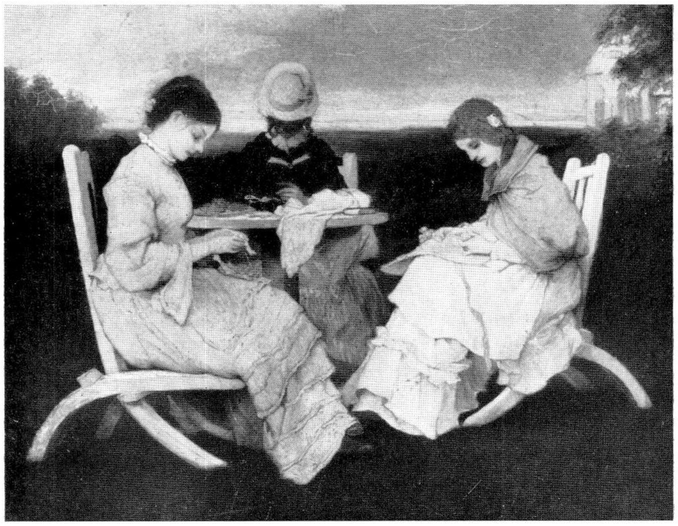

297

298

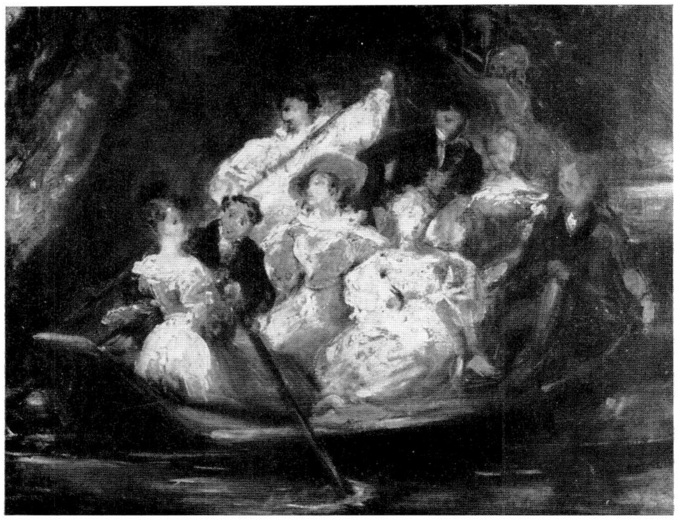

301

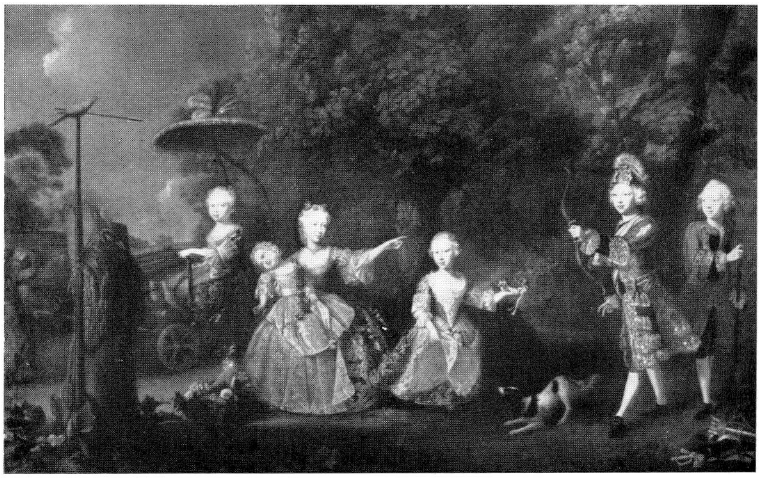

302 attr. to JOHN DOWNMAN (c. 1750-1824), *The Children of John and Elizabeth Mordaunt*. Godmersham Park, Canterbury (Kent), collection of Mr. and Mrs. Robert Tritton (see p. 150).

303 PER KRAFFT THE YOUNGER (1777-1863), *Lovisa Albertina Bohnstedt and her Children*, 1812. Stockholm, collection of Mrs. L. Wicander (see p. 154).

304 FRANÇOIS GÉRARD (1770-1837), *Marshall Lannes' Wife and Children*, 1818. Versailles, Musée de Versailles (see p. 152).

305 GIUSEPPE (JOSIP) TOMINZ (1796-1866), *The Children's Go-cart*. Gorizia, Museo Provinciale di Palazzo Attems (see p. 156).

306 HENRI GUILLAUME CHATILLON (1780-1856), *The Children of Jérôme Bonaparte in the Garden*. Rome, Spalletti Collection (see p. 152).

307 PIETRO BENVENUTI (1769-1844), *The Children of Prince Corsini*, 1808. Florence, Palazzo Corsini (see p. 154).

308 JOHN FERNELEY (1781-1860), *The Rev. and Mrs. Henry Palmer with their Children*, 1838. Washington, D.C., collection of Mr. and Mrs. Paul Mellon (see p. 156).

309 GEORGE CHINNERY (1748-1847), *The Artist's Brother with his Children and their Chinese Nurse* (sketch). Formerly the property of G. Schrijver; Sotheby's sale, July 1966 (see p. 159).

310 WILHELM FRIEDRICH HERBIG (1788-1861), *The Artist's Family*, 1824. Berlin, Nationalgalerie (see p. 156).

311 GEORGE CHINNERY (1748-1847), *The Family of the Artist's Brother*. Washington, D.C., collection of Mr. and Mrs. Paul Mellon (see p. 159).

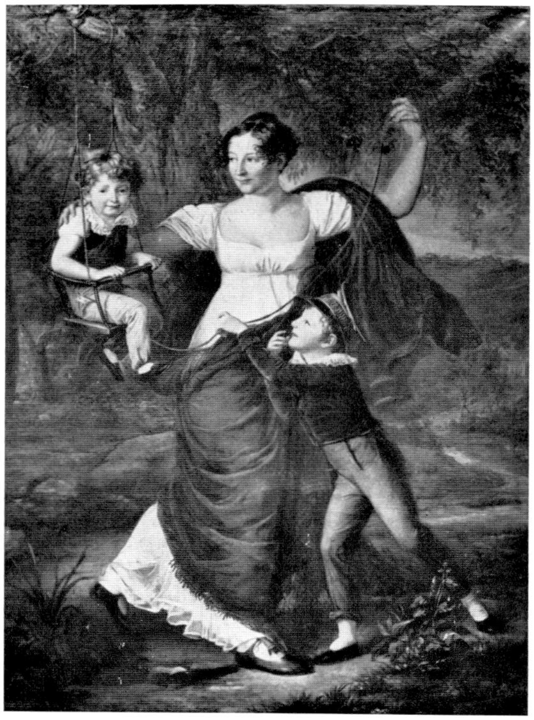

303

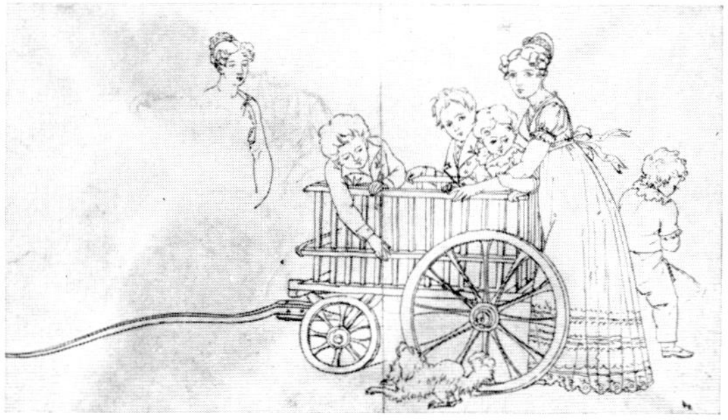

305

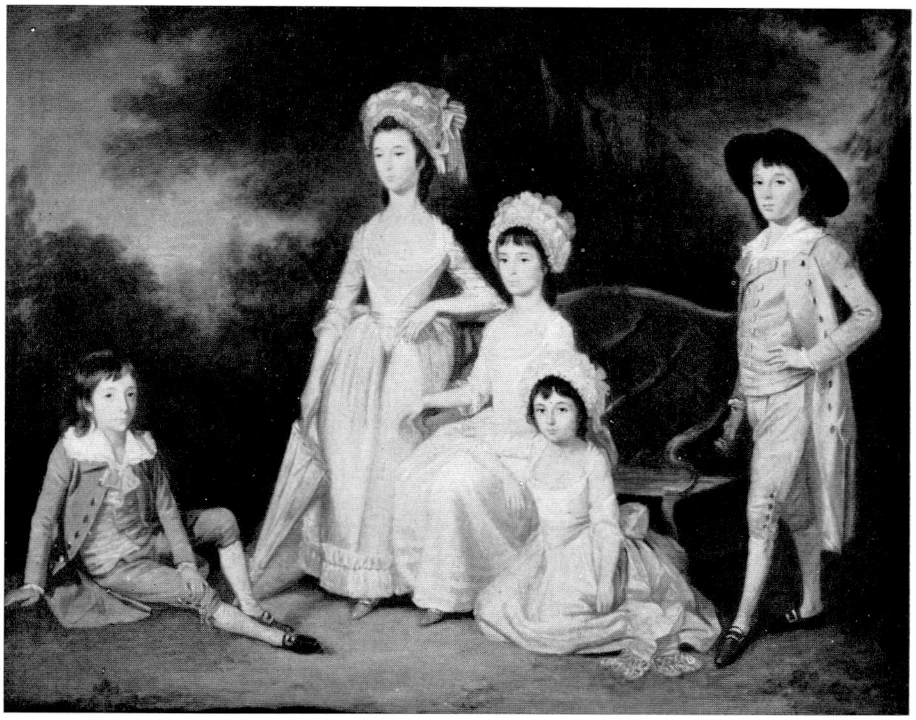

302

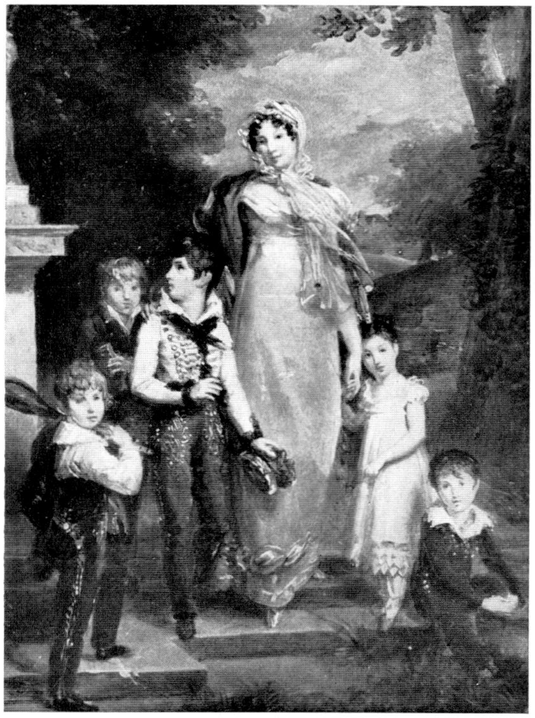

304

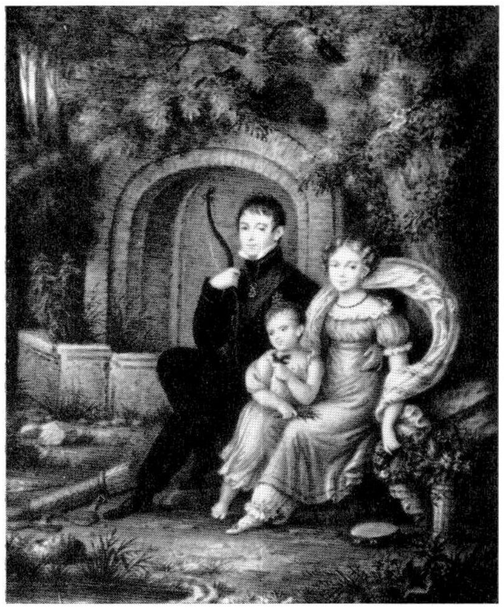

306

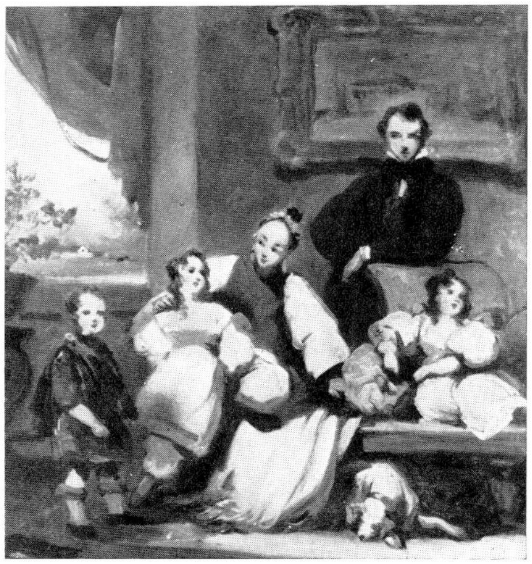

309

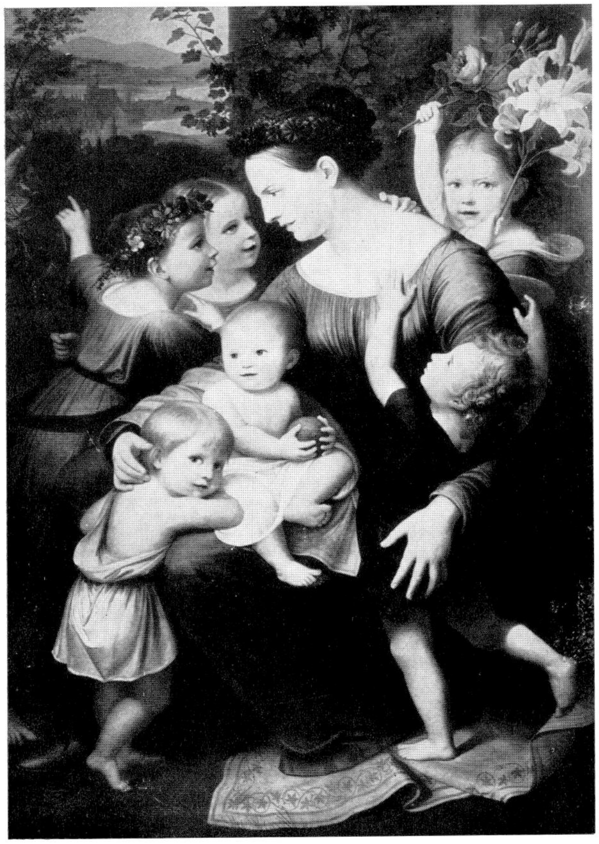

310

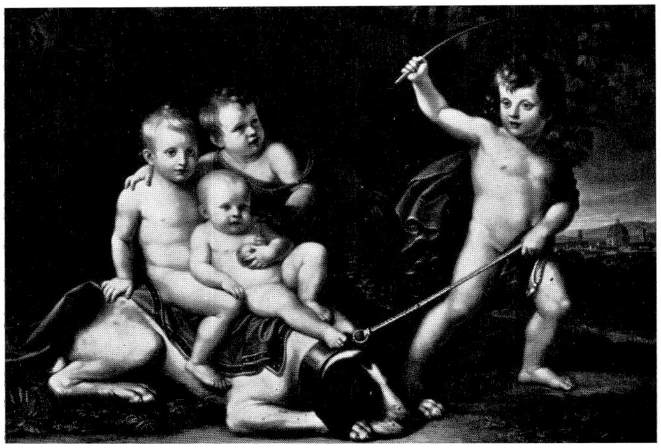

307

308

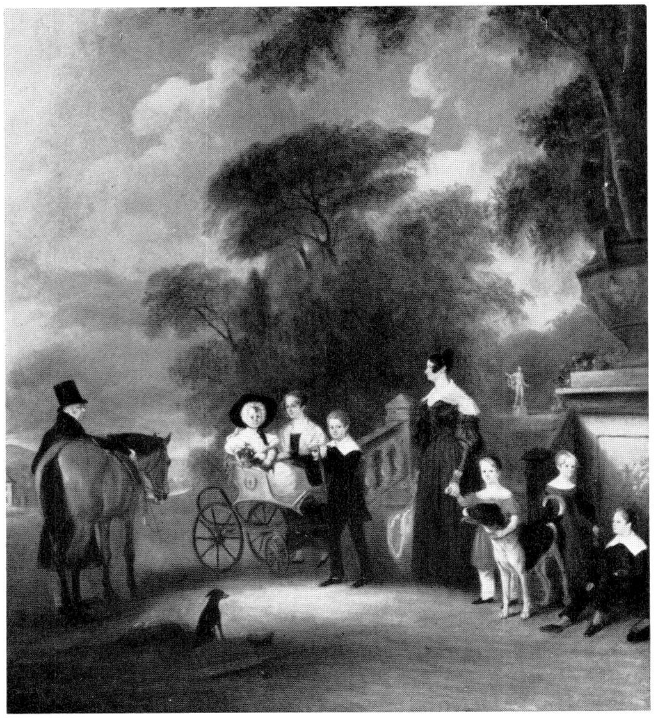

311

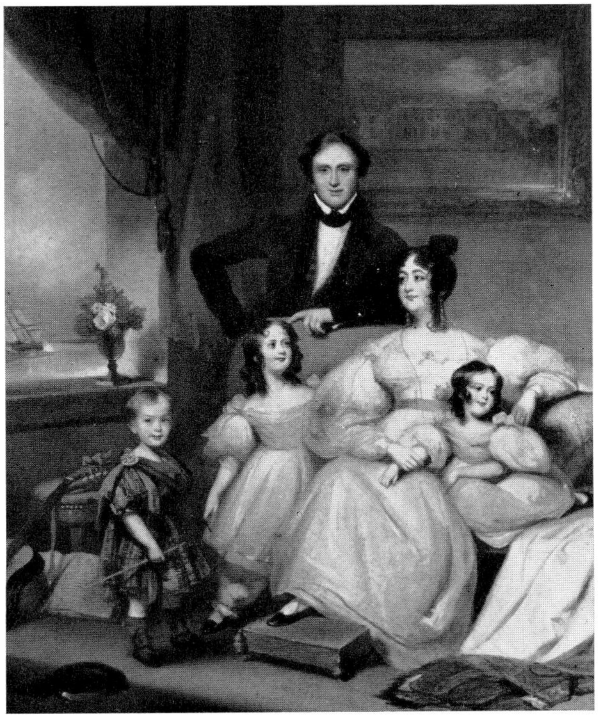

312 ARTHUR DEVIS (1711-1787), *Mr. and Mrs. Atherton*. Liverpool, Walker Art Gallery (see p. 162).

313 ARTHUR DEVIS (1711-1787), *The Lyttelton Family*, 1748. Godmersham Park, Canterbury (Kent), collection of Mr. and Mrs. Robert Tritton (see p. 162).

314 CASPAR NETSCHER (1635/6?-1684), *A Scholar at a Desk Delivering a Paper to a Young Man*. Exh. Agnew's, London, 1938; photo Witt Library, Courtauld Institute of Art (see p. 170).

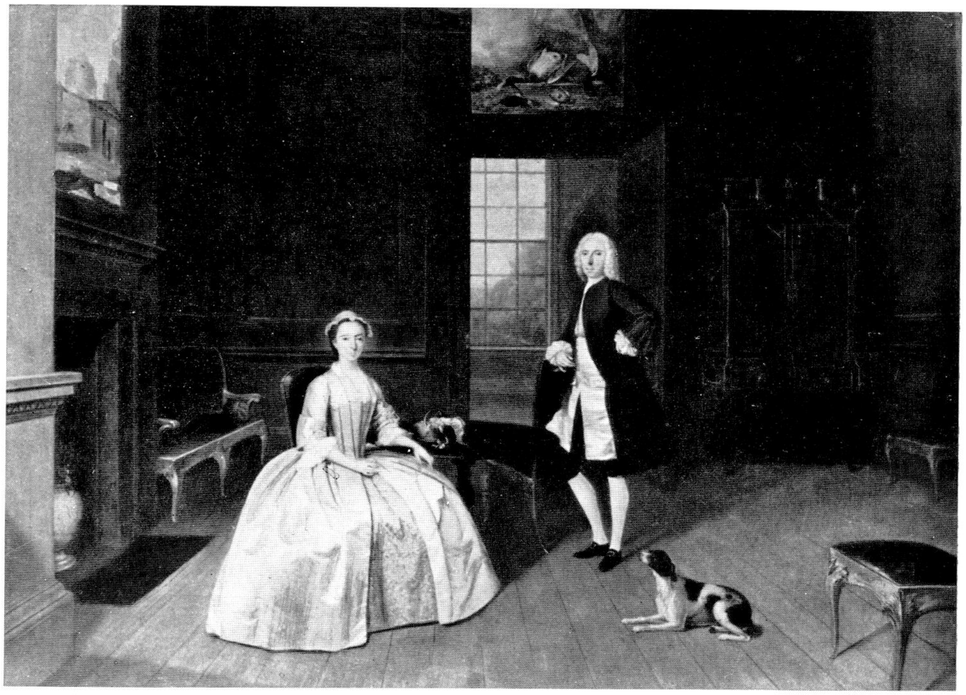

312

313

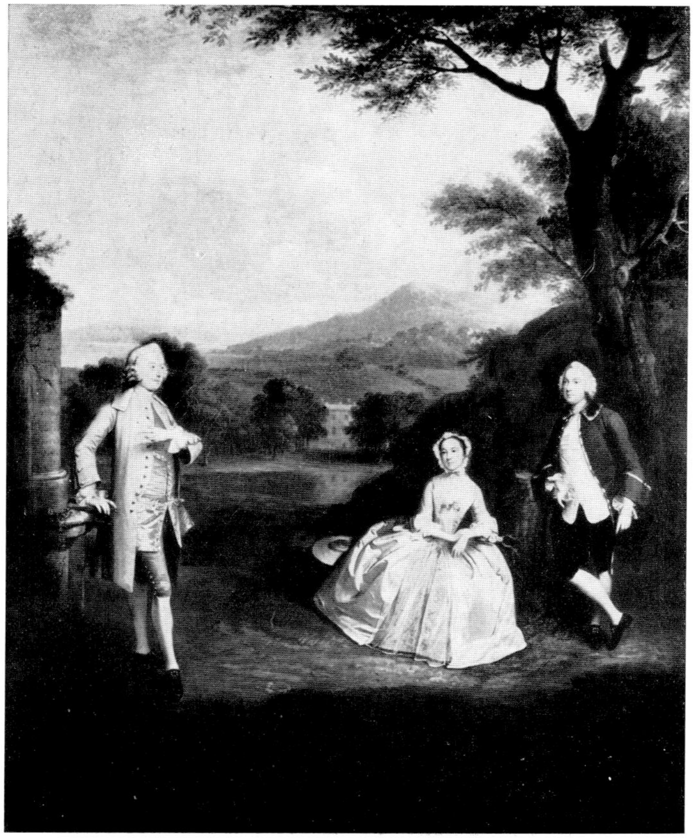

314

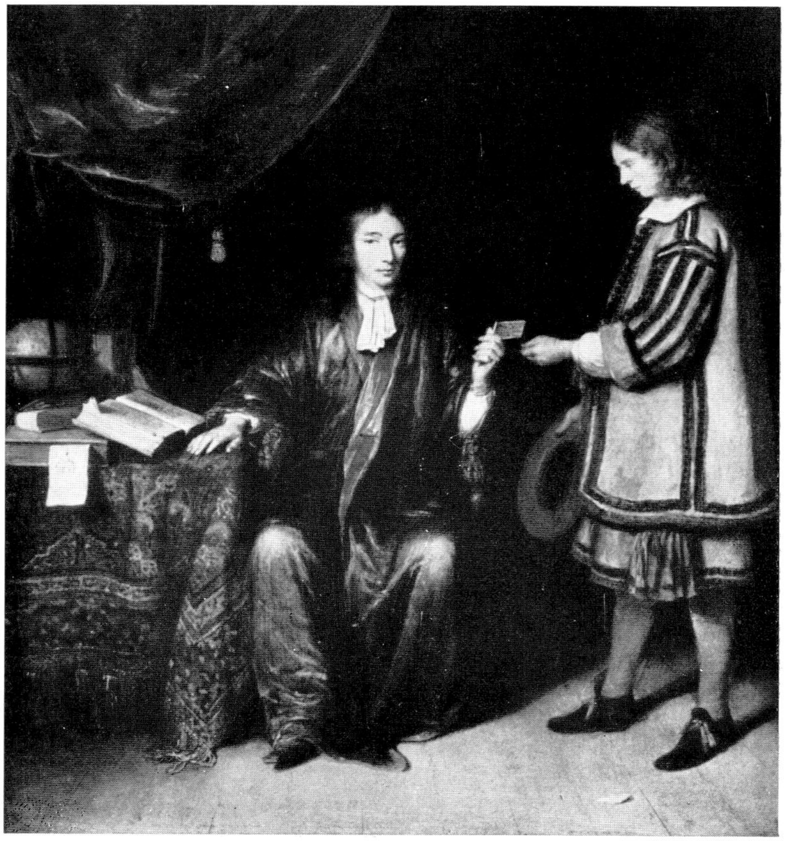

315 NICHOLAS BIDDLE KITTELL (1822-1894), *Mr. and Mrs. Charles Augustus Carter*, 1845. New York, Museum of the City of New York (see p. 170).

316 WILLIAM HOGARTH (1697-1764), *David Garrick and his Wife*. Windsor Castle, Royal Collections; copyright reserved (see p. 170).

317 GIUSEPPE (JOSIP) TOMINZ (1796-1866), *A Betrothed Couple*, c. 1832. Gorizia, Museo Provinciale di Palazzo Attems (see p. 170).

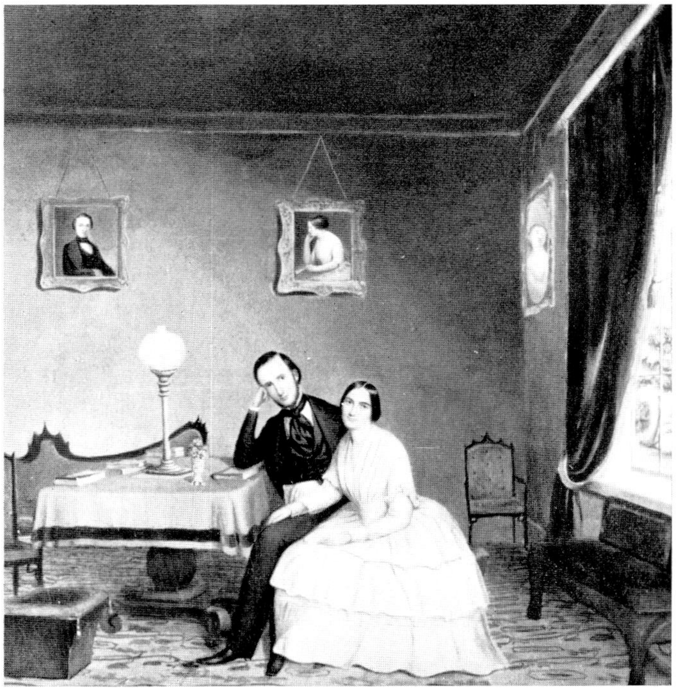

315

316

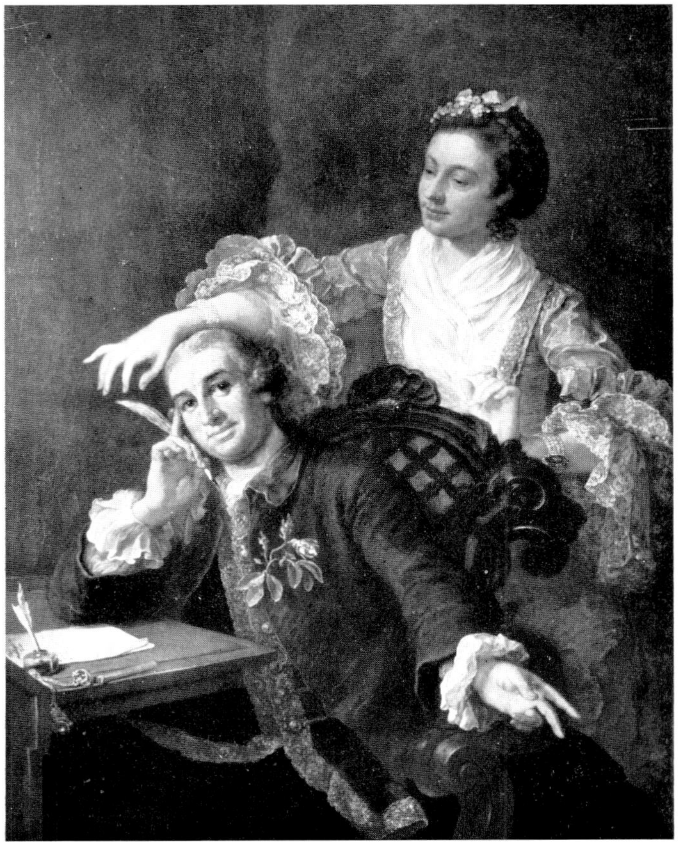

317

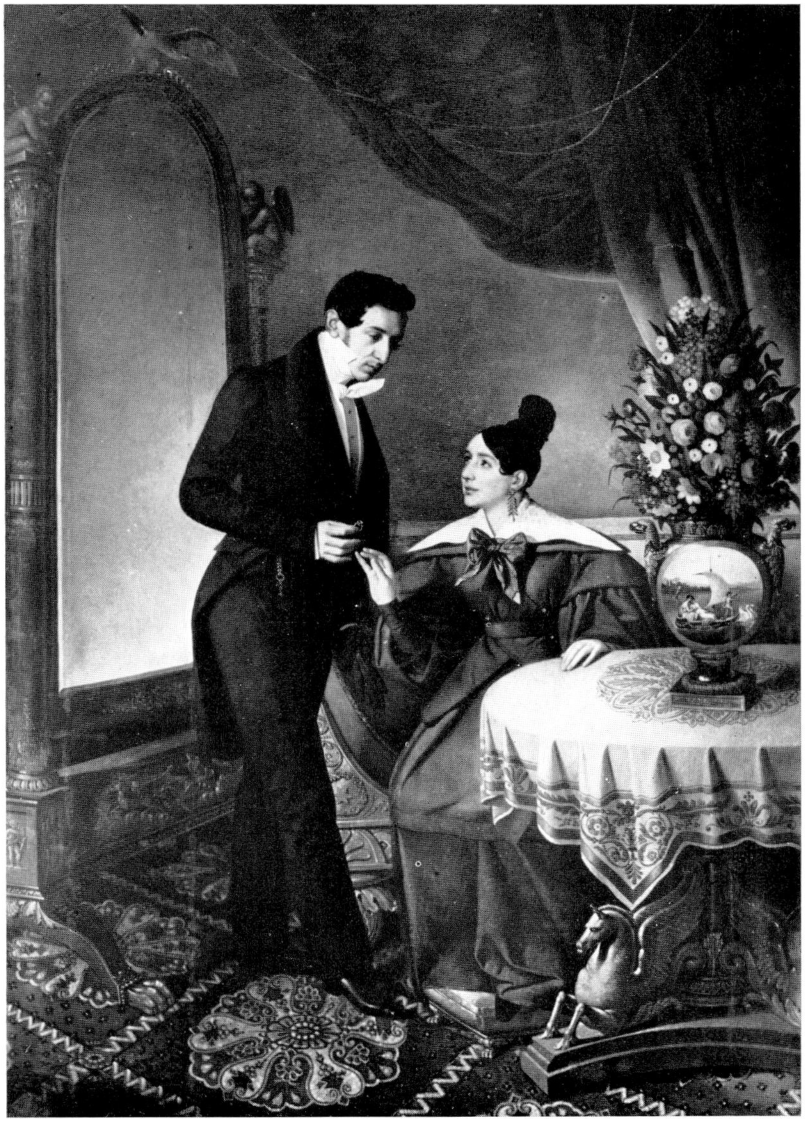

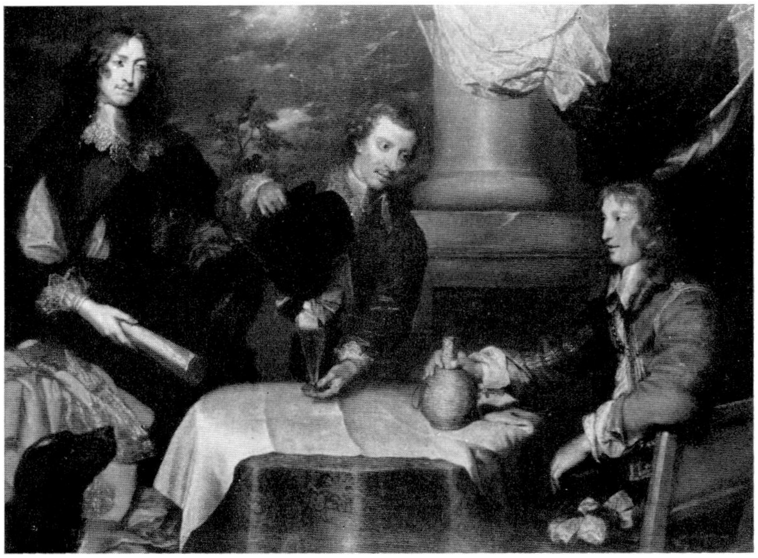

318

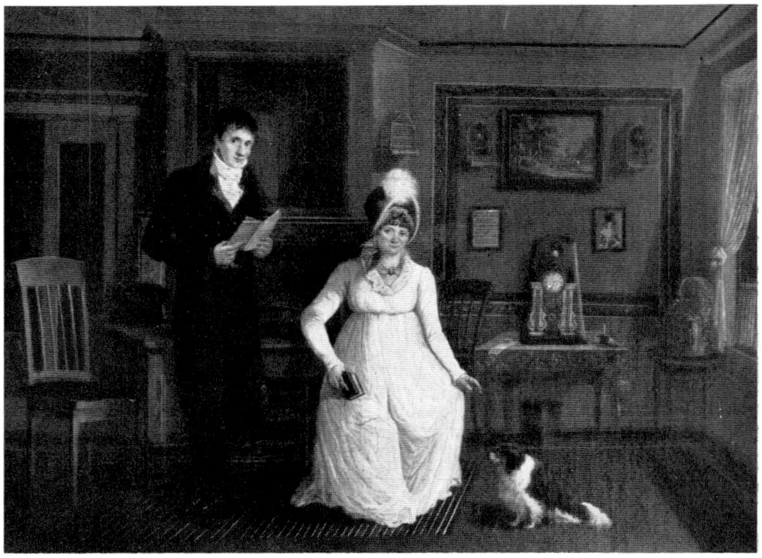

320

319

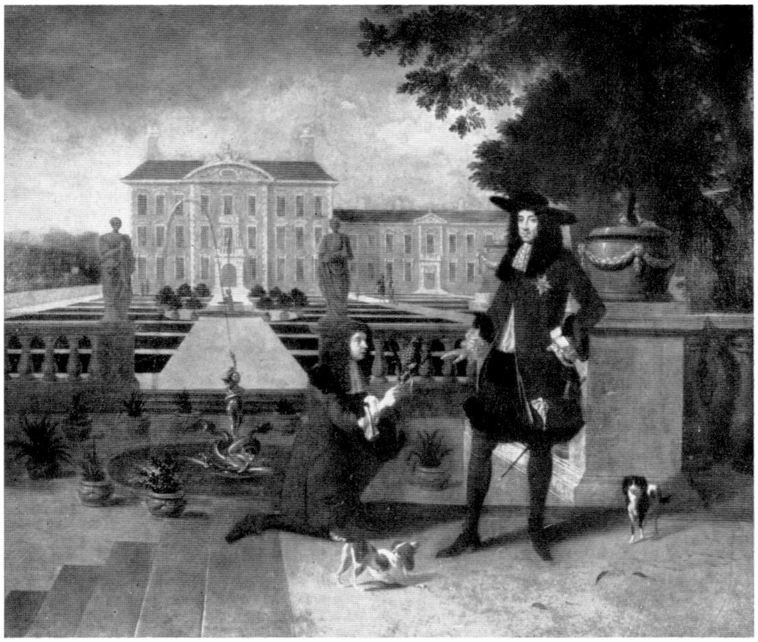

321

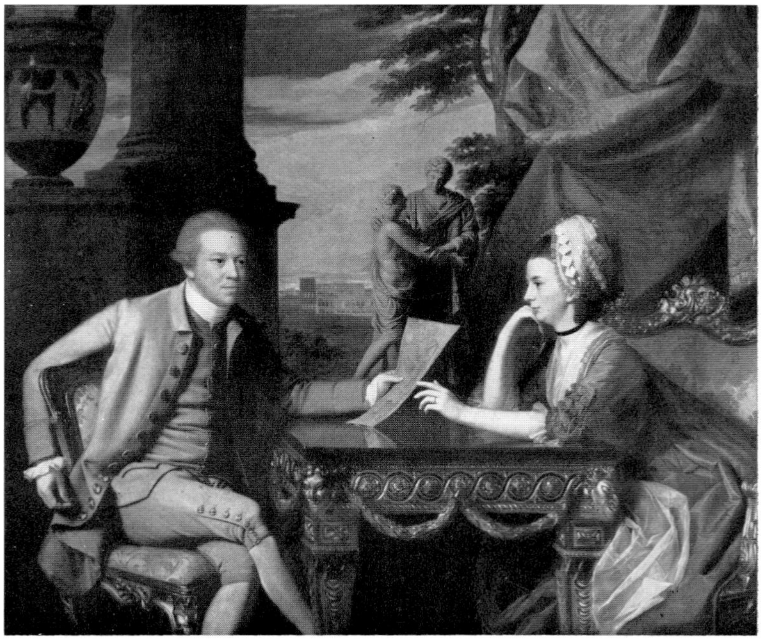

318 WILLIAM DOBSON (1611-1646), *Prince Rupert, Colonel William Murray, and Colonel John Russell*. Ombersley Court, Droitwich (Worcestershire), collection of Lord Sandys (see pp. 170-72).

319 HENDRIK DANCKERTS (c. 1625-1679?), *Charles II Being Presented with a Pineapple by Rose, the Royal Gardener*. Houghton Hall, Norfolk, collection of the Marchioness of Cholmondeley (see pp. 137 and 172).

320 HARMEN OTTEN (1773-?), *The Artist and his Wife*, c. 1810. Holland, private collection (see p. 175).

321 JOHN SINGLETON COPLEY (1738-1815), *Mr. and Mrs. Ralph Izard*, 1775. Boston, Museum of Fine Arts (see p. 173).

322 WYBRAND HENDRIKS (1744-1831), *Mevrouw van Walré-Kops*, 1787. Domburg, collection of Mevrouw van Eeghen-van Walré de Bordes (see p. 175).

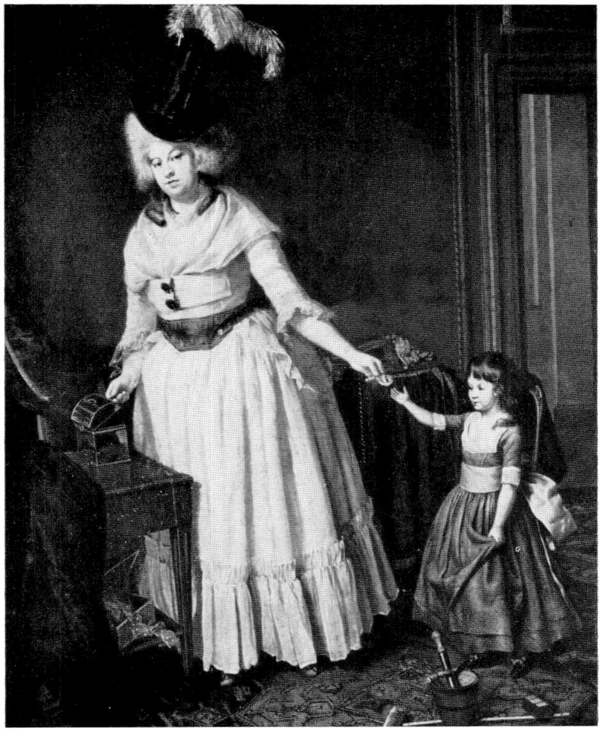

322

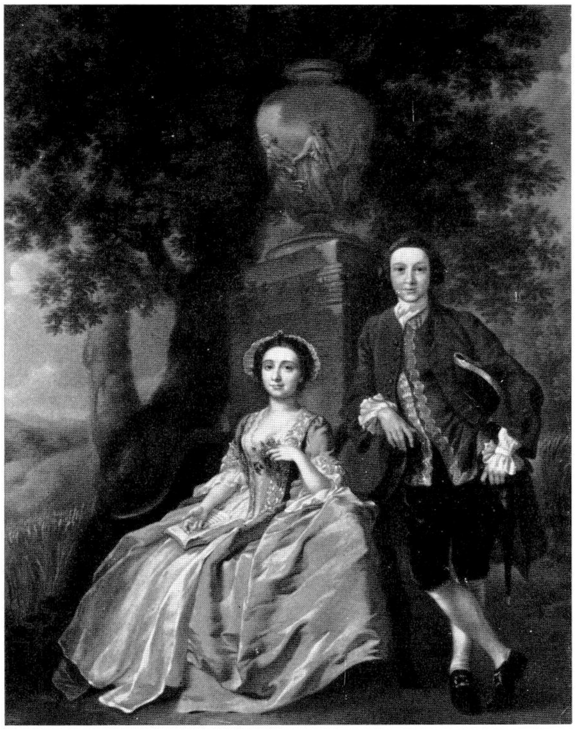

324

323

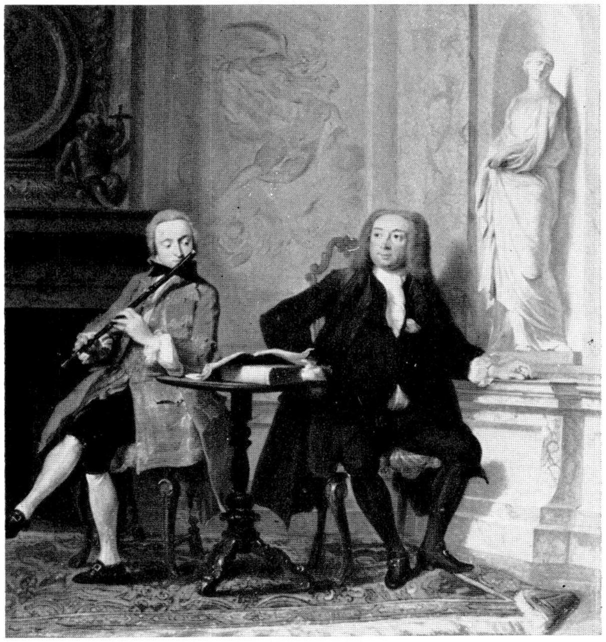

325

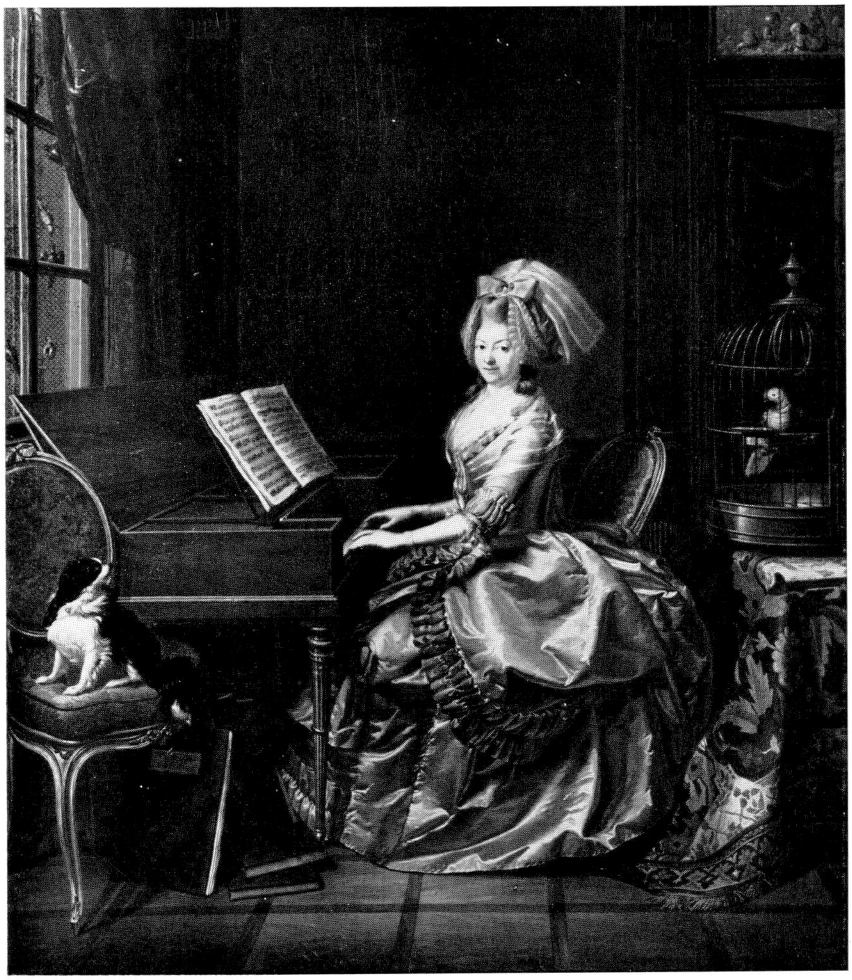

323 CORNELIS TROOST (1697-1750), *Jeronimus Tonneman and his Son*, 1736. Dublin, National Gallery of Ireland (see p. 173).

324 FRANCIS HAYMAN (1708-1776), *Margaret Tyers and her Husband* (?). Washington, D.C., collection of Mr. and Mrs. Paul Mellon (see p. 172).

325 LOUIS-FRANÇOIS-GÉRARD VAN DER PUYL (1750-1824), *A Conversation with Animals*. In 1966 the property of Beets en Fontein, Bennebroek (see p. 177).

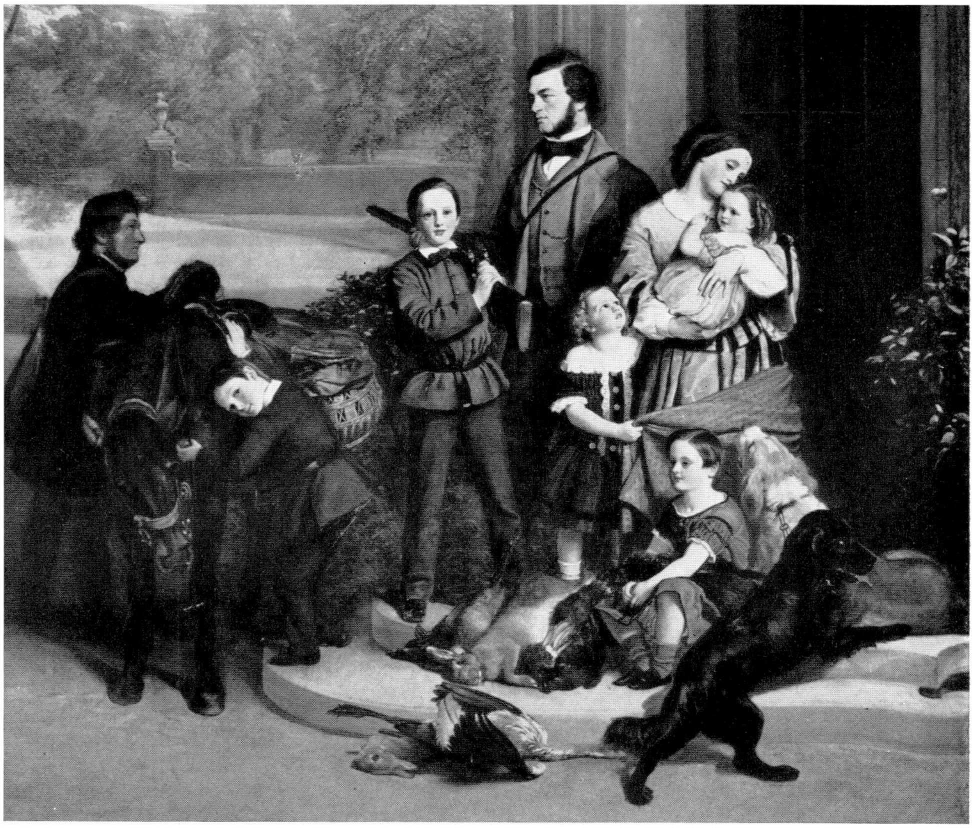

327

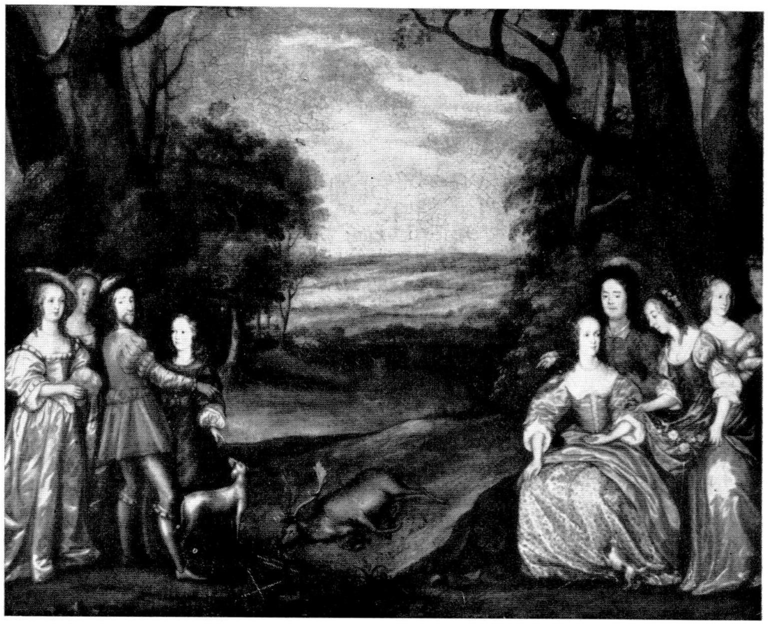

328

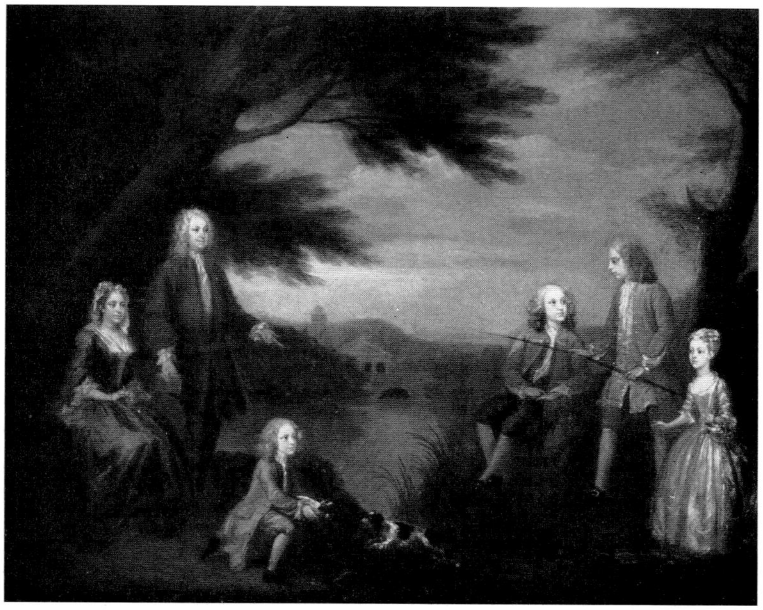

326

326 WILLIAM HOGARTH (1697-1764), *The Jeffreys Family*. Washington, D.C., National Gallery of Art (on loan from Mr. William H. Jeffreys) (see p. 179).

327 SIR EDWIN LANDSEER (1802-1873), *The First Game-bag*. Rome, private collection (see pp. 180-81).

328 JOAN CARLILE (1606-1678/9), *The Stag Hunt*, 1649-50. Lampton Hall, Northampton, collection of Sir Gyles Isham, Bart. (see p. 179).

329 ARTHUR DEVIS (1711-1787), *John Ord and his Family*, c. 1750-1. Washington, D.C., collection of Mr. and Mrs. Paul Mellon (see p. 180).

330 ALLAN RAMSAY (1713-1784), *Thomas Mansel and his Half-brothers*, c. 1740, collection of C. Methuen Campbell (see p. 180).

331 JOHN WOOTTON (1686?-1765), *The Beauchamp and Rivers Families and Sir Nevil Hickman*, 1749. Ulting Lea, Maldon (Essex), collection of the Rev. Sir Ivor Proctor Beauchamp (see p. 180).

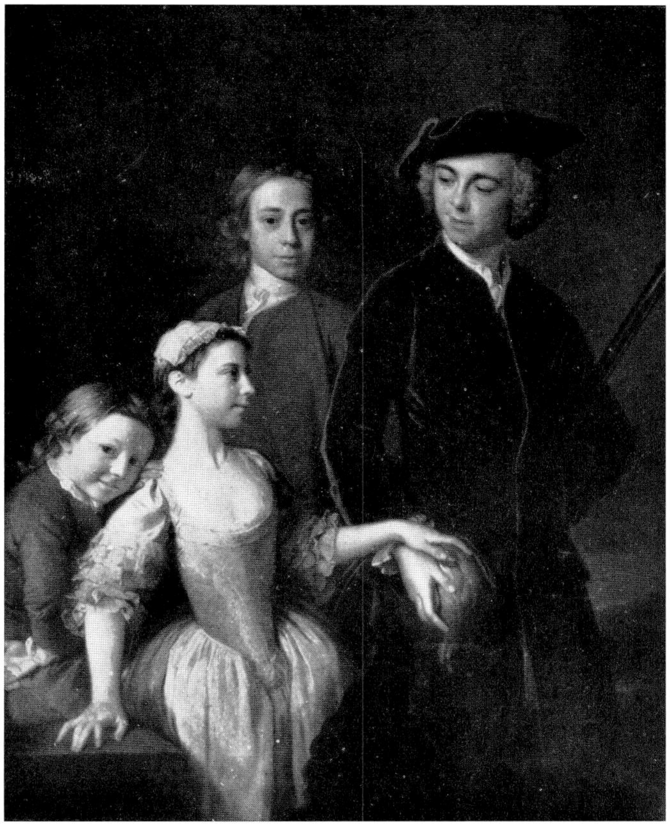

330

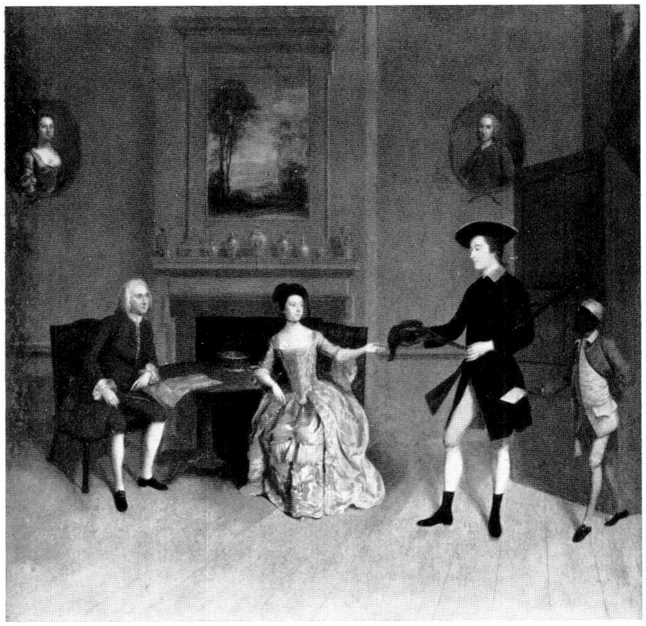

329

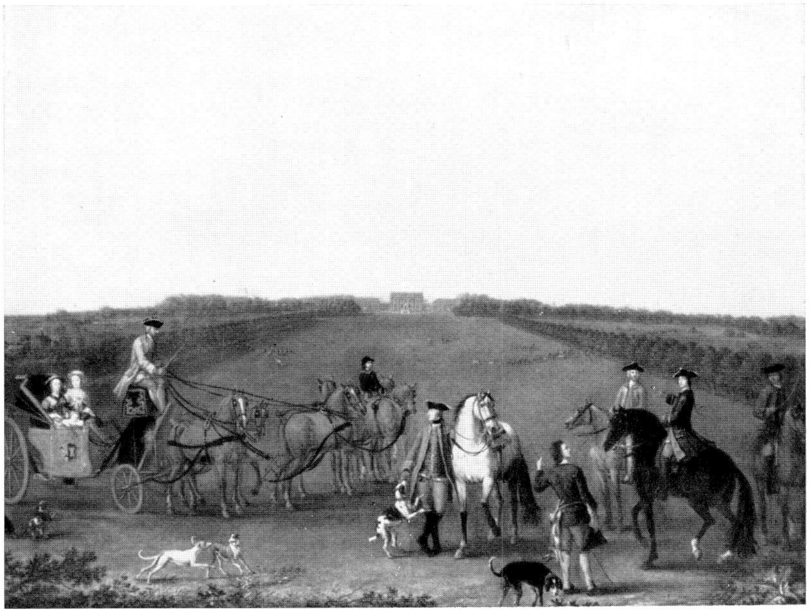

331

332 FRANCIS WHEATLEY (1747-1801), *The Earl of Carlisle in Phoenix Park, Dublin*, 1780-2. Castle Howard, York, collection of Mr. George Howard (see p. 180).

333 GEORGE STUBBS (1724-1806), *The Melbourne and Milbanke Families*, c. 1770. Little Durnford Manor (Wiltshire), collection of the Hon. Julian Salmond (see p. 180).

334 WILHELM LEIBL (1844-1900), *Leibl and Sperl Hunting*. Munich, Neue Staatsgalerie (see p. 181).

335 attr. to MARCO RICCI (1676-1729), *Rehearsal of an Opera*. Washington, D.C., collection of Mr. and Mrs. Paul Mellon (see p. 184).

336 DANIEL PREISLER (1627-1665), *Self-portrait with his Family*, 1665. Nuremberg, Germanisches Nationalmuseum (see p. 184).

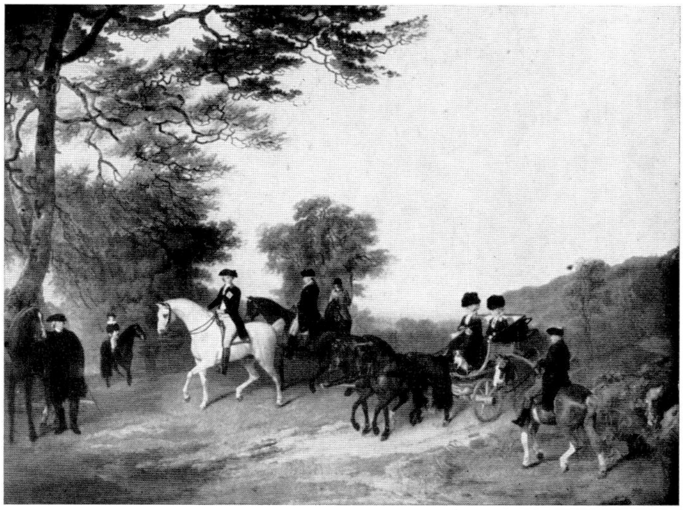

332

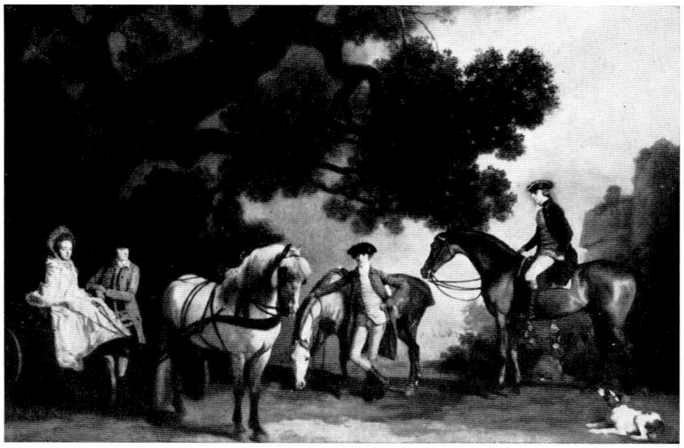

333

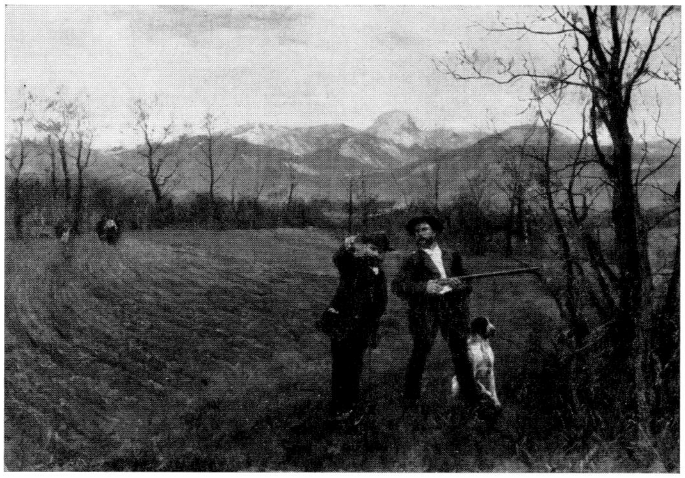

334

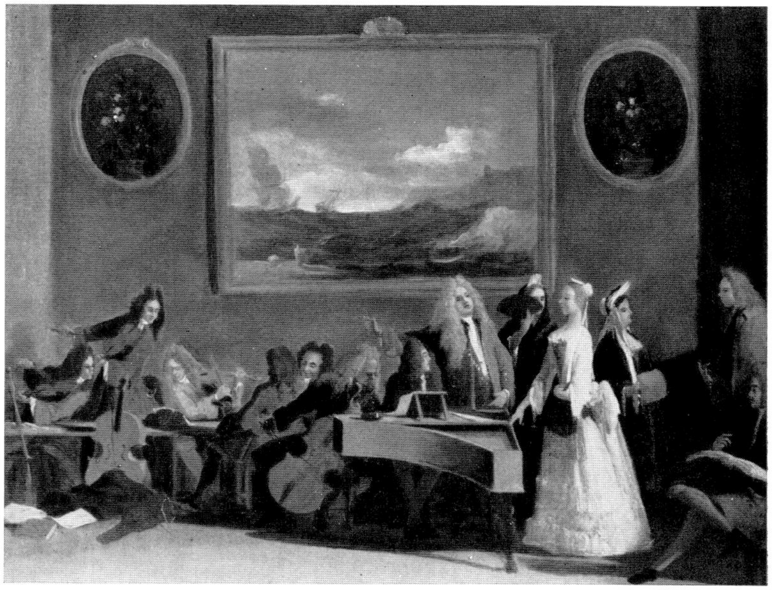

335

336

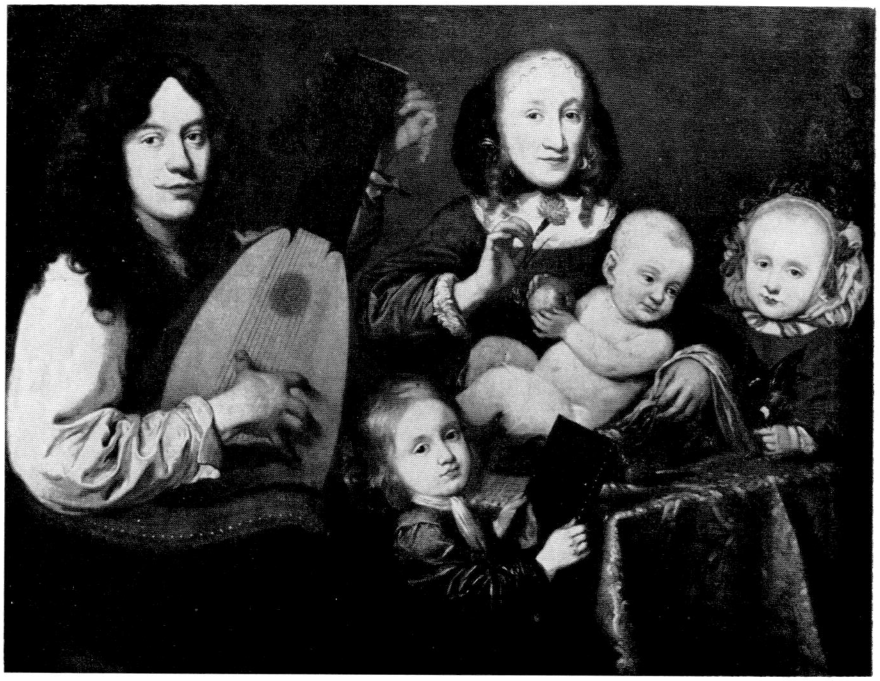

337 attr. to MARCO RICCI (1676-1729), *Rehearsal of an Opera.* Washington, D.C., collection of Mr. and Mrs. Paul Mellon (see p. 184).

338 JOHANN ZOFFANY (1734/5-1810), *The Cowper and Gore Families at Villa Palmieri, near Florence.* Henfield Place, Henfield (Sussex), collection of Lady Salmond (see p. 184).

339 JOHANN ZOFFANY (1734/5-1810), *Mr. and Mrs. Blew and their Children.* London, Sotheby's sale, 6 July 1966 (see p. 184).

340 PIETRO BENVENUTI (1768-1844), *Princess Corsini and Signora Scotto.* Florence, Corsini Gallery (see p. 184).

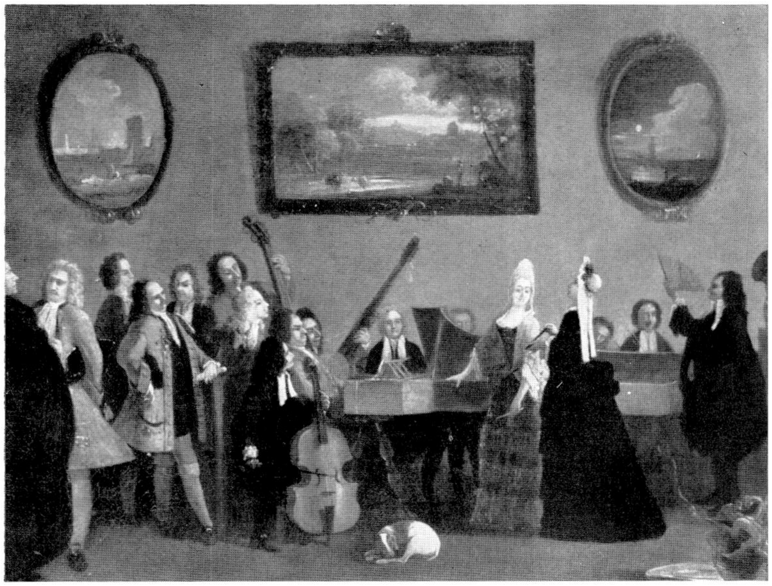

337

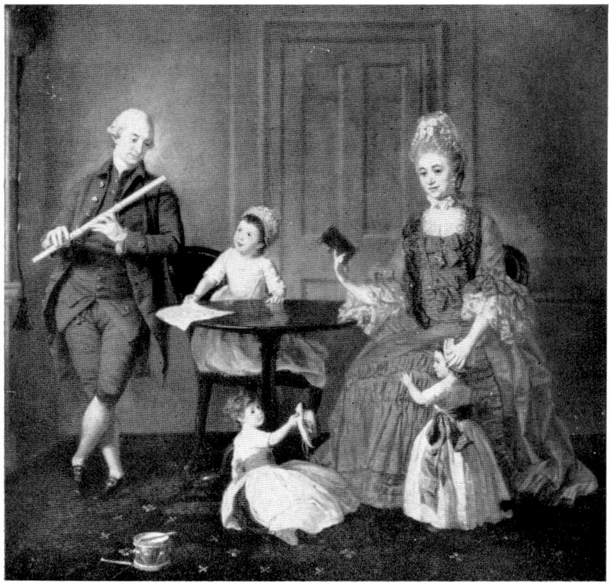

339

338

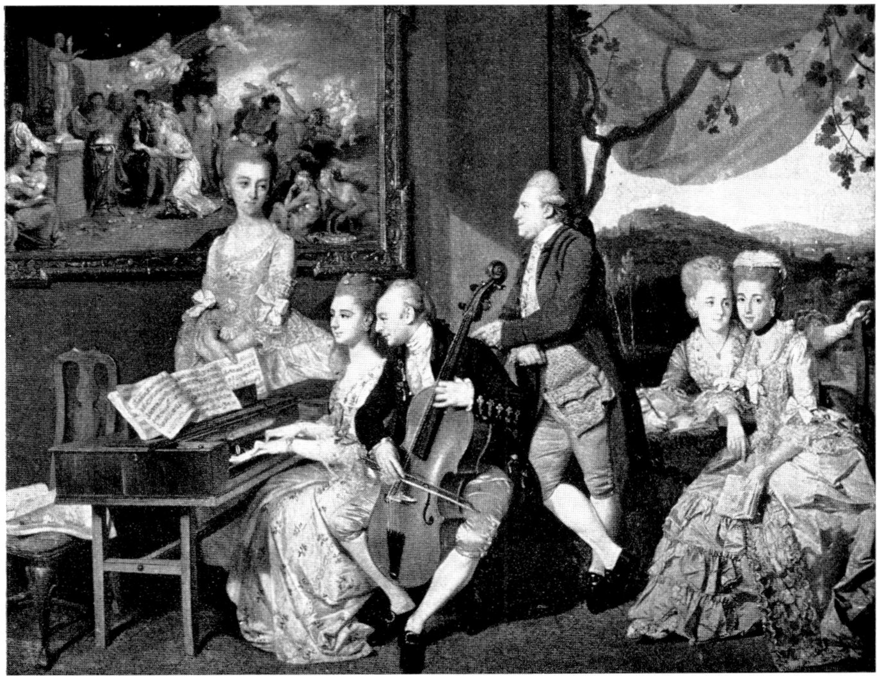

340

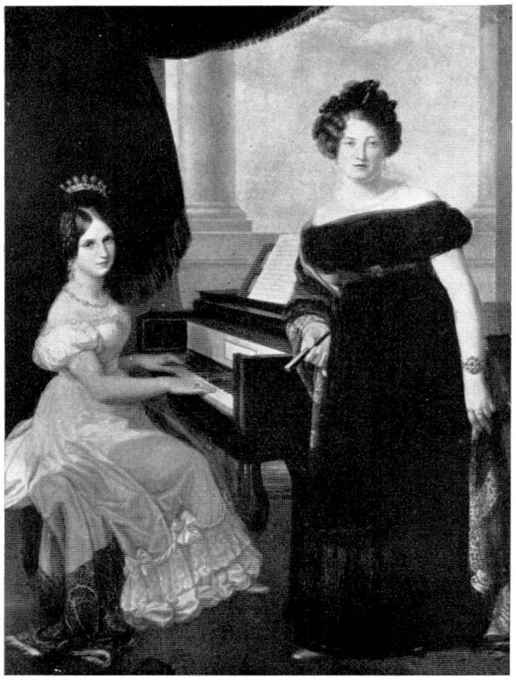

341 TEODORO MATTEINI (1754-1831), *A Family in a Garden*, 1805. Present location unknown; formerly the property of Col. E. Francis Hutchinson (see p. 184).

342 RAFFAELE D'AURIA (19th century), *The Children of Francis I of Naples*. Naples, Museo di San Martino (see p. 184).

343 JOHN FAED (1819-1902), *The Children of Dr. Archibald Bennie*, 1847. Edinburgh, National Gallery of Scotland (see p. 184).

344 GIUSEPPE MARIA CRESPI (1665-1747), *The Painter's Family*. Florence, Uffizi (see p. 186).

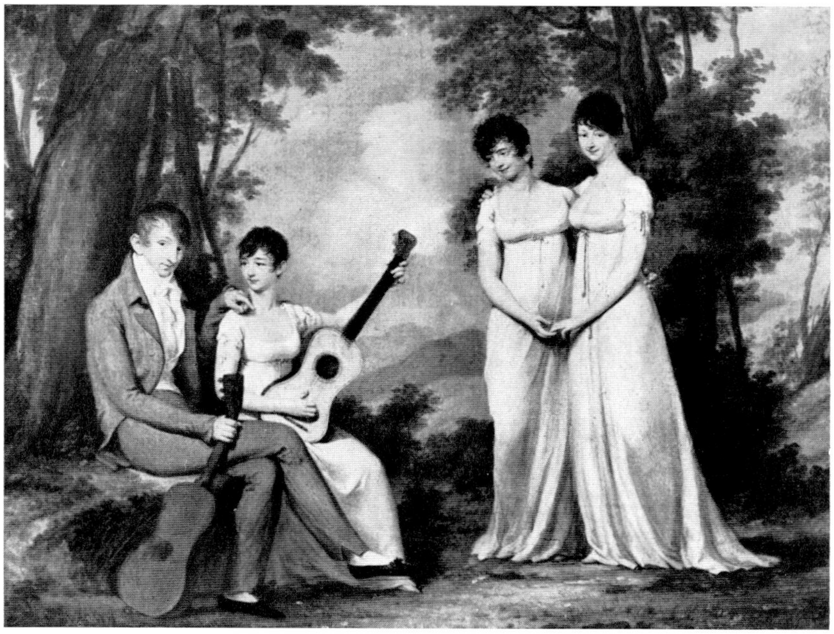

341

342

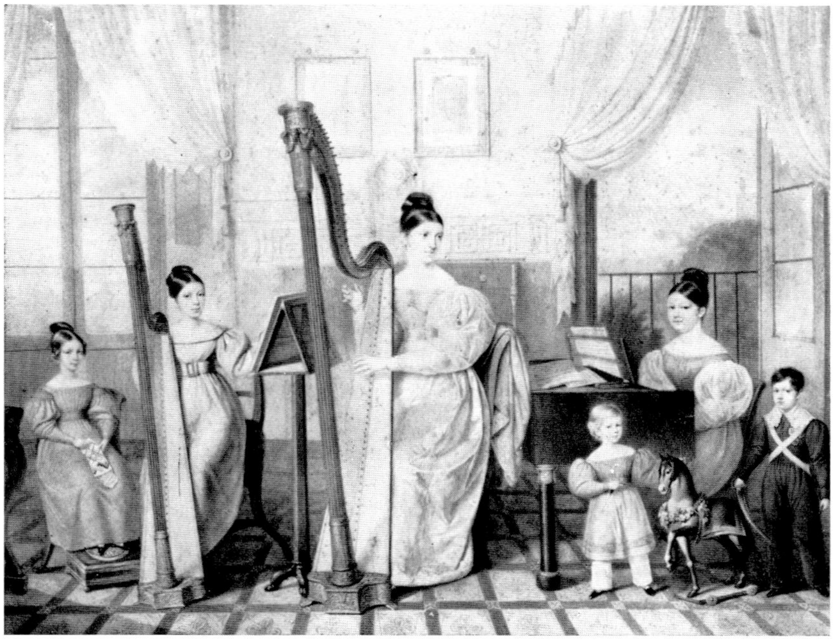

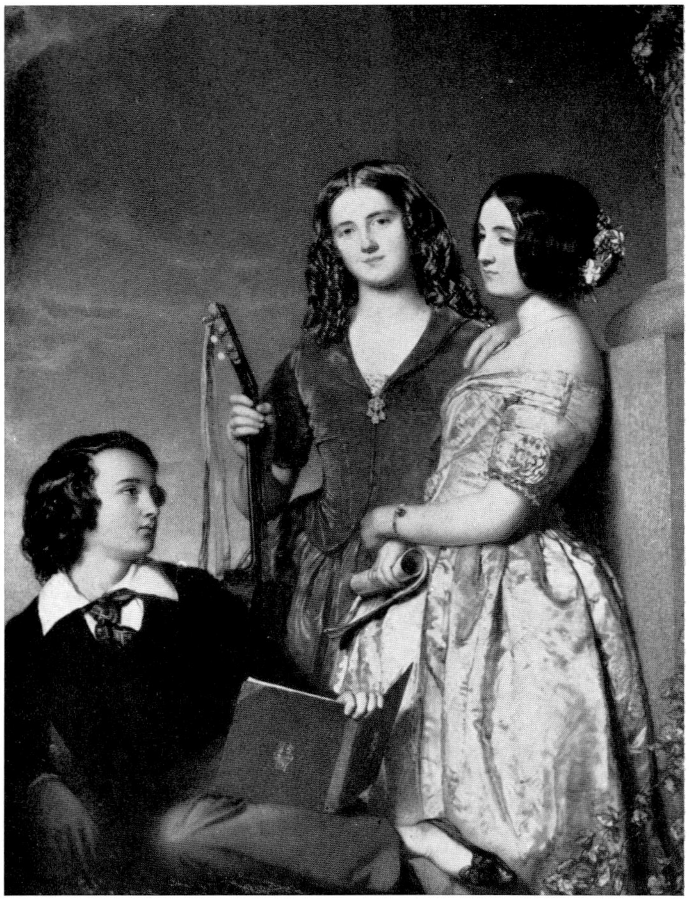

343

344

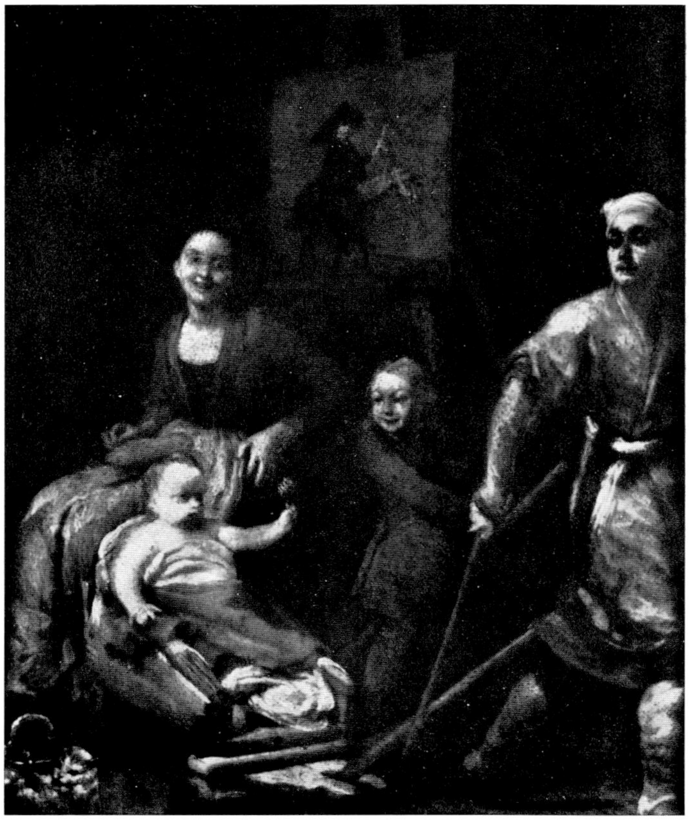

345 JOHANN ZOFFANY (1734/5-1810), *The Painter's Family*. Present location unknown; photo Witt Library, Courtauld Institute of Art (see p. 189).

346 JOHANN ZOFFANY (1734/5-1810), *The Family of the Painter*. One half of a large composition, sold at Christie's 23 July 1954; photo Witt Library, Courtauld Institute of Art (see p. 189).

347 JOHN HAMILTON MORTIMER (1741?-1779), *The Artist and his Teacher*, c. 1760. London, Royal Academy (see p. 189).

348 JOHANN ZOFFANY (1734/5-1810), *The Family of the Painter*. The second half of the above composition (no. 346), sold at Sotheby's 20 January 1957; photo Witt Library, Courtauld Institute of Art (see p. 189).

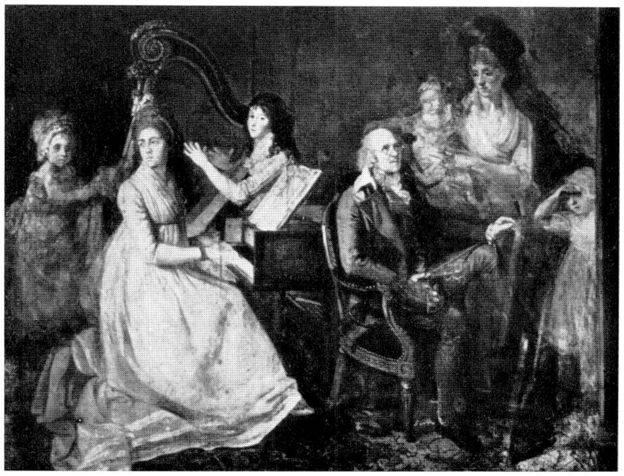

345

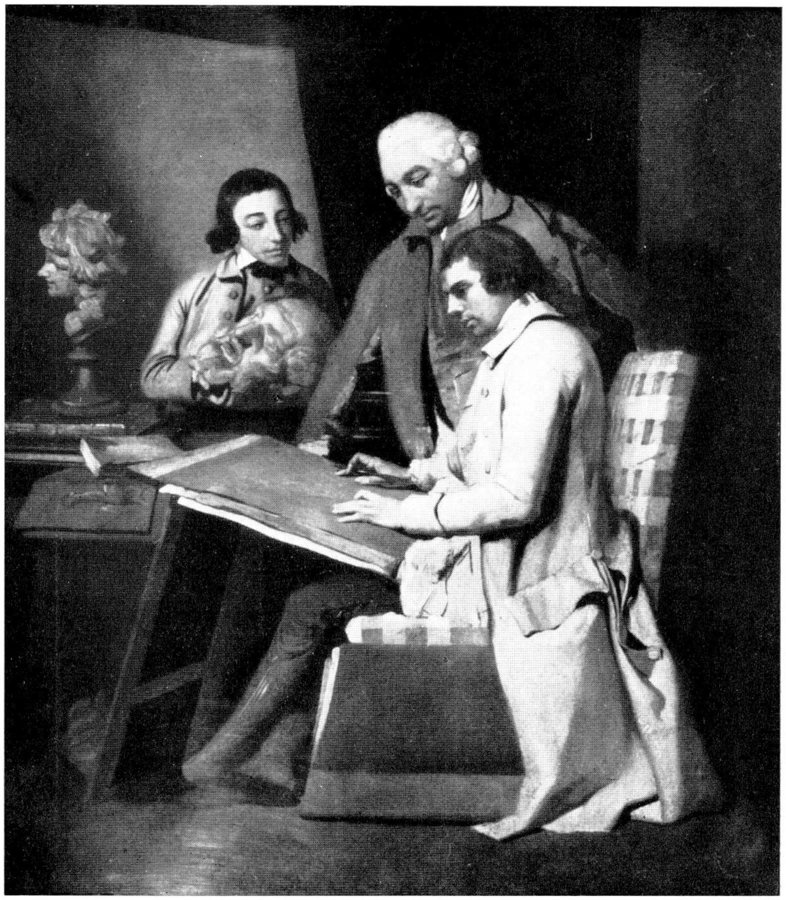

347

346

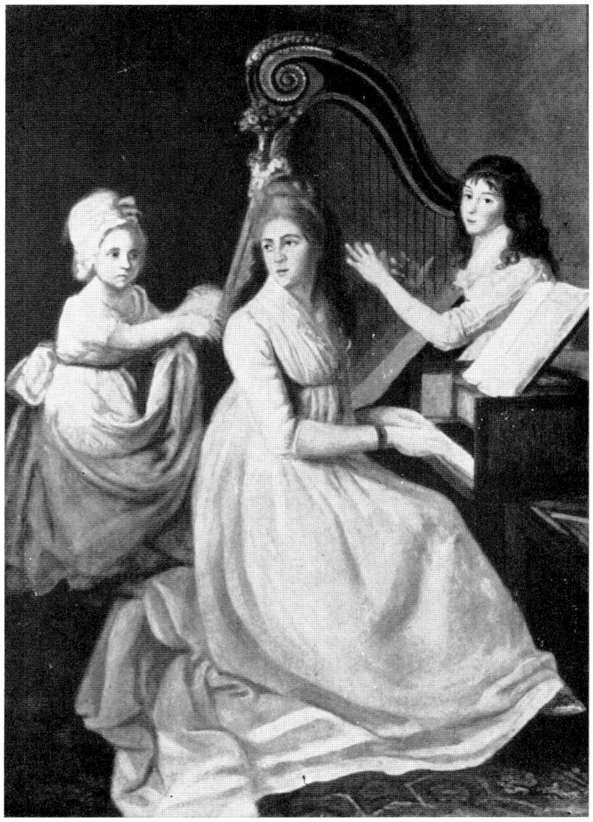

348

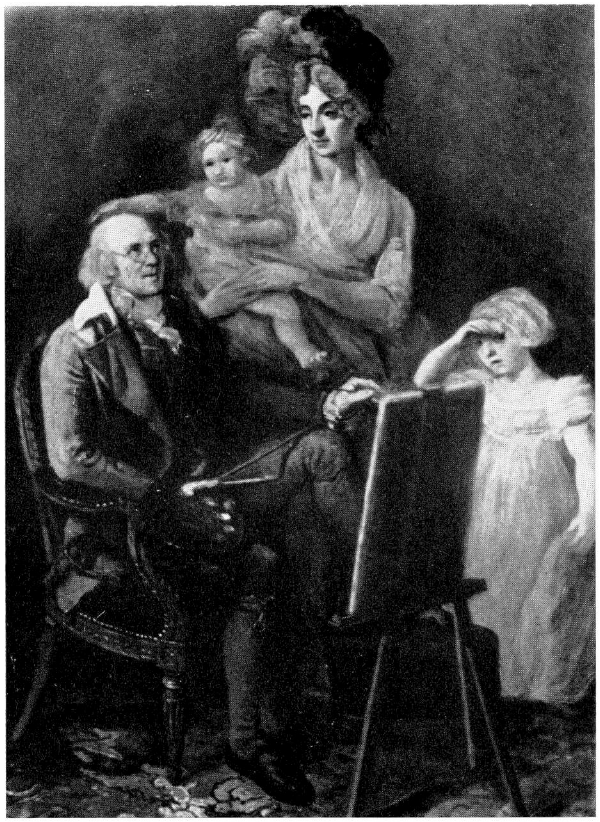

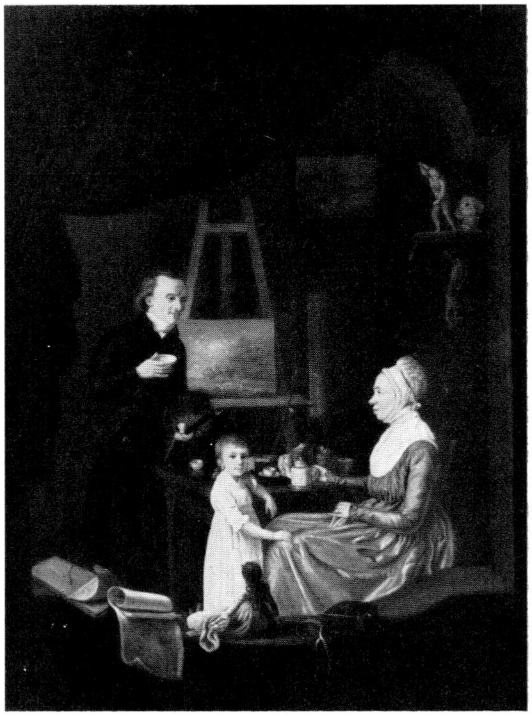

349

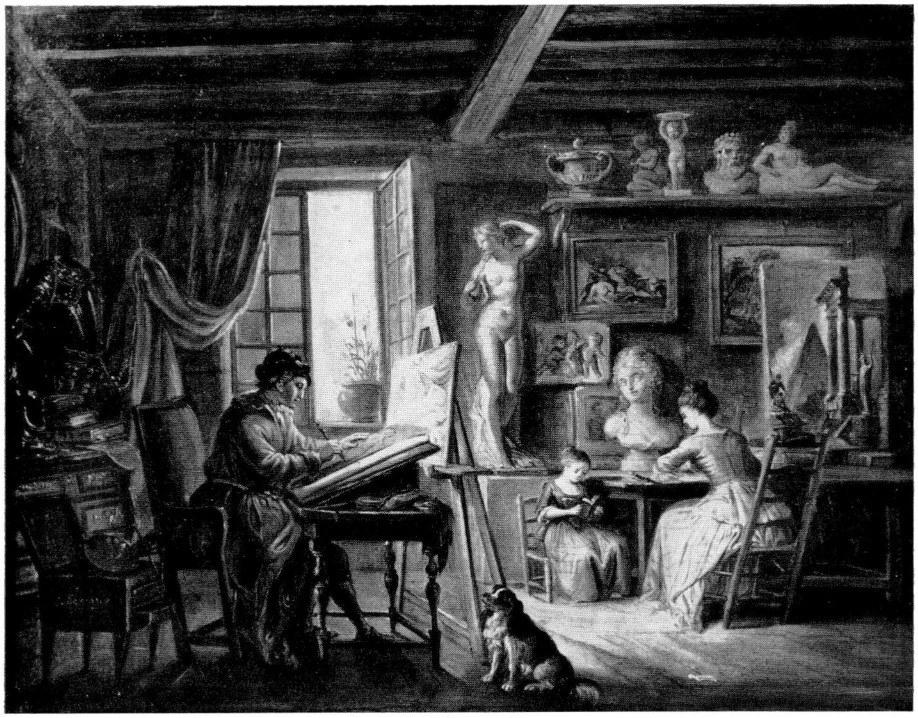

351

350

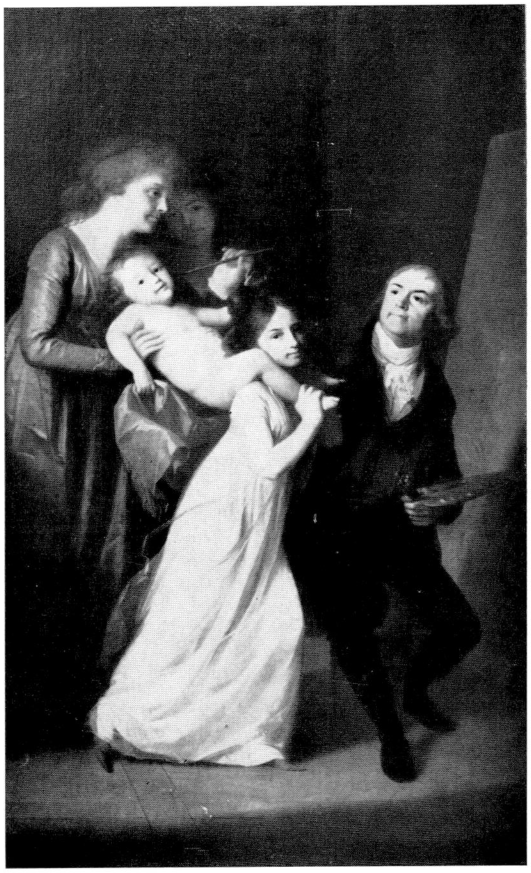

352

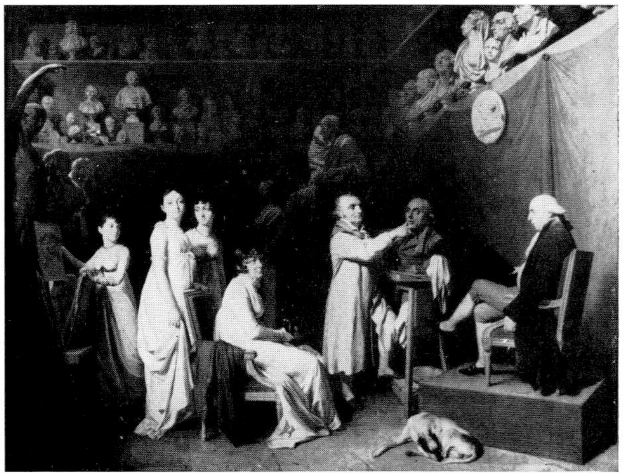

349 HENDRIK JAN VAN AMERON (1777-1833), *Self-portrait with his Wife and Small Son*, 1804. Arnhem, Gemeentemuseum (see p. 195).

350 JOHANN FRIEDRICH AUGUST TISCHBEIN (1750-1812), *The Artist's Family*, 1800. Leipzig, Museum der bildenden Künste (see p. 195).

351 JEAN-BAPTISTE LALLEMAND (1716-1803), *The Painter's Studio*. Dijon, Musée des Beaux-Arts (see p. 192).

352 LOUIS-LÉOPOLD BOILLY (1761-1845), *Houdon's Studio*. Paris, Musée des Arts Décoratifs (see p. 195).

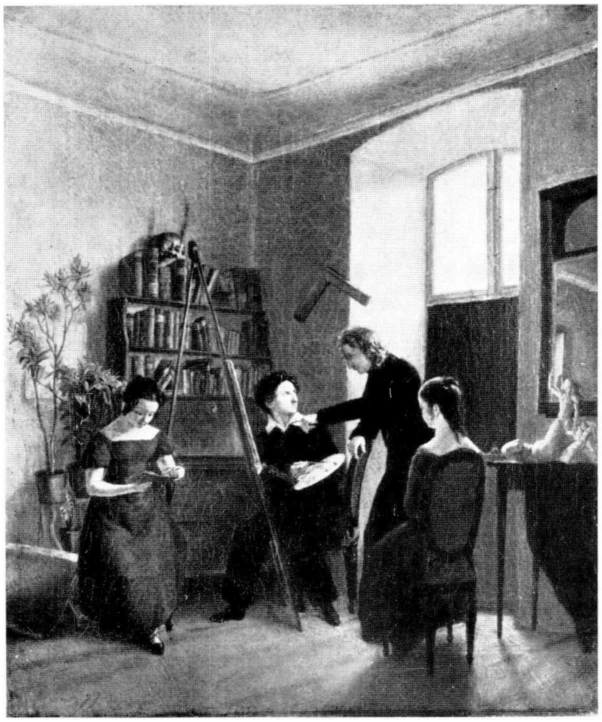

353

354

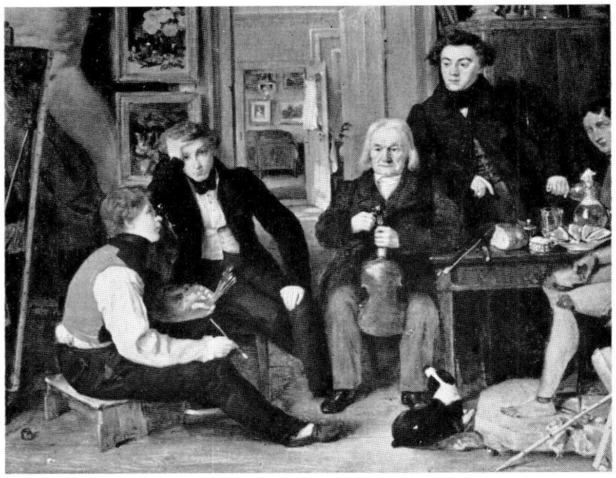

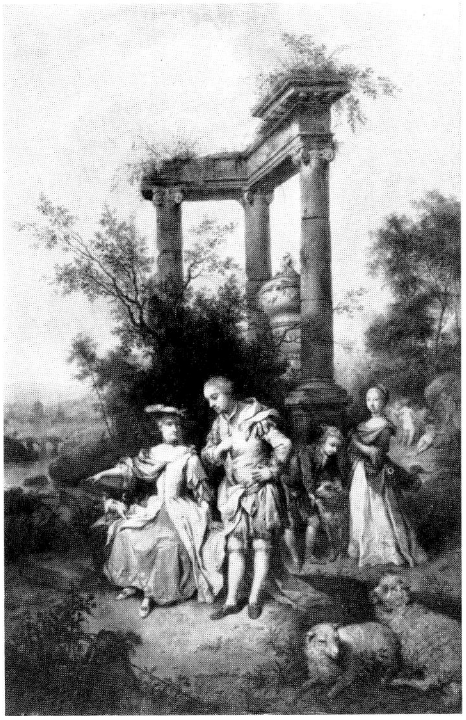

355

356

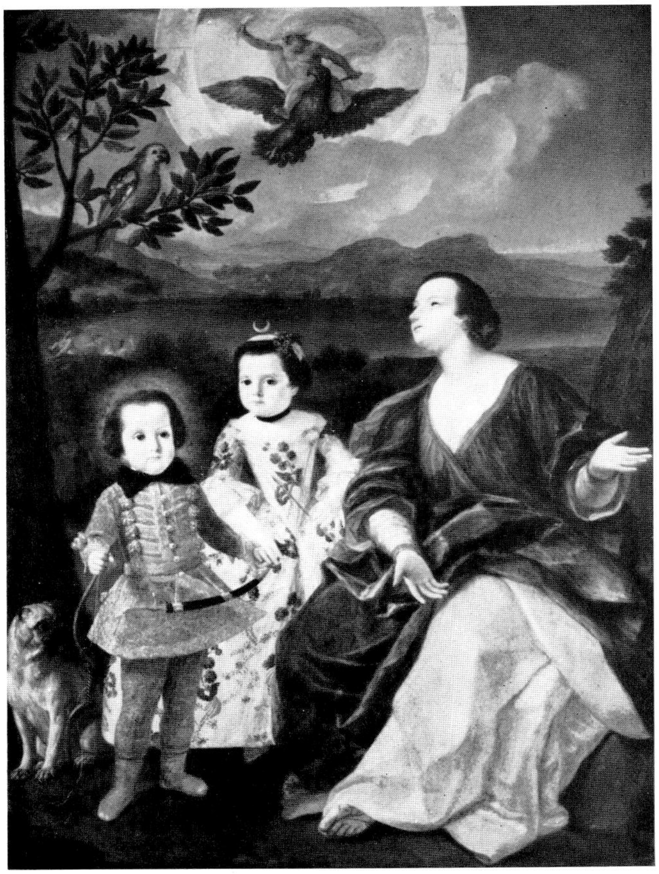

353 JULIUS LOUIS ASHER (1804-1878), *The Painter in his Studio*, 1828. Hamburg, Kunsthalle (see pp. 187 and 195).

354 JOHANN BAPTIST REITER (1813-1890), *The Artist's Studio*, c. 1832-40. Vienna, Historisches Museum der Stadt Wien (see p. 195).

355 JOHANN CONRAD SEEKATZ (1719-1768), *The Goethe Family in Pastoral Costumes*, 1762-3. Weimar, Goethe-Nationalmuseum (see p. 202).

356 MARCO BENEFIAL (1684-1764), *The Two Orsini Children as Apollo and Diana*, 1746. Rome, Museo di Roma (see pp. 200-2).

357 JOHANN JACOB POSNER (17th century), *Anna Maria de' Medici, the Widow of the Elector Palatine Johann Wilhelm, Showing the Portrait of her Dead Husband.* Florence, Soprintendenza alle Gallerie (see p. 213).

358 NICOLAAS MAES (1634-1693), *The van den Brandelaer Family*, 1672-3. Geneva, Musée d'Art et d'Histoire (see p. 210).

359 GEORGE VAN DER MIJN (1723-1763), *The Family of Pieter Cornelis Hasselaer*, 1763. Amsterdam, Rijksmuseum (see p. 213).

360 DAVID DES GRANGES (1611/2 - after 1670), *The Saltonstall Family*, c. 1637. Saltwood, collection of Lord Clark of Saltwood (see p. 210).

361 PETER PAUL RUBENS (1577-1640), *Portrait of Caspar Gevaerts*, c. 1628-30. Antwerp, Musée Royal des Beaux-Arts (see p. 214).

362 FOLLOWER OF VAN DYCK, *Nicholas Rockox, Burgomaster of Antwerp*, 1621. Baltimore (Md.), Museum of Art (Mary Frick Jacobs Collection) (see p. 214).

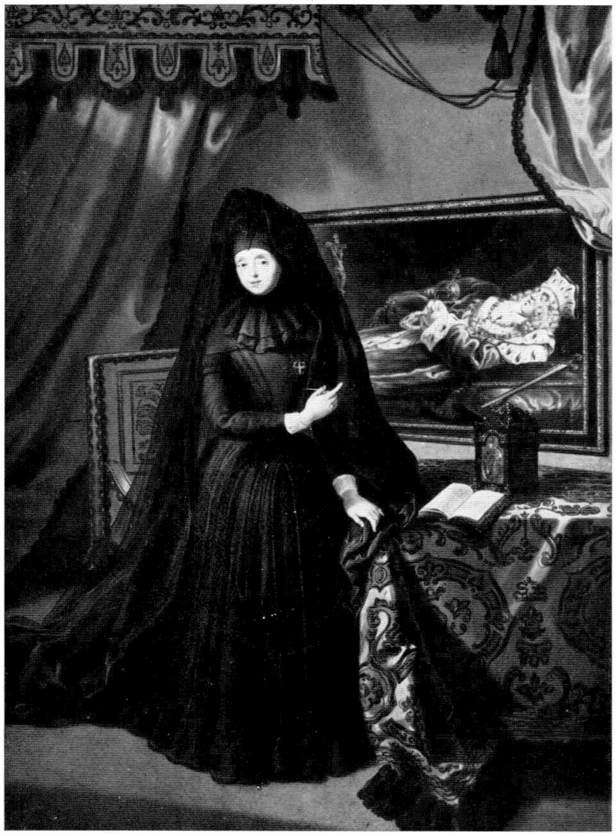

357

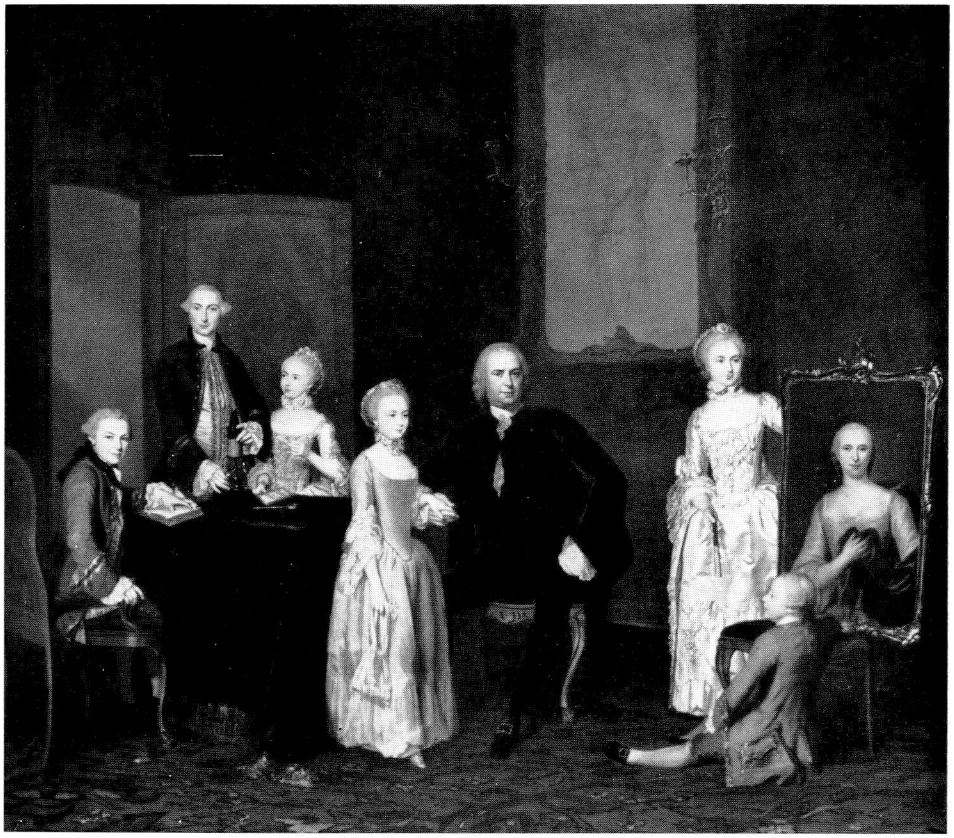

359

358

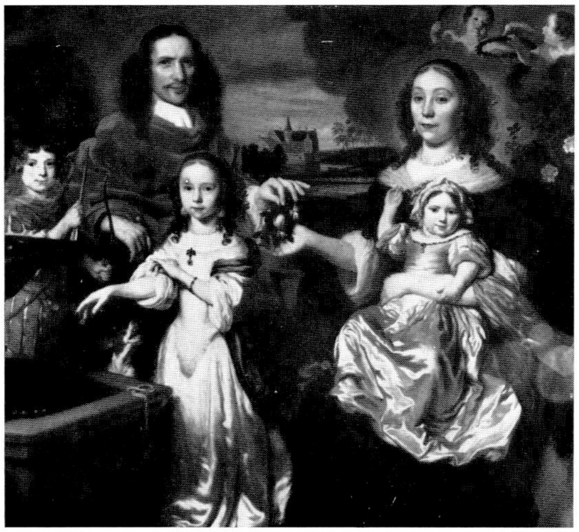

360

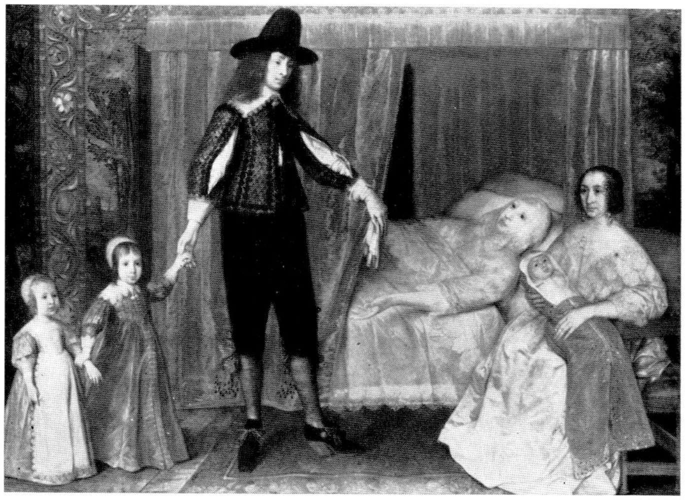

363 GIUSEPPE SOGNI (1790-1874), *Camilla Besozzi Figliodoni, Marchioness Lunati, Showing the Portrait of her Husband*, 1854. Milan, Ospedale Maggiore (see p. 216).

364 JOHANN HEINRICH FÜSSLI (FUSELI) (1741-1825), *Self-portrait Conversing with J. J. Bodmer*. Zurich, Kunsthaus (see p. 215).

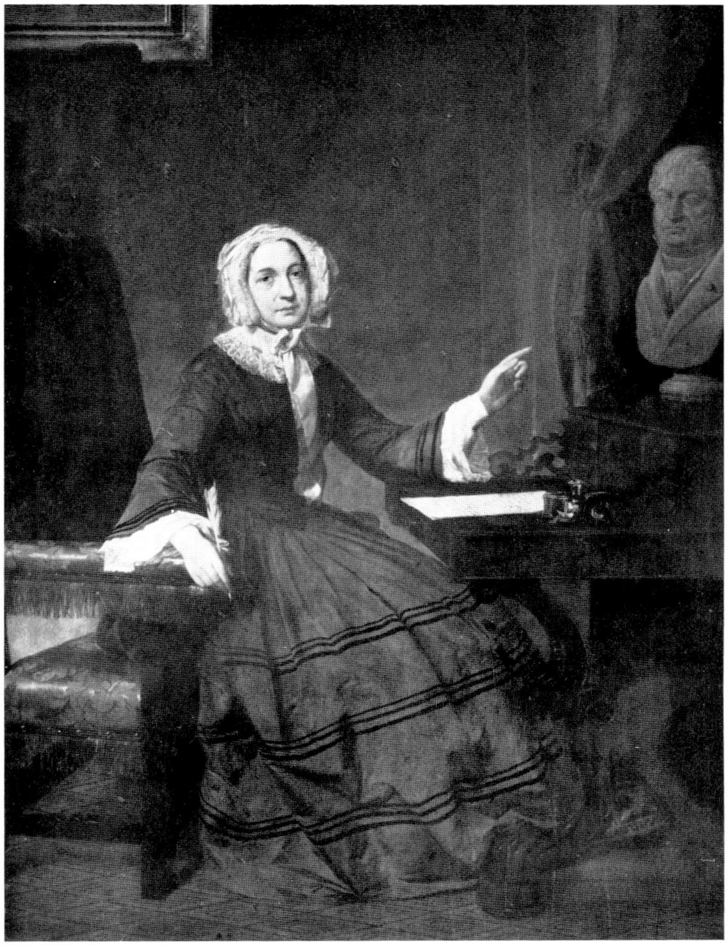

363

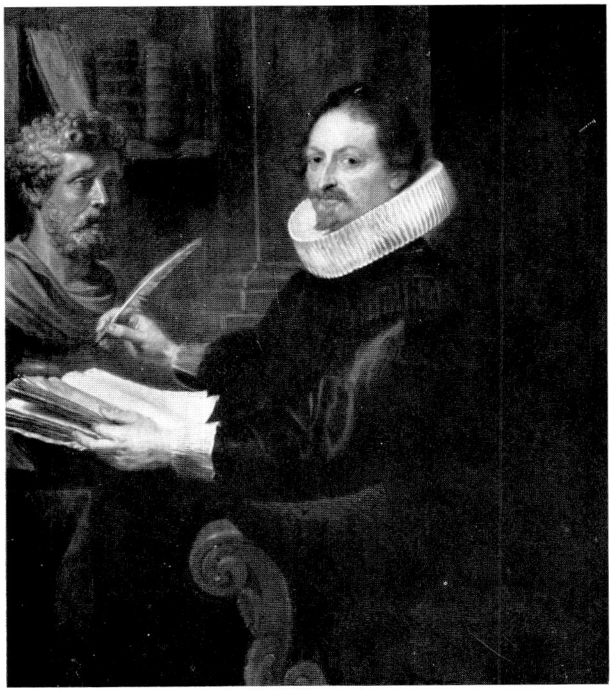

361

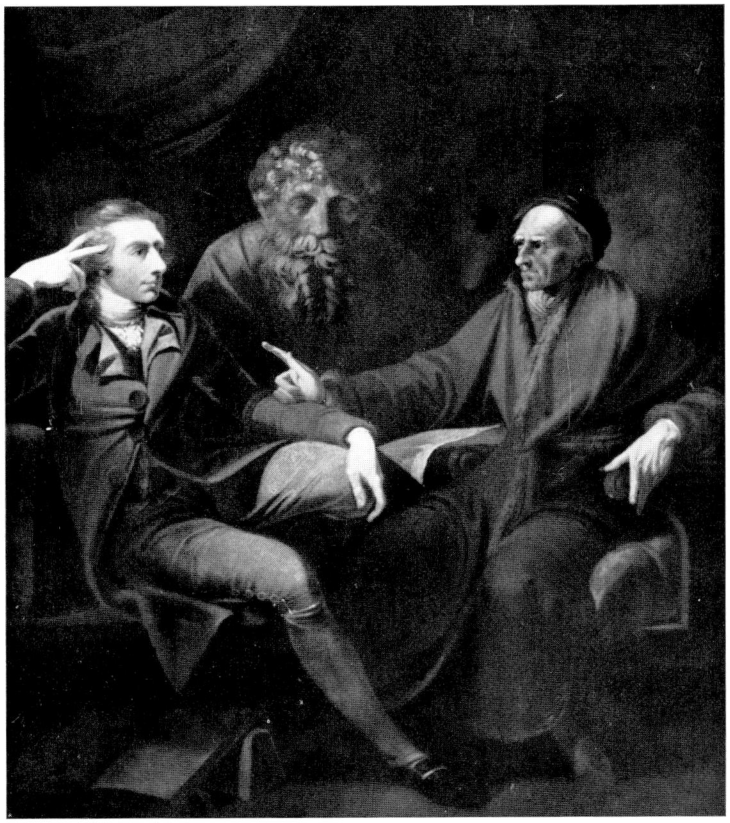

364

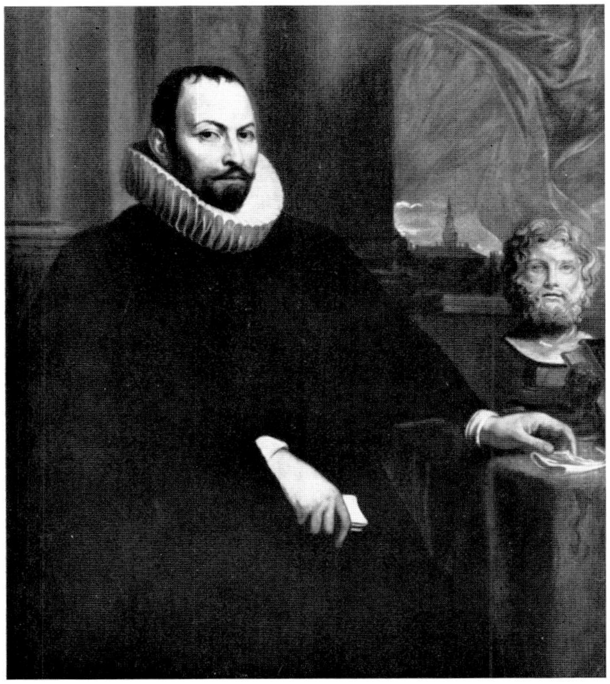

362

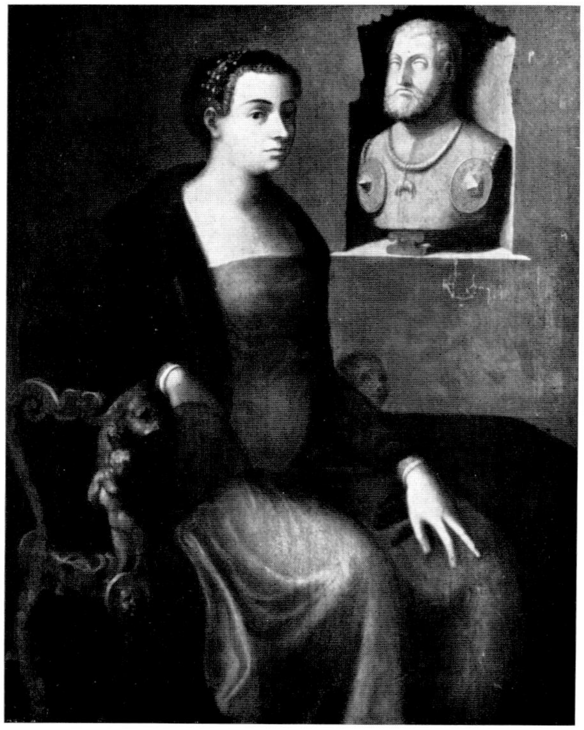

365

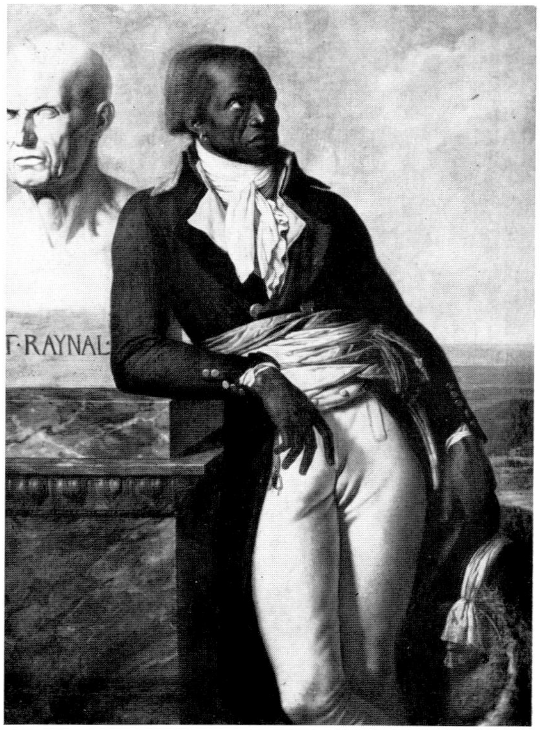

367

366

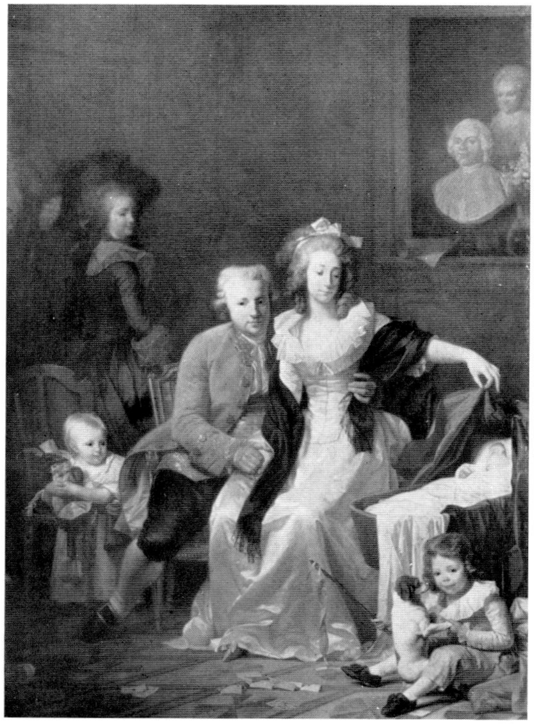

368

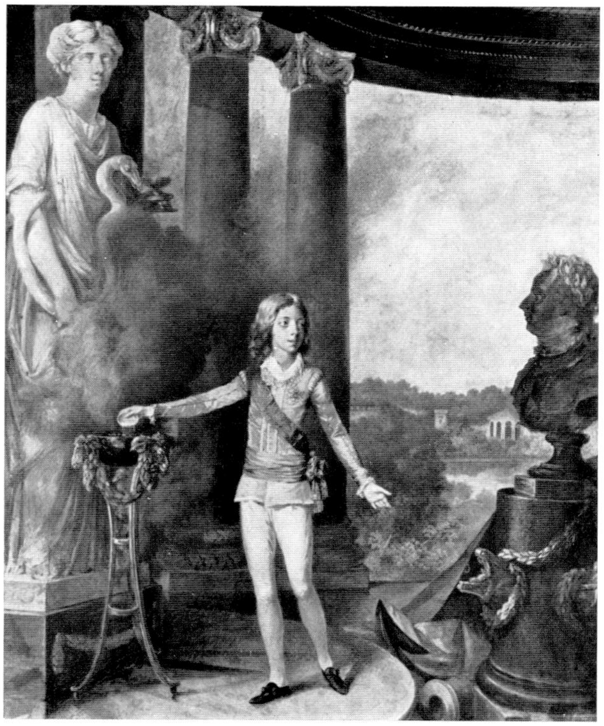

365 ITALIAN SCHOOL (16th century) (attr. to SEBASTIANO DEL PIOMBO), *Margaret of Austria near the Bust of her Father, Charles V*. Parma, Galleria Nazionale (see p. 215).

366 HENRI-PIERRE DANLOUX (1753-1809), *The Family of Mégret de Sérilly*. Private collection; photo courtesy of the Galerie Charpentier, Paris (see p. 215).

367 ANNE-LOUIS GIRODET-TRIOSON (1767-1824), *Portrait of Jean-Baptiste Belley*, 1797. Versailles, Château de Versailles (see p. 216).

368 NIKLAS LAFRENSEN THE YOUNGER (1737-1807), *Gustavus Adolphus IV of Sweden and the Bust of his Father, Gustavus III*, 1792. Stockholm, Nationalmuseum (see pp. 215-16).

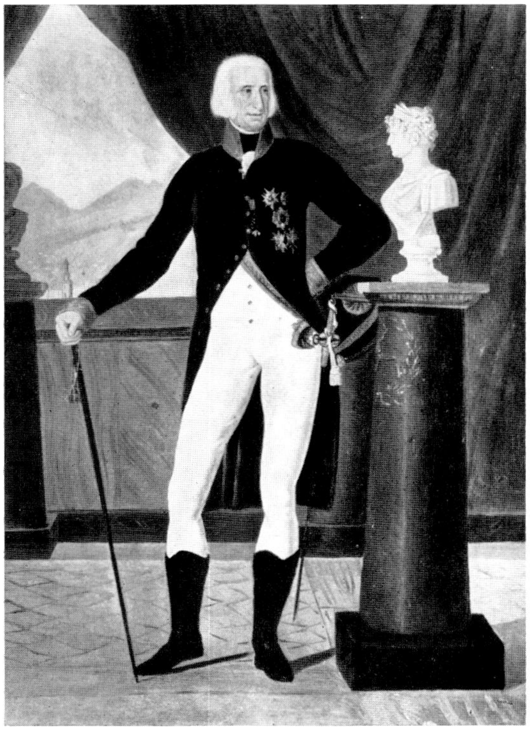

369

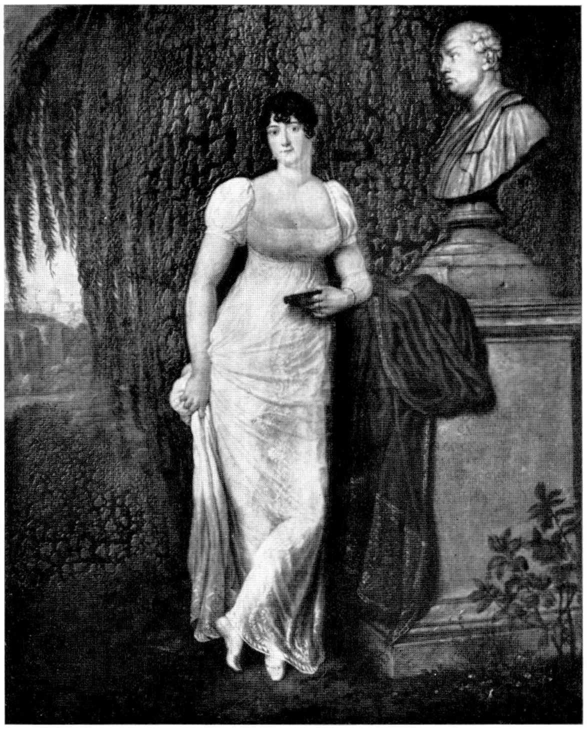

371

370

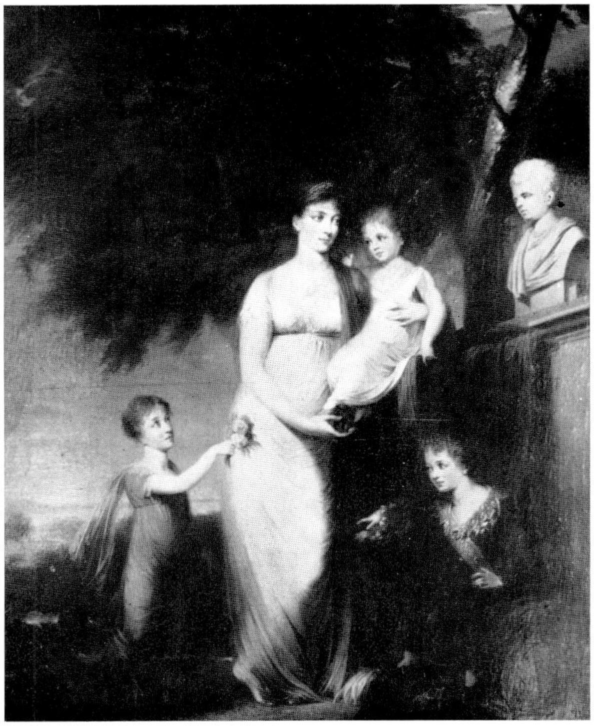

372

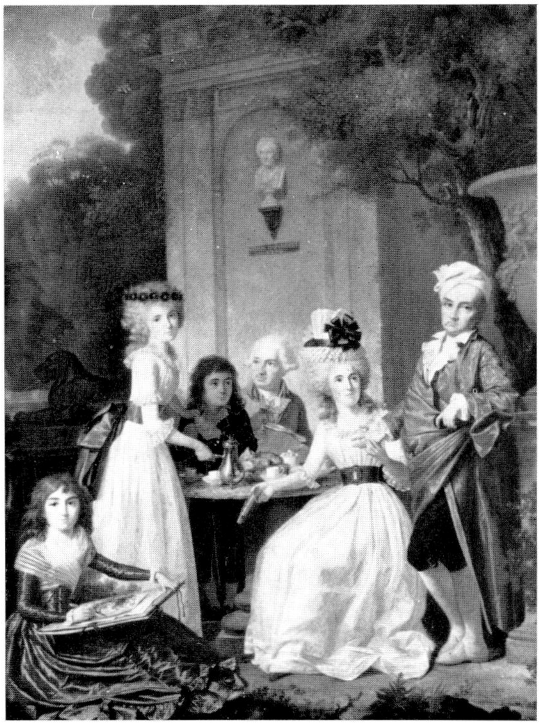

369 ANONYMOUS, *Ferdinand IV near the Bust of Maria Carolina*. Rome, private collection (see p. 215).

370 CARL FREDRIK VON BREDA (1759-1818), *Queen Fredrika of Sweden with her Children Gustavus, Sophia, and Amalia*, 1807. Formerly in Dresden, Residenzschloss; photo Svenska Porträttarkivet, Nationalmuseum, Stockholm (see p. 216).

371 PIETRO LABBRUZZI (1739-1805), *Teresa Pikler Monti with a Bust of her Father*. Florence, Pitti Palace (see p. 216).

372 JEAN-CLAUDE NAIGEON (1758-1832), *The Painter with his Family*, 1793. Paris, private collection; photo courtesy of the Galerie Charpentier (see p. 215).

373 ANONYMOUS (19th century), *Carlo Lodovico di Borbone Parma with his Wife, his Sister, and the Future Carlo III of Parma Offering Flowers to the Bust of Maria Luisa di Borbone*. Viareggio, archducal estate; property of the Bourbon-Hapsburg heirs (see p. 216).

374 NATALE CARTA (1790-1884), *Carlo Filangieri and his Family*. Naples, Museo Civico Gaetano Filangieri (see pp. 216-18).

375 BRONZINO (1503-1572), *Lodovico Capponi*. New York, Frick Collection (see pp. 218-221).

376 JEAN-BAPTISTE CLAUDE ROBIN (1734-1818), *Marquis Trophime-Gérard de Lally-Tollendal Removing a Black Veil from the Bust of his Father*, 1779. New York, Kendl Galleries, auction 3-4 Oct. 1951 (see p. 218).

377 GIUSEPPE (JOSIP) TOMINZ (1796-1866), *The Artist's Father*, 1848. Ljubljana, National Gallery (see p. 221, note 21).

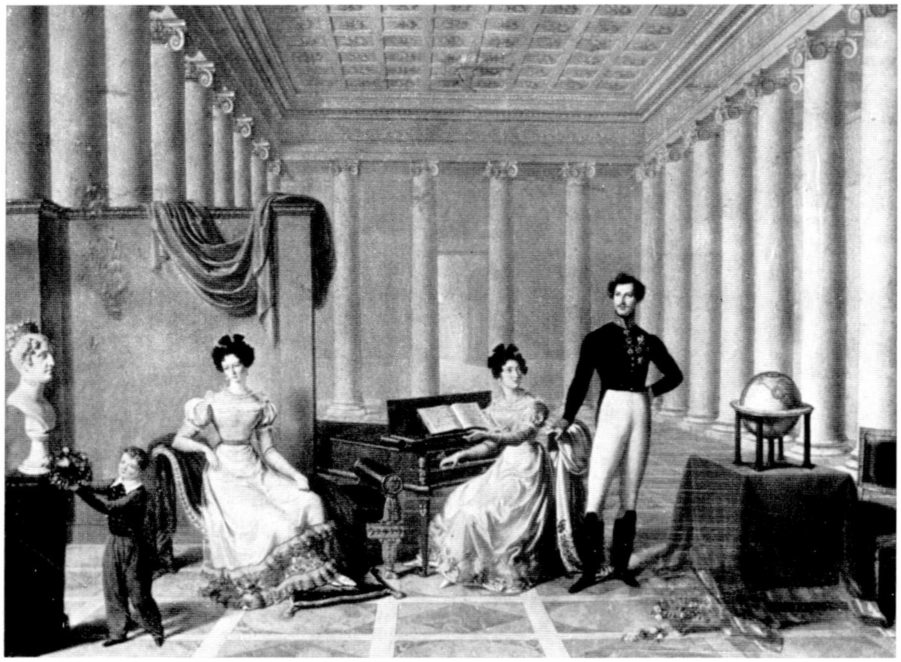

373

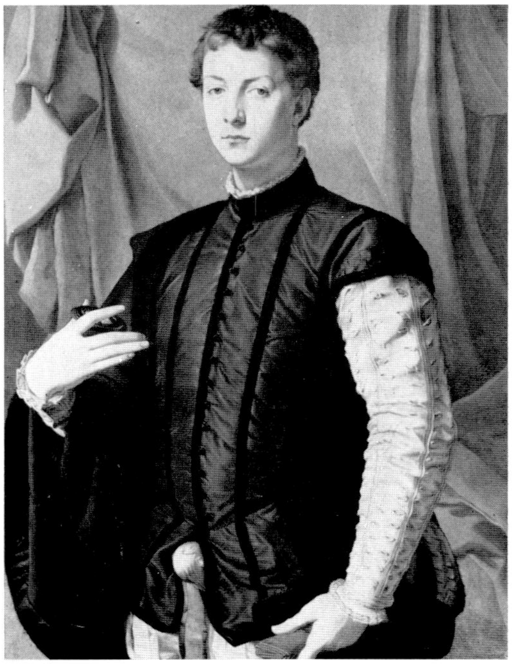

375

374

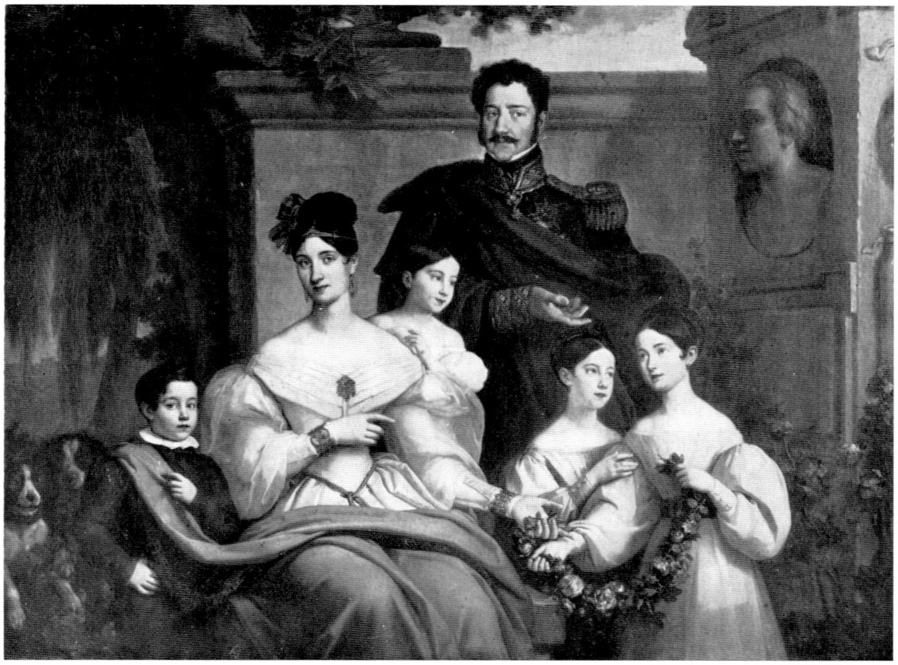

376

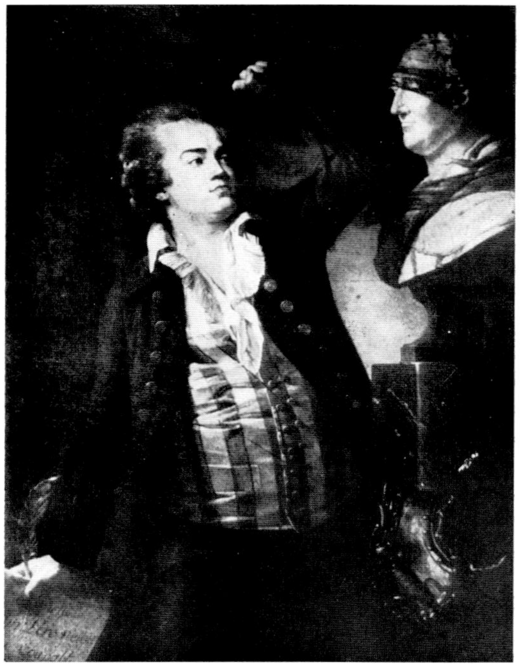

378 CONSTANCE MAYER (1778-1821), *The Artist and her Father in her Studio*, 1801. Present location unknown; on the art market (Seligmann) in 1930 (see p. 216).

379 FOLLOWER OF SANCHEZ COELLO (1531/2-1588) (formerly attr. to FELIPE DE LIAÑO [d. 1625]), *The Infanta Isabella Clara Eugenia with the Court "Loca" Madalena Ruiz*. Madrid, Prado (see p. 221).

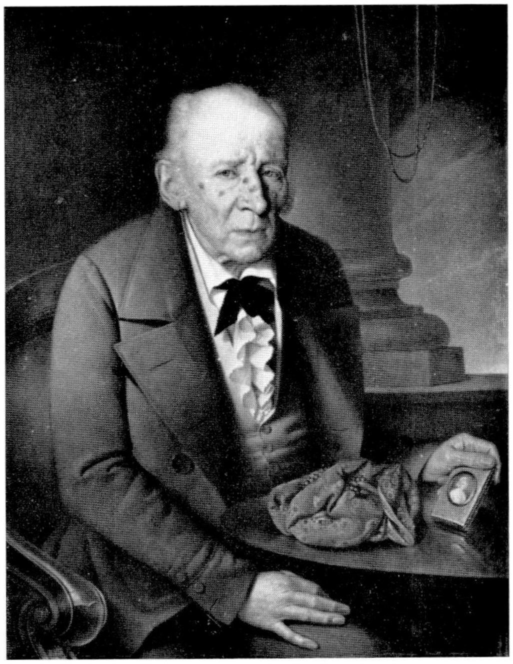

377

378

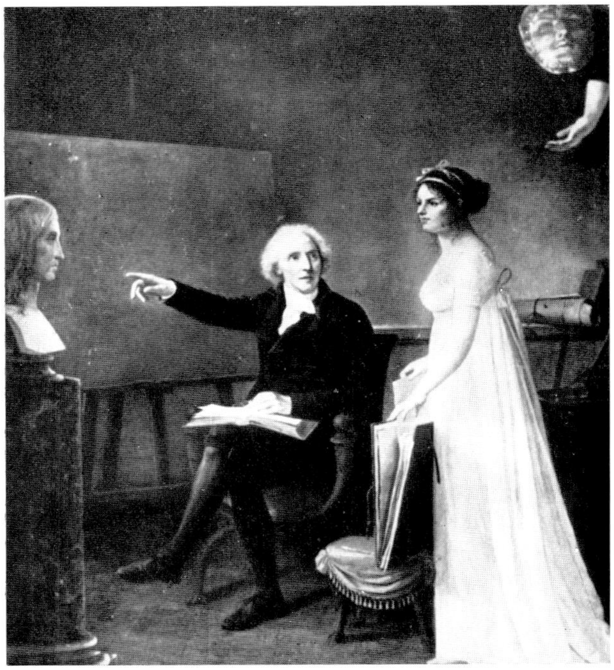

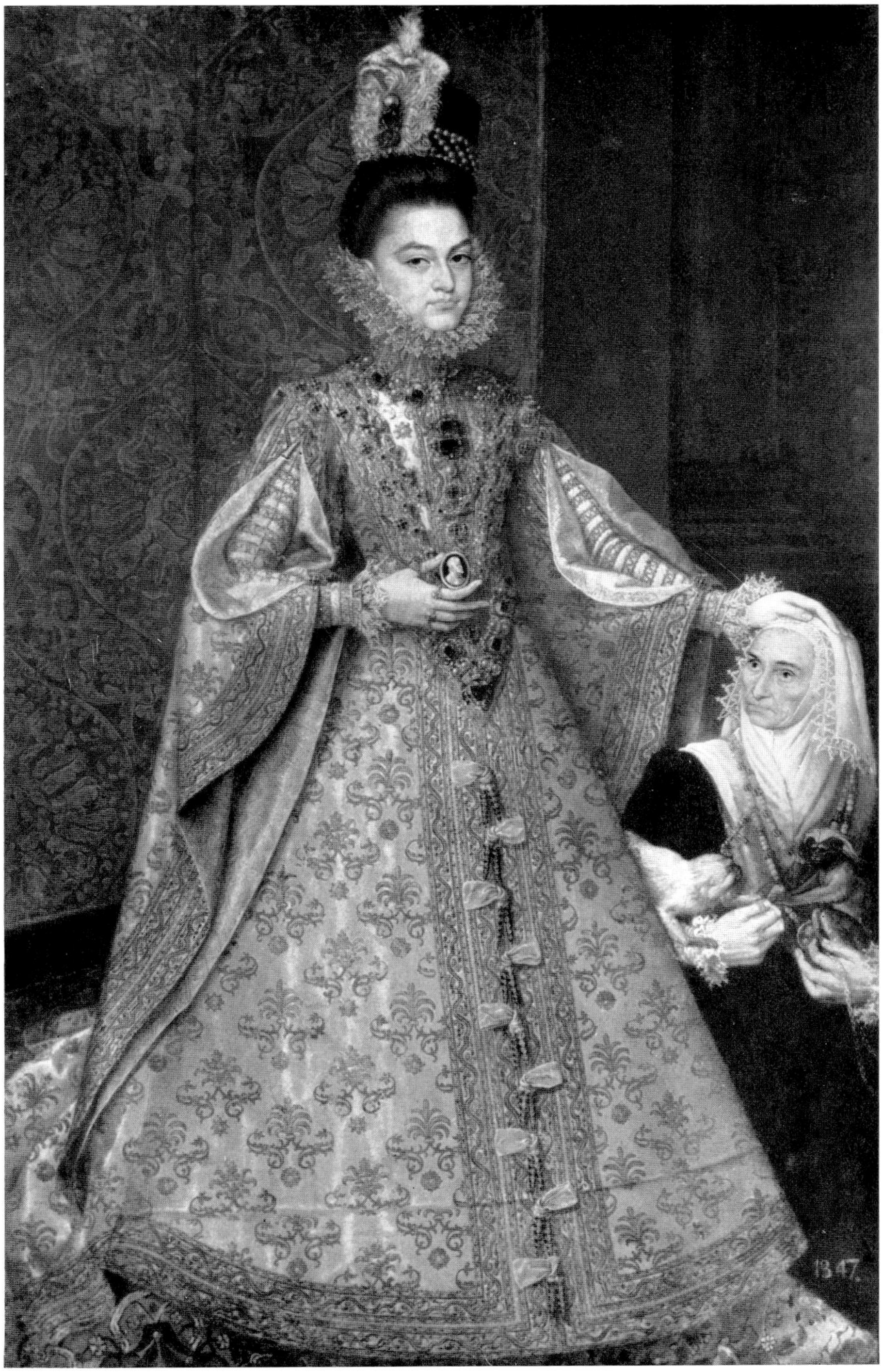

379

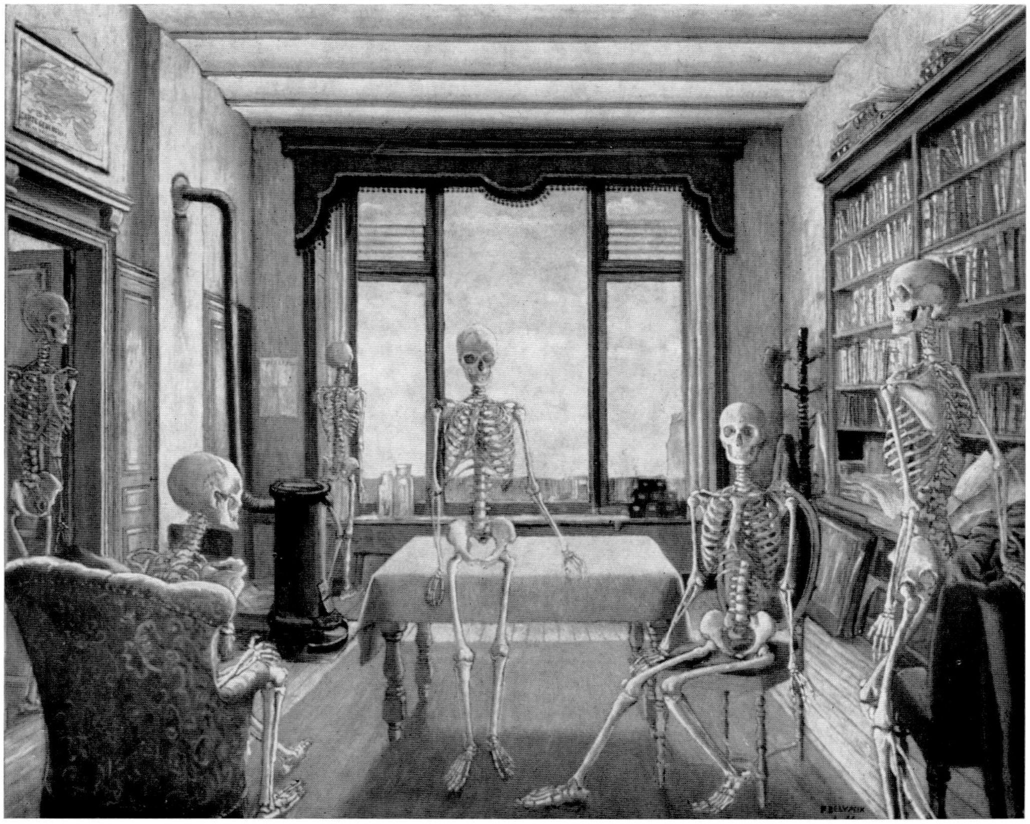

380

380 PAUL DELVAUX (1897-), *Squelettes dans un bureau*, 1944. New York, collection of Jerome L. Stern (see p. 36).

INDEX

Printed in Milan by I.T.E.C. - Type from Monotipia R. Olivieri. Photoengravings by Fotoincisioni d'Arte, Rome. Paper manufactured especially for this volume by the Burgo Papermills. Binding by the Legatoria Torriani.